The Routledge Handbook of New Security Studies

The Routledge Handbook of New Security Studies

Edited by
J. Peter Burgess

LONDON AND NEW YORK

First published 2010
by Routledge
2 Park Square, Milton Park, Abingdon, Oxon, OX14 4RN

Simultaneously published in the USA and Canada
by Routledge
270 Madison Avenue, New York, NY 10016

Routledge is an imprint of the Taylor & Francis Group, an informa business

© 2010 J. Peter Burgess for selection and editorial material; individual
chapters, the contributors

Typeset in Bembo by
HWA Text and Data Management, London

All rights reserved. No part of this book may be reprinted or reproduced
or utilised in any form or by any electronic, mechanical, or other
means, now known or hereafter invented, including photocopying
and recording, or in any information storage or retrieval system,
without permission in writing from the publishers.

British Library Cataloguing in Publication Data
A catalogue record for this book is available from the British Library

Library of Congress Cataloging-in-Publication Data
Handbook of new security studies / edited by J. Peter Burgess.
     p. cm.
  1. Security, International. 2. National security. I. Burgess, J. Peter.
JZ5588.H36 2010
  355'.033—dc22   2009031233

ISBN10: 0-415-48437-5 (hbk)
ISBN10: 0-203-85948-0 (ebk)

ISBN13: 978-0-415-48437-4 (hbk)
ISBN13: 978-0-203-85948-3 (ebk)

Contents

List of Contributors	viii
1 Introduction *J. Peter Burgess*	1

Part I: New Security Concepts

5

2 Civilizational Security *Brett Bowden*	7
3 Risk *Oliver Kessler*	17
4 Instruments of Insecurity: Small Arms and Contemporary Violence *Keith Krause*	27
5 Human Security: A Contested Contempt *Taylor Owen*	39
6 Critical Geopolitics and Security *Simon Dalby*	50

Part II: New Security Subjects

59

7 Biopolitics of Security *Michael Dillon*	61

CONTENTS

8   Gendering Security — 72
    Laura J. Shepherd

9   Identity/Security — 81
    Pinar Bilgin

10 Security As Ethics — 90
    Anthony Burke

11 Financial Security — 100
    Marieke de Goede

12 Security and International Law — 110
    Kristin Bergtora Sandvik

Part III: New Security Objects — 121

13 Environmental Security — 123
    Jon Barnett

14 Food Security — 132
    Steve Wiggins and Rachel Slater

15 Energy Security — 144
    Roland Dannreuther

16 Cyber-Security — 154
    Myriam Dunn Cavelty

17 Pandemic Security — 163
    Stefan Elbe

18 Biosecurity and International Security Implications — 173
    Frida Kuhlau and John Hart

Part IV: New Security Practices — 185

19 Surveillance — 187
    Mark B. Salter

20 Urban Insecurity — 197
    David Murakami Wood

21	Commercial Security Practices *Anna Leander*	208
22	Migration and Security *William Walters*	217
23	Security Technologies *Emmanuel-Pierre Guittet and Julien Jeandesboz*	229
24	Designing Security *Cynthia Weber and Mark Lacy*	240
25	New Mobile Crime *Monica den Boer*	253
	References	263
	Index	310

Contributors

Jon Barnett is a Reader in the Department of Resource Management and Geography at Melbourne University. He is a human geographer whose research investigates the impacts of and responses to environmental change on social systems. This includes research on climate change, environmental security, water and food.

Pinar Bilgin is Associate Professor of International Relations at Bilkent University, Turkey. She is the author of *Regional Security in the Middle East: a Critical Perspective* (Routledge, 2005). Her articles have appeared in various academic journals, including, *Political Geography, European Journal of Political Research, Third World Quarterly, Security Dialogue* and *Geopolitics*. Her research agenda focuses on critical approaches to security studies. Further information is available at: http://www.bilkent.edu.tr/~pbilgin/.

Brett Bowden is Associate Professor of Politics and International Studies. He holds appointments at the University of Western Sydney, the Australian National University and the University of NSW at the Australian Defence Force Academy. He is the author of *The Empire of Civilization: The Evolution of an Imperial Idea* (University of Chicago Press, 2009) and editor of the four-volume major work *Civilization: Critical Concepts in Political Science* (Routledge, 2009).

J. Peter Burgess is Research Professor at PRIO, the International Peace Research Institute, Oslo, where he leads the Security Programme and edits the interdisciplinary peer-reviewed journal *Security Dialogue*. In addition, he is Adjunct Professor at the Norwegian University of Science and Technology, Trondheim (NTNU), and Senior Research Fellow at the Institute for European Studies, Brussels. His current research focuses on the ethical implications of the changing nature of threat and insecurity, particularly in Europe.

Anthony Burke is Associate Professor of Politics and International Relations, University of New South Wales, at the Australian Defence Force Academy. He is the author of *Beyond Security, Ethics and Violence: War Against the Other* (Routledge, 2007) and *Fear of Security: Australia's Invasion Anxiety* (2nd edn, Cambridge, 2008), and is editor, with Matt McDonald, of *Critical Security in the Asia-Pacific* (Manchester, 2007).

LIST OF CONTRIBUTORS

Roland Dannreuther is Professor of International Relations and Head of the Department of Politics and International Relations, University of Westminster. His research interests include security studies, the international politics of the Middle East and Central Asia, energy politics, and the role of historical sociology in international relations theory. His recent publications include *International Security: The Contemporary Agenda* (Polity, 2007).

Simon Dalby is Professor of Geography, Environmental Studies and Political Economy at Carleton University in Ottawa. He is author of *Creating the Second Cold War* (Pinter and Guilford, 1990), *Environmental Security* (University of Minnesota Press, 2002) and *Security and Environmental Change* (Polity, 2009) and co-editor of *Rethinking Geopolitics* (Routledge, 1998), *The Geopolitics Reader* (Routledge, 1998, 2nd edn, 2006) and the journal *Geopolitics*.

Marieke de Goede is Associate Professor at the Department of European Studies of the University of Amsterdam. She is author of *Virtue, Fortune and Faith: A Genealogy of Finance* (University of Minnesota Press, 2005) and co-editor of *Risk and the War on Terror* (Routledge, 2008). Her current research project *Datawars*, with Louise Amoore, enquires into the deployment of commercial (financial) data for security decisions. De Goede is member of the advisory board of *Environment and Planning D: Society and Space*.

Monica den Boer holds the Police Academy Chair on the Internationalization of the Police Function at the VU University Amsterdam on behalf of the Police Academy of the Netherlands. Her publications are on European law enforcement cooperation, with a recent focus on the ethical aspects of security and international counter-terrorism governance. She is a member of the Dutch Advisory Board on International Affairs and Vice-Chair of the Board of the Clingendael Institute on International Relations, and was appointed member of the Dutch Iraq Investigation Committee on 1 March 2009.

Michael Dillon is Professor of Politics at the Department of Politics and International Relations of the University of Lancaster. His research examines the problematization of security and war from the perspective of continental philosophy. He has written extensively on security and war, international political theory, continental philosophy and cultural research – including *Politics of Security: Towards a Political Philosophy of Continental Thought* (Routledge, 2007), *Foucault on Politics, Security and War* (ed. with Andrew Neal, Palgrave Macmillan, 2008), and most recently, *The Liberal Way of War: Killing to Make Life Live* (with Julian Reid, Routledge, 2009).

Myriam Dunn Cavelty is Head of the New Risk Research Unit at the Center for Security Studies, ETH Zurich, and Lecturer in the Department of Social Sciences and Humanities at ETH Zurich, Switzerland. Her recent publications include *Cyber-Security and Threat Politics: US Efforts to Secure the Information Age, Securing the Homeland: Critical Infrastructure, Risk, and (In)Security* (ed. with Kristian Søby Kristensen, Routledge 2009), and *Handbook of Security Studies* (ed. with Victor Mauer, Routledge, 2010).

Stefan Elbe is Reader in the Department of International Relations at the University of Sussex, after holding positions at the University of Essex, the University of Warwick, the International Institute for Strategic Studies, and the London School of Economics, where he also obtained his doctorate in the Department of International Relations.

Emmanuel-Pierre Guittet is Lecturer in Politics at the School of Social Sciences, University of Manchester (UK). He is an Associate Researcher at the Canada Research

ix

LIST OF CONTRIBUTORS

Chair in Security, Identity and Technology of the University of Montreal (Canada), a member of the International Political Sociology section at the International Studies Association (ISA) and a member of the Critical Approach to Security in Europe network (CASE Collective).

John Hart is Head of the SIPRI Chemical and Biological Security Project. He co-edited *Chemical Weapon Destruction in Russia: Political, Legal and Technical Aspects* (Oxford University Press, 1998); and co-authored *Historical Dictionary of Nuclear, Biological and Chemical Warfare* (Scarecrow Press, 2007) and 'WMD inspection and verification regimes: political and technical challenges', in Nathan Busch and Daniel H. Joyner (eds), *Combating Weapons of Mass Destruction: The Future of International Non-Proliferation Policy* (University of Georgia Press, 2009). He is a doctoral candidate in military sciences.

Julien Jeandesboz is a doctoral candidate at Sciences Po on the government of borders in the European Union. He is an Associate Researcher at the Centre d'Études sur les Conflits in Paris and a Researcher in the FP7 integrated programme INEX, as well as a member of the CASE Collective.

Oliver Kessler is Acting Professor for Political Sociology at Bielefeld University. His most recent publications are 'International relations between anarchy and world society: towards a sociology of the international?', *International Political Sociology* (2008) and 'Is risk changing the politics of international legal argumentation?', *Leiden Journal of International Law* (2008).

Keith Krause is Professor of International Politics at the Graduate Institute of International and Development Studies in Geneva, and Director of its Centre for Conflict, Development and Peacebuilding (CCDP). He is also the founder and Programme Director of the Small Arms Survey project, the main source of information and analysis for international public policy on small arms issues, and has jointly edited its annual yearbook since 2001. His current research is concentrated in three areas: the changing character of political violence, concepts of security and state formation and insecurity in the post-colonial world.

Frida Kuhlau is a PhD student at the Centre for Research Ethics and Bioethics at Uppsala University, Sweden. She holds a degree in political science and was previously a research associate in the chemical and biological warfare project at SIPRI. Her recent publications include F. Kuhlau, S. Eriksson, K. Evers, and A. T. Höglund, 'Taking due care: moral obligations in dual use research', *Bioethics*, 22/9 (Nov. 2008).

Mark Lacy is Lecturer of International Politics at Lancaster University. His publications include *Security and Climate Change: International Relations and the Limits of Realism* (Routledge, 2005) and *The Geopolitics of American Insecurity: Terror, Power, and Foreign Policy* (co-edited with Francois Debrix, Routledge, 2009). He is currently working on a project on design and security.

Anna Leander is Professor of International Political Economy at the Copenhagen Business School. She works with sociological approaches to international political economy and international relations and has focused on the security practices. For a list of publications and further information see www.cbs.dk/staff/ale.

Taylor Owen is a doctoral candidate and Trudeau Scholar at the University of Oxford. He was a Post-Graduate Fellow in the Genocide Studies Program at Yale University, has received a MA from the University of British Columbia and has worked at the International Peace Research Institute, the Liu Institute for Global Issues and the International Development Research Center. His work is on the concept and operationalization of human security, the causes and consequences of conflict, and EU, Canadian and US foreign policy.

Mark B. Salter is Associate Professor at the School of Political Studies, University of Ottawa. He is editor of *Politics at the Airport* (University of Minnesota Press, 2008), and *Global Policing and Surveillance: Borders, Security Identity* (Willan Publishing, 2005) with Elia Zureik. He is the sole author of *Rights of Passage: The Passport in International Relations* and *Barbarians and Civilization in International Relations* (Pluto Press, 2002, also published in Chinese). Recent research appears in *Geopolitics, Citizenship Studies, International Political Sociology, Alternatives, Security Dialogue*.

Kristin Bergtora Sandvik is a senior researcher at the PRIO Security Program. Her research is on the socio-legal aspects of humanitarian governance, international organizations and international law in the African Great Lakes region and Southern Sudan. Sandvik received her doctorate for 'On the everyday life of international law: humanitarianism and refugee-resettlement in Kampala' from Harvard Law School in 2008.

Laura J. Shepherd is Lecturer in International Relations at the Department of Political Science and International Studies (POLSIS), University of Birmingham. She teaches and researches in the areas of gender politics, international relations and critical security studies. Recent publications include *Gender, Violence and Security: Discourse as Practice* (Zed Books, 2008), and articles in *International Studies Quarterly*, *Review of International Studies*, *Critical Studies on Terrorism* and *Political Studies Review*.

Rachel Slater works in the Social Protection Programme at the Overseas Development Institute in London where she leads work on food security, social protection and rural growth. Her work on food security sits within a portfolio of research and policy advisory activities encompassing rural and urban livelihoods, social protection and hunger safety nets, and poverty and vulnerability analysis. She has worked extensively in southern and eastern Africa, particularly Lesotho, Zambia, Malawi and Ethiopia, and more recently in South Asia.

William Walters is Professor in the Department of Political Science and the Department of Sociology and Anthropology at Carleton University, Canada. He is author of *Unemployment and Government: Genealogies of the Social* (Cambridge University Press, 2000), co-author of *Governing Europe: Discourse, Governmentality and European Integration* (Routledge, 2005) and co-editor of *Global Governmentality* (Routledge, 2004) along with numerous journal articles and chapters on themes of power, governance, borders and citizenship. He is currently writing a book about Foucault and global politics (Routledge, 2011), and researching the work of standardization in the construction of global security networks.

Cynthia Weber is Professor of International Politics at Lancaster University and co-director of the media company Pato Productions. She is the author of numerous books and articles on sovereignty, intervention, US foreign policy, feminism, post-structuralism and film. She currently has two research projects under way – a critical design and security project called 'New Sciences of Protection: Designing Safe Living' (with Mark

Lacy and Adrian MacKenzie) and a filmmaking/gallery exhibition project called '"I am an American": Video Portraits of Unsafe US Citizens'.

Steve Wiggins is an experienced agricultural economist with interests in rural livelihoods, poverty, food security and nutrition in Africa, Latin America and other parts of the developing world. In food security and nutrition, his work in recent years has concerned the food crisis that broke out in Southern Africa in 2002, nutrition in Bangladesh, and most recently the implications of the 2007–8 spike in international food prices.

David Murakami Wood is Canada Research Chair (Tier 2) Associate Professor of Surveillance Studies in the Department of Sociology, and member of the Surveillance Project, at Queen's University, Canada. He is the Managing Editor of *Surveillance and Society*, and a trustee of the Surveillance Studies Network (SSN). He is currently working on two books: *Global Surveillance Societies* (Palgrave, UK) and *The Watched World* (Rowman & Littlefield, USA).

1

Introduction

J. Peter Burgess

This volume appears just as the dust begins to settle over a period of rich, productive and stimulating transformation in the field of security studies.[1] Since the late 1980s and the receding of the Cold War, a flurry of research and scholarship has nurtured new theoretical positions, generated a treasure trove of new empirical material, and developed new methodologies to unite them. Though there are signs of a levelling-out of this flood of activity, it is unlikely that the evolution of security thinking will diminish. Indeed, much suggests that this vigorous development will continue.

It is therefore a crucial time for stock-taking, a moment to pause and reflect on the newness of this new thinking, its premises and ambitions, its explicit and hidden values, its politics, the continuities and discontinuities with what remains of the Cold War tradition, and the meaning of the apparent transition from the one to the other. It is a milestone where we can ask how the field of security studies has structured itself, how certain methods are naturalized while others remain exotic, how certain theorizations of security crystallize while others resist or wane.

The *Routledge Handbook of New Security Studies* is in this sense not intended as a survey of the latest and greatest in security studies. A number of admirable books currently play this role, and new and coming books will certainly continue to do so. Instead, this book is meant as a contribution to a self-critique of the field of security studies. It is motivated by the principle that the renewal of the field carries with it as many pitfalls as it does creative or productive moments. Like any developing field, its coherence depends on its self-reflection and self-critique.

This volume does not carry out such a critique but instead aims to provide a certain point of departure for doing so. No case for the novelty of New Security Studies will be made here. This work represents neither a school nor a movement, neither theory nor empirical field. Instead of reviewing the major theoretical positions, empirical fields and methodological schools, the volume is organized along four pragmatic or applied axes of security. Instead of trying to account for the approaches and methods of security studies, it is organized and structured according to a number of variables in the way security is enacted, given meaning through its application.

If the rapid evolution in security theory has today calmed somewhat, some scholars see a kind of regression to a new-militarization of the concept, in large part due to the nature of political responses to the attacks of 11 September 2001 (Fierke 2007: 28–9). The canonical positions of post-Cold War security theory are also well-studied. Most begin with the tried and true distinction between theoretical realism and liberalism, the bulwarks of security thinking through most of the twentieth century, formulated in the works of Morgenthau (1948), Bull (1977) and many others, critiqued and developed into a variety of forms of neo-realism and neo-liberalism by even more (Doyle 1997; Keohane 1986; Mearsheimer 2001; Oye 1986; Waltz 1959).

In the late 1980s and 1990s a sea change passed over security theory in general, provoked by the exhaustion and decline of the Cold War bi-polar security complex. During this period conventional theories of security were widely regarded as inadequate to the task of accounting for a new landscape of security issues and actors and a new set or principles began to emerge (Aggestam and Hyde-Price 2000; Alkire 2003; Baldwin 1995, 1997; Booth 2005; Brown 1997; Buzan 1991a; Dalby 1997, 2000; Buzan 1991b; Derian 1993; Dillon 1996; Huysmans 1998; Kaldor 2000; Lipschutz 1995; Rothschild 1995; Tickner 1995; Ullmann 1983; Wæver 1997, 2000; Williams 1994; Wyn Jones 1999). These interventions cover a wide range of concerns, but their uniting theme and interest is a critique of realist and neo-realist perspectives through a radical, linguistically based 'constructivist turn' in which social theories of security, linguistics and performativity become progressively more important to theoretical approaches. In addition, questions of identity and culture are seen as keys to understanding security and to supporting the translatability of security between social and political settings. This expansion also broadens the remit of security and links to nationalism studies, political philosophy and conflict studies.

Much of this scholarship coalesces around the advent of securitization theory that grew out of a research group at the Copenhagen Peace Research Institute in the 1980s and culminated in a number of influential works by Wæver, Buzan and others (Buzan et al. 1990, 1998; Buzan & Wæver 2003; Wæver et al. 1993). Securitization theory is a self-proclaimed 'speech act theory' of security that focuses on the means by which security issues are constructed through language. According to the theory, a given object becomes securitized by virtue of the pronouncement of a securitizing actor, appropriately positioned, permitting it to be shifted from the order of ordinary politics to one kind or another of exceptional politics.

The subjectivization of security through securitization theory has had distinct consequences for the objective side of the security equation. Through applications of this highly subject-oriented theory a number of new objective components of security are revealed. One important consequence of the theory is thus: that it is able to take cognizance of the broader field of security threats. The widening application of securitization theory reveals the process by which new objects of security are constituted. Thus the 'new security objects' discussed in this volume, and others again, are indebted to the realization that the security status of any object is a correlate of its situation within a field of political action, authority and democracy.

It is the aim of this volume to intervene in this evolution by giving it one structured presentation among several possible ones. This presentation does not have the ambition of an exhaustive coverage of themes, methods and objects of the field of security studies. Such a project is neither feasible nor useful. Instead, it organizes a selection of material in the form of four types of strategies for understanding and advancing research on the changing landscape of security and insecurity. These types differentiate and focus on (1) new concepts of security, (2) new subjects of security, (3) new objects of security and (4) new security practices.

New security concepts can be understood as ways of coupling ideas or principles of security with the empirical basis that supports them. They refer to the combinatory possibilities for synthesizing subject positions or perspectives from which security and insecurity is lived or operationalized with new empirical objects or areas of study. The chapters in this section focus on challenges of correlation. They seek to understand objects of security by making sense of how they are conceptualized, and how they are linked to those ideas, actors, institutions, etc., that have an interest in how they play out their positions. They deal with the forces of correlation and the antagonisms mobilized by conflicts between idea and world, high politics and fieldwork. This section includes five analyses all of which reflect the challenge of conceptually correlating subject positions and objects of security, perspectives and empirical scope, actors and fields. 'Civilizational security' (Bowden), 'risk' (Kessler), 'small arms' (Krause), 'critical human security' (Owen) and 'critical geopolitics' (Dalby) all present constellations of security thinking and the surrounding tension between how the empirical world of security is experienced as a heterogeneous challenge to the very principles of that seeing. These chapters, each in their own way, present concepts as unities of the facts they conceptualize and the principles that give them their empirical validity.

New security subjects assemble a range of subjective positions relative to the empirical world of security and insecurity. To evoke the subject of security encompasses not only the perspective of the subject, but its value premises, interests, political valence and its situation in other discourses of security that participate in governing its validity. The collection of new security subjects in this section attempts to account for the changes in subject positions from which security is assessed, asserted and treated, increasingly made between analytic positions and a changing world. The chapters in this section present six subject orientations that have emerged in recent years, giving new and alternative meanings to the security objects that have traditionally been understood according to traditional models. 'Biopolitics' (Dillon), 'gendered security' (Shepherd), 'identity security' (Bilgin), 'security ethics' (Burke), 'financial security' (de Goede), and 'international law and security' (Sandvik) advance analyses that explicitly and implicitly put into question the transparency of the security subject, and document the analytic consequences of intensified focus on the subject position in security analysis.

New security objects assembles a set of studies that document and explore the character of emerging security threats to empirical objects traditionally not considered to be under threat. The six chapters in this section explore the direct and indirect consequences for conceptual analysis of these non-traditional security objects. The contributions, 'environmental security' (Barnett), 'food security' (Slater and Wiggins), 'energy security' (Dannreuther), 'cyber security' (Dunn Cavelty), 'pandemic security' (Elbe) and 'biosecurity' (Kuhlau and Hart), thus confront conventional premises and expectations of status quo security concepts, by suggesting how securitization processes can shift focus to objects outside of conventional approaches.

New security practices gathers a series of chapters illustrating the effects of construing security as practice, as a mode of operation or of implementation of security measures through means that are themselves governed by a variety of structures and drives. In contrast to the three previous sections, which explore security as positions in a subject–object equation, these chapters regard security as a management function with in a logic of governance. These chapters, 'surveillance' (Salter), 'urban security' (Wood), 'privatization of security' (Leander), 'migration' (Walters), 'security technologies' (Guittet and Jeandesboz), 'designing security' (Weber and Lacy), and 'new mobile crime' (den Boer) examine security less as a strategy aimed at ideally erasing insecurity from society than as a project of overseeing and regulating insecurity in society, integrating it into the social system, and administering resources that give it a role in the overall governance of society.

Note

1 The realization of this volume has been supported through the invaluable editorial assistance of Monica Hanssen, Marit Moe-Pryce and Jonas Gräns.

Part I
New Security Concepts

2

Civilizational Security

Brett Bowden

The Idea of Civilization

The idea of civilization occupies a prominent and complicated place in the history of ideas and world history more generally. It has played no small part in shaping history; the demands of civilization have long been employed to describe, explain, rationalize, and justify all manner of interventions and socio-political engineering (Bowden 2009a). The significance of civilization is captured in the suggestion that it is one of a small number of 'essential' ideas intimately linked to the 'whole history of modern thought and the principal intellectual achievements in the western world' (Benveniste 1971: 289). One might add to this claim that, while civilization is a distinctly Western idea, perhaps its greatest impact has been felt in the non-Western world, where much of the aforementioned intervention and socio-political engineering has taken place, particularly since the Spanish 'discovery' and conquest of the New World.

In the context of a century that gave rise to two World Wars, the Great Depression, and the Holocaust, it seemed for a time as though the very idea of civilization might be rendered something of an anachronism. But that was not to be the case, for the end of the Cold War brought with it a revival in the use of the term *civilization* – and its plural, *civilizations* – as tool for describing and explaining a wide range of events and issues in the social and behavioral sciences. Nowhere was this more the case than in politics and international affairs. Given that the term *civilization* has been with us since the mid-eighteenth century, it is noteworthy that it was not until its post-Cold War revival that people began to think explicitly about the concept of civilization in relation to security. The catalyst for this turn in thinking can in large part be attributed to Samuel P. Huntington's provocative article and book in which he developed his version of the clash of civilizations thesis (Huntington 1993a, 1996).

In order to explore the issue of civilizational security and the range of ways in which it is interpreted, it is first helpful to have a good understanding of what civilization means and how it applies to human affairs more generally. This exercise, however, is not as straightforward as one might hope; because from the time it was coined the term *civilization* was imbued with a range of meanings. And in the time since then so much

7

analysis has fallen under the broad umbrella of civilization that it often lacks any specific or readily graspable meaning. This in turn means that civilizational security can be conceived of in a number of distinct ways, as will be explained further below. Serving as something of a 'synthetic' or 'unifying concept', *civilization* is used to describe both a process through which individual human beings and nations became civilized, and the cumulative outcome of that process. As Jean Starobinski states, the 'crucial point is that the use of the term, *civilization*, to describe both the fundamental process of history and the end result of that process established an antithesis between civilization and a hypothetical primordial state (whether it be called nature, savagery, or barbarism)' (Starobinski 1993: 5).

This account suggests that the term *civilization* is used to more than simply describe the civilizing process and the state of civilization that is achieved through that process. It implies that the idea of civilization also has an inherent value-laden or normative quality. Thus, the term and idea of civilization has widely been thought of and applied in two distinct senses. First, it is used to identify and describe what are thought to be quantifiable traits and values held in common by a distinct group of peoples – a civilization. Second, civilization is also a 'normative concept on the basis of which it was possible to discriminate the civilized from the uncivilized, the barbarian, and the incompletely civilized' (ibid. 7–8). These two uses of *civilization* are neatly expressed by Lucien Febvre, who noted that the 'same word is used to designate two different concepts'. Referring to the first sense, Febvre writes:

> In the first case civilization simply refers to all the features that can be observed in the collective life of one human group, embracing their material, intellectual, moral and political life and, there is unfortunately no other word for it, their social life. It has been suggested that this should be called the 'ethnographical' conception of civilization. It does not imply any value judgement on the detail or the overall pattern of the facets examined. Neither does it have any bearing on the individual in the group taken separately, or their personal reactions or individual behaviour. It is above all a conception which refers to a group.
>
> (Febvre 1973: 220)

In this sense *civilization* is said to be largely a 'descriptive and neutral' term that is used to describe specific civilizations such as those of ancient Greece or contemporary Western civilization. Furthermore, it is this sense of the term with which the plural – *civilizations* – has been so readily associated.

Following the ethnographic account of civilization, Febvre offers a second definition of civilization as an ideal or value.

> In the second case, when we are talking about the progress, failures, greatness and weakness of civilization we do have a value judgement in mind. We have the idea that the civilization we are talking about – ours – is itself something great and beautiful; something too which is nobler, more comfortable and better, both morally and materially speaking, than anything outside it – savagery, barbarity or semi-civilization. Finally, we are confident that such civilization, in which we participate, which we propagate, benefit from and popularize, bestows on us all a certain value, prestige, and dignity. For it is a collective asset enjoyed by all civilized societies. It is also an individual privilege which each of us proudly boasts that he possesses.
>
> (Ibid. 220)

While these two definitions appear straightforward enough, as stated above, the idea of civilization (and its plural, civilizations) is complex, and does not readily lend itself to a simple or concise definition. Particularly important here is the fact that Febvre's ethnographic definition of *civilization* is more than just descriptive; it too has an (unacknowledged) normative-evaluative component. The label civilization is not usually used to describe the collective life of just any group, as culture sometimes is; rather, it is reserved for social collectives that demonstrate a degree of urbanization and organization. This normative assumption is evident in that Febvre's ethnographic markers all relate, either directly or indirectly, to a group's socio-political organization (Bowden 2004b). The point to be emphasized here is that the study of civilizations, that is, ethnographic civilizations, cannot be readily divorced from a concern with the normative demands of civilization.

In essence, *civilization* is an 'evaluative-descriptive' term in that it is used both to describe and evaluate; or pass judgement in the very act of describing. In contradistinction to Febvre's supposedly purely ethnographic account of *civilization*, such terms have no neutral reading, they at once describe and evaluate, commend and condemn.[1] This important point is overlooked by Huntington who simply notes, 'To be civilized was good, to be uncivilized was bad.' While he acknowledges that there evolved a distinction between the use of *civilization* and *civilizations*, this is oversimplified to the point that the arrival of the latter marks the 'renunciation of a civilization defined as an ideal, or rather as the ideal' (Huntington 1996: 40–1). But as explained above and as Fernand Braudel notes, the 'triumph' of one over the other 'does not spell disaster' for one or the other, for they are necessarily tied together in 'dialogue' (Braudel 1980: 213).

Civilization and its plural are interrelated terms and subjects of study that have been examined both independently and with reference to one another. An initial concern with the concept of civilization gave way in the nineteenth and twentieth centuries to detailed comparative studies of civilizations, in large part instigated by the foundation and development of the fields of anthropology and ethnography (Spengler 1926–8; Toynbee 1934–61). Such a shift led to claims that a broader concern with the normative-evaluative aspects of civilization had 'lost some of its cachet' (Huntington 1996: 41).[2] The result of this shift was a preoccupation with narrow definitions, such as the suggestion that a 'civilization constitutes a kind of moral milieu encompassing a certain number of nations, each national culture being only a particular form of the whole' (Durkheim and Mauss 1971: 811). This is the conceptualization of civilization that is central to the clash of civilizations thesis that has done so much to get people thinking in terms of civilizations and their respective security requirements, particularly in relation to other civilizations.

One of the leading and most influential exponents of the comparative study of civilizations was the historian, Arnold Toynbee. In his *Study of History* and related works, however, he did not completely set aside the ideal of civilization, for he stated that 'civilizations have come and gone, but Civilization (with a big "C") has succeeded' or endured. That is, while particular civilizations might rise and then fall, other civilizations rise in turn to advance the lot of humankind. So, despite the persistence of war, famine, and pestilence, Civilization keeps 'shambling on' (Toynbee 1948: 24). Toynbee also sought to articulate a link between 'civilizations in the plural and civilization in the singular', noting that the former refers to 'particular historical exemplifications of the abstract idea of civilization'. This abstract idea of civilization is defined in 'spiritual terms', which 'equate civilization with a state of society in which there is a minority of the population, however small, that is free from the task, not merely of producing food, but of engaging in any other of the economic activities – e.g. industry and trade – that have to be carried on to keep the life of the society going on the material plane at the civilizational level' (Toynbee 1972: 44–5). This line of argument concerning the organization of society has long been held in connection with the advancement of civilization. It is found in the work of Thomas Hobbes for instance, for although his life and work preceded the term civilization, it is argued that 'the primary theme of Hobbes' studies in civil history is the distinction between barbarism and civilization' (Hobbes [1651] 1985: 683; Kraynak 1983: 90). Some semblance of this general line of argument has been made time and again throughout history. One of the earliest to do so was Aristotle in *The Politics*, in which he posited that 'society [meaning the *polis* or state] ... contains in itself ... the end and perfection of government: first founded that we might live, but continued that we may live happily' (Aristotle 1912: 3, para. 1252b).[3]

In essence, the idea of civilization can be conceived of as both a process and a destination or state of being; this account of civilization is inextricably linked to the ideal of civilization as a comparative benchmark against which other human collectives are measured and evaluated. These variations on the idea of civilization are important when it comes to distinguishing and articulating the various ways in which civilizational security is conceived, pursued, and threatened.

Civilization and Security

Following on from the range of ways in which the idea of civilization can be conceived, so too civilizational security can be conceptualized in at least three distinct ways, as introduced briefly below and elaborated on in the following sections. First, directly related to the ethnographic account of civilization, or civilizations, civilizational security can be thought of in terms of the stability and security of any given civilization, whether it is Western civilization, Islamic civilization, ancient Greek civilization, or some other recognized civilizational collective. This conceptualization of civilizational security includes both external and internal threats to security. The former includes threats such as other civilizations, as outlined in the clash of civilizations thesis, and as will be explored further below. Internal threats to stability, cohesion, and security are generally associated with long-held ideas of preserving civilizational purity or national-civilizational identity. This is a notion that is long-associated with thinking about racial purity and the dangers of immigration and intermingling. In many societies there exists a long history of opposition to the large-scale influx of migrants who might be seen as posing a threat to cultural homogeneity. To take just one example from the Western world, it has been suggested that, based on the 'fear of civilizational decomposition', the 'immigrant as a security threat to American civilization is again being articulated'. Immigrants who are unable to assimilate are increasingly regarded 'as an ongoing threat that must be contained in the name of national-civilizational security' (Persaud 2002: 77–80).[4] Such thinking has only intensified in the wake of the extremist terrorist threat and the rise of the 'home-grown' terrorist phenomenon.

The second manner in which civilizational security can be conceived relates to the evaluative-normative dimension of civilization. It is perhaps best thought of in terms of the security of sovereignty – state sovereignty in particular – that is conferred on any given collective when it is considered to be civilized or a sovereign member of civilized international society. Historically, those societies, peoples, or other human collectives that have been deemed by the civilized world to be lacking in civilization, that is, those characterized as uncivilized, savage, or barbaric, have been particularly vulnerable to external intervention, even conquest. This has been the case for centuries, from the English domination of its Celtic neighbors in Scotland and Ireland, to the Spanish conquest of the supposedly uncivilized Amerindians of the New World, to the European scramble for Africa in the late nineteenth century. A considerable factor in the justification of such interventions, occupations, and conquests was that they took place under the guise of the burden of civilization. As will be elaborated below, in the twenty-first century, interventions continue to take place in those societies that are deemed to be less than civilized, and hence, less than fully sovereign members of civilized international society.

The third significant way of thinking about civilizational security relates to the survival and ongoing viability of (big C) Civilization in the face of global concerns that potentially threaten the very existence of humankind and other species. At the very least, some of these threats pose serious challenges to our ongoing ways of life, and our capacity to continue to inhabit and exploit planet Earth as we have become so accustomed to. In the recent past, the greatest threats to Civilization have been seen as most likely to come from catastrophic human generated dangers such as nuclear holocaust. More recently, the most serious threats are seen as emerging from less immediate, but no less serious in the medium to longer term, human initiated phenomena such as climate change. Other serious threats to Civilization are posed by a variety of deadly pandemics associated with highly virulent human and trans-species viruses.

1. The Security of Civilizations

In his *Foreign Affairs* article of 1993 in which he introduces his take on the clash of civilizations thesis, Samuel Huntington writes:

> It is my hypothesis that the fundamental source of conflict in this new world will not be primarily ideological or primarily economic. The great divisions among humankind and the dominating source of conflict will be cultural. Nation states will remain the most powerful actors in world affairs, but the principal conflicts of global politics will occur between nations and groups of different civilizations. The clash of civilizations will dominate global politics. The fault lines between civilizations will be the battle lines of the future. Conflict between civilizations will be the latest phase in the evolution of conflict in the modern world.
>
> (Huntington 1993a: 22)

The new world Huntington was referring to was that of the post–Cold War; a world that Francis Fukuyama claimed had witnessed not just 'the passing of a particular period of postwar history, but the end of history as such: that is, the end point of mankind's ideological evolution and the universalization of Western liberal democracy as the final form of human government' (Fukuyama 1989: 4). The airing of Huntington's clash of civilizations thesis was a direct response to the publication of Fukuyama's end of history thesis. As with Fukuyama's response to the end of the Cold War, Huntington's account of the future of world politics generated much interest and debate. Some of the many criticisms leveled at Huntington's thesis concerned his identification of eight or nine distinct civilizations, the constituent parts of those civilizations, and the use of civilizations as a unit level of analysis more generally.[5] Huntington is not the first to go down this particular path. Decades earlier, Arnold Toynbee suggested that when it comes to the study of world history, the most appropriate or sensible units of study are civilizations, not nations, states, or even epochs or periods of time, all of which are prone to lead one to ill-considered or incomplete conclusions (Toynbee 1934–61).[6]

Touching on the topic of civilizational security during the Cold War, Lester B. Pearson has argued, 'In the past all great civilizations have in their periods of growth tended to be expansive – "imperialistic," if you will ... Hitherto the normal relation between such expanding civilizations has been conflict and war, or at best an uneasy truce.' He went on to state, 'We are now emerging into an age when different civilizations will have to learn to live side by side in peaceful interchange, learning from each other, studying each others' history and ideals and art and culture, mutually enriching each other's lives. The alternative, in this crowded little world, is misunderstanding, tension, clash, and catastrophe' (Pearson 1955: 83–4). In reference to Pearson's observations, Huntington wrote in *The Clash of Civilizations*:

> The futures of both peace and Civilization depend upon understanding and cooperation among the political, spiritual, and intellectual leaders of the world's major civilizations. In the clash of civilizations, Europe and America will hang together or hang separately. In the greater clash, the global 'real clash', between Civilization and barbarism, the world's great civilizations, with their rich accomplishments in religion, art, literature, philosophy, science, technology, morality, and compassion, will also hang together or hang separately. In the emerging era, clashes of civilizations are the greatest threat to world peace, and an international order based on civilizations is the surest safeguard against world war.
>
> (Huntington 1996: 321)

The interest the clash of civilizations thesis generated in respect to civilizational security was reinvigorated with the terrorist attacks of September 11, 2001 on New York and Washington DC, and subsequent terrorist attacks in London, Madrid, and elsewhere.[7] These terrorist attacks also generated considerable discussion and debate in relation to Huntington's speculations about the 'real clash' between Civilization and barbarism. For instance, in a speech to the Congress on September 20, 2001, United States President George W. Bush stated, 'Every nation, in every region, now has a decision to make. Either you are with us, or you are with the terrorists.' He further declared that the terrorists responsible for the attacks on New York and Washington were 'the heirs of all murderous ideologies of the twentieth century ... they follow in the path of fascism, and Nazism, and totalitarianism'. Bush went on to cast the war as a 'fight *for* civilization'. He confidently added that 'the civilized world is rallying to America's side' (Bush 2001).[8] As will become clear in the following section, this notion of civilizational security in face of the threat of barbarism is closely linked to the discussion of the security afforded to those societies classified as civilized.

2. The Security that Comes With Civilization

The version of civilizational security discussed immediately above can be best thought of as evolving out of the ethnographic conception of civilizations already described, that is, the idea that there exists a plurality of civilizations. As suggested at the end of the preceding section, closely related to this is the idea of civilization as a benchmark or ideal, which informs another aspect of civilizational security. Throughout much of our history, particularly since the evolution and expansion of the Westphalian states system, our world has been divided between a sphere of civilized international society made up of fully sovereign states, and a less than civilized cacophony of barely legitimate quasi-states.[9] Between the extremes of civility and chaotic savagery, and the barbarism of terrorists for that matter, are a range of states that occupy intermediate positions on the scale; some developing ever-more characteristics and institutions that are the hallmark of fully civilized states, others sliding further away from the civilized ideal model. Those deemed as occupying the uncivilized end of the scale are said to have failed the test of modernity in that they are seen as collapsed states, rogue states, or something in between or approaching one of these conditions. These states and societies lack or are denied the security of civilization in that they fall short of meeting the standards of civilization required for the granting of absolute sovereignty by the full and sovereign members of the international society of states. One of the consequences of the construction of the uncivilized other, who is at once both subject to international law's sanction but deprived of any real measure of protection afforded by it is that it 'creates an object against which sovereignty may express its fullest powers by engaging in an unmediated and unqualified violence which is justified as leading to conversion, salvation, civilization' (Anghie 1996: 332–3).

The so-called civilizational confrontations (Gong 1984) and the consequences that flowed from them were not meetings between equal sovereigns; rather, they were between the sovereign states of Europe and the non-sovereign or quasi-sovereign Amerindians and other indigenous peoples of the world. Once it was determined that these newly discovered peoples lacked civilization and thus lacked sovereignty, it was almost inevitable that European international law would create for itself 'the grand redeeming project of bringing the marginalized into the realm of sovereignty, civilizing the uncivilized and developing the juridical techniques and institutions necessary for this great mission'. As a critical concept both entrenched in, and as a tool for extending international law's ambit, the standard of civilization 'is mired in this history of subordinating and extinguishing alien cultures' (Anghie 1996: 333)[10] by way of violent civilizing missions that were intended to civilize the uncivilized.

In the colonial era, the classical standard of civilization was associated with a tendency to intervene in the uncivilized world; to conquer and colonize it, to coax and train it toward civilization. More recently, the existence of uncivilized states has not always been a pressing concern for the security of broader international society. So long as they posed no immediate threat they could be isolated, or at least kept at arm's-length, and presented a problem only for themselves. But this was a short-lived exception to the long-standing general rule, for the terrorist attacks of September 11, 2001 and the ongoing threat of terrorism have had dramatic ramifications. Once again a similar interventionist tendency has taken hold; and once again, as outlined above, the language of civilization and barbarism is a prominent force behind the justifying rationale of such foreign policies in the name of security. The fleeting deference to political correctness has been passed over as troubled states are again seen as posing a threat to the security of civilized states, in part because of what they are, but more so because of what they might harbor, the primary concern being terrorists and other rogue elements.

For some commentators on international affairs, the drawing of a line between these worlds is an exercise in normative theory, but this is also how international politics effectively works in practise. Given that such divisions persist, this means that aspects of contemporary world politics inevitably continue to be regulated by contemporary standards of civilization; employing much of the same language to bar membership, deny sovereignty, and justify intervention. This intervention, ranging from humanitarian intervention to pre-emptive and preventative war is undertaken with the aim of extending civilization to those societies that are deemed less than civilized by modern standards of economic civilization, legal civilization, cultural civilization, and socio-political civilization (Bowden 2005).

3. The Security of Civilization

As the aforementioned aspects of civilizational security have touched on, there is also a greater concern about threats to the security of (big C) Civilization. That is, threats to the ongoing viability of all humankind along with the other occupants and systems of life that share planet Earth. As to whether threats such as extremist terrorism fall under this category and pose a serious threat to Civilization, or even Western civilization, as some have hinted, is highly debatable. And few are likely to argue vigorously that this is the case. But there does exist a range of other threats that are increasingly seen as posing a serious danger to Civilization. Some of these are existential, such as the threat posed by near Earth objects that are closely monitored by NASA. Such scenarios have often been played out by Hollywood to dramatic effect.

Other threats not just to civilizations but to Civilization that are more within the bounds of human control include the threat and fear of nuclear holocaust (United States Congress 1979). This was particularly the case during the Cold War when the United States' nuclear arsenal reached as high as about 30,000 warheads in the mid-1960s, while the Soviet Union's arsenal peaked at around 40,000 warheads during the 1980s. As many have observed, this represents enough firepower to more than guarantee nuclear annihilation. The *Bulletin of the Atomic Scientists* determines and sets the risk of such a scenario through its Doomsday Clock, which in 2007 was advanced from 7 minutes to midnight to 5 minutes to midnight. This is the closest we have come to midnight since 1984, when two-way communications between the two superpowers, the United States and the Soviet Union, practically came to a halt, resulting in the clock being set at 3 minutes to midnight. The riskiest moment prior to that was in 1953 in the early years of the Cold War when the clock was set at 2 minutes to midnight (www.thebulletin.org, May 2009). While the threat of nuclear holocaust might have diminished somewhat with the end of the Cold War, the general concern persists into the twenty-first century. Today there are concerns about renewed regional arms races and the dangers posed by rogue regimes and non-state actors that are seeking to acquire nuclear weapons capabilities.

The Doomsday Clock now also includes considerations of climate change and biosecurity; two emerging and pressing concerns that are increasingly seen as threats to Civilization and the viability of maintaining certain ways of life. The impacts associated with climate change are many and varied. They include melting ice and rising sea levels, variations in air and sea temperatures, extended periods of drought in some parts of the world while others experience increased rainfall and flooding, and increasing frequency of extreme weather phenomena, just to name a few. These in turn impact on our capacity to continue to inhabit certain parts of Earth and our capacity to continue to utilize and exploit resources as we have done for centuries. Shortages of essential resources such as food, water, and energy in turn bring with them another set of security issues (Homer-Dixon 1991, 1994, 2001). As no country or region of the world is immune to the impacts of climate change, it is seen as a serious threat to the way of life of virtually every inhabitant of Earth. And thus it is deemed as a serious threat to the economic, physical, and general security and sustainability of Civilization, as is evidenced by Maurice F. Strong's statement to the United States' Senate Committee on the Environment in July 2002:

> All people and nations have in the past been willing to accord high priority to the measures required for their own security. We must give the same kind of priority to civilizational security and sustainability. This will take a major shift in the current political mind-set. If this seems unrealistic in today's political context we should recall that history demonstrates that what seems unrealistic today becomes inevitable tomorrow.
>
> (Strong 2002, http://epw.senate.gov)

Throughout history, the health and general well-being of significant populations in various parts of the world have been threatened by flu pandemics and major outbreaks of disease. The Black Death or the Black Plague of the fourteenth century, which is estimated to have killed as many as 75 million people (or more according to some estimates) worldwide is a particularly prominent example (Benedictow 2004). More recently, the Spanish Flu pandemic of 1918 is estimated to have infected half of the world's population and been responsible for as many as 50 million deaths (Potter 2001). In the increasingly connected and globalized world of the twenty-first century, a new yet similar range of biosecurity threats abound. Recent outbreaks of Severe Acute Respiratory Syndrome, or SARS, and avian influenza, or bird flu, particularly highly pathogenic strains that can potentially cross species, have given us a hint of how rapidly biosecurity threats can spread around the world. These are just a few of the known pathogens that have the potential to spread far and wide to virtually every corner of the globe. Similar to the effects of climate change, it is near impossible for any nation or part of the world to shut itself off from such threats; migratory birds do not abide by geopolitical boundaries. The impact of HIV/AIDS, which has claimed more than 25 million lives since it was first recognized, including as many as 2 million in 2007, is a good indicator of the devastating impact that pandemics can have on the social infrastructure and general well-being of certain states (Hunter 2003; UNAIDS 2007). Given the potentially devastating worldwide impact of pandemics in a worst case scenario, such biosecurity threats are increasingly treated by state and international authorities as a genuine threat to civilizational security.[11]

Conclusion

As outlined above, the idea of civilization can be conceived or interpreted in a number of different ways. This in turn has led to civilizational security being conceptualized in a range of different ways from a range of different perspectives. Generally speaking, the explicit concept of civilizational security is relatively new, really only surfacing following the rise of interest in the clash of civilizations thesis following the end of the Cold War. Throughout history, it is unlikely that many people have actually thought in terms of civilizational identity, civilizational loyalty, or civilizational belonging. As such, civilizational security is not something that one often personally contemplates. Instead, humans have been more likely or more inclined to think in terms of personal security, including physical, emotional, economic, or some other aspect of our individual security needs.

When we come to think in terms of the security of a collective, we are more likely to think first about family, or the various other communities or smaller social collectives to which we belong. Included among these are collectives such as our workplace and colleagues, ethnic and religious affiliations, and other such social groups. The largest, most obvious, and most widely discussed socio-political collective in terms of security, is the collective security of the citizens of the nation to which we belong – that is, traditional state security. Rarely do humans think first of themselves as members of this or that civilization; our daily circumstances simply do not promote such thinking, we tend to move in far smaller circles and operate on a much lower level of affiliation. Furthermore, it would be a rare circumstance in which people have thought of their own personal security in relation to or as being immediately dependent on the security of the civilization (or civilizations) to which they might belong. And it is probably even rarer that we think of our own security and that of friends and loved ones in terms of the security of big C Civilization. That said, given the range of new and emerging threats and dangers that are facing all of the inhabitants of Earth and the ecosystems of which we are a part, thinking and strategizing in terms of Civilizational security has become a necessity.

Notes

1 On 'evaluative-descriptive' terms, see Skinner 1999: 61; 1988: 122.
2 Important exceptions include work on standards of civilization, of which, two of the earliest are Schwarzenberger 1955: 212–34; and Gong 1984. See also Bowden 2009b: vols 2–3.
3 For more on the concept of civilization, see the range of sources compiled in Bowden 2009b: vol. 1.
4 See for instance Huntington 2004a: 30–45; 2004b.
5 Some prominent critiques include Said 2001: 11–14; Sen 2006.
6 See Toynbee 1934–61. Across history, Toynbee identified 21 distinct civilizations and a further 5 'arrested' or 'abortive' civilizations.
7 See for instance Scruton 2002. Similar terminology to the 'West and the rest' was used much earlier by the anthropologist Marshall Sahlins, and the historian Arnold J. Toynbee, see esp. Toynbee 1953.
8 On this issue, see Bowden 2007.
9 For a discussion of quasi-states post-Second World War, see Jackson 1993.
10 For more on standards of civilization, see Bowden 2004a.
11 For a general review of the issues, see Fidler 2004. See also Siegel 2006. See also Greenfeld 2006 and Abraham 2007.

3

Risk

Oliver Kessler

Introduction

When Ned Lebow *et al.* (1994) argued 'we all lost the cold war', they showed that well established theories based on balance of power, MAD, and instrumental rationality were simply inadequate to grasp the end of the Cold War – and were potentially even less useful to understand the things to come. A point that increasingly became evident with the global implementation of 'precautionary' and 'pre-emptive' security measures in the aftermath of 9/11: the resulting 'war on terror' cannot be confined to states' practices without excluding some of its crucial aspects, rendering a confinement of security studies to states' transaction and military conduct highly problematic. At this point, the notion of risk became attractive to describe security practices in our post-national era (Aradau *et al.* 2008; Huysmans and Tsoukala 2008). While 'security' points to dangers located 'between' states, risk irremediably leaves behind the confines of the state system to point to global and transnational threats like diseases or the pollution and destruction of the environment. Risk applied to security thus emphasizes a shift in the formation of security policies: not the avoidance of threats or the deterrence of enemies but the management of risks constitutes the specific rationale, defines current operations, and provides the background for future development of technology and strategies (Daase and Kessler 2007). Risk shows that threats are increasingly transnationalized and privatized, embedded in global financial structures and answered by new illiberal practices challenging the private–public and national–international distinction. Of course, that does not mean that states are to vanish or are about to become unimportant, but that the stories one could tell with sovereignty alone become increasingly limited.

Despite this overall interest and burgeoning literature referring to risk, this contribution argues that in fact there is no 'risk' approach to security studies. This might seem to be an odd point to make given that this contribution is supposed to be all about risk. However, risk is a contested concept that takes on different meaning in different contexts and is by itself meaningless. Looking at the semantic field and the changing significations, the debate appears to be more about different notions of uncertainty, probability and contingency than about risk in itself. Although the notion of risk is certainly widely used, it is the counter-concept, the concept that risk is differentiated from, that does the explaining. What the current interest in risk *does* highlight, however, is a systemic shift within the world polity challenging established dogmas rooted in an individualistic philosophy of science and thereby calling for a different understanding of how the world is (made) known. It calls for a different vocabulary detached from the state and thus changes the way we read, write and do security.

This contribution is divided in two parts. The first part provides an overview to different approaches to risk and their basic propositions. It points to the work of Beck, Foucault and Luhmann to argue that the risk approach is actually more about contingency, uncertainty and probability than about 'risk' itself. The second part asks for the social presupposition of the use of risk for understanding security and argues that these presuppositions can be found in the changing reproduction process of contingency. Taking this systemic shift as a vantage point, this part then highlights three sites of changes associated with the risk approach: a semantic shift in our political vocabulary, the emergence of new actors and redefinition of already established actors, and changing practices of security partially based on a changing temporality of security politics.[1]

Risk, Uncertainty and the Social Construction of Danger

The notion of risk has entered the field of security studies by three different approaches: via Beck's notion of risk society (Beck 2002, 2003, 2007), via Foucault's notion of 'dispositif' (Aradau and van Munster 2007; Lobo-Guerrero 2007, 2008; Neal 2004), and via contributions inspired by Niklas Luhmann's autopoietic systems theory (Daase and Kessler 2007; Kessler and Werner 2008; Petersen 2008a, b). In this part I will first outline the basic propositions of these three approaches before in a second step I highlight the maybe unnoticed importance of uncertainty.

What is today characterized as post-industrial, post-colonial, post-modern and post-Fordist is for Beck nothing less than the transformation from the industrial into risk society. The differences between industrial and risk society touch upon the most basic assumptions about social reality. Industrial society is characterized by its modern convictions of progress, linearity and the controllability of both nature and social systems that were cemented in modern societal institutions and practices. Yet just as modernity dissolved the agricultural, hierarchical and class-defined society to pave the way for industrial society, the modernization of the industrial society dissolves the confines of the industrial society itself and, by continuing the project of modernity, creates and forms the new risk society where previous held convictions are unmasked as unjustified beliefs (Beck 1992: 14). Risk society requires us to rethink science, technological progress and the political project of the nation state.

With the terrorist attacks of 9/11, Beck shifted the focus from his original thesis by proclaiming the emergence of a *world* risk society. The world risk society differs from his previous 'model' in at least three respects.[2] First, it is characterized by its temporality. Not the presence but the *anticipation* of possible risks provides the rationale for counter-measures: the mere possibility of risks such as for example a terrorist attack, cancer from genetically modified food or flooded cities due to the meltdown of the polar regions feed back on present decision-making and puts the present in the 'conditional tense' (Beck 2007: 62; see also Elbe 2008b). It's the anticipation of some risk that challenges the spatial and temporal conditions of world society. While a terrorist attack is a spatially and temporally bounded incident, the anticipation and the prevention of it transform the risk into a global 'beginning without an end' (Beck 2007: 62).

Second, the world risk society develops further the distinction of risk and danger that has a somewhat longer trajectory in the sociology of risk (Douglas and Wildavsky 1982). For Beck, and quite different to other scholars, risk and danger stand in opposition to each other: the larger risks are, the more they become uninsurable. While an insurance company can cover the cost of a potential car accident, it cannot pay for the consequences of life extinction or a nuclear catastrophe. That is – the larger the risk, the more 'controllable' risks become indistinguishable from uncontrollable dangers. In this sense, global risks such as terrorism are per se uncontrollable, dislocated and a 'beginning without an end'. But that does not mean that they are beyond politics. Quite to the contrary: they demand states to transform 'fortuna of the classical political theory and that is not controllable by politics into virtue, for whom political instruments and institutions need to be invented' (Beck 2007: 85). States then embrace and implement anticipatory and preventive measures to provide the image of control where there is none.

Third, the world risk society emphasizes the role of non-knowledge.[3] Non-knowledge for Beck takes on different forms and ranges from a not-wanted-to-be known over the outer-limits of knowledge to the non-knowledge unknown to us, the unknown unknown (ibid. 231). The consequences of non-knowledge are twofold. On the one hand, it constitutes a cosmopolitan moment as it requires acknowledging the otherness of different perspectives, cultures and interpretations. On the other hand, it is non-knowledge in the form of unintentional consequences of individual and institutional decisions that ultimately feeds back on society and brings risk society about. Non-knowledge gives rise to a societal struggle over the very definition of risks that becomes indistinguishable from the reality of those risks themselves. This struggle ranges from the definition of potential harm, the identification of causal chains, the proof of evidence and the determination of some possible compensation. What risks 'are' are thus result from specific modes of knowledge and non-knowledge inscribed in their definition. This struggle in other words holds the same position as the mode of production in the industrial society: in both cases, they establish power relationships.

At this point, it is interesting to note that it is *uncertainty* that creates these 'regimes of non-knowledge'. As just mentioned, while global risks are uncontrollable, states are not released from their responsibility of addressing them. Yet insofar as states do act, they counterfactually presuppose a control over risks even when the classical policy measures fail. What has changed, according to Beck, is the uncertain environment within which states have to act. It is the social force of uncertainty that does not allow states to just sit and wait irrespective of whether such an action improves or worsens the actual conditions. Global risks need to get a face in order to re-establish ontological security that was lost when one of the foundations of security calculus, actor, intention, potential, became unknown (ibid. 83, 85).

At the same time, the notion of uncertainty Beck invokes is actor-centric in the sense that risks require decisions and actors who make those decisions when faced with risks. Indeed, Beck subscribes to a notion of inter-subjectivity where states and other social actors engage in a struggle over a definition of risks. But these actors are prior to their interactions. Risks exist between actors when they define and formulate expectations under uncertainty. Even more, the ontological status of risk and uncertainty remains unclear. Although Beck argues that risks are indistinguishable from their definition, the actors' expectations and anticipations refer to an objectively existing risk: the risk of a terrorist threat does exist and even though there are different definitions of causal chains, possible compensation, etc., it is the risk that produces the force to redefine the basic contours of world society.

Risk as Dispositif

A different approach is proposed by scholars inspired by Michael Foucault where the war on terror introduces risk as a new *dispositif* of security politics (Foucault 1976). The term *dispositif* refers to the ways in which a 'heterogeneous ensemble consisting of discourses, institutions, architectural forms, regulatory decisions, laws, administrative measures, scientific statements, philosophical, moral and philanthropic propositions' (Foucault 1977c: 194) is configured and assembled into a specific 'apparatus' or 'gaze' and reproduced by both discursive and non-discursive practices (also Aradau and van Munster 2007: 97). However, while the notion of *dispositif* points to the production of subjectivity by a network of statements and the creation and formation of objects, it points to more than just the episteme of historically specific truth regimes: the *dispositif* is an apparatus of power interweaving what is said and what is not said (Foucault 1977b: 300). It captures the discursive and non-discursive practices by highlighting the ways in which populations, institutions and places are made by disciplining bodies. In this setting, risk is not a thing or cognitive capacity subject to rational decision, but a heterogeneous, contradicting and constantly changing set of discursive and non-discursive practices (Dillon and Lobo-Guerrero 2008). Risk shifts the boundary between the sayable and unsayable and between the visible and invisible. It creates new heterotopias such as Guantanamo and new utopian political projects (Neal 2004).

These ideas have been applied, for example, by Aradau and van Munster in their analysis of the impact of precautionary measures on the relationship between the present and the future and the ways in which this relationship is controlled (Aradau and von Munster 2007, 2008). They thereby criticize Beck's view on an assumed inability to insure and calculate risks: Beck would thereby neglect the politics and lobbying of the insurance companies leading to the Terrorism Risk Insurance Act (TRIA). This Act effectively provided a temporary bail out as catastrophic risks are actually insured by insurer and reinsurer. Risks are thus not beyond control by proclaiming their incalculability signed in the U.S federal law, but made subject to the art of governance (Aradau and Munster 2007: 97); Lobo-Guerrero 2008). Furthermore, holding on to a realist ontology, Beck would underestimate the constructedness and thus political contestation over risks. Through an assemblage of material and discursive elements risk enact actors and is therefore not just a characteristic of our society, but 'ordering our world through managing social problems and surveying populations' (Beck 2007: 97). In particular the employment of precautionary measures acting on the 'limits' of knowledge or probably even beyond knowledge, allow for the governance of the unknown. Precautionary risk is based on four rationalities: zero risk, worst case scenario, shifting the burden of proof and serious and irreversible damage – replacing traditional rationalities of risk insurance (risk identification, risk reduction and risk management) (ibid. 102; also Daase and Kessler 2007). As a result, the 'global risks' are divided and controlled by proactive security policies, surveillance of populations and movements (or circulations).

It is interesting to note, though far from being accidental, that also in Aradau and van Munster's discussion on precautionary measures, it is the notion of uncertainty that redefines security measures. As they argue:

precautionary risk introduces within the computation of the future its very limit, the finity of uncertainty and potential damage. It is therefore exactly the opposite of prudence. If the latter recommended what 'precautions' to take under conditions of knowledge, the former demands that we act under scientific and causal uncertainty.

(Aradau and van Munster 2007: 101)

It is this uncertainty beyond secure knowledge that makes terrorism a '"risk beyond risk", of which we do not have, nor cannot have, the knowledge or the measure' (ibid. 102). Precaution addresses the uncertain, the unknown we try to prevent. The precautionary principle works at the boundary of risk and uncertainty and is not just a change within the notion of 'risk' itself. And as this reference to 'beyond measure' indicates, uncertainty signifies a realm where rationalism breaks down but where we try to impute rational calculus.

Risk as Mode of Observation

A third avenue to the 'risk and security' *problématique* derives from Luhmann's radical constructivist rewriting of systems theory.[4] Of course, this is not the place to engage in a lengthy discussion on systems theory, but it might be sufficient to highlight that systems are not things in an ontological sense, but only constituted and reproduced by the observation and use of distinctions inscribed in communication. Systems exist only in their continuation, in the moment of the constantly reproducing connectivity of the present to a possible future communication.

Insofar as systems operate by the continuing enactment of distinctions, risk has no existence outside of communication. Risk is neither a psychological attribute nor some ontological sequence. There 'is' no 'risk' that could execute force on the nation state or that somehow demands states to act in a certain way. Rather, risk is a mode of observation based on specific distinctions. As every 'thing' or unity results from temporary condensation of meaning using and reproducing distinctions, the meaning of words and concept is not located 'inside' but 'between' concepts. This includes the very term of risk itself. The notion of risk in itself is meaningless until it is separated from and differentiated from counter-concepts. One cannot simply observe risk without at the same time differentiating it from something else. To know what risk 'is' or what it 'does', one cannot simply look at it but needs to reconstruct the hidden and (in)visible semantic distinctions. And it is this setting apart that gives meaning to risk.

In this sense, whatever distinction one chooses to start with, risk remains an ascription and a specific mode of observation that creates and performs its own reality (also MacKenzie 2006). From this perspective, risk is not simply a form of knowledge or some material force or necessity, but equally characterized by our non-knowledge. Risk marks the boundary between knowledge and non-knowledge and the way in which this boundary might be made known. At the same time, this boundary between knowledge and non-knowledge and the knowledge about our non-knowledge are of a different kind than simply the knowledge of some fact. The question can only be what the use of risk *does* and what societal preconditions a specific use of this semantic there are – and not what risk 'is' in an ontological sense. The notion and its use inevitably rest and reproduce societal meaning structures concerning the social, time and reality that are inscribed in the connectivity of communications.

This opens the way to see risk embedded in and reproduced by a multiplicity of overlapping and conflicting discourses. What the risk of 'pollution' means is different in each functional system such as law, health, economy, religion, etc. Each system, based on its own rules of significations, sense-making and logic, reconstructs and endows risk with a different meaning. The societal observation of some risk, for example of a terrorist attack, then presents itself a flux of contradictions and a multiplicity of logics simultaneously at play.

Exactly this multiplicity or polycontextuality of risk instantly refers back to a constitutive uncertainty. As every discourse reconstructs some assumed 'objective' risks in its own terms and logic, uncertainty refers to the specific way in which communication is connected. It is not simply some residual category, but the constantly reproduction of uncertainty absorption and production provides the space of *the possible* where variety and evolution of communication and its semantics forms become possible. Uncertainty is always reduced to risk by social systems (i.e. by processes of categorization, world disclosure, interpretation and observation, etc.) thereby producing new internal contingencies and uncertainties in the form of other excluded alternatives, other possible worlds and perspectives that always makes one's own position contingent and fluid. Uncertainty is the noise allowing the construction of order that depends on forms of social differentiation.

Having argued that the risk approach to security studies could equally be called the 'uncertainty' approach, one could instantly wonder why then there is so much noise about risk these days when uncertainty is a well-known concept in 'traditional' approaches to security anyway. As I will argue in the second section, the notion of uncertainty used by risk approaches differs fundamentally from the one we are acquainted with in international relations (IR) with important theoretical and methodological consequences.

Uncertainty and Risk

The last section has argued that, within the risk approach, it is more the notion of uncertainty than the notion of risk itself that signifies the current changes. At the same time, the notion of uncertainty in itself hardly justifies current interests as it has a long trajectory in IR. Decades ago Hans Morgenthau emphasized the 'uncertainty' of the balance of power warning for overconfidence in our scientific concepts (Morgenthau 1948: 223ff.) and John Herz referred to a structural uncertainty when he noted that: 'no one can ever feel entirely secure in such a world of competing unity, power competition ensures, and the vicious circle of security and power accumulation is on' (Herz 1950: 157). IR as a discipline is almost founded upon the conviction that the international is characterized by the lack of a fixed set of signs, giving rise to uncertainty about the motives or intentions of other states. Under conditions of uncertainty, there is no 'absolute' security and attempts to 'maximize' security can lead to negative feedbacks, with everybody worse off (see in particular Jervis 1978).

Yet, as the common representation of uncertainty in terms of the security dilemma and operationalization by game and contract theoretical models reveals, the notion of uncertainty used in 'security studies' is deeply embedded in a positivist philosophy of science. Uncertainty neither challenges the imperatives of instrumental rationality, nor has it any epistemological connotation. Uncertainty exists only within given games and logically prior to any interaction. The categories and rules of the game remain, thus allowing for change only within the confines of given categories and games.

To capture the relevance of risk and uncertainty for contemporary security practices, it is therefore necessary to leave behind the positivist notion of uncertainty where uncertainty is always equated with and squeezed into the paradigm of 'risk' decisions. At this point, the distinction of uncertainty and risk as introduced by Knight and Keynes shows some promise (Keynes 1937; Knight 1921). In situations of genuine uncertainty, we need to answer the question 'what is the case', pointing to questions of world making and world disclosure where we first have to ask ourselves in what game and in what model we actually are. This knowledge is fundamentally different from comparing costs and benefits *within a model* simply because these categories do not have any meaning until epistemological questions are settled. The kind of knowledge that Keynes or Knight therefore envisage is not to be found in propositions, laws and theories, but the ability to follow rules or what Polanyi called the knowing-*how*. This knowing-*how*, in contrast to the knowing-*that,* points to underlying social norms and conventions allowing for interactions and the *construction* of probabilistic knowledge.

Focusing on genuine uncertainty indicates that our knowledge, models and ideas bring reality about, that knowledge is not simply a passive insight or a mirror of reality but always part of the social world. Not only what we know but also what we do not know are 'socially' constructed. Non-knowledge and the knowledge about our non-knowledge is of a different kind than the knowledge 'about' the world, opening the space for a different logic that breaks free from the identity principle, its hierarchical relationship of sentences and quest for some foundation, and embraces paradoxes, contradictions and a plurality of worlds.

Starting therefore from a completely different concept of knowledge, the 'uncertainty as risk' and 'uncertainty vs. risk' approaches differ in their understanding of *contingency*. For the positivist 'uncertainty as risk' approach, contingency is a *natural* product like the drawing of some variable or the result of a lottery while for the 'risk vs. uncertainty' *contingency* is a *social* product. Genuine uncertainty is reduced by 'technologies' of risk management and disciplinary rationalities and in the moment of uncertainty reduction, new contingencies and new uncertainties are produced generating the realm for new contingencies.

From this perspective, the current interest in risk as an approach to security studies has three legs: a redefined concept of (not) knowing (knowledge as practice), an abandonment of a positivist philosophy of science and methodologies, and the identification of a *redefined production of social contingency*.[5] I assume that this reference to a *systemic shift* may also explain *why* the work of Ulrich Beck, Michel Foucault and Niklas Luhmann attracts attention. Despite their fundamental differences, they all have in common this reference to some 'systemic' shift. For Ulrich Beck, for example, the terrorist attacks have led to a 'death of distance' and a silence of words that do not capture today's reality: 'the difference between war and peace, the military and police, war and crime, and national and international security are, from within and without, completely annulled' (Beck 2007: 255). Writings inspired by Foucault use risk to highlight new technologies of self, new inclusion and exclusion mechanisms reproduced by a (redefined) set of discursive and non-discursive practices. A discursive shift that produces new political spaces (heterotopias and utopias) and new discursive practices as represented for example by the precautionary principle. Writings inspired by Niklas Luhmann argue that the shift from 'security' to 'risk' represents a shift in the social differentiation, i.e. a functional differentiation, of world society where discourses alter their constitutive boundaries. The shift alters the very relation between the political, the economic and the law and thereby goes beyond the image of a 'broadening' of the security concept. In the end then, it is the systemic shift and not the existence of some objective 'risk' that a risk approach to security highlights.

This raises a further conceptual problem that I think these attempts all struggle with: how can the systemic shift be described? How can this newness be apprehended without losing it right away by squeezing it into well-known concepts? What kind of vocabulary do we need? On the one hand, as all three 'avenues' highlight, the war on terror for example addresses genuinely inter-subjective phenomena that are beyond the individual calculus or 'rational' choice. On the other hand, our political vocabulary of sovereignty, security, interests instantly point back to the state as an autonomous actor where the inter-subjective is ultimately reduced to the subjective level. It is this de-coupling of the political vocabulary from the state in order to capture the de-coupling from 'the political' from the state that the risk approach tries to achieve. A point to which I will turn now.

The Saying and Doing of Security

The terrorist attacks of 9/11 are widely perceived to be neither crime nor an act or aggression that by itself could trigger the law of war. It was not a private act, but nor was it just something that happened between public actors. Terrorist networks might have supporters but not a constituency, they might have camps but no embassy, they might have spokespersons sending video messages, but no addresses where a protest note could be sent. Of course, terrorism itself is a long-known phenomenon and would by itself not raise that many eyebrows. However, the meaning transnational terrorism and the 'war on terror' acquired does challenge some 'traditional' convictions. This feeds back to the meaning we ascribe to our political concepts such as the state, sovereignty and the concept of security itself.

The notion of security in international relations is tightly connected to the nation state and used to point to an existential threat, a state of exception set apart and differentiated from everyday life of the state's citizens. Risk on the other hand is all about the control, management and shape of everyday practices, the routinization and normalization of the 'exception' (Bigo 2002; Neal 2004). It transforms contingency into a calculative practice where security is transformed from a public into a private good (Leander 2005a). As a result, security is commodified and transformed into a business, a product that can be produced by private companies not by reducing but by managing and controlling contingency. With the commodification comes the idea that private military companies (PMCs) are the more efficient and appropriate actors augmenting the neo-liberal governmentality to security provision where demand can be 'generated' by marketing strategies and 'positioning' in the market. 'As such, security becomes increasingly a question of the right technical solutions, and not a question of justice or social and political reform' (Abrahamsen and Williams 2007: 135).

The management of risk is big business: Risk allows the hedging, spread and even the deliberate exposure to security threats and catastrophic events by buying or selling risks over the capital market by issuing bonds and derivatives. In the end, with the rise of the private sector in security provision, the state has lost its pivotal role in interpreting data. While the state was the key authority for security concerns, risk points to a transnationally organized discourse, shaped by a multitude of rationalities including insurance companies, banks, hedge funds, private business (Aradau and van Munster 2008; Peterson 2008b).

These changes are not simply a shift from 'the state' towards the market, but highlight the different rules of formation and correlation, a redefining constellation between these various discourses, where for example international law is increasingly used not to restrain but to legitimate violence and has a hard time to regulate these private actors and businesses (Kessler and Werner 2008).

Risk changes not only the social dimension, but the temporality of world politics as well. Risk shows how security practices turn from a reactive towards preventive and proactive measures managing not the actuality but the potentiality of some 'risk'. Consequently, new methods like scenario planning or targeted sanctions are invoked to provide meaning to an open future. Third, risk changes the 'factual dimension' as risk reaches beyond state boundaries towards everyday life (Dillon and Lobo-Guerrero 2008; Dillon and Neal 2008; Lobo-Guerrero 2008). While the security technologies were concerned with border-management and coincide with modern forms of knowledge and freedom, today security practices are directed at the biopolitics where, as Mick Dillon and Luis Lobo-Guerrero summarized, 'biological entities understood in these terms will not be secured through the practices traditionally favoured by the geopolitical discourses of political subjectivity. They cannot be secured in such ways because, representing a differently understood referent object of both freedom and power, living entities pose a quite different kind of security problematic. For one thing their very presence is not fixed' (Dillon and Lobo-Guerrero 2008: 270–1). It is not the human being 'in itself', but the self is constructed by a multiplicity of technologies, rationalities or discourses. All three changes, the commodification of security by risk, the acceleration of time and the biopoliticization highlight a parcel of current changes under way but, at the same time, point to the limitedness of a state-based, rational approach to security.

Conclusion

This contribution has argued that there is not 'the' 'risk' approach to security studies. Rather, different avenues with different conceptual schemes try to capture the changing mode of contingency production within the world polity. With the notion of risk, scholars try to capture the overall transformation of the political landscape with its 'private' and 'transnational' actors and the production of new uncertainties resulting from their interplay. From this perspective, the current interest in risk highlights the different kind of (un)certainties prevalent in world politics, the changing contours of dangers and threats and consequently a necessary shift in the knowledge structure of world politics. In other words, Beck, Foucault and Luhmann provide entry points from where the change of the inter-subjective meaning structures can be reconstructed without falling back on a vocabulary that reinforces the individual actor and loses the inter-subjective from sight. And it is probably the promise of the risk approach to explore this terrain. Having said that, this contribution sought to trace some changes of the 'saying' and the 'doing' of security, the semantic and structural shifts we can witness, in order to see what a risk approach highlighting the systemic shift encompasses. Of course, this transformation includes changes in ethics, aesthetics, and further the rules of formation and correlation of discourses I could not talk about but instead only highlight a small proportion of this still emerging field.

Notes

1 Of course, the systemic shift identified in part two has more implications and affects diverse fields from aesthetics, ethics, design, art, competition and collaboration between military companies that this contributions unfortunately cannot talk about. For a discussion see e.g. *Lacy* (2008). For an analysis of the 'ethics of risk' see Peter Burgess, Ethics of Risk, unpublished manuscript, and Burgess *et al.* (2007).
2 I refer to the German edition because, as Beck said, the German version became a completely different and updated book than the English version.
3 A point he now shares with Niklas Luhmann's systems theory. It might be too much to claim that he has accepted Luhmann's previous critique, but the notion of non-knowledge and how Beck uses it is surprisingly similar to systems theory. See below on p. 8.
4 Niklas Luhmann's understanding of risk is best encapsulated in Luhmann (1993). For an introduction to his systems theory see Luhmann (1996). Unfortunately, I cannot go into detail about the promises of the notion of autopoiesis for overcoming many dead ends of traditional systems theory. On the distinction between open and closed systems theories see Kontopoulos (1993).
5 In Daase and Kessler (2007) and Kessler and Daase (2008) we tried to develop two typologies of the changing contours and interplay of knowledge and non-knowledge give rise to different security practices in the war on terror.

4

Instruments of Insecurity
Small Arms and Contemporary Violence

Keith Krause

Introduction

The risk of violent conflict has long been at the centre of reflections on security and security studies. Traditionally, this has been translated into the study of war or legally recognized 'armed conflict' between organized groups. As far back as Quincy Wright's *A Study of War*, the central object of analysis was defined as 'a form of conflict involving a high degree of legal equality, of hostility, and of violence in the relations of organized human groups' (Wright 1964: 7).[1] More recently, Steven Walt defined the field of security studies as 'the study of the threat, use, and control of military force ... the conditions that make the use of force more likely, the ways that the use of force affects individuals, states and societies, and the specific policies that states adopt in order to prepare for, prevent, or engage in war' (Walt 1991: 212).

Within this perspective, weapons – as the *instruments* of insecurity and violence – were not exactly invisible, but they were seldom at the centre of analysis of the causes of conflict, war and insecurity. The major exceptions, of course, were studies of arms racing and arms acquisition behaviour, of nuclear weapons and deterrence theory, and, somewhat less prominently, of arms control and disarmament. But the overwhelming Clausewitzian bias to the field – which regarded war as a continuation of politics by other means – meant that weapons themselves were seldom regarded as having a particular explanatory interest in and of themselves, except perhaps as a technological change that transformed the landscape of modern warfare (McNeill 1984). Politics and the pursuit of power 'explained' violent conflict, and everything else (its scope, scale, intensity, etc.) was a residual.

Within the last two decades, the landscape of security studies has been – at least in Europe and parts of North America – almost entirely reshaped. Contributions to this volume demonstrate the breadth and depth of the topics that are now part of the canon of security studies, even if this vision is not widely shared among American scholars and university curricula. Most of these efforts at broadening and deepening move far away from the threat of physical violence as their central concern, yet still there has to date been little focus given to the actual 'instruments' of insecurity (broadly defined).[2] Subsequently, although these contributions represent important conceptual and practical moves, it can be

27

reasonably argued that this shift in attention to new approaches and topics has once again surrendered the terrain of the core concerns of war and peace – of violence and conflict – to realist or rationalist approaches to security studies.

This state of affairs is problematic for three reasons, all of which will be addressed in more detail in subsequent sections in this chapter. First, many strands of 'new thinking' follow the lead of Ole Wæver and other scholars in the Copenhagen School, in acknowledging that securitization requires, among other things, the invocation of an existential threat to a particular referent object. The nature of the existential threat is indeterminate (and socially constructed), but given that life-threatening physical and violent threats are often at their core existential in nature both to individuals and communities, it is surprising that the bulk of research on securitization has *not* focused on issues of violence, but on such things as migration, HIV/AIDS, the war on terror and so forth.[3]

Secondly, the threat of physical violence has hardly disappeared, even if the threat of violence from armed conflict has diminished significantly. Even without war, the threat of physical violence (political or non-political) in some parts of the world still represents one of the major public (and private) sources of insecurity, and can be reasonably compared to other forms of insecurity (food, health, environmental). Arguably, the opening of security studies to new issues such as identity, ontological security, or risk analysis reflects more the unprecedented condition of safety from the threat of physical violence that is enjoyed by most Northern societies (and scholars). It also rests upon an implicit acceptance that the threat of large-scale organized conflict is the only way in which international relations and security studies can apprehend physical insecurity, while other forms of more 'internal' violence fall into the realm of sociological and criminological analysis.

Finally, a focus on small arms and light weapons as the primary *instruments* of contemporary armed violence allows one to grasp the different actors involved in framing responses to the threat of physical violence around the world, and perhaps to better situate the (mainly European) preoccupations that dominate this volume. A focus on small arms parenthetically also allows one to situate the instruments of violence as one leg of the Weberian triangle that also includes the *agents* (violence entrepreneurs) and the *institutions* designed to use and/or regulate the use of violence within and between societies and states (Krause 1996). Although critical or constructivist scholarship shies away from a focus on the material aspects of insecurity (and hence the 'instruments'), there are important socio-cultural and symbolic dimensions to the use and misuse of small arms and light weapons that provide fertile topics for research, and that can highlight the relationship between ideas about, and the instruments of, armed violence.

The subject of this chapter – small arms proliferation and misuse – thus provides a useful perspective onto the larger issue of how we study contemporary insecurities, as well as representing an interesting (and new) topic in its own right. This chapter will unpack the issue of small arms in three parts: first it will briefly describe the scope and distribution of small arms; it will then highlight their lethal effects in different contexts; finally, it will explore what we know (and do not know) about the role of weapons in the broader etiology of contemporary violence. Overall, the twin goals of this chapter are to erase or blur the analytic distinctions between different forms of violence in order to bring violence – in all its social and political forms – back into the new thinking on security, and to provide a general overview of contemporary scholarship on arms and insecurity.

There are two broad framing questions about small arms and light weapons that can facilitate critical reflections on the contemporary use and threat of violence. First, how many weapons are there, where and in whose hands? And secondly, how much death and destruction is caused by small arms? Unpacking the first question requires a brief summary of available information on the global distribution of weapons holdings in order to illustrate the links (or not) between small arms and contemporary insecurities.

Where are the Weapons?

According to research by the Small Arms Survey, there are approximately 875 million small arms and light weapons worldwide, held by state institutions (military, police), private individuals and various organized (or disorganized) non-state actors (armed groups, private security agents, community defence forces, militias, etc.) (Small Arms Survey 2007: 39).[4] The most common instruments of violence are thus far more widely distributed than 'major conventional weapons' (aircraft, tanks, armed vehicles, etc.) which are not only held almost exclusively by states, but are also held along a fairly hierarchical (and rigid) distribution of power (Krause 1992). In fact, and as Figure 4.1 illustrates, of the approximately 875 million small arms and light weapons worldwide, only about 226 million – just more than one-quarter of the total – are in the hands of state institutions. Of these, about 200 million (less than one-quarter) are in the hands of national armed forces, and about 26 million with national police or public security forces. That leaves about 650 million (almost 75 per cent) in civilian possession, and less than 1 per cent in the hands of organized insurgent groups (Small Arms Survey 2007: 39–71).

What are we to make of such figures? First, they highlight that the Weberian state, in most parts of the world, possesses exactly what Weber postulated: a *legal* but not a practical monopoly over the use of force. It is likely true that weapons held by the state are more 'lethal', in the sense that a military-style automatic weapon has considerably more killing power than a single-shot pistol or shotgun. In an absolute sense, however, lethal means are widely available in many societies. The category of so-called 'civilian weapons' is also rather broad in that it covers not only weapons legally held by individuals for sport, hunting or

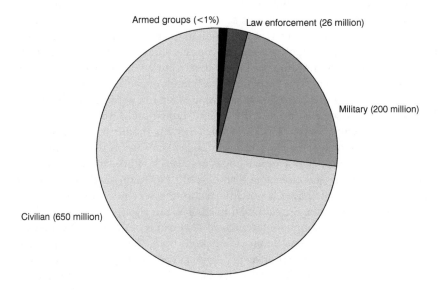

Figure 4.1 Distribution of weapons among different actors

other traditional and 'non-threatening' uses, but also weapons held illegally by criminal individuals and groups, weapons that move from legal to illicit circuits, and weapons that remain in society after large-scale conflicts.

The potential significance of non-state weapons possession becomes clear when we note that most violent exchanges in contemporary armed conflicts involve at least one actor who is not a state agent, ranging from armed groups to large-scale politico-criminal gangs (often called 'warlords'). As the Uppsala Conflict Data Program has noted, of the more than 122 conflicts that have taken place since the end of the Cold War, more than 90 per cent (115) involved at least one non-state actor – only seven were classic inter-state conflicts (Harbom 2007). Although the number of weapons formally in the arsenals of non-state armed groups is very small (based on the estimates in terms of membership in armed groups, plus some reasonable estimates of weapons holdings per combatant), these are the weapons that are most often used to sow death and destruction in places such as the eastern Democratic Republic of Congo, Sri Lanka, Darfur, Afghanistan, and elsewhere. Essentially, a tiny proportion of the world's weapons account for most of the killing. At a minimum, analysts need to keep in mind that the state in many parts of the world does not have a practical monopoly over the instruments of violence and use of force, with all the implications that this may have for efforts to prevent or reduce large-scale armed violence in both war and non-war contexts.

It is difficult to get a picture of how small arms and light weapons are distributed geographically, but there are at least three conclusions that can be drawn from available data. First, around 40 per cent of civilian weapons worldwide are in the hands of American citizens, meaning that between 260 and 290 million firearms are held by 5 per cent of the world's population. This makes the United States completely *sui generis*, for historical and constitutional reasons (the interpretation of the Second Amendment to the US constitution as enshrining an individual right to possess weapons). Not surprisingly, given the global policy reach of the USA (both governmental and non-governmental), this has had specific implications for international and multilateral efforts to tackle the proliferation and misuse of small arms. Second, the distribution of the remaining 60 per cent of civilian-held small arms is extremely 'lumpy' and does not seem to follow any particularly strong pattern. Countries such as Finland, Switzerland and Yemen, with particularly strong traditions of civilian firearms ownership, rank among the top ten states in terms of weapons per 100 members of the population. Countries highly affected by armed violence, such as Mexico or Brazil by contrast, do not have particularly high levels of civilian ownership of weapons.

There does appear, however, to be a relationship, albeit not a strong one, between overall levels of wealth in a society (measured by GDP/capita) and levels of civilian weapons possession (Small Arms Survey 2007: 57–60). That this should be the case is not that surprising. In very poor societies (or groups in society), a weapon would represent one of the largest, if not the single largest, capital goods possessed by a household. Even inexpensive but functioning weapons still cost more than US$100. Not surprisingly, such an inefficient (in productive terms) capital asset is not attractive to the very poor. Once other assets are acquired, however, (say, cattle, agricultural implements, a small shop or other capital goods), the need for protection becomes important, and a firearm is both 'affordable' (in household capital terms) and more 'efficient' (in providing protection). Certainly such a pattern can be seen in weapons holdings among shopkeepers in inner cities, or in pastoralist communities in East Africa. At the other end of the spectrum, wealth and relatively high disposable income is required in order for guns to be seen as leisure or sporting goods, suitable for collection and acquisition, or use in hunting, target shooting and so forth. Weapons also have a long life span, and their relative accumulation in Western Europe and North America reflects a decades-long process of diffusion of guns within societies that began in the eighteenth and nineteenth centuries, but which only spread to the rest of the world with nineteenth-century colonial conquest or contact (Headrick 1981).

Obviously, seeking individual or personal 'security through the gun' may be ineffective, and it is certainly less desirable than a functioning and reliable security sector. It also has significant 'negative externalities', to use the somewhat antiseptic economic language. The presence of guns in a household, for example, increases almost threefold the risk of women becoming homicide victims, regardless of why the weapon was in the household in the first place (Campbell *et al.* 2003; Kellermann *et al.* 1993). Other insecurities such as the risk of accidental death and injury, or other forms of interpersonal violence, are also related to the presence of weapons. At a micro-level, one could regard this as analogous to the risk of accidental war posed by the proliferation of weapons of mass destruction; the existential threat is merely personal rather than national or societal.

Similarly, the level of suicide by firearms is a good proxy for overall levels of firearms ownership in society, suggesting that the availability of a particular *means* has an impact on spontaneous decisions to use violence (whether interpersonal or self-inflicted). Perhaps less intuitively, however, the level of civilian weapons ownership is *not* correlated with overall suicide levels – in some places, such as Japan, with very low levels of weapons possession, suicide rates are still high and other means are used (Killias 1993). This 'substitution effect' by which one means of (in this case personal) destruction is used in place of another finds its expression also in communal conflicts, with the oft-cited example of the genocide in Rwanda being used to highlight that even common agricultural implements can be used for mass killing. Of course, matters are more complex in both cases: for suicide (assuming a society wished to minimize the social and personal costs), the availability of weapons increases the likelihood of success, and also results in permanent disabilities, which is not the case with all alternative means.[5] In the Rwandan genocide, small arms and light weapons were used to round up and terrorize the population so that massacres could be undertaken. These examples highlight that few if any generalizations can be made about the circumstances under which weapons act as a specific vector of violence, exacerbating or accelerating the intensity of violent exchanges.

Less is known about the distribution of weapons among state arsenals, and the available figures (roughly 200 million military-held weapons) are based on estimates derived from a few states, related to the size, mobilization strategy and military doctrine of different armed forces. Four broad categories of armed forces can be identified: 'trinitarian' militaries that follow the Clausewitzian triad of state–military–society and have a broadly Western war-fighting strategy (Canada, South Africa, USA); 'people's armies' reliant on mass mobilization of the population (Albania, Yugoslavia); 'constabulary' armed forces mainly designed for internal security and border policing functions (Jamaica, Cambodia); and 'reserve' armies (Switzerland, Finland) (Small Arms Survey 2006). Tremendous variation in weapons holdings follow from these strategies, with states such as Albania or the former Yugoslavia on one side having had more than five small arms and light weapons per active-duty soldier, versus Western armed forces which have roughly two or so weapons per soldier.[6] In very many states, however, the restructuring of the armed forces following the end of the Cold War or changes in national strategy have resulted in large estimated surpluses of weapons: one estimate is that approximately *76 million* of the 200 million military small arms and light weapons are surplus to national requirements (Small Arms Survey 2008).

This somewhat schematic and anecdotal account of the global distribution of small arms and light weapons does, however, at least alert us to the way in which small arms possession by both states and non-state actors may be driven by factors other than high levels of armed conflict and insecurity, internal violence, or predatory and criminal motivations. At a minimum, strategies for regulating civilian possession or misuse of weapons would have to take account of the diverse factors feeding the demand for small arms at these different analytic levels (Brauer and Muggah 2006). Perhaps more importantly, the lack of any simplistic and linear explanation of the link between weapons and violence highlights the importance of more constructivist approaches to violence that emphasize cultural or social factors conditioning weapons use, and the norms towards the use of force to regulate conflict and resolve disputes, an issue discussed in more detail below. Just as a constructivist account of inter-state insecurity emphasizes that threats cannot be 'read off' the material distribution of destructive power under the security dilemma, so too are threats and insecurities at a sub-national and even micro-level conditioned not just by the availability of weapons, but also by the way in which the gun is mediated through social exchange relationships.

Death by the Gun

Numbers of weapons do not in themselves create insecurity; their use is mediated through violence entrepreneurs who mobilize and use force, and via the institutions designed to channel, direct and restrict the use of violence in modern states. But it is also worth highlighting that small arms and light weapons are responsible for the overwhelming majority of casualties in contemporary conflicts and non-conflict settings. Just how significant are small arms in different forms of violent death?

Most analysts agree that levels of armed violence and conflict deaths have declined, perhaps dramatically, since the end of the Cold War, although the wars in Afghanistan, Iraq and elsewhere have halted the downward trend that was evident in the late 1990s. Although there is less agreement over 'how low' the totals are, the best estimate for 2004–7 is that an average of 52,000 people were recorded as killed each year in the roughly 40 armed conflicts that were ongoing or occurred around the world in that period (Geneva Declaration 2008). This figure is higher than that reported in many 'single' source reports (such as the *Human Security Report*), but it captures reports from a wider variety of data sources. One important limitation, however, is that most data sets on armed conflicts only count *recorded* deaths – deaths that appeared in media or NGO reports, or in official government records. In many contemporary war zones, such as Somalia or Northern Pakistan, media and NGO coverage is limited, official statistics are not kept and survival takes priority over data gathering. Existing data sets almost certainly undercount actual conflict deaths.[7]

It is difficult to pin down exactly what proportion of the 52,000 average annual recorded violent deaths in conflict zones are committed with small arms and light weapons; but one study of eight conflicts suggests that 'between 60 and 90 percent of violent conflict deaths, depending on the nature of the fighting, are caused by small arms and light weapons' (Small Arms Survey 2005: 248). The lower figure may understate the actual role of small arms, since large-scale killing by crude weapons such as machetes (as in the Rwanda genocide) is only made possible once people have been rounded up, terrorized and contained by the use of small arms (Verwimp 2006). And other forms of killing, such as roadside bombs or other forms of bombing attacks, also often implicate the use of small arms and light weapons (to halt vehicles, sow panic, create a distraction, etc.).

When we widen our perspective beyond what are formally considered as 'armed conflicts', the picture changes radically. Estimates derived from figures from out of the United Nations Office of Drug and Crime, the World Health Organization, and national or regional sources, show that approximately 490,000 people die in non-conflict or so-called criminal contexts each year – a figure that dwarfs that of contemporary war zones (Geneva Declaration 2008). Similarly to armed conflict, approximately 60 per cent of these deaths are from small arms and light weapons (Geneva Declaration 2008). It is a mistake, however, to think of these deaths as simple 'criminal homicides' (as one sees, for example, in Western Europe or North America) for at least two reasons. First, in many regions of the world the distinction between armed conflict and non-conflict violence is blurred. In some cases, political violence such as that witnessed in Kenya after the 2007 election, in which more than 1,000 people died, is more important than in many contemporary 'armed conflicts', and well above the threshold for 'battle deaths'. In other situations, large-scale criminal violence, such as that which gripped Mexico in 2007 and 2008, makes certain cities such as Cuidad Juarez resemble war zones. More than 4,000 people were killed in drug-related violence alone in 2008, and during one month in the summer of 2008 almost as many people died violently in Mexico as in Iraq or Afghanistan.[8] While Mexican violence may not be 'political' in the narrow sense, it certainly has political/security implications, and can arguably be considered to have been securitized, with the deployment of more than 40,000 soldiers in 2007–8 to tackle the drug cartels, and with 68 per cent of the public agreeing with the deployment of the armed forces in the 'war on drugs'.[9]

Such violence is hardly simple homicide, although from a purely domestic legal point of view, it is categorized as criminal violence. The Mexican example and similar situations in places such as Brazil, Thailand, Guatemala and elsewhere highlight that large-scale killing occurs in many places that are not formally considered to be at war or in an armed conflict. The problem of classifying different forms of violence creates problems on both sides of the domestic–international divide. On the domestic side, large-scale violence is often not economic or criminal in nature, and can have profound political roots and implications, whether it is the result of political factions or leaders establishing and arming militias, the creation of community self-defence forces (either by the state or the communities themselves), paramilitaries working parallel to state forces, or criminal gangs that have infiltrated or corrupted state security institutions.

Already in the 1990s, the use of the label 'international' or 'inter-state' proved inadequate to describe most contemporary armed conflicts, as seen in the post-Cold War rise of communal (so-called 'ethnic') and intra-state conflicts. Most researchers, however, treated these as analytically similar, with the contest over power or the distribution of political 'goods' serving as the touchstone (Posen 1993). The rise of greed-based conflicts over economic goods, and the phenomenon of warlordism, in which taking and holding state power was not a principal goal, shattered this easy equation of large-scale violent conflict with political ends (Berdal and Malone 2000; Collier 2000; Marten 2006–7; Reno 1999). The Clausewitzian vision of war as the continuation of politics by other means is today an obstacle to understanding contemporary violent exchanges. As Michael Brzoska points out, the standard definition of 'what constitutes an armed conflict – with the elements of battle, political objectives and government participation at its core – … is too narrow to facilitate an understanding of the trends in peace and security' (Brzoska 2006: 94–5), especially if one adopts a human security perspective that puts individuals at the centre of the picture. In short, conventional conceptual categories hinder a broader appreciation of the scale and diverse forms of contemporary violence.

One way to capture this is to compare the risk of dying violently in different conflict and non-conflict contexts. Table 4.1 provides several comparisons between levels of lethal violence in conflict and non-conflict contexts. It is immediately obvious that armed violence in many non-conflict countries is greater than that in many war zones. Even if one acknowledges that most victims of war die 'indirectly' or non-violently through easily preventable causes such as disease and malnutrition, the number of deaths that can be attributed to armed conflict is still much smaller than in non-conflict countries, and the rate of dying (directly or indirectly) in armed conflict is still lower for all but the most intense wars.[10]

This relative (and shifting) balance of conflict and non-conflict armed violence must be placed in a broader historical/comparative perspective. Beginning roughly in the seventeenth century, Western European states successfully evacuated violence from the 'domestic' sphere, through what Norbert Elias called the 'civilising process', which included rising education levels, increased state capacities for surveillance and social control, especially in urban spaces, urbanization, and changed norms towards the use of lethal violence.[11] Murder rates dropped roughly by half from late Middle Ages to the early seventeenth century, and by the nineteenth century, had dropped five to ten times further (Body-Gendrot and Spierenburg 2008; Krause 2008). The threat of violence was externalized, and increasingly associated with large-scale (and increasingly violent) inter-state wars, in part fuelled by technological revolutions that increased the intensity of killing power (McNeill 1984). This reached its bloody apotheosis in the twentieth century, which was almost certainly the most violent in human history (Lacina *et al.* 2006; Reid Sarkees *et al.* 2003). The end of the Cold War and the 'democratic peace' now means that the problem of external violence has also receded – at least for a lucky few who live in advanced industrial states.

But there is no teleology here, and in much of the rest of the world, these twin processes of declines in domestic then external violence do not follow a similar path. One obvious reason for this is that the easy availability of small arms and light weapons makes it increasingly difficult for the state (especially in the post-colonial world) to provide internal security,

Table 4.1 Comparing the risk of dying violently in conflict and non-conflict settings, per year

Country	*Direct conflict death rate (battle deaths per 100,000)*	*Non-conflict violent death rate (homicides per 100,000)*
Iraq	65	–
El Salvador	–	59
Guatemala	–	47
South Africa	–	40
Venezuela	–	37
Somalia	24	–
Afghanistan	10	–
Sudan	9	–

Note: Direct conflict death rates are the annual average for the most lethal conflicts, 2004–7 (Geneva Declaration 2008: 27). Non-conflict (homicide) rates are for most recent year in the 2005–7 period (various sources). Data is not strictly comparable but is indicative.

or to eliminate threats to its practical monopoly on violence, with all the implications this has for the creation of reciprocal bonds of loyalty and legitimacy between state and society. Conversely, while the risk of external inter-state violence may have diminished, the mutation of forms of armed conflict means that the domestic–international divide is largely irrelevant to contemporary large-scale armed violence.

Small Arms and the Etiology of Violence

The many examples offered above highlight that there are no simple relationships or linkages between arms and violence, whether between or within states, or in conflict and non-conflict settings. Weapons use and misuse is mediated through a variety of pathways of social and economic interaction, and violent exchanges involve complex relationships (both constraining and fostering violence) between agents and socio-political or normative structures. But critical scholarship on contemporary armed violence can do more than simply assert that violence is a complex and highly contextual social phenomenon, and weapons play an indeterminate role. Such a conclusion is consistent with a broadly constructivist approach to security studies, with its emphasis on the social rather than material dimension of threat construction, and it certainly undermines rationalist arguments that would read off the threat and insecurity posed by weapons from their global patterns of distribution. However, unless treated as the starting point for a research agenda, it could lead to disengagement from some of the larger socio-political questions that are raised by contemporary violence.

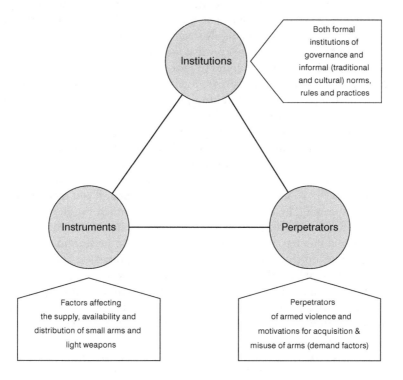

Figure 4.2 Thinking about armed violence

There are both micro and macro avenues for moving beyond contextualist arguments, focusing at the micro level on the specific role of weapons in social exchanges, and at the macro level on attempts to unpack more systematically the etiology of different forms of violence. These could be labelled the 'gun culture' and the 'contagion of violence' approaches. Both are captured in Figure 4.2.

The bottom axis of the triangle captures the micro-level relationship between violence entrepreneurs and their 'tools of the trade'. Scholars such as Bernard Harcourt or Deanna Wilkinson have studied the 'language of the gun' to uncover the symbolic meanings and roles attributed to weapons, and the 'power', 'protection' and 'prestige' that they convey (Harcourt 2006; Wilkinson 2003). The meanings that violence entrepreneurs give to their weapons condition not only the demand for weapons (and particular types of weapons), but also their responsiveness to efforts to control and regulate small arms availability and misuse. Understanding the role of these meanings in shaping demand is a precondition for effective conflict and violence reduction programmes. But beyond the way in which weapons possession and use is drenched in meaning lurks the larger issue of how the presence, use and misuse of weapons shapes social (and individual) identities – in particular those associated with violent masculinities – making certain ways of dealing with or resolving conflicts more or less possible (Myrttinen 2003, 2004). Despite little work being done on this topic internationally, frequent invocations of the role of 'gun cultures' in conjunction with such places as South-Eastern Europe, the Middle East and elsewhere facilitates a greater understanding as to the importance of such analyses within security studies more generally (Florquin and Stoneman 2004; Small Arms Survey 2005; South Eastern and Eastern Europe Clearinghouse 2006).

Most often violence entrepreneurs are members of gangs, non-state armed groups, or other formal and informal social groups, and the meanings they attribute to the possession and use of weapons are embedded in highly structured social contexts. Given the nature of contemporary conflicts, most of which involve non-state armed groups, it is important to employ the same methods and techniques to examine the symbolic meanings of weapons and violence in these wars. Certainly anecdotal evidence is that armed groups in West Africa adopt the trappings of 'hood culture', including the cell phones, sunglasses and uniforms of the North American subculture, while street gangs from Rio de Janeiro to Chicago have codes and norms governing weapons holding and use (Cook *et al.* 2007; Dowdney 2003). Beyond simplistic motivational categories for armed violence, such as 'greed' and 'grievance', the violence in places such as Colombia, Lebanon, Sri Lanka or Peru also must be apprehended in conjunction with its symbolic and social context.

At the macro level, two sets of research questions of practical and theoretical relevance require further research. The first concerns the way in which the institutions designed to channel and punish the illegitimate use of violence themselves encode weapons in particular social and cultural ways. An obvious example can be seen in the impact of the Second Amendment on the understanding of weapons possession and use in the USA. Another example would be the role of weak or non-existent security institutions in 'privatizing' the provision of security, thereby creating (and legitimizing) individual and social incentives to seek security through the private use of force, and through institutions ranging from community self-protection groups to vigilante groups or private security forces.

The second, somewhat larger question is whether or not different forms of violence are 'layered' on top of each other, each following a different set of social channels, and obeying a different normative and strategic logic, or whether or not (and how) the diverse forms of violence in a society are linked, as in a cobweb, into one larger 'culture of violence'. One aspect of this concerns the 'social contagion of violence', in which 'individuals within social networks ... turn to each other for cues and behavioural tools that reflect the contingency of specific situations' (Fagan *et al.* 2007: 689). On this account, violence, like other social phenomena (adolescent alcohol and drug use, trends in fashion), is spread socially, shaping preferences and actions well beyond the ways that can be captured by rational action models (Fagan *et al.* 2007). Another concern is the way in which violence in high-intensity conflicts (armed conflict, high levels of gang or localized violence) can 'spill over' into such things as extreme levels of gender-based and sexual violence. Evidence is often anecdotal, but the situations in post-conflict countries in West Africa, or high-violence countries such as Guatemala, or war zones such as the Democratic Republic of Congo, point towards significant – and destructive – linkages between different forms of violence (Bastick *et al.* 2007; Millard and Stevenson 2009).

In all of these cases, the instruments of violence play a crucial role in shaping the potential for violence, and are carriers of particular meanings that legitimize or normalize certain kinds of behaviour, often with negative or even pathological consequences for the security of individuals and communities. Uncovering these meanings is as important as analysing the simple availability of weapons and the costs and benefits associated with possession and (mis)use.

Conclusions

This exploration of the role of small arms and light weapons in contemporary violence and armed conflicts provides a useful lens that challenges the way in which security studies understands and studies weapons and violence. First, it highlights the inadequacy of equating armed violence solely with war – in either its inter-state or internal variants, by emphasizing that the majority of victims from armed violence die or are injured in non-conflict settings. This realization opens the way to examining the different socio-cultural contexts in which the availability and use of weapons shapes social interactions, and in turn the way in which the meanings associated with weapons shape their use and the identities of their users. Second, by blurring the boundaries between political and non-political violence, it opens the way to a broader understanding of 'the political' that includes not only the use of violence for political ends, but the way in which the boundaries of the political are used to classify and categorize certain forms of violence as criminal, while others are understood as political, and still others (in particular intimate partner violence) are viewed as beyond the realm of the political.

This analysis also questions the adequacy of using a practical version of the Weberian vision of the state, by showing that the state does not in many cases actually possess a practical monopoly on the instruments of 'ordinary violence', although its potential to use massive force and repression remains largely intact. This points the way to the need for closer examination of how the institutions of the state that are designed to provide internal or external security actually function to channel the legitimate and illegitimate uses of violence by different social actors. Finally, it points the way to a constructivist or critical research agenda on contemporary violence that has not been taken up within new approaches to security studies.

In short, a focus on the instruments of violence can 'bring violence back in' to security studies, and into a wider vision of contemporary international politics.

Notes

1　He added that it was 'the legal condition which equally permits two or more hostile groups to carry on a conflict by armed force' – an important restriction on the analysis that would exclude a wide range of contemporary political violence.

2　Exceptions would be Price 1997; Mutimer 2000; Tannewald 2005.

3　See Wæver 1995: 46–86; Buzan *et al.* 1998: 21–47; Elbe 2006: 119–44. Most critiques have focused on the nature of 'speech acts'; few have challenged the idea of existential threats and urgency that are intimately linked with physical violence.

4　The definition of small arms and light weapons follows that of the United Nations group of governmental experts: small arms include revolvers and self-loading pistols, rifles and carbines, sub-machine-guns, assault rifles, and light machine-guns, while light weapons include heavy machine-guns, hand-held under-barrel and mounted grenade launchers, portable anti-aircraft guns, portable anti-tank guns, recoilless rifles, portable launchers of anti-tank missile and rocket systems, portable launchers of anti-aircraft missile systems, and mortars of calibres of less than 100 mm.

5　There is good evidence for a substitution effect in suicides, but matters are less clear for other forms of violence.

6　The figure per soldier for the former Yugoslavia was 4.4 weapons per soldier, for the USA 1.1, and for Canada 2.3.

7　The actual number of direct conflict victims is probably two to four times higher, depending on the intensity of the conflict and access of media and NGOs to war zones. See Geneva Declaration 2008: 9–30.

8　See <http://news.bbc.co.uk/2/hi/americas/7721608.stm>; <http://news.bbc.co.uk/2/hi/americas/7625195.stm>. According to figures from the government's public security office, there were a record 443 drug-related murders across the country in July alone. In Iraq e.g. there were 669 civilian deaths in June according to the Iraq Body Count. In Afghanistan, Human Rights Watch estimates there were 540 civilian deaths in the first seven months of 2008.

9　See <http://news.bbc.co.uk/2/hi/americas/7625195.stm>.

10　An estimated three to ten times more people die indirectly than directly in armed conflict, although this depends critically on the intensity of the fighting, levels of displacement, access to basic services and the baseline health of a population. For an overview see Geneva Declaration 2008: 31–48.

11　'Domestic' here means internal; another article entirely could be devoted to the shifting public–private distinction, in particular as concerns intimate partner and so-called 'domestic' violence.

5

Human Security

A Contested Contempt

Taylor Owen

From the State to the Individual

There are many interpretations of how and why the concept of human security emerged in the early 1990s. While some have rooted the discourse in the origins of liberalism (Leaning and Arie 2001; Rothschild 1995), and others in the post-war human rights discourse (Axworthy 2001a), most of the literature on human security rightly identifies the end of the Cold War as the geopolitical turning point from which the concept emerged. In these accounts human security is understood as a response to the proliferation of new security threats which fit awkwardly within the relatively narrow confines of the traditional, state-centric national security paradigm.

While this undoubtedly tells part of the story, the reality is multifaceted. Because the issues generally included within the purview of the concept of human security encompass such a diverse range of academic disciplines and policy discourses (e.g. development studies, international relations, environmental studies and public health), it is difficult to identify a linear narrative of what precisely instigated the discourse. Instead, it is useful to think of human security as emerging from the changing nature of insecurity that became increasingly apparent at the end of the Cold War, and from a corresponding changing discourse around how best to explain these new phenomena.

In the early 1990s the geopolitical stability provided by the Cold War gave way to a new understanding of the causes of human vulnerability. An array of harms that had been marginalized due to the prioritization of macro threats during the Cold War were suddenly in view, and the nation state was often found to be incapable or unwilling to protect citizens from these widespread vulnerabilities. The primary threat to people's lives was not nuclear war, but rather stemmed from a mix of health, environmental and economic vulnerabilities as well as new forms of conflict which had become a greater human threat than the inter-state war that had long dominated the field of security studies.

The result of this new security context was a period of adjustment in the way in which the international community, policy-makers and academics talked about and responded to insecurity. For example, establishment security scholars began to question the scope of their discipline, advocating the inclusion of all major threats to human survival, not just

39

military threats (Tuckman 1989; Ullman 1983). Environmental security scholars argued that environmental preservation should be included in national security planning due to both the direct threat posed by degradation and by its potential indirect link to conflict escalation (Deudney 1990; Deudney and Matthew 1999; Thomas 1992; Homer–Dixon 1991). Liberal internationalists who saw the primary tool of realism, a balance of power amongst states, as being insufficient to mitigate the increasing and varied harms threatening individuals (Weiss and Gordenker 1996), argued that the rule of law, international institutions, and in some cases, military intervention be drawn on to promote international security (Pettman 2005). Finally, a diverse range of critical security studies emerged to not simply challenge the state as the best security provider, but also state relations as the best means of understanding insecurity. Instead, this critical school argued that attention should be paid to gender, history, race, ethnicity or economic relations when seeking to understand the causes of insecurity (Buzan *et al.* 1998; Krause and Williams 1997; Lipschutz 1995).

Out of this context, new concepts of security began to proliferate, including cooperative, common, comprehensive, societal, and global security (Baylis 1997). For many, however, it led to a belief that the best way of adjusting the security concept was not just to include more harms or to alter the analytic perspective with which they were viewed, but to shift the actual referent object of security away from the state and onto the individual. The concept of human security takes the most dramatic step by making the referent object of security not the state, society or community, but the individual person. Table 5.1 summarizes the shift to the individual implicit in all definitions of human security.

This shift in the referent of security from the state to the individual is the core attribute of the concept of human security. It is what separates the concept from the wide range of other security conceptualizations, it is the central characteristic that is shared by all definitions of the concept, and it is uncontested within the human security literature. But while there may be agreement on the referential shift of human security, there is fierce debate over which threats to the individual should and should not be considered as a threat to human security. This debate is unique in that it is not rooted in an academic discipline, and is made up of a mix of scholarly articles, government policy papers and reports from international organizations. All, however, specifically engage with the challenge of defining the concept of human security, in particular, on the question of what threats should be included once the referential shift to the individual is made.

And perspectives on this question are diverse. For example, in a 2004 issue of *Security Dialogue*, twenty-one academics and policy experts who had previously written about the concept of human security were asked what they believed it entailed. The result was twenty-one highly divergent responses (Burgess and Owen 2004). Some argued for a broad development-focused definition, while others pushed for a narrow conceptualization focused on violent threats. Some stressed the practical utility of the concept based on its

Table 5.1 Traditional versus human security

Type of Security	Referent Object	Protection	Possible Threats
Traditional security	The state	The integrity of the state	Inter-state war, nuclear proliferation, revolution
Human security	The individual	The integrity of the individual	Disease, poverty, natural disaster, violence, landmines, human rights abuses

UNDP: Safety from chronic threats such as hunger, disease and repression, and protection from sudden and hurtful disruptions in the patterns of daily life whether in jobs, home or communities. A combination of freedom from want and fear. Threats are categorized into seven groups: economic, food, health, environmental, personal, community and political security (1994: 22–5).

Canadian Government: Freedom from pervasive threats to people's rights, safety or lives with a focus on increasing people's safety from the threat of violence (DFAIT 2002: 7).

Sabine Alkire: Safeguarding the vital core of all human lives from critical pervasive threats, in a way that is consistent with long-term human fulfilment (2002: 2).

Commission on Human Security: To protect the vital core of all human lives in ways that enhance human freedoms and human fulfilment. The protection of fundamental freedoms, from critical (severe) and pervasive (widespread) threats and situations using processes that build on people's strengths and aspirations. Creating political, social, environmental, economic, military and cultural systems that together give people the building blocks of survival, livelihood and dignity (Ogata and Sen 2003: 4).

Amartya Sen: Protection from the menaces that threaten the survival, daily life and dignity of human beings and strengthening the efforts to confront these threats (2002: 2).

Leaning and Arie: The protection of social, political, psychological and economic factors that enable human well being over time, combining basic physical human needs, such as water, food and shelter, with more intangible concerns, such as identity, recognition, participation and autonomy. A product of hazards combined with coping mechanisms (2004).

Caroline Thomas: A condition in which basic human needs are met, and in which dignity and community participation are realized. Divides the concept into quantitative material sufficiencies and qualitative measures of livelihood (1992).

GHECHS: A state in which individuals have the options, capacity and freedom to mitigate or adapt to threats to their human, environmental and social rights, and actively participate in doing so (Lonergan 2000: 1).

Kanti Bajpai: An equation between temporally and regionally dependent threats and capabilities (2004).

Japanese Government: Comprehensively seizing all the menaces that threaten the survival, daily life and dignity of human beings and strengthening the efforts to confront threats (MOFA 2007).

Gary King and Christopher Murray: The number of years of future life spent outside a state of generalized poverty (2002).

Andy Mack and the Human Security Report: The protection of individuals and communities from violence (2005).

Sverre Lodgaard: Protection from violent threats to the individual, mitigated in three ways: the rule of law, public order and peaceful management of conflicts (2000).

Neil MacFarlane and Yuen Foong Khong: Protection from organized violence (2005).

Figure 5.1 Sample of human security definitions

early policy successes, and others urged its theoretical utility as a critical tool with which to assess perceived gender, state, and economic power imbalances in the traditional security discourse. It is therefore difficult to compile a list of all human security definitions, as there are many. Figure 5.1 outlines thirteen of the most commonly cited.

Organizing the Definitions

Seeking to make sense of this diverse range of definitions, various scholars have proposed schemas for categorizing the human security discourse.

Sagaren Naidoo sees the human security literature as being split between two schools of theoretical origin, both rooted in international relations theory. The neo-realists argue that security conceptualizations must be broadened to include non-military threats, such as political, economic, social and environmental threats. Critical or postmodern approaches, on the other hand, while also advocating for a broadening of included threats, add a deepening of the concept to include a wider range of security referents, including individuals, ethnic groups, cultural groups, multi-national cooperation and NGOs (2001).

Claude Daudelin depicts the range of human security conceptualizations as existing along three parallel axes. The first, 'definitions of threats', encompasses all attempts to broaden the list of harms that should be included under the security label. The second, 'new objects of security', advocates for various shifts in the referent object of security, whether it be to the individual or groups, super or supra national. The third axis, 'new security instruments', describes the best mitigating mechanisms to deal with a new broadened list of threats falling under the human security mandate (Daudelin 2001).

Fen Osler Hampson organizes the literature in three conceptual categories. First, the rights-based approach is anchored in international human rights law, and champions the right of the individuals to live in safety above and beyond the sovereign rights of states. Second, the cluster on 'safety of the people' consists of articulations which focus on the wide range of violent threats to the individual. These can come from either traditional state-based threats or, more commonly, from new forms of violence including civil war and insurgency. Third, the 'sustainable development' grouping includes those interpretations that are rooted in the broad 1994 UNDP conceptualization. These definitions include a very wide range of harms including many issues traditionally considered in the development rubric (2002).

Edward Newman provides four typologies of human security which demonstrate clear tensions in the literature. First, 'basic human needs' approaches are rooted in the UNDP conceptualization and focus on the basic welfare of individuals and their protection from sudden and hurtful disruptions. Second, 'assertive interventionist' approaches focus on the challenging of state sovereignty in the face of gross violations of human security, and the subsequent use of the concept as a means of justifying breaches of sovereignty. Third, the wide range of 'social welfare and development' focused conceptualizations, unlike the human needs approach, go beyond minimum survival needs to consider just, equitable and sustainable levels of development. Fourth, 'new security' approaches look at non-traditional threats such as HIV/AIDS, drugs, terrorism, small arms, landmines, and put their impact in the context of traditional security threats (Newman 2001).

Paul Oquist (2008) sees four groups of human security conceptualizations. First, development analysts who have broadened their analysis to include a wider range of metrics. Second, environmental analysts and activists who use human security as a means of promoting environmental issues both as a source of potential threat as well as a requirement for human sustainability. Third, international relations theorists who seek to broaden the range of threats included in the security mandate, bringing focus to civil conflict, and move away from the dominance of sovereign rights in the international system. Fourth, peace activists who see human security as a precondition for both intra- and inter-state peace and stability.

Finally, by far the most widely used categorization of the literature bifurcates definitions into those that include a broad range of threats to the individual, and those that include only a narrow range. Descriptions of this broad versus narrow dichotomy – also known as freedom from fear versus freedom from want – generally use the UNDP and the Canadian definitions as the poles under which all other conceptualizations can be clustered.

The 1994 UNDP Human Development Report is generally seen as the first significant attempt at articulating the broad approach to human security. The report describes human security as having two principal aspects: the freedom from chronic threats such as hunger, disease and repression, coupled with the protection from sudden calamities. The report concedes that it is broad, but explains that that this is simply a reflection of the number of significant harms that go unmitigated. As a conceptual structure, the UNDP proposes seven human security components: economic, food, health, environmental, personal, community and political security (1994). What is important about this categorization is that it sets the 'boundaries of the tent' very broadly, clearly separating itself from past security reconceptualizations. Also, it forces other definitions of human security to justify their narrowing from this very broad starting point.

On the other end of this perceived dichotomy is the narrow approach, often labelled the Canadian definition. The Canadian government acknowledges the UNDP conception as a phase in the development of human security, but envisions a much more focused definition, one centred on violent threats, as an instrument of policy. While, the definition is relatively clear and concise, 'Human security means freedom from pervasive threats to people's rights, safety or lives', it does not stipulate that these threats need be violence-based until, in a subsequent paragraph, they narrow the focus of the concept as it relates to Canadian policy: 'Canada's agenda focuses on increasing people's safety from the threat of violence.' Indeed, on the surface, there is little differentiation between this articulation and that of the UNDP. Where the intentions of the Canadian approach become clear are in the policy priorities which fall under the human security mandate of the Department of Foreign Affairs, which include public safety, protection of civilians in armed conflict, conflict prevention, governance and accountability, and peace support operations. The Canadian definition, therefore, restricts the parameters of human security to violent threats against the individual. This can come from a vast array of threats, including the drug trade, landmines, ethnic discord, state failure, trafficking in small arms. And all must, as former foreign minister Lloyd Axworthy points out, be countered primarily by the use of soft power, such as diplomatic resources, economic persuasion, and the use of intelligence and information technology (2001a).

The Definitions

Using the broad versus narrow categorization, it is possible to cluster definitions in either group. First, of the definitions listed in Figure 5.1, the following should be placed in the broad category: Sabine Alkire, the Commission on Human Security, Amartya Sen, Leaning and Arie, GECHS, Caroline Thomas, Kanti Bajpai, and the Japanese government.

Sabine Alkire, who later became the lead researcher for the Commission on Human Security, wrote perhaps the most substantive definitional discussion to date (2002). Alkire defines the objective of human security as 'safeguarding the vital core of all human lives from critical pervasive threats, in a way that is consistent with long-term human fulfillment' (2002: 2). She expands on the meaning of the terms used at length. By 'safeguard' she is implying that human security is deliberatively protective. 'Vital core' focuses the concept on a specific severity of threat, defined by Alkire as fundamental human rights, basic capabilities and absolute needs. 'All human lives' both centres the concept on people, as opposed to states, and shifts that focus away from any distinguishing characteristic such as race, religion, ethnicity or citizenship – the protection of the individual's vital core is paramount. This protection, however, is exclusively from 'critical and pervasive threats' meaning they require urgent address, and that they are both large-scale and non-anomalous (2002). The latter is particularly important as it excludes natural disasters, which are included in other broad definitions, notably Kanti Bajpai's. Finally, the protection of human security, by individuals or institutions, must be mindful of 'long term fulfillment' and the potential negative repercussions of short-term alleviation policies.

Not surprisingly, as Alkire's work fed directly into the Commission on Human Security (CHS), established in 2001 by Kofi Annan and led by Sodako Ogata and Amartya Sen, it uses a very similar definition. The key difference is that they appended a notion of dignity to Alkire's definition. They argued that this was important because human life extends beyond survival, 'to matters of love, culture and faith' (2003: 4). This broadening, however, dramatically changes the implication of the definition, and the report was widely critiqued for being expansively vague.

The Japanese government, having partially funded the Human Security Commission, and with its co-chair Sadako Ogata being named Japan's International Development Minister, have largely adopted the report's definition. Following the publication of the Commission's report, the Japanese government announced the creation of a Human Security Trust Fund, operating out of the Ministry of Foreign Affairs. Due to their broad interpretation, however, the use of human security within the Japanese government remains largely attributed to its development, rather than foreign policy (MOFA 2007; Ogata 1999; Ogata 2004).

While Amartya Sen was a co-chair of the Human Security Commission, he has also written widely about the concept. He frames his discussions of human security with what he argues are its four distinct elements: a clear focus on individual lives, a focus on social and societal elements of human livelihood, a focus on downside risks over general expansion of freedoms, and a focus on elementary human rights (2002: 2). In combination, these factors lead to an expansive conceptualization, but one which is differentiated from the concepts of human development and human rights via a subjective assessment of threat severity and a focus on downside risks. Whereas human development, Sen argues, is focused on progressive gains in the human condition, human security is the ability to absorb potential downturns. This vulnerability can be heightened by unequal opportunity for economic growth and development. He argues that, while there is complementarity between the concepts, their objectives are notably different. His conceptualization, however, remains broad. He endorses Obuchi's focus on human security as the 'menaces that threaten the survival, daily life, and dignity of human beings and to strengthening the efforts to confront these threats', which notably includes the dignity element of the Commission on Human Security's definition (2003).

Leaning and Arie take a decisively different approach, arguing that human security should be concerned with social, political, psychological, and economic factors that enable human well-being over time (Leaning 2004). This articulation combines basic physical human needs, such as water, food and shelter, with more intangible concerns, such as identity, recognition, participation and autonomy. Leaning and Arie argue that human insecurity is a product of hazards combined with coping mechanisms. The sum total of this equation is one's capability to remain secure, a concept they root in Jean Drèze and Amartya Sen's theory of social security, which led to subsequent work by Sen on the Capability Approach (Drèze and Sen 1989: 12). The three aspects of psycho-social well-being that Leaning and Arie propose (relationships with location, community, and time) render their definition very broad, but metrics are proposed for assessment (Leaning and Arie 2001: 18–31).

Similarly, Caroline Thomas (2004) argues that human security is a condition in which basic human needs are met, and in which dignity and community participation are realized. She divides the concept into quantitative material sufficiencies and qualitative measures of livelihood. Basic human needs, she argues, are necessary but not sufficient conditions of human security. It is important to note that, by explicitly bringing quality of life issues under the umbrella of human security, Thomas is broadening the definition dramatically. She is not simply arguing that quality of life is related to human security, but that a relatively high livelihood is a precondition for human security.

The Global Environmental Change and Human Security project (GHECHS) takes a notably environmentally focused perspective in their definition, but the core attributes have far wider implications. They see human security as a state in which individuals have the options to 'end, mitigate or adapt to threats to their human, environmental and social right' have the capacity and freedom to do so, and actively participate in doing so (Lonergan 2000: 1). While this is very broad, the focus of their definition is derived from a link to environmental degradation. They argue that there is a cumulative causality between environment and security, that responses to environmental insecurities may heighten other vulnerabilities, and that broader concepts underpinning human security (social, economic, environmental, or institutional) are often root causes for conflict, both environmental and more general (ibid. 2).

Kanti Bajpai (2004), in an extensive work advocating for a Human Security Audit, has argued that human security should be defined as an equation between threats and capabilities. While both will vary in time, and in any one location, the calculation is decipherable. As the elements of this equation are both temporally and regionally dependent, he argues, any uniform definition is futile. Bajpai's articulation is therefore the only one to introduce regionally and temporal subjective factors, which as will be discussed below is critical to overcoming the limitations of laundry-list style threat assessments.

In addition to the Canadian approach, on the narrow end of the spectrum, there are three principal articulations: Andy Mack, Sverre Lodgaard, and Neil MacFarlane and Yuen Foong Khong.

Andy Mack advocates for a narrowly defined understanding of human security, limiting its scope for pragmatic and methodological reasons (2002). He suggests a shift in referent to the individual, but a limitation of threat to those of political and criminal violence. He argues that the Human Development Report already addresses the freedom from want side of the spectrum, so another such report would be redundant. Methodologically, Mack argues that understanding the relationship between underdevelopment and violence necessarily requires a separation of dependent and independent variables. While Mack recognizes the potential in 'securitizing' a range of issues in order to increase their political urgency, he is not willing to do so at what he argues are severe analytic costs (HSC 2005).

Sverre Lodgaard sees violent threats to individuals as being analogous to military threats to states, and therefore proposes a very narrow, violence-based articulation of human security. Like Mack and the Human Security Report, he sees human security as a shift in the unit of analysis rather than a broadening of threats. Operationally, however, his conceptualization becomes quite broad. He sets out three general categories (the rule of law, public order and peaceful management of conflicts), which each encompass long lists of actionable policy areas (mitigation against physical torture, arbitrary arrest and detention of crime and street violence, rape and other domestic violence directed at women, child abuse, mishandling of refugees and so on). Each of these then have a host of social, political, economic and cultural root causes which would have to be addressed as part of any policy solution (Lodgaard 2000: 6–10). What is important to note from Lodgaard's conceptualization is that he has separated the original threat identification (violent threats to the individual) from the mitigation mechanisms, which are much more diverse.

MacFarlane and Khong present what are arguably the most sophisticated of the narrow conceptualizations. They argue that a definition must meet two challenges. First, it must achieve conceptual clarity by remaining true to the shift in the referent from the state to the individual. Second, it must analytically delineate and justify which threats are included and which are not (2005). The proposed organized violence conceptualization has two components. The first is to limit the horizontal extension of legitimate human security threats to those that are physical and violence-based. However, MacFarlane and Khong build on these earlier narrow definitions by adding the source of the violence, a perpetrator. What makes violence particularly potent, they argue, is that it is organized. Using this definition, the threat to individuals has to be violent and has to come from other organized individuals (2005). Therefore, a tsunami would not count as a threat to human security, but an al-Qaeda attack would. Also included would be genocide, internal/civil wars/terrorist attacks, inter-state war, ethnic cleansing, organized mass rape, torture and the laying of landmines. While MacFarlane and Khong state that environmental threats and disease are important, they argue that there is a cost to treating them as security issues, 'a mistake that not only dilutes the meaning of a useful concept but also complicates the process of prioritising the more deadly threats to human beings'. They believe that these 'most deadly' or 'gravest' threats are perpetrated by leaders of organized groups, including state elites, functionaries, outcasts or non-state actors such as terrorists (2004: 253).

Four Categories of Use

This conceptual diversity and obvious lack of agreement on which threats to the individual should be included as human security threats has led to the concept being used for a wide range of purposes. So much so, that it is difficult to consider the multifaceted uses of the concept as fitting in a single paradigm of research, activism or policy. Academics, governments and international organizations have all appropriated the term for markedly divergent reasons and uses. This has led many to reach dramatically different conclusions on its utility both as an analytical and policy tool. It is useful to catalogue the uses of human security in four clusters: human security as a policy tool, as a means of issue appropriation, as an exercise in measurement and as a critical tool.

First, human security has been used as a guiding principle for foreign policy and as a rationale for the mandates of international organizations. In the 1990s Japan, Canada and Norway began to see human security as a potentially attractive foreign policy doctrine.

In all three countries, human security was seen as a useful way of promoting issue areas in which there was a desire to have influence (in Canada landmines, in Norway conflict negotiation and in Japan international development). It was also seen as corresponding with a set of policy tools that each country had at their disposal. Following some early successes by each of these early adopters the creation of the Human Security Network widened the policy discussion further, to what a group of like-minded states could accomplish using the concept (Axworthy 2001a; Bosold and Werthes 2005; Roy and Baranyi 2005; DFAIT 2002; MacLean 2000). More recently, the Barcelona Report has identified human security as a guiding principle for a common EU foreign policy (Kaldor 2004; Kotsopoulos 2006). International institutions have also developed policy agendas based on human security. The UNDP's Human Development Reports, UNESCO's regional Human Security Assessments, the ICRC's work on protecting civilians in the late 1990s, and a wide range of Secretary General reports have all used human security as a conceptual framework (Annan 1999, 2000; Ogata and Sen 2003; UNDP 1994; UNESCO 2005). In addition, there has been a wide range of academic discussions on the validity and utility of human security as a guiding policy principle focusing on the feasibility and scope of the concept (Debiel and Werthes 2006; Hampson and Daudelin 2002; Kaldor 2007; MacLean 2006; McRae and Hubert 2001; Newman and Richmond, 2001; Suhrke 1999; Thakur 1997) as well as its regional applicability (Arevena and Goucha 2001; Bah 2004; Bedeski 2007; Burgess 2007; Glasius and Kaldor 2006; Tow 2000).

Second, human security has been used as a means of labelling a wide range of issues. A number of research and advocacy organizations have used the concept in order to promote their specific area of concern. Instances of this usage of the concept are vast, and include small arms (CHD 2003), landmines (Matthew *et al.* 2004), education (Sen 2002), international criminal law (Sembacher 2004), public health (Chen and Vasant 2003; Curley and Thomas 2004), food security (Clay and Stokke 2000), human trafficking (Nadig 2002; Friman and Reich 2007), globalization and development (Picciotto 2007), HIV/AIDS (Kristoffersson 2000), gender and peacebuilding (Lemmers 1999; Khagram 2001), water and conflict (Wolf 2001; Onduku 2004), security sector reform (Brzoska 2003), non-state actors (Bruderlein 2000), the environment (Bhattacharya and Hazra 2003; Brauch 2005; Dalby 2002a; Liotta 2003; Page and Redclift 2002), conflict prevention (Arevena 2001), refugees and forced migration (Adelman 2001; Graham and Poku 2000), conflict diamonds (Smillie 2000), and civilian protection in armed conflict (Annan 2001). Some of this literature links human security to a larger debate over the feasibility and scope of the concept, but most cases in this category of use simply appropriate the concept as a means of enhancing the advocacy position of the issue in question.

Third, there have been a series of projects aimed at measuring human security and a corresponding debate on the feasibility and utility of such efforts. These exercises range from econometric models, to large-N national-level statistical analyses, to more subjective threat local assessments (Bajpai 2001; Brecke 2003; Buttedahl 1994; King and Murray 2002; Leaning and Arie 2001; Lonergan 2000; Mack 2002; Owen 2002, 2003; Restrepo and Spagat 2004). Efforts at measurement are often quite closely linked to the definition debate, since what one chooses to measures can often be seen as a good indication of how the concept is being interpreted. But because most of the proposed measuring methodologies have not been implemented using real data, and none have been implemented by an organization or government to influence policy decisions, thus far, the methodological side of the this debate is largely an idiosyncratic exercise.

Fourth, the concept of human security has been used by a range of theoretical schools as a critical lens through which to analyse and critique state power. First, constructivists have used human security to challenge the central focus on the state in both neo-realist and liberal theorizing. They argue that this overemphasizes one security actor (the state) while diminishing a range of others, such as individuals, groups, NGOs and transnational organizations. They also argue that too much focus is placed on materialism and positivism, while failing to fully account for subjective, psychological, human elements of the security discourse (Tadjbakhsh, and Chenoy 2005: 87; Bellamy and McDonald 2002; Conteh-Morgan 2005; McDonald 2002; Newman, 2005). Second, advocating fundamental transformations to state and institutional systems, neo-Gramscian theorists have used human security to argue that a state-entrenched hegemonic elite promotes a global power structure and state-centric security discourse that marginalizes and undermines the true vulnerabilities of individuals (Conteh-Morgan 2004). Third, postmodernists use human security as a means of critiquing dominant knowledge theories, and subsequently the state as an all-encompassing security actor (Duffield and Nicholas 2004; Grayson 2004; Mendlovitz and Walker 2006; Seng 2001; Thomas 2001). And, fourth, feminist theorists use human security as a means of critiquing the patriarchal theory and practice embedded in the mainstream security discourse (Hoogensen 2006; Hudson 2006; McKay 2004; Nuruzzaman 2006). All four theoretical perspectives use human security as an agent of social change against dominant security processes.

Contested Concept

It is clear that human security is a contested concept. Aside from a consensus that the concept represents a referential shift from the state to the individual, proponents and critics alike are deeply divided over which threats should be included in the human security agenda. It is important to remember, however, that following the traditional definition of security, a security threat is defined as something that poses an existential threat to the state. This has led to a focus on a long, but manageable list of harms, including inter-state war, WMD proliferation, revolution and, recently, some global environmental threats such as climate change and desertification. But how the boundaries are drawn on this list of threats when the referent of security is transferred to the individual human being is far less clear. Are all potential existential threats to the individual to be included? Are all threats to all humans in all locations to be prioritized to the level of prescience that the security label commands? And, perhaps most critically, how serious does a threat have to be, and how many individuals must it harm, before the security label is evoked? In short, the literature on human security is contested on which humans are to be protected, when, and how, as well as on what, precisely, their security entails. This has led to a proliferation of definitions, numerous conceptualizations for categorizing the literature, and to a proliferation of its use for widely varying purposes.

But perhaps this is of little concern. When asked critically about the level of uncertainty, debate, conjecture, and outright scepticism regarding the concept of human security, former Canadian foreign minister Lloyd Axworthy responded assertively: 'The world had no idea what sovereignty and the security infrastructure would look like immediately following the signing of the treaty of Westphalia. Norms evolved through decades of debate, thought, action, conflict and compromise' (2001b). This is worth considering as we address the state and future of the concept of human security. There is no doubt that the majority of human vulnerability is not the result of inter-state war but rather is caused by disease, extreme poverty, natural disasters, civil conflict and small arms. As the primary threats have changed, so too must our security mechanisms.

6

Critical Geopolitics and Security

Simon Dalby

Geopolitics

Geopolitics is a term traditionally used to refer to great power rivalries and the geographical dimensions of global political power. Sometimes used as a synonym for political geography it supposedly captures the importance of context and scale in considerations of politics, but links this to an awareness of the weighty matters of international politics (Dodds 2007). Indeed the utility of geopolitical reasoning in the speeches and pronouncements of politicians and pundits is often precisely in its apparent simultaneous invocation of intellectual gravitas and political acumen. Geopolitics is a matter of serious consideration in the halls of power, in the institutes for studying foreign policy as well as in political speeches that invoke geographical languages to specify the world in particular ways that have political effect.

The term has traditionally been applied to matters of foreign policy-making, and to the frequently implicit coding of the world used by foreign policy elites and politicians in decision-making (Dodds and Atkinson 2000). These themes continue to permeate discussions of world order (Kearns 2009), only most obviously in contemporary discussions of great powers and the geographical aspects of their grand strategies (Grygiel 2006). Partly in response to alarms about nuclear war in the 1980s, and partly because of the new intellectual concerns with discourse, culture and in particular the then nascent discussions of Orientalism (Said 1978) in other disciplines, a critical engagement was stimulated with the geographical representations used in politics (Dalby 2008a). What became known as critical geopolitics grew out of this combination of intellectual concerns in parallel with similar critical currents in international relations and security studies (Campbell 1992; Der Derian and Shapiro 1989; Walker 1993).

Critical Geopolitics

In drawing explicitly on Edward Said's (1978) formulation of imaginative geographies the early critical geopolitics literature looked to the taken-for-granted mappings of the arenas

CRITICAL GEOPOLITICS AND SECURITY

of international politics (Ó Tuathail and Agnew 1992), and in traditional realist security studies (Dalby 1990). In John Agnew's (2003: 3) words: 'The world is actively "spatialized", divided up, labeled, sorted out into a hierarchy of places of greater or lesser "importance" by political geographers, other academics and political leaders. This process provides the geographical framing within which political elites and mass publics act in the world in pursuit of their own identities and interests.' But in doing so such 'geopolitical reasoning' frequently simplifies and obscures the subtleties and local circumstances of political struggle, war and globalization.

Through the 1990s geographers used the term critical geopolitics to encompass a diverse range of academic challenges to the conventional ways in which political space was written, read and practiced (Ó Tuathail and Dalby 1998; Ó Tuathail *et al.* 1998). The emphasis was on deconstructive readings of geopolitical reasoning, in leading author Gearoid Ó Tuathail's (1996a: 68) words, from his key book on the subject simply titled *Critical Geopolitics*:

> Critical geopolitics is distinguished by its problematization of the logocentric infrastructures that make 'geopolitics' or any spatialization of the global political scene possible. It problematizes the 'is' of 'geography' and 'geopolitics', their status as self evident, natural, foundational, and eminently knowable realities. ... In contrast to the strategic ambition of imperial geopolitics (which is about the establishment of place or proper locus), critical geopolitics is a tactical form of knowledge. It works within the conceptual infrastructures that make the geopolitical tradition possible and borrows from it the resources necessary for its deconstruction.

Rather than a single analytical or methodological endeavor, critical geopolitics encompassed various ways of unpacking the geographical assumptions in politics, asking how the cartographic imagination of here and there, inside and outside, them and us, states, blocs, zones, regions, or other geographical specifications, worked to both facilitate some political possibilities and actions and exclude and silence others. These writings all challenge common-sense and 'modern' assumptions that national identities and the states that govern populations are the necessary starting point for either policy discussion or scholarly analysis.

A key part of such analyses aims to understand both how such assumptions have come to be taken for granted and what political possibilities are silenced by this modern geopolitical imagination which can invoke such concepts as 'Europe' (Heffernan 1998), without reflection on either their complex discursive heritage or the political implications in such designations. Who is European has been an especially complicated political question in recent years (Kuus 2007). The challenge is to problematize the practices of geographical knowledge production, whether in terms of the 'formal geopolitics' of scholarly texts, the more 'practical geopolitics' of policy-makers and practitioners of statecraft, the 'popular geopolitics' in media representations of contemporary events and in popular entertainment genres (Ó Tuathail and Agnew 1992), or in the resistance to conventional designations in 'anti-geopolitical' protests (Routledge 1998). These critical concerns increasingly melded with larger concerns in the geographical discipline that explained in the 1990s how spaces are anything but natural phenomena (Lewis and Wigen 1997). This research showed that the geographical constructions of everything from large-scale maps that define property boundaries, to the small-scale maps of states and empires, are modes of reasoning with powerful political effect.

51

Such considerations focus attention on how important spatial assumptions are to modern discussions of administration, whether at state or other 'levels'. Territory is basic to conventional political, legal, and social science definitions of states. Jurisdiction is first and foremost a territorial matter in the modern world. At the largest of scales the taken-for-granted political constructions of North and South, developed and developing, zones of peace and zones of turmoil, failed states, and so on structure how governance is usually considered. As even writers in *The Economist* magazine (1999) came to understand by the end of the 1990s, when discussions of global problems appear in policy deliberations and scholarly texts, their implicit geopolitical representations shape the discussion by providing the ontological categories that literally 'geo-graph' or 'write the earth'.

The conceptual inadequacies of these ontological schemes are often immensely politically productive. The ability to specify the world in simple geographic terms has political utility when these terms are accepted as the common-sense parameters for political reasoning. In terms of American foreign policy in the 1990s the basic distinction between democratic and non-democratic states structured many of the discussions. Coded in terms of zones of peace and zones of turmoil, danger could be specified as external; its origins somewhere out there beyond 'our' borders (Ó Tuathail and Luke 1994). Categories of rogue states defined particular places as in need of military containment. Such cartographic practices suggested a separateness to them, and their place, that operates politically to remove obligation and responsibility across these borders (Campbell 1993). The specification of states in terms of these categories shapes the policies that are deemed appropriate by the rich and powerful who make state foreign policy, and by most other people who use these categories. It also constructs particular political identities in these spaces and in conjunction with these identities appropriate modes of conduct for these identities in their own spaces and elsewhere.

Such insights spawned a diverse range of scholarly investigations in the 1990s examining identities and places in terms of the implicit spatial formulations that structured them in many genres. Many of these studies involved examining fairly clear geographical specifications of danger and insecurity. Notably Joanne Sharp (2000) looked to popular culture representations of American identity in the Cold War as articulated in numerous articles in the *Reader's Digest*. Her longitudinal study of these texts which she wrote about as exercises in *Condensing the Cold War*, showed a remarkable persistence of themes of American virtue and Soviet threat regardless of the specific topic of the story. Klaus Dodds's (1997) analysis of Antarctica focused on how one single place was understood differently as the discursive practices through which it was represented changed as international politics and science were reinvented. At various times Antarctica was understood as a place of geopolitical rivalry in the Cold War. In the 1950s it became a scientific arena for cooperation in geophysical research. Subsequently it has been a place for tourism, with agreements to ban mineral prospecting and mining, more recently a place to monitor climate change. How its attributes are specified is intimately related to how governance structures are formulated to deal with this space. These change but Antarctica remains.

The popular articulation of identity, and the invocation of geographical tropes to situate actors in political dramas complements this analysis of the technical practices of governance; who is rendered insecure by precisely what threat to their social and political identity is a matter of culture understood broadly and critical geopolitical analysis focused on movies (Sharp 1998), cartoons (Dodds 1998), and popular culture in many places as well as on protest movements that challenged the dominance of official scripts of place and territory (Routledge 1998) and the geographical imaginations implicit in the use of

CRITICAL GEOPOLITICS AND SECURITY

violent opposition to state power (Sparke 1998). This literature also engaged with gender as a mode of critique focusing on the gendered dimensions of war and peace (Ó Tuathail 1996b) and the larger questions of violence tied into numerous gendered spaces and practices which rendered people, and women in particular, insecure (Dowler and Sharp 2001; Hyndmann 2001).

Concerns about environmental dangers also proliferated in the 1990s, with some of the most highly cited texts drawing links between traditional Malthusian scenarios of disaster and more contemporary angst concerning migration and the crossing of numerous boundaries. The links to the broader agenda of environmental security also drew critical comment on the spatial assumptions structuring discussions of dangers related to resources and ecological politics (Dalby 2002b). More recently the discussion of resource wars and the links between consumption practices in the metropoles and the violence tied into the production of many consumer products has extended such concerns into analysis of the complex political economies of diamonds, petroleum, tropical timber, and other commodities (Le Billon 2008).

Critical Geopolitics and the Global War on Terror

In the aftermath of the events of September 11 2001 and the American declaration of a 'global' war on terror as the overarching framework for the conduct of American foreign policy, the importance of critical geopolitics as a mode of tackling the taken-for-granted assumptions in American security policy in particular, and more generally Western security thinking, has become even more pronounced (Dalby 2003). But simultaneously the literature published under this label has also continued to become more diverse and interconnected with social theory and security studies elsewhere. Only some of the more salient lines of inquiry can be highlighted here; but the problematization of the spatial categories and the invocations of dangers in political discourse remains a major thrust of literature under the rubric of critical geopolitics in recent years (Ingram and Dodds 2009; Pain and Smith 2008). Hence its continued importance to matters of security, the new agendas of human security, and the broader themes of critical security studies.

Four themes are especially salient in the profusion of analyses that have emerged from the discussion of the war on terror and contemporary political violence. First the reinvention of colonial tropes in political discourse and the imperial motifs that run through the discussion of American power; second the proliferation of discourses of danger into numerous practical dimensions of everyday life and the implicit and sometimes very explicitly geographical tropes of endangerment that run through the popular political discussion; third the practical application of power in the war on terror, the redrawing of boundaries, the reinvention of prison camps at Guantanamo and such security practices as the formulation of 'homeland security'; and fourth the remilitarization of North American culture and the related matter of citizenship, how it is now understood in geographical terms in the face of globalization and apparently global threats from terrorists and the imprecisely mapped dangers of the current 'new wars'.

Derek Gregory's (2004) book *The Colonial Present* reprises some of the early themes of critical geopolitics when he returns to Michel Foucault for theoretical inspiration, and specifically to Edward Said's (1978) analysis of Orientalism and the powerful construction of the Middle East in antithesis to Occidental modernity. Gregory does so to investigate how such formulations are rearticulated in contemporary times in the constitution of

53

various places in the Middle East as arenas in the war on terror. Arguing that many of the colonial formulations of earlier times are reappearing in discourses of superior Western civilization confronting non-Western threats, of barbarism of various kinds, he examines in detail the cases of the invasion of Afghanistan in 2001 and its aftermath, the invasion of Iraq and the subsequently violent aftermath of the occupation, as well as the Israeli occupation of Palestine with all the colonizing rhetoric and practices involved in that conflict.

The Cold War Manichean division of the world into them and us, civilization and barbarism, their place and ours (Dalby 1990), was quickly reprised in George Bush's rhetoric in late 2001 as 'with us or with the terrorists', and subsequently codified in official national security doctrine the following year. How the fear generated from 9/11 was subsequently invoked as a justification for the invasion of Iraq is also focused on, but the key point here is ironically precisely the lack of geographical specificity which allowed the global war on terror to conflate Osama bin Laden with Saddam Hussein, while simultaneously there was an intense debate about the legalities of violating the territorial integrity of Iraq (Elden 2007). All violence is subsumed under a global war script that in this case ignored the geographical practicalities in specific places in favour of an overarching vision of a global geopolitical struggle to eradicate the wild zones on the fringes of civilization (Dalby 2007).

In part, this worked rhetorically because fear of threatening others, terrorists, migrants and imprecise dangers of many other things were part of the larger rearticulation of American culture in the 'culture wars' of the previous generation (Williams 2007). But the other part of Derek Gregory's geographical analysis points precisely to the technical specification of the world into military terms, into geographies of targets, nodal points, secure spaces, battlespaces, regional commands and a huge repertoire of geographical terms, nearly all of which work to remove people from the potential landscapes of combat (Gregory 2006a). Targets are designated in the technical terms of missile sights/sites not in terms of residents, local cultures, histories and prior inhabitation. Here the specific designation of contemporary cities as the terrain of military action in the future is an especially important matter as the war on terror morphs into occupation and pacification of the cities of the South and the policing of cities of the North in the new militarized versions of contemporary security thinking, another important matter for research in contemporary critical geographical scholarship (Graham 2004, 2010).

This policing is related to the popular fears of numerous threats to everyday life in the metropoles of the global economy (Pain and Smith 2008). The proliferation of numerous fears of many things, not only the immediate dangers of terrorist attacks, but fears of poisons, economic disruptions, diseases, cultural change, natural hazards, moral depravities of all sorts, are prevalent in numerous genres in contemporary life. Risk management has become a dominant formulation in social policy as well as business and insurance. The uncertainties of life have become commodified in informational capitalism, and are persistent themes in advertising discourse too where protection from numerous vagaries is an important theme in selling all manner of things and services. These fears are politically useful as well as profitable for corporations which can marketize fear effectively (Dillon 2008).

Implicit in much of this discourse are geographical definitions of proximate safety and external threat. The violation of in here from out there is directly related to policing strategies of territorial control (Herbert 2007). Hence the intertextuality of geopolitical threat with all manner of contemporary fear has provided a rich vein of inquiry for geographers interested in how danger works as a political strategy, and how insecurity is a cultural phenomenon with variations dependent on specific context (Ingram and Dodds

2009). This works from the macro geopolitics of the war on terror, through the security landscapes of gated communities at various scales (van Houtum and Pijpers 2008), to the micro geographies of bodily encounters coded in the Orientalizations of 'Muslims' or 'Turks' on the streets of metropolitan cities (Haldrup *et al.* 2008), the slums of Southern cities (Graham 2008) and through numerous other modes of political violence in many places (Flint 2004; Gregory and Pred 2007).

The fear of cultural others and the specification of Muslims as potential terrorists in the cultural articulations of danger in the aftermath of 9/11 play into larger geopolitical concerns with migration and the supposed necessity of controlling entry into Europe and the USA in particular (Coleman 2003, 2007; Noxolo 2009). Likewise the extraordinary measures that the US government has gone to in specifying the prison facility in Guantanamo Bay as outside court jurisdiction also points to the complete inadequacies of the conventional mapping of the nation state as an unproblematic geographic entity with responsibilities for ensuring security against internal subversion and external threat (Gregory 2006b; Hannah 2006). In none of these cases do Weberian definitions of state sovereignty based on precise territorial demarcations and patrolled borders make sense in the lived world of people in contested places.

Nonetheless the remilitarization of citizenship; the laudatory language used by political elites concerning the actions and sacrifices of military personnel in the occupations of Iraq and Afghanistan, has proceeded apace and drawn the attention of geographers interested to tease out how the professional militaries of Western states rearticulate loyalties and obligations in the conditions of contemporary warfare (Cowen and Gilbert 2008). Where these professional soldiers are deployed and the practical politics of how their activities relate to the politics of the states who send them to distant places also requires some careful geographical analysis to specify who is fighting for what where. The geographies of all this are especially fraught where NATO now deploys troops in Afghanistan and the UN doctrine of the responsibility to protect remind critical commentators of the logic of empire despite the sophisticated rationales of human security and the apparent need for humanitarian interventions in many places, whether as a matter of fighting a 'new war' or aiding a population suffering the after affects of a 'natural disaster' (Hyndman 2008).

Once again the key point from a geographical analysis here is the sheer complexity of interconnections across boundaries in sharp contrast to how simple cartographic practices of naming states and regions as supposedly separate entities structure the narratives justifying intervention while simultaneously upholding territorial integrity (Elden 2007). What critical geographical analysis, and the persistent focus on the taken-for-granted spatial assumptions in contemporary geopolitical reasoning in particular, has revealed is the irony of territory in all these formulations of dangers and insecurities. Territorial entities are simultaneously essential and contingent; regimes in Afghanistan and Iraq were removed, only to require immediate reconstitution, whether under the rubric of nation building, development, democracy, human rights or the responsibility to protect. In Stuart Elden's (2008: 158) summation: 'Territorial preservation is almost an absolute, because of the perceived dangers to stability of secession or fragmentation; yet territorial sovereignty is now held to be contingent, for humanitarian reasons, the harboring of terrorists, or the production of weapons of mass destruction.' Hence the appropriateness of asking geographical questions concerning the location of power and the representational practices of claims to legitimate authority. Geographical common sense, the modern mapping of states, nations, boundaries, and territorial jurisdictions is itself now very obviously insecure!

Popular Culture and Tabloid Geopolitics

The ironies of territory and the inescapable point that popular representations of danger and of the spaces of safety and threat implicit in these formulations are part of the contemporary geopolitical imaginary has led to a focus on popular geopolitics that runs in parallel with the literature that explicitly engages contemporary practices of violence (Shapiro 2007). This in part is because of the widespread recognition that geographical formulations are key to contemporary practices of legitimation and are so not least because geographical understandings render the cultural constructions of modernity as the natural given ontological context for discussion. These landscapes are in turn populated with numerous exemplary figures, warriors and civilians, evil doers and heroes who rescue innocent victims, contextualized in narrative structures that are amenable to the analytical tools of contemporary cultural studies quite as much, and frequently much more, as by the more formal tools of spatial analysis (Dalby 2008b).

This focus on popular culture has lead to analyses of movies and the geopolitical settings invoked in popular entertainment (Crampton and Power 2007) as well as such things as the cartoon strip adventures of Captain America as a means of investigating the popular imaginary of American identity set in antithesis to many imaginary foes (Dittmer 2005). To work as a culturally believable narrative such superheroes have to invoke articulations of national identity and endangerment which provide an interesting fictional counterpoint to conventional political rhetorics (Dodds 2005; Ó Tuathail 2003). In doing so they also provide legitimations to particular forms of behaviour, acceptable conduct in the face of dangers to that social order, and common cultural framings of the contexts for those behaviours. Most recently these textual themes have begun to link up with more conventional analysis of politics by looking at the reception of key movies, examining the online movie databases where movies are ranked by audiences and discussed at length online (Dodds and Dittmer 2008). This research extends the focus in contemporary cultural analysis of security on identity and endangerment by explicitly examining the contextualizations of internal safety and external threat, and all the complicated geographies of empire, combat and 'interventions' (Dalby 2008b).

Analyses of fictional representations of contemporary geopolitics, and in particular those linked to contemporary religious dimensions of geopolitics in American popular culture, add an additional important dimension to contemporary popular geopolitics and articulations of danger (Dittmer 2009). This is especially the case with the 'fundamentalist' religious themes of prophecy and widespread beliefs that the world is entering 'end times' and will soon see warfare and tribulation predicted in various biblical texts. In particular this matters in so far as it facilitates particular American foreign policies justified by religious rather than geopolitical calculation (Sturm 2006). Given the explicit invocation of geographical themes as justification for the interpretations of prophecy in widely read commentaries on contemporary politics analysis of these apparently banal matters of popular culture has political import in so far as such religious systems have influence on policy-making.

This focus on popular culture is also important when discussing other forms of fear including those of disease and the dangers of biohazards (Hartmann *et al.* 2005). The popular cultural repertoire provides the scripts wherein danger is understood and the cultural logics of threats to the social and moral order articulated. How anxieties are channeled in facing threats of pandemics matters in terms of how specific dangers are used to justify particular responses which may target certain groups as the carriers of disease (Ingram 2008). Such

CRITICAL GEOPOLITICS AND SECURITY

themes too have led to some of the most famous parodies and spoofs of danger and its responses in popular culture. The genre of Zombie movies, and recently such productions as *Shaun of the Dead*, and in particular *Fido*, rearticulate widespread anxieties while examining how danger causes social change, and in turn provide more grist for the mills of academic commentary linking cinema to geopolitical analysis (Molloy 2009).

Contemporary popular formulations rely on geographical oversimplifications and repetition of simple story lines and shocking media images, such as the bodies of American servicemen being dragged through the streets of Mogadishu in 1993 or airliners crashing into the World Trade Center to construct what Debrix (2008) calls 'tabloid geopolitics'. 'Tabloid geopolitics is the form taken by the medium and its discourse, particularly in the United States, in the early twenty-first [century] in matters regarding national security, the survival of the state (the United States first and foremost), war, and global terror' (Debrix 2008: 5). Interrogating this through the implicit geographical categories used to structure the discourse thus offers a continuing mode of critique that challenges the categories through which insecurity is articulated and dangers are made efficacious in ways that can be used to mobilize forces and prepare for various kinds of emergencies, threats and wars. The point of such a critique is not that these wars, emergencies, and threats are entirely fictitious; diseases, bombs, and challenges to the political order of modernity are many. But how they become a matter of security, dealt with by practices of warfare, and emergency actions are unavoidably tied into these practical matters of tabloid scripts and geopolitical representation. Security is unavoidably about culture (Williams 2007); now too it is unavoidably about how television portrays violence, and does so in ways that are no longer entirely dominated by Western channels (Khatib 2009).

Global Insecurities/Geographical Theories

Contemporary anxieties about climate change and the potential for dramatic disruptions in the biosphere in coming decades have also recently reintroduced some of the themes from the environmental security discussion with all its fears of refugees, political violence and disruption as a result of climate change-induced shortages. This too brings with it a geopolitical imagination in how sources of danger are represented. But what is clear is that the simplistic cartographic assumptions of national security states and internal safe spaces to be protected from external depredations, which have for so long structured the narratives of tabloid geopolitics, are no longer tenable given the unavoidable facts that the metropolitan states are the sources of the majority of greenhouse gases and the disruptions of many of the natural ecologies of the planet (Dalby 2009). The conventional geography of national security no longer holds in these discourses of danger.

Nor do the geographical categories of social theory hold in contemporary discussions; indeed some of the intense disputes about post-modernism and post-colonial studies can be understood precisely as attempts to grapple with the now impossible cartographies of identity. As Matt Sparke's (2005) lengthy analysis of the 'space of theory' suggests, the founding myths of stable modern states and communities that can be easily mapped have given way to a recognition that post-modern spaces are more about flows, connections, and changes than stabilities. Hence, too, the discussions of empire and the possible geographical vocabularies of imperialism as a better designation of contemporary power (Dalby 2005). But Sparke's (2007) more recent discussion of the responsibilities of geography now takes these arguments further by arguing that post-foundational critique requires the refusal

57

to take any geographical categories for granted; indeed his argument is that it is precisely in challenging these categories that an ethic of responsibility emerges for contemporary scholars.

The key point in all this which links Sparke's (2005, 2007) theoretical concerns and Gregory's (2004, 2006a) more empirical investigations of contemporary practices of violence is a focus on the explicit spatializations of politics that structure the narratives that legitimate the violence. This crucial theme runs through the chapters in Ingram and Dodds (2009) which pose critical geopolitics analyses of many places in the securitized contexts of the war on terror and the militarization of modes of governance in the aftermath of 9/11 mostly outside the USA. All this matters because the territorial language of sovereignty and security cannot now be taken for granted in any analysis of security; identities and places are unavoidably political formulations with practical effect in the geopolitical language of contemporary political anxieties (Debrix and Lacy 2009). Critical geopolitics renders the spatial vocabularies of insecurity part of the larger task for critical security studies; it does so by making the ontological categories of security thinking part of the analysis, rather than simply allowing them to specify taken for granted contexts for articulations of danger.

Part II
New Security Subjects

7

Biopolitics of Security

Michael Dillon

> Nothing is more important than a revision of the concept of security as a basic principle of state politics.–
>
> (Giorgio Agamben)

> Freedom is nothing but the correlative development of apparatuses of security.–
>
> (Michel Foucault)

Introduction

There are now several schools of biopolitics. In addition to those inspired by the work of Michel Foucault and Giorgio Agamben, others include that of Paolo Virno (2005), Negri and Hardt (2000, 2004) and, more recently, Roberto Esposito (2008). This chapter leaves the detailed task of differentiating between these different schools of biopolitics for another occasion. It nonetheless does offer a summary overview of the two most prominent accounts of biopolitics. The first of these is the original one supplied by Foucault. The other is that supplied by Agamben. In explaining how Foucauldian biopolitics fundamentally differs from Agamben's, the chapter also indicates how, taking these different projects as their inspiration, Foucauldian biopolitics focus on the micro-practices and governing technologies of contemporary biopolitics, exploring in addition how these change along with changing accounts of the nature of life itself, while biopolitical analysis inspired by Agamben tends, instead, to focus on the nihilism of modern politics, the juridical reduction of 'natural' life to bare life and the ramifications of the claim that the juridical exception is the rule and 'the [concentration] camp' the *nomos* of rule (Agamben 1999, 2000).

Foucauldian biopolitics has in many respects been overshadowed by Agamben's in the last ten years. Although Foucault's *The History of Sexuality* (1981) first broached the idea of biopolitics for the Anglo-American world, the lectures in which he extensively explored biopolitics have only recently been published and translated into English (Foucault 2003b, 2007, 2009). For that reason, Foucault's account of biopolitics remains in many respects less well developed in the English-speaking world than that of Agamben; and this despite the significantly more esoteric and philosophically difficult account which Agamben provides. Whereas Foucault's account is genealogical, clearly influenced in addition by Nietzsche's emphasis on the importance of relations of force, Agamben's biopolitics is very much more concerned with interrogating 'the originary' relation of law to life. In consequence, Agamben's biopolitics is driven much more by his engagement with the German jurist and political theorist Carl Schmitt and, in particular, with pursuing Walter Benjamin's critique of Schmitt's theory of the correlation of sovereign power, the law and the exception (Benjamin 2004; Schmitt 2008, 2007, 2005a). 'In fact', as Catherine Mills observes in her excellent study of *The Philosophy of Agamben*, Agamben's 'account of biopolitics is more accurately read as an attempt to fulfil or complete Benjamin's critique of Schmitt's theory of sovereignty than it is an attempt to "complete" Foucault' (Mills 2009).

Foucault's biopolitics is thus a direct extension of his genealogical analysis of the diverse and heterogeneous domain of modern power relations, in which the issue of the originary nature of things is displaced by differentiation of the concrete micro-practices through which historically different apparatuses or technologies of modern power and governance work. Agamben's project is instead a direct extension of his preoccupation with language (Agamben 1993, 1999c), sustained critique of the nihilism of Western metaphysics (Agamben 1991, 1999b), the workings of its 'anthropological machine' (Agamben 2004b) and his politics of the messianic (Agamben 2005b). If Foucault's project can therefore be said to be that of interrogating the power of truth-telling in the modern period, and the collateral effects which different orders of power/knowledge have on the simultaneous empowerment and subjection of the modern subject, Agamben's project is in many ways more traditionally philosophical; however idiomatic every philosophical voice may be, and Agamben's is quite distinctive.

Less concerned with the ethos and power of the truth-teller, Agamben is more concerned with the traditional philosophical pursuit of 'truth' and the ethos it demands. Understanding that the human does not simply have language but is had by language, the 'truth' in Agamben's case therefore lies in the unspeakable or the ineffable which lies at the heart of the taking place of language as such (Mills 2009). Deeply influenced also therefore by Heidegger, as Foucault admitted that he was too, the Heidegger in Agamben is, however, not leavened by Nietzsche in the way that it is in Foucault. Agamben's concern for history similarly also, then, conflates more than it discriminates. It is the history of Western metaphysics, its nihilism and the prospect of a new taking place of the experience of language.

For both thinkers, nonetheless, biopolitics may in general be said to be the interrogation of what happens to politics and power when the biological properties of the human species become the referent object of politics and power. Whereas Foucault did address himself directly to the reproblematization of security which occurs when security discourses and practices also take the biological properties of human species as their referent object of security (2007), Agamben does not directly address the biopolitics of security as a 'politics' of security. His work has nonetheless influenced many concerned with, for example, the camp as the *nomos* of Western society and politics (Diken and Lausten 2005; Edkins 2003), with the vast increase in powers of surveillance by Western governments (Lyon 2006), and in the unlawful holding of suspected 'terrorists' in a wide variety of 'camps' worldwide, the most notorious of which is Guantanamo (Munster 2004).

Biopolitics of Security: Foucault

One cannot understand Foucault's account of biopolitics – and thereby of the biopolitics of security – unless one first addresses Foucault's generic understanding of power. Foucault teaches that power is less a commodity that can be held than a force which comes into circulation when human beings – who he considers to be free beings – come into relation with one another. To be crude, power as a force that circulates is more like electricity than it is like a lever or a sword. From Foucault's perspective, human beings are also extraordinarily good conductive material for the generation and circulation of power. However energizing and conductive they may be, it is also fair to say that Foucault does not think that human beings were made for the sole purpose of generating and conducting power. Since Foucault scrupulously avoids saying what they are I suspect he thinks that the question is not only radically undecidable but also the wrong place to begin any analytics of power, at least if it does not recognize that the way the question is posed and answered is radically historical. Human conductivity to any individual form of power has limits.

Foucault's understanding of power is relational and strategic. Relational because it arises in the context of networks of relations established when human beings relate to one another; and to 'things'. Strategic because relations of power are structured by different generative principles of strategic formation. The result is not only a field of formation, in which the dynamics of the logic of strategic formation can be conjugated, but what Foucault also calls a 'field of intervention'. Fields of intervention are where the problems addressed by different strategic formations of power find their specific problematization. These in turn allow power to discover what Foucault also calls their specific 'points of application'. A good example, in each instance, for biopower, would be 'population'.

For Foucault modern power relations are also distinguished by the fact that they seek to ground themselves in truth, specifically the regional truths or rationalities of their referent objects or fields of intervention and points of application. Thus, for example, the rationality of sovereign power in the modern period was raison d'état. Correspondingly we might say that biopower seeks to ground itself in 'the truth' of human being as biological being and more generally now, in the twenty-first century, in the 'informationalized truth' of what is said now simply to be a living being as such.

In his earlier lectures on *Society Must Be Defended* (2003b) and *Security, Territory, Population* (2007), Foucault had detailed how biopolitics arises as one of the principal means by which liberal response to sovereign absolutism sought both to constrain sovereign power and themselves to offer their own distinctive account of how power might best operate to rule more effectively. In *The Birth of Biopolitics* (2008) he further details how biopolitics is not the only characteristic of liberal regimes of power, but how they also bring economic criteria to bear on the problematic of rule – introducing a homo oeconomicus disruptively into the sphere of the subject of rights established under sovereign rule – and suffer successive 'crises of governance' as well (Foucault 2008).

Foucault is concerned with how this 'truth', a truth in the emergence of modern power relations which was once distinctive of liberal regimes of power, gets applied to every aspect of life. Here one can also observe an unexamined connection between species life and economy. Foucault's lectures *The Birth of Biopolitics* (2008) are almost exclusively concerned with the application of the truth of economy to the problematization and operation of government and governance (it is of course also a changing truth), and with the successive 'crises of governance' which liberal regimes experienced throughout the twentieth century. What he doesn't say directly and explicitly, although the point is obvious in retrospect, is that if circulation and contingency characterize species existence (Dillon 2006) so also does economy. Species existence is in other words also said to be a reproductive economy of continuous transaction and exchange between the organism (in this case human being) and its environment; to which the truth or rationality of economy – essentially different forms of utile means–ends analysis – can also be rigorously modelled and applied. Little wonder, therefore, that risk should become such a prevailing biopolitical security practice; since risk makes contingency fungible and commodifies the exposure to danger and opportunity for advantage which, together, now describe what risk is (Dillon 2008a).

A fundamental shift occurs here in the kind of questions asked of government and governance. Respecting the truth of economy as a metric which itself could be applied to the evaluation of the rule of rule, the task of rule acquired a new criterion biopolitically and was thereby construed differently. Subject to the truth of economy, both as a metric of rule as well as a separate domain of social behaviour, it was no longer sufficient, for example, to ask if rule was legitimate. It also became necessary to ask, biopolitically, if rule was effective and successful. Indeed, it became obligatory to make rule as effective and successful as it could be if the biopolitical project of rule to make life live was to be pursued and realized (Foucault 2008: 17). The criteria of success were now to be found in how well power regulated these domains of life, navigating between regulating too little and regulating too much, seeking to discover how much regulation was enough for successfully promoting life in pursuit of making life live.

When power comes to take species existence as its referent object, and when the biopolitics of security come to take species life as their referent object as well, then the *dispositif* of power relations follows suit and begins to revolve around the properties of species existence. There is little space to go into what the properties of species existence are said to be, or explain in detail how the account of species existence has been changing over the last two hundred years. Suffice to say that it has, and that as it has done so biopolitics and the biopolitics of security in particular have followed suit (Dillon and Lobo-Guerrero 2008; Dillon 2008a). But we can say that, whereas for Foucault circulation and contingency were the primary characteristics of species existence, so also, in fact, is economy. Species are now said to survive through the operation of a continuously and contingent economy of circulation in which the living entity emergently co-evolves with its environment. Moreover, when the truth of economy begins to be applied systematically to the governing practices of security and war – to the very transformation of cognition brought to the reproblematization of the entire space of security and war through transformation of military strategic discourse and security talk, as well as operational concepts and doctrines and equipment acquisition – further radical conflation of the civil and the military takes place throughout the governing practices of liberal societies.

What is species existence according to Foucault? The discourse of life understood as species existence (*espèce humaine*) differs fundamentally, he observed in his lectures on *Security, Territory, Population*, from life understood as 'le genre humain' (Foucault 2007). The root of *le genre humain* – *gens* – refers to the *jus gentium* of Roman and medieval law. Usually translated as 'the law of nations', and extensively treated in the work of two early modern international jurists, Hugo Grotius and Emmerich de Vattel, the *gentium* of *jus gentium* invokes the juridico-political and cultural notion of a 'people' or 'peoples' belonging together in respect of law and custom, and not the biological notion of 'species' (the root of *espèce*, or *être biologique*), in which the principle of belonging together is furnished by shared biological properties. *Être biologique* is not then, for example, Machiavelli's Renaissance republican idea of *civere civile*. The move from *gentium* to *espèce* thus effects a transformation in the very discursive understanding of what it is to be a living being and, correspondingly also therefore, of how the governmental regulation of such a living thing will operate.

What followed, then, in that shift from *gentium* to *espèce* was a transformation not only in the referent object of power relations, in the very mechanisms by which power operates and circulates, but also in the very understanding of the 'nature of the nature' from which politics and power are said to follow; what Foucault calls the political rationalities as well as the governing technologies of power. Specifically, in relation to *espèce humaine*, power comes to be exercised on, in and through the biological mass which constitutes the 'species', an empirical example of which is 'population', rather than the juridico-political and cultural processes of belonging and rule said to constitute the *gens* of *gentium*, or of 'le genre humaine' (Dillon and Lobo-Guerrero 2008).

Foucault argues that the eighteenth century witnessed a historically unique event, that is, 'the entry of phenomena peculiar to the life of the human species into the order of knowledge and power, into the sphere of political techniques' (Foucault 1981: 141–2). He goes on to claim that 'for the first time in history, no doubt, biological existence was reflected in political existence' (p. 142). Thus the administration of life became the central characteristic and defining rationale of the regime of power operative in the modern world. From this, Foucault suggests that the conception of man proposed by Aristotle as a 'living animal with the additional capacity for a political existence' should be revised to acknowledge that 'modern man is an animal whose politics places his existence as a living being in question' (p. 143). From there he goes on to argue with some force that wars made in the name of making life live make massacres and genocide vital and that the threshold of modernity is reached when it comes to wager the life of the species on its own political strategies; strategies by means of which war is not the extension of politics by other means but strategies, rather, in which politics is construed as the extension of war by other means (Dillon and Neal 2008; Foucault 2003b). Security discourses and practices thus become the means by which the logos of war is deeply inscribed into the logos of peace. Indeed, security discourses simply are the logos of war written as the logos of peace (Dillon and Neal 2008; Dillon and Reid 2009).

Foucault sees security as integrally involved with the biopoliticization of politics. Like discourses and practices of power, security discourses and practises similarly also revolve around the properties of their referent object. Biopolitical security practices revolve around the properties of biological being. Other security practices do not. Geopolitical security practices, for example, revolve around sovereign territoriality, its properties and exigencies.

Traditional security discourses and practices tend to suppose the existence of preformed subjects comprised of more or less fixed properties or values which it is the job of security practices, in the main prophylactically, to preserve. Just as sovereign power, for example, has not disappeared, nor has this account of security and the institutions and practices which characterize it. But things are different biopolitically because the referent object of biopolitical security practices, life, is different. Biological beings are not comprised of preformed bodies characterized by more or less fixed attributes. Biologically speaking, especially since life, what it is to be a living thing, has become so radically informationalized, defined in terms of informational processes, biological beings are said to be complex adaptive and continuously emergent. Their properties are not pre-given. They are always under formation because biological beings evolve and adapt, not just their behaviours but ultimately also their very constitutive features. They consist as much in potential as they do in actuality and the actuality of their potentiality is also space-time dependent. It depends among other things, even in respect of the expression of their genetic composition, on the correlations of time and place.

The very problematization of security and the very mechanisms of security are thus radically transformed when their referent object becomes that of making life live. Foucault makes this point directly in the very early lectures of *Security, Territory, Population* (2007). There he explores how the early empirical object of the biopoliticized referent object of security becomes population and how population is characterized, among other features, by its radical contingency and by circulation (Dillon 2005, 2006). He also states quite baldly that biopolitics is a *dispositif de sécurité* designed to promote the multiple transactional freedoms which comprise biological existence, and that, therefore, 'freedom' – this transactional account of freedom – is nothing but 'the correlative of the development of apparatuses of security' (2007).

Biopolitics of Security: Agamben

As Catherine Mills observes: 'The entry of life into the mechanisms of power and correlative organization of political strategies around the survival of the species constitutes the "threshold of modernity" for Foucault' (Mills 2009: 59). His biopolitical analytic is, typically, an analytic of the advent, plural and heterogenetic character of modern power relations, however much they continue to correlate with sovereignty. This is precisely where the two most currently prominent accounts of biopolitics, those of Foucault and Agamben, not only meet but also differ, and they do so fundamentally.

Agamben claims instead that, rather than being characteristic of the modern era, biopolitics and sovereignty articulate in much more fundamental and pre-modern ways going back to the very originary definition of politics supplied by Aristotle. For Foucault, biopolitics emerges in complex correlation and competition with sovereign power, as each form of power developed out of the political, economic, religious and intellectual revolutions which so transformed European civilization from the seventeenth century onwards. Agamben claims, however, that rather than being characteristic of the modern era, biopolitics and sovereignty articulate in such a way that 'production of a biopolitical body is the original activity of sovereign power'; that biopolitics is therefore 'at least as old as the sovereign exception'; and that 'the sovereign exception' goes back to the Aristotelian account of man as an animal which has politics (Agamben 1998: 6).

Just as these rival accounts of biopolitics begin with quite different conceptions of the origins of biopolitics, so also do Foucault and Agamben differ in the mechanisms by means of which they operate. In Foucault, those mechanisms tend to be plural because they proliferate according to what historical truths and rationalities are told about species being; essentially, although not exclusively, they are epistemically driven.[1] If species being is construed as operating within an economy of radical contingency, for example, then risk-based strategies of biopolitical regulation will be a natural consequence. If species being is said to be existence in time whose horizons are fundamentally futural, then preventive and pre-emptive security strategies will be a natural consequence. Finally, if species existence is said to be adaptive and emergent, then the sciences of emergence will furnish biopolitics with strategies of regulation and control designed to breed the right kinds of animals (Dillon 2007, 2008a, b). Liberal biopolitics has, for that reason, always been naturally given to eugenics (Agar 2004). In Agamben there is only one mechanism, albeit that mechanism will find different sites of operation. Agamben's biopolitical mechanism is that of sovereign law itself.

BIOPOLITICS OF SECURITY

Agamben's heritage is not so much the Nietzschean emphasis on relations of force that so deeply informs Foucault's genealogical approach to biopolitics of security, but the metaphysical or ontological concerns of Aristotle, Heidegger, Benjamin and Schmitt, even though these are critically reformulated by Agamben. Nor is Agamben interested in the specification of species life or the historical transformations in the life sciences which so concerned Foucault and whose further development into the twenty-first century have so influenced other Foucauldian inspired interrogations of the biopolitics of security (Amoore 2006; Amoore and Goede 2007; Cooper 2006; Elbe 2005; Lobo-Guerrero 2007, 2008; Masters and Dauphiné 2007; Reid 2004, 2007). In a sense Agamben is not interested in the changing accounts of the specification of the biological properties of living beings at all. Indeed, Agamben's account of the referent object of power, biopolitically, is not the product of those discourses of power/knowledge concerning the changing truths told about the nature of species being which so concerned Foucault; deeply informed as he was also by his teacher Canguilhem (1988, 1991). Alongside his fundamental preoccupation with language, Agamben is concerned with law.

Apart from his cursory identification of biometrics as a digital version of the tattooing which took place in the camps, therefore, Agamben has shown little if any sustained interest in the historical development of the life sciences and the power/knowledge effects of their truth-telling. He begins instead with a reappraisal of the structural character of sovereign power which takes him back to a reconsideration also of Aristotle's base distinction between *Zoē* and *βios*; in which *Zoē* stands for politically qualified life and *βios* stands for biological life. Resisting Foucault's account of biopolitics as a distinctively modern operation of power, Agamben therefore finds the source of biopolitics in an 'originary', rather than historical, relation. Moreover, that originary condition does not lie in the relation between changing historical orders of power and life, but in a preordinate relation between law and life that has obtained throughout the history of Western metaphysics, its political imaginary and the *nomos* which has governed its existence. Deriving from this base Aristotelian distinction, Agamben also finds the biopolitics of the West operationalized through the 'exceptional' structure of sovereign law.

According to Agamben, political order in the West arises out of a certain manœuvre which institutes the law itself. The order of Western politics is considered as if it were dissolved so that the legal power that institutes and preserves it may be specified and continuously reinstituted. Also engaging the contract theorists of the seventeenth century, Hobbes in particular for example, Agamben maintains that the state of nature, which he also says stands for the state of exception, is 'not a real epoch chronologically prior to the foundation of the city but a principle internal to the city, which appears at the moment the city is considered tanquam dissoluta' (1998: 105). Moreover, the foundation of sovereign power which occurs through this manœuvre 'is not an event achieved once and for all but is continually operative in the civil state in the form of the sovereign decision' (p. 109). This ensures the 'survival of the state of nature at the very heart of the state' (p. 106).

By virtue of its very formal structure, the political topologizing of sovereign power tends towards the indistinguishability of the spheres of inside/outside, *physis/nomos*, norm/exception which it claims to establish and preserve. The state of nature (in Agamben's terms that of 'the exception') expresses two aspects of a single topological juridical manœuvre in the process of which what was 'presupposed as external (the state of nature) now reappears, as in a Mobius strip or a Leyden jar, in the inside (as state of exception)' (p. 109) In its political topologizing, sovereign power in fact becomes a-topic as this 'very impossibility of distinguishing between inside and outside, nature and exception, *physis* and *nomos*'

67

(p. 37). Which is why the search for the definitive place in which sovereignty ultimately resides is always a mythic, a-topic or even u-topic, one. Indeed, it is integral to the way in which Agamben understands the functioning of sovereign power that it cannot be located in a material place since it is itself the principle that does the locating and differentiating of inside from outside as such.

Precisely speaking, the political topology of sovereign power is not a space at all but a mode of operation. As such it does work. That work is not simply or even exclusively, however, to command and preserve the domain of the inside of law and order, or to promote the interests of the inside externally with and against sovereign outsiders. Rather, it is to operate as a switching mechanism that effects a passage between inside and outside, law and violence, *physis* and *nomos*, norm and exception. In commanding the trafficking thus instituted, sovereign power thereby continuously institutes and reinstitutes itself. It is the mode of power which juridically both establishes and regulates this trafficking. The state of exception is not so much a spatio-temporal suspension, therefore, as a complex topologizing figure in which not only the exception and the rule but also the state of nature, exception and law – outside and inside – pass in and out of phase with one another. Sovereign power – as a generative principle of formation that institutes a strategic ordering of relationships, thereby instituting itself through that very manœuvre as the arbitrator of the play of the relations thus established – is simultaneously premised, then, both, 'on the violence that posits law and the violence that preserves it' (p. 40).

Here then also lies another key point of distinction between Agamben and Foucault. The life whose biopolitical regulation comprises the very object of Agamben's account of biopolitics as the operation of sovereign law is not biological life at all. It is not the politically qualified life of β*ios*, of course, but neither is it *Zoē*. It is, in fact, a life constituted by the law for the purposes of remaining always amenable to the writ of the law. If the life which informs Foucault's account of biopolitics refers to changing understandings of species existence provided in particular by the life sciences, the life which underwrites Agamben's biopolitics is a life constituted by the operation of sovereign power itself. The name of that life is what he calls 'bare life'. And what characterizes bare life most is not any account of its biological properties but the fact that the operation of sovereign power places it in the position of being continuously exposed to death. Bare life is not biological life. Bare life is, as Agamben says quite precisely, *homo sacer*. And *homo sacer* is a form of 'legally' constituted life which arises out of the remorseless operation of the very structure of sovereign law as such. One might therefore say that, if the project of Foucauldian biopolitics is to secure making life live, the project of Agambenian biopolitics is to secure the continuous reproduction of this bare life of *homo sacer*.

As Catherine Mills pithily summarizes the point, for Agamben, 'the state of exception, law without significance, passes into life while life always subsists in relation to the law' (Mills 2009: 64). She emphasizes the point in a way that deserves further emphasis: 'Importantly, Agamben is not simply suggesting that natural or biological life founds the existence of law. Rather the key figure in the exclusive inclusion is bare life, understood as "the zone of indistinction" or hinge through which political and natural life articulate' (Mills 2009: 64). As Agamben himself states, 'not simple natural life, but life exposed to death (bare life or sacred life) is the originary [bio] political element' (1989: 88). Moreover, this bare life is no modern invention. It has been, he says, foundational to the very political imaginary and operation of the West since its earliest inception.

Thus, if we characterize Foucault the analyst of power as constantly asking the question what truths and rationalities inspire modern power relations, Agamben is quite differently inspired. When addressing himself to Western biopolitics, the question he asks was that first formulated in Walter Benjamin's celebrated essay 'Critique of Violence' (Benjamin 2004): 'From whence does the force of law arise?' His answer is 'biopolitical' in the sense that the force of law derives from the way in which law reduces 'natural' life (in Aristotelian terms *Zoē*) to *nuda vita* or bare life. It does this, he says, following but reformulating Schmitt, by deciding the exception. The exception is not some chaos preceding order. The exception is the outcome of a decision which institutes the law by determining where and when, or to be precise in the form of *homo sacer*, to whom, it does not apply.

The formal structure of sovereign law, understood as a strategic principle of formation rather than a metaphysical point of origin, is therefore precisely this: 'the excluded included as excluded'. By virtue of that inclusion as excluded, bare life is simultaneously both produced by the exercise of sovereign law and subject to it in a particular way. As excluded life, bare life the product of the strategic ordering of sovereign law is life exposed to death – life available to be killed – *homo sacer*. Mundanely, it is life that is disposable – at the disposal of the law which disposes of it. Thus created, *nuda vita* is included in the political order 'solely through an exclusion' (Agamben 1998: 11). It is that 'included as excluded' which produces bare life, allowing Agamben to maintain, as we observed earlier, that: 'The production of bare life is the originary activity of sovereignty' (Agamben 1998: 83). Only by effecting a zone of indistinction between *nomos* and *physis* – inside and outside, law and nature – does the force of sovereign law therefore come into operation.

All force of law, all power, requires material upon which it can gain traction. It requires material that is, in fact, peculiarly amenable in its composition and formation, to that traction. Without such traction there is no force of law. Agamben's point is, in effect, that the force of sovereign law lies in the way in which it produces the very material that it requires to gain traction for itself. A form of life is thereby instituted that is capable of continuously bearing the rule, of being 'included as excluded' as a correlate of the power which produces it. The name which Agamben gives to this 'securing' of bare life – and by now it is evident that what is being 'secured' here is continuous exposure of life to death via the force of law – is biopolitics. This is not a deliberately obscure account of biopolitics of security. It is a different one. For Agamben also claims that all life is captured through this manœuvre: 'life ... [is] the element that, in the exception, finds itself in the most intimate relation with sovereignty' (1998: 67). Since the law, he argues, 'is made of nothing but what it manages to capture inside itself through the inclusive exclusion', it exists in the 'very life of men' (1998: 27). Indeed life becomes what sovereign law makes of it, and nothing falls outside the all-encompassing manœuvre by means of which sovereignty secures a peculiar status for life, that ultimately of being at the disposal, alone, of sovereign law. It is this state of exception, he concludes, which has become the norm not only of Western biopolitics, but of sovereignty as biopolitics. Thus whereas Foucault continued to discern a distinction between the security politics of sovereign and biopower, Agamben detects an epochal conflation of crisis proportions. What is more, for Agamben, sovereign law has no purpose or function other than the operation of this continuous biopolitical securing of life. It is, he says, 'in force without significance' (Agamben 1998: 51). Biopolitically, for Agamben, life is reduced to being that which is required for the force of sovereign law to continuously reinstitute itself. While this 'law without significance' passes into life, life passes out of itself biopolitically for Agamben into 'law without significance' (Mills 2009: ch. 3). Biopolitics of security becomes the living death of life which characterizes late modern times after Auschwitz for Agamben, and in ways which, while intersecting with, nonetheless also differ from, the necropolitics integral to the biopolitical appeal of Foucauldian biopolitics.

Conclusion

Foucault and Agamben's biopolitics therefore do intersect on a variety of issues. Those intersections serve less to conflate the two accounts of biopolitics, however, than they serve to further illuminate their key differences. And so, for example, where these two accounts intersect in relation to the problematic of sovereign power one might say that Agamben's account of sovereign power is far more philosophically sophisticated than that of Foucault's. But one can also see from Agamben's account of it that sovereignty is not only nothing to do with the expression of a will, but the operation, instead, and in a curiously Foucauldian way, of a kind of manœuvre or strategy.

In respect of the biological being Agamben has little to say about how accounts of its properties translate into apparatuses of regulation of population and global circulation of every conceivable kind of material description, from people to information and money, or how these also impact on health care strategies designed to regulate the incidence and circulation of disease, military strategic discourse and the operational concepts, doctrines and burgeoning surveillance techniques of network-centric warfare, homeland security and national resilience strategies designed around global/local circulation and flows as well. Once it is understood how pervasively the account of species existence has become radically informationalized – such that what it is to be a living things is almost defined in terms of being in informational exchange, hence the interest in cyborg life and theorizations of the post-human – it is possible also to recognize how contemporary accounts of biological existence emphasize its complex adaptive and emergent character. Here life unfolds in radically contingent emergent ways. But, as was explained earlier, such emergence is also an emergency since as it unfolds such life is continuously also engaged, and necessarily so, in destructive as well as a productive processes. This state of emergency also differs radically from the Agambenian understanding of the permanent state of emergency instituted by sovereign law through its operation of the manœuvre of inclusion by exclusion or permanent 'state of the exception' that Agamben derives from his Benjaminian torsioning of Schmitt. The emergency derives from the way biological life is said to be contingently adaptive. The permanent state of exception is instituted by the structural manœuvre that characterizes sovereign law.

It is, however, in relation to securing the 'ontopolitics' that the relation between Agamben and Foucault's accounts of biopolitics remains in many ways significantly underexamined. Foucault is generally coy where ontology or metaphysics is concerned. His instinct is for the historical and the micro-practical. But, like Agamben, Foucault is nonetheless also a kind of philosopher and when he philosophizes in his own distinctive way he does directly address the historical a prioris and transcendentals which underwrite modes of historical being of which liberal biopolitics is a direct expression (Han 2002). This he did with supreme skill in *The Order of Things* (1989). Here, nonetheless, it is possible to observe that Foucault's account of the analytics of finitude, a direct expression of which is the biopolitics of security, contrasts once again with Agamben's analytics of sovereign exception, a direct expression of which is a biopolitics dedicated to securing the bare life of homo sacer as that form of life which sovereign law requires if it is continuously to enact and institute itself.

Note

1   *The Order of Things* is e.g. an account of the historical a prioris or quasi-transcendentals (specifically life, labour and language) which such epistemic power/knowledge must 'retroject' in order to sustain itself. They thereby become the unacknowledged assumptions on the basis of which modern power/knowledge currently operates (Foucault 1989; Han 2002).

8

Gendering Security

Laura J. Shepherd

In June 2008, the United Nations Security Council voted unanimously to accept Resolution 1820, in which the Council '*Notes* that rape and other forms of sexual violence can constitute a war crime, a crime against humanity, or a constitutive act with respect to genocide' and, further, '*Demands* the immediate and complete cessation by all parties to armed conflict of all acts of sexual violence against civilians with immediate effect' (UNSC 2008: Articles 3-4, emphasis in original). Building on the adoption and implementation of Resolution 1325 (UNSC 2000; see Shepherd 2008a), it is clear from the adoption of Resolution 1820 that the Security Council considers sexual violence during periods of armed conflict to be a matter of grave concern for the international community. Acknowledging that sexual violence matters in the study of security is, however, different from understanding what it means and how, as scholars of security, we might endeavour to engage critically with, for example, rape as a weapon of war. From the camps housing internally displaced persons in Darfur come distressingly familiar tales of rape being used by the Janjawid militia as a disciplinary measure and as a collective deterrent: 'They took K.M., who is 12 years old ... More than six people used her as a wife; ... K, another woman ... was captured by the Janjawid who slept with her in the open place, all of them slept with her' (A., a farmer from Um Baru, cited in Amnesty International 2004: 12; see also UNOHCHR 2007; Amnesty International 2008: 8–11). It does not take an expert on gender and security to point out that the rape of a 12-year-old girl by more than six people is abhorrent. However, in this chapter I use this example to illustrate three different ways in which rape in war, and, by extension, gender and security, can be understood.

In the first section below, I outline a broadly empiricist approach to gender and security, which I identify as the study of 'violence against women'. This is followed by a constructivist approach that seeks to explain rape in war as an aspect of 'gender violence'. In the third section I introduce a post-structural approach that understands gender as performative, drawing on the works of Judith Butler (1993, 1999), which suggests that we might conceptualize rape in war and other gendered security practices as acts of violence that are reproductive of gender identity: security as 'the violent reproduction of gender'. Rather than illustrate through critical engagement with conventional accounts of security the ways in which gender has been written out of and in to security studies, this chapter proceeds on the assumption that security practices are performed by and upon gendered bodies, whether the practice in question is the Israeli Defence Force staffing checkpoints in the West Bank, the President of the USA presenting the country's most recent 'National Security Strategy' or the gang-rape of a 12-year-old girl. Gender may not always be central to the study of security's analytical optic, but it is always there, productive of – and a product of – the ways in which we think about security in global politics. In this chapter, I hope to show that whatever the ontological, epistemological or methodological commitments of the researcher, the serious scholar of security needs to acknowledge that gender matters.

Violence Against Women

The adoption of the 1993 Declaration on the Elimination of Violence Against Women (DEVAW) was triumphed as a landmark achievement for women's rights activists, as it sought 'to ensure the elimination of violence against women in all its forms, a commitment by states in respect of their responsibilities, and a commitment by the international community at large to the elimination of violence against women' (United Nations 1993: Preamble). As I have argued elsewhere, 'DEVAW preceded the appointment of the first UN Special Rapporteur on Violence Against Women in 1994 and is recognised as foundational to contemporary theorising and policy-making that seeks to articulate gendered violence as a "security issue"' (Shepherd 2005: 380). In the discourses of international organizations, non-governmental organizations and the majority of media sources, framing rape in war as an instance of 'violence against women' remains the dominant mode of understanding and thus influences how we think about gender and security. Several assumptions characterize this approach, among them: women suffer at the hands of male violence; male violence is related to patriarchal privilege; and understanding gender and security means understanding the reality of patriarchal power.

On this view, gender matters in the study of security because practices of security and violence impact upon gendered bodies. Further, these bodies are disproportionately female. According to Amnesty International, global statistics suggest that '[a]t least one out of every three women has been beaten, coerced into sex, or otherwise abused in her lifetime' (2008). With this in mind, this literature draws strong links between violence against women in times of peace and the violence experienced by women and children during conflict. Liz Kelly defines sexual violence as 'a collective noun to encompass all forms of male violence against women and girls' (Kelly 1988 cited in Kelly 2000: 62), conceiving of it as 'one of the most extreme and effective forms of patriarchal control' (Kelly 2000: 45), an approach that lends itself equally effectively to the study of spousal abuse or war rape. Kelly further argues that violence against women is a means by which men gain and retain power: the perpetrators of such acts of violence are 'men who presume power refusing to give up one iota of historical privilege' (ibid.) and the victims are women. I label this approach 'empiricist' because this literature assumes that men and women are easily identifiable as knowing/acting subjects and that the experiences of these men and women can serve as the foundation for knowledge about social/political reality. That is, men enjoy 'historical privilege', women are universally subordinated and the militiamen who raped the 12-year-old girl in Darfur were exercising a form of 'patriarchal control'.

Contrary to the conventional approaches to security that see the appropriate referent object of security policy as the sovereign state, this approach insists that security should apply to the human subject, and, moreover, that state practices of security frequently function to render women and children *in*secure. Derived from feminist critiques of the state and of the assumption of a distinction between the spheres of public and private, scholars working on 'violence against women' illustrate how masculinist policies and practices of governance (practices that are defined by a belief in the superiority of masculinity) sanction the dismissal of sexual violence as a personal matter, thereby removing such acts from the political realm and, ultimately, rendering them permissible. Feminist insights into the ways in which 'the personal is political' demand that acts of violence, even those that take place behind the closed doors of private homes, must be recognized as political and deemed worthy of study in the scholarship of security, as no individual can be fully secure as long as such violence occurs. This meta-level analytical commitment, however, usually translates into a focus on how women in particular are at risk of victimization by men's violence. The privilege enjoyed by men (manifested in masculinist governance and masculinist war-waging) extends to the ability to use violence against women with impunity, both at the individual level and collectively.

Conceptualizing rape in war as an aspect of patriarchal privilege means that to understand fully the complexity of gender and security we must understand patriarchal power. This analytical approach demands that we see the rape of K. not only as a violation of her sovereign rights over her own body but also as an act committed by men; that is, not committed by individual militia who happen to be men but by men acting as men, benefiting from the privilege of being men. Conversely, it is not incidental that K. was a woman-child, as it is women and children who are persecuted, victimized, violated in and through the patriarchal order. Sylvia Walby identifies male violence as one of six structures of patriarchy (1989: 212), patriarchy itself being 'a system of social structures, and practices in which men dominate, oppress and exploit women' (ibid.). Employing these analytical insights in the study of gender and security means that scholars must recognize the wider social context of acts of sexual violence in times of armed conflict and, further, trace the connections between rape in war and, for example, sexual harassment in the workplace: both are assumed to happen predominantly to women and to happen as a result of the systematic and universal subordination of women by men.

Gender Violence

It is of course not the case that rape in war, or sexual harassment in the workplace for that matter, happen only to women. It is also not necessarily the case that individuals are subjected to sexual violence as a direct manifestation of the universal subordination of women. In studying gender and security through the lens of 'gender violence', we can acknowledge different explanations for and understandings of rape in war, which are based on a constructivist theory of gender. Whereas some scholars claim that there are gendered social behaviours that issue directly from biological sex – for example, women are inherently more peaceful than men, mothering comes naturally to women, men are usually more aggressive than women and so on – a constructivist account argues that sex is biological (that is, 'natural') and gender is social (or 'cultural'). Such theories accept that gendered behaviours are largely a product of socialization, i.e. they are constructed through interaction with society and vary according to social and historical context. Scholars of security will be familiar with constructivism from Alexander Wendt's highly influential essay 'Anarchy is What States Make of it' (1992); however, constructivism as applied to gender and security is more complex and potentially more challenging to orthodoxies of security than that advanced by Wendt. The core assumptions that characterize this approach are as follows: violence can affect men as well as women and children (i.e. men may be targeted as victims of violence because of their masculinity just as women are targeted because of their femininity); violence is best conceived of as a continuum linking acts of interpersonal violence through societal violence to structural violence such as poverty and oppression; and understanding gender and security means understanding power/ powerlessness, equality/inequality and justice/injustice at a global level.

This literature suggests that there are two ways in which violence such as rape in war is seen as gendered. The first, as in the first approach discussed above, sees rape in war as gendered because it happens to gendered bodies. Moreover, different forms of violence are more likely to happen to bodies gendered in a particular way: bodies gendered female are more likely to be raped, for example, than bodies gendered male, which are more likely to be affected by direct violence. Taking this view ensures that 'gender violence' does not see rape in war as 'violence against women' but as a specific form of violence that mostly happens to women, although it sometimes happens to men (see Bracewell 2000; Hansen 2000; Koo 2002). Rape in war is a means of inscribing economic, political and organizational violence on the (mostly female) body. For example, in her discussion of the political economy of rape, Meredeth Turshen identifies several ways in which rape was used during the wars in Mozambique and Rwanda, drawing the conclusion that 'armies use rape systematically to strip women of their economic and political assets' (Turshen 2001: 56). Both the threat of rape and the act itself were used to terrorize communities during the conflict, and to further threaten already insecure subjects. Conversely, sex-selective massacres, for example, are another form of violence that mostly happens to men, although it sometimes happens to women. Researchers such as Adam Jones (2000) have argued that it is empirically verifiable that 'non-combatant men have been and continue to be the most frequent target of mass killing and genocidal slaughter, as well as a host of lesser atrocities and abuses' (2000: 186). Drawing on examples from Kosovo, Kashmir, Colombia, Rwanda and Sri Lanka, Jones argues that 'the most vulnerable and consistently targeted population group, through time and around the world today, is non-combatant men' (ibid. 191).

The second way that violence is gendered is directly related to the constructivist theory of gender that underpins this account. This literature argues that specific forms of violence happen to differently gendered bodies because of widely accepted ideas held about those bodies, ideas about masculinity and femininity. Further, contextually specific ideas about masculinity and femininity are identified as a potential cause of violence. Whereas the approach outlined in the first section holds patriarchal privilege to account for 'violence against women', this approach sees 'gender violence' as the result of pathological power relations, of which gender relations are a part. The rape of K., on this view, should be understood in the context of socially constructed beliefs about masculinity (that e.g. performing such an act is 'manly') and femininity (that the social value placed on the body of a 12-year-old girl is such that violating that body is permissible, or that the honour of K.'s family is bound up with the purity of her body). This account recognizes that the perpetrators of violence may not be male, nor the victims female (see Moser and Clark 2001), but that gender plays a crucial role in determining how and why violence is used against individuals and communities.

The conceptualization of violence that best characterizes this approach is, as mentioned above, is that of a continuum, as on this view specific acts of violence such as rape in war cannot and should not be analytically separated from their wider political, economic and organizational context. Much attention is paid to forms of structural violence within this account, forms of violence where there is no necessary agent but as a result of which human subjects are nonetheless rendered less secure. The domestic political situation in Sudan and the dynamics of conflict in Darfur are both key to understanding K.'s experience and, crucially, understanding how it became possible that K. would be subjected to such an attack. One level further up the analytical chain, the refusal of the international community to intercede effectively on behalf of the terrorized local communities is also culpable according to this account. Gender and security cannot be understood without reference to 'the men and women who make war, and also those who are complicit in it, support it, benefit from it, or suffer from it' (El Bushra 2000: 84).

Envisioning acts of violence as complex, interlinked and variant results in the adoption of a broad and multifaceted analytic and the recognition that, to effectively combat 'gender violence', scholars and activists must work simultaneously on strategies for wider social and political change. Rape in war cannot be stopped simply by punishing those responsible, although this is a necessary component, nor is it reducible to an instantiation of patriarchal power that universally privileges men over women. There are many forms of power at work in that one act, many forms of power productive of and written on K.'s body at that time. This approach endorses many different methodologies in the study of gender and security. These range from large-N quantitative studies that seek to tell us something important about, for example, how ideas about masculinity and femininity affect a propensity for violence at state level (see Caprioli and Boyer 2001; also Caprioli 2005; Melander 2005), to qualitative accounts of gendered dynamics of particular conflicts (see Cockburn 2001; Jacobson 2000, 2005). Based on the assumption that gender and other social identities are socially constructed, this literature examines how such constructions come to be widely accepted and, moreover, how identity constructions intersect and interact with other forms of political relationships. On the widest view, this approach seeks to answer questions relating to global justice: rape in war is an act of violence perpetrated against the structurally disadvantaged and neither the act nor the existence of inequality is just.

The Violent Reproduction of Gender

Whereas both of the two approaches discussed above take the difference between genders as their starting point for the analysis of gender and security (a difference assumed to be biological, as in sex difference, and socially constructed, as in gender difference), this approach turns the question around. Rather than only asking how particular acts of violence are *gendered*, this approach asks also how such acts are *gendering*. That is, this literature conceives of violence as a site at which gender identities are reproduced. Gender identities are seen as discursive, rather than social constructions, where a discourse itself is understood as a system of meaning-production, a system that fixes meaning, albeit temporarily, and enables us to make sense of the world. There are multiple and competing discourses about gender, and a similar variety of discourses about security; this approach interrogates the ways in which these discourses articulate specific subjects, ascribe identities to these subjects and position them in relation to each other. The rape of K., on this view, can be represented as an obscene act of violence, as a reasonable privilege of soldiering in a militia or as the unfortunate effect of a legacy of colonial oppression. The assumptions that characterize this approach, which I would label as post-structural, include: violence produces (rather than affects) men, women and children; violence is productive not only of gender but also of other social identities and regulatory schema, as it is a technique of power and, following Foucault, power is productive; and understanding gender and security means paying careful analytical attention to the representations we use in constructing our narratives about the world, as well as recognizing that values that we might hold to be universal may be culturally and contextually specific.

While there are multiple representations of K.'s rape that are possible, and indeed would be intelligible, within various discursive contexts, this approach seeks to understand how the particular violence committed against K.'s body functions to perpetuate her gendering as female while simultaneously reinscribing the masculinity of her rapists. Involved in the physical act of rape, there are two individuals who exist within a specific cultural context. The cultural conditions that sustain and permit rape are also in part reproduced by such instances of violence. The articulation of the subjects affected by the rape – both victim and perpetrator – is produced through discourses of gender at the same time as it is productive of them. According to widely held beliefs about gender, 'women' are assumed to be subservient, subordinate and femininity is assumed congruent with passivity, peacefulness and emotion. Thus when individuals are forced into a passive position, the individual is feminized and the feminization of passivity is reinforced. The penetration that occurs is an artifice, mocking the 'natural' (read: safe and secure) heterosexual union and exposing the asymmetrical power relations embedded in that gendered construction that sees the masculinity of the perpetrator reaffirmed through the feminization of the victim. In the case of K., her femininity is an immature one, constructed in part through our (Western) discourses of childhood, innocence and purity. This immaturity means that K. is doubly violated: according to our cultural understandings of childhood, K.'s innocence renders her asexual, so her childishness as well as her femininity are transgressed by the rape as she is forced to become a sexual being.

It is not just the case of rape that can be subjected to critical scrutiny using this approach. On this view, what we study as scholars of security is violence, both material and discursive, and violence is always both gendered and gendering (see Shepherd 2008b: 49–54), productive of gendered identities and other regulatory schema such as reputation, legitimacy and morality. It is gendered because different forms of violence tend to be perpetrated against, and have different impacts on, male and female bodies, both materially as people experience violence differently depending on their gender (and race, class, sexuality and so on) and also discursively, as what we expect of men and women in terms of their behaviours, violent and otherwise, is limited by the meaning(s) ascribed to male and female bodies by society. Violence is gendering as our understandings of subjectivity, security and identity are in part reproduced through violent actions, as described above. To illustrate this view, as well as exploring the example of K.'s rape that is used throughout this chapter, we can consider a range of other violences that more traditionally fall within the remit of security studies: the 2003 invasion of Iraq, for example, or the international concern over nuclear proliferation.

Whereas the issue of rape in war might easily be understood as relevant to the study of gender and security, I wish to emphasize that the remit of studies of gender and security is in no way limited to interpersonal violences that are conventionally understood as relevant to gender studies (or, given the tendency to slip between 'gender' and 'women', relevant to women). Marysia Zalewski once asked, 'what is the feminist perspective on Bosnia?', to illustrate the disciplinary expectations, first, that feminist approaches would have little to contribute to the study of 'hard' issues such as intervention and armed conflict and, second, if there was a contribution to be made, that there would be a single, coherent feminist perspective on the conflict. One of the core insights of feminist theory is that gender is one of the most influential logics through which we make sense of the world. It is the only identity that is announced at birth, even prior to birth, in Western societies, and from that initial inscription follows a whole range of behaviours, ideas and techniques that discipline the individual to ensure that they perform their gender appropriately. These assumptions about bodies are intrinsically, inherently related to the study and practices of security, because security is studied and practised by gendered bodies.

With this in mind, what can this approach tell us about the invasion of Iraq? The representations used in the preparation and prosecution of war must be opened to critical scrutiny.

> [A] popular caricature of Saddam Hussein [during the first Gulf War] depicted the Iraqi president on all fours, his posterior high in the air, seemingly 'inviting' a US missile draped in the American flag strategically aimed at his rear end. This particular depiction exemplified the discursive construction of Saddam Hussein and Iraqis in general, as submissive (read: woman), inferior (read: ethnicity/ race and animal-like) and deviant (read: homosexual).
>
> (Masters 2005: 118)

In the case of the US discourse about Saddam Hussein in the months preceding the war on Iraq, the identity of Hussein was systematically and often violently represented as Other, implicitly – and sometimes explicitly – articulated as different from the identity of the US President, 'ordinary decent citizen' and nation, and from the identity of an assumed Iraqi people. This difference was made intelligible in part through the deployment of gendered imaginings. Similarly, with regard to the invasion of Afghanistan, discourses of gender were central to the production of a recognizable and legitimate narrative of war (see Shepherd 2006). The identities of 'the nation', 'the enemy' and 'the intervention' were not only discursively constructed in particularly gendered ways but also subsequently made permissible certain responses, actions and attitudes and censored others.

And what of nuclear weapons? In 1987 Carol Cohn published an article that was to inform decades of scholarship on nuclear weapons technology and the institutional politics of security organizations, with the iconic title 'Sex and Death in the Rational World of Defence Intellectuals'. This article, and Cohn's subsequent research, illuminates quite brilliantly how speaking security among security experts – the 'defence intellectuals' of the title – relies upon abstraction for its intelligibility and, moreover, relies on the ordering functions of gender metaphors and mythology to situate the experts as experts. It is worth quoting at length this account of a strategy meeting told to Cohn by a made by a white male physicist:

> At one point, we re-modelled a particular attack, using slightly different assumptions, and found that instead of there being 36 million immediate fatalities, there would only be 30 million. And everybody was sitting around nodding, saying, 'Oh yeah, that's great, only 30 million,' when all of a sudden, I heard what we were saying. And I blurted out, 'Wait, I've just heard how we're talking – Only 30 million! Only 30 million human beings killed instantly?' Silence fell upon the room. Nobody said a word. They didn't even look at me. It was awful. I felt like a woman.
>
> (Cited in Cohn and Ruddick 2003: 14)

Feeling 'like a woman' compromised this interviewee's masculinity, but also his professionalism: the underlying assumption is that women (irrational, emotional creatures) have no place in the hard-headed world of defence strategy. Crucially, Cohn's research draws attention to the ways in which gender functions in security by not only interrogating the actions of physical bodies but also by asking what work gender is doing to organize and make sense of security discourses. For example, Cohn witnessed a country without tested nuclear capacity being referred to as a nuclear 'virgin' (Cohn 1987: 687). Similarly, phrases such as 'more bang for the buck', 'the Russians are a little harder than we are' and the assertion that 'you're not going to take the nicest missile you have and put it in a crummy hole' all rely on gendered imaginings to render them intelligible (Cohn 1987: 683–4).

Given the productive power of discourse and the ontological commitments that characterize this approach – that all subjects and objects materialize through discourse, that no subject or object can be rendered intelligible (and therefore be said to exist in any meaningful fashion) outside of its discursive conditions of emergence – the representations we as scholars use to construct our studies is of central importance. Indeed, it is not possible to fully understand issues of gender and security, such as rape in war, without attending to how such issues are represented, in media coverage, policy documents and in our own academic analyses. Paying close analytical attention to language is often derided as 'political correctness' in contemporary social debate, a term that has become synonymous with pointless and often ridiculous reworkings of gendered language (the example I often hear from my students is the renaming of a fictitious Mr Chapman as Mr Personperson). Quick to dismiss the importance of not allowing the masculine subject to stand for the universal (as in 'Chairman' or 'manhole'), or attributing feminine characteristics to objects under discussion (referring to boats – or states – as 'she'), such antagonists of 'political correctness' are convinced that it can't possibly matter how we label things, that such concern is trivial in comparison to the 'big issues' with which scholars of security should be concerned. However, to paraphrase Angel, if nothing we say matters, then all that matters is what we say.[1]

Conclusion

In this chapter, I have outlined three different ways to think about gender and security, using the analytical vehicle of rape in war, specifically the rape of 12-year-old K. by Janjawid militia in Darfur. Characterized by different ontologies, epistemologies and often methodologies, the three approaches all offer a way to understand K.'s rape, a way to make it meaningful to the conventional study of security. Rather than mapping the development of feminist security studies, I proceeded from the assumption that feminist critiques of the human subject in security studies, the state and the international system as conventionally represented within the discipline have facilitated the proliferation of approaches to gender and security. '[I]f all experience is gendered, analysis of gendered identities is an imperative starting point in the study of political identities and practice' (Peterson 1999: 37). Analysis of gendered identities is an integral part of understanding security because, as mentioned above, while we may lapse into using the analytical abstractions of 'the state' and 'the United Nations', for example, political practices are performed by gendered bodies. Moreover, *analyses* of such political practices are also performed by gendered bodies. Conventional security studies are characteristically silent about the existence of human subjects and about the relevance of experiential subjectivity to matters of security. 'Messy bodies' are absent, as are many of the socio-political relations that fall outside of those relations designated international. Power may be central to the conceptual armoury of international relations, but orthodox studies consistently marginalize the different forms of gender and power relations that are both produced by and productive of practices of security.

Rectifying this disciplinary tendency entails not only acknowledging that gender matters to the study of security but also engaging with the vibrant and varied feminist literature that advances debates on this subject. Whether we are looking to understand war (see Skjelsbæk and Smith 2001; Cockburn and Zarkov 2002; Mazurana *et al.* 2005), human rights (see Agosín 2001; Caprioli 2004b; Merry 2006), weaponry (see Das 2002; Peach 2004; Schroeder et al. 2005), political violence (see Skaine 2006; Struckman 2006; Cunningham 2007; Sjoberg and Gentry 2008), conflict resolution (see Corrin 2000, 2003; Moser and Clark 2001; Handrahan 2004; Kandiyoti 2004; Rajasingham-Senanayake 2004; Zuckerman and Greenberg 2005) or security theory (see Hudson 2005; Hoogensen and Stuvoy 2006; Sjoberg 2006), quality feminist scholarship is available on the topic. Ranging from analysis of violent conflict and political violence using a gendered framework to critiques of the policies and practices governing post-conflict reconstruction, and encompassing strong and vital interjections on debates over securitizing development, migration, health and human rights, feminist security studies scholarship is accessible, innovative and by no means limited to 'women and war' (although this is of course an aspect of the same). Much of the work mentioned here might fall outside strict disciplinary boundaries of what constitutes security studies, but this is part of the remit of feminist security studies, alongside other critical scholars of the subject: to challenge such arbitrary divisions and to illustrate that security not only means different things in different contexts but also functions in different ways to constitute particular social/political realities. Locating gender and security scholarship at the centre of the discipline and, crucially, listening to the voices of those human subjects long exiled from the academic study of security brings new challenges but also new opportunities for collaboration, with the sighting and citing of gender by other critical scholars.

Note

1 The original quote is from the popular television series *Angel*, a spin-off from *Buffy the Vampire Slayer*. The entire narrative arc of the series can be read as an existential quest for understanding destiny and free will. Repeatedly, Angel and his team, which includes a number of *Buffy* crossovers, attempt to negotiate the right path between good and evil in Los Angeles, eventually concluding that 'if nothing we do matters, then all that matters is what we do. 'Cause that's all there is' (Angel to Kate, *Angel*, 2. 16).

9

Identity/Security

Pinar Bilgin

Identity is a social construct. So is security. Conventional approaches to security have, for long, denied the constructedness of both, offering instead a conception that takes identity as pre-given and its relationship to security as negative – i.e. identity concerns as a source of insecurity. Increasingly since the 1990s, critical approaches to security have revealed the identity/security nexus as one of co-constitution, which allowed for considering identity as a source of security as well. In doing so, critical approaches have looked into identity dynamics in broader terms – i.e. not only in terms of ethnic, religious, linguistic differences, but in terms of a wide range of 'self–other' dynamics.

The Return of Identity?

It is a characteristic of wisdom in the field of security studies that identity has, for long, been absent. In the early 1990s, as the post-Cold War euphoria turned into despair following the proliferation of violent conflicts in various parts of the world (e.g. the Balkans, Africa), they were popularly viewed as related to concerns with identity. The end result was portrayed in the scholarly world as the 'return' of identity to the study (Lapid and Kratochwil 1996) and practice (Brown 1993; Henderson 1997; Lacina 2004; Rogers 2002; Rogers and Dando 1992; Seul 1999) of international relations and security studies. This trend was later reinforced by the September 11 attacks that were popularly framed as a clash rooted in cultural differences.

Emblematic of the so-called 'return' of identity has been Samuel P. Huntington's *Foreign Affairs* article, 'Clash of Civilizations?' (Huntington 1993a; see also, Huntington 1993b, 1996) where the author identified clashes between groups and states with different civilizational affiliations as 'the next pattern of conflict'. Notwithstanding its numerous loopholes, which were identified by many (see e.g. Henderson and Tucker 2001; Chiozza 2002; Gartzke and Gleditsch 2006; Gusterson 2004; Sen 2006), Huntington's article served as a catalyst for effectively bringing identity concerns back into security debates.

Here, it is crucial to distinguish between the absences of identity in the study of security and in security practice. Whereas concerns with identity were indeed missing from conventional approaches to security, this absence marked a past presence – the legacy of previous generations' violent practices justified with reference to differences in identity (as with the 'Thirty Years' War' in Europe). The absence of identity concerns from the study of security thus was a response to the insecurities of an earlier era. As Michael C. Williams (1998a: 205) underscored, the progenitors of the 'liberal sensibility' sought to 'confute these beliefs in theory, to marginalise them in practice, and to replace them with new forms of understandings and political action, and in doing so transform fundamentally the politics of violence and the nature of security'. Understood as such, the absence of identity from the conventional approaches to security constituted a 'negative identity practice'; by way of limiting the definition of 'knowledge' to knowledge about the material world warranted by an empiricist epistemology, an attempt was made to transform practice, thereby '[removing] the destructive conflict engendered by irresolvable questions of religious truth from the political realm' (Williams 1998a: 211).

That said, identity was never totally absent from the study of security. A literature developing on the margins of security studies highlighted the roles culture and identity played in shaping Cold War dynamics (Booth 1979; Kaldor 1990; Klein 1990; Shapiro 1990). Furthermore, security in the developing world was often studied through the prism of ethnic or religious differences (see e.g. Horowitz 1985; Levine 1986; Gurr et al. 1994). A third line of research pointed to gender as a factor shaping the dynamics of the study (Cohn 1987) and the practice (Enloe 1989) of security worldwide.

Taken together these three sets of literature serve to remind that the 'negative identity practice' of the more conventional approaches to security was not fully successful. While such practice has indeed 'confuted' concerns with identity in conventional security theory, it failed to 'marginalize' them in practice. Accordingly, scholars employing conventional approaches to security had to face the limits of their conceptual and methodological toolkit as they encountered concerns with identity in their research. Consider, by way of illustration, Stephen Walt's *The Origins of Alliances* (1987), where the author portrayed the practice of balancing between Arab states as 'different'. The difference stemmed from the ways in which Arab actors responded not (only) to changes in the balance of military power, but also challenges to their image. Yet Walt was not able to analyse such 'representational power-balancing' (Mattern 2000: 306), for he relied on the materialist-empiricist framework of neo-realism. As Michael Barnett (1998) has highlighted, non-material aspects (as with identity) also demanded close attention in studying inter-Arab relations. Security in the Arab world was often 'not tied to material power but presentational politics' as 'few alliances among Arab states were a response to shifts in material power, and many more were efforts at impression management' (Barnett 1998: 2).

To recapitulate: it would be inaccurate to say that identity concerns were missing from the study and practice of security during the Cold War. While conventional approaches to security suffered from the limits of their conceptual and methodological toolkit that disallowed systematic study of the identity/security nexus, a rich literature began to emerge on the margins of security studies (see e.g. Acharya 1998; Booth 1991a, 1991b; Campbell 1992; Campbell 1998; Krause and Williams 1997; McSweeney 1999; Tickner 1992, 1995; Weldes et al. 1999). The latter has offered fresh insight into the study of the identity/security nexus in two main ways: (1) through revealing identity as a social construct; (2) through revealing the relationship between identity and security as one of co-constitution thereby opening up room for understanding identity as a source of security as well. As such, this new literature has come against the received wisdom in conventional approaches to security. The following presents an overview of this burgeoning literature in terms of the two axes of insight it offers.

Where Do Identities Come From?

Conventional approaches to security give either one of two standard responses to this question. Whereas neo-realists take state identity to be exogenously given and constant (all are egoists as a product of the push and pull of the anarchical system), neo-liberals allow for exogenously given identities to change (egoists seeking to cooperate under conditions of anarchy) (cf. Walt 1987; Keohane 1988). In treating identities as exogenously given, 'the idea that taking questions of identity seriously may require a different understanding of group formation and interaction is never raised' by either of the two conventional approaches (Krause and Williams 1996: 240). While it is indeed possible to understand such neglect of identity concerns as a product of the 'liberal sensibility' of 'seeking liberty and security from the 'enthusiasm' of others' (Williams 1998a: 211), the resulting treatment of identity by these very approaches have produced analyses that seem to have betrayed the same 'liberal' sensibilities.

Consider Barry Posen's article 'The Security Dilemma and Ethnic Conflict' (1993). Different from Walt, Posen sought to integrate national identity as a factor in analysing the conflicts that followed the Yugoslav and Soviet break-up. Yet, in the absence of conceptual and methodological tools that would have allowed him to analyse identity differently, Posen relied on a primordialist notion of identity. This proved problematic in two ways. First, Posen sought to provide an explanation that took into account the role group identity and collective memory played in shaping conflict dynamics, while his choice of method only allowed for the study of material factors. Accordingly, as he took identity as pre-given, Posen proposed an explanation that was – as Paul Roe (1999: 189) highlighted – 'rather Wendtian', thereby revealing a contradiction in his framework. Second, Posen, through bringing in identity in the way that he did (i.e. introducing a primordialist notion of identity into neo-realism) ended up reinforcing the determinacy of material factors (i.e. military power) with the determinacy of non-material factors (i.e. national identity).

The point being, the ways in which conventional approaches have sought to integrate identity concerns into their materialist-empiricist framework have served to highlight why the progenitors of the 'liberal sensibility' had excluded them in the first instance. In seeking to respond to the 'return' of identity concerns to security practice, conventional approaches have bought into primordialist notions of identity and ended up offering research that betrayed its roots in overcoming the practices of those who justify resort to violence with reference to presumed differences in identity. Whereas, as Roland Bleiker has argued,

> Difference does not necessarily lead to violence. The source of conflict is located in the political manipulation of the tension between identity and difference, in attempts to isolate a few arbitrary selected elements of the past in order to construct around them a mythological division between inside and outside ... Once these artificial demarcations of identity have become internalized in language, school curricula, political institutions, moral discourses, and the like, their mythical origin appears more and more real until the ensuing worldview, and the conflicts that they generate, seem inevitable, even natural.
>
> (Bleiker 2005: 116)

Alexander Wendt took issue with conventional approaches 'that take identities and interests as pre-given, and revealed them to be products of an inter-subjective structure. Echoing Mary Kaldor's (1990) characterization of the superpower rivalry as 'imaginary war', Wendt made the point that

> The Cold War was a social structure in virtue of which the United States and the USSR had certain identities. They were embedded in 'national security worldviews' (in terms of which each defined self and other) and in role positions in a social structure ... The content of national interests was in part a function of these structurally constituted identities (as well as of domestic ones).
>
> (Wendt 1994: 386)

Having revealed identity to be endogenous to state interaction, Wendt went on to show that 'self-help and power politics do not follow either logically or causally from anarchy and that if today we find ourselves in a self-help world, this is due to process, not structure' (Wendt 1999a: 394). In line with Barry Buzan's (1991b) notion of 'mature anarchy', Wendt offered that

> There is no 'logic' of anarchy apart from the practices that create and instantiate one structure of identities and interests rather than another; structure has no existence or causal powers apart from process. Self-help and power politics are institutions not essential features of anarchy. *Anarchy is what states make of it.*
>
> (Wendt 1992: 394–5)

Recognizing identity as a social construct has significant implications for the study of international security as it opens up room for inquiring into identity change transformative of security relations. Viewed through the lens of conventional approaches, egoist state identity does not allow for security beyond manœuvres of power balancing and deterrence (neo-realism) (Walt 1987) or temporary cooperation beyond security regimes (neo-liberalism) (Jervis 1982). Whereas recognizing identity as a social construct allows considering 'how social processes and international community may transform security politics' (Adler and Barnett 1998: 12). Calling for recognizing identity as a social construct, therefore, is not a mere plea for the formation of security communities, but rather a plea for adopting a theoretical framework that does not render invisible already existing ones (see the contributions to Adler and Barnett 1998).

That said, recognizing the constructedness of identity also allows for imagining the formation of security communities worldwide. While the existence of a security community in Western Europe is widely recognized, its formation is popularly understood to be rooted in and eased by a pre-existing 'European' identity. Whereas, as Bill McSweeney (1999) has argued, identity in 'Europe' has been reconstructed through the formation of the European Community (later the European Union) which, in turn, allowed for the institutionalization of non-war relations among a group of states that had fought two very destructive wars in the first half of the twentieth century. It would therefore be historically inaccurate to give causal power to 'European' identity in the formation of a security community in Western Europe for it also worked the other way around. 'European' identity was (re)constructed by the transformation of identities and interests of various actors through the development of the European Community (Wæver 1998; McSweeney 1999). Denaturalizing the role identity played in the formation of Western European security community and laying bare the role human agency played in the process thus allows for imagining the transformation of security relations in other parts of the world.

Conventional approaches' understanding of identity as exogenously given is problematic not only because it disallows security communities in theory and practice, but also (perhaps more so) because it disallows capturing the very dynamics they seek to explain – as with the 'security dilemma'. Considered to be the 'perennial dilemma' of world politics, the security dilemma is defined as the 'irresolvable uncertainty' state B faces when interpreting state A's weapons acquisition programme – 'defensive' or 'offensive'? Choosing to err on the side of caution, policy-makers in state B often assume A's actions to be 'offensive' and start (or hasten) their own weapons acquisition programme. In the end, state A's search for security through rearmament results in insecurity as it triggers an arms race. Conventional approaches to security explain the security dilemma dynamics with reference to egoist state identity and the problem of uncertainty in world politics, which increase policy-makers' lenience towards worst-case thinking. Yet, as Ken Booth and Nicholas J. Wheeler (2007: 60–1) have shown, worst-case scenarios as such persist only because conventional approaches assume a 'logical convergence of external interests and weapons acquisition'. Whereas 'the material facts of weapons never speak for themselves; weapons speak through the cognitive system of interpreters' (Booth and Wheeler 2007: 61). What shapes (and is shaped by) the cognitive system of actors is identity. Even a seemingly primal response such as fear is mediated through identity. To quote Booth and Wheeler,

> Policy-makers always bring something to an encounter, and, in the twentieth century, ideological convictions were often decisive in resolving dilemmas of interpretation and response. In some cases this led to ... ideological fundamentalism ... which assigns enemy status because of what the other is – its political identity – rather than how it actually behaves.
>
> (2007: 64–5)

Conventional accounts that take identity as pre-given cannot imagine a way out of the security dilemma, for they fail to capture the role politics plays in the (re)construction of those very identities.

To reiterate: recognizing the constructedness of identity has immense significance for security. Through recognizing identity as a social construct, critical approaches to security have opened up room for a transformation in security relations through responding differently to the condition of anarchy (Wendt 1999b), transcending the security dilemma (Booth and Wheeler 2007), creating security communities (Adler and Barnett 1998), 'crafting international order' (Mattern 2005), reconsidering relations in/with the developing world (Doty 1996a), the 'eastern' other (Neumann 1999), Bosnia and the 'Balkans' (Campbell 1998; Hansen 2006), Australia (Burke 2001), the Soviet Union/Russia (Hopf 2002), 'Divided Korea' (Bleiker 2005), the 'Middle East' (Bilgin 2005), and 'migrants' in Europe (Huysmans 2006).

How to Study Identity/Security?

Even as they agree on the constructedness of identity, critical approaches to security differ in the study of identity/security. To pick up an example from feminist approaches, while some have sought to unveil how notions of security are not gender neutral and that they do not relate positively to women's security (Caprioli 2004a; Enloe 1989; Tickner 1992, 1995), others have highlighted the patriarchal philosophy that empowers statism in the study and practice of security and warrants narrow definitions of democracy and human rights (Agathangelou and Ling 2004, 2005). Such differences crystallized in a debate dubbed the 'Copenhagen Controversy' (Williams 1998b) concerning the study of 'societal security'.

The notion of 'societal security' was introduced by Ole Wæver (1993) to highlight the insecurities of societies as they differed from (if not caused by) the insecurities of states. He wrote:

> In the contemporary international system, societal security concerns the ability of a society to persist in its essential character under changing conditions and possible or actual threats. More specifically, it is about the sustainability, within acceptable conditions for evolution, of traditional patterns of language, culture, association, and religious and national identity and custom.
>
> (Wæver 1993: 23)

While Wæver (1993: 23) declined to start with an 'objective definition of when there is a threat to societal security' and expressed preference for studying 'situations when societies perceive a threat in identity terms', some others who used the concept in their empirical studies fell back upon treating identity almost as a 'fact of society' (see the contributions to Wæver et al. 1993), thereby eliciting McSweeney's (1999) criticisms regarding 'objectivism'. The debate that ensued highlighted what is at stake in how one responds to the question heading this section.

In contrast to Wæver et al. (1993) who focused on 'the politics around the established identities' (Buzan and Wæver 1997: 243), McSweeney highlighted the problems of treating any form of identity as a 'thing'. He wrote:

> Identity is not a fact of society; it is a process of negotiation among people and interest groups ... a conflict of interests and a problem of security have coexisted with a conflict of identity between unionists and nationalists in Northern Ireland, between Serbs and Croats in former Yugoslavia, between Jews and Palestinians in Israel, between republics in the former USSR. The security problem is not there just because people have separate identities; it may well be the case that they have separate identities because of the security problem.
>
> (McSweeney 1999: 73)

What is out there to be studied, insisted McSweeney (1999: 77–8), is not collective identity, but 'identity discourse on the part of political leaders, intellectuals and countless others, who engage in the process of constructing, negotiating, manipulating or affirming a response to the demand – at times urgent, mostly absent – for a collective image'.

McSweeney and the Copenhagen School debated whether collective identity could (even momentarily) be treated as a 'thing' or whether it is narrative all the way down. Janice Bially Mattern recast the debate at the macro-level. While the 'Copenhagen controversy' had consequences for understanding conflicts and the potential for their resolution, Mattern's discussion addressed the subject of 'ordering' world politics.

In a way not dissimilar to McSweeney, Mattern (2005: 10, 14) distinguished between those who assumed 'a socially settled foundation' in the study of identity and those who 'begin and end with narratives and their authors'. Contra Wendt and other 'conventional constructivists' who theorize about international identity 'as though it develops only in situations where states already share an epistemological order, that is, where they are already mutually oriented toward each other's "nature" or "essence"' (also see Hopf 1998), Mattern (2005: 10, 12) developed an account of international identities as 'power-laden narrative constructs'. She explained the need for this move as follows:

> For constructivism, the identity-formation and maintenance process takes place only against the backdrop of settled social facts, so it logically follows that when those social facts are unsettled – during crises – identity formation and maintenance cannot occur. Thus, if one proceeds from the constructivist model, the only logical conclusion is that international identity cannot be a source of international order.
>
> (Mattern 2005: 9–10)

Recognizing identity as a narrative, argued Mattern (2005: 15), allows for understanding how identities are reproduced even during times of crises, i.e. how identity provides 'the shared knowledge sufficient to impose international order upon disorder'. Accordingly, it becomes possible to understand how security communities are maintained – through recourse to 'representational force' that reconstructs actors' identities.

McSweeney and Mattern's call to study collective identity as a narrative revealed how much is at stake in choosing how to study identity/security. Taking identity as a 'thing' with a 'socially settled foundation', while heuristically powerful in security analysis (see e.g. Katzenstein 1996), renders impossible capturing the process of co-constitution between identity and security. Failing to capture the mutually constitutive relationship between identity and security, in turn, renders incomplete our understanding not only of the processes through which security communities are constructed (Adler and Barnett 1998) and maintained during times of crises (Mattern 2005), but also the production of insecurity through the process of constructing and maintaining communities at the local or international level (see the contributions to Weldes *et al.* 1999; Mattern 2001).

Consider, by way of illustration, Jutta Weldes's (1999b, 1999a) study of the Cuban Missile Crisis. What rendered the 'Cuban Missile Crisis' a crisis, argued Weldes, was not the mere presence of Soviet missiles in Cuba or the strategic threat posed by those missiles. 'After all, the Soviet Union lived with U.S. missiles in Turkey without insisting on a "Turkish missile crisis", so, crises are not inherent in the presence of enemy missiles, even nuclear ones, near one's borders' (Weldes 1999b: 36). What the US policy-makers found particularly threatening was the challenge those missiles posed to US identity as the 'leader of the Free World'. It was not merely the destructive (material) capability of the Soviet missiles but the destructive political consequences of the Soviet and Cuban daring and ability to transfer and plant those missiles in the US 'backyard' that constituted a threat to its security. Hence the conclusion of Weldes *et al.* (1999: 11): 'insecurity, rather than being external to the object to which it presents a threat, is both implicated in and an effect of the very process of establishing and re-establishing the object's identity'.

Pointing to the insecurities produced through the construction of identity need not be taken as conflating difference with otherness (Connolly 1991) or otherness with insecurity (Campbell 1994; Rumelili 2004). Nor is it to assume that insecurities to one's identity could only be found elsewhere. One's identity could be constituted *vis-à-vis* geographically distant others (Neumann 1999), 'strangers' (Huysmans 1998) or one's own forefathers (Wæver 1998). Study of the latter is currently burgeoning in the critical literature under the title of 'ontological security'.

Initially articulated by Jef Huysmans (1998: 241–4; also see McSweeney 1999) in counter-distinction to 'daily security' (as in security policy), ontological security

> is a strategy of managing the limits of reflexivity – death as the undetermined – by fixing social relations into a symbolic and institutional order. It does not primarily refer to threat definition – in the sense of enemy construction – or threat management but concerns the general question of the political – how to order social relations while simultaneously guaranteeing the very activity of ordering itself.
>
> (Huysmans 1998: 242)

The search for ontological security, then, can threaten the very physical security of states because they find security in the uncertainty in a self/other relationship institutionalized by the security dilemma (Mitzen 2006) or the 'humanitarian' acts of intervention abroad (Steele 2007). As such, the research agenda of 'ontological security' turns on its head the very assumptions upon which conventional approaches have rested: that is, security as the avoidance of physical harm caused by 'others'.

To recapitulate: scholars who converge on recognizing the constructedness of identity have differed on their approaches to the study of identity/security dynamics. While some chose to study identity at a 'frozen' moment in time, others researched the very fluidity of identity/security dynamics. The latter group of scholars have produced significant insights as they turned on its head the age-old assumption of conventional approaches through unveiling insecurity as a source of identity and the potential for ontological security to rest on a degree of physical insecurity. As the same time, scholars have engaged in lively debates that furthered the critical agenda into territories long neglected by the conventional approaches as with 'post-colonial insecurities' (Abraham 1998; Krishna 1999; Muppidi 1999), East–West relations beyond the US–USSR rivalry (Ling 2002a, 2002b), religion and secularism (Lautsen and Wæver 2003).

Conclusion

Various contributors to new thinking about security are often dismissed for being interested in 'soft' security as opposed to its 'hard' (i.e. military) aspects. Putting aside the patently gendered hierarchy that is sought to be created between conventional and critical approaches to security, what is significant in such dismissal is the way in which it overlooks how critical approaches 'better' account for the material through considering the non-material as well as the material. This is nowhere better explained than in the following excerpt by McSweeney:

> *si vis pacem, para bellum* – serves to deflect attention from the question of identity, which is central to our conception of security and to any attempt to match security policy to the threats to which it is a response. If the identity of states is externally fixed in egoism, the preparation for war must indeed be the indispensable basis of security policy. If the structure which determines the relations between states is objectively and inescapably anarchic, then insecurity is an environmental constant and the condition of peace must be eternal vigilance of military autarky. But then, how did the Cold War end?
>
> (McSweeney 1999: 5)

The question on which this quote ends had initially encouraged students of security to (re)turn to identity. It was the failure to explain (but not to predict) the end of the Cold War that had driven the conventional approaches to security to disrepute (Booth 1991a; Gusterson 1999). More than two decades after the end of the Cold War, critical approaches have made significant headway in exploring the identity/security nexus. In doing so, they have returned security studies to the central position they had previously come to occupy in international relations debates.

10

Security As Ethics

Anthony Burke

Every vision of security has an ethic, but not all are equally ethical.

In late 2008, as this chapter was being written, Presidential candidates John McCain and Barack Obama toured the United States campaigning for election to an office that – more than any other – has the potential to shape the global security environment and affect the very possibility of security for millions of human beings. The statistics are familiar. The USA has the world's largest economy, and the world's largest military. Its powerful position in the governance of major global institutions shapes the social and financial landscape of the world economy. Its web of alliances influences the security calculations and doctrines of multiple states, and its use of force, or even the merest threat of it, affects crises from Iraq to North Korea. It has helped to prevent genocides, and stood by as they were perpetrated, and its powerful position in the United Nations has both driven, and frustrated, normative and institutional innovation. As the just war theorist Jean Bethke Elshtain (2004: 6) is fond of saying, with great power comes great responsibility.

Despite this, the vast importance of the electoral race seemed perversely mirrored in the abjection of its foreign-policy discourse. Both candidates vied to boast of how they will 'protect America' and best preserve its 'national security', rather than the security of states and human beings outside America. Both vowed to protect Israel and prevent Iran obtaining nuclear weapons, and, despite setting out an admirably cosmopolitan vision of US leadership in a powerful speech in Berlin, Obama vowed to 'take out' Osama Bin Laden in Pakistan if necessary. The war in Afghanistan was important not to prevent the return of the Taliban – a vicious regime that had slaughtered thousands and abolished the rights of women – but because al-Qaeda may be plotting new attacks against Americans (CNN 2008). These were, to be sure, legitimate foreign policy concerns, but their self-regarding nature spoke volumes about the ethical problems posed by security policy and discourse. The issues raised during the year reflected the gamut and changing nature of international security concerns – climate change, nuclear proliferation and disarmament, poverty, terrorism, genocide and military flashpoints – yet all of them are global in nature and raise concerns for billions outside the United States. Inside the USA, it seemed impossible for Obama to repeat his paean in Berlin that 'there is no challenge too great for a world that stands as one' (Obama 2007).

Affirming, Questioning, Ethics

Linking security and ethics is not a simple matter. Debates about security have rarely been framed in explicitly ethical or moral terms, and it is hard to point to any self-consciously ethical theory of security as such, in contrast to the role that the just war tradition performs for studies of war and peace, for example. This does not mean, however, that ethics are foreign to questions of security; they are in fact central to them, however submerged or disavowed. Every vision and practice of security has an ethic: an ideal of the good and the right, even if it is buried in a story about the facts. Every vision of security poses an ideal vision of human nature, societal priority and international order, even if they state them as fixed, ahistorical givens. This is one vision of the ethical, one that is all too often collapsed into ontology, into claims about what is true, what exists and what cannot exist.

Yet another vision of the ethical, which we could call 'critical', seeks to make ethical judgements about ethical visions. It refuses to collapse ethics into ontology, to reduce ethics to timeless visions of what is or to a set of fixed and rigid principles. It does not eschew principles, but subjects them to a test of their effects and implementation, to the practices they generate and the results – in terms of security or insecurity – that they produce.

However a serious obstacle is posed by the way in which the idea of security itself shapes the terrain upon which we can think and achieve the ethical. The historical terms upon which we have understood and conceptualized security – and with it, political and moral community – constrain the very basis upon which we can achieve anything 'ethical' with security. In the wake of recent reformulations that have sought to 'broaden' or 'deepen' security to new threats or new objects of concern, powerful questions press in. Who or what is the object of security concern? How is security defined? What practices, methods and goods does security name, and how do we evaluate them? And could security, by overriding other goods that societies deem to be of value, unnecessarily constrain the worlds we can make under the name of the ethical? In short, does security have ethical worth at all?

National Securities: Statism

Realist approaches are primarily statist, or state-centric, in nature. This is also true of some liberal security policy outlooks, particularly those that frame global commitments under the banner of 'good international citizenship', where national interests take priority and shape international commitments, which are seen otherwise as acts of charity. Such approaches view 'national security' as a fundamental objective and role of government, and the nation-state as its beneficiary. In the language of security studies, the state is the 'referent object' of security.

In the realist ontology of international relations, insecurity is a permanent condition because of either the innate human tendency towards violence, power-seeking and aggression, or – as John Herz's analysis of the 'security dilemma' contends – the structural conditions of international anarchy (Donnelly 1992). Upon this consensus realists then divide on their policy outlooks, especially with regard to the utility of force, the dilemmas of deterrence and the role of morality in foreign policy. These differences tend to be most stark between some strategists and classical realists, and matters have become more complex with the rise of neo-conservatism (which combines a particularly hawkish view of force with aggressively liberal visions of Western-led global transformation) and realist-liberal hybrids of just war theory and international intervention.

Many Cold War strategists – perhaps best exemplified by Robert Osgood and Robert Tucker (1967), Thomas Schelling (1966), and Henry Kissinger (1969), who were using a conceptual template laid down by Carl Von Clausewitz (1975) – saw force as a natural tool of American statecraft and sought to develop hard-boiled doctrines for its use. Out of these efforts came the doctrines of limited war (including, controversially, the limited use of nuclear weapons), and conflicts in Vietnam, Iraq, Lebanon, Afghanistan, Panama, Nicaragua, Cambodia and East Timor, among others. Often quite ruthlessly, national security was premised on the insecurity and suffering of others – on what Schelling called 'the power to hurt' (1966: 4). This consensus quickly evaporated however, with early limited war thinkers such as Morton Halperin (1987) and Robert McNamara (2003) becoming critics of nuclear strategy and sceptics of hawkish positions.

Here a statist ethics divided: while the hawks viewed force as a politically and morally unproblematic servant of the national interest, other realists saw US and European security as closely intertwined with that of its adversaries and developed profound moral qualms about the humanitarian costs of war in Vietnam or potential nuclear war. Such thinking was also reflected in more liberal European ideas of 'common security' and 'non-offensive defence' (Booth and Wheeler 2008: 137–45). More recently, John Mearsheimer and Stephen Walt criticized the USA's 2003 invasion of Iraq and uncritical support of Israel as detrimental to US security and interests, and as lacking a compelling strategic basis (2003, 2007). Walt also elucidated a broader vision of US foreign policy that abandons a desire for primacy for an effort to act on the basis of 'greater knowledge, wisdom and self-restraint' (2005: 26). While they were not indifferent to violations of human rights principles and universal norms, their central concern was about strategic damage to US interests. Here a statist ethic raises profound questions about the utility and costs of force.

Given the liberal, Wilsonian tinge of much neo-conservative foreign policy after 2001, such realists were implicitly reviving a classically realist concern with excessive moralism in foreign policy because of its detrimental impact on mutual security. While such arguments have been deployed against the view that foreign policy should not be distracted by morality at all (Kennan 1954), writers like E.H. Carr (1969) and Hans Morgenthau (1954: 245–9) have argued for a complex balance of realism and morality, with Morgenthau making the prescient argument that Western policy-makers are too often tempted to assume that all moral virtue lies with their own states and allies and all perdition with their enemies, which can intensify conflict and dehumanize the other side (see also Schmitt 1996: 54).

These concerns with mutual security have informed liberal efforts to promote cooperation, confidence-building measures, security dialogues and regional institutions that can build upon the original normative framework of the United Nations more effectively. Here statist ethics jostle for room with more deontological, cosmopolitan perspectives, a set of tensions captured in liberal arguments about 'good international citizenship' and in much constructivist scholarship on security. Here scholars have extended Karl Deutsch's idea of the 'security community' to examine the processes of 'socialization' that create systems of states that eschew the use of force to resolve disputes, and create normative webs that can prevent conflict and solve common security problems (Acharya 2001; Adler and Barnett 1998). However concerns have been raised that constructivist scholarship, such as on ASEAN, neglects the coexistence of good and bad norms that legitimize coercive responses to intra-state threats, and that security communities have the potential to be transformed into 'regional fortresses' that contain the potential for new conflicts with outsiders (Bellamy 2004; Burke and McDonald 2007).

Profound ethical issues have also been raised by late twentieth-century realist scholarship and policy that 'broadens' the national security agenda to take in new 'transnational' and 'non-traditional' threats such as those posed by disease, the environment, crime, terrorism, illegal immigration, economic instability, piracy, cyber-attacks and more (Buzan *et al.* 1998; Dupont 2001). This framework builds on older Asian models of 'comprehensive' security, which are still state- and regime-centric but focus on a wider range of threats, including those from within. This agenda certainly incorporates legitimate concerns, but has been criticized for its focus on states as objects of security and for legitimating repressive or inappropriate policy responses that undermine international law, or compromise human rights (Burke 2007a). In this regard the work of the Copenhagen School has been important, if ethically ambiguous. It rightly seeks to illuminate and question the process of how new threats are 'securitized', and in some cases advocates their 'de-securitization'. However it tends to see security in very realist (and even Schmittian) terms as being about existential threats to the 'survival' of the state, the 'special nature' of which 'justif[y] the use of extraordinary measures to handle them'. Furthermore, by reifying the state as the prime referent of security, Copenhagen School analysis blocks any path to human security (Doty 1998–9: 80; Fierke 2007: 110). In his key 1995 article, Ole Wæver insists that 'there is no literature, no philosophy, no tradition of security in non-state terms … neither individual nor international security exist' (1995: 48–9).

Human and Environmental Securities: Cosmopolitanism, Feminism and Critical Theory

The most profound, and ethically promising, move in the redefinition of security came in the 1990s as feminist, post-Marxist and peace movement perspectives came to influence security analysis. In the academic sphere, R. B. J. Walker (1988) argued for a security inclusive of all human beings in his book, *One World, Many Worlds*; Ken Booth published his article 'Security and Emancipation' in a 1991 issue of the *Review of International Studies*; and J. Ann Tickner published her book *Gender and International Relations: Feminist Perspectives on Achieving Security*, in 1992. In reinterpreting security as 'emancipation', Booth argued for 'a holistic and non-statist' approach that would achieve 'the freeing of people' from 'physical and human constraints … war and the threat of war … poverty, poor education, political oppression and so on' (1991a: 317–19). Tickner argued that security should be based upon 'the elimination of unjust social relations, including unequal gender relations'. It must address the 'multiple insecurities' represented by ecological destruction, poverty and (gendered) structural violence, rather than the abstract threats to the integrity of states, their interests and 'core values' (1992: 127–44). Her perspective has been echoed by her student, the revisionist just war scholar Laura Sjoberg, who argues for a replacement of 'the need for security with an affective attachment to others' needs for security' (2006: 212).

On the policy side, the United Nations Development Program (UNDP) placed what it called 'human security' on the UN agenda in its 1994 *Human Development Report*. There it defined human security as 'safety from constant threats such as hunger, disease, crime and repression … [and] from sudden and hurtful disruptions in the patterns of our daily lives' (1994: 3). The 2003 UN Commission on Human Security in turn defined human security in terms of a twofold set of freedoms: 'freedom from want and freedom from fear … protecting people's vital freedoms from critical and pervasive threats, in ways that empower them'. To do so, it continued, 'means creating political, social, environmental, economic, military and cultural systems that together give people the building blocks of survival, livelihood and dignity'. Its report, *Human Security Now*, also argued that 'the security of one person, one community, one nation rests on the decisions of many others – sometimes fortuitously, sometimes precariously'; an insight which stresses the irreducibly interconnected and interdependent nature of security, and strongly implies a cosmopolitan ethic and architecture of response (Commission on Human Security 2003: 4, 2).

The 'deepening' move made by human security analysis – the shift in the referent of security from the state to the human being – is of profound ethical importance. Not only is it a sharp challenge to the ethics of statism and its restrictive moral community, it challenges the emphasis on military and defence issues along with the 'broadening' move of more recent realisms in ethical terms. It incorporates threats *from* states to their own populations, and challenges states to find non-repressive and just solutions to internal challenges to their security. Human security thus challenges states and international organizations to deal with a broadened range of threats in less self-regarding and coercive ways. If the security of human beings is everywhere intertwined, national security cannot be an exclusive priority and cannot be achieved by depriving others of security. To the extent that national security remains valid, it must be based on human security. Approaches that are genuinely holistic also stress preventive, long-term and structural solutions to insecurity, which places a premium on transnational cooperation and justice. It is possible that human security can improve a statist ethic – by showing pragmatically how to achieve more sustainable national security outcomes – but its central ethic embraces human beings everywhere, in both their diversity and common humanity.

This is where arguments for the narrowing of human security to questions of conflict and human rights – to the 'freedom from fear' agenda – raise potential ethical problems. This is the approach taken by the Human Security Report Project at Canada's Simon Fraser University, and by some realists who seek to limit human security to questions of political violence and intervention (Thomas and Tow 2002). While one can appreciate the pragmatic rationale for this – which seems to be based around a concern with how new issues can be effectively securitized – it opens up dangers. While granting that the emphasis of new normative frameworks for intervention (such as the 'responsibility to protect') is on prevention, it risks undermining a genuinely holistic analysis of how insecurity processes are interrelated and threats arise, and must thus be addressed. It also risks associating human security too closely with intervention, which in the post-Iraq era has become controversial and, in some quarters, deeply suspect as a new liberal version of imperialism. Indeed, in some liberal and just war accounts, controversial new arguments for intervention are made in terms of human rights and security, even as they affirm Western security agendas and statist ethical frameworks (see *Ethics and International Affairs* 2005, and *International Relations* 2005). It is likewise possible for governments to absorb human security rhetorics into (otherwise unchanged) statist frameworks, to reduce human security to a political discourse of disciplinary power rather than an ethically rich series of emancipatory practices. Human security, I would argue, should not be reduced to 'good international citizenship'; it is far more challenging and transformative than that.

Good international citizenship, or what the Australian Labor government of Kevin Rudd calls 'multilateral realism', is merely a modification of a statist ethic which prioritizes national security, and only seeks human security and sustainable development when it is in the national interest, or can be constructed as a form of cost-free altruism (Burke 2008: 232–3). While national security cannot be disregarded, good international citizenship blocks the transformative potential of human and critical security approaches and obscures the profundity of their demand. It also obscures the advantages for national security of the sustained stability that human security provides. At the policy level, human security needs to be thought as broadly as possible, uniting the freedom from fear and want agendas. It demands a genuinely holistic and long-term policy approach that builds interlocking systems in which the basic underpinnings of security – from systems of health and social security, stable and sustainable economies, the prevention and resolution of conflict within and across borders, to the protection and promotion of human and cultural rights – can be assured in forms that preserve human dignity rather than lock people into new, and ethically suspect, webs of disciplinary power. This latter concern, as I explore below, is something of which post-structuralists rightly warn.

In this way it is unsurprising, and welcome, that critical security approaches emphasize a cosmopolitan reconstruction of world order so it is less violent and more just. Booth argues that reconceiving security as emancipation offers 'a theory of progress for society and a politics of hope for a common humanity' (2005: 181), and in his *Theory of World Security* seeks to imagine a vision of transnational political community that is not 'synonymous with homogeneity'. This, in Gandhi's terms, is a challenge to 'reconcile the singular *I* with plural *We's*'. 'World security', writes Booth, 'asks us to celebrate the possibility of human equality; this alone, if put into consistent and universal political practice, offers hope of eradicating universal human wrongs' (2007: 138, 140). How as a world we construct and enact such cosmopolitanism, and the challenges of power and responsibility it would bring into play, open ups a whole series of new ethical dilemmas in turn.

Mitigating and preventing damage to natural ecosystems, animal and plant life, and human activities that are vulnerable to environmental disturbances, has also become an ever more important part of a broadened security agenda. Examples include a UN Security Council meeting in February 2007 that discussed climate change, the US Congress's commission of a national intelligence estimate on the implications of climate change for US security, and the UK government's listing of climate change as a major security threat (Burke 2007a; Eckersley 2009). Yet we have a right to ask how well the discourse about human security has been 'deepened', and whether aligning environmental with human security really captures the ethical challenge it evokes.

The ethical problem raised by environmental security is twofold. First, to what security 'referents' is the environment linked: states, individuals or ecosystems? And secondly, what are the implications of 'securitizing' environmental problems: will they be effectively addressed or are new injustices possible? Arguments that climate change poses a serious threat to international security do have great weight (Dupont and Pearman 2006), but there is an all too real danger that they will simply be statized: that they will stimulate militarist and exclusivist responses, rather than the far more profound transformation of policy and concepts that they demand. The report that stimulated Congress's vote for the NEI, by a group of retired admirals and generals for the CNA Corporation, made a number of important warnings about how US defence policy would need to change (CNA Corp 2007). However it was narrowly focused on US security and interests: on the instability posed by climate refugees and environmental stresses on weak states, rather than on their human security impacts and attendant ethical obligations. Reflecting such thinking, Al Gore said in his speech to the 2008 Democratic convention that 'military experts warn us our national security is threatened by massive waves of climate refugees destabilizing countries around the world' (Gore 2008). If Western policy aims merely to block, warehouse and detain refugees, and to quarantine unstable regions, the climate change future will be one of both physical and moral disaster.

In this light, the holistic and cosmopolitan impulses of critical security approaches have rarely been more relevant: dangerous climate change must be prevented by a profound transformation of global energy economies, land use patterns and approaches to growth – and where it cannot be prevented, we must manage its impacts humanely and without regard for harsh Westphalian norms, rather than wall ourselves into violently defended islands of greater and lesser security. In turn, we can ask whether climate change and other forms of environmental degradation do not demand an ethical displacement of both the national *and* human egos? Here, animals and ecosystems become prime objects of moral concern, and the post-Cartesian human pretence to mastery and calculation yields to a sense of debt to, and interconnection with, nature (Dalby 2002: 160).

Post-structuralism: Security Politics and the Human

Post-structural writings raise important questions for security studies through what might be called an ethics of conceptual destabilization. Here the 'linguistic turn' in twentieth-century social science is linked with a 'deconstructive' tradition in continental philosophy that places the entire structure of concepts under scrutiny, and excavates *practices* from the claims to necessity and truth that naturalize them.

Where traditional and critical approaches settle on a fixed set of referents for security, seeing it as a thing and an end, post-structural writings see a *politics*: a struggle for power, and a process for constructing social life and thus shaping the possibilities for determining ethics. As Jef Huysmans argues, 'security knowledge is a political technique of framing policy questions in logics of survival with a capacity to mobilise politics of fear in which social relations are structured on the basis of distrust'. This, as he and others have argued, is to see security as a form of Foucauldian 'governmentality' and a 'political technology' that links strategies of 'individualising' and 'totalising' power into a working whole (Burke 2007b: 1–53, 2008: 8–12; Huysmans 2006: pp. xii, 9, 97). This enables us to identify and critique concrete practices that claim to promote and defend security, by denaturalizing them and questioning their ethical effects.

In addition, post-structural theory has pointed out how, more deeply, claims about security are embedded in ahistorical claims about the nature of politics and life. As R. B. J. Walker has written, security is linked to a 'constitutive account of the political' that reduces humanity to citizenship (1997: 69–71). In this light, security is a *metaphysical* discourse, an overarching political goal and practice that guarantees political existence as such, that makes the possibility of the world possible. However since the settlement of Westphalia was developed into a hard series of norms structuring international society, alongside a tradition of statist political thought deriving from the social contract theories of Hobbes, Locke and Rousseau, these possibilities have been limited to an exclusive moral community existing in fundamental (and often violent) alienation from a range of internal and external Others (Burke 2007b: 28; Dillon 1996: 13; Neocleous 2008: 11–38). This is where post-structural thought can challenge the way that the idea of security itself shapes the terrain upon which we can think and achieve the ethical.

Both of these moves have been very productive in enabling a sociological analysis of the way in which security has naturalized violence, cramped the ethical potential of political community and structured the creation of a 'security politics' in which human bodies and minds can be appropriated, constructed, harmed, disciplined, utilized and discarded in both 'normal' and 'emergency' practices of bureaucracy, war, justice, intervention and capital accumulation. Following Foucault (1987) and Agamben (1998), this process – termed biopolitics – has been placed under sustained scrutiny because of the seizure of life at its roots that it implies. Profound ethical problems are raised by even the routine question of how, in the national security state, subjects can find the agency to negotiate daily webs of power; when coercive powers are legitimated and lives are placed directly at risk, the ethical stakes are raised even further.

Warfare obviously raises such issues, but even apparently routine practices of immigration policy and population management highlight the ethical dangers of biopolitics. These were put powerfully by Elizabeth Dauphinée, in her conclusion to *The Logics of Biopower and the War on Terror*, where she links her own story of immigration processing – 'a process through which one becomes politically human in the United Kingdom' – to the suicide of an Angolan asylum seeker, Manuel Bravo. Bravo had killed himself both out of despair and as a tactic to ensure that his 13-year-old son Antonio could not be deported. In this 'final, astonishing act of parental love', and in his 'instrumental use of his own bare-life-in-death, Manuel Bravo exercised political subjectivity in a place where he was presumed to have none and thus reclaimed, for a time at least, the subjectivity of his son' (Dauphinée and Masters 2007: 230–2). Experiences of suicide, self-harm, brutality and depression were also common for those confined in immigration prisons in Australia, where they were victims both of the securitization of migration and the very structure of the political – national sovereignty and the social contract – in which modern systems of security are embedded (Burke 2008: 207–21). How then can a better ethical response be conceived?

It would take many books to adequately answer such a question, but, put briefly, in seeking an answer it is possible to see both affinities and tensions between those critical approaches informed by post-structuralism and post-Kantian critical theory. Post-structuralists have generally been reluctant to speak the languages of emancipation and cosmopolitanism, but it also seems clear that both traditions have been palpably concerned with systematic injustices, evils and human wrongs that cause grave and avoidable suffering. While post-structuralists would do well to (critically) reconnect with cosmopolitanism, by drawing on ethical traditions from Jacques Derrida, Emmanuel Levinas, Martin Buber and others they have conducted a profound rethinking of security, sovereignty and being; one that displaces the sovereign Cartesian ego of the post-Westphalian state in favour of a vision of political being and transnational community based on a fundamental interdependence, and structure of responsibility, between selves and others (Burke 2007b; Butler 2004; Campbell 1998; Dauphinée 2007).

This offers two forms of ethical promise. The first is a route out of the system of existential alienation that is the social contract and the anarchic world of power-seeking states. This would break Kant's vision of a pacific federation of liberal republics into something more complex: to reduce national sovereignty to a construct of legal equality in international affairs and a principle of self-determination, while dramatically softening, if not abandoning, its claim to make and remake being, which is now thought in terms of complex relations of commonality and difference in a culturally, economically, politically and ecologically interconnected world. We may still make our identity in relation to the local and the near, but never in abandonment of our fundamental, and global, relation to Others, without whom we do not meaningfully exist.

The second is a perspective on biopolitics. Post-structural thought has done the great service of making biopolitics *visible*, and thus making it challengeable as a system of power. Harder is the question of whether, and how, a decent politics of the human can be detached from its systems of making human being political. Any such project must negotiate a minefield of contradictions. Traditional efforts to codify and enforce universal human rights standards are worth pursuing, but are often attenuated, in both domestic and international law, by sovereign 'interests'. At the same time the era of counter-terrorist wars, humanitarian interventions and liberal imperialism has shown that biopolitics operates even where 'humanity' is the object of concern. On the other hand, it seems self-defeating to devalue the human as such, out of fear of its ever-potential reducibility to 'bare life', or to hope for a world where biopolitics – and thus power itself – disappears as a possibility (Owens 2008: 45). Every criticism of a biopolitical abuse rests implicitly on an ethic of the human and a humanism of the ethical, and the dark connection between what Michel Foucault called 'life insurance and death command' cannot be escaped (2002: 405). It can only be made subject to a more stringent ethic of responsibility: its powers contained in a critical political economy where life is affirmed, emancipated and protected on the most general basis possible. Whether this should take the name of 'security' remains an open question.

War and Security: Strategy and Just War Theory

By exposing combatants, civilians and – increasingly – entire populations to the danger of death, injury and displacement, war raises profound ethical questions that exhaust what can be discussed here. Here I wish to evaluate how critical and post-structuralist orientations to ethics and security raise some tough questions for the most influential ethical approach to war: the just war tradition.

This tradition – which specifies principles for legitimate resort to war (*jus ad bellum*) and conduct in war (*jus in bello*) – has stimulated both an enormous literature in moral and political philosophy, and been influential in shaping the international law of war and international security norms, along with the ways governments justify war and militaries conduct operations (Coady 2008; Nardin 1996). What is striking about this literature is how rarely it relates its analysis systematically to a theory or practice of security, even in writers who have written incisively about security (Bellamy 2006). The notable exception here is Laura Sjoberg, who anchors her revision of just war theory in a 'security ethic' that 'gives attention to individual and collective security at the political margins'. This ethic, importantly, seeks to synthesize a Kantian 'ethic of justice' and a relational 'ethic of care' for Others, in opposition to an ethic that would secure the autonomous, egoistic self (whether that of a nation or individual) against a range of threatening others (2006: 45–6).

To be sure, just war theory has much to recommend it and has certainly helped to reduce civilian suffering in war. However the link of a given just war orientation (and they are diverse) to a given security paradigm is rarely clear. They are most commonly marked by a disdain for an ethics of the Kantian or Levinasian kind, resting instead in a realist ontological foundation in which the state is the privileged structure of political community and war remains a politically (and morally) satisfying way of resolving conflict in the last resort. Moral and generous behaviour is possible, and force may be a way of performing it, but peace is not (Elshtain 2004, 2005). In this way it moderates Clausewitz's amoral vision of strategy, but does nothing to challenge his modernist assumption that force can be an effective way to achieve political ends.

Just war doctrines are thus nested in the same fundamental ontology of alienation that post-structuralists have been at pains to unpack in the national security state. Hence they tend to add an ethical supplement to national security policy, rather than support a more profound reorientation of security as holistic, human–centred and emancipatory. Broader questions of the antecedents to and aftermath of war have thus received little attention, and where just war argument has been utilized to support liberal interventions, it risks moralizing war and politics with exaggerated claims about truth and justice, at the same time as some of its principles – such as the double-effect and proportionality – excuse the killing of innocents (Elshtain 2003, 2004, 2005). Here just war is complicit with biopolitics, and both critical and post-structuralist approaches have questioned the ethical effects of a schematic, modernist application of moral principles that lack the important moral qualities of self-critique and respect for undecidability (Burke 2007b: 160–5; Campbell and Shapiro 1999; Zehfuss 2007).

We could, perhaps, ask that just war theorists account for their arguments in security terms. However if this takes place uncritically, a new danger appears: the securitization of morality.

Conclusion: An Ethic of Progress, or Perpetual Critique?

There is a final feature of security analysis that has ethical implications: its attitude to history and time. It is my feeling that most theories of security fail to adequately grapple with the radical break with the past that modernity makes, with the tremendous ability to destroy, make and remake worlds that is the stuff of modern politics and constitutes both the nightmare and possibility of security as a set of practices and powers. For example, Ole Wæver (1995) appeals to a tradition in which state security is the only one with historical continuity, and must thus limit our ethical horizon; Elshtain (2005: 95) offers a vision of historical recurrence where alienation and war are ever tragic possibilities, and perpetual peace is a 'solipsistic dream' that would eliminate politics as such; and, at the other pole, Ken Booth insists on the normative necessity of an idea of progress – both moral and historical – even as he insists it must be self-reflexive and not be read in teleological terms (2007: 124–33).

While Booth's insistence on agency and responsibility is welcome, when used at such a metaphysical level progress retains its historicist force, and risks underplaying the dangers of acting in the service of even the best ends. Thus it is intriguing, in the wake of the critique of biopolitics, to read Booth advocating an open orientation to what humanity might become: emancipation as 'inventing humanity' (2007: 256). I have trouble seeing progress as much more than the most cynical of signifiers, always obscuring the concrete contradictions of its past. However enlightenment can continue to inspire us, if it changes from a dialectic of history, however critical, to what Foucault called 'a permanent critique of our historical era' (1984: 42). The terrible powers mobilized under the name of security suggest that we dare invent a better humanity only if we perpetually criticize the ways humanity is being invented. How security is about the human thus becomes the crucial question of ethics for security.

99

11

Financial Security

Marieke de Goede

Introduction: Security and Economy

During the 2008 US Presidential campaign, the Republicans raised substantial questions about Obama's capacity to deal with imminent terrorist threats and to command the national security apparatus. Obama's strategy to counter this line of attack was to draw the economy in general, and the credit crisis in particular, into the domain of security. 'We often hear about two debates – one on national security and one on the economy – but that is a false distinction,' said Obama in a October 2008 speech in Virginia. He rephrased finance as one of the greatest national security 'challenges facing our nation', and concluded: 'We are in the midst of the greatest economic crisis since the Great Depression. … To succeed, we need leadership that understands the connection between our economy and our strength in the world' (Obama 2008b). The news media picked up on Obama's reformulation of security, and, increasingly, the language of war became used to understand the credit crisis. Even one of the war on terror's most central and controversial concepts – *preemption* – was redeployed to the financial domain, so that by early 2009 new Treasury Secretary Geithner could encourage G20 finance ministers to move '*preemptively* to get ahead of the intensifying pressures … across national financial systems' (Geithner 2009; emphasis added).

Obama's campaign move can be understood as a process of 'securitization' as described by literatures in critical security studies. Securitization, in this sense, refers to the discursive and political processes through which societal phenomena become understood and addressed as security issues (Buzan *et al.* 1998; Williams 2003). 'Before an event can mobilize security policies and rhetoric', Jef Huysmans (2006: 7) has pointed out, 'it needs to be conceived of as a question of insecurity and this conception needs to be sustained by discursively reiterating its threatening qualities.' Obama's securitization of the financial crisis seems to have been effective on two levels. By rephrasing security as *financial* security, Obama was able to divert attention away from doubt and discussion concerning his abilities and agenda regarding the war on terror. Simultaneously, Obama was working to garner support for his ambitious but costly economic bail-out plans by phrasing these as an issue of national security, requiring bold and immediate, yes even preemptive, action. Thus, it is clear that the new links drawn between finance and security in the midst of the credit crisis work to legitimate unpopular and, until recently, unthinkable political agendas, including the effective nationalization of banks and mortgage providers across the European Union (EU).

Recent developments suggest that there is no more pressing time to explore finance as a security concept than in the midst of the credit crisis and the political agendas surrounding it. As the security of citizens' everyday financial lives seems to evaporate in the wake of practices of securitization gone wrong (Langley 2008), it is important to raise questions concerning the conceptual and empirical relations between 'finance' and 'security'. With some exceptions, the discipline of international relations (IR) has traditionally worked with a division of labor in which questions of national security, sovereignty and war are addressed within a different set of literatures than questions of economy and finance, which have come to belong to the domain of international political economy (IPE). Simply put, finance and security have been relegated to different conceptual and professional domains both within and beyond IR. That this is a relatively recent development, however, will be shown in this chapter. As Randy Martin (2007: 17) has recently put it, 'pressing on the political meaning of security' inevitably brings 'its economic double to the surface'.

This chapter places our understandings of finance and security into historical and theoretical perspective. It explores three avenues for thinking about security's economic double. The first avenue understands the relation between finance and security to be an *instrumental* one, where finance is deployed in the service of security, war or foreign policy. The second avenue understands the relationship between finance and security to be a *causal* one, where finance produces societal (in)securities. A third avenue of study emphasizes the history of *conceptual* finance/security entanglements. Here, it becomes clear that finance and security are virtually inextricable as techniques acting in the name of the uncertain future. In conclusion, this chapter assesses to what extent financial security is to be understood as a *new* security concept.

Security and Finance

The first avenue for studying 'financial security', or the relationships between finance and security, is to look at the instrumental deployment of financial instruments in the service of national security and foreign policy. One example is provided in Emily Rosenberg's study of early twentieth-century 'dollar diplomacy' as a way in which the USA tried to leverage (mainly South American) governments that it considered unstable. Dollar diplomacy involved close cooperation between government officials, private bankers and financial experts, in order to arrange loans in exchange for financial supervision. This process was regarded as a 'cornerstone of progressive foreign policy': in the words of then-US President Taft, the policy entailed a substitution of 'dollars for bullets'. Taft continued, 'It is [a policy] that appeals alike to idealistic humanitarian sentiments, to the dictates of sound policy and strategy, and to legitimate commercial aims' (quoted in Rosenberg 1999: 1). However, as Rosenberg demonstrates, this deployment of finance as foreign policy entailed specific operations of power that advanced a New York-centred global financial order, while establishing 'control' without 'outright colonial possession' in the countries affected (1999: 32). Dollar diplomacy, then, is an early incarnation of IMF conditionality in development processes which is further discussed below.

A different example of the harnessing of finance in the service of war and security is provided in the study of war bonds, which, as Rob Aitken has convincingly argued, do *more* than pursuade the population to part with their savings for the sake of the national war effort. They also visualize the nation and its enemies in order to cast the investor as a responsible patriot. Thus, writes Aitken (2003: 306), 'mass investment comes both to serve the national war project and to assume a kind of national security function by constituting the nation in distinction to the dangerous "other."' More generally, the financial profit to be had by war has been an important strand of analysis in the literature, with acute political relevance in light of subcontracting practices in the war on terror in general and Iraqi war in particular – even if these authors do not necessarily identify an outright instrumental relationship between war and finance (Avant 2005; Leander 2005b; Rosén 2008).

These themes point to a much larger historical and political interweaving of finance, sovereignty and security. One of the starting points for international political economy (IPE) as a field of research in the 1970s was an increased interest in finance and economics as sites of power in the service of but also exceeding national sovereignty. Early work in this domain researched the relationship between the investment positions and foreign-policy interests of national states, in order to understand the dynamic interactions between security and property in world affairs (e.g. Frieden 1993). Marxist readings of this research agenda have emphasized the deployment of military violence in defence of financial interests and in the expansion of colonial possessions (van der Pijl 2006; Hilferding 1981). More recent readings point to the presumed financial capitalist class interests behind the development of contemporary information and surveillance technologies (Gill 1995).

Thus, from an exploration of finance as an instrument of sovereign states, this axis of study has frequently reconceived finance as 'master' of international affairs (Helleiner 1994; Sinclair 2005). It has become widely observed that the end of the Bretton Woods agreement and the liberalization of capital flows from the 1970s onwards changed the landscape of global power to the extent that sovereign states now had to operate under structural constraints caused by globalized capital markets (e.g. Helleiner 1994; Strange 1986; Gill and Law 1993; Pauly 1997). An important author in these debates was Susan Strange, whose 1986 *Casino Capitalism* emphasized the active role played by key states, notably the USA, in fostering financial liberalization and globalization. Others ascribe a more autonomous self-expanding logic to contemporary financial markets, and conceptualize it as a 'Phoenix' rising from the ashes of Bretton Woods (Cohen 1996). According to Hardt and Negri's influential discussion of Empire, moreover, money operates as one of three 'global and absolute means' of 'imperial control' (2000: 345). Where historically capital has relied on the sovereign and security structures of national states for its expansion, in the current age of Empire capital operates as transnational disciplinary power: 'capital sweeps clear the fixed barriers of the precapitalist society – and even the boundaries of the nation-state tend to fade into the background as capital realizes itself in the world market', they write (2000: 327).

Furthermore, the deployment of financial conditionality in development processes illustrates this first axis along which the contemporary finance–security conjunction can be studied. Such conditionality has been widely criticized as a manifestation of new imperialism, whereby intervention in domestic policies of debtor states serves the neo-liberal ideological agendas of the West (Strange 1998; George and Sabelli 1994). Increasingly, it is emphasized that development policy and debt conditionality are now being securitized, in the sense that they are understood and conducted in the name of security policy and may serve the security aims of donor states more than the development aims of receiving states (Duffield 2007; Harrison 2004: 117–27). Here, according to Duffield (2001: 312), 'the security concerns of metropolitan states' and the 'social concerns of aid agencies ... have become one and the same thing'. 'This security paradigm', Duffield (2001: 310) concludes, 'is not based upon the accumulation of arms and external political alliances between states, but on changing the conduct of populations within them.' Here, Duffield points us in the direction of more fundamental, conceptual links between security and finance as techniques of governing through the unknown future that will be explored in the third section of this chapter.

Finance and Security

A second avenue for exploring financial security would emphasize not the financial elements in security policy, but the security aspects of finance. Here, the relationship is thought to be a *causal* one, where the sphere of finance produces societal (in)securities. Security, of course, is a properly financial term – one that emerged prior to, and in conjunction with, our current understandings of (national) security and safety. The *Oxford English Dictionary* (OED) notes the usage of 'security' as denoting a pledge or a property deposited to secure the fulfilment of an obligation as far back as the fifteenth century. 'Security' as a pledge or property guaranteeing the repayment of debt emerges in the late sixteenth century, with the *OED* offering the following entry from 1592: 'Without good securitie they will lend Nobody mony.' Here, then, we have one of the first usages of security as a bond or credit document that became current in the nineteenth and twentieth centuries. For our purposes, then, it is important to note that the meaning of *security* as 'the safety or safeguarding of (the interests of) a state [or] organization' on the one hand (*OED* §1b), and that of *securities* as 'stock, shares' or other forms of credit documents on the other (*OED* §10), was not stabilized until into the twentieth century.

Remarkable as it may seem in the midst of the credit crisis, finance regards itself primarily as a *security technology*: one that seeks to secure a fickle future, tame uncertainty and insure against disaster. As any introductory finance textbook will affirm, the rationale of complex financial instruments, including futures and options, is to offer certainty and security to business participants. Thus, the international trader can insure himself against the risk of currency fluctuation by buying currency futures; the citizen can insure his financial future by pension investment; and the speculator himself can hedge his bets with index futures. The work of financial instruments, in this reading, is to provide certainty and predictability within uncertain business environments. Rather than economic logic however, this rationale is a historical and political construct, in need of continuing rearticulation and reaffirmation – especially in times of financial crisis. For example, Aitken (2007) has explored the visual and discursive histories through which finance and investment became cast as techniques through which responsible individuals (most often gendered male) were able to secure their family's financial futures. Moreover, and as I have argued elsewhere, such articulations countered the historically durable criticism of speculation as nothing but mere gambling. From the early twentieth century onwards, investors and speculators became cast as rational providers of secure futures, rather than reckless gamblers. In this argument, speculators are cast as 'responsible men who anticipate the wants to the market and take the risks on their own shoulders', thus facilitating the day-to-day operation of business practice (Charles O. Hardy quoted in de Goede 2005: 83).

Securitization, of course, is also a financial term, as well as a term deployed to refer to processes by which social phenomena become regarded as security issues. In the financial sense, securitization refers to the process by which financial assets, for example loans, mortgages and credit card receivables are repackaged and resold in the financial markets – thus, turned into tradable securities. This practice became increasingly important in the financial markets from the 1980s onwards, driven by a twinned rationale of profit and security: the bundling and resale of risky assets from small banks and mortgage companies to large financial institutions was supposed to mitigate risk as well as yield handsome profits. If premised on the promise of 'real' protection against uncertainties for each individual participant, Adam Tickell (2000: 88) has argued that 'the aggregate impact of derivatives for the financial system is to increase [risk]'. Securitization has been analyzed from the perspective of the concomitant importance of new financial practices such as credit rating in rendering these new financial products liquid (Sinclair 2005).

At the same time, securitization has been widely understood to foster the primacy of the 'virtual' over the 'real' in financial capitalism, in the sense that repackaged and reassembled financial promises, that were *themselves* based on promises to repay, have become the drivers of growth in the financial markets. Derivatives, as Martin (2007: 31, 33) has pointed out, not only 'remove reference' from the underlying commodity, but also 'delocalized debt' in the sense that it no longer depends on a (personal) creditor–debtor relation localized in time and space. According to Lipuma and Lee (2005: 412) moreover, 'the speculative capital devoted to financial derivatives' here has developed a 'directional dynamic towards an autonomous and self-expanding form' that is increasingly divorced from the 'real' economy of production and trade (also Arnoldi 2004). Generally, the 1973 abandonment of the dollar–gold standard is seen as the starting point of this new age of virtual capital: in the words of Mark C. Taylor (2004: 6), 'going off the gold standard was the economic equivalent of the death of God', as it pertains to human certainty and security.

Paradoxically, then, it is the securitization of finance that has helped introduce spectacular *in*security in economic life, according to many observers. Increasingly built on faith in algorithmic models too complex for even financial managers to understand, the edifices of securitization come tumbling down with some regularity. These regular financial market crises wreak havoc in the seemingly secure lives of pension holders, stock purchasers and, most recently, home owners (Galbraith 1993; Chancellor 1999; Langley 2008; Sassen 2008a). As Susan Strange put it as far back as 1986 in *Casino Capitalism*: '[T]he great difference between an ordinary casino which you can go into or stay away from, and the global casino of high finance, is that in the latter all of us are involuntarily engaged in the day's play' (109–10). However, signalling a new era of virtual money – or alternatively, casino capitalism – starting with the end of the gold standard is unsatisfactory for a number of reasons. First, such readings cast the gold standard retrospectively as a 'golden era' of financial certitude and stability. Nothing could be further from the truth: even if popular financial participation was less widespread during earlier phases of financial crises, the questions raised concerning the in/securities of finance, the justness of financial profit and the morality of speculation and were no less pressing in earlier crises. Secondly, it is easily forgotten that gold, as much as paper money, requires faith and social affirmation for its effective functioning *as money* (Carruthers and Babb 1996). Third, even if it were the case that financial markets have become more volatile since the 1970s, it is still important to analyse the precise socio-cultural histories of each phase of securitization (cf. MacKenzie 2007b).

Instead of locating a breaking-point in the 1970s, then, it could be more fruitful to say that a dynamic of *security/insecurity* runs as red thread through the history of modern financial markets. Simply put, if financial technologies and profit are premised on the provision of security, the commercial logic of the markets is to identify *more and more* insecurities to be hedged. This goes for the commodifying logic of early insurance, that offered fire and life insurance alongside bets on the longevity of kings and captives, or protection against losing at the lottery (Clark 1999; Daston 1988). Indeed, one early modern objection against paper credit and speculative instruments was their ability to unsettle the secure social orders of the time (Dickson 1967). And it goes for more recent financial market theory. For example, the vision of financial market innovator and founder of the hedge fund Long-Term Capital Management (LTCM) Robert Merton entailed the ideal of continuous and complete markets in which every thinkable uncertainty can be bought and sold at an intrinsic fair price (Merton 1998; cf. de Goede 2001). Such complete market utopia had been earlier proposed by Stanford economist and Nobel laureate Kenneth Arrow who, as one journalist put it, 'had a vision of a world in which everything was assigned a value on a market. In this utopia, every possible state of the world, past, present and future, from a stormy July evening in Patagonia to England winning the World Cup had a financial payoff associated with it' (Dunbar 2000: 42). Financial calculative models, in particular the infamous Black–Scholes formula, enable this transformation of life's contingencies into calculable and, most importantly, *tradable* risk (MacKenzie 2006).

The current credit crisis illustrates this logic of commodification in the markets. The securitization of consumer credit and family mortgages took place in the name of a redistribution and reallocation of risk in the markets: from small mortgage companies and building societies towards large reinsurers and investment banks. Theoretically, as small loans were bundled and resold in the markets, risk was redistributed to those financial parties better able to bear it. However, as Saskia Sassen (2009) explains, this logic of financialization acquired its own dynamic: 'Whether people pay the mortgage or the credit-card matters less than securing a certain number of loans that can be bundled up into "investment products,"' she writes. This process transformed the modest debts and 'meagre savings' of ordinary households into investment vehicles of the financial markets (Sassen 2009; Aitken 2006; Foud *et al.* 2006). As Paul Langley (2008: 233) has put it, the crisis is 'profoundly related' to the ways in which 'unprecedented relationships between Anglo-American everyday borrowing, on the one hand, and the capital markets of global finance, on the other', have developed. For Sassen (2009), the process of financialization eventually runs against its natural limits. 'When everything has become financialised,' she writes, 'finance can no longer extract value. It needs non-financialised sectors to build on.' However, the boom and bust histories of modern markets suggest that the limits of financialization are not easily reached. A socio-cultural perspective would be required in order to understand *which* contingencies become commodified and securitized at different moments in history (e.g. Langley 2008; Aitken 2006).

It is not the case, then, that financial technology renders the uncertain future calculable and predictable. Put bluntly, the tamed future is not commercially profitable. Rather than an eradication of risk in the markets, financial instruments are more properly understood as a modern *embracing* of risk, whereby the identification of uncertain futures enables commodification in the present. It is this embracing of risk that allows and fosters business practice (Baker and Simon 2002; Lobo-Guerrero 2007). Strange (1986) herself was aware of this paradox of in/security in finance, and concluded: 'A speculative market therefore actually *requires* uncertainty.' Indeed, Ulrich Beck (1992: 56) has called risk a '"bottomless barrel of demands," unsatisfiable, infinite'. Beck continues: 'Demands, and thus markets, of a completely new type can be *created* by varying the definition of risk, especially demand for the avoidance of risk' (emphasis in original). In sum, there is a circular argument propping up the financial sphere: while professing to provide security for an uncertain future, the financial industry invents more and more uncertainties to be hedged. Financial markets simultaneously celebrate uncertainty and seek to redistribute it; simultaneously profess to effect security and multiply insecurities.

Finance/Security

A third avenue for studying finance and security now follows logically: this avenue emphasizes that the domains of finance and security are connected not just in an instrumental sense (where finance is put in the service of security or vice versa), or a causal sense (where finance causes societal (in)security), but demonstrate a much more profound conceptual entanglement. Finance is security's economic double, as is evidenced in the etymological affiliations between security as safety and securities as tradable debt that have been briefly discussed above. Here, it becomes clear that finance and security demonstrate conceptual and historical interrelations that would make the one unthinkable without the other in modernity. For example, it would be difficult to disentangle historically the domains of security and finance as technologies of dealing with the uncertain future. The histories of colonial conquest and financial innovation are inextricable, and jointly premised on novel time horizons and commodifications of the future that had been unthinkable in the Middle Ages (Campbell and Dillon 1993: 6–7). As financial historian Larry Neal (1990: 9–10) has observed, the origins of financial instruments like tradable shares derive from 'overseas discoveries and the emergence of long-distance trade' (also Leyshon and Thrift 1997; Burch 1998). Stocks and shares as we now know them were first issued by joint-stock companies such as the VOC in Holland and the East India Company in England in the seventeenth and eighteenth centuries. It would be an anachronism to understand these companies as *private* enterprises: they operated in conjunction with the nascent European national states. On the one hand, joint-stock companies were authorized to act in the name of the national state, for example in establishing forts and settlements, monopolizing trade routes and combating colonial competitors (Burch 1998: 107–35). The 'security' of the early modern state, then, was defended and expanded through one of the first organizational forms of modern finance. On the other hand, the emergence of the modern national state would be unthinkable without the institution of the national debt (Germain 2004). If the national state, in Hobbes's famous metaphor, is like a body (Campbell 1992), then the circulation of money has been envisioned as its *blood*.

We are accustomed to thinking about *finance* as the first modern domain squarely oriented to the uncertain future as both a source of threat and an opportunity. As discussed above, financial speculation rationalizes itself as a security technology that tames the uncertain future. We are less accustomed to understanding the domain of *security* as a technology of the future; one that works through a probabilistic comprehension, calculation and colonization of uncertain futures. However, this is precisely how the apparatus of security under liberalism ought to be understood, according to Michel Foucault's recently transcribed 1978 lectures at Collège de France. Security, for Foucault (2007: 19), is a technology of *risk*: 'one that works on probabilities' in order to '[maximize] the positive elements ... and [minimize] what is risky and inconvenient'. It is in this sense that the 'specific space of security' *works on the future* and 'refers to a series of possible events; ... to the temporal and the uncertain' (ibid. 20). Akin to the domain of finance, then, security as a practice of government pivots not so much on a forbidding or enclosing of phenomena, but on an 'embracing' of the uncertain future, by acting on its variations and circulations through a series of probabilistic interventions (also Burke 2007b: 43; Dillon 2007; Lobo-Guerrero 2007). I do not mean to argue here that finance and security – or even less so, capital and empire – have historically worked in flawless conjunction. Instead, it is my purpose to draw attention to the joint histories, philosophies and technologies of governing through uncertain futures in what are often thought to be the separate domains of finance and security.

What new or rephrased questions arise if we understand both finance and security through the lens of their joint embracing of uncertain futures? One avenue of inquiry here could pursue the genealogy of disciplines and ask how, given their etymological and historical inextricability, did finance and security become relegated to different conceptual, professional and political domains in late modernity. Studies are also starting to appear on the shared technological histories of finance and security; for example, the algorithmic decision-models deployed both in war situations and in the financial markets (Martin 2007; Der Derian 2001; Taylor 2004). Related, we could enquire into the financial and economic work done to constitute the nation: not in the narrow sense of financing war, although that is important, but in the broad sense of the constitutive role that the economy played in imagining the nation (Miller and Rose 1990; Helleiner and Gilbert 1999).

Indeed, Foucault has affirmed many times the centrality of economy to practices of security insofar as they act on the population, emphasizing that the statistical knowledge practices of political economy were central here (e.g. Foucault 2007: 77; also 2003a). Different conceptualizations of power come into focus here, calling not just for a determination of the primacy of market over state, or vice versa, but for investigation into the making of the modern investment subject and the securing of the self through articulations of financial responsibility and rationality (e.g. Langley 2007; Campbell 2005). For example, Rosenberg shows how dollar diplomacy took place within a larger cultural context that associated financial discipline with civilization, control and manliness. 'Manly restraint,' writes Rosenberg (1999: 33), 'both in monetary and sexual matters, would bring capital accumulation and family (thus social) stability'.

Furthermore, it is important to emphasize that rather than seeking to tame or reduce uncertainty in the world, finance/security technologies effect governing *in the present* in the name of the uncertain future (Dillon 2008a). Put differently, the imagination of the uncertain future shapes and constrains action in the present, both in the realm of finance and in the realm of security. As Jakob Arnoldi (2004: 37) explains, in the logic of financial markets, 'randomness becomes accessible as a space of possibilities ... and thus also becomes the object of practice: something that can be acted upon' (cf. Anderson 2007; O'Malley 2004). Such recognition would shift enquiry towards, for example, the contingent articulation (un)imaginable futures and their disciplining effects (Salter 2008c; de Goede 2008a). Here, I would not be the first to emphasize that *risk* comes into focus as a technique that bridges finance and security (Baker and Simon 2002; O'Malley 2000; Aradau *et al.* 2008; Kessler this volume). However, current developments, both in finance and security, have begun to exceed the logic of risk-calculation and have turned to non-actuarial technologies of imagining the future, including scenario planning, stress testing, attack simulation and premediation (e.g. Bougen 2003; Der Derian 2001; Grusin 2004). Scenario planning is one example of shared techniques whereby specific futures are actualized so that we may act upon them in the present (Harmes 2009).

At the beginning of the twenty-first century, then, can we observe new incarnations of the historically durable finance/security relationship? Could we say that Obama's securitization of the credit crisis exceeds his own political agenda and is symptomatic of a larger tendency, in politics as well as academia, to explicitly recognize and theorize the mutual dependence of finance and security? Tentatively, we can answer affirmatively here. First, the deepening of the credit crisis leads not just to a securitization of the problem whereby its analysis and solution become considered a matter of (national) security. In addition, questions are being raised concerning the lasting geopolitical effects of the credit crisis. Will US indebtedness finally cause a decline of American hegemony (Nesvetailova and Palan 2008)? Will high rates of savings coupled with low rates of consumer credit in China and other parts of Asia foster an Asian ascent (Ferguson 2008)? Do the highly leveraged and under-regulated Western financial systems, awash with 'toxic assets', demonstrate the corruptness of financial capitalism and predict its demise (Sassen 2008a)?

It is perhaps the war on terror, however, that has fostered the most worrying contemporary manifestations of the finance/security complex – in at least two ways. First, as Jacqueline Best (2003) – among others – has pointed out, the US-led invasion of Iraq very clearly had an 'central economic dimension' as well as a self-professed security logic (Klein 2008). This dimension was to 'integrate Iraq into global financial markets' and to govern its space through the logic of the international financial institutions including the IMF and the World Bank. The moral discourses deployed by these institutions, Best (2008: 84) argues, mean that increasingly, 'global economic institutions are policing the definition of political community'. If security is by definition a technology of community, regulating the boundaries of in- and exclusion, then the policing of community by financial institutions presents us with a remarkable new finance–security conjunction.

The war on terrorism financing, finally, fosters new spaces of governing within the finance–security complex, because it effectively draws the domain of mundane financial transactions into the sphere of security and preemptive security action. The objective of this domain of the war on terror is, ostensibly, to cut off money flows to terrorists and thus disable violent groups and even preempt terrorist attacks (e.g. Levitt and Jacobson 2008). Through freezing assets, blocking accounts, regulating financial transactions, discouraging financial business with particular clients or geographical areas, political adversaries are targeted, disabled and economically isolated As Sue Eckert (2008: 103) has recently put it, 'such non-military measures have become increasingly attractive and, in fact, the policy instrument of choice'. The fight against terrorist financing is attracting considerable academic attention for its impact on the institutions of global governance and for its (lack of) effectiveness (Biersteker and Eckert 2007; Biersteker 2004; Heng and McDonagh 2008). Less attention has been directed towards the ways in which this axis of the war on terror draws everyday spaces of charitable donation, political affiliation and personal remittances into the domain of security (de Goede 2008b). In effect, the identification of suspect financial spaces in the wake of 9/11, including – but not limited to – Islamic charitable giving, informal remittance networks and particular kinds of wire transfers, enables scrutiny, intervention and regulation of these spaces in the name of security (McCulloch and Pickering 2005). A logic of transactions data mining and preemptive security intervention becomes legitimate here (Amoore and de Goede 2008). In this sense, the 'war on terrorist finance' is not just, and perhaps not even primarily, about a global financial (re)bordering (Andreas and Biersteker 2003), but more about enabling new domains of security that work through the spaces of everyday financial life.

Conclusion

This chapter has considered three avenues of studying 'financial security' or, more precisely, the empirical and conceptual conjunctions between 'finance' and 'security.' The first avenue prioritizes an instrumental relationship between these concepts, where finance is deployed in the service of national security and sovereignty, or indeed whereby the national security apparatus has become an instrument in the service of financial interests. The second avenue understands this relationship to be a causal one, whereby modern financial instruments are ascribed the ability to engender business security, or alternatively, to cause spectacular societal insecurity. The third avenue emphasizes the conceptual closeness of finance/security as historically and technologically related human practices of confronting the uncertain future. In this latter sense, it becomes clear that the relations between finance and security cannot be considered incidental or instrumental, but depend upon a conceptual and historical interweaving that makes the one unthinkable without the other.

In conclusion, then, finance cannot be understood to be a *new* security concept. From a realist perspective within security studies, recognizing economic and financial security as legitimate goals – above and beyond defending the nation – would certainly seem novel. But any enquiry into the constitution of the modern nation that functions as a given to realists would *have to* grapple with the role of the joint-stock company in national history and, more generally, the imagination of *currency* as the blood of the modern nation. Alternatively, from the perspective of economy and finance, questions concerning national security would seem remote or even inappropriate: if there is any domain of human endeavour that works to challenge, transcend and overturn national boundaries, many would argue, it is modern finance. However, any enquiry into the rationale and purpose of modern financial instruments would inevitably lead to questions of security and risk management. The etymological history of security/securities serves to underscore this inextricability of finance/security in history. Rather than a new security concept then, finance may be one of the oldest security concepts around, with the finance/security double operating at the heart of modernity.

12

Security and International Law

Kristin Bergtora Sandvik

Introduction

The events of the present decade have revealed international law to be an ambiguous force with respect to the distribution of security in global governance. Despite intensive legislative efforts on national, regional, and international levels to ensure greater environmental security, the effectiveness of the international environmental law regime, such as that of the 1997 Kyoto protocol, remains acutely vulnerable to the political priorities of nation states. The liberalization of world trade agreements and the codification of patents within the intellectual property law regime have had highly adverse effects on food security for communities in the Global South. The celebrated codification of women's international human rights has sometimes meant that women's advocates on the ground have been attacked as emissaries of the West and traitors to their own culture. The string of humanitarian interventions that culminated with the 2003 invasion of Iraq showed us that the relationship between what is legal and what is legitimate under international law remains convoluted, and that political appropriations of human rights discourses have pervasive and serious ramifications for the well-being of individuals and communities. After 9/11, international legal frameworks have been essential and controversial elements of national and regional 'anti-terror' strategies.

Throughout the Cold War, international law scholarship primarily considered security matters in the context of intra-state arms control and disarmament efforts, such as the Nuclear Non-Proliferation Treaty (1968) and the SALT I (1972) and II (1979) agreements. During the 1990s, mainstream international law scholarship viewed the globalization of legal liberalism, the emphasis on achieving social change through law-making, as a clear ideological indicator of progress: rule of law and good governance agendas were seen as having legitimate and largely benevolent popular effects. Critical legal scholarship has gone some ways towards unpacking the neo-liberal biases of these agendas. Less scholarly attention has been given to how international law became a way to manage and distribute security between institutions, actors, norm-systems, and administrative processes at local and transnational levels.

While the Westphalian model of international law that was hegemonic during the Cold War retains much of its salience for a security analysis of these developments, this chapter aims to identify new sites for the study of security and securitization in international law. The focus will be on fleshing out critical linkages between developments in the fields of international human rights law, humanitarian law and international criminal law, and the organization of security in global governance, linkages that so far have been the subject of little scholarly attention (as noted by Oberleitner 2005; Von Tigerström 2007). This chapter aims to map out possible lines of inquiry by focusing on the interplay between the sites of doctrinal production of international law and their social and political context. Emphasis has been put on offering a broad outline. A note of caution is warranted: in carving out these links, it is necessary to be cognizant of the way differences in disciplinary vocabularies shape the understanding of conceptual and empirical issues. For example, a problem of human security in the context of armed conflict may or may not respond to a violation of the 1949 Geneva conventions, just as a finding of a breach of state obligations by the European Court of Human Rights may not indicate the existence of a security issue.

The interrogation of international law as a security framework is structured around the discussion of three major trends in international law, followed by a brief reflection on the politics of knowledge construction. First, the *legalization* of global governance, including the emergence of non-state actors as players in international law, the growing prominence of international organizations as standard setters, and the increased significance of soft law. Second, the *humanization* of international law at the institutional, procedural, and material level. This section maps the institutionalization of international human rights adjudication and the proliferation of individual complaint mechanisms under treaty body law, before looking at the intensifying 'merger' or 'co-application' of human rights and humanitarian frameworks, including the emergence of the so-called 'human security treaties'. Then attention is shifted to two aspects of *the rise of the individual* in international law: the section considers emergence of a set of 'soft' and 'hard' individual and collective legal identities in international refugee management and international criminal law, and the testimonial practices that underpin the production of these regulatory subjects. Starting from the contrast between the internal critiques of international law's 'imperial character', and the events of the post-9/11 period which have exposed the fragility of the international law structure, the fourth section reflects on which possibilities the modes of knowledge construction available in international law offer for the interrogation of the relationship between international law and security. The chapter ends with a brief recap of the interfaces to be explored.

The Legalization of Global Governance

This section discusses the security implications of the recent shifts in the formats and infrastructure underpinning international law. Traditionally, public international law was deployed as a means to regulate relations between states, and to protect sovereignty. States were bound by obligations incurred through the international agreements they entered, but also by the evolving norms of international customary law. The period after the Second World War has seen a gradual turn to *non-state actors* in international law. Today, the world is faced with a rapidly expanding range of new regulatory subjects such as international organizations (IOs), transnational corporations (TNCs), NGOs, and individuals. Attendant to these subjects are new institutional frameworks and new ways of producing and organizing normative approaches and administrative processes (see generally Shaw 2003).

As IOs have become ever more powerful actors in global governance, international law plays an increasingly prominent role in their activities, both as a framework for governance, and as a strategy to address questions of accountability and democratic participation (Karns and Mingst 2004). The institutional structures and practices of IOs have gradually become more legalized, and they themselves have turned into important producers of soft law, so-called 'secondary international law'. These proliferating soft-law regimes, which are non-binding in their form, include recommendations, guidelines, codes of practice, and standards (Alvarez 2005). Scholars have also begun to pay attention to the element of public authority embedded in the forms of 'internal soft law' (Smrkolj 2008) or 'internal administrative law' (Goldmann 2008) generated by international organizations to regulate their own internal activities. These consist of administrative handbooks, bureaucratic guidelines, codes of conduct, and standards of procedure that are formally non-binding but which in practice affect the legal situations of individuals directly or indirectly, such as listings by the UN Taliban and Al Qaida Sanctions Committee or the Refugee Status Determination undertaken by the United Nations High Commissioner for Refugees (UNHCR) (Goldmann 2008).

In the late 1980s and early 1990s, serious questions were raised about the procedural legitimacy of expanding international bureaucracies (Barnett and Finnemore 2004). The answer to the anxiety about law and bureaucracy seems to have been to bring in more of both, in an effort to make the administrative bodies of the international community more efficient. Today, there is again growing unease among commentators about how these transnational expert-run bureaucracies of international law, including the regulatory schemes devised to generate greater degrees of accountability and transparency, impact not only the nature and content of international law in itself, but also conditions on the ground. Rather than lying in the background of global politics, the everyday decisions made by the professionals who manage norms and institutions now appear as instrumental to the distribution of material resources and the making of policy agendas (Kennedy 2005). This development has been accelerated by the resort to soft and non-binding instruments, whose factual impact may be as significant as that of formal and legally binding instruments, but which makes the control of bureaucracies as they engage in 'interpretive change' or 'mission creep' more difficult (Venzke 2008).

In the present context, this account of the legalization of global governance points to the perception of a relative decline in the ability of Third World states, states in transition, *and* welfare states to be the exclusive guarantors of security, coupled with the notion that the emergence of new types of de-territorialized threats and risks require international and transnational management. As this observation suggests, in addition to a continued focus on how international law governs relationships between states, the mandates of international organizations, their organizational cultures, and the administrative and norm-engendering aspects of their activities ought to be central frameworks for the examination of how security is manufactured in legal discourse.

The Humanization of International Law

This section focuses on a particular thematic turn emanating from the general legalization of the international sphere: the focus is on the centering of the human condition, which includes not only the establishment of a host of judicial and quasi-judicial protection mechanisms, but also the gradual move towards institutional parity between the regimes of economic, social, and cultural rights, and civil and political rights, and the normative rapprochement between human rights and the law of armed conflict, formerly separate bodies of international law.

The section begins with a brief look at two facets of the institutionalization of human rights frameworks, a process which has been one of the most important advances in international law in the post-Second World War period. The first is the emergence of regional human rights courts. The European Court of Human Rights established under the European Convention on Human Rights of 1950, the Inter-American Court of Human Rights established in 1979 under the American Convention on Human Rights and the African Court on Human and Peoples' Rights established under the 2004 African Charter on Human and Peoples Rights (not yet operational) are mandated to adjudicate on a range of civil, political, social, cultural, and economic rights (see Steiner *et al.* 2008: ch. 11). The second is the rapid institutionalization of individual petition rights. Currently, five of the UN human rights treaty bodies have quasi-judicial mechanisms composed of committees of independent experts which may consider individual complaints alleging treaty violations, although the views and recommendations on remedies are not legally binding on the state concerned. They include the Human Rights Committee, which considers petitions relating to the First Optional Protocol to the International Covenant on Civil and Political Rights (1966, 1976), the Committee on the Elimination of Discrimination against Women which considers petitions relating to the Optional Protocol to the Convention on the Elimination of Discrimination Against Women (1999, 2000), the Committee against Torture which considers individual petitions under article 22 of the Convention against Torture and Other Cruel, Inhuman or Degrading Treatment of Punishment (1984, 1987), the Committee of the Elimination of Racial Discrimination which considers petitions under article 14 of the Convention on the Elimination of Racial Discrimination (1965), and the Committee on the Rights of People with Disabilities which consider petitions under the Optional Protocol to the Convention on the Rights of Persons with Disabilities (2006, 2008). The Optional Protocol to the International Covenant on Economic, Social and Cultural Rights establishes individual complaint mechanisms. The protocol was adopted by the UN General Assembly on 10 December 2008, and will enter into force when ratified by ten state parties.

While the move towards humanization represents an important thematic reorientation, this development also constitutes a significant shift in *how* and *through which sites* security is to be allocated: individuals and communities are now asked to pursue protection against government interference as well as their active intervention against third parties through the language of law and rights in forums *outside* the structures of the nation state. This point is illuminated by looking at the socio-legal critique of this thematic turn.

The European and Inter-American courts of human rights have been highly effective in reshaping the procedural and material landscapes of domestic jurisdictions. Both the courts and the complaint mechanisms have significantly influenced the evolvement of international human rights law. Nevertheless, there is a high threshold for succeeding in this type of claims-making: access is disproportionately available to individuals with sufficient legal literacy, adequate material resources, and available social connections. In addition, the benefits of resorting to international legal institutions are uncertain and often at best symbolic. The institutions in question are overwhelmed by their caseload, and state parties frequently remain reluctant to change their sanctioned behavior (although they may pay out compensation to claimants). In addition to the observation that the promise of justice – and increased security – through international human rights institutions may prove elusive for marginal groups, what are the implications of devoting scarce resources to the pursuit of justice through international law for marginal individuals and communities? How may the recourse to human rights discourses and legal tactics marginalize social movement strategies and other forms of political mobilization which aim towards structural change, rather than the fulfillment of individual needs and rights?

A substantive and institutional 'merger' is taking place between international human rights and humanitarian law, and occurring in the work of courts, tribunals, and international organizations (Meron 2000), although the implications of this rapprochement remain unclear (Kretzmer *et al.* 2007). There is an intensifying 'co-application' of human rights law and humanitarian law in international case law, most recently in the International Court of Justice's advisory opinions on *the Consequences of the Construction of a Wall in the Occupied Palestinian Territory* (2004), and *Armed Activities on the Territory of the Congo (Democratic Republic of the Congo v. Uganda)* (2005). A number of newer international treaties and instruments incorporate or draw from both human rights and international humanitarian law provisions. These include the Convention on the Rights of the Child (1989), the Rome Statute of the International Criminal Court (1998), and most recently the Convention on the Rights of Persons with Disabilities (2006) (Droege 2007). The so-called 'human security treaties', the Mine Ban Treaty and the Convention on Cluster Munitions, place obligations on countries to clear affected areas and destroy stockpiles, and to offer assistance to survivors and their communities. Disagreement persists as to the current status of the Responsibility to Protect (R2P), which on a legal level attempts to reconcile two sometimes diverging principles of international law: state sovereignty and human rights. The R2P codification agenda is to some degree driven by the idea of an integrated, rights-based humanitarianism. While commentators propose that R2P *already* is a principle of international law (Evans 2008), with a firm basis in human rights law and international humanitarian law, others argue that that the extent to which these regimes provides the basis for the R2P framework fails to transform R2P from a policy initiative to a legal doctrine (Focarelli 2008).

Legal commentators remain divided in their assessment of the rapprochement between human rights and humanitarianism, with some arguing that this 'merger' has 'bad' political consequences for the human rights regime or conversely that it compromises the non-derogability and universality of humanitarian law and humanitarianism (Douzinas 2007; Teitel 2002). From a security perspective, it is useful to read these diverging approaches as modes of ranking values and risks. Making the long-term fulfillment of human rights a priority in field interventions may come at the expense of fulfilling urgent short-term humanitarian needs.

The Rise of Individuals: Victim Categories and Testimonials

This section examines the rise of individuals and human suffering in international law. The past two decades have witnessed the emergence and consolidation of a host of legal identities in international law, through treaty-based law-making, soft law arrangements, adjudicative practices, and judicial proceedings. It has already been noted how the thematic orientation towards humanization simultaneously represented a transformation of the relationship between citizens and the state, where collective political struggles to establish agreements on societal security were shifted towards juridical and individualized formats in the international sphere. This section explores different aspects of the transnationalization of security, namely the rise of individuals-as-victims, of mass suffering as the preeminent mode of insecurity in international law, and the globalization of how imageries of suffering are to be mediated.

Although the codification of individual responsibility for transgressions is central to this process, it is the expansion of victim categories that has been the most spectacular. The definition proposed by the UN Basic Principles and Guidelines on the Right to a Remedy and Reparation for Victims of Gross Violations of International Human Rights Law and Serious Violations of International Humanitarian Law (2005) defines victims as 'persons who individually or collectively suffered harm, including physical or mental injury, emotional suffering, economic loss or substantial impairment of their fundamental rights, through acts or omissions that constitute gross violations of international human rights law, or serious violations of international humanitarian law'. While driven by the humanization of international law, this expansion has also been accelerated by three parallel developments: the globalization of 'risk society', the institutional soft law-production of contexts of 'large-scale victimization', and the emphasis on individual participation as the symbolic constituent of international justice.

The globalization of 'risk society' has generated the idea that we are all potential victims of mass suffering (Ewald 2002). This development can be illustrated by the growing number of classifications of individuals as victims of 'gender-based violence', here illustrated by the function of the 'Women-at-Risk' category in refugee resettlement. Third-country resettlement under the auspices of UNHCR is one of three durable solutions to the refugee problem, and involves the selection and transfer of refugees from a state in which they have initially sought protection to a third state that has agreed to admit them with permanent residence status. During recent decades, the focus on the extent and gravity of gender-based violence in situations of unrest and displacement has led to the recognition of refugee women as a particularly vulnerable group. 'Women-at-Risk' has evolved gradually from the 1980s, when, as a result of political lobbying, the protection of women refugees became a topic for UNHCR. Particularly significant were the 1991 Guidelines on the Protection of Refugee Women, which recognized the link between refugee protection and human rights. In 1995 this connection was specified and reinforced by the Executive Committee Conclusion no. 73, *Refugee Protection and Sexual Violence* (Kneebone 2005). These developments have had great significance for refugee women's formal access to resettlement: according to the 2007 UNHCR Resettlement Handbook, the category 'Women-at-Risk' is designed to provide a remedy for women who are single heads of families or who are accompanied by an adult male who is unable to support them, and assume the role of the head of the family. They may suffer from a wide range of problems including expulsion, refoulement and other security threats, sexual harassment, violence, abuse, torture, and exploitation.

At the same time, there has been an institutional production of contexts of 'large-scale victimization' as fields of intervention (Ewald 2006). This can be illustrated by the gradual cementation of a soft-law norm concerning the plight of internally displaced people (IDP). As of 2008, twenty-six million people were internally displaced in their own countries (IDMC 2009). The dire predicament of the world's IDPs raises sensitive questions regarding sovereignty and intervention. The UNHCR has traditionally argued that it does not have a 'general competence for IDPs' even though at least since 1972 it has had relief and rehabilitation programs for those displaced within a country (Goodwin-

Gill 1996). Consequently, achieving international consensus about their legal status has been difficult. While international refugee movements are regulated by the 1951 Convention relating to the Status of Refugees, no international treaty applies specifically to IDPs. In 1998 the former special representative on IDPs submitted the draft principles on internal displacement as a text produced by international experts, rather than as a draft convention on the human rights of IDPs. Today, the most authoritative statement by the international community remains the 1998 Guiding Principles on Internal Displacement, which restates the responsibilities of states before, during, and after displacement according to the human rights and humanitarian law relevant to internally displaced persons. While these principles have been widely endorsed, they remain non-binding for states, and they have had a mixed impact on national legal standards and on actual state behavior. Strategically, in the quest for protection of IDPs, legalization has to a certain extent been replaced by institutional reform. In September 2005, responding to a call by the General Assembly for a more predictable, effective, and accountable humanitarian system, the Inter-Agency Standing Committee (IASC) established a 'cluster approach', under which the UNHCR assumed the lead responsibility for protection, emergency shelter, and camp management for internally displaced people (FMR 2008).

The third development concerns the idea of individual agency as intrinsic to the legitimacy of international justice. Espousing a broad definition of victims, the 1998 Rome Statute of the International Criminal Court, and the 2002 ICC Rules of Procedure and Evidence enshrine groundbreaking provisions with respect to victims' rights to participation, protection, and reparation (Gioia 2007). As the tribunals for Rwanda and Yugoslavia attempted to put proper emphasis on witness accounts in their proceedings, the outcome was often feelings of disempowerment and factual increases in the security problems faced by individual victims. In the Rome statute, for the first time, victims were granted the right to representation. Article 68(3) gives victims the right to participate in all stages of the proceedings determined to be appropriate by the Court, and they are to be assisted in obtaining legal advice by the Registrar pursuant to procedural rule 16(b). Furthermore, mechanisms have been established to provide victim protection at all stages of the proceedings. Article 43(6) establishes a Victims and Witnesses Unit to provide 'protective measures and security arrangements, counseling and other appropriate assistance for witnesses, victims who appear before the Court, and others who are at risk on account of testimony given by such witnesses'. Article 68(2) provides for in camera hearings, entailing the non-disclosure of victims' identities. Article 79(2) establishes a Trust Fund to make financial reparations to victims and their families according to rules of procedure 98, in the form of physical or psychological reparations, or material support. According to the 2005 Regulations of the Trust Fund for Victims, the Trust Fund is mandated to focus on two aspects of situations where the prosecutor has opened investigations. First, the Trust Fund will support the court in the implementation of reparations awards. Second and more controversially, the Trust Fund will also assist victims in areas under the jurisdiction of the Court *without* any link to the alleged crimes or suspects/perpetrators and at *any* stage of the proceedings. This extremely wide mandate raises important questions about which ideas of victimization and insecurity will form the basis for the distribution of resources.

The discursive properties of 'mass-suffering' are produced through particular globalized templates that detail not only the range of available imageries, but also circumscribe permitted formats. In this context, storytelling and personal narrative have become important in the establishment of legal facts about suffering. Such testimonies about abuse, exploitation, and violence are intrinsic to the inclusion of an increasingly broad range of individual and collective attributes of victimhood in international legal discourse and practice. From the late 1980s and onwards, a proliferating number of international and national tribunals, commissions, and administrative entities have been created to deal with the need for legal protection, transitional justice, restoration, and allocation of criminal responsibility in the aftermath of internal and international conflict (Sandvik 2008). Successful transnational 'circuits of suffering' (McLagan 2005) have come into being by way of the specialized communication structures of the human rights community, and take place on a proliferation of international and transnational stages.

Perhaps the most prevalent and popularized source of narratives of suffering are the highly mediated eyewitness accounts produced by advocacy groups such as Human Rights Watch and Amnesty International (Dudai 2008). Victims in such varied locations as Argentina, South Africa, and Morocco have given testimonies to truth commissions and participated in truth and reconciliation hearings. Some of these processes of reconciliation have involved formalized apologies or monetary compensation (Slyomovics 2008). Other processes, such as the South African Truth and Reconciliation Commission, aimed to achieve a more abstract form of restorative justice (Wilson 2001). Finally, to allocate individual responsibility for atrocities, the international community summons victims to testify about their personal experiences in front of the International Criminal Court and the tribunals for the former Yugoslavia, Rwanda, and Sierra Leone.

Fulfiling the contemporary cosmopolitan preference for personal narrative, as well as the interdisciplinary academic emphasis on qualitative data, these testimonies have come to constitute a particular cosmopolitan practice that reproduces global imageries of suffering in a plethora of settings (Colvin 2004; Segall 2002). Hence, attention must also be paid to how notions of suffering link up with globalized imageries of insecurity: what kind of insecurity will trigger the interventions of the international community?

Knowledge Construction in International Law

The topic for this final section is how the processes of knowledge construction in international law affect ideas about security and securitization. Consider the tension between the following developments: since the mid–1990s, international law scholars on the left have suggested that international law is going through a disciplinary crisis, and that mainstream doctrinal scholarship is characterized by limited reflexivity with respect to knowledge construction. These critics have argued that the legalization global governance represents a form of Americanized 'Imperial law' developed by an elite group of professional bureaucrats, who serve the ends and interests of a transnational capitalist class (Sklair 2001; Mattei 2003; Nader 2005). Describing the rule of law as 'plunder', they have argued in favor of a fundamental reassessment of the project of international law (Mattei and Nader 2008).

However, the geopolitical events of the past decade throw this theoretical critique into sharp relief: in the wake of the terror attacks on New York, Madrid, and London, a pervasive displacement of the values and legal principles underpinning the international human rights framework, humanitarian law, and the refugee regime has taken place. The doctrine of 'preemptive strikes' remains highly problematic under international law. There have been widespread extensions of emergency powers in domestic jurisdictions, with the consequence that universal freedoms of movement, expression, and assembly have been abrogated in the name of anti-terror legislation, with severe substantive and procedural consequences. These so-called 'terror laws' have allowed for torture, extraordinary renditions, targeted killings, and the establishment of secret detention camps. The attempt by the Bush administration to exempt their prisoners of war from the protection of the 1949 Geneva conventions by reclassifying them as enemy combatants represents a particularly grievous example of denial of procedural justice. Thus, it might be argued it is rather the *vulnerability* of international legal norms, and the degree to which they have been undermined by domestic policy agendas, that has been most striking, and which has constituted the greatest threat to regional security

This development has placed critically minded legal scholars in the difficult position of having to do two things at once: the need to be continually engaged in assessments of the ideological underpinnings of international law has combined with the imperative to produce strategic interventions against misappropriations of international law. The challenge is thus to be both critical *and* part of a reconstructive project (Craven *et al.* 2004). In the security context, the need remains for scholars to deploy a theoretically and empirically informed awareness of international law's tendency to reify its own projects, categories, and master concepts such as accountability and transparency (see also Franceschet 2006). Hence, the challenge in the present context is to find ways to explore how the institutions, norms, and methods of international law intersect with geopolitical events to produce processes and outcomes that reshape security situations on the ground, while at the same time privileging particular security agendas in policy-making and in scholarship.

Non-doctrinal methodological approaches in international law offer some possibilities for combining ongoing methodological reflexivity with a critical interrogation of the relationship between law and security. While supporting the globalization of the women's human rights project, international feminist legal scholarship has pointed out how the emphasis on formality and doctrinal interpretation has promoted interventionist and patriarchal approaches in international law (Chinkin and Charlesworth 2000). This may be a useful starting point for assessing how an ostensibly gender-neutral international legal discourse may in fact produce highly gendered interventions on the ground. More ambivalent about the potential of human rights to provide the foundation for universal emancipation, TWAIL (Third World approaches to international law) scholars criticize international law for being a vessel for *perpetuating* dominance as well as the *tools* for domination, by preserving the hierarchical relationships between nations and peoples in the North and the South (Gathii 2000). Their critique of the way international law defines the parameters of *how* the world is projected discursively is highly relevant for the analysis of how international law forges connections between *legitimate* social, political, or economic standards and sites of security and insecurity. Finally there is the challenge of vantage point: critical explorations of law and security necessitate knowledge about how international law is constituted on a formal level *and* how it is reshaped through bureaucratic practice and field-interactions. The answer may be found by turning to socio-legal approaches to international law, which combine the traditional top-down perspective with a 'from below' approach which focuses on social movement activities and transnational advocacy (Rajagopal 2003).

Exploring the Interfaces

This chapter has interrogated four potential linkages between security and international law. The first line of inquiry looked at changes in the format and infrastructure of international law, and the significance of attuning the analysis of the discursive and empirical security implications of international law towards these newly created sites of power. The second inquiry examined the transnationalized protection regimes engendered by the humanization of international law, and the potential democratic and social costs of these institutional and normative shifts. The third inquiry concerned the link between the rise of individuals and the standardization of templates for communicating suffering, and the role of international law in triggering assessments of security and insecurity. The fourth inquiry considered the methodological implications of how we study international law as a site of security, securitization, and insecurity, including how the methodology of international law in itself may transform political and social ideas about security and risk-situations. Brought together, these linkages suggest a possible way forward for the critical study of the role of international law as a framework of security in global governance.

Part III
New Security Objects

13

Environmental Security

Jon Barnett

Introduction

Environmental change poses risks to the territorial integrity and economic growth of states, to the health and welfare of people and communities, and it may increase the risk of violent conflict. In these ways environmental change can be seen as generating problems for national and human security. This chapter describes these effects of environmental change on security. It locates them in broader historical and spatial patterns of development and charts their effects on the biological, physical and chemical components and systems necessary for the process of life (hereafter 'the environment'). It then explains the way in which growing recognition of this problem of material and ecological interdependencies gave rise to the concept of environmental security. It discusses in turn the ways in which environmental change may increase the risk of violent conflict, undermines the territorial integrity and economic growth of states, and creates human insecurity.

The Trajectory of Environmental Insecurity

The broad history of human–environment interactions has been one of increasing population growth, increasing use of resources per capita and increasing inequality between the richest and poorest people in the world in terms of consumption and pollution. These trends, combined with the development of industrialization as the dominant mode of production, capitalism as the near-universal economic order, the emergence of the nation state as the dominant political institution, and the centralized control of the means of violence (Giddens 1985) have given rise to a condition where environmental change increasingly poses risks to people, states, and peace.

The world's population has grown from approximately 5 million people in hunter-gatherer times (up to 12,000 years ago), 100 million people 5,000 years ago, a billion people at the start of the Industrial Revolution in the late eighteenth century, 2.5 billion in 1950, to around 6.7 billion in 2008, and will most likely peak at 9 billion people in

2050 (after Boyden 1987; PRB 2008). The vast majority (80 per cent) of people live in developing countries.

Whereas in hunter-gatherer times production and consumption of material possessions was minimal and restricted mainly to perishable foods and tools, today enormous quantities of resources are produced, for example, the world's population now consumes: 3,953 million tons of oil (in 2007) (BP 2008), 148 million tons of fertilizer (in 2002), 259 million tons of meat (in 2004), 118 million tons of marine fish species (in 2005), 1,250 million tons of steel (in 2006), and 352 million tons of paper and paperboard (in 2005) (BP 2008; IISI 2007; WRI 2007). The 20 per cent of the world's population that lives in the developed countries consumed 57 per cent of the oil, 36 per cent of the fertilizer, 43 per cent of the meat, 32 per cent of the marine fish species, and 40 per cent of the steel.

The massive consumption of resources leads to very significant amounts of pollution, including annual emissions in excess of 150 million tons of sulphur dioxide (45 per cent from developed countries), 24,760 million tons of carbon dioxide (60 per cent from developed countries), and 2,200 tons of mercury (UNEP 2002; WRI 2007). The consequences of increasing population, consumption and pollution has led to massive interference and unprecedented changes in the earth system (Crutzen and Steffen 2003).

These unsustainable changes in environmental processes coincide with dramatic changes in the organization of social life in the past 12,000 years. As Western civilization has moved from the hunter-gatherer to early farming, early urban and now modern high-energy phases, population densities have increased, systems of control over societies have become more complex and hierarchical, the volume and value of trade has increased faster than the rate of growth in production, trading networks have become increasingly dense and critical to welfare, and permanent armed forces have become institutionalized. Yet social systems vary in form and function, and the distribution of human well-being among them varies enormously, for example there are 854 million people in the world who are undernourished (96 per cent in developing countries) and 1.4 billion people living on less than $1.25 a day, while there are over 10 million people whose net worth exceeds US$1million, and whose total assets are worth more than US$40 trillion (slightly more than the annual income of all developed countries in 2006 (Capgemini and Merrill Lynch 2008; Chen and Ravallion 2008; FAO 2006a; World Bank 2008).

Poverty is a powerful driver of vulnerability to environmental change as the poor have few means at their disposal to avoid, reduce or adjust to risks to livelihoods created by environmental change. In an average day, environmental degradation and poverty combine to cause the death of 5,200 children due to diarrhoea, and 2,300 children due to malaria (Bryce et al. 2005). Undernutrition is an underlying cause of over 4.6 million child deaths each year (Black et al. 2008), and inadequate access to clean water and sanitation results in the death of 1.4 million children each year (Bartram et al. 2005). The vast majority of these deaths occur in low-income countries in Africa and Asia. As well as the chronic problems, the poor are most severely affected by environmental hazards: it has recently been estimated that 98 per cent of the people in the world affected by climate disasters live in developing countries (UNDP 2007), and per capita mortality rates from disasters are far higher in developing countries (Kahn 2005). Poverty and environmental change therefore combine to create environmental insecurity, which is the vulnerability of individuals and groups to critical adverse effects caused directly or indirectly by environmental change (Barnett 2001: 17). Environmental security is achieved when individuals and groups have the ability to avoid or adapt to environmental change so that their basic needs, rights, and values are not undermined.

Environmental insecurity is therefore the product of the global political economy, which sustains a situation where the wealthy consume a disproportionate amount of resources and produce a disproportionate amount of pollution, yet remain relatively far less vulnerable to the impacts of environmental change. It follows, then, that environmental security will be achieved when the aggregate impact of human consumption does not exceed the capacity of the earth's systems to provide resources and absorb wastes now and for future generations, while ensuring that everyone enjoys a minimum standard of well-being which can be maintained despite periods of perturbation and change in environmental and social systems. Yet most often the practices and policies on environmental security are oriented towards quite different outcomes. Indeed, in as much as security is about protecting something valued from change, then in practice environmental security seems to be about protecting the consumption of the wealthy and/or the longevity of security institutions from these imperatives for ecological sustainability and equity (Dalby 2002b).

Environmental Security into Policy

The environment has been a political issue in developed countries since the late 1960s, and has been the subject of international summits and agreements since the early 1970s. In this time the number of local, national and international non-governmental organizations concerned with environmental issues has massively increased (Raustilia 1997), and environmental issues have been increasingly understood as products of – and as risks to – various other international issues, including development, security and human rights.

The issue of inequalities in consumption and well-being in the world, the processes that sustain it, and the proposed solutions (hereafter called 'development') has had less domestic political salience in developed countries than the environment, although it has long been a pressing concern of people in developed countries. It has been an important concern of the international community and non-governmental organizations since the end of the Second World War, and the subject of many summits, reports and agreements. In the 1970s, at the same time as the environment was linked to development, so too was the issue of military spending and the arms trade (highlighting their opportunity costs to welfare and social progress). These issues were highlighted in reports such as *North–South: A Programme for Survival* (ICIDI 1980), and *Common Security: A Blueprint for Survival* (ICDSI 1982).

Thus, throughout the 1970s and 1980s there was growing awareness of the links between environmental change, development and security, as reflected in the rise in international agreements, reports and government and non-governmental organizations dealing with one or more of these issues. These three pillars came together in the 1987 World Commission on Environment and Development Report (*Our Common Future*), which is most recognized for its definition of sustainable development as 'development that meets the needs of the present without compromising the ability of future generations to meet their own needs' (WCED 1987: 87). However, chapter 11 of the WCED report also had much to say about security and disarmament, and appears to be the first document to coin the term 'environmental security', arguing that 'the real sources of insecurity also encompass unsustainable development' (p. 334), 'environmental stress can thus be an important part of the web of causality associated with any conflict' (p. 335), 'poverty, injustice, environmental degradation and conflict interact in complex and potent ways' (p. 335), and that 'threats to environmental security can only be dealt with by joint management and multilateral procedures and mechanisms' (p. 345).

The WCED process gave rise to the most significant international conference on the environment, the United Nations Conference on Environment and Development (UNCED), which was held in Rio in 1992, at which a number of the world's major environmental treaties (such as the UN conventions on climate change, biodiversity, and desertification) were signed. However, while the development dimensions of this sustainable development agenda were at the forefront of debates between the developed and developing countries (with the latter arguing for a more 'development first' approach), the security dimensions were of peripheral concern. Indeed, security aspects have remained largely peripheral to UN processes on the environment and development, and it was the Security Council that most forcefully forged the link with a high-level debate on climate change in April 2007 (Podesta and Odgen 2007).

For the most part the rise of environmental security as an international issue occurred outside the UN system, and was stimulated by the USA and its allies' response to the end of the Cold War. With the collapse of the Soviet Union the principle reason for NATO and its force structure ostensibly disappeared. For the US armed forces, which were at the time receiving US$422 billion from the government, the demise of the principal reason for this spending represented a threat to the sustainability of budget allocations. Indeed, between 1989 and 1991 US military spending fell by $68 billion (data adjusted for inflation, from the SIPRI Military Expenditure database). The material risks the end of the Cold War posed to security institutions was matched by the ideological and doctrinal vacuum: it was no longer clear what risks there were to national security (assuming of course that there had to be some), and how it was to be obtained. Thus, as Klare (1995) describes it, the USA and its allies began to 'search for a new foreign policy'. Environmental issues began to figure prominently in this search to fill the threat vacuum.

Thus, writing about the connections between the environment and security predated the end of the Cold War by at least a decade, and was far less concerned with the ways in which environmental change might cause conflict and far more concerned with the kinds of impacts environmental change can have on people and states, and highlighting the inability of armed forces to meet these challenges. After 1989, however, there were many more articles on environmental security in high-profile journals, most of which were concerned with the potential for environmental change to cause violent conflict (Dalby 2002b). The end of the Cold War therefore marked a turn towards an appropriation of environmental concerns to justify traditional security institutions, and these institutions, such as the US Department of Defense, NATO and the US National Security Strategy, began to incorporate environmental issues in ways that did nothing to challenge their pre-existing values and practices (Barnett 2001). There are now at least thirteen countries with policies and practices relating to environmental security in some way – all of which are developed countries, most of which are members of NATO, as well as eight intergovernmental organizations (Kingham 2006), although each differs in terms of the relative emphasis they give to the environmental, conflict and development dimensions of the issue.

The risk that powerful mainstream national security institutions in the developed world would 'securitize' environmental issues (see Floyd 2007) was foreseen by a number of more critical thinkers, including Brock (1992), Deudney (1991), and Dalby (1992), all of whom warned that environmental security would work to secure the state and its security institutions more than it would help advance the resolution of environmental problems.

Yet there remain arguments that environmental change does pose risks that are so severe that they can be likened to war, and that it is a factor in causing conflicts, and so there may be some substance to the idea of environmental security even though the effect of the idea on policy is problematic. It is therefore important to examine these issues in a little more detail.

Environmental Risks to Security

Security is a plastic word that means different things according to who talks about it and the entities at risk and the nature of the risks they identify. If the volume of academic articles and government spending is any indication, then the prevailing meaning of security must certainly be the security of a country against the risk of attack from a hostile group. Within this, however, there is debate about whether what is being secured is the people of a country or its state apparatus (e.g. Klein 1997), whether the attack comes from other states, rogue elements within other states, rogue elements with the state, or terrorist networks, and then, depending on how these two issues are resolved, which responses will maximize security. Given this prevailing concern for national security, it is not surprising that environmental security has been interpreted to mean the security of countries from violent conflicts induced in some way by environmental change.

Environmental Change and Violent Conflict

Thus there has been a considerable amount of effort devoted to understanding if, and to what extent, environmental change may be a cause of violent conflict. There have been four major approaches (some less coordinated than others) to understanding this issue: the Project on Environment, Population and Security (see Homer-Dixon 1999), the Environment and Conflicts Project (ENCOP) (see Baechler 1999), work seeking generalizable findings based on statistical data (see Diehl and Gleditsch 2001) and qualitative case studies using a political ecology framework (see Peluso and Watts 2001). All of this research shares two common findings: environmental change does not and is highly unlikely to ever cause war between countries; and environmental change is never the sole or principal cause of violent conflicts.

Beyond these common findings, however, there is some disagreement about the circumstances under and degree to which environmental change is a factor in violent conflicts. Homer-Dixon (1999) argues that environmental change increases the scarcity of renewable resources and when consumption of scarce resources is unequal, violent conflict is more likely. He also argues that such environmentally induced conflicts are more likely in low-income resource-dependent societies, and that population pressures are a contributing factor. Yet these insights are not unchallenged, with critics arguing that because the studies lacked appropriate controls and contrasts, and downplayed many other important risk factors, they tend to overemphasize the environmental and demographic factors in violent conflicts (Barnett 2001; Gleditsch 1998; Matthew 2000).

The findings of the ENCOP project were similar to those of the Project on Environment, Population and Security, albeit with more emphasis placed on structural inequalities generated by development processes as the more important underlying condition, which is exacerbated by unequal outcomes arising from environmental change. ENCOP differed too in its use of syndromes of environmental change and development to illustrate pathways to conflict, and it identified areas most susceptible to environmental conflicts, such as drylands, tropical forest belts and low-income urban areas.

Quantitative analyses of data generally suggest that poorer states with relatively low levels of trade and states undergoing significant economic and political transitions are less capable of managing environmental change and its social consequences, and are more at risk of violent internal conflict (Hauge and Ellingsen 2001). There is good reason to think that it is not scarcity of renewable resources, but rather the abundance of lootable non-renewable resources that drives conflict (de Soysa 2000). Some studies show a connection between rainfall variability of violent conflict, for example Miguel *et al.* (2004) find that decreases in rainfall strongly increase the likelihood of conflict in the following year. Nel and Ringharts (2008) find that natural disasters increase the risk of violent civil conflict in low-income countries. There are no studies of this kind suggesting that water will be a cause of war between countries, and a number, such as Yoffe *et al.* (2003), which show that cooperation between countries sharing rivers is the prevailing outcome. These studies are only as good as the data they rely on and they have methodological problems. While they do suggest that under certain circumstances environmental change may increase the risk of environmental conflict, they do not suggest that environmental factors are paramount, that there is nothing that can be done (there is no biological determinism at play here), nor that a *risk* of a violent outcome is a *prediction* of a violent outcome.

Political ecology approaches are largely dismissive of the idea that environmental change is an important cause of violent conflict, but they recognize that when the distribution of capital among people becomes more skewed due to resource extraction activities or environmental perturbations, it stimulates grievances that may transcend into violence. They suggest that the configurations of material and institutional power in a society create the preconditions in which environmental change may, or may not, lead to violent conflict.

Many of the debates about environmental causes of conflict have been revisited in the wake of a number of sensationalized reports about the ways in which climate change may cause violent conflicts. There is much that is familiar about these arguments, and their proponents, for example, studies from the USA security policy community argue that climate change may lead to 'skirmishes, battles, and even war due to resource constrains' (Schwartz and Randall 2003: 2; see also CSIS 2007). There is very little that is new in these studies of climate change and conflict, and much of what has been learned about environmental conflicts has been overlooked. The more sober assessments do not consider climate change to be likely cause of war between states, nor do they consider it to be a major driver of civil wars (Barnett and Adger 2007; Buhaug *et al.* 2008).

So, at worst, environmental change may exacerbate the risk of violent conflict under certain circumstances, and this is most likely to occur in low-income countries with governance problems. This conclusion hardly justifies claims that environmental change is a risk to the national security of the developed countries, despite past – and under the auspices of climate change more recent – attempts to argue that strong security institutions are required to respond to environmental conflicts. However, environmental change may undermine the territorial integrity and economic growth of states, although this may have nothing to do with violent conflict, and it is a problem that armed forces cannot address.

Environmental Change and Territorial Integrity

For some countries, environmental change is the major risk to their national security. For example, there are a number of low-lying small island states (such as Kiribati and Tuvalu) which may cease to be habitable given likely future changes in climate, including sea-level rise, increasing rainfall variability, decreasing abundance of fish, and more severe storms (Barnett and Adger 2003). For others, environmental change can lay waste to large swathes of territory. Examples of this abound: diversion of waters that previously flowed into the Aral Sea (spanning Uzbekistan and Kazakhstan) has exposed 33,000 km^2 of lake area to drying and 5 million people living in a 2 million km^2 area to widespread diseases arising from water and airborne pollutants (Glazovsky 1995; Small *et al.* 2001); drying of the Yellow River between 1972 and 1997 has affected 4.7 million hectares of crop land and caused a loss of some 9.86 billion kg of cereal production worth RMB12.2 billion (Changming and Shifeng 2002; Fu and Chen 2006); the Chernobyl accident spread carcinogens across 100,000 km^2 of land (Marples 1993: 39); degradation of 10 million hectares of land in Africa has caused an 8 per cent reduction in agricultural yields (Dregne and Chou 1994; Lal 1995); and smoke pollution from forest fires in Indonesia in 1997 cost Singapore between US$163 and US$286 million in lost production (Quah 2002: 429).

Were these kinds of impacts due to armed aggression from another country, the countries concerned would consider these to be national security issues and mobilize resources on a scale and in a time frame commensurate with war. Yet they are rarely so conceived, because in most cases the culprit is less easily identified and the impact is unintentional, and, because there is no obvious role for them in addressing these problems, it does not benefit the propagators of national security discourse to identify them as security issues. Yet environmentalists such as Lester Brown (1977) have long argued that for all intents and purposes these problems are national security problems because they undermine the territorial integrity and functional capacity of the nation state and its inhabitants, and this justifies responses commensurate with war in terms of urgency and resources.

Environmental Change and Human Security

In many of the instances where environmental change undermines territorial integrity people suffer too, through, for example, contractions in income, loss of land, illness and death. Most of the people whose human security is affected by environmental change are dependent on local stocks of natural resources for their food and their incomes, and they have low financial capital. Their resource dependence makes them sensitive to changes in the environment, and their poverty means their shelters may be unable to withstand storms and floods, they live in hazardous environments where there is less demand for land and their health status and educational attainment may be low. So it is the pastoralists, farmers, fishers, refugees and the urban poor living in informal settlements in developing countries who suffer most during periods of gradual and sudden changes in the environment.

Environmental insecurity is, therefore, very much a function of social factors such as the size and structure of the economy, labour markets, health and education services, urban and rural planning, infrastructure, access to finance, political voice and social networks. It is typically less (although, as Hurricane Katrina showed, not zero) in countries where the government is democratically elected, growth is sustainable and equitable, there is widespread access to social services such as education and health care and there is no armed conflict. It is, therefore, the case that insecurities created by environmental change are not equally distributed between and within countries, with the most insecure being the poorest people in the poorest societies.

The health effects of climate change are one example of the way in which environmental change undermines human security. According to the World Health Organization (2002), climate change is already responsible for over 160,000 deaths per year around the world, largely through the way it exacerbates hunger and diarrhoea (as a result of impacts on food production and prices and water quality), particularly in developing and Least Developed Countries in Asia and Africa. These deaths are those that occur above and beyond baseline levels of mortality caused by interacting effects of poverty, hunger, and environmental changes. The World Health Organization also estimates that, in addition to causing excess deaths, climate change is causing the additional loss of some 5.5 million disability-adjusted life years (the sum of years of healthy life lost due to illness). Climate change will exacerbate the incidence of infectious diseases such as malaria, waterborne diseases such as diarrhoea and cholera, and cardio-respiratory diseases. In Africa, for example, one estimate suggests that malaria exposure will increase by between 16 and 28 per cent under a range of climate change scenarios, which is significant given that 445 million people are already exposed to malaria each year in Africa, leading to over 1.3 million deaths per year in Africa (Nchinda 1998). Slightly over half of all the disease already caused by climate change is due to malnutrition. Malnutrition is the product of a range of factors that may be affected by climate change, notably: food production and imports; the ability to access food, which is a function of incomes and food prices, and in the case of subsistence farmers this is also a matter of food production; and the ability to utilize food, which is a function of the availability of clean water and energy for preparing food, and the body's ability to effectively utilize food, which is often impeded in developing countries by common illnesses such as malaria and gastro-intestinal disorders.

Conclusions

There are three main reasons for considering environmental change to be a security issue: it may under some circumstances increase the risk of violent conflict within if not between states, it can undermine the territorial integrity of states and reduce economic growth, and it can undermine the needs and rights of people. There are degrees of empirical validity associated with these claims: the first is uncertain, whereas the second and third are well documented. There are degrees of relevance to different policy constituencies too. The first claim about environmental conflicts is most relevant to, and supports, the mission of national security institutions. The second claim, about environmental impacts, justifies the concerns and activities of environmental institutions. The latter claim, about human security, is most relevant to and aligned with the mission of development agencies.

However, this pairing of issues and policy constituencies should not be overstated. There are important interrelationships among these three concerns, for example, human insecurity increases the risk of violent conflict (and violent conflict certainly increases human insecurity) (Barnett and Adger 2007), and military activities are a major cause of environmental degradation (Renner 1991). This therefore gives rise to some interesting policy tensions, for example when national security institutions seek a mandate to address human security issues, and environmental policy seeks to regulate the activities of the military.

This plurality of issues and institutions impedes the development of a coherent set of responses to enhance environmental security. For some, environmental security can be achieved through military practices to respond to the anticipated effects of environmental change on population movements and on violent conflict. For others, environmental security can be achieved through reducing consumption and pollution (especially where levels of both are high), including a reduction in the military's use of resources and pollution. For others, environmental security can be achieved through changes in social systems that reduce people's exposure to risk (e.g. by ending violent conflicts), and enhance their capacity to adapt to environmental change (e.g. respecting and upholding human rights). Those in favour of environmental and human security interpretations share a concern that traditional national security institutions are more of a threat than a solution to environmental security, and when it is understood in these ways, environmental security presents a radical challenge to conventional understandings of security.

14

Food Security

Steve Wiggins and Rachel Slater

Food Security: Concepts and Definitions

Food security is about assuring individuals of their capability to lead their lives, by being able to move physically for work and leisure. It also means that as infants and children they were fed well enough to allow development of their physical and mental powers. Conversely, when people are food insecure, they cannot fully function, and this may entail additional insecurity since they may respond in dangerous ways. For example, a hungry person may undertake commercial sex work, engage in crime, or migrate to find work and assistance regardless of the dangers of the route or the destination.

Food security also embraces the idea that not only should a physical state be achieved, but that anxieties and fears that one may be hungry and in discomfort, unable to function fully, and prone to potentially dangerous responses, should be removed. It can thus be seen as one of the cornerstones of human existence: without food security other securities are undermined. At the most basic level, a hungry and malnourished individual is less able to fight, or flee from, physical danger.

Given the importance of food security for functioning, do people have a right to food? Many would agree they should, indeed most countries have formally recognized the right to food. Assuring the right to food is no mean task for governments. Unlike some human rights whose enforcement may be largely one of preventing actions that infringe rights, assuring the right to food involves positive action. Food security is a combination of physical and psychological security, expressed at individual level, and thus although it may seem a fairly straightforward matter of ensuring that people have access to an adequate diet, in reality it entails more than this. While diet may be important for good nutrition, equally so is health. Furthermore, the psychological dimensions take the matter well beyond the bounds of food and health.

This leads us to the two key challenges relating to the right to food. The first is that few countries have the capacity to operationalize the right to food and lack the required combination of strong advocates, information and assessment systems, legislation and accountability processes and benchmarks and monitoring (FAO 2006b). Second, human rights are interrelated so achieving the right to food will only happen alongside the achievement of other rights including access to water, health, education, minimum living standards and so on.

Food security applies to all individuals, no matter their place in the family, household or society. Food security is a continuing state: it applies at all times, through life cycles and through seasonal and other temporal variations. Satisfying these conditions is thus challenging for policy-makers.

Turning to definitions and their implications, a commonly used definition states that 'Food security exists when all people at all times have physical and economic access to sufficient, safe and nutritious food to meet their dietary needs and food preferences for an active and healthy life' (FAO 1996, www.fao.org). Food insecurity is the converse.

Physically, food insecurity ultimately results in malnutrition through undernutrition. Malnutrition varies by degree, from severe to moderate conditions. Its impacts on welfare vary amongst individuals by age, sex and maternity. Some conditions are temporary, others are chronic. Sudden increases in food insecurity on a large scale – populations at district level and above – produce food crises that in severe cases can be classed as famine.

Politically, it is sudden deterioration of food security, or anxiety that this may be about to happen, that tends to attract the attention of leaders, media and the public. It is the drama of food emergencies and famines, typically rarely affecting more than ten million persons at a time, that makes the news; while the continuing shame of more than 900 million persons across the world being regularly and often seasonally undernourished, and of more than 150 million infants being underweight, many of them with lifelong physical and mental disadvantage, goes little remarked.

This chapter sets out the current extent of food insecurity, examines the causes, and considers the policy implications. Future challenges are set out before concluding with considerations of the interaction of food security with other forms of security.

Current Extent of Food Insecurity

Worldwide, FAO (2008) estimate that 848 million, 13 per cent of the world's population, were undernourished in 2003–5: a figure that has been revised upwards to 923 million for 2007 as a result of the increase in food prices on world markets. As many as 27 per cent of children under 5 years in developing countries are underweight (UN 2008), more than 152 million; an even larger number is stunted. Around two billion persons suffer from deficiencies in iodine micro-nutrients, primarily of vitamin A, iodine and iron (UN SCN 2004). Figure 14.1 explains how nutrition is measured in national and international statistics.

The consequences can be severe and long-lasting, above all for young children who can see their full physical and mental development compromised.

> Malnutrition is implicated in over half of all child deaths and contributes significantly to morbidity and cognitive underdevelopment. About 1 billion adults in developing countries are underweight, and an estimated 1.6 billion are anemic. They suffer from lowered resistance to infection, impaired work capacity and reduced economic productivity. In addition, there is growing evidence that fetal malnutrition has significant consequences, not only for survival, growth and development in childhood, but also with respect to the risk of contracting various chronic diseases such as diabetes and coronary heart disease in later life.
>
> (Gillespie and Haddad 2003: 1)

Undernutrition is a measure of access to food. FAO produce estimates of those not getting access to enough food by the following computation:

- Assess the calories available in a country, through food balances showing production, net trade, losses, use for seed, feed and industry;
- Distribute the available food energy log-normally across households – according to surveys of household income or expenditure; and,
- Compare the distribution seen to a calorie cut-off point, based on a consideration of needs of individuals by age and sex.

There is no direct measurement of individuals: much then depends on the quality of the data on food production, trade and use; on assumptions about the distribution of food; and about the thresholds to define nutritional adequacy. In many developing countries, data on food availability are unreliable and the FAO measures are broad estimates at best. Since the estimation method has been consistent through time, however, trends in the statistics may be more reliable than the estimates themselves. (Svedberg 1999 is particularly critical of the results for Africa.)

Malnutrition is generally measured by weighing and taking the heights and ages of individuals sampled from populations. Four sets of statistics are commonly reported.

1 For infants, aged either 5 or 3 years, the following three measures are computed:

- Height for age – low scores indicate stunting, the long-term cumulative result of inadequate nutrition or health or both;
- Weight for height – low scores indicate wasting, the consequence of recent acute starvation or sever disease or both; and,
- Weight for age – low scores indicate underweight, a combination of stunting and wasting.

In all cases, scores that are two standard deviations below the international reference median refer to moderate problems, more than three standards deviations below the reference point are severe conditions.
The UN Millennium Development Goal for hunger, indicator 1.8, is measured by the prevalence of underweight children under 5 years of age.

2 Adult nutrition, although less commonly surveyed than that of infants, is usually reported in terms of body mass indices, or thinness, computed as weight (kg) divided by height (m) squared. These indices are particularly important for pregnant women since their nutrition affects that of the unborn child.
3 The percentages of population suffering from micro-nutrient deficiencies, the most common ones surveyed being those of iodine, iron, vitamin A, and zinc.
4 The percentages of babies with birth-weights considered low, less than 2.5 kg.

Sources: Allen and Gillespie 2001; Svedberg 1999; UN SCN 2004.

Figure 14.1 Measuring undernutrition and malnutrition

Progress Towards Food Security

In 1996, the UN World Food Summit (WFS) agreed a target of halving the number of undernourished people in the world to 415 million, or 6 per cent of the population, by 2015. By the end of the decade it was already clear that this target would not be met. Consequently, the Millennium Development Goal (MDG) target for food security is the less ambitious one of halving the proportion of undernourished people over the same period, from 20 to 10 per cent (Slater *et al.* 2008).

Prior to the food price spike of 2007–8 the overall number of undernourished people stagnated in the 1990s, after reductions of 37 million in the 1970s and 100 million in the 1980s. With the increase of 75 million more in undernourished from the food price spike, the WFS target is increasingly unreachable. On the previous projections, the MDG target would be met at a global level: however, this masks considerable variation among regions.

Asia and Latin America have made significant progress. Vietnam is a notable success story where the proportion of people undernourished has declined from 31 to 17 per cent. In China nearly 50 million people moved out of food insecurity in the 1990s and the undernutrition rate fell from 16 to 12 per cent, largely due to strong economic and agricultural growth (FAO 2006a). In Africa, by contrast, the number of undernourished people increased between 1995 and 2005, and is actually expected to be higher in 2015 than in 1990–2 (although the *proportion* will be lower) (Slater *et al.* 2008).

Looking at nutrition statistics, specifically those of children underweight, UN statistics show that, while progress has been made since 1990 in reducing the fraction underweight from 33 to 26 per cent in the developing world, this is not fast enough to meet the target of halving the rate by 2015. Some regions have improved faster than others, with East and South-East Asia, Latin America and the Caribbean and North Africa likely to reach their targets (East Asia has already done so); whereas other regions, most notably South Asia and sub-Saharan Africa, are making slow progress.

Variations between countries are even greater than those between regions. Given that countries that are similar in many other economic and social characteristics show different levels and trends of child nutrition, this suggests that policy choices can make a difference.

Temporary Food Insecurity: Famines and Food Crises

Famines, defined as events where mortality rises suddenly in association with increased hunger, are relatively uncommon. Indeed, so unusual is outright famine that John Seaman (1993) wrote that the chances of an African dying of famine were 'vanishingly small'.

Mortality in famines is rarely from starvation: the majority of victims die from disease. While in some cases this may be linked to the effects of hunger, the connection may not always be so close. For example, severe drought struck in Darfur in 1984–5, ruining harvests and leaving livestock hungry. Faced by the prospect of destitution, farming families left their homes and headed for the towns where they hoped they could get either work, aid or both. Once gathered in camps, with poor sanitation, their children mixed closely with other children. Epidemics broke out: malaria, measles and enteric diseases. As many as 100,000 perished, the large majority being children aged 5 years or under. There was, apparently, no correlation with their nutrition. It was disease that killed them, not hunger (de Waal 1989).

Progress is being made in reducing the incidence of famines. Some parts of the world that regularly saw famine in the past are probably unlikely to see a repetition, unless catastrophe occurs. South Asia is the prime example where the last famine seen was that of Bangladesh in 1974. Indeed, contemporary famines are mostly in Africa, and even within Africa, these have been concentrated in the Horn, the Sahel and some pockets of southern Africa such as the south of Malawi. Recent famines in Africa have been closely linked to conflict. War and strife can comprehensively and suddenly close down livelihoods, destroy savings and assets, and force people to move with little means of support.

Food crises and emergencies are more common events where outright starvation and mass mortality may be avoided, but people endure hunger, impoverishment – this may have longer term implications when productive assets such as livestock are sold off and people undertake migrations to find temporary relief. The numbers of such events, as logged by FAO, has been rising since the early 1980s.

It seems that in the early 1980s most food crises stemmed from natural disasters, whereas by the 1990s human causes were equally problematic. Natural disasters with sudden onset – floods, hurricanes, earthquakes, etc. – are increasingly important compared to those with slower onset, principally drought. The composition of human issues is changing as well, with an increasing fraction attributable to economic and social failures compared to outright war and conflict.

The numbers affected by food crises can be large, although compared to those suffering from chronic undernutrition, they are fewer. For example, even in one of the most frequently regions of the world, the Horn of Africa, the average number of persons affected is around 20 millions. This can be compared to 35 million people who are chronically undernourished in East Africa as a whole.

Causes of Food Insecurity

A much-used framework proposes that food security will be achieved when there is sufficient food available, when people have access to it and when it is well utilized – and some would add when availability and access are reliable.

The emphasis on these different dimensions has changed. In the 1960s and 1970s Malthusian fears that the rapid growth of world population would outstrip food production and lead to widespread famine meant that global food production was the focus. Matters came to a head in 1973–4 when a combination of poor harvests and reduced food stocks led the prices of maize, rice and wheat to rise by 140, 250 and 260 per cent respectively within little more than a year. At the same time famine broke out in Bangladesh. Leaders were sufficiently alarmed to convene a World Food Conference in Rome in late 1974 to agree how to manage what was perceived as global crisis of insufficient food production (Slater *et al.* 2008).

The price spike, however, proved temporary as farmers responded strongly to the higher prices on offer, thanks in part to the success of the 'green revolution' in the irrigated lands of Asia and Latin America. Improved varieties of maize, rice and wheat that took full advantage of plentiful applications of fertilizer, supported by adequate water and crop protection, led to average yields per hectare doubling and tripling. By the end of 1970s, it was clear that the world, as well as low-income countries with large numbers of hungry households such as India, could produce the food needed to feed growing populations.

But success in overall food production did not eliminate hunger nor prevent famines breaking out. It was increasingly clear that people could go hungry while food was available. What mattered was what Amartya Sen (1981) called entitlement to food. His main illustration was the Bengal famine of 1943 when more than three million persons, mainly landless labourers, fishers and artisans, perished as rice prices more than tripled, while rural wages increased by no more than one quarter, leaving them without the means to acquire food.

If this suggested access to food as being the most important factor, evidence from medical and demographic studies – including de Waal's analysis of the Darfur famine of 1984–5 – showed that the majority of famine deaths are caused by disease rather than outright starvation.

Approaches to food security have thus shifted from national and international concerns about food supply and self-sufficiency to ensuring household and individual access to food, and that individuals are healthy enough to make full use of nutrients in their diet. Others have proposed adding additional conditions for food security. These include the reliability of access and the absence of fear that food will not be available; that the food available is acceptable to the hungry; and that people should not feel deprived or have to acquire their food in demeaning ways (Maxwell 1996). What then determines whether these three conditions for food security are fulfilled?

Food Availability

Sheer availability of food globally is hardly the problem in modern times. For much of the twentieth century, despite the historically unprecedented rapid rates of population increase, production of staple foods outstripped population growth. For more than half of this period, the growth of cereals output – at an average of 2.8 per cent a year – was well ahead of world population growth that peaked at 2.1 per cent a year in the early 1970s, and is reflected in a gradual increase in cereals production a head during the 1960s and 1970s. But since the mid-1980s cereals production has grown at less than half the previous rate and just below population growth rates. The amount of cereals produced a head has thus fallen back, although the amount, at just under 350 kg/capita, is still more than adequate to satisfy the energy needs of everyone, were the grain equitably distributed and used to feed people.

Since the early 1960s for most years supplies of cereals have been available in sufficient quantity, and at prices that have fallen in real terms. The two outstanding exceptions to this have been the price spikes of 1973–4 and of 2007–8. Both events were the result of an unusual combination of circumstances – involving a background of rising demand for commodities triggered by fast growth of the global economy, harvest failures, policy decisions that exacerbated the situation,[1] and low stocks that meant adjustment took place through large price rises. Since the unusual and unexpected will happen occasionally, the lesson to be learned is to have more resilience in the system to cope with such circumstances: in the case of food, that means having adequate physical stocks and better management of them.

Access to Food

In a world where cereals can readily be transported, international markets exist and communications mean that traders are well informed of supplies and prices, then global physical availability equates to local availability as well. If a country, region or district is short of food it is not so much a problem of supply as of access, the means to acquire supplies from other areas. During famines, local food deficits may be much larger: but there has not been a famine in more than half a century when the world as a whole did not have enough food stored somewhere or other to break the famine several times over. Access by households and individuals to food can be seen, using Sen's entitlements approach, as a function of their production of food, what they can obtain in markets through exchange, and through transfers from governments, charities, family, friends, and neighbours.[2]

Individuals lose access to food under several circumstances, and sometimes with more than one of these applying at the same time. Natural disasters can undermine people's entitlements. Events such as drought, floods and cyclones destroy harvests, reducing the implicit incomes of farmers and herders, as well as depriving farm labourers of work. When farmers lose their harvests, it often means less trade and income for those providing services and goods to them, such as village barbers, potters, blacksmiths, masons and carpenters.

Harvest failures are of course local failures of supply, apparently a matter of food availability. But it is more useful to see the effects on access since this helps to identify the households and individuals most at risk from such events, and to assess what can be done to mitigate harm to them. A harvest failure in a remote region may involve a sharp decline in local availability, at least for as long as it takes for supplies to be brought in. But looking only at availability suggests generalized distress, whereas food crises and famines have differing impacts on individuals and households depending on their access to food. Put simply, rich households rarely go short of food, no matter how bad the local harvest; whereas very poor households regularly endure hunger, again regardless of the local harvests.

Policy failures can deprive people of access. The sheer mismanagement of food policy, as was seen in China 1958–61 under the 'Great Leap Forward',[3] would be an example, as would the decision to restrict inter-provincial trading in India in 1943 at the time of the Bengal famine. Beyond such evident sins of commission lie those of omission, including failures of government or the international community to react sufficiently or promptly to calls for help during food crises and the early stages of famine.

More contentiously, some argue that policies that encourage farmers to grow cash crops have led to local food supplies being neglected and have thus undermined local food security. While localized cases of more commercialized cropping being associated with malnutrition can be found, there is little evidence for this being generally true. On the contrary, to the extent that producing cash crops raises incomes, such policies can enhance food security (Maxwell and Fernando 1989; von Braun 1995).

Closely related to policy are instances of strife and warfare when people may find their crops burnt, livestock slaughtered or requisitioned, granaries, savings and other assets seized or destroyed. They may also be forced to flee conflict zones without money or the means to continue their livelihoods. In such cases, their access to food falls catastrophically.

Changes in prices, employment and wages can be powerful factors affecting food security. For example, in his analysis of the 1943 Bengal famine, Professor Sen argues that the primary cause was not a failure of supply, since the cyclone of late 1942 and the consequent harvest losses still left Bengal with more food in 1943 than in 1941 when the harvest had also been poor, but when famine had not broken out. Instead he blames the workings of a booming economy, pumped up by wartime public spending, that caused the rice prices to rise by four or more times. Those poor whose earnings lagged behind the rice price, including farm labourers, fishermen and artisans, found themselves unable to buy enough food and thus starved. Famine deaths were concentrated amongst members of their households.

Food Utilization

Concerns here include the way in which food is distributed within the household between individual members, the preparation of food, and the health of those eating. Fears that in patriarchal households adult males will get most and the best of the food, leaving females and children to eat last and little, have frequently been voiced. Evidence for this is mixed: in East and South Asia girls under 5 years are more likely to be underweight than boys. But in Africa the reverse is true,[4] with more of the boys underweight than the girls –perhaps since the latter help their mothers in the kitchen and get titbits in the process.

The preparation of food for infants post-weaning can be a problem. In some cases, working mothers have too little time to prepare food with the frequency that infants require (Moore and Vaughan 1987). Weaning foods, such as watery maize meal, can be thin in nutrients (Walker and Pavitt 1989). One of the arguments for breastfeeding for at least six months is to delay weaning with its risks of too little intake and of food contamination.[5]

Perhaps the most important element of food use, however, is the health of the person eating. Those with high temperatures and stomach complaints, for example, may lack appetite. Some enteric problems, most notably dysentery and diarrhoea, can lead to rapid loss of nutrients and water before the body has had time to use them.

The importance of health is reflected in UNICEF's framework for thinking about child malnutrition, mortality and disability. In this scheme, the immediate causes of malnutrition are inadequate dietary intake and disease. Access to food is one of three underlying causes of malnutrition, the other two being child care practices and health conditions.

How important are the various underlying causes to malnutrition? Smith and Haddad (2002) examined the relation between income and child underweight rates for the period from 1970 to 1995. Almost 60 per cent of the reduced prevalence of underweight infants could be attributed to rising incomes. But the influence of higher incomes was not directly a matter of access. Instead it affected malnutrition through interactions with increased food availability, more female schooling, better access to safe water and improvements in the ratio of female to male life expectancy (a proxy for female status) – factors that responded in part to higher incomes, but only in part. In order of their contribution to reducing malnutrition, female schooling was the strongest factor followed by food availability, safe water and the life expectancy ratio.

Addressing Food Insecurity

Since food insecurity and malnutrition has several causes, applying in varying combinations in different circumstances, the solutions are various and varied by context. That said, the policy agenda is not that complicated and consists of measures in the following areas:

- reduce extreme poverty that deprives people of access to food;
- keep the prices of basic foods low and stable;
- educate girls and improve the status of women;
- ensure reasonable public health and hygiene;
- complement health programmes with nutritional programmes to monitor the growth of infants and the nutrition of pregnant mothers, to use therapeutic feeding where necessary and to tackle micro-nutrient deficiencies; and
- mitigate shocks and provide safety nets to reduce the risks that vulnerable households face of temporary food insecurity.

Poverty can be reduced and quite rapidly, given economic growth with reasonably well distributed benefits, as the experience of China since the late 1980s shows. But even when growth is less rapid and poverty reduction is halting, the other measures can make a difference to malnutrition.

Keeping food prices low is best done through increased farm output, rather than by price controls and subsidies. Staple food prices do fall when production outruns population and income growth. The rates needed to do this are not that high – no more than 3 per cent a year – and were achieved on a world scale by a comfortable margin from the early 1960s for two decades: a feat that has been replicated by many individual countries in recent history. In Bangladesh, for example, increased output from the green revolution helped halve real food prices between the 1980s and 2000.

Investments in education, primary health care, water and sanitation are as straightforward as they are well known. So are specific programmes for nutrition (see e.g. Allen and Gillespie 2001 on nutrition interventions). Young mothers and children under 3 are particularly vulnerable to malnutrition. Health programmes are needed to monitor their nutrition, immunize infants, provide oral rehydration to treat diarrhoea, de-worm children, combat malaria through measures such as use of treated bed-nets, and to deliver safe water and sanitation.

The 'hidden hunger' of micro-nutrient deficiency can readily be tackled through fortifying staple foods where these are commonly processed (e.g. bread and salt); by providing supplements to young mothers and infants; and by encouraging dietary diversification through home gardens, raising chickens, fish ponds and the like. There is also the potential, now being realized, of increasing the vitamin content of some staple crops through crop breeding.

In mitigating the effect of shocks on the vulnerable, lessons in effective social protection are not lacking. Programmes ranging from Maharashtra, India's guaranteed employment scheme, to Mexico's conditional cash transfers to the rural poor, to South Africa's universal old age pension have been largely successful. Once again, options exist.

Under extraordinary stress that overwhelms official responses and household coping, threatening famine, food distribution may be needed. Food aid can be essential when local food supplies have collapsed, but in other cases people who have suffered sudden falls in their entitlements may be better served by cash transfers (Harvey 2007). Food aid is not only difficult and costly to transport, but often takes long to arrive. In addition, its impact on local markets and livelihoods has long been questioned (Barrett and Maxwell 2005). Children are particularly vulnerable, and may need supplementary feeding and inoculation. Clean water, sanitation and medical supplies are often critical in averting famine deaths.

Most of the above measures are neither technically difficult, nor hard to implement, nor even that costly. Most are not specific to food security and nutrition either: reducing poverty, investing in schooling and health care, and mitigating shocks are central to development. Fighting food insecurity does not require major investments that would otherwise not be made.

The challenge is summoning the political will to make a difference. Moreover, the returns to some of these interventions are rated as some of the highest in the world. The Copenhagen Consensus (Behrman *et al.* 2004), in considering global challenges, included no less than four nutrition actions amongst the top half-dozen in terms of returns to investments: supplements of vitamin A and zinc for children; iron fortification and salt iodization; bio-fortification of staples; and de-worming and school nutrition programmes.

The very large numbers of people who suffer from chronic hunger or from temporary food crises could be reduced very considerably and rapidly, if there were the political will to commit resources and undertake programmes. The food price spike of 2007–8 has brought food issues into the limelight and prompted the UN to convene a Task Force on the Global Food Security Crisis. This may make some difference.

Prospects, Challenges and Changes

The prospects for improved food security are probably good in the long run, so long as incomes rise in the developing world, allowing people to access the food they need. With matching improvements in sanitation and education, and some basic health programmes, great inroads on food insecurity could be made. But it remains frustrating that this could happen within a few years, rather than a few decades, if the political will were there. Equally frustrating is the glacial pace of nutritional improvement in so many parts of Africa and South Asia; and above all in India, about to be classed a middle-income country yet with some of the worst nutritional indicators in the world.

Set against these prospects are the twin challenges of HIV/AIDS and climate change. High rates of HIV prevalence in Eastern and Southern Africa introduce new vulnerabilities for affected households, often depriving them of earnings and drawing down on their assets (Jayne *et al.* 2004). Some have even worried that the pandemic could lead to new variants of famine (de Waal and Tumushabe 2003). While fortunately this has not come to pass, households affected by HIV/AIDS are more susceptible to food insecurity. Time spent caring for the sick reduces labour time on productive activities such as agriculture, while money that would otherwise be spent on productive investments is diverted to pay for medicines and funerals. Similarly, urban households unable to work lose entitlement to food (Slater *et al.* 2008).

HIV/AIDS and nutrition are, moreover, interlinked. People with poor diets are more vulnerable to HIV infection; once infected they develop AIDS more quickly; once they have AIDS their nutritional requirements increase; and anti-retroviral drugs are more effective when coupled with an adequate diet (Gillespie 2006).

Climate change is expected to affect both food supply and access. Even under scenarios with limited climate change, agricultural yields may fall where crops are near their maximum temperature tolerance; decreased rainfall could affect agriculture regardless of latitude; and there may be significant negative effects for small farmers and pastoralists weakly integrated into markets (Parry *et al.* 2005). African farming, heavily reliant on rainfall, may be particularly vulnerable. If to mitigate carbon emissions, transport of food is more heavily taxed, local food supply may re-emerge as a focal point of food security policy (Slater *et al.* 2008).

Across the world, food systems are changing as urbanization, technology and industrialization change the way food is produced, marketed and consumed (Maxwell and Slater 2004). Food businesses, such as supermarkets, play new roles in moving food between countries and in establishing new kinds of supply chains within developing countries. Small farmers and producers may be squeezed out of supply chains by larger producers and supermarkets. Poor consumers may find themselves paying higher prices for less healthy food, or being socially excluded because they cannot afford a diet that society considers normal (Slater *et al.* 2008).

More integrated economies and supply chains means that changes in systems tend to transmit internationally and affect distant economies and societies that may not be well prepared to address the challenges or take up opportunities. Urbanization is changing dietary patterns and preferences, leading to a 'nutrition transition' towards increasing proportions of proteins and fats in people's diets. Town-dwellers, especially poor people, are consuming more food outside the home.

These dietary changes are not limited to the industrialized world. Non-communicable diseases linked to diet such as diabetes, obesity, high blood pressure and heart disease are emerging in developing countries. Obesity rates are as high in Mexico and South Africa as they are in the USA: diabetes is at epidemic levels in urban Ethiopia (Slater *et al.* 2008).

It thus likely that concerns over food will broaden in the future, with major challenges in handling market power, health dangers and regulation.

Security and Food Security

Finally, how much does food security affect other dimensions of security? Although hungry people may constitute a reservoir of disaffected persons liable to insurrection and extreme political action, there is little evidence to support this. Indeed, in a country such as India, not to mention on a global scale, it is precisely the passivity of the hungry that allows scandalous levels of malnutrition to persist with scarcely a ripple on the political agenda.

Political effects tend to rise when there is relatively sudden change in circumstances. Hence when world food prices rose in 2007–8, there were frequent reports from developing countries of popular discontent. At least one government, that of Haïti, fell as a result. At a more local level, crime can increase when food crises strike rural societies. Theft of livestock and harvests rose, for example, in rural Malawi in 2002 (Devereux 2002).

The political motivation of crises is however not primarily the fear of revolt, but more a combination of humanitarian concern, and the desire of both states and multinational agencies to be seen as being capable of dealing with disasters as part of their legitimacy.

If food insecurity does not generally exacerbate other forms of insecurity, the reverse does not apply. Other dimensions of security affect food security strongly. Conflicts, especially when protracted, in areas of high poverty dislocate economies and societies and provoke food crises and famines. Health insecurities, such as the HIV/AIDS pandemic, aggravate food insecurity.

Notes

1 In 1973–4 the USSR imported grains to feed its livestock after a crop failure, whereas a decade earlier it had slaughtered stock to economize on feed. In late 2007 India restricted exports of non-basmati rice, a move that was emulated by other rice exporters.
2 Transfers are not just gifts and loans: they can be a matter of taking food or the means to acquire it away from people through legal taxes, social pressure, and theft.
3 The Chinese government decided to stimulate rural industry and go for regional self-sufficiency in cereals production. Trading between provinces was restricted. Trying to grow cereals in inappropriate lands, plus a series of droughts, floods, typhoons and attacks of pests and diseases drove down per capita food availability by around 25%, with daily food availability on average in 1960 at around 1,535 kcal per person. Policy failure was exacerbated by reluctance of regional officials to report bad news to Beijing. Estimates of deaths range from 15m to 30m.
4 Source: UN MDG database, data on underweight infants, by region and sex.
5 See: http://www.who.int/topics/breastfeeding/en/index.html

15
Energy Security

Roland Dannreuther

With the turn of the millennium, energy security has risen inexorably up the security agenda. In the late 1990s, two decades of cheap energy prices and abundant supply had erased the memories of the oil crises of the 1970s and fostered a belief that the age of 'cheap oil' would extend indefinitely into the future (Jaffe and Manning 2000). But instead of the $5 per barrel which some predicted, crude oil prices rose fivefold from 2000 to 2008, reaching well over $100 per barrel. Oil was now more expensive than it had ever been, greater even than the period of the Iranian Revolution and the second oil crisis in 1979–80.

During this period of sharply rising oil prices, geopolitical tensions and conflicts increased significantly between the West and key oil-producing states. In 2003, the United States and Great Britain intervened into Iraq and overthrew Saddam Hussein after a decade of political pressure and economic sanctions. The ensuing chaos in Iraq, which undermined any swift resurrection of its oil industry, was paralleled by growing Western suspicions of Iran and its nuclear programme, leading to intensification of sanctions and fears of military escalation. Tensions with other key other oil-producing states, such as Russia and Venezuela, have intensified the fear of a new global axis of confrontation between energy-rich and energy-dependent countries (Leverett and Noel 2006). But these dividing lines are not so simple as China and India, the fast growing Asian economies with rapidly expanding energy needs, have aggressively sought to secure oil supplies from around the world, often in direct competition with Western international oil companies (IOCs) (Andrews-Speed *et al*. 2002). This has in turn fostered distrust and suspicions, including the fear of a new Sino-Russian anti-Western alliance. The sunny optimism of the 1990s and the hope of an 'end to history' have become increasingly a dim and fading memory. The renewed concern for energy security is central to this, leading many to argue for the need for a new 'energy paradigm' (Helm 2007).

To all these growing fears and concerns must be added the environmental dimension. The near-universal consensus that climate change is occurring and needs to be reversed has brought into fundamental perspective our modern dependence on fossil fuels. The use of these abundant and cheap fuels has been the essential pre-condition for the exponential growth, both in population and wealth terms, over the last two centuries. But as John

McNeill has aptly written, in so doing the 'human race, while not intending anything of the sort, has undertaken a gigantic uncontrolled experiment on earth' which raises real fears that our dependence on fossil fuels might irreversibly damage the complex global ecosystems on which our civilization is dependent (McNeill 2000: 4). A key further question is, therefore, whether energy security will prove to be compatible with 'climate security', which demands ultimately a shift away from our addiction to fossil fuels.

This chapter provides an overarching assessment of these key critical challenges for energy security. In doing this, it will concentrate primarily but not exclusively on oil. This is partly due to limitations of space as there are complex and differentiated security issues raised in relation to other energy resources, such as gas, coal, nuclear, biomass and alternatives. But oil does also rightly assume primacy of place in terms of energy security as it is the most internationally traded energy commodity (65 per cent traded against 30 per cent for gas and 15 per cent for coal); it is the main fuel used in transportation and is not easily substitutable; and it remains the key commodity which excites most significant geopolitical concerns and anxieties.

The Conventional Approach to Energy Security

The dominant approach to energy security prioritizes the interests of the rich, primarily Western, energy-importing states (see e.g. Barton *et al.* 2004; Kalicki and Goldwyn 2005). From this perspective, it is whether these states are able to obtain secure supplies of energy at reasonable prices which is taken as the almost unquestioned definition of energy security.

Within this dominant conventional approach of energy security, there are two diverging accounts of the causes of energy insecurity and the means to overcome them. These reflect in turn differing traditions within the study of the international political economy. The first draws from a neo-mercantilist and realist tradition, which sees the international struggle for energy security as a zero-sum game where energy-dependent states are deeply vulnerable to energy-rich countries. Such an acute perception of energy vulnerability has been a significant factor in the historical developments of both imperialism, as in the post-Ottoman carving up of the Middle East, and of modern warfare, as in the Japanese involvement in the Second World War. Ensuring access to oil supplies was a critical causal factor in these geopolitical developments (Yergin 1991; Parra 2004). For some analysts, it is precisely such current fears of energy insecurity among Asian states which are likely to lead to conflict and war over energy resources (Calder 1996). Such neo-mercantilist thinking was also evident in the strategic calculations of the G. W. Bush administrations, 2000–8. Bush frequently espoused the objective of US energy independence so as to be free from vulnerability to external supplies, particularly from the Middle East. The neo-conservative vision for the Middle East, which underpinned the US intervention into Iraq, also had a clear energy-driven agenda, seeking to destroy or undermine OPEC, overthrow the anti-Western oil-wealthy authoritarian states, and usher in an era of cheap and plentiful oil. US military power, it was believed, would achieve these ambitious energy security and geopolitical goals (Morse 2003).

The alternative and contrasting approach to energy security draws from the liberal political economy tradition. Instead of seeking independence, preferential market arrangements and politico-military solutions to gain energy security, this approach promotes interdependence, markets and integration. This is based on the fundamental assumption that energy independence is not a strategic option in the contemporary world.

Even Saudi Arabia imports some of its energy needs and it is simply not realistic for the USA, or other major Western states, to seek energy independence (Crooks 2007). Energy security should not be seen narrowly as being solely about supply but critically also about managing demand. High oil prices are not, in themselves, necessarily bad as they should act to improve domestic energy efficiency and thus reduce energy dependency. More fuel-efficient cars are one key example. Measures to improve energy efficiency at home need also, from this liberal perspective, to be matched externally by expanding and improving the operation of the international energy markets. One of the most consistent supporters of this more liberal approach is the European Commission, which has sought to persuade reluctant member states that the solution to Europe's energy security problem lies in the liberalization of markets so as to create a truly unified and interconnected energy network within Europe (European Commission 2006). Liberalization, diversification of fuels, ensuring that there is strategic storage in the event of emergencies, along with consistent attempts to improve energy efficiency, all help to ensure energy security in a globally interdependent world (Yergin 2006; Verrastro and Ladislaw 2007).

From the perspective of liberal interdependence, neo-mercantilist approaches exacerbate rather than resolve the situation. Rather than military force, the most effective way to undermine the ability of the oil-producing states to use oil as a political or geostrategic weapon is through making oil a freely and internationally traded commodity. The failure of the Arab states to use the 'oil weapon' even at the height of the oil crisis in the 1970s highlights the significant constraints of translating oil wealth into political power (Al-Sowayegh 1984). Indeed, the way in which the USA has been able to use the weapon of sanctions against key oil-producing states, such as Iran, Libya and Iraq, suggests that political power rests more with the energy-importing than exporting states (Morse 1999). More generally, it is this belief in the pacific benefits of liberal interdependence which leads many analysts to project that China's energy dependence will actually foster the further integration of China into global markets and underpin its accommodative and non-conflictual rise to great power status (Manning 2000; Andrews-Speed et al. 2002).

Alternative Security Perspectives

Traditional security studies have tended to privilege the security interests of 'the West' – the rich industrialized countries of the North – and this is reflected in the principal prevailing approaches to energy security as described above. However, the post-Cold War security agenda has increasingly challenged and questioned such a prioritization (see e.g. Buzan 1997; Buzan et al. 1998; Dannreuther 2007). New ways of conceiving of security have included the promotion of concepts like human security, societal security and environmental security. Utilizing these competing conceptions of security and applying them to the issue of energy security is helpful in moving beyond the limitations of the conventional debate with its competing realist and liberal approaches.

This section does this in the following ways. First, it takes the concept of human security, which privileges the interests of the poor and disadvantaged, and applies this to the issue of energy security. Second, the concept of societal insecurity is developed in relation to the citizens of many oil-producing states who lack many fundamental civic and political rights. Third, the notion of security of demand, as against the conventional emphasis on security of supply, brings out the legitimate security concerns of oil-producing states and the complex historical legacies and memories which underpin much of the insecurities found in these countries. Finally, the concept of environmental security is utilized to address the challenges of the environment to develop energy security in ways which do not further damage the global environment.

Human Security

The human security dimension is arguably one of the most neglected dimensions of the energy security debate. The conventional focus on rich oil-importing states fails to recognize that the citizens of these wealthy states generally enjoy the benefits of a continual and assured access to reliable, cheap and modern energy. The extent of their energy insecurity comes in the form of fluctuations in prices, which can admittedly affect the poorest in these societies, and the threat of intermittent but generally relatively rare disruptions in supply. In general, though, the citizens of the developed world enjoy a level of energy security of which the poorest of the people in the world can only dream. It is estimated that 1.6 billion people – one quarter of the world's population – have no access to electricity. Over 2.4 billion – a third of the world's population – still rely on traditional biomass, such as wood, agricultural residues and dung, for their cooking and heating. A further third of the world's population has access to modern energy supplies but on an irregular and intermittent basis. It is only the citizens of developed countries, the third most wealthiest portion of the world's population, who enjoy affordable and reliable energy supplies (World Energy Council 1999; World Bank 2000; IEA 2002).

The human security consequences of this endemic energy insecurity amongst the world's poorest and most vulnerable people are considerable. Economic and social development is constrained as people, mainly women and children, are forced to spend hours gathering fuel wood and other forms of biomass. In India, two to seven hours each day can be devoted to the collection of fuel for cooking (UNDP 2002). Such gathering of wood leads to local scarcity and ecological damage, particularly in areas of high population density, increasing inter-communal tensions and conflict (Homer-Dixon 1999). Furthermore, the biomass fuels tend to be burned in inefficient stoves which leads to serious health damage from indoor smoke pollution. These health and other negative consequences particularly affect women, who are the primary users of household energy and who are the ones who are often excluded from decision-making on poverty alleviation programmes.

The challenges to deal with energy security from a human security framework include, first, the need to increase the number of people with direct access to electricity supplies. China is a developing country which has shown how this can be done with an electrification rate of 98 per cent. Second, more efficient biomass technologies are required so that not only there is greater energy efficiency in biomass use but also the potentially damaging health effects are limited. All of this requires substantial investment (an estimated $2.1 trillion over the next three decades for India and sub-Saharan Africa); energy prices which make such energy affordable both for the individual family unit and for the local economy; and promoting market reforms, such as reducing subsidies, which provide incentives for continuing investment. These are significant challenges for countries which are not only in the tortuous process of development but where large numbers are migrating from the countryside to the cities. But focusing on the challenges of energy security for the world's poorest provides a good corrective to the tendency to focus on the considerable less existential energy security concerns of the richest in the world.

Societal Security

There is a further dimension to a more comprehensive energy security framework which conventional accounts tend to ignore. This is the security interests of the citizens of the energy-rich oil-exporting states themselves. On the surface, this is an improbable and unexpected source of insecurity as a country's natural resource wealth should be a blessing for any society. The empirical evidence shows, though, that such wealth and power tends to be poorly and unequally distributed, with state elites benefiting far more than the broader society. To capture the security implications of this, it is useful to follow the distinction made between state security and societal security, which highlights the fact that security for the state is not necessarily the same as security for society as whole (Buzan *et al.* 1998).

A disparity in quality of life and security between those with and those without access to the patronage of the state is a generic problem in many developing countries and not limited to resource-rich countries. There is, though, evidence that the problem is particularly acute for societies in resource-rich states. There are three main factors which are generally brought out to explain this particularly high level of societal insecurity. The first comes under the rubric of the 'resource curse', which seeks to explain the empirical evidence that the developmental record of resource-abundant developing states has been substantially worse than the record for resource-poor countries (Karl 1997; Ross 1999; Sachs and Warner 2000). A good example of this is the contrast between the economic stagnation of the resource-rich Middle East and the economic dynamism of resource-poor East Asia. The 'resource curse' theory argues that much of this poor economic performance is linked to the capital-intensive and enclave nature of natural resource exploitation which tends not to generate positive linkages to other parts of the economy, such as agriculture or industry. Unlike in East Asia, there have not been the same set of incentives in the Middle East (or similarly in Latin America) towards the shift to export-oriented industrial development that so invigorated the East Asian economies. Instead, industry and agriculture stagnated and became increasingly internationally uncompetitive and dependent on state hand-outs and subsidies. For the general economy in the Middle East as a whole, natural resource wealth often appeared to be more of a curse than a blessing.

A second more political factor is what has been called the 'rentier state' phenomenon. This is the term which has been coined to highlight that resource-rich states, most notably oil-rich states, structurally have a less dependent relationship with their society. Unlike resource-poor countries which need to promote the economic dynamism of their societies in order to raise taxes and obtain the resources for the functioning of the state, resource-rich countries enjoy the immediate 'rents' of their natural wealth and focus on the distribution of that resource wealth to garner support and legitimacy. Society, in this context, is much more dependent on the state. The political consequences of this is that, as Ross (2001) demonstrates, oil-rich states tend towards authoritarianism and are poor at promoting democratic forms of governance with protection for civil and political rights. To reverse the well-known saying, 'with no taxation, there is no representation' in such states. The preferred form of politics is neopatrimonialism, with complex networks of patron–client relations, and a heavy reliance on internal policing and extensive security forces. The consequence is that many citizens in oil-rich countries fail not only to receive a fair share of the country's resource wealth but also lack some basic civic and political rights.

Violence in the form of daily state repression is, therefore, one further aspect of the societal dimension of energy security. This leads to the final set of factors which connects to the substantial academic research on how resource wealth is seen to be linked to generalized violence in the form of civil war. The literature on the 'political economy of war' highlights how primary commodities, such as oil, diamonds and timber, have been significant causal factors behind the multiple post-Cold War civil wars (Keen 1998; Collier and Hoeffler 2001; Klare 2001). A good example of this is Angola where the government's control of the oil resources and the guerrilla opposition's control of the country's diamonds led to a brutal and lengthy civil war (Le Billon 2001). Although there is a debate about the extent to which it is the struggle to gain control of these primary commodities which causes such conflicts, or whether greater account needs to be given to political and ideological factors (the so-called 'greed versus grievance' debate), it is undoubtedly the case that an abundance of lootable resources contributes to the prolongation of conflict and the creation of a political economy of war which is difficult to reverse (Berdal and Malone 2000; Ballentine and Sherman 2003).

Security of Demand

The conventional approach to energy security focuses almost exclusively on security of supply. But this does not mean that security of demand is irrelevant. Oil-producing states, despite their often poor engagement with their broader society, still have legitimate energy security interests. This security of demand essentially boils down to the need for stable and secure revenues for development. In practice, oil-producing developing states have an even greater interest in stable oil prices than oil-importing states. While most Western states have limited the exposure of their economies to the effects of higher oil prices, such as by high levels of taxation on gasoline prices, oil-producing states suffer dramatically when oil prices drop significantly, as during the 1980s. In such periods of low oil prices, public expenditure on health, education and a whole host of other services have to be cut and the economies of these states contract severely. While there is obviously an interest in higher-than-average prices for oil producers, there is an even greater concern for stable and predictable prices which can be relied upon for future developmental planning.

The oil-producing states have a vested interest in a longer term future for oil. This limits their interest in prices being too high since that accelerates the process by which alternative energy resources will displace oil. This concern for security of demand also influences the extent to which states with plentiful oil reserves are willing to make the vast investments necessary to meet projected future demand. The IEA estimates that over $17 trillion needs to be invested in oil and gas exploration and production to meet demand for 2025. A large part of that investment will need to provided by oil producers in the Persian Gulf region, as the larger part of future reserves are to be found there. However, these states naturally question the wisdom of investing such sums if, as is often stated by Western leaders, the ambition is to reduce substantially dependence on the conflict-prone Persian Gulf region. The dilemma here is that, if such dependence is reduced through successful energy diversification, the Middle East oil-rich states will have no market for their expensively extracted energy. As these states logically counter, 'no security of demand, no investment'.

In this context, some recognition needs to be given to the extent to which the Gulf States, in particular Saudi Arabia, have historically contributed and continue to contribute to the global security of supply. Saudi Arabia's single great contribution to energy security is its maintenance of 'surplus capacity' which can be utilized at any moment to manage unexpected disruptions or outages. It was the erosion of surplus capacity in the 1970s which was a significant cause for the oil price spikes at that time. Since then, Saudi Arabia has provided this key public good underpinning energy security of supply and has paid the economic costs for this, in part in exchange for the military security provided by the USA (Morse 1999). In a fundamental way, the core of global energy security, and the sources of its fragility, are captured by this US–Saudi convergence of interests.

As with the Saudi–US alliance, there is no necessary conflict in interests between oil exporters and importers and between the requirement to ensure security of supply and security of demand. Stability of oil prices, conditions for future investment and the provision of surplus capacity reflect mutual and shared interests. However, there do remain two sets of interests of oil-rich states where such convergence is more difficult. The first relates to the sense of obligation for future generations. For many oil-rich states, there is no necessary requirement to maximize production, even if the immediate or prospective demand seems to call for it, since 'oil in the ground' remains valuable, not least for future generations (Stevens 2008). In addition, a fast depletion policy can often exacerbate the 'resource curse' problems noted above. The second set of factors relates to the complex set of historical legacies and memories of many of the oil-producing states in relation to the West. Much of the collective memory is of a rapacious West subjugating and exerting direct control of their natural resources for the benefit of the imperial metropolis. Some of these perceptions of Western malpractice can be quite recent, as in Russia where the economic chaos of the 1990s is popularly viewed as inspired and promoted by the West to weaken Russia. Overall, though, this continuing suspicion of the West tends to promote 'resource nationalism', which includes a desire to limit the engagement of Western IOCs and to strengthen local national control. Such resource nationalism does not necessarily lead to the most economically efficient and mutually beneficial conditions for large-scale investment in future energy needs. This North–South dimension of energy security needs, therefore, to be included as a further critical element of energy security.

Environmental Security

The issue of environmental security is a large and complex topic in itself and is dealt with elsewhere in this volume. In relation to energy security, there are though a few key aspects. The first is a further dimension in North–South relations, involving the need to recognize that the South, with its need for plentiful and cheap energy to promote its developmental ambitions, naturally has a greater relative interest in energy security than in environmental security. This places a particular obligation on the North to provide incentives and direct support to the South's environmental policies, which not only reflect the North's historic responsibility for global climate change but also the need to ensure that the South's path to prosperity is not impeded by the costs of environmental adaptation. A complex North–South bargain needs to be constructed where development, energy security and environmental protection are incorporated into a meaningful and mutually beneficial package.

A second aspect is that there needs to be a clear recognition that there are tensions between energy security and environmental security which need to be taken into account. For instance, the fuel of choice for ensuring energy security is coal, since coal is generally plentiful and found in ample quantities in many energy-importing countries. This is the case, for example, in both Western Europe and in China and, in the latter case, most of the new power stations being built to meet surging demand are coal-fired. This drive towards exploitation of coal for energy security reasons, and the potentially negative environmental consequences of this, highlights the need to give priority to reducing these environmental costs and moving forward on technologies for 'clean coal'. In this regard, there is a strong argument for developing these technologies, most notably carbon capture and storage, as one of the most effective climate change mitigation measures. However, it is difficult for environmentally image-conscious governments to admit that dirty coal still has an energy future and that resources should be focused on developing clean coal technologies rather than more fashionable alternatives such as wind farms.

A final factor is the longer term inter-connection between environmental security and energy security. The evidence so far is that energy security still trumps environmental security as far as the policies of governments around the world are concerned. However, there is the likelihood that, at some point, the balance will shift and that energy security will be driven by the environmental demand to make a decisive move away from our long-term dependence on fossil fuels. That would usher in a very different conceptualization and understanding of energy security, where the environment assumes primacy over economic efficiency. As such, the end of the oil age will probably not come, as is popularly believed, from us running out of oil but from the excessive environmental costs of its profligate use. This provides a context for understanding the quip of Shaykh Yamani, the former Saudi energy minister, that 'The stone age did not end because the world ran out of stones. In the same way, the oil age will not end due to us running out of oil.'

Scarcity and Energy Security

This also puts into perspective the broader issue of the future scarcity of oil. Ever since the oil price rises of the 1970s, there have been regular alarming projections of the imminent precipitous decline in oil production (Gever 1986; Roberts 2004). Geologist Colin Campbell and his associates have been highly influential in promoting the idea of 'peak oil', which involves the projection that global oil production has, or is just about to peak and that the world will have to cope with a fairly rapid decline in supply (Campbell 1997; Campbell and Laherrere 1998).

The precipitous rise in oil prices since 2000 has added to the seeming credibility of these claims (Hoyes 2008). However, the majority view is that this fear of an imminent geological peak is misguided. Past experience of high oil prices is that it actually leads to increases in oil reserves, as oil companies have new commercial incentives to explore for new oilfields and to exploit additional oilfields that have become economically viable at the higher oil price. The peak oil hypothesis also applies strictly to the supply of conventional oil and ignores the plentiful supply of non-conventional oil, such as oil sand, oil shales and tar sands. The problem here is not the scarcity of these non-conventional oil supplies, as they are plentiful, but that the environmental costs of securing these supplies are currently very high. As Peter Bijur, the former chairman of Texaco, has noted, 'It is true that we have probably been able to harvest most of the proverbial low-hanging fruit. But the higher fruit coming within reach is equally plentiful.'

The fact that a geological peak to conventional oil is not imminent, and will probably not occur until the middle of this century, is not though a reason for complacency. There still remains a real danger of an upcoming oil supply crunch, which is well set out by the energy analyst, Paul Stevens (Stevens 2008; see also Horsnell 2000). He puts forward a convincing case that the real danger is not of reaching a peak of oil production but rather a temporary, but still very damaging, discontinuity between supply and demand in the period around 2013 which would lead to both a supply crunch and a price hike.

The fundamental causes of this will not be due to a geological scarcity of oil in itself, but the failure of oil companies and oil-producing states to invest sufficiently to be able to meet future demand, particularly with the fast growth of developing countries like China and India. This failure in investment is due in part to the changes in the economic strategies of Western countries, where economic liberalism has limited the role of state-directed intervention, and where IOCs have adopted 'value-based management' strategies, returning money to their shareholders rather than investing. Due to this obsession with maximizing share prices, there have been serious cuts in manpower in these oil companies, limiting the managerial capabilities for expansion in exploration and production (Yergin 2008). A further set of factors is located in the oil-producing states who, as noted above, have increasingly espoused resource nationalism, have been willing to leave oil in the ground for future generations and have limited access for IOCs in preference to their national oil companies (NOCs), who often lack the necessary managerial and project skills for developing new fields.

The negative consequences of this combination of factors, which is constraining the investment necessary to support future projected demand, is already evident in the substantial reduction in surplus capacity, that critical foundation stone of energy security, as noted above. In 2004 surplus capacity was completely eroded as a series of geopolitical events and weather accidents created a perception of outage and forced prices to rise. If Stevens's analysis of a continuing fundamental discontinuity of supply and demand holds true, further price hikes can be expected, with major macro-economic and geopolitical repercussions. This, rather than the issue of 'peak oil', is the real immediate threat to energy security.

Energy Security in a Nutshell

Energy security is a multifaceted and complex phenomenon. At its heart, it is about ensuring that there are sufficient energy supplies at reasonable prices to meet the socio-economic needs of society. But, within this broad definition, there are multiple differing perspectives. There is the perspective of the poor and the perspective of the rich of the world; of the producers of energy and the importers of energy; those who benefit from energy-derived wealth and those who do not; of the perceived needs of the present and the obligations to future generations; and the economic benefits of fossil fuel consumption and the longer term environmental consequences. All of these differing perspectives and tensions become even more critical as energy becomes more expensive and the era of cheap energy fades from memory.

By way of conclusion, one can make a temporal division of the energy security equation and the key short-term, medium-term and long-term challenges. The short-term challenges are essentially to ensure that the national and regional economies are capable of managing a temporary disruption of supply, which might be caused by war, terrorism, accident or other geopolitical events. Here, the main challenges are to ensure that there are sufficient oil stocks and spare capacity to provide the necessary immediate replacements of supply; to promote the diversification of energy supplies so that alternative energy sources, if available, can be utilized; and to build as robust and inter-connected an energy supply system as possible, with appropriate international agreements and institutions and well-regulated but flexible markets, so that effective collective responses can be made to any immediate energy supply challenges.

ENERGY SECURITY

The medium-term challenges are more complex and demanding. First, there is a need to create the incentives and to foster the conditions for increased energy efficiency, so that the demand for energy is reduced, which is both necessary for climate change mitigation as well as for improving energy security. Second, there is a critical need, as argued above, for ensuring that there is sufficient investment in future oil supplies so as to avoid future oil supply crunches. This will involve both measures to reduce resource nationalism in oil-producing states and to provide IOCs a better set of incentives for large-scale investment. More generally, this involves a greater success in overcoming historic tensions and conflicts and significantly improvement in the degree and quality of the mutual cooperation between oil-exporting and oil-importing countries. These two key sets of medium-term challenges – decreasing or managing demand and increasing supplies – need also to be pursued with other complementary goals. These include the moral obligation to prioritize the developmental objectives of ensuring access to clean and modern energy supplies among the poorest in the world; the need to improve state governance and enhance civil society among many energy-rich countries; and to reduce of the risks of climate change and global environmental damage by increasing energy efficiency and developing alternatives.

Finally, the longer term challenge is to prepare for that point in time, which is inevitable, where we do reach a geological peak for oil. As mentioned above, the timing of this juncture will probably be intimately linked with the perceptions and reality of the state of the global environment. But, whenever the peak is reached, there is the need to be prepared, through the necessary research and investment, to ensure that this momentous transition away from a dependence on fossil fuels can be made without engendering severe economic or political conflicts. In part, this will require the necessary technological advances to have adequate and affordable alternative non-fossil fuel-based energy sources. But, in larger part, it will require the political will and wisdom to establish the conditions for, and to persuade all sections of society to support, the complex and inevitably economically and politically costly shifts in societal preferences that will be required to make such a dramatic shift in the very foundations of our modern civilization. Probably the biggest longer term question for energy security is whether the political norms, structures and institutions that we currently have will be capable to rise to this complex and demanding set of challenges.

16

Cyber-Security

Myriam Dunn Cavelty

Introduction

> Every American depends – directly or indirectly – on our system of information networks. They are increasingly the backbone of our economy and our infrastructure; our national security and our personal well-being. … As President, I'll make cyber security the top priority that it should be in the 21st century.
>
> (Remarks of Senator Barack Obama – as prepared for delivery, Summit on Confronting New Threats, Purdue University, 16 July 2008)

With this statement, Barack Obama continues the American policy tradition of portraying attacks by means of computers as one of the graver threats to national security along with nuclear and biological threats and of calling the protection against them – by ways of cyber-security – a top priority for the future. Even though (or rather because) this inclusion into the threat-triptych has become so widely accepted in the security policy community and is hardly ever questioned or challenged, it is worth taking a closer look at why (and how) cyber-security is conceived as a key national security task today.

The fact is that there is nothing inherently 'national security' about cyber-security. It is mainly concerned with analysing the risk to information networks of all sorts and then mitigating the identified risks with technical (and at times organizational) means (Gordon and Loeb 2006). It is argued in this chapter that cyber-security is only included among key tasks for national security and only discussed in a volume on 'new security' because the representation of the issue is based on well-accepted, normalized 'threat clusters', in which typical security issues have been successfully interlinked with less typical ones. Like other 'new' threats, the key question in the case of cyber-threats/cyber-security is how this elevation to the national security level and the inclusion on the security policy agenda happened, what the consequences of this are, and how they challenge conventional thinking on security.

This chapter first sets out to define what cyber-security is and what the concept connotes. It then shows how a convincing case for security is argued in various instances of cyber-security in the USA. This focus is justified by the fact that both the threat perception and the envisaged countermeasures were shaped almost exclusively by the USA, with a great influence on how the issue is treated in other countries. This sheds some light on threat clustering over the years and shows how and why two rationales – a business rationale and a national security rationale – became interlinked. The result of this is that cyber-security is imagined as a shared responsibility that cannot be accomplished by the government alone: The maintenance of 'business continuity' for an individual, corporate or local actor is often regarded as equally important as national or even international security efforts in the cyber-realm, as the one ensures and reciprocally influences the other. The chapter then specifically focuses on countermeasures as the consequence of these threat representations (cf. Balzacq 2005). It will be shown that cyber-security emerges as a strange animal: nothing known quite fits, either conceptually or theoretically. Because of persuasive threat clustering, it has become more than just a technical issue, but there is also nothing exceptional or extraordinary about it. These might also be the prime reasons for why there is hardly any literature on the topic in the field of security studies or IR, and especially no theoretically based analyses. Even though an 'existential threat' (Wæver 1995) is frequently invoked, and the politics of security are often said to depend on the exceptional, much of the actual practice of cyber-security is very commonplace in character. This inevitably focuses our attention on the question what security is and how it is practised, but also on how we should approach it theoretically, which is addressed in the concluding section.

What is Cyber-Security? Striving for a Definition

'Cyber-' is a prefix derived from the word cybernetics and has acquired the general meaning of 'through the use of a computer'. It is also used synonymously with 'cyberspace'. Cyberspace connotes the fusion of all communication networks, databases and sources of information into a vast, tangled and diverse blanket of electronic interchange. Thus, a 'network ecosystem' is created, a place that is not part of the normal, physical world. It is virtual and immaterial, a 'bioelectronic environment that is literally universal: It exists everywhere there are telephone wires, coaxial cables, fiber-optic lines or electromagnetic waves' (Dyson et al. 1994). As this quote nicely shows, cyberspace is also grounded in physical reality. As one observer argues, 'the channelling of information flows … occurs within the framework of a "real" geography' (Suteanu 2005: 130) made up of servers, cables, computers, satellites, etc.

Cyber-security is concerned with making this 'bioelectronic environment' safe. It refers to a set of activities and measures, technical and non-technical, intended to protect the 'real geography' of cyberspace but also devices, software, and the information or data they contain and communicate, from all possible threats. Threats that could potentially damage information are categorized as 'failures', 'accidents' and 'attacks' in information security, even though these categories are not necessarily mutually exclusive or always easily distinguishable (Ellison et al. 1997; Whitman and Mattord 2002). Failures are caused by deficiencies in the system or in an external element on which the system depends; they may be due to software design errors, hardware degradation, human error or corrupted data. Accidents, on the other hand, include the entire range of randomly occurring and potentially damaging events, like natural disasters. Usually, accidents are externally generated events (i.e. originate from outside the system), whereas failures are internally generated events. Finally, attacks are orchestrated by an adversary. This category, even though not necessarily the most prominent one in terms of frequency of occurrence or impact, is of prime importance in the cyber-threats debate because of the actor dimension.[1]

System intrusion can be seen as the main goal of attacks and are also to be considered the most 'dangerous' occurrence; in comparison, denial-of-service attacks, which gain a lot of publicity in the media, are relatively harmless in terms of effect. If the intruder gains full system control, or 'root' access, unrestricted access to the inner workings of the system is granted (Anonymous 2003; Hack FAQ 2004). Due to the characteristics of digitally stored information, an intruder can delay, disrupt, corrupt, exploit, destroy, steal and modify information (Waltz 1998). Depending on the value of the information or the importance of the application, function or service for which this information is required, such actions can have severe impacts. To ensure that such degradation does not occur, cyber-security and information security measures have three goals: confidentiality, integrity and availability of information (Dhillon 2007; Stoneburner 2001). 'Confidentiality' refers to the protection of the information from disclosure to unauthorized parties, while 'integrity' refers to the protection of information from being changed by unauthorized parties. 'Availability' means the information should be available to authorized parties when requested. Sometimes, 'accountability', or the requirement that the actions of an entity be uniquely traceable to that entity, is added to the list.

It can be argued that cyber-security and national security do not differ in their core: both connote a condition that is free of (real or imagined) danger. The word 'security' in general usage is synonymous with 'being safe', but especially as a technical term 'security' means not only that something is secure, but also that it has been secured. It refers to the degree of protection resulting from the application of these activities and measures (Fischer 2005). The notion of security thus includes the practice of making something secure by 'securing' it. It therefore is both a state of being and an activity or practice. It can further be argued that cyber-security and national security are even concerned with the same threat subjects ranging from terrorists to enemy states (though this has something to do with threat clustering, as we shall see, and has not necessarily been the case from the beginning).

However, cyber-security and national security differ most decisively in scope, in terms of the actors involved, and in their so-called 'referent object', or the thing they aim to protect. They differ in scope, because national security entails quite a different league in terms of resources (monetary, personnel, etc.) and mobilization of emotions. They also differ in terms of who the actors involved in the two securities are: computer experts on the one hand and 'professionals of (in)security' (Bigo 2001, 2002) on the other. And while the security of information systems is, in its pure form, concerned with technical measures to ensure that information flows as it should, national security measures include much more, such as the maintenance of armed forces, the maintenance of intelligence services to detect threats and civil defence measures. However, with the advent of cyber-security on the security policy agenda, the two notions begin to merge in strange ways. National security today is also concerned with attempts to create resilience and redundancy in national infrastructure through cyber-security measures and cyber-security is included as a top priority on the national security agenda. This means that measures that are generally regarded as being within the purview of information security may now also be included among measures to ensure national security and vice versa. In the next section, I try to explain how this merging of the two notions happened.

Cyber-security Threat Clustering

Threat clustering in the case of cyber-security happened along chronological steps because technical development played a decisive role in how the threat could be represented. At first, there was a particular focus on cyber-crime and attacks on business networks. This was discursively interlinked with classified information and the foreign intelligence threat and thus elevated to a national security level. At the same time, two different notions of security clashed when the National Security Agency (NSA) and the academic/business community butted heads over how to treat encryption technology. The debate basically centred on the question of whether 'security' meant the security of US society as a whole, or whether it only referred to the security of individual users or technical systems, and should therefore be handled by authorities other than national security bodies.

In the mid-1990s, the issue of cyber-security was even more firmly anchored on the security political agenda when it was persuasively interlinked with both terrorism and critical infrastructure protection. During that time, it was established that key sectors of modern society, including those vital to national security and to the essential functioning of industrialized economies, rely on a spectrum of highly interdependent national and international software-based control systems for their smooth, reliable and continuous operation. This critical information infrastructure (CII) underpins many elements of the critical infrastructure (CI), as many information and communication technologies (ICT) have become all-embracing, connecting other infrastructure systems and making them interrelated and interdependent. This reasoning made it more than clear that cyber-security was to be one of the key tools when it came to protecting national key assets.

Cyber-crime and the Foreign Intelligence Threat

As the 1970s gave way to the 1980s, the merger of telecommunications with computers meant that everybody with a computer at home became theoretically able to make use of the slowly emerging computer networks. The introduction of the personal computer created a rapid rise in tech-savvy users, many of whom would dial into bulletin board systems with a modem and download or disseminate information on how to tinker with technology. Together with this emerging cyber-counter-culture, the notion of cyber-crime was born. During this period, the amount of attention given to cyber-security issues grew incrementally in response to highly publicized events such as simple pranks, computer viruses but also politically motivated attacks and penetrations of networked computer systems for criminal purposes (cf. Bequai 1986; Parker 1983).

According to some statistics, by the mid to late 1970s, scores of such crimes were turning up every year, and losses were estimated to be as high as US$300 million (Kabay 1998; Parker 1976, 1980). From early on, the discussion about computer misuse was determined by notions of computer-related economic crimes, which are still regarded as the central area of computer crime (Sieber 1986). But even though it was called crime, the issue was also linked to the topic of espionage and thus elevated to the level of urgency required for an issue to become a national security topic. Mainly by referring to incidents which involved data theft by foreign individuals from government computers (cf. Stoll 1989), computer intrusions were successfully framed at an early stage as a national security issue. Key documents at the time specifically addressed the problem with a focus on 'classified national security information' (cf. Reagan 1984: §2). It was also stated that information security was a vital element of the operational effectiveness of the national security activities of the government and of military combat-readiness (Reagan 1984), thus making the national-security connotation even more explicit.

At this stage, cyber-security was discussed in two largely separate discourses. One was related to cyber-crime and concerned mainly the business sector and certain companies like financial institutions that were becoming digitalized. The second was about the protection of government networks and the classified information residing in them. However, the technological substructure still lacked the quality of a mass phenomenon that it would acquire once computer networks turned into a pivotal element of modern society, with the result that cyber-threats did not receive much attention from the wider public nor were they seen as a problem for it. For a change in the threat representation, technological development was highly decisive, as was the linkage between the two discourses.

The Encryption Debate: Clash of Two Worlds

While still based on the same technological substructure, this interlinkage happened in a related but different domain: cyber-security became a culmination point in a conflict between the academic and government cryptography communities. The science of cryptology is the practice of converting information to an obscured form to prevent others from understanding it, often applied to ensure secrecy of important communications. Up until the 1970s, cryptography had been the sole province of a few groups with exceptional needs for secrecy. Cryptology was on the Commerce Control List (Export Administration Act of 1969, 50USC.App. 2401–20) as well as on the Munitions List (until 1996), along with other items that are 'inherently military in character', and was thus treated as a dangerous good whose export needed to be closely monitored by the national security apparatus (Office of Technology Assessment 1987: 142; Committee on Science, Engineering, and Public Policy 1982). The key player in this field was the NSA, an agency responsible for both collection and analysis of message communications, and for safeguarding the security of US government communications against similar agencies elsewhere. Because of its listening task, the NSA had been heavily involved in cryptanalytic research for a number of years.

By the 1970s, interest in cryptography was growing not only in commercial, but also in academic circles, and academic research in cryptography had achieved several major breakthroughs (Dam and Lin 1996; Diffie and Hellman 1976). This led to direct confrontation with the NSA and other national security bodies. The Reagan administration's concerns about damaging disclosures of classified information were closely interlinked with questions of cryptology. That concern presented itself in documents such as Executive Order 12356 (Reagan 1982a, 1982b; Schroeder 1982), as well as in a number of national security decision directives (NSDD). The most controversial of these security directives was NSDD 145 (Reagan 1984). Through this directive, the NSA was assigned responsibilities that fell outside of the scope of its traditional foreign eavesdropping and military and diplomatic communications security roles, such as authorization to 'protect' communications and computer systems in the private sector. This development gave rise to considerable concern within the private sector and in Congress as well as academic circles, especially since the NSA quickly began to exercise its newfound authority. Through heavy opposition, these groups progressively restricted the main focus of the NSA's activities to the protection of defence systems, and the NSA was forced to scale back its interaction with commercial organizations (Electronic Privacy Information Center 1998; Knezo 2003; Landau 1994).

The struggle was (and still partly remains to be) mainly related to the meaning of 'national security' and about the continued securitization of cryptology. This particular struggle can be seen as a securitization move that was thwarted: the argument that national security and economic security had become one and the same, and that therefore, the protection of economic information also fell under the purview of the national government, was not accepted by 'the audience'. Many of the fundamental advances in personal computing and networking during the 1970s and 1980s were made by people outside government, influenced by the technological optimism of the new left, best expressed in Marshall McLuhan's predictions that new technology would have an intrinsically empowering effect on individuals (McLuhan 1964). The emergence of the so-called 'Californian Ideology' mirrored their passionate belief in electronic direct democracy, in which everyone would be able to express their opinions without fear of censorship (cf. Barlow 1994, 1996). This was so fundamentally opposed to what the US security establishment wanted to establish as 'truth' that various exponents of this counter-culture began to forcefully react by promoting their own ideas of reality. With the rapidly developing technological substructure, this position became even stronger.

Cyber-threats and Critical Infrastructures

In the late 1980s and especially the 1990s, documents started to appear that made a clear link between cyber-threats, cyber-security and critical infrastructures (cf. Computer Science and Telecommunications Board 1989; National Academy of Sciences 1991). The Department of Defense (DoD) was probably the strongest driving factor behind this threat representation. On the one hand, information technology had been firmly coupled with military matters since at least the Second World War, and specifically so in the wake of the more general debate in the Cold War about technological innovation and warfare (Hables Gray 1997; Hinsely and Stripp 2001). On the other, the cyber-threats debate was decisively influenced by the larger strategic context after the Cold War, in which the notion of asymmetric vulnerabilities, epitomized by the multiplication of malicious actors (both state and non-state) and their increasing capabilities to do harm, started to play a key role.

As a result of this, the advantages of the use and dissemination of ICT that had fuelled the revolution in military affairs (Metz 2000; Rattray 2001) were no longer seen only as a great opportunity providing the country with an 'information edge' (Nye and Owens 1996), but were perceived as constituting a disproportionate vulnerability *vis-à-vis* a plethora of malicious actors, especially terrorists and 'rogue states'. Widespread fear took root in the strategic community that those likely to fail against the American war machine might instead plan to bring the USA to its knees by striking vital points at home: critical infrastructures. It was established in various reports and publications that the information revolution had made the USA asymmetrically vulnerable, due to the disappearance of borders and the dependence of military forces on vulnerable civilian infrastructures. The information revolution is thus responsible for transforming the issue into a topic of high saliency. With the growth and spreading of computer networks into more and more aspects of life, the object of protection changed. Whereas it had previously consisted of limited government networks, it now encompassed the whole of society. This way, cyber-threats came to be seen as a threat to society's core values, and the economic and social well being of the entire nation – and cyber-security as ensuring critical infrastructure protection (CIP) a key task of national security. In contrast to earlier stages of threat clustering, the two discourses were no longer separate but had become one and the same.

But while military documents were influential in shaping threat perceptions and in bringing the issue of cyber-threats to the attention of a broad audience, several factors made it impossible for traditional national security bodies to play larger role in countering it. On the one hand, the 'Californian Ideology' as described above had become much stronger in the course of the 1990s, as practically all the relevant advances in ICT were happening in the commercial domain. Furthermore, the nature of cyber-attacks also restricted the involvement of traditional national security actors. If detected, it is often impossible to determine whether an intrusion is an act of vandalism, computer crime, terrorism, foreign intelligence activity or some form of strategic (military) attack. The only way to determine the source, nature, and scope of the incident is to investigate. And the authority to investigate such matters and to obtain the necessary court orders or subpoenas clearly resides with law enforcement (Hamre 1998; Vatis 1998).

What's more, national security countermeasures stress deterrence or the prevention of attacks, and only attribute secondary importance to the investigation and pursuit of the attackers, since the concept of compensatory or punitive damage is rarely meaningful in the context of national security. Law-enforcement (as well as private-sector) countermeasures, however, are frequently oriented towards detection, which means developing audit trails and other chains of evidence that can be used to prosecute attackers in court. In addition, US domestic law also limited the possibilities of the military establishment. Because an attack on US infrastructures could originate overseas as well as in the USA, a military counter-strike through cyberspace might unwittingly constitute an operation of US armed forces on domestic territory, which is prohibited by the *Posse Comitatus* Act of 1878 (§. 1385 of Title 18, United States Code).

On top of this comes a very 'practical' issue which also defeats a larger involvement of the law-enforcement community. Through privatization and deregulation of many parts of the public sector since the 1980s and the globalization processes of the 1990s, 85–95 per cent of the critical infrastructure are now owned and operated by the private sector. Therefore, much of the expertise and many of the resources required for planning and taking better protective measures lie outside the federal government. What emerged from this threat representation in the late 1990s was an 'uncomfortable' situation. On the one hand, security professionals had clearly framed the issue of cyber-security (in connection with cyber-threats and critical infrastructures) as a key national security task requiring action. On the other hand, state institutions saw themselves unable to tackle this task by themselves.

Distributed Security and the Risk Rationale

Given the growing importance of information and knowledge that resides within the private sector, and given that overly intrusive market interventions are not a valid option either in liberalized societies, the state has just one option: try to get the private sector to share some of the responsibility. But calls for cooperation with the private sector could only be legitimized on the basis of a convincing argument to the effect that the interests of the national security apparatus and the private sector were one and the same. Therefore, many arguments can be found in official documents and statements that try to fuse the realms of economy and security, as well as the private and the public sectors. The crucial difference from the older attempts as discussed above is that the private sector is approached as an equal partner and that the national security rationale is scaled back.

The key document in the field (which has established a lasting framework for CIP and whose reasoning is still followed today) seeks to convince the business community that the interdependent nature of infrastructures creates a shared risk environment and that managing that risk will require close cooperation between the public and the private sector. This is done by an appeal to responsibility: 'Because the infrastructures are mainly privately owned and operated, we concluded that critical infrastructure assurance is a shared responsibility of the public and private sectors' (PCCIP 1997: p. i). The responsibility must be shared, because the threats are shared: 'the line separating threats that apply only to the private sector from those associated with traditional national security concerns must give way to a concept of shared threats' (PCCIP 1997: 20, esp. fig. 4). These shared threats are terrorism, industrial espionage and organized crime. The appeal to the self-interest of owners and operators of critical infrastructures argues that they are on the front lines of security efforts, as they are the ones most vulnerable to cyber-attacks (PCCIP 1997: 20).

Thus, the distinction between the private and public spheres of action is dissolved. It is implied that national defence is no longer the exclusive preserve of government, and economic security is no longer just about business. The private sector must focus on protecting itself against the tools of disruption, and should be encouraged to perform a periodic 'quantitative risk-assessment process' (PCCIP 1997: 69), a process that corporations are already very familiar with. In addition, the report advocates a strategy of cooperative 'information-sharing'. Mutual win–win situations are to be created by exchanging information that the other party does not have: 'government can help by collecting and disseminating information about all the tools that can do harm. Owners and operators can help by informing government when new tools or techniques are detected' (PCCIP 1997: 20). In other words, the government flags the proprietary information it requires about potentially hostile groups and nation states and which it intends to acquire through its intelligence services, while the private sector is to give up technological knowledge that the public sector does not have. The approach of the PCCIP report (and other similar reports) is therefore to rally for the idea of 'distributed security'. The problem owner is no longer only the military or the state; responsibility is distributed.

This notion of 'distributed security' closely follows the rationale of risk management. It is argued (truthfully) from the side of government that it is technically and economically impossible to design and protect the infrastructure to withstand any and all disruptions, intrusions or attacks, i.e. that absolute security in the field of cyber-security is not possible. The logical consequence of this is that one has to manage the residual risks. Managing risk is essentially about accepting that one is insecure, but also constantly patching this insecurity, and thus working towards a future goal of more security. This way, grey zones of security become possible: security is no longer inherently binary – meaning that either one is secure, or one is not – but the future state of being secure is continually approached through risk management, creating a sense of security that never fully exists, but is always becoming, like the technological substructure on which critical infrastructures rest.

Through this, the responsibility for creating security can be and must be put on the shoulders of non-state actors, not least because any involvement of the state in cyber-security matters is undesirable and subject to much scrutiny since the information revolution and economic growth are so closely interrelated. Second, one can argue that in the cyber-security community it has long been acknowledged that absolute security is not possible. The traditionally sovereign act of making society secure has moved into the domestic space, and this 'moving security into society requires engagement with the civilian and private actors of society' (Kristensen 2008: 69). The concept of risk in the CIP discourse thus functions as a door opener that allows the government to engage in security policy based on domestic/economic logic.

Conclusion

This chapter has tried to show that cyber-security is a manifestation consistent with the line of reasoning that the challenges faced 'inside' and 'outside' of the state have become blurred in the new threat environment to the point where they have become the same. Today, national security is also concerned with attempts to create resilience and redundancy in national infrastructure through cyber-security measures and other means. This means that measures that are generally regarded as being within the purview of information security may now also be included among measures to ensure national security. In this new logic of security, two formerly different notions of security merge as technical security and safety and national security become one.

Not everything about these practices is new: protection concepts for strategically important infrastructures and objects have been part of national defence planning for decades, though at varying levels of importance (Collier and Lakoff 2008). Today, however, both the context and their significance have changed. It is indeed a 'new' phenomenon that certain practices in connection with cyber-security/critical infrastructure protection have made grey zones of security possible. Due to the nature of what is to be secured, these policies are conditioned on negotiation and shared responsibility with the private actors of domestic society. These practices are expressions as well as causes of the breakdown of the central political distinctions between inside/outside, public/private, civil/military and normal/exceptional.

As a result, the kind of security that this chapter looks at is no longer a 'special' and extraordinary issue. This discourse is not primarily about threats and battles against an enemy, but is characterized by an inward-looking narrative about vulnerability (Bigo 2006: 89). This means that the traditional and normal conditions for day-to-day politics are intermingled with the exceptional dynamics of national security; and new forms of (in)security and protection emerge. Cyber-security (linked to CIP) is a kind of security much embedded into the everyday routines and technologies of actors who are not even necessarily professionals of security. This shifts the focus of attention from 'utterances referring to dangerous futures' to the technologies and strategies by means of which any kind of security is sought and produced (CASE Collective 2006: 469). To see CIP as belonging to the politics of protection helps let security analysis 'run more flexibly across traditional and less traditional security agencies' and ultimately serves to open up security studies 'to the importance of everyday practices and routines in security practices' (Huysmans 2006: 14).

Note

1 In their seminal contribution to security studies, Buzan and his colleagues speculate whether actor-based threats are a pre-condition for a security problem or not. By pointing briefly to insights from 'attribution theory', they come to the conclusion that 'probably, they usually are' (Buzan *et al.* 1998: 44). Though a largely under-researched question, evidence suggests that securitizing actors have the tendency to 'actorize' threats, even though threats might originate in structural conditions. Threat frames linked to a (human) actor, i.e. enemy, seem to have a higher mobilizing potential (cf. Dunn Cavelty 2008: 32).

17

Pandemic Security

Stefan Elbe

Treating the international spread of infectious disease as a matter of 'high' politics is nothing new. As early as 1851 infectious diseases already became the subject of international diplomacy when delegates of the first International Sanitary Conference gathered in Paris to consider joint responses to the cholera epidemics that overran the European continent in the first half of the nineteenth century. During the course of the twentieth century, though, this concern with controlling potentially pandemic microbes gradually receded. It was overshadowed by the more pressing imperatives of avoiding the specter of renewed wars and the ever-present potential for a nuclear confrontation. The twentieth century's deep addiction to war, coupled with important advances in medicine and public health, reinforced the view in the West that that the world was moving in a direction in which infectious diseases would eventually be controlled – something exemplified by the bold declaration made by US Secretary of State George Marshall in 1948 that the conquest of all infectious diseases was imminent. Our concept of security began to mirror this shift, becoming ever narrower in its focus on the deployment of military force in international relations.

More recently this medical confidence has been profoundly shaken. At the outset of the twenty-first century there is once again considerable international anxiety about a host of potentially lethal 'rogue' viruses circulating the planet – ranging from relatively new ones such as the highly pathogenic H5N1 strand of avian influenza and the corona virus responsible for severe acute respiratory syndrome (SARS), through to the globally much more entrenched human immunodeficiency virus (HIV) that causes AIDS. The medical optimism of the twentieth century has been displaced, giving way to a renewed and deep sense of microbial unease. Perhaps nothing reflects this shift more poignantly than the fact that many national and international responses to these microbes are today being articulated in the language of security. Our concept of security is thus in flux once more. Following its severe contraction in the twentieth century, the notion of security is expanding again by acquiring an important epidemiological dimension.

The ongoing securitization of infectious disease can be traced back at least as far as 1992 when, amidst the shifting geopolitical tectonics of the end of the Cold War, an influential report issued by the Institute of Medicine in the USA, *Emerging Infections: Microbial Threats to Health in the United States,* warned: 'some infectious diseases that now affect people in other parts of the world represent potential threats to the United States because of global interdependence, modern transportation, trade, and changing social and cultural patterns' (Lederberg *et al.* 1992: p. v). This, according to the report, was the uncomfortable lesson the USA needed to take away from the rapid emergence and spread of the AIDS pandemic. By the end of the decade such anxieties had reached sufficiently high levels for the US government to take the bold move of officially designating infectious diseases as national security threats. As part of this effort the US National Intelligence Council produced a widely cited national intelligence estimate entitled *The Global Infectious Disease Threat and its Implications for the United States.* The findings of the report, declassified in January 2000, confirmed many of these fears by pointing out that since 1973 at least thirty previously unknown disease agents have been identified (including some for which there is no cure such as HIV, Ebola, Hepatitis C, and the Nipah virus). It also found that during this same period at least twenty older infectious diseases have re-emerged, frequently in drug resistant form – most notably amongst them tuberculosis, malaria, and cholera. 'New and reemerging infectious diseases', the report thus concluded, 'will pose a rising global health threat and will complicate US and global security over the next 20 years. These diseases will endanger US citizens at home and abroad, threaten US armed forces deployed overseas, and exacerbate social and political instability in key countries and regions in which the United States has significant interests' (NIC 2000). Three infectious diseases in particular have been singled out as constituting wider threats to national and international security: HIV/AIDS, SARS, and avian flu.

The AIDS Pandemic: An International Security Threat?

Amongst this group of securitized pandemics, AIDS represents the pandemic that 'is' – in the sense that AIDS-related illnesses continue to claim more than 2 million lives annually, and have already caused more than an estimated 25 million deaths over the past three decades. As early as 1990 a few pioneering analysts at the US Central Intelligence Agency began to systematically analyze the likely impact of the AIDS pandemic on the political stability of foreign countries and US interests abroad. To be allocated the time and resources necessary for examining this issue was a unique and unprecedented opportunity, as a similar request made only three years earlier in 1987 had been turned down on the grounds that this was not an appropriate area to deploy CIA resources, and that any impact on US interests abroad would likely be benign (Gellman 2000). In 1991 the agency nevertheless produced a classified interagency intelligence memorandum (91-10005) projecting – reasonably accurately in retrospect – some 45 million HIV infections by 2000, but the report was still largely met with indifference as the critical mass of policy-makers willing to embrace this new security dimension of HIV/AIDS did not yet exist (Gellman 2000). Nor had this situation changed much by 1994 when the Center for Strategic and International Studies produced another analysis of the wider social implications of the AIDS pandemic, including its security ramifications (CSIS 1994).

Things did begin to change by the late 1990s when security arguments about HIV/AIDS began to be harnessed in a much more concerted manner by those with a specific interest in the international politics of HIV/AIDS – in part as a way of raising the profile and resources devoted to fighting the pandemic. The past few years have thus witnessed a deliberate attempt by policy-makers to move beyond the health and development

PANDEMIC SECURITY

frameworks previously used to address HIV/AIDS, and to reposition the disease as a much more urgent matter of international security. By early May 2000 the Clinton administration even made the unprecedented gesture of designating HIV/AIDS a threat to the national security of the USA. Reports by organizations such as the International Crisis Group (ICG 2001, 2004) and the Civil–Military Alliance to Combat HIV/AIDS (Yeager and Kingma 2001) corroborated this relationship, as did a series of articles in prominent security and international relations journals (Eberstadt 2002; Elbe 2002; Ostergard 2002; Singer 2002).

How have the links between HIV/AIDS and security been drawn in these analyses? Arguments linking HIV/AIDS and national security include that the social, economic, and political stability of communities (and even entire states) could be undermined in the long run by a large disease burden. Armed forces are also argued to be particularly susceptible to HIV/AIDS, with controversial estimates indicating prevalence rates in some African armed forces ranging between 40 and 60 per cent – raising concerns about combat effectiveness. Such security arguments about HIV/AIDS have not fallen on deaf ears. Speaking before a Senate intelligence panel in 2003, the director of the Central Intelligence Agency George Tenet (2003) openly discussed the threat posed by HIV/AIDS alongside other pressing security issues ranging from terrorism and Iraq through to North Korea. 'The national security dimension of the virus is plain,' he insisted, 'it can undermine economic growth, exacerbate social tensions, diminish military preparedness, create huge social welfare costs, and further weaken already beleaguered states.' In a historically unprecedented gesture, the threat of HIV/AIDS to international peace and security has even been the subject of six separate United Nations Security Council meetings held since January 2000 (meetings 4087, 4172, 4259, 4339, 4859, 5228), rendering the AIDS pandemic the latest in a long line of wider social issues to become securitized.

With the passage of time, however, both of these prominent arguments linking the AIDS pandemic and national security have been subject to greater analytical scrutiny by researchers. In terms of the impact of HIV/AIDS on the armed forces, for example, much uncertainty remains about the extent to which the armed forces are affected by HIV/ AIDS, especially given the lack of publicly available information of HIV prevalence rates in military forces. In the absence of the latter, a set of declassified estimates by the Armed Forces Medical Intelligence Center (AFMIC), cited in the 2000 report by the National Intelligence Council (NIC 2000), proved both shocking and influential; they indicated HIV prevalence rates in some African armed forces in excess of 50 per cent. These figures were widely cited and constituted the main basis for many arguments about the national security implications of HIV/AIDS. They also seemed to broadly corroborate a claim frequently advanced by policy-makers at UNAIDS – the specialized United Nations agency tasked with addressing the international spread of HIV/AIDS. UNAIDS has frequently claimed throughout the past decade that rates of sexually transmitted infections are two to five times higher among the military than amongst the general population, and that it therefore expected this to be true in relation to HIV as well.

How accurate are these claims? The estimates initially published by the National Intelligence Council contained considerable margins and consisted of classified sources. It is therefore unclear whether these estimates were based on actual testing or on anecdotal evidence. Some of the countries mentioned in these estimates, such as Congo, Eritrea, and Nigeria, reported at the time that they had not yet carried out force-wide surveillance on HIV/AIDS, raising questions about the reliability of these figures. Angola actively disputed the veracity of the figures at the time. The widely cited NIC figures about military HIV prevalence rates in sub-Saharan Africa are also at odds with other data that have been

165

subsequently generated in other parts of the US government. Richard Shaffer, executive director of the US Department of Defense HIV/AIDS Prevention Program based in San Diego, and who works on a military-to-military basis with many African countries, has presented quite different figures about the prevalence of HIV/AIDS in some of these same countries. These figures point to differences between the national and civilian populations that are not this stark (see Elbe 2009). Although there is indeed some evidence of elevated levels of HIV in some African armed forces based on figures made publicly available (Ba *et al.* 2008), the fact that such divergent figures are circulating within various US government agencies means that much uncertainty remains about the actual HIV prevalence in the many of these armed forces. What is more, there are also grounds to suspect, on the contrary, that HIV prevalence rates in some armed forces may increasingly become lower than in comparative civilian cohorts because studies show that the male age cohorts from which militaries predominantly recruit (males aged 17–22) generally have lower HIV prevalence rates than women cohorts of the same age, and because many militaries have introduced mandatory testing at recruitment stage and have ceased to recruit those who are HIV-positive (Whiteside *et al.* 2006). Arguments about the impact of HIV/AIDS on the armed forces, though intuitively plausible, thus remain shrouded in a high degree of uncertainty, and there is very little publicly available and verifiable evidence to corroborate them at present (McInnes 2006).

The same is true about the impact of HIV/AIDS on state capacity and fragility. 'Declining health, particularly in the form of the spread of infectious diseases', one report (CBACI 2000: 13) concluded, 'will work in combination with other factors to promote instability.' As parts of its efforts in the early 1990s, the CIA decided to add AIDS incidence to the list of variables that should be considered when analyzing which states were likely to become unstable or collapse in future (Gellman 2000). UNAIDS has similarly warned with reference to sub-Saharan Africa that 'the risks of social unrest and even socio-political instability should not be under-estimated' (UNAIDS 2001: 18). How could HIV/AIDS weaken a state to the point of instability or failure? Discounting some of the more outlandish speculations that have surfaced, there are four separate arguments claiming that in heavily affected states HIV/AIDS might: (i) undermine the national economy, (ii) weaken political institutions, (iii) produce new political tensions over access to life-prolonging medicines, and (iv) generate a socially unsustainable high number of orphans.

Yet in this case, too, more systematic analysis of these arguments undertaken in recent years has raised doubts about whether such direct links between HIV/AIDS and state stability can be postulated in all but the worst affected communities (de Waal 2006; Elbe 2009). The macro-economic effects of HIV/AIDS are not yet properly established, with different studies conducted even in the same country generating very different projections. Nor has a rise in the number of orphans generated further political instability. Nor, for that matter, have conflicts broken out over access to life-prolonging medicines. Such medicines have also become more widely available in many countries, and this too serves to mitigate any potentially detrimental impact that the AIDS pandemic could have on state stability. Increasingly it is therefore thought that HIV/AIDS is rather unlikely to generate political instability in the isolation of other causes. This last realization also has important implications for many of the stark predictions made in recent years about HIV/AIDS creating insecurities outside of the worst affected regions of sub-Saharan Africa. In an influential *Foreign Affairs* article Nicholas Eberstadt (2002: 22) warned that the coming 'Eurasian' pandemic in China, India, and Russia will 'derail the economic prospects of billions and alter the global military balance'. Others have similarly predicted a 'second wave' of HIV/AIDS undermining these 'big' states outside of Africa, such as India, China and Russia (CSIS 2002: 2).Yet again, epidemiologists today believe that these countries are actually rather unlikely to follow this trajectory and that in these countries HIV/AIDS is more likely to remain concentrated in various risk groups (Chin 2007).

On the back of much research that has been undertaken on HIV/AIDS and security in recent years, these complex relationships are becoming understood in a much more nuanced manner, with a greater array of case studies and multiplicity of methodological approaches being brought to bear by research on this issue – including a large number of studies commissioned by the Social Science Research Council in the USA within the context of its AIDS, Security and Conflict Initiative (ASCI). Nevertheless, HIV/AIDS will go down in history as one of the first diseases to become securitized in the twenty-first century and marks the first time in the history of the Security Council that a health issue was officially deemed to constitute such a threat to international peace and security. It broke the mold in terms of highlighting the epidemiological dimension of security.

SARS: The Epidemiology of the Twenty-first Century Takes Shape

If AIDS represents the pandemic that 'is', SARS very much represents the pandemic that 'was'. Unlike the many lives that continue to be claimed every day by the AIDS pandemic, the threat of SARS has been successfully averted – at least for now. Widely regarded as the first infectious disease epidemic of the twenty-first century, SARS is thought to have first emerged in the Guangdong Province of China in November 2002 – a region known for its lively markets where human and livestock mingle in close proximity. Symptoms of the new disease included a high fever, a dry cough, and shortness of breath or other breathing difficulties.Yet it was not until 11 February 2003 that the Chinese Ministry of Health forwarded reports of 305 cases of acute respiratory syndrome to the World Health Organization (WHO), by which time at least five deaths had already been reported in Guangdong Province.The new disease appeared to confirm all the earlier fears about how a newly emerging infectious disease could rapidly spread across the globe on the back of a complex transport infrastructure – irrespective of where it first emerged. If anyone personified this fact, it was a local Chinese doctor by the name of Liu Jianlun who initially treated patients infected with the new disease. He subsequently traveled from Guangdong Province to Hong Kong to attend a wedding. Once in Hong Kong, he stayed on the ninth floor of the four-star Metropole hotel (in room 911), where the disease he was carrying quickly began to spread to other guests staying on the same floor. In epidemiological terms he is now referred to a 'superspreader', in that the WHO ultimately attributes more than 4,000 worldwide cases of SARS to this doctor alone (NIC 2003: 10).Those who became infected by him subsequently traveled internationally as far as Singapore, Hong Kong, Vietnam, Ireland, Canada, and the USA where they, in turn, infected more than 350 people directly or indirectly.Another doctor who had treated the first cases of SARS in Singapore also reported symptoms before boarding a flight from New York back to Singapore on 14 March, and had to disembark prematurely in Frankfurt, Germany, for immediate hospitalization and isolation. Wide-ranging international cooperation amongst scientists and laboratories eventually revealed that SARS was caused by a new coronavirus believed to have crossed over from the animal to the human population.This is because evidence of infection with the coronavirus could also be found in several animals groups, including Himalayan masked palm civets, Chinese ferret badgers, raccoon dogs, and domestic cats.

By the time the last human chain of transmission was broken in July 2003 there had been 8,098 reported SARS cases causing 774 deaths in 26 different countries. In the end SARS thus killed about 10 per cent of those infected, although the chances of survival in the event of an infection were heavily dependent upon the age of the victim. Less than 1 per cent of persons aged 24 years or younger died from the disease, while up to 6 per cent of those aged 25 to 44 years died, as did 15 per cent of persons aged 44 to 64 years. Persons aged 65 years or older were at greatest risk, with 55 per cent of those succumbing (NIC 2003: 16). Geographically, SARS left its deepest mark in Asia, with China, Taiwan, and Singapore accounting for more than 90 per cent of cases, although notable outbreaks also occurred in Toronto. As with HIV/AIDS, moreover, the effects of SARS were not confined to these deaths alone. The disease also caused widespread fear amongst populations around the world, especially as there was no cure readily available, and its transmission patterns remained unclear for a considerable period of time. People began to wear masks covering their noses and mouths, shunned public places like restaurants and cinemas, and ceased to travel. In conjunction with the decision of many investors to put investment plans in the region on hold, the SARS outbreak also had considerable economic consequences for the region. The travel and tourism sectors were hit particularly badly, with room and airline seat bookings being down in several cases by more than 50 per cent compared to previous years. In countries such as China, Singapore and Canada public health agencies also implemented quarantine and isolation measures, restricting the movements of those perceived to be at risk of being infected with the virus. Some countries even introduced thermal scanners at airports in order to detect people with symptoms of fever.

The SARS outbreak coincided with wide-ranging diplomatic efforts to improve and tighten international regulations governing the spread of infectious diseases. In 1951 member states of the newly formed WHO had adopted the International Sanitary Regulations. These regulations sought to balance two contradictory needs: protecting populations from the international spread of infectious diseases whilst causing as little disruption to international traffic and trade as possible. Renamed the International Health Regulations in 1969, these provisions initially pertained to six diseases: cholera, plague, yellow fever, smallpox, relapsing fever and typhus. The regulations made several demands of states, including that they must notify the WHO of any outbreaks of these diseases. States also agreed to implement a set of hygienic measures at key locations (such as airports, ports, etc.) to monitor the international movement of goods and cargo, including the maintenance of isolation facilities. Moreover, states could now demand certificates relating to the health and vaccination status of travellers moving from infected to non-infected areas (Gostin 2004: 2624). Yet despite clearly spelling out these obligations on paper, the regulations worked far from effectively in practice, which is why the 48th World Health Assembly passed a resolution in 1995 calling for their eventual revision.

Following a ten-year round of negotiations, the World Health Assembly subsequently adopted a revised set of International Health Regulations on 23 May 2005. These new regulations, which entered into force on 15 June 2007, are binding on 194 countries, as well as all members of the WHO. In responding to the lessons of HIV/AIDS and SARS, these new International Health Regulations have an expanded remit, applying to public health emergencies more generally. Rather than being restricted to a fixed list of specific diseases, the new regulations apply to *any* public health issue that could pose a risk to other states through spreading internationally and that requires a coordinated international response. States have also agreed to undertake further new obligations, such as having to establish national focus points for communicating information relevant to these regulations with the WHO on a seven day a week, twenty-four hours a day basis. The regulations set out the minimum public health capabilities that states must ensure in terms of reporting and responding to international public health risks, while the WHO has also received additional powers to make temporary recommendations to mitigate any such threat.

The success in reaching widespread agreement on these regulations, in conjunction with the fairly rapid containment of SARS, has prompted some analysts to argue that – at a deeper level – the entire SARS episode also points to the emergence of a post-Westphalian system of international health governance. According to David Fidler (2004) the SARS episode represents a break with the nineteenth and twentieth centuries during which the notion of state sovereignty was paramount, and the internal sovereignty of states remained closely guarded. The post-Westphalian era of public health inaugurated by SARS, in contrast, is marked by a much stronger emphasis and role for international organizations. The WHO in particular is now seen to have emerged as the central player in the control and dissemination of epidemiological information. Fidler thus shows how the WHO has been empowered by the development of the Global Outbreak Alert and Response Network (GOARN) – a system of technical collaboration for rapidly identifying and responding to disease outbreaks of international importance, as well as by a new electronic information systems constantly collecting a variety of epidemiological information originating from state as well as non-state sources. The last point is crucial because it means that information about the outbreaks of new infectious diseases is no longer under the sole control of sovereign states; it can also be picked up by the WHO through other information sources. WHO can then use this information to pressure member states for faster disclosure, which Fidler argues was the case with China's slow initial response to the emergence of SARS.

Beyond information gathering, the WHO played an important role serving as a central link in various international efforts to locate and identify the causative agent of SARS, as well as disseminating treatment options and containment protocols. Furthermore, WHO undertook bold and unprecedented actions during the SARS crisis by issuing travel advisories – even though this power was not explicitly stipulated in its constitution. The Canadian government, subject to some of these advisories, was largely reduced to the role of a spectator; it had little choice but to make very vocal complaints to WHO given the economic repercussions. According to Fidler, these aspects of the SARS crisis collectively point to the emergence of a wider system of post-Westphalian global health governance. Irrespective of whether one agrees with this thesis, it is certainly true that many policy-makers felt in light of the SARS outbreak that the writing was now on the wall, and that things could have gone much worse, especially if the coronavirus had achieved more efficient human-to-human transmission. The SARS episode, in short, represented a wider warning about what could happen in the event of a renewed flu pandemic ravaging the human population in the twenty-first century. It showed that the epidemiological dimension of security warranted greater attention.

A Flu Pandemic: Fearing the Future

If AIDS represents the pandemic that 'is', and SARS signifies the pandemic that 'was', then human influenza very much marks the pandemic that 'might be'. Of the three, it is the pandemic that has not yet occurred. However, there were three such human flu pandemics in the twentieth century alone – in 1918, 1957, and 1968. The first of these was particularly severe, breaking out in the harsh conditions of the First World War and leading to the deaths of tens of millions of people around the world. Policy-makers at the WHO and in several national governments remain concerned that the H5N1 strand of avian flu has the potential to eventually evolve into such a renewed pandemic, and are framing avian flu as a threat to national security. Writing in the *New York Times* in 2005, Richard Lugar and Barak Obama – who at the time were both members of the Senate Committee on Foreign Relations – argued: 'When we think of the major threats to our national security, the first to come to mind are nuclear proliferation, rogue states and global terrorism. But another kind of threat lurks beyond our shores, one from nature, not humans – an avian flu pandemic. An outbreak could cause millions of deaths, destabilize Southeast Asia (its likely place of origin), and threaten the security of governments around the world' (Obama and Lugar 2005). In that same vein the US National Security Strategy (NSS 2006) points to the dangers posed by 'public health challenges like pandemics (HIV/AIDS, avian influenza) that recognize no borders', arguing that 'the risks to social order are so great that traditional public health approaches may be inadequate, necessitating new strategies and responses' (NSS 2006: 47). The National Security Strategy of the United Kingdom similarly cites pandemics alongside terrorism and weapons of mass destruction as part of a 'diverse but interconnected set of threats and risks, which affect the United Kingdom directly and also have the potential to undermine wider international stability' (NSS 2008: 3). The specter of a renewed flu pandemic is thus becoming securitized even before such a pandemic has emerged.

The scenario that policy-makers are particularly concerned about is that of a zoonic (animal-to-human) transmission of H5N1 which subsequently recombines or mutates to achieve efficient human-to-human transmission. If such a virus emerges it will, in all likelihood, be spread through coughing and sneezing, and people will probably become infectious before they actually become aware of any symptoms. This latter fact is crucial and would make a future flu pandemic much more difficult to contain than SARS, when people mostly became infectious only after developing symptoms. The first step in this chain – the zoonic 'leap' from the animal to human populations – was already documented in Hong Kong in 1997. Officials sought to deal with this danger quickly and at great costs to the animal population by ordering virtually the entire poultry population of Hong Kong (some 1.5 million birds) to be destroyed. Although these measures appeared successful, there was a further outbreak in February of 2003, again in Hong Kong. By September 2008 there had been 387 confirmed cases of bird flu according to the World Health Organization, of which 245 died. The fatality rate for human cases of avian influenza is thus much higher than in the case of SARS, with just under two-thirds of infected persons dying. Like SARS, however, the geographical region most seriously affected is again Asia, with China, Indonesia, Thailand, and Vietnam (but also Egypt) accounting for the majority of cases. On rare occasions it has also been possible for H5N1 to become transmitted between people, but usually only in situations of very close contact with this person during the acute phase of the illness, and even when this spread has occurred it has not gone beyond one generation of close contacts. Despite the anxieties that these development generate, it is worth bearing in mind that, given the wide geographic spread of the virus in birds, as well as the high number of cases of infection in poultry, the numbers of human infections are at the moment comparatively 'low', indicating that the virus does not 'jump' the species barrier that easily.

Nobody can predict in the end when – and indeed if – another human influenza pandemic will emerge. It could be years before it happens, and it could conceivably also be caused by a different strand of influenza virus from H5N1, although the latter is widely thought to be the most likely candidate to mutate in a way that would allow it to achieve more efficient human to human transmission. If it does, the estimates used by the WHO and the Centers for Disease Control in the USA indicate that there could be between 2 and 7.4 million deaths worldwide, with many more becoming ill and requiring hospitalization. Policy-makers have therefore resorted to stockpiling antiviral medicines, and drawing up lists of who should receive priority access to such medicines in the case of a renewed pandemic. Many questions remain, however, about the efficacy of these drugs, and governments are therefore simultaneously trying to increase the worldwide capacity for producing vaccines so that once the latter is developed, more doses can be manufactured and distributed more quickly.

What is more, ongoing efforts to prepare for a possible influenza pandemic also raise questions about the effectiveness of the new International Health Regulations, and to what extent global health governance can in fact be said to have now decisively entered a post-Westphalian era. Perhaps the greatest challenge to this thesis presently comes from the rise of the idea of 'viral sovereignty'. This notion has recently been advanced by the Indonesian government in order to assert its rights over any developments that are made on the basis of flu strains that originate in Indonesia and that the government passes on to other international agencies. Indonesia's role in these international efforts to prepare for an influenza pandemic is crucial because many of the recent avian flu outbreaks have occurred within that country. Yet since 2005 the Indonesian government has only shared samples of less than a handful of the more than one hundred people who are known to have died from avian flu in that country with the WHO. Indonesia is also no longer notifying the WHO of outbreaks of avian or human forms of influenza. The argument of the Indonesian government is that because these viruses originate in Indonesia, the country should be entitled to control this information and the commercial uses to which it is put. Clearly, the Indonesians are concerned about the prospect of them freely sharing such genetic information, only to be later charged high prices for products developed on the basis of information they provided. The old Westphalian notion of sovereignty has therefore reared its head once more once again, testifying to the persistent difficulties in securing international cooperation – including in the field of international health.

Conclusion

This chapter showed how a group of three pandemics – both real and imagined – have recently acquired a greater security salience in world politics. In the course of 2009, they were joined by a yet another unexpected pandemic that began to spread rapidly across the globe – H1N1 swine flu. How is this recent merger of pandemics and security to be conceptualized? Most analysts to date have followed the broad tenets of securitization theory (Buzan *et al.* 1998) in identifying this emerging health–security nexus as the 'securitization' of health. In this view pandemics such as AIDS, SARS, and avian flu are the latest in a long line of wider social issues – such as drugs, migration, the environment, and so on – to become securitized, i.e. framed as existential threats requiring the adoption of emergency measures. Yet there are also other ways of interpreting the emerging nexus between pandemics and security. Scholars working outside the disciplines of security studies and international relations, most notably in sociology, have for many years been tracing the progressive 'medicalization' of societies, whereby more and more social problems are becoming considered and responded to as medical problems. One important result of these medicalization processes is that they also create substantial material benefits for the medical professions broadly conceived (including pharmaceutical companies), as well as elevating the social position of these professions (Conrad 2007). Viewed from this perspective the recent merging of pandemics and security could be understood not just as the securitization of health, but, on the contrary, also as the latest manifestation of progressive medicalization of society – which is now also beginning to include the practice of security. Put differently, these security debates on AIDS, SARS, and avian flu are also sites in contemporary world politics where security is itself becoming partially redefined in medical terms requiring the greater involvement of the medical professions. The deeper conceptual question that the emerging nexus of pandemic security gives rise to, in the end, is whether it is best understood as the securitization of health, or, in fact, as the medicalization of security.

18

Biosecurity and International Security Implications

Frida Kuhlau and John Hart

Introduction

Biosecurity is an important component to protecting international peace and security from biological warfare threats. Analysts, government officials, and others have given increased attention to the concept of 'biosecurity' in recent years partly because of the anonymous mailing of anthrax spores to politicians and members of the media through the US post in 2001. The term is related to 'biosafety' and, in some languages, a single word can mean either biosafety or biosecurity, leading to some confusion (e.g. in French, Russian, and Swedish). While biosafety is well-established in the research community and industry in terms of protection of the environment and workplace safety, it has not been generally implemented within a national security paradigm. Governments and various international institutions are continuing to consider and to develop a variety of overlapping initiatives and measures in the field of biological weapons prevention and response partly by establishing and implementing biosafety and biosecurity measures. Such activities are carried out, for example, by the World Health Organization (WHO), within the framework of the 1972 Biological and Toxin Weapons Convention (BTWC) and under the United Nations Security Council Resolution 1540 (2004). Some states and institutions can be reluctant to 'securitize' activities that have traditionally been viewed principally as health and safety issues, rather than measures that may be useful for countering perceived bioterrorism or other bio-crime threats. This reflects broader disagreement among the states on whether or how to 'securitize' select measures. Efforts to identify and mitigate perceived biological weapon threats that fall under biosecurity include the further development of inventories of sensitive materials and the implementation of measures to make more safe and secure high-level containment facilities (BSL-3 and BSL-4 level) and awareness raising (e.g. of generic scientific and technological developments). Some of these activities are carried out as part of biosafety measures. Conversely, some biosafety measures, such as waste handling and minimizing aerosols during manipulation, can be viewed as part of biosecurity. Finally, it is important to consider differences between political and legal commitments, where they exist, to biosecurity measures and their actual implementation.

Definitions of Biosecurity

The concept of biosecurity is relatively new within the national security context and states interpret the term differently. This complicates reaching an agreement on terminology and measures to be taken. Biosecurity can be viewed broadly or more narrowly. If viewed narrowly, biosecurity measures are confined to those administrative and procedural steps that can be taken at the laboratory or facility level only. In a broader sense a biosecurity system includes elements of preventive security measures, and disease surveillance, preparedness, and response in the event of biosafety or biosecurity breaches. Some have argued that 'biosecurity' is sometimes inappropriately used too broadly, including a range of measures to prevent and respond to possible biological attacks, particularly bioterrorism committed by non-state actors. Negligence should be viewed within a reasoned and balanced perspective and penalties should not be such that breaches of biosecurity will go unreported. Otherwise, there is a risk that efforts to address biosecurity failings will become an exercise in protecting an individual's or facility's reputation and funding. Another concern is that biosecurity is sometimes used as a motivation to obtain increased funding for bio-defence research, thereby draining resources from important public health research (Roffey and Kuhlau 2006). Finally, biosecurity can be viewed in terms of protecting and sustaining health and safety by supporting national and international peace and security.

A standard, internationally accepted definition of biosecurity is given in the WHO's 2006 laboratory biosecurity guidance which states that 'laboratory biosecurity describes the protection, control and accountability for valuable biological materials ... within laboratories, in order to prevent their unauthorized access, loss, theft, misuse, diversion or intentional release' (WHO 2006: p. iv). Another useful definition has been provided by Japan which defines biosecurity as 'measures taken for preventing the illicit development, acquisition and use of pathogens and toxins and relevant information and technology for purposes that run counter to the aims of the BTWC. In ensuring biosecurity, the approaches of non-proliferation and counter-terrorism are employed' (GoJ 2008: 2). In December 2008 the Meeting of States Parties to the BTWC defined biosecurity (in the context of the convention only) as 'the protection, control and accountability measures implemented to prevent the loss, theft, misuse, diversion or intentional release of biological agents and toxins and related resources as well as unauthorized access to, retention or transfer of such material' (BTWC Meeting of States Parties, 4–5). Finally, in 2007 the Organization for Economic Co-operation and Development (OECD) issued best-practice guidelines for biosecurity above the laboratory level, including incident response planning, security management for personnel and visitors and control and oversight of valuable biological materials (OECD 2007).

Biosecurity could also be considered within a broader context of related terms and concepts. The term biosecurity is closely connected to the terms 'biosafety' and, in some instances, 'bioethics' (e.g. when considering dual use/dual purpose dilemmas). The WHO guidance states, for example, that 'laboratory biosafety describes the containment principles, technologies and practices that are implemented to prevent the unintentional exposures to pathogens and toxins, or their accidental release' (WHO 2006: p. iii). Many argue that biosafety is a prerequisite for biosecurity to function. Bioethics, referring to ethical responsibility, is presented as a related strategic approach to assist in preventing bioterrorism (ibid.). The WHO's 2006 laboratory biosecurity guidance describes biosecurity within an overarching 'biorisk management' approach which includes various other concepts such as accountability, bioethics, biorisk, biorisk assessment, biorisk management, biosafety, codes of conduct, ethics, or practice, control, dual-use, hazard, misuse, threat, and valuable biological material (ibid., pp. iii–v).

Finally, the term biosecurity has different meanings for those involved in human, animal or plant health. For example, in the agricultural field, 'biosecurity' is generally understood as the protection of plants from invasive species. Within the BTWC context, the term is broadly understood as the maintenance of security and oversight of pathogenic micro-organisms and toxins. Given the increasing overlap between chemistry and biology, the term may also be understood to include any biologically active chemicals (i.e. biochemicals). It should also be noted that the 1993 Chemical Weapons Convention (CWC) covers toxins.

Although the measures to implement the various terms and concepts overlap, there are two main underlying reasons for implementing them. One is to ensure the health and safety of humans, animals, and plants, while the other is to prevent the *misuse* of biological material.

International Threats and Concerns

In the 1990s, issues of proliferation of biological weapons and the threat of bioterrorism became the focus of international attention for several reasons, including the uncovering of Iraq's biological weapon programme, revelations about the extensive offensive biological weapon programme of the Soviet Union and the perceived increased threat of bioterrorism. Attacks, such as the bombings in Madrid in 2004, in London in 2005 and in Glasgow in 2007, have also contributed to a heightened perception of threat from terrorism against international peace and security in general and bioterrorism in particular. An analysis in 2004 of potential threats from the present to 2020 indicated that most terrorists will continue to use primarily conventional methods, but that there is concern that smaller, well-informed terrorist groups, in particular, might use biological agents to cause mass casualties (National Intelligence Council 2004). The increased importance of future biological threats and of biosecurity as a key security concern was also highlighted in the December 2004 United Nations Report of the High-level Panel on Threats, Challenges and Change (UN 2004). In 2007 the European Commission issued a Green Paper stating: 'Europeans regard terrorism as one of the key challenges [to] the European Union ... Terrorists may resort to non-conventional means such as biological weapons or materials' (Commission of the European Communities 2007: 2). Finally, a 2008 report by the US National Intelligence Council stated: 'We are especially concerned about the potential for terrorists to gain access to WMD-related materials or technology' and 'We also are concerned about rogue or criminal elements willing to supply materials and technology ... without their government's knowledge' (McConnell 2008: 11).

Security specialists and governments are continuing to consider whether and how various initiatives and measures should be implemented, both in terms of general policy and in terms of specific technical or operational-level challenges. Much of this focus has been on how to prevent and respond to acts of bioterrorism or bio-crimes committed by non-state actors or attacks carried out without claims of responsibility, including those with possible clandestine state involvement. The principal generic threat scenarios that biosecurity measures are designed to meet are an al-Qaeda affiliate, a disgruntled domestic individual or group, or a non-state actor with clandestine state support. Although some al-Qaeda material such as the *Encyclopedia of Jihad* refer in passing to chemical and biological weapons, the technical capacity of al-Qaeda affiliates to carry out such attacks or to choose to use chemial and biological weapons (CBW) over conventional weapons remains disputed. This is partly because such 'grey' literature has almost invariably contained inaccuracies. Also explosives and bullets are easier to acquire and use effectively. Some cases have initially gone unnoticed, such as the 1984 Rajneesh cult's use of salmonella to poison a salad bar at restaurants in Oregon in order to prevent people from participating in a local election (Wheelis and Sugishima 2006). Other incidents are essentially closer in nature to more ordinary poisoning of individuals as a method of murder.

Biosecurity is an important component in the 'web' of preventive mechanisms to manage biological weapon threats. However, the threat from such weapons is not new. What is new is rather the shift of focus from states as perpetrators to individuals (i.e. terrorists or other criminals) as the principal danger. This has made it more difficult to identify and define the threat and to deter such actors. Possible threat scenarios encompass both traditional security interests, such as protecting borders from external military (or terrorist) attacks, as well as human health security interests due to the potential use of disease as a weapon. Challenges that affect achieving effective biosecurity include: the transfer and widespread availability of biological material, the dual-use character of materials and equipment, the small amounts of agents initially needed due to their ability to self-replicate, their availability from natural outbreaks, and the dynamic nature of biotechnology. These challenges differ substantially from the corresponding measures used to curtail the spread of nuclear or chemical weapons. Biological security therefore requires a different set of measures for non-proliferation, deterrence, and defence (Roffey 2005). Another challenge concerns terrorism's change of focus from 'traditional' efforts to kill people to attacking economic targets and the increased awareness about the extensive economic and psychological damage outbreaks of epidemics among farm animals can cause (e.g. foot-and-mouth disease (FMD) and 'mad cow disease') (Zanders 2002). There is also widespread concern about disease outbreaks such as those caused by rapidly changing strains of influenza which have the potential to disrupt economies or to cause a pandemic. These factors could inspire terrorists to use disease-causing agents as their means instead of conventional means and methods. A third concern and a potential future challenge is that the rapid advancement of new and refined technologies and methods within biology will enable the development of novel pathogens and more effective or easily accessible dissemination methods and techniques. If misused to develop biological weapons, biotechnology could become a driving force in promoting standby biological weapon programmes creating concerns of, for example, potential misuses of neurosciences for military application to enhance soldier performance and to develop non-traditional biological weapon agents (US National Academy of Sciences 2008; Wheelis and Dando 2005). It is also possible that existing, but rare, pathogens could be developed and used for hostile purposes.

Assessments concerning the probability and magnitude of a bioterrorist attack have been debated and some have argued the threat to be greatly exaggerated (Leitenberg 2004, 2007; Tucker and Sands 1999). It is often stated that the risk of an attack with biological agents is low, while the consequences would be high or even catastrophic, at least in terms of economic and social disruption. However, it is difficult to assess the risk of terrorists acquiring, manufacturing, and using biological agents because specific and sufficient information is not publicly available. In addition, the historical record of successful (and unsuccessful) attempts of misuse of biological weapon agents is limited and may, in any case, not accurately reflect the current situation or be suitable for predicting the future.[1] Finally, the number of casualties would depend on the agent and the delivery system that was used. States' perceived vulnerabilities, combined with the limited understanding of the consequences of an attack, largely determine how the threat is understood (Zanders 1999).

The threat analyses and risk assessments associated with bioterrorism prevention, preparedness, and response and their implementation are also inherently more diffuse, uncertain, and open-ended than 'traditional' state-based military threats involving conventional weapons. This is partly because of the variety and type of actors involved in such activities (e.g. the public health and security sectors), the lack of clear, quantifiable or otherwise 'objective' criteria to assess such threats and a lack of agreed and operationally meaningful criteria with which to evaluate the effective implementation of measures to address them. These efforts are further complicated by a lack of authoritative, public information with which to carry out such analyses. Many states do not feel directly threatened by bioterrorism and some of the consideration of measures to meet bioterrorism threats can lack resonance with them, especially when limited resources must be prioritized and actually implemented at the working level (Roffey and Kuhlau 2006). At the facility level biosecurity breaches may go unreported or unnoticed within the bioterrorism or international security context (e.g. laboratory break-ins by animal rights activities). Finally, many national police organizations and intelligence services have little knowledge or appreciation of biological weapon-related issues.

The Role of Biosecurity in the Effective Implementation of the International Prohibition Against Biological Warfare

The international prohibition against chemical and biological warfare are based on the BTWC and CWC. The BTWC, which currently has 163 states parties, prohibits the member states to 'develop, produce, stockpile or other wise acquire or retain: 1. microbial or other biological agents, or toxins whatever their origin or method of production, of types and in quantities that have no justification for prophylactic, protective or other peaceful purposes, [and] 2. weapons, equipment or means of delivery designed to use such agents or toxins for hostile purposes or in armed conflict' (BTWC 1972: Article I).

The BTWC and CWC both cover toxins. Also the conventions' language banning CBW is phrased in a manner that prohibits biological agents or toxins and toxic chemicals and their precursors, *except where for permitted purposes*. Thus the prohibitions embody a so-called general purpose criterion whereby all activities involving toxic chemical and biological substances are prohibited unless for permitted purposes. The prohibitions against CBW are, therefore, not restricted to lists of agents and the prohibitions can remain fully applicable in the face of scientific and technological developments.

UNSC 1540 obliges states to refrain from supporting by any means non-state actors from developing, acquiring, manufacturing, possessing, transporting, transferring, or using nuclear, chemical, or biological weapons and their delivery systems (UNSC 2004). It does so partly by imposing binding obligations on states to establish and effectively implement domestic controls and encouraging enhanced international cooperation in accordance with and through the promotion of universal adherence to existing international non-proliferation treaties. This resolution is adopted under Chapter VII of the United Nations Charter, meaning that it is legally binding and that a breach constitutes a threat to international peace and security. A temporary committee at the United Nations in New York assists with the implementation of UNSC 1540.

Biosecurity is an important element in the effective implementation of prohibitions against CBW. In particular, states are obligated to take measures to ensure that biological or biochemical agents are not misused for hostile purposes or as a method of warfare. To do so states have typically developed lists of agents deemed to pose a risk to public health and safety. Scientists who work with such agents may then be required to undergo a background criminal and mental health checks (although this varies widely). Facilities and institutions that transfer such agents may have to report them to their government for vetting, while those that receive such agents may be required to complete end user certificates. The implementation of lists-based control and oversight regimes typically incorporate a 'catch all' provision for agents not listed but which are deemed, based on specific law-enforcement or intelligence information, to pose a specific risk. At the international level, the Australia Group (AG) is an informal export control arrangement that considers the effectiveness of measures, including biosecurity measures, to prevent the transfer of agents for CBW purposes. The AG currently having 41 participants was established in 1984 in response to the use of chemical weapons during the Iran–Iraq War (ww.australiagroup.net), 8 Oct. 2008). Certification controls are also placed on hazardous material and genetically modified organisms (GMO) and for quality control reasons.

In 2008 the parties to the BTWC met to consider: (*a*) national, regional, and international measures to improve biosafety and biosecurity, including laboratory safety and security of pathogens and toxins; and (*b*) oversight, education, awareness raising, and adoption and/ or development of codes of conduct with the aim of preventing misuse in the context of advances in bio-science and bio-technology research with the potential of use for purposes prohibited by the Convention. Also in 2008 the EU Commission completed taking comments on a draft Green Paper on Biopreparedness it had issued in July 2007 (Commission of the European Communities 2007). The paper was tabled in order to initiate a process of consultation throughout Europe on how to reduce biological risks and to enhance Europe's biopreparedness capacity, including proactive measures, emergency management of bio-related events, and establishing investigative capabilities. It also posed the question whether a publication procedure should be applied where sensitive biological dual-use research is concerned. In April 2008 the Commission formed a working group to develop a biopreparedness strategy. The group consists of representatives from the Directorate for Justice, Freedom and Security and representatives from the EU member states. The formal taking of comments is between states, while stakeholders and industry have reacted more informally. The EU is currently developing a chemical, biological, radiological, and nuclear (CBRN) Action Plan on the basis of draft recommendations issued by a CBRN Task Force in 2009. Biosecurity will almost certainly be retained in this plan.

Biosecurity Developments and Oversight

The 2001 anthrax letter attacks, which resulted in 22 confirmed cases of exposure of which five died from pulmonary anthrax, have prompted widespread speculation on whether the perpetrator(s) were domestic or international and whether they were 'state-sponsored'. In 2008 the Federal Bureau of Investigation (FBI) announced that a research microbiologist who had worked for more than 28 years at the US Army Medical Research Institute for Infectious Diseases (USAMRIID), located at Fort Detrick, Maryland, was solely responsible for the attacks. The case has resulted in a renewed focus on biosecurity, especially in the US biodefence establishment. In August 2008 the US Army initiated a 'biosurety' programme

BIOSECURITY AND INTERNATIONAL SECURITY IMPLICATIONS

review at USAMRIID. This programme was started in 2003 and consists of four main elements: physical security, agent accountability, biological safety, and personnel reliability. Access to laboratories is allowed only after the person has completed laboratory safety training, undergone a physical examination, received the necessary immunizations, and passed a security background check by the FBI. The microbiologist's mental health was called into question, but this did not result in his losing clearance to work with biological select agents and toxins (Clevestig and Hart 2008). As a consequence of the case, some have argued that psychological assessments should be carried out more frequently.

Since 2001 the USA has increased focus on strengthening the physical containment of pathogens and vetting personnel working with dangerous 'select' agents (Rappert 2007). This resulted in the USA PATRIOT Act (2001) and the Public Health Security and Bioterrorism Preparedness and Response Act (2002). The PATRIOT ACT criminalizes possession of biological agents unless justified by a 'prophylactic, protective, bona fide research, or other peaceful purpose' and prohibits the possession, transport, and receipt of select agents by convicted felons, foreign nationals from terrorism-sponsoring nations, etc. (www.cdc.gov, 23 Oct. 2008). The Public Health Security and Bioterrorism Preparedness and Response Act aimed at preventing the deliberate theft or misuse of pathogens from US laboratories requires that the Secretary of Health and Human Services maintain and expand by regularly updating a list of select agents, requires research facilities possessing select agents to register their possession to the CDC, requires background checks of those in possession of select agents to ensure that they are not, among other things, convicted felons, and requires the 'establishment of safeguard and security measures to prevent access for such agents and toxins for use in domestic or international terrorism of for any other criminal purpose' (Fischer 2006: 20–1).

The National Science Advisory Board for Biosecurity is an often-cited model for biosecurity oversight of unclassified research. It was established in 2004 in order to provide advice to US agencies on ways to minimize the possibility that knowledge and technologies from biological research are not misused to threaten public health or national security (http://oba.od.nih.gov/biosecurity) June 2009). In addition, the US Department of State currently implements a Biosecurity Engagement Program as part of the 1991 Nunn–Lugar Cooperative Threat Reduction (CTR) program under which partnerships between US and international institutions are funded with a view towards strengthening biosafety and biosecurity partly by promoting the training of scientists, upgrading laboratories, and enhancing disease surveillance. For example, in January 2008 US scientists shipped bubonic and pneumonic plague strains from Kazakhstan to the US Centers for Disease Control and Prevention (CDC). The agreement, which took five years to negotiate, was done within the framework of the CTR Program. Kazakh and US researchers will conduct joint research on the material in order to develop diagnostics and treatments for plague, which is endemic to parts of Kazakhstan (Lugar Letter 2008).

Among biosecurity measures implemented by states are background checks on some natural sciences students to prevent or maintain oversight over the spread of 'sensitive' knowledge. For example, in 2007 the UK introduced the Academic Technology Approval Scheme that requires all graduate students from outside the European Economic Area and Switzerland who intend to study natural sciences to complete a questionnaire which is then vetted by British security services. The survey is being used to assist with the implementation of a programme to prevent the spread of sensitive knowledge (Brumfiel 2007; British Foreign and Commonwealth Office). Some students' applications for such postgraduate study have reportedly been denied under the programme.

179

In 2007 the British Health and Safety Executive investigated failures in bio-containment and biosecurity occurred at a farm near Pirbright in Surrey, UK, where an outbreak of foot-and-mouth disease (FMD) was discovered. The source of the virus was the Institute of Animal Health where small quantities of the virus are studied, as well as two nearby private biotechnology companies one of which manufactures FMD vaccines. Bio-containment failures can occur at even apparently well-funded and well-organized facilities. Achieving effective biosecurity requires sustained effort.

Laboratory and Facility-level Biosecurity

It is not fully known internationally which laboratories and facilities work with dangerous pathogens or toxins and where some potentially dangerous pathogen might be located (Tucker 2001: 136–7). Most researchers working in laboratories are at least generally familiar with standard safety procedures such as protective clothing and the safe handling of biological materials in order to protect personnel from exposure to pathogens and preventing accidental releases. The threat of deliberate releases has also resulted in biosecurity measures being focused on the prevention of unauthorized access, negligence, loss, and theft.

Traditional security programmes have ususally focused on physical protection that is most effective against external threats. Physical security measures include, for example, surveillance systems, locks, and fences (Roffey 2005). However, other elements are also necessary in order to take into consideration internal threats. Mechanisms have therefore been introduced at BSL-3 and BSL-4-level facilities such as controls and background checks on personnel, registration of personnel, pathogens and research and employment of appropriate organizational routines. BSL-1 and BSL-2-level facilities remain largely little affected by such measures internationally and therefore represent a gap in effective biosecurity implementation. Others include control and background checks on counterparts and visiting researchers, informing scientists, practitioners, and students about potential security implications of their research and product as well as educating personnel about security standards and guidelines (Kuhlau 2007: 4). According to some, biosecurity should encompass more than just physical security measures and also include such elements as carrying out periodic risk assessments, psychological evaluations, and reviewing the control and oversight of dangerous pathogens and toxins. Such a broad concept would also include ensuring the verified and secure transfer of infectious materials between facilities, internal and trans-boundary accountability, information security, licensing and accreditation, oversight of research and well-developed standards and codes of practice (Roffey and Kuhlau 2006; Sandia 2005).

In 2007, a report co-authored by the J. Craig Venter Institute, proposed that biosafety offices and committees also be given responsibility for biosecurity matters (Garfinkel *et al.* 2007). At the 2008 meeting of BTWC states parties, Japan proposed that regulations for risk management could be divided according to the control of pathogens and toxins, a domestic monitoring system and controls on the import and export of pathogens and toxins. It recommended that measures for strengthening the capacity of states to handle pathogens and toxins can be divided according to the physical protection of research facilities; and education and training for personnel for handling pathogens and toxins at such facilities. It also proposed that biosecurity could be strengthened through various regional and international actions, including by coordinating work with international organizations, convening meetings and establishing networks among researchers (GoJ 2008). Whether and how this might be applied in developing countries is somewhat unclear and open to debate.

Biosecurity and Dual Use Research in the Life Sciences

Much life science research has dual-use applicability, which refers to its potential to be used for harmful as well as for legitimate and beneficial purposes. Traditionally the term 'dual use' has concerned technologies that can have both civil and military applications. However, the term can have multiple dimensions. One interpretation of the term is that it involves equipment, technologies, and biological material that could be misused for biological weapons purposes and the generation or dissemination of scientific knowledge and know-how that could be misapplied for such purposes (Atlas and Dando 2006). Since the events of 2001 a growing concern has emerged regarding the international security threats posed by dual-use life science research should it be misused for biological weapons purposes. Research and equipment that are used to improve public health can also be used for hostile purposes in the hands of malicious actors. The research sector and the private sector (such as biotechnology industry, university laboratories, medical institutes, and the like) are important actors in developing and disseminating biological material, technology, and knowledge, yet they are actors who have largely been excluded from broader security analysis (Kuhlau 2006). Discussions have emerged requesting that scientists consider the security implications of their work and by doing so assist in preventing potential misuses of scientific research for weapons purposes. However, such discussions do not include consideration of possible threats posed by classified research.

In 2005 discussions intensified regarding research recreating the 1918 Spanish influenza virus. During 1918 and 1919, this virus killed an estimated 40–100 million people in a worldwide pandemic. Today's population moreover lacks immunity against the influenza (Johnson and Mueller 2002). Although some reports of the research project were positive, citing it as a breakthrough in virology, others raised concerns that the dangers of resurrecting the virus were perhaps too great. The risks that the recreated strain might escape were considered and the publication of the full genome sequence was seen as providing 'rogue' nations or bioterrorist groups with sensitive information to make their own version of the virus (Rappert 2007; van Aken 2006). This is one example which has been raised about security threats in relation to the life sciences (www.fas.org, Sept. 2008). Lists of 'research of concern' have also been created with the intention to identify research areas where security and health risks are considered increased. These include, for example, experiments that would render a pathogen more deadly or transmissible, able to infect additional species, resistant to existing vaccines or therapeutic drugs, or capable of evading existing diagnostic or detection techniques (Committee on Research Standards 2004: 5).

The advances and benefits from the rapid developments in biotechnology including genetic engineering are immense, but they can also pose potential risks when mistakes or misuse occur (Chyba and Greninger 2004).[2] These advances have arguably increased the risk that research could be used against us by individuals or groups of individuals with intent to harm. It is therefore perceived as important that life scientists increase their awareness of biosecurity issues and to assess their research in terms of modern security concerns to minimize this threat (www.fas.org, Sept. 2008). Much of the debate about increased scientific participation in minimizing concerns has been formulated around awareness-raising of potential security risks and the development of codes of conduct, ethics, and practice. Codes of conduct and other guidelines are, as opposed to the more operational and physical biosecurity measures, voluntary mechanisms intended to increase the security consciousness among life scientists. 'Codes of practice' is a term that refers to practical guidance and advice on how to achieve a certain standard. Such codes are considered enforceable, in contrast to 'codes of conduct', which are often interpreted to be advisory and to apply to individuals only (Hart and Kuhlau 2005: 8; University of Exeter and University of Bradford). A number of codes of practice exist in, for example, good manufacturing practice, which is used by the pharmaceutical industry (World Health Organization 2004). The content, promulgation, and adoption of codes of conduct were discussed in 2005 by the state parties of the BTWC, a topic revisited in 2008 (BTWC; University of Bradford). Research carried out by Malcolm Dando and Brian Rappert also revealed that researchers to a great extent are unaware of the fundamental international prohibition against biological warfare expressed in the BTWC (Dando and Rappert 2005; Dando and Revill 2006: 55–60).

The debates on researcher responsibility and the possibility of developing and implementing codes of conduct, ethics and practice and education are continuing as are security concerns about whether potential risks with scientific research conflict with fundamental scientific values such as the freedom to do research, share and publish one's results (Kuhlau *et al.* 2008: 477–87). Whether and how to integrate security aspects into legitimate life science research is a new challenge, to both the security and research communities, which will have to be tackled over the coming years. It can be argued that in conjunction with other biosecurity measures, codes of conduct and practice for scientists and technicians can affect how current and future threats from the use of biological materials are handled. Individual responsibility, an increased awareness of biosafety and biosecurity measures, how research could be misused and a culture of integrity and responsibility – including through scientific oversight, peer review, pre-publication review and 'whistle-blowing' mechanisms – are important (Interacademy Panel on International Issues 2005; Somerville and Atlas 2005: 1881–2).

Conclusions

The changed international security environment has resulted in a need for broader non-proliferation and disarmament activities that focus more on concerns such as the risks posed by bioterrorism and outbreaks of infectious diseases. The emphasis of many activities has therefore moved from threat reduction to terrorism prevention. Bioterrorism prevention implies complex threat analysis and assessments due to its more diffuse, uncertain, and open-ended nature when compared to 'traditional' state-based military threats involving conventional weapons. The number of issues and actors involved in related prevention and response activities also contribute to the complexity. Examples of this include public health-related issues and environmental protection, which have been increasingly viewed within a security paradigm.

Biosecurity measures are important components in managing biological weapon threats. The concept of biosecurity is relatively new and there is currently no universally agreed or applied definition. Biosecurity can be viewed narrowly, in terms of a process of operative mechanisms at the biological laboratory and facility level. It can, however, also be viewed more broadly as an element within a comprehensive bio-risk management approach in which the goal is to achieve absolute security against the misuses of biological agents.

Traditional security programmes have mainly focused on physical protection against external threats. More generally, however, biosecurity is facilitated not only by physical measures, but by mechanisms protecting against internal threats together with the establishment of a culture of responsibility and accountability among those who handle, use, store, and oversee work with pathogens and other valuable biological materials. This would also be true for life science research in general where greater emphasis on scientists' roles and responsibilities for potential security implications of research has emerged over the past years. There is, however, concern that the adoption and implementation of biosecurity measures in the life sciences will needlessly restrict the free flow of information necessary for scientific research, thereby impinging on the core scientific values and risks stifling research and development. Partly for these reasons, any measures and programmes to promote biosecurity should be 'reasoned' and 'balanced' and efforts should be periodically taken to understand the reasons why some states and analysts believe such measures and programmes are insufficient or overly ambitious.

Notes

1 The most cited cases of successful and attempted events include the Rajneesh using salmonella on food in The Dalles, Oregon, in 1984, the Japanese group Aum Shinrikyo, which unsuccessfully attempted to procure, produce, and disseminate anthrax and botulinum toxin in 1990–4, the unsuccessful efforts to obtain anthrax and to prepare a facility for microbiological work by al-Qaeda in 1999 and 2001, and the successful distribution of high-quality dry powder anthrax spores in 2001 (Leitenberg 2004).
2 Examples include the reconstruction of Spanish influenza virus, the synthesis of poliovirus and the inadvertent creation of a lethal mouse pox virus.

Part IV
New Security Practices

19

Surveillance

Mark B. Salter

Surveillance is the organized observation of behavior with the intention of care or control of the observed, and forms an important object of study in new security studies. Traditional security studies are organized by the state/anarchy and the inside/outside dichotomies: domestic policing inside and international, military war-fighting outside. Surveillance in this traditional context was of markers of military power through reconnaissance, intelligence, espionage, international observation, or diplomatic maneuvering (Der Derian 1992). Domestic policing and surveillance of international private actors were the domains of criminology and sociology or comparative politics and really outside the scope of mainstream research programs (Andreas 2003). Security, however, does not stop at the water's edge or the territorial border. New threats to the state, society, and economy are now much more diffuse: global mobility and migration, international organized crime, drug, or terrorist groups, capital flows and networks of financial institutions, to name a few. As Bigo (2006b) and others demonstrate, contemporary security practices are no longer strictly divided by the border: police and intelligence agencies increasingly cooperate regionally and internationally, while the strict division between military and domestic policing operations is increasingly blurred. For example, the Schengen Information System (SIS) and Eurodac are fed by and provide information about visa and asylum seekers to European border authorities, immigration agencies, police, and intelligence agencies (and are under pressure to share that data with other countries). Also in the European area, military tactics, hardware, and personnel are often used for border policing, both at the immediate level and at a distance. The expansion, internationalization, and securitization of surveillance is due to the empirical increase in mobility and capital flows enabled by economic, social, and political globalization and the technological innovation of the information and communications revolutions. In short, the threats to security are conceived by policy-makers and practitioners as less traditional and more asymmetric, risk management has come to dominate deterrence as a strategy (see Kessler this volume): more people, more information, and more things are moving and there is a greater capability to track and monitor those movements.

To give a sense of the scope of contemporary international surveillance, here are some figures. Surveillance is 'focused, systematic and routine attention to personal details for purposes of influence, management, protection, or direction' (Lyon 2007: 14), and is not limited to state actors. Consumer organizations, such as banks, marketers, advertisers, service providers, insurers, have long monitored their customers to better sell products (see Leander this volume). However, what is new is that the government is making use, not only of those private databases, but also of those tactics. JetBlue, Delta Air Lines, Continental, America West Airlines, and Frontier Airlines, and a large global distribution system, Galileo International, shared information with a DHS subcontractor, and at least 5 million passenger name records (PNR) were collected from JetBlue, 'augmented ... with Social Security numbers and other sensitive personal information, including income level' to test out a passenger profiling system (Singel 2003). The centralized US Terrorism Screening Centre coordinates 'no-fly' and border watch-lists, a government audit reports that 'the overall size of the consolidated terrorist watch-list has quadrupled in size since the TSC's inception, increasing from about 150,000 records in April 2004 to over 700,000 as of April 2007' (Office of the Inspector General 2007: 67), and tens of thousands of individuals have used the redress mechanism to correct errors in the list, including Senator Edward Kennedy and two other congressmen. A similar consolidated database in Europe, the Schengen Information System, holds more than 700,000–800,000 records of third category nationals, and the second iteration of that system extends into the tens of millions of records (House of Lords 2007: 20). The US-VISIT program registered over 25 million entries in its first year of operation including biometric information, personal data, and encounter information (Weins 2005: 2). While borders are crucial for understanding new security studies, there is an increase in domestic surveillance for security purposes. The average Briton is captured on CCTV (closed-circuit television) over 300 times per day (Norris and Armstrong, 1999: 67), and CCTV aided in the investigation of the 7/7 attacks on the London transport system. New surveillance is not limited to European countries, with 'smart' national identity card schemes, which include personal and medical information, planned or implemented in Malaysia, Thailand, Japan, China (Bennett and Lyon 2008). Surveillance has long been a staple of military action, but new kinds of technology have led to greater capacity and inclination to intervene. The military 'Echelon' system monitors satellite communications, while the FBI 'carnivore' system 'checks millions of email messages' for suspect phrases (Lyon 2007: 42). Over 750,000 Iraqis have been biometrically captured in a US Army database (Electronic Privacy Information Center 2007). Mobile phones with global positioning systems (GPS) have been used to target precise individuals for military action. Airports, borders, and other sites of public–private interface have become increasingly important in surveillance studies, because the technologies of monitoring and control have been made possible and necessary by the delocalization of borders and the deterritorialization of personal data. The disappearing physical state boundary is replaced with a dispersed virtual border composed of databases, decisions, and 'remote control'. The changing nature of surveillance technology, global mobility, and the telecommunications revolution make new strategies and practice of control possible. It is clear also that the widening scope of data collection has the effect of securitizing new areas of formerly private information, such as health care, travel arrangements, financial transactions, consumer spending patterns, and social relations. This chapter will provide an overview of contemporary surveillance strategies, models, and suggest a research program for surveillance in the new security studies.

Traditional security studies is primarily concerned with the relations between sovereign states or between states and their competitors. As a consequence, state surveillance over other states was figured in military and strategic terms, epitomized by Regan's oft-repeated maxim: 'Trust but verify.' Within an anarchical, self-help system of states, as demonstrated by the prisoner's dilemma, there is sometimes an incentive to defect, to break agreements or treaties, or to simply preempt the strategic actions of other countries. The Cuban Missile Crisis is a plain example: American forces discovered the placement of mid-range nuclear missiles on Cuban soil through over-flights of spy planes, and in response created a blockade of Soviet ships to ensure no further missiles would be transported. The advantage of surprise was undone through surveillance and then policed through the blunt instrument of the blockade. Two superpowers engaged in surveillance to limit the strategic advantage of their opponent. Similarly, American and Soviet forces exchanged inspectors to oversee the decommissioning of nuclear weapons after the START I treaty. Surveillance is not simply reconnaissance of an opponent's position, but also includes the attempt or intention to control the behavior of the observed. Verification – whether through international inspectors, satellite imagery, communications intercepts, or espionage – increases the costs of defection and incentivizes a predictable set of behavior. Traditional security studies, then, takes the state as its primary lens through which it sees surveillance as a strategic tool in the arsenal of intelligence gathering, reconnaissance, verification, and diplomacy.

While other disciplines examined surveillance practices, they were mostly understood in a domestic frame and so not linked extensively to international security. We must admit that in the current strategic environment, inter-state warfare is less significant than in the past. Even the wide-scale military interventions of the post-9/11 era have demonstrated much more complex, not to say chaotic, battle-spaces in an environment of asymmetric threats. President Bush gave a graduation address to the West Point military academy that he said himself was the most important foreign-policy speech of his administration. In it, he articulates the changing strategic environment for the USA: 'Enemies in the past needed great armies and great industrial capabilities to endanger the American people and our nation. The attacks of September the 11th required a few hundred thousand dollars in the hands of a few dozen evil and deluded men. All of the chaos and suffering they caused came at much less than the cost of a single tank' (Bush 2002). In this speech, he articulates a foreign-policy doctrine that sets the standard for military intervention by the USA: 'new threats also require new thinking. Deterrence – the promise of massive retaliation against nations – means nothing against shadowy terrorist networks with no nation or citizens to defend. We cannot defend America and our friends by hoping for the best. If we wait for threats to fully materialize, we will have waited too long' (Bush 2002). In addition to connecting state sponsors of terrorism to the war on terror, and indeed arguing that any state which harbored terrorists would be considered an enemy of the USA, Bush in this speech radically changed the standard of proof for justifying military action and signalled that terrorist groups would be a legitimate target of state attacks. The war on terror is a powerful discourse, precisely because the object of the conflict is not a particular group (although al-Qaeda clearly holds pride of place), but the ideology of anti-Americanism. Thus, to 'know' or preempt an attack of a few dozen people and a few hundred thousand dollars fuelled by anti-Americanism, surveillance of the total population of potential terrorists and all international financial movements – in short all transactions – must be undertaken (Amoore and de Goede 2008; de Goede this volume). Surveillance, as a crucial strategy of risk management, becomes a dominant strategic trope of American post-9/11 policy, providing the intelligence and analysis that justifies preemption.

New security studies makes three key observations about contemporary practices of surveillance. We can observe: the expansion of the practices, objects and impact of surveillance; the internationalization of the means and objects of surveillance; and the securitization of surveillance. A quick survey of surveillance technologies indicates the degree of ubiquity and invasiveness of observation for the object of security control in everyday life (Guittet and Jeandesboz this volume). CCTV systems are used in public and private spaces, such as airports, borders, shopping malls, main streets, government offices, private homes, gated communities, highways, trains, and so on. Satellites can now identify objects as small as 10cm and image license plates from space (Privacy International 2007). Programs for data-mining use open-ended searches to identify complex patterns of ownership, consumption, relation, or affiliation within and between enormous private and public databases (i.e. rather than assume to know the question for which the data has the answer, the program tries different kinds of solutions and lets the data organize its own question). The widespread use of biometric technology, such as fingerprints, facial or iris recognition, in identity documents such as ID cards, visas, and passports, secures the abstract information to a particular body, from biological body to data-double (Bilgin this volume). Radio-frequency identification (RFID) technology, in which a passive chip is embedded in an object, is being used currently in shipping containers, passports, visas, and more benign consumer items. In the case of identity documents, this can help with document authentication and identity certification; for shipping containers, border authorities can track the movement of objects through the global transport grid or more locally. As RFID chips are integrated into more and more objects, we may arrive at an 'internet of things' (Gershenfeld *et al.* 2004) that can monitor not just the GPS in our satellite navigation systems, cars or trucks, and mobile phones (which some companies have required of their employees and many rental companies also require of drivers), but also examine the things in our home, office, and public space (den Boer this volume). These technologies make possible new circuits of power, new methods of analysis for vast quantities of new data, and create new security dynamics in everyday life.

Expansion

Any shelter that state-centricism gave security studies was shattered by the 19 hijackers on 9/11, however much foreshadowed by other attacks or movements. Contemporary uses of surveillance are oriented not solely towards states and state agents, but individuals, organizations, and groups, not solely at forensic or investigatory efforts but at preemption and suspicion. At root, because the quality and quantity of intelligence about terrorist and criminal groups is so thin, government actors attempt to gather as much information as possible. The new security is not about deterrence, but about preemption: stopping the enemy before the attack. In the absence of actual evidence of wrong-doing, policing and intelligence agencies (and the assorted constellation of border authorities, visa and immigration agencies, even aviation security and private companies) use large statistical databases to construct profiles of individuals who may pose a risk (Bigo 2002). The reduction of data storage costs and the increased ability of computer systems to analyze and integrate data mean that preemption is also applied to the gathering of intelligence: it is never clear what information might be useful, and so as much information as possible is collected. The US-VISIT system, for example, records the biometrics of every foreign national entering the USA at the airport, and checks this information against both visa applications and criminal/terrorist watch-lists. CCTV cameras on Britain's A roads track license tags for all movements. While signals intelligence (SIGINT) has long been a staple of military and intelligence work, new advances in surveillance have vastly increased the ability of the government to capture, process, and analyze many different forms of personal communications. While the Echelon program was able to intercept large amounts of telecom traveling by satellite and 'automatically filter all telecommunications traffic passing thorough the UK for key words and phrases' (Wood 2006: 18), new strategies have been needed with the advent of fiber optics. According to a lawsuit by the Electronic Frontier Foundation, in a secret room in San Francisco, all internet traffic from AT&T customers going through a main trunk-line of the internet was copied to the National Security Agency's computer system, while the Central Intelligence Agency and other counter-terrorist groups gained access to the SWIFT (Society for Worldwide Interbank Financial Telecommunication) database, which records global financial transactions, as part of its counter-terrorist financing campaign. This information was not limited to the collection of data about American citizens, but rather an attempt to take a snapshot of all internet and financial transactions that could trace terrorist and criminal networks. These individual programs are mere shadows of the proposed Total Information Awareness system, which aimed to mine all government databases and privately and publicly held information to monitor counter-terrorist activities. Though this project was shut down after public outcry, the revised Terrorist Information Awareness program or an analogue is reported to continue as part of the 'Black' or secret Pentagon budget. The collection of vast amounts of security-related data is not simply limited to governments: private firms, such as WorldCheck, have established their own watch-list of 'politically-exposed persons' or suspected criminals and terrorists. These private watch-lists are being sold to banks, governments, international companies, and even higher educational institutions as part of their 'due diligence' vetting of new and current employees. The actual efficacy of these programs can be questioned, because the number of actual prosecutions for terrorist or financing offensives is extremely small, although the number of lesser charges, such as identity theft or immigration violation is larger. However, these programs are not justified or evaluated in terms of success, but rather in terms of the cost of failure. The logic of preemption and risk management thus creates both pressures and rewards for greater surveillance.

Internationalization

The object of surveillance has also been internationalized: contemporary threats will not necessarily cross the Rubicon with an army to march on Rome, roll across the plains of Central Europe, or fly across the Arctic. And so, with disaggregated threats, surveillance must happen at a distance. Rather, the doctrine of preemption impels agencies to collect information about the global population, in order to find their targets or rather to generate the profile of a target. In the global war on terror, under the sign of preemption, intelligence agencies, the military, and police must increase their knowledge about the *global* population. From a possible pool of more than 6 billion individuals, the threat vector is no longer 194 states (and of those only great powers and regional rivals), or even a smaller group of failed or rogue states, but networks of three to fifteen individuals. This requires the gathering as much information as possible. The internationalization of surveillance can be seen in the launch of the US-VISIT program, in which the US Department of Homeland Security gathers personal information and biometric data about every visitor to the USA (arriving by air and sea, land borders are due to be integrated into the system by 2009). Personal information about all foreign nationals traveling to the USA is thus stored in an American database. While allies have often shared intelligence, a practice continued today with perhaps more unidirectional sharing with an insistent USA as the chief global consumer, this represents a different kind of surveillance: rather than post-facto, forensic policing that gathers data about particular suspects, the current modality is preemptive data collection from any and all sources. In the current environment, data collected about benign travelers simply contributes to the statistical significance and reliability of profiles that are generated about risky or dangerous individuals. As a consequence, the USA in particular has become an avid collector of information, even to the extent of using the technique of extraordinary rendition to outsource torture. Bigo argues that some parts of the American government aim to create a database of the whole global population with as much information as possible. Through extraordinary rendition, suspect individuals are taken from countries in which torture is illegal to countries in which tame intelligence or police services will use exceptional measures to extract information: two signal cases include Canadian-Syrian Maher Arar and Egyptian Abu Omar. Arar was deported from the USA to Syria, where he endured over a year of torture, on the basis of weak and mishandled intelligence from the Canadian authorities; Abu Omar's abduction from Milan occurred without the knowledge of the Italian government. We can conclude that more of the global population is coming under the scrutiny of security officials through surveillance of financial transactions, social connections, political affiliations, and foreign government observation. More than that, it is clear that the intelligence community is enjoying widespread cooperation on the front of counter-terrorism, and particularly in the case of extraordinary rendition but also in the normal lines of security cooperation, foreign governments are increasingly tasked to perform surveillance and control of suspects.

Securitization

Older forms of international surveillance, such as intelligence, signal interception, or satellite imagery, were clearly related to state-based, military threats. However, what is new about contemporary uses of surveillance is the expansion of the kinds of information now considered a matter of security. This may be seen as a classic example of 'function creep' where available tools and programs expand to meet the technical capabilities of the system rather than the intended goal of the policy. Because information systems can generate, analyze, and in effect produce more connections, more data are collected. Industry experts boast as to how data-mining software can connect phone records, credit card information, driver's license information to recreate the 9/11 terrorist cell. While, forensically, this represents a real revolution in the ability to investigate crimes, when applied to forecasting relationships it represents something far more worrying. Financial information – particularly international transactions, charity donations, or even informal banking systems such as hawala – can reveal networks of money laundering, criminal operations, or support for terrorism and so are now being monitored by private and public authorities; those records can also indicate networks of family migration, community or religious allegiance, or the circuits of labor migration which are not threats. Financial surveillance is being conducted by both counter-terrorism and policing, and also by banks themselves as part of their risk management strategy. Although surveillance is a regular tool of epidemiology, within the increasingly popular discourse of biosecurity (Kuhlau and Hunt this volume) and the threat of pandemics such as avian flu and SARS, health information is also becoming an important element of security information (Elbe 2008a;

Elbe this volume). For its national identity card, Thailand is including a large set of personal information: 'The personal data to be on the cards consists of name, address(es), date of birth, religion, blood group, marital status, social security details, health insurance, driving license, taxation data, the Bt.30 healthcare scheme, and whether or not the cardholder is one of the officially registered poor people' (Kitiyadisai 2005: 22). Accompanying this scheme, the government is now registering SIM cards for mobile phones, in part because they have been used to detonate Improvised Explosive Devices (IEDs) (Kitiyadisai 2005: 24). The Thai example demonstrates, first, the expansion of the amount and kind of information that is gathered about the population, and, second, the expansion of new technologies that are monitored. Because the new definition of national security threats have expanded, and the possibility of generating new patterns of criminal and terrorist association has become more real with data-mining technologies, so too have the categories of information that come to be considered relevant for security agencies to monitor increased.

Strategies of Surveillance

Surveillance has been coupled with the growth of modern, bureaucratic state. The tools of the government to 'know' and thus better care for and control its population have become more pervasive over time. These tools, such as the census, geographical survey, public health records, welfare rolls, voting register, national identity cards, passports, visas, etc., provide a statistical foundation of population management. Foucault describes how these statistics, in effect, create a population, and a particular kind of governmentality (Foucault 1997: 73). He argues that this leads government to manage the population in terms of statistics, birth and death rates, poverty rates, recidivism and epidemiology data, and so on, what he terms 'biopolitics' (Foucault 2008; Dillon this volume). Surveillance becomes a primary modality of governmental control, through the tactic of visibility, which can be seen in the architecture of lecturing halls, prisons, clinics, public spaces that are monitored by CCTV cameras, and the generation of government programs that require the submission of extensive personal information (Haggerty and Ericson 2006). The organization of space, policies, and institutions maximizes the individualized data collected, analyzed, and then applied. Lyon describes how one of the chief effects of widespread surveillance is social sorting, which is also illustrated by the mobility turn in sociology and geography (Lyon 2003). In technological terms, the automation and digitalization of surveillance leads to social sorting by profile and statistics, rather than by direct human judgment. Underlying the widespread use of surveillance is a shift from a post-crime investigation model of policing towards a preemptive risk-management model of security. The preemptive labeling of 'youths' as young as 10 as at risk for antisocial behavior in the UK epitomizes this perspective. Analysts argue that the contemporary mode of surveillance – whether private or public – is structured by the model of risk management, which entails an orientation of resources towards those threats which have the greatest impact and frequency. As a methodology for decision-making, however, this doctrine of risk has the effect of increasing the amount of surveillance done on the object population, precisely to generate profiles of the different risk categories (Ericson and Haggerty 1999). Within the field of critical social theory, this has also been associated with insurance and the adoption of the precautionary principle (Aradau and van Munster 2007). For all kinds of institutions, not simply intelligence agencies, militaries and police, but also banks, schools, local governments, are increasing their surveillance under the rubric of risk management, public security, and customer relations. This folds into discussions of neo-liberalism and the privatization of many state functions, even the security field. Within the framework of risk management, both preemption and profiling create a pressure for more surveillance.

Models of Surveillance

We can identify two dominant models of surveillance: the panopticon and the assemblage, although the theoretical discussion has expanded recently (Lyon 2006). Foucault uses the model of a prison, originally designed by Jeremy Bentham, to demonstrate the operation of power in creating systems of self-discipline. In the panopticon, a central tower is able to observe equally all of the prison cells, arranged as a transparent screen in front of them, but crucially, prisoners in their cells cannot tell if they are being observed. The result of this system, Foucault argues, is the perfect operation of power: the architecture itself induces the prisoner to self-police their behavior: 'surveillance is permanent in its effects, even if it is discontinuous in its action [consequently] the perfection of power should tend to render its actual exercise unnecessary' (Foucault 1977a: 201). He extends this metaphor and argues that the networks of knowledge and power generated by this quest for governmental control, such as the census, employment and welfare rolls, public health records, credit rating agencies, etc., create a disciplinary society. For Foucault, though the effect of the panopticon is directed at the obedience of the individual, there is a centralized 'will to know and to govern' that structures these institutions. Modern panopticism can be seen in the use of centralized CCTV systems, or the 'joining up' of e-government services that connect personal identity certification with different entitlements or regulations. One can see the persuasiveness of this model in the centralization of global surveillance in the central pillar of American intelligence gathering. The American no-fly list, for example, prevents individuals from flying not simply in the USA or to the USA, but also along other parts of the global aviation system. Furthermore, the new Electronic System for Travel Authorization (ESTA) – modeled on a similar Australian system – will require potential third-country passengers (even from Visa Waiver Program countries) to submit personal information to the US DHS before even starting their journey. Similarly, the Schengen Information System collects personal, criminal, and visa/asylum information from all member countries (including whether or not the individual is suspected of serious crime). One of the prominent uses of the SIS was the monitoring of anti-globalization protesters and football hooligans. These centralized collection points have the effect of making certain kinds of movement and activity impossible, or pressuring them to become clandestine. International economic migration comes to be policed as human smuggling.

The assemblage, presented by Haggerty and Ericson (2000), presents a less centralized model of surveillance. They argue, from Deleuze and Guattari, that independent actors each making uncoordinated decisions to engage in surveillance has the effect of creating a rhizomatic system of surveillance that reduces the range of freedom for individuals and groups. The assemblage 'operates by abstracting human bodies from their territorial settings and separating them into a series of discrete flows. These flows are then reassembled into distinct 'data doubles' which can be scrutinized and targeted for intervention. In the process, we are witnessing a rhizomatic leveling of the hierarchy of surveillance, such that groups which were previously exempt from routine surveillance are now increasingly being monitored' (Haggerty and Ericson 2000: 606). This happens without a centralized intention to care and control, but through disaggregated and unconnected actors each making individual choices to engage in surveillance that has the result of constraining the freedom and choices of individuals and groups. The surveillance assemblage can be seen in the surveillance practices of an individual traveling internationally: consumer data is gathered by credit card companies; travel data is gathered by airline global distribution systems (such as SABRE or Galileo); frequent flyer, fare, schedule data, and meal preference are collected by airlines; advanced passenger information is collected by airlines or online-agents and distributed to foreign governments for prima facie 'fly/no fly' decisions, often administered by off-shore border staff or airline representatives (Bennett 2008). Border guards and immigration inspectors have access to globally aggregated databases that bring together disparate information with no sense of pedigree or reliability. Without assuming a centralization of control or a common 'conspiracy', each of these different systems engages in greater surveillance of the individual and groups. The assemblage of surveillance practices is rhizomatic, in that it expands where there is space for surveillance and a perceived need or benefit. Thus, the EU–US negotiations over the transmission of passenger name record and advanced passenger information data revolved around the question of what information was necessary for immigration, criminal, and counter-terrorism activities. Because of the American adoption of the preemptive model of risk management, and an acute sensitivity about the vulnerabilities of the air border, US officials wanted as much information as possible; the EU, on the other hand, with a European Court of Human Rights judgment in hand, were far more conservative in their balance between personal rights and national security.

These two models, panoptic and rhizomatic, focus our analytical attention on the effect of surveillance practices on the targeted individuals and groups. In particular, there is an acknowledgement from both schools that, whether discrete or overt, surveillance has an effect – that is increased pressure and incentivization of self-government, self-discipline, and self-censoring. Within each of these models, surveillance expands to fill the social and political space available. Security is a common political appeal that justifies the expansion of these surveillance practices, whether that justification is made by political and bureaucratic elites or by the populace.

Research Program

The most important topic for new security studies in the field of surveillance is the analysis of the relationship between the increased surveillance of everyday life and the protection afforded. Dramatic increases in domestic and global surveillance have been justified in terms of security, and more international political sociological work needs to be undertaken to understand the development of new tactics and practices of surveillance, and in particular the political-cultural-economy of surveillance. Graham argues rightly that more attention must be paid to the connections between surveillance studies and international relations (2006). Some surveillance practices, such as the panopticon itself and fingerprinting, were developed in the colonial scene, and new schemes are being rolled out in the post-colonial present. Equally, science and technology studies must be engaged to understand how biometrics, RFIDs, data-mining programs, and other technologies are used in surveillance (Monahan 2006). Work on the bureaucracies and private companies of surveillance can demonstrate how governments and political elites are sold these risk management or technological systems, with what justifications, and at what cost. The increasing militarization of police activities, and the role of surveillance in both military and police spheres, must be examined further, taking particular advantage of work done in criminology, law and society studies, and geography. Recent publication of Foucault's *Security, Territory, Population* indicates that his concern had moved to notions of circulation, and the proper governance of flows of population, capital, ideas, and other elements of the state, matching the mobility turn in human geography and sociology (Adey 2006; Foucault 2007). More work must be done on how global surveillance can be seen as a way of monitoring and controlling circulation of populations, capital, ideas, diseases, etc. New security studies overcomes the state-centricism of traditional analyses, and surveillance is an important part of the study of these new circuits of power, control, and management in the name of security.

20

Urban Insecurity

David Murakami Wood

Varieties of Insecurity

In this chapter, I consider the relationship between insecurity and the city.[1] Previous chapters have dealt with an enormous variety of definitions, forms and objects of security and insecurity. My approach here is multidisciplinary, historical and rooted in a philosophical position holding that all sentient beings should be able to flourish or unfold, to reach a full positive potential (Naess 1989).

Whatever conception of security one uses, insecurity can be argued to be a far simpler concept. For David Roberts (2008), human insecurity is easier to define than human security, and means a focus on avoidable deaths and suffering. Insecurity is clearly negative and connected to material vulnerability. This has its ultimate expression in the miserable state of 'bare life' (Agamben 1998), where nothing more than day-to-day bodily survival is possible and death is ever-present. Richard Ericson (2008: 4) has defined security 'as both safety and a capacity for taking action to secure a better future'. However, contemporary society has also been defined as one in which we live 'with risk' (Beck 2002). Insecurity can thus have any of three aspects: *a state* approaching 'bare life', *a risk* of approaching that state, and *a lack of capacity* to alter either state or risk. This schema recognizes both *actual* material insecurity and *psychic* or *existential* insecurity, which Freud argued was a fundamental feature of human existence (Wolstein 1987).

Urban insecurity is therefore multidimensional. For the purposes of this chapter, I will make a division between two scales: between urban insecurity as the insecurity *of* the city, and insecurity *in* the city. This division is heuristic rather than categorical. As I shall show, in drawing the threads back together, urban insecurity and security are unevenly and inequitably distributed: the insecurity of the city is almost always the insecurity of the poorest and the most marginal in the city before it is anything else.

The Insecurity of the City

Most theories of city formation agree that the origin of cities lies in responses to insecurity. The most basic of these was food insecurity: analysis of ancient Mesopotamian city formation has confirmed the key role of granaries to store surplus grain to protect against the possibility of famine (Reader 2007). Another was insecurity in the face of attack. Defence, exemplified by the 'city wall', or 'enceinte', played an important role in the origins of many, although not all, cities (Tracey 2001; Weber 1921). Of course, these insecurities are also consequences of the existence and success of cities: the city as a walled granary represents a clear target, and the concentration of population means that the effects of natural disasters are as much magnified in scale as mitigated in effect (Mitchell 1999).

However, the contemporary concern with resilience and security takes it for granted that entities *should* persist. This has not been the case throughout history and in all places. Pre-modern worldviews often included an acceptance of the inevitability of change. Later eschatological religious and secular revolutionary ideologies developed more active opposition to cities, demanding the tearing down existing cities in favour of either an anti-urbanist rural idyll or an alternative, 'heavenly' city (Cohn 2001). Often cities have been associated with 'evil', from the biblical Sodom and Gomorrah or the Tower of Babel, through the ambivalent Victorian 'city of dreadful delight' (Walkowitz 1992) to the destruction of New York's World Trade Center by Islamic extremists on 11 September 2001. This perceived immorality has been blamed for many natural disasters, a tendency which only began to decline following the 1755 Lisbon earthquake that saw the rise of more 'scientific' explanations (Dynes 1997).

The Enlightenment saw the origin of the concept of 'progress' and the generation of change as a goal in itself. Insecurity, even disaster, often came to be portrayed as necessary for development and growth: Vale and Campanella (2005) show how disaster can act as a 'stimulus' to encouraging post-disaster innovation and Torrence and Grattan (2002) have gone further and argued that disasters may be fundamental to cultural change.

Natural geological hazards (volcanoes, earthquakes, landslides, tsunamis, floods, hurricanes, etc.) have destroyed or severely damaged many cities (see de Boer and Sanders 2000, 2005; McGuire *et al.* 2000). Earthquakes have been by far the most destructive. Lisbon, which killed up to 300,000 (Chester 2001), might have been the most important in Europe, but the most devastating for cities have all been in China, for example the Shaanxi earthquake (1556) which killed 830,000 people and destroyed several cities. Flooding has been a constant threat to cities in riparian civilizations, particularly Egypt, China, India and the Netherlands, and has been used deliberately in war: the tactical destruction of dykes overwhelmed several southern Chinese cities in 1642 and again in 1938, each attack resulting in the deaths of almost one million people (Heberer and Jakobi 2002).

The annihilation of cities in wars has been relatively frequent. Some city-state cultures developed effective siege tactics, particularly the Assyrians, the Romans, Chinese, and in medieval Europe, increasingly elaborate technologies and rules of siege warfare emerged (Campbell 2006; Tilly 1992). However, stories of razing cities to the ground were often exaggerations or referred only to the destruction of walls or towers (Kern 1999).

The security or insecurity of cities is strongly related to their place in wider political and economic networks. In earlier times, cities flourished only so long as their links to a central authority could be maintained, as in the Eastern Roman Empire after the fall of Rome (Haldon 1999). Where cities were less densely distributed, their fall could lead to civilizational collapse, as in the invasions of the Americas after 1492 (Wright 1992; see also

Chapter 2). The development of 'world systems' from the eleventh century onwards (Abu-Lughod 1993; Braudel 1986) meant individual cities were less vulnerable to some forms of destruction, but also generated new threats. Trading routes intensified disease transmission vectors, transforming outbreaks into pandemics, as in the plagues of the European Middle Ages that wiped out a third of the population of some countries (McNeill 1976).

Cities have, however, tended to become increasingly obdurate. One reason has been the reduction of existential or actual threat, whether through an imposed peace like the *pax Romana* (Owens 1999) or the very success and expansion of cities individually and collectively. However more important for the decreasing insecurity of cities have been changes to technologies and practices of warfare. Geoffrey Parker's 'military revolution' hypothesis (1996) argued that the massive increase in army size and the rapid development of firearms and the development of the *trace italienne* transformed early modern Europe. Better urban defences meant that smaller states could hold out against imperial powers (McNeill 1984), thus shifting wars away from urban sieges to pitched battles (Fuller 1992), and also generating economic pressures for expanding proto-nation-states to look outside of Europe for resources and markets.

However, by the early 1900s, the networks of economic relationships linking cities in the medieval and early modern period had started to become more integrated into a single world system of capitalism (Wallerstein 1989) which before the First World War was dealing in volumes and values of trade that were greater than at any time before or indeed for many years afterwards (Hirst and Thompson 1996). Thus, the 1906 San Francisco earthquake resulted in a regional economic recession that changed both preparation for disaster and the management of the wider economy, leading, for example, to the creation of the Federal Reserve banking system (Odell and Wiedenmeir 2004).

War and disaster remained strongly linked, but the implications were increasingly global. The 1923 Great Kantō Earthquake and fire that struck the largely wooden centre of Tokyo, killing around 140,000, led directly to the US strategy of fire bombing Japanese cities in the Pacific war. US General Billy Mitchell argued that 'these towns are built largely of wood and paper to resist the devastations of earthquakes and form the greatest aerial targets the world has ever seen' (Sherry 1987: 58). Industrial war (Ruttan 2006) meant that cities became targets for destruction from above, first by aircraft, and then by inter-continental ballistic missiles (ICBMs). Moral warnings against the killing of non-combatants began to disappear almost as soon they were formalized. British Conservative Party leader, Stanley Baldwin, warned in 1932 that 'the bomber will always get through', and that 'the only defence is in offence, which means that you have to kill more women and more children more quickly than the enemy if you want to save yourselves' (*Hansard*, 10 November 1932).

This marked a period of renewed insecurity that threatened to overturn the general trend towards urban obduracy and resilience. The terrorization of the civilian population was to be one of the most significant features of war from the 1930s onwards, with the return of sieges (e.g. Stalingrad, Berlin), the threat of annihilation of cities through fire (of Dresden, London, Tokyo and others) and the atomic bomb (Hiroshima and Nagasaki). Abandonment of cities became, once again, a possibility, as H. G. Wells speculated in *The Shape of Things to Come* (1933), with its rationalist defensive vision of cities reconstructed underground. In the post-Second World War period, except in the most secure and neutral nations such as Switzerland, plans for shelter and civil defence were largely abandoned or reduced to pathetic public relations exercises (Campbell 1982; Coaffee *et al.* 2008; Vale 1987) and evacuation and retreat became strategic priorities (McCamley 1988; Vanderbilt 2002). Post-war 'anxious urbanism' partially derailed the optimism of the 1930s skyscraper boom, and prompted the decentralization of military and civil urban functions. For example, Matt Farish (2003) shows how one clear function of the US interstate highway system was to facilitate the mass evacuation of cities.

However, 'Mutually Assured Destruction' (MAD) theoretically meant that no rational government would ever use nuclear missiles (Freedman 2003). For the most part, apart from threatening retaliation, it was as much as any state could do to develop early warning systems of aerial assault (Stocker 2004). Early warning was far from civilian or purely defensive however, and as satellite technologies developed, became more and more connected with strategic purposes and international power-projection to threaten the cities of other nations as much as to defend their own (Richelson 1999).

Insecurity in the City

Just as insecurity has been involved in an intimate relationship with the development of the city as a whole, so it has also been vital within the city. Medieval German patricians might have claimed that 'stadtluft macht frei' (city air makes you free) (Notestein 1968), but cities, as a means of concentrating populations in a space, have also always had the function of social control over otherwise dispersed and therefore potentially unruly people (Mumford 1961). As cities come to dominate the economic as well as the political landscape, they act as magnets attracting increasing numbers of people. They therefore concentrate both relative and absolute poverty, creating new forms of marginality, exclusion and insecurity. The concentration of population also allows politics to develop, citizens to organize and revolt to ferment amongst the disenfranchised and dispossessed, generating fear and insecurity in the ruling classes.

These systems of ordering, or securitization, were often intimately bound up with both war and defence against natural hazards. In the former case, in the famously unwalled ancient Greek city of Sparta, the very existence and increasingly reputed cruelty of the *krypteia* (hidden ones) had a chilling effect on political opponents inside the city as well as being a defence against invasion (Coaffee *et al.* 2008). In the latter, in Tokugawa-period Edo (Tokyo), ordinary people were responsible for dealing with the threat of fire, which also served as an intense, mutual regulation of behaviour (Murakami Wood *et al.* 2007). In medieval Europe, measures to prevent the spread of plague were not designed around medical priorities but 'were aimed at containing the panic, social breakdown and civil disorder which the epidemic threatened to create' (Porter 1999: 37), a process contributing ultimately to the consolidation of power in new national bureaucracies.

In pre-industrial times, with smaller more contained cities, urban authorities were able to identify and control 'outsiders' in the city, often creating special areas for traders. In many places, even more permanently resident outsiders were closely controlled: in Venice, Jews were restricted to the *ghetto nuovo* ('new quarter') from 1516, adding to other non-territorial measures like the compulsory wearing of yellow hats. Ironically, ghettoization gave rise to a greater security for Jews compared to the insecurity of generalized persecution they suffered in other parts of Europe at the time (Ravid 1976). In other places, like China and Japan, it was the separation and control of class and caste distinction that mattered: Beijing was divided concentrically, with walls between different residential and occupational areas, and further more intimately divided with curfews and gated alleyways (Steinhardt 1999).

Such protection of elite interests became even more important as cities grew larger with the rise of industrial capitalism. In the USA, the growing flight of the wealthy to privately constructed suburbs meant that 'the old urban centres increasingly became the domain of newcomers divided by language, religion and tradition, but often united in poverty and a pitiful lack of preparation for urban existence' (Bower 1978: 124). Poor living conditions for the urban working classes throughout the industrial world inevitably gave rise to insecurity, crime, gang warfare, and to massive labour unrest, leading to their characterization by the elite as 'dangerous classes', 'criminal classes' or the 'residuum' (Jones 1971).

Some responses were to deal with this as a problem of moral order (cf. Hunt 1999). In the newly urbanizing USA, this produced movements from temperance and anti-gambling leagues, societies to deal with 'idleness' like the Young Men's Christian Association (YMCA) and model communities (Bower 1978; Smith 1995). However, combining Enlightenment rationalism and absolutist authority (Raeff 1975), new forms of policing also became more important. Initially, these were not much more than a formalized version of the long extant systems of informers (see e.g. Williams 1979, on Paris). These formed the base for more interventionist nineteenth and twentieth century nation-states. In the USA, police were employed to break up the growing numbers of strikes and demonstrations, culminating in the bloody struggle in 1886 at Haymarket Square in Chicago (Smith 1995). In Britain, one of the main and most unpopular roles of the police was to target those already most economically insecure through 'moving on' ordinary people in the street (Taylor 1997). Victorian London was also full of divisions, gates and toll-barriers operated by private police employed by the wealthy elites (Atkins 1993), and the USA, with its 'rugged individualism' and strong private property rights, saw the construction of entirely private streets and neighbourhoods, particularly in the divided cities of the south, like St Louis and New Orleans (Savage 1987).

These developments did not happen in isolation from the rest of the world. The colonies acted as test beds for urban spatial and social order; for the UK in particular, India and Ireland (Palmer 1988; Porter 1987). The British experimented with policing, urban design and prison construction, for example, the rebuilding of Zanzibar (Bissell 2000), the use of fingerprinting for identification in India (Higgs 2004), and the Benthamite colonial prisons of Hong Kong and Singapore that so influenced Meiji-era Japanese prison reformers (Botsman 2005). Prison rapidly replaced outcasting, exile and execution, as the preferred method of punishment here as elsewhere (Foucault 1975).

However, responses to elite insecurity also generated more subtle methods of control. Johann Gottlieb Fichte, wrote in 1796 that 'no one must remain unknown to the police' (Groebner 2007: 229), and although Groebner shows that establishing individual and group characteristics and identity had been a concern for a long time, it started to become far more important at the end of the nineteenth century. The new 'social sciences', aimed at applying natural science methods to the problem of the 'dangerous classes' or newly discovered 'criminals' (Wetzell 2000), ranging from the identification techniques of Alphonse Bertillon in Paris to the attempts to find the 'criminal type' through composite photography of Francis Galton in London (Sekula 1987).

Repression and control always went hand in hand with philanthropy and altruism. As Clive Ponting (1999) argued, the twentieth century was in fact characterized by a seemingly inescapable iteration between striving towards better conditions and the utmost violence. For a while during the twentieth century, and especially during the 'golden age of capitalism' from the 1950s to the early 1970s, with the ending of colonialism and the construction of welfare states, there was an optimism that insecurity might be overcome (Hobsbaum 1994). Norbert Elias's vision of 'the civilizing process' (2000), as the growing mutual interdependence of peoples and the assuaging of fear and insecurity, might be shown to be a living empirical truth.

In contrast, Mumford (1961) argued that as an expression of the insecurity of the sovereign, the city had always tended to a generalized pathology. Whether this was true or not, as war and preparation for war came to dominate the twentieth century, as Zygmunt Bauman astutely remarked, the era was increasingly characterized by 'fast and efficient killing, scientifically designed and administered genocide' (Bauman 1995: 183). Paranoia grew up around the safeguarding of the state, which one can see in a whole range of state activities from the control of trade union activity in the UK in the use of the 1920 Emergency Powers Act (Bonner 1985), through the rise of McCarthyism and internal espionage in the USA (Davis 1992), to the extremes of the gulags of the Soviet Union (Applebaum 2006) and the Nazi regime in Germany (Agamben 2005a).

Contemporary Urban Insecurity

However, the elite insecurities of the Cold War period in the USA also prefigured a new model of order: the 'threats' of communism, civil rights and black radical activism and anti-Vietnam protests, as well as the more diffuse threats to moral order of the 'sexual revolution' and feminism. The moral panic especially after the Watts Riots (Loo and Grimes 2004) generated several responses. One was a new emphasis on architecture and urban design with the idea that crime was something that could be 'designed out', whether through the creation of 'better environments' that would improve moral character or more defensive and repressive schemes (cf. Newman 1972). Another lay in new means to provide an infrastructure for multiple forms of surveillance with proposals for a new central state database of personal information first by President Lyndon B. Johnson, and then again in the 1970s by President Gerald Ford (Solove et al. 2006). This was the basis of the contemporary 'surveillance society' (Lyon 2001) or 'control society' (Deleuze 1990) with the database as its exemplary mechanism that threatened to enable older Fichtean dreams of the 'ideal police state'.

It is at this time that we see a stronger separation between the forms and intensities of insecurities afflicting cities in different parts of the world, with a new form of capitalist development, individualization and privatization that would come to dominate responses to insecurity in the late twentieth and early twenty-first centuries. The new period of post-Fordist capitalism and globalization externalized capitalist class divisions on a global scale, producing massive inequalities and an uncontrolled expansion of cities in the global south that was unprecedented in world history (see Montgomery et al. 2004). Industrialization and the restructuring of the economy on a global scale had made cities increase rapidly in size, further concentrating population and resources, which led to natural events becoming correspondingly more disastrous. Direct destruction tended to be the greater where cities were expanding rapidly onto unsuitable terrain, vulnerable to flooding and landslides, with poor infrastructure and informal settlement with inadequate building standards. This was particularly true of the rapid urbanization that took place in Asia from the 1950s and Latin American and Africa from the 1970s (Mitchell 1999; Montgomery et al. 2004).

For a while, these underlying trends were hidden by the Cold War. However, it became clear soon afterwards that both new forms of insecurity and new forms of urbanism were emerging. For example, from very different disciplinary backgrounds, Scott Lash and John Urry (1994) and Barry Buzan (1999) both adopted a 'two worlds' model to describe security and insecurity in the advanced capitalist, post-Cold War world. Lash and Urry described 'tame and wild zones', whereas Buzan referred to zones of peace and conflict. Crucially, rather than being a simple inside/outside model, both also recognized that these were not separate but what Buzan called 'interleaved zones of living' (Buzan 1999: 10).

This juxtaposition of security and insecurity is crucial to understanding the contemporary urban condition. To compete in a global economy and move up the league table of 'world' or 'global cities' the contemporary city requires openness to flows. External fortification or abandonment and retreat are out of the question, but this does not represent a new era of urban security: the divisions *between* and *within* cities are both sharper and wider than ever before. The interleaved tame and wild zones of living generate socio-economic and physical landscapes at global and urban levels that have been described as 'splintered' (Graham and Marvin 2001) or 'fractured' (Koonings and Kruijt 2007) from both global north and south perspectives.

This is clear with respect to both the insecurity of the city and insecurity in the city. There remain many places some way outside the emerging global networks that have helped make cities in the global north more resilient. The 2003 earthquake that levelled of the city of Bam in Iran was a clear demonstration that, despite the development of earthquake-mitigating building technologies, such developments were not evenly distributed (Bilham 2004). In many cases, it was a co-evolution with, but almost total exclusion from, the global economy, as Pelling (2003) shows of the devastating Payatas landslide of 2000 in Manila. Payatas is not just a site of marginal housing; it is based entirely around the city's garbage dump – merely an extreme example of insecurity generated by marginality in the new global economy.

However, even in the supposedly most advanced nations, cities remain vulnerable to natural hazards. The devastation of New Orleans from flooding resulting from Hurricane Katrina in 2004 could not have provided a clearer example of structural insecurity that came from judgements of risk and value of particular areas and people. As Spike Lee (2006) argued more clearly and directly than anyone else, New Orleans was flooded not only because of its location but also because it was largely poor and black. Similarly it was the poorer areas of the city of Kobe in Japan that were most affected by the great Hanshin earthquake in 1995. Japan, despite all its experience with earthquakes and destruction of its cities and its reputation for social homogeneity and trust, did not develop a workable disaster preparedness law until 1971, and when tested by a real disaster, these laws – and the state – were found wanting (Shaw and Goda 2004).

These modern disasters demonstrated three things. The first was that cities reliant on a state to provide security proved to be riddled with insecurity. The second was that, just as the military revolution helped to 'externalize' European war and economic expansion, so Katrina simultaneously showed the effects of externalizing the economic bads of contemporary inequality and prefigured a future where the environmental profligacy of northern urban lifestyles and consumer capitalism returns with the destructive effects of climate change. However, there is also a more direct link to the politics of risk and conceptions of the relative importance of different types of threat. As Steve Graham (2006a) has argued, Hurricane Katrina demonstrated that the concentration on protecting the asset-rich urban financial centres of world cities from the unlikely and much less deadly threat of terrorism has led to the corresponding relative lack of concern for the fate of the poor, marginal and already insecure.

Garland's influential thesis in *The Culture of Control* claims that late modern capitalism generates 'a generalised insecurity deriving from the precariousness of social and economic relations' (Garland 2001: 133). Hall and Winlow (2005) argue that psychic insecurity is magnified during periods of instability and that economic inclusion is essential for security, thus if the ethic of inclusion is replaced entirely by entrepreneurialism then permanent insecurity results. This however matters less and less to contemporary capital, which has reached a stage where the control of desires and stable communities inhibits growth.

This was perhaps first identified by the studies of Los Angeles in the 1980s and 1990s, particularly by Mike Davis (1998) and Steve Flusty (1994). Los Angeles was seen as exemplary in many ways because of its contradictions: a massive modern metropolis faced with the permanent threat of a devastating earthquake that could wipe it out completely; a city of the global north, with a massive immigrant population from the global south; a playground for neo-liberal capitalism riven with inequalities. Davis identified the key bourgeois activity in this frontier example of neo-liberal urbanism as 'padding the bunker' (1998: 364). This he further described as a paranoid securitizing reflex, characterized by the privatization of public urban space through commercial management, public space video surveillance (CCTV), private security, and gated communities. This was driven by bourgeois moral panic, a generalized sense of insecurity, which expressed itself in things that were felt to be controllable (personal safety) even though the fundamental causes were psychic insecurities generated by the real threat of total devastation.

The relative certainties hoped for by Elias are gone. Dutch architect Lieven De Cauter (2004) divides contemporary fears into six types: first, *demographic fear*, the fear of the human species out of control in its own numbers and its environmental effect on the world; second, *dromophobia*, the fear of the pace of change, or more accurately the fear of being left behind 'left in the wake of acceleration' (p. 119) of the information society; third, *economic fear*, the fear of losing out in the competitive neo-liberal economy; fourth, *xenophobia*, the fear of outsiders, foreigners and 'others'; fifth, *agoraphobia*, the fear of the disintegration of the space of politics at every level from economic globalization to the incivility of public spaces; and finally, the *fear of terrorism*. What is interesting is the rhetorical and policy movement that constantly occurs between these types. Emotive and militarized rhetoric talks of not only the war on terror but a war on drugs, crime, binge-drinking, antisocial behaviour and so on – as Ericson (2008: 208–9) argues, solutions to crime become a 'war on everything' leading to 'the undermining of law as a democratic institution' and 'the unravelling of civil society'. Agamben (2005a) characterized this as the increasing normalization of a 'state of exception'. In a state of exception, everything and every person is a potential threat. This means a constant modulation between the three modes of governance identified by Foucault (Rose 2000): the responsibilitization of moral control, the exposing discipline of surveillance, and the authoritarianism, violence and territorial control of sovereign power.

Even conservative commentators like Hank Savitch (2008: 49) recognize that 'cities are the soft underbelly of an aggressive capitalism' and that the restrictions on civil liberties attack 'freedom of movement, tolerance, and the compatibility of diverse populations' without which 'urban life withers' (ibid., 60). It is thus both the goal of terrorists and the outcome of repressive reactions to generate 'Constant intimidation and fear [which] can wear down civil society' (ibid., 63).

This is supported by many recent empirical studies of crime and urban violence. For anthropologist, Caroline Moser (2004: 3), introducing a special issue of *Environment and Urbanisation* on the subject, urban violence was 'rapidly, dramatically changing', not only in the informal *suburbios* (low income communities) of Ecuador that she has observed for over 20 years but throughout the global south. However, she continues, 'in cities across the world, relentless, "routinized" violence dominates the lives of local populations. The fear of such violence isolates the poor in their homes and the rich in their segregated spaces' (ibid., 13).

In the north, Hogan *et al.* (2005) argue that the circumstances of industrial restructuring of the US and global economy has led to economic insecurity and a sense of 'social threat' that results in a culture of blame of 'others' for the situation. Likewise Hall and Winlow's studies of youth crime in Britain (2005) led them to argue that social insecurity caused by the breakdown of traditional (or at least industrial) class/community solidarities and the rise of hyper-individualized consumer capitalism has led to a kind of instrumental, utilitarian approach to interpersonal relationships. For these people, permanently excluded from the consumerist dream, there is fatalistic acceptance of *total insecurity* as normal, leading to lack of conscience and an acceptance of violence and crime as normal:

> the inhibiting norms that permeated working class cultures in Britain's classical capitalist phase are now being rapidly displaced by the sort of rugged hyper-individualism that is more readily associated with North American culture, and instrumentalism is being enacted in a more radical, non-consequential and ruthless manner by individuals who feel trapped.
>
> (Hall and Winlow 2005: 40–1)

Psychic insecurities may be to some extent shared, but material vulnerabilities are not. One can contrast the terrible situation of the poor of Medellin in Colombia (McIlwaine and Moser 2007), the new ghettos of Chicago (Wacquant 2008), or the banlieus of France (Body-Gendrot 2003) with the incredible growth of the secured, gated communities of Sao Paulo (Caldeira 2000), or even whole new towns and cities where it is guaranteed that only 'people like you' will be allowed to live. These are the nostalgic 'retroscapes' (Brown and Sherry 2005) or 'dreamworlds' (Davis and Monk 2007) of places like Celebration or Seaside, or whole new walled cities to house the emerging elites in India, whose residents' only experience of the poor will be their fleeting daily contact with bussed-in servants generating an entirely unreal social imaginary that appears to be unable to appreciate the reality of life outside (see e.g. Shukla 2008). Of course, there are those still more marginal: those cast out into Agamben's 'bare life', the limbo of refugee and resettlement camps, detention and transit centres, never truly 'inside' (Huysmans 2006).

It could be countered that such studies provide a very strong and perhaps overly pessimistic argument generated by ideological motivations. Some researchers associated with the 'social cohesion' agendas of the European Union in contrast claim that 'urban safety is a very basic precondition for urban economic and social development. Or, to put it negatively, insecurity, caused by whatever factors, seriously hampers it' (Van den Berg *et al.* 2006: 2). They link insecurity largely to fear of crime, and consider its main problem to be not simply the effect on individuals but its effect on what has come to be called 'reputational risk' in the competition for global capital and inward investment. It should also be recognized that security is increasingly being leveraged within neo-liberal urban regeneration agendas, and that increasingly security is part of a place-branding process used to market cities and generate competition between places (Coaffee and Murakami Wood 2006).

Van den Berg *et al.* argue that the biggest problems are the impact of structural political changes (especially in Eastern Europe) and the short-term insecurity that comes with increased freedom and lack of state support; and media-generated misconception and 'sensational stories or robberies, burglaries or even murders' (2006: 277). Fear of crime, they claim, does not reflect reality, 'most cities in this study have safety perceptions that [do] not reflect the actual security situation' (ibid. 268). Drawing on Crawford's (2002) distinction between micro- and macro-level security, they claim that both macro- and micro-insecurity in Europe are decreasing almost everywhere. However better official figures and the 'the safety paradox' of' improving actual security with simultaneously more fear of crime' means that 'in all cities, decreasing crime rates did not lead to improved safety perceptions (yet)' (ibid. 276).

However, the suggested responses in such studies are all too often timid, or amount to weak restatements of the 'broken windows' thesis (Kelling and Wilson 1982). Van den Berg *et al.* argue that a good balance is needed between repressive, preventive and proactive structural changes, yet what they identify as 'proactive' and 'structural' is hardly justifiable as such, in particular the use of CCTV, which they claim based on a study of Glasgow is a 'community resource' (2006: 286). Despite stressing the problem of low economic prospects, the only strong common factors that they identify in all cases are that 'the quality and the maintenance of the built environment and the media appear both to have a large influence on fear of crime in all cities' (ibid. 298).

Hall and Winlow (2005) in complete contrast reject that idea that fear is simply a media-generated image, claiming that in fact that it is a result of the real experience of life lived in conditions of insecurity. It is not that 'fear' is not important, but fear does not create the conditions of actual material insecurity. As 9/11 and Katrina show, contemporary states, urban authorities and the media do not create fear out of nothing, rather they draw on a variety of insecurities, including material insecurity, as resources for governance, which generally does nothing to address the insecurities themselves.

Conclusion

There is a tension at the heart of considerations of urban insecurity between those studies whose object of study is prompted by a more empathic concern for those structurally most at risk, which tend to start from 'vulnerability', and studies of insecurity that emphasize crime and terrorism (Roberts 2008). Particularly, studies of cities in the global south tend to posit insecurity as a more political-ecological concept, involving a multidimensional relationship between people and their environment (Bankoff *et al.* 2004). For these approaches, insecurity is usually qualified by a relationship to 'food', 'water', 'housing', 'employment', 'income' and so on (see Part III). However when 'urban insecurity' is used as a specific term, it more often refers to a lack of security of the person (and of property), and therefore relates more specifically to crime and violence (Crawford 2002).

Roberts (2008: 184), asks:

> How may we reconcile the imbalances in, for instance, the attention paid to terrorism, which kills a few people periodically, and which receives the highest priorities within many western polities, with the attention paid to global impoverishment, which kills millions of people, every year, but which is rejected as a significant security concern?

This chapter has tried to provide some answers. It involves a rejection of the 'cosmic alarmism' (Mueller 2004: 45) of those who argue in the post-9/11 world that civilization is at stake from highly unlikely and infrequent events, such as acts of terrorism. In this sense, it is more the hyperbolized response to terrorism and crime that leads to the creation of feelings of insecurity than the acts themselves. As Mueller argues, 'the constant, unnuanced stoking of fear by politicians and the media is costly, enervating, potentially counterproductive, and unjustified by the facts' (ibid. 46).

The results can be seen in processes as diverse as the privatized reconstruction of Iraqi cities, the massive increase in secure gated communities in cities from Sao Paulo to Tokyo, the popularity of overlarge 'safe' 4×4 automobiles, and publications which link defence against global threats through 'homeland security' right down to personal safety as one continuous spectrum of fear and response (e.g. Safir and Whitman 2003).

Most would agree that security is most effective and acceptable when it involves a mutual and accountable network of civic institutions, agencies and individual citizens working towards common goals within a framework of democratic and accountable government (Pelling 2003). As Richard Ericson (2008: 219) concludes, we need 'conditions of trust, in which people are allowed to be themselves, experiment with the boundaries of acceptable behaviour, take risks, and make mistakes, without fear of exclusions as the criminal other when things go wrong'. However, in the current state of structural inequality, defensive isolationism and rejection of human empathy that this encourages, this seems an unlikely prospect.

Note

1 This chapter draws heavily on work I did with Jon Coaffee and Peter Rogers for an ESRC New Security Challenges project, *The Everyday Resilience of the City*, and the book of the same name (Coaffee *et al.*, 2008), however the considerations and mistakes here are entirely my own and do not reflect the views of my co-investigators.

21

Commercial Security Practices

Anna Leander

Introduction

The significance of commercial security practices is no longer news. The death of 17 civilians shot by Blackwater employees in Nisour Square Baghdad in September 2007, the diffusion of the Aegis 'trophy' video showing firm employees shooting at random while 'driving in Iraq' in 2004, the involvement of TITAN and CACI employees in the abuse of Abu Ghraib inmates in 2003–4, or the role of Executive Outcomes in the Sierra Leone civil war 1995–6 are only some of the many spectacular events that have drawn attention to the growing role of commercial security practices in international security. Security commercialization has changed from being a rather obscure issue to being a highly publicized political bone of contention. Policy-makers, NGOs, journalists, lawyers and academics strive to impose an understanding of commercial security, its problems and their possible solution. The result is an explosion in publications, including filmed documentaries and other media reports, about security commercialization. Voices from all political and academic horizons are striving to draw attention to the issues and questions they find most significant and pressing with regard to the development of security.

This chapter gives an overview of the resulting cacophony. It cannot pretend to cover everything in equal detail. It is geared to highlight the parts of the discussion about commercial security practices that are of most immediate interest to new security studies. Very succinctly put, the chapter shows the pertinence of the emerging research agenda where commercial security practices are part of a broader analysis of evolving insecurities, of (in) security spaces and of everyday practices, insisting on the scope for further developments with regard to these issues. The chapter also suggests that, although the more conventional literature on the subject—mostly framed in terms of privatization—has made valuable contributions to the debates about commercial security, it has limited analytical clout for analyzing the politics of commercial security. Worse it sometimes obscures it. It is therefore not surprising that commercialization is currently tending to replace privatization as the vantage point from which analysis is taking place.

From Privatization of Security to Commercial Security Practices

The end of the Cold War ushered in a profound change in the role of commercial security. Although private firms had had important roles in arms production, logistics and even security provision, the magnitude of their presence increased exponentially. The peace dividend the reduction of military expenditure was expected to generate with the end of the Cold War was channeled into the emerging market and kept it growing. In the process, the roles firms took on changed. Military training and consultancy, intelligence and planning were outsourced to degrees unthinkable during the Cold War. But perhaps the most significant change is that military firms were increasingly expected to behave as private-sector firms, to compete in markets and make a profit (Kaldor *et al.* 1998; Markusen *et al.* 2003; Susman and O'Keefe 1998). This entailed detachment from the state. Although this process is still incomplete and patchy—many firms remain closely tied to states and states weigh heavily on the markets—a global market for force has developed. In this market private business is *private,* acting for commercial reasons and not merely as extensions of their home states. The process of 'discovering' this market has been a gradual one, driven by a practical need to respond to the challenges of the market and an academic concern with its implications for the future of the state.

Security Privatization as a Practical Challenge

Not only NGOs, academics, and lawyers but also the policy-makers, administrators, and security professionals have come discuss security privatization largely in response to the practical challenges it poses. Three recurring challenges dominating the debate are introduced here.

A first practical challenge has been (remains) to get basic knowledge about the private-security sector, to get a grasp of how big it is, what activities firms engage in, where, and why. There has been a striking shortage of adequate information about the private military/security sector. Estimates, more akin to wild guesses, have circulated and been used to convey the rapid expansion and growth of the market. The private military sector reportedly doubled in size between 1990 and 1999 ($55 to $100 bn) and is expected to double again by 2010 (reaching $200 bn). The increased ratio of contractors to US soldiers is another figure often brandished to drive home the point. It said to have been 1:60 in the 1991 Gulf war and to have become 1.3:1 in Iraq 2007. The guess work in these figures is considerable. The overall industry figures are produced without a clear understanding of the boundaries of private military/security and based on figures that neither firms nor states are interested in providing. Figures about soldier:contractor ratios are just as uncertain. Most states do not publish information on contractors (most do not collect that information) and even when they do (as the USA has started to) these figures do not include the contractors that are hired (subcontracted) by contractors or hired by firms, international organizations, NGOs, or journalists. Considering the debilitating effects of this lack of clarity about the nature, scope, and activities of the private military/security market for any practical engagement with the market, it is far from surprising that much energy has gone into raising awareness about privatization and simply documenting commercial military/security or an aspect thereof. The numerous reports and books striving to reveal private security, to show its origins, spell out the range of its activities, and create awareness of its implications are attempting to fill this lacuna (Rasor and Bauman 2007; Scahill 2007; Singer 2003; Shorrok 2007; Pelton 2006).

A second practical challenge that has been central in the discussion of security privatization is the role of managing and controlling economic efficiency. The promise of increased effectiveness, of diminished red tape and possibly even of more proficient and professional soldiering played no small part in motivating the turn to commercial military/security; checking whether this promise is realized has been correspondingly important. This is true in the journalistic world but also inside public institutions and in academia. Markusen (2003) criticizes the criteria and information used compare public and private military service providers. She shows that the while the private sector enjoys a strongly positive bias which makes it possible to turn failure into exception and to use anecdotal examples as evidence of success, public service providers suffer an inverse fate. But more than this, their costs are systematically ignored as is the role played by social and political rules established for good reasons in creating the 'lack of flexibility' of they stand accused. Similarly, exploring and deploring the deficiencies in the management of contracts and the perverse consequences of this in terms of costs incurred to the public and damage done to the armed forces is central in the work of Rasor and Bauman. With regard to the USA, the possibly most informative source in this regard is the discussion inside state institutions and particularly the reports of the GAO (government accountability office), the Congressional hearings on contracting, and the reports issued by DoD. Regretably no other country publishes comparable information, which does not mean that they do not outsource or that there are no problems.

Finally, the practical challenge of legal accountability has taken on a pivotal role in the debate. There has been a 'mad scramble' to bring private companies to justice (Kierpaul 2008). First, there is a prolific production of scholarly articles debating how private companies may be held responsible for their impact in war zones – in particular for their treatment of civilians – under international human rights law (Coleman 2004; Human Rights First 2008) or under alternative regulations, including military regulations, self-regulation or the development of international standards (Chesterman and Lehnardt 2007). In practice companies still benefit from a 'culture of impunity' (War on Want 2007; Leander 2007). The concerted efforts by the International Committe of the Red Cross (ICRC) and Swiss government to alter this by pushing through the adoption of the Montreux Document (2008)—encouraging states to shoulder their International Human Rights Law obligations—signal a growing political willingness to tackle this problem. Second, the accountability of the firms towards their employees is receiving attention. Blackwater's responsibility towards its employees who were lynched and burnt in Fallujah as well as the court case against the company in relation to a helicopter crash killing three of its employees in Afghanistan epitomize a trend which is also being extended to cover the fate of employees from 'third countries' such as Namibia, Tanzania, Peru, Columbia or the Phillipines (UN Working group reports). Third and finally, the relations between the military and the market raise a range of accountability issues. The extent to which market actors are accountable to the military—for example, the extent to which they have to deliver services and obey orders independently of the conditions—is unsettled. Contractors are ruled by contracts usually allowing them to stay out of 'harm's way' but they are also an integral part of military operations (Zamparelli 1999). Inversely, whether or not the military can be held accountable for the fate of contractors, and has an obligation to devote resources to protect them, remains unsettled.

Reactions to the practical challenges of security privatization are bound to remain essential in reflections about security privatization. So far they constitute the bulk of the literature on the topic and provide invaluable insights. Without interest in tackling practical challenges we would hardly know anything about military/security privatization.

Security Privatization and the Transformation of States

As awareness of military/security privatization has increased the discussion has slowly made its way into academic political science and international relations (IR). The time is past when a senior Harvard scholar could answer a PhD student who wanted to write on the topic that it was suited for fiction and fantasy but hardly for academic work. The statism in IR and political science combined with the focus on *privatization* means that the resulting scholarly production has concentrated on the question of how privatization transforms states. Three key themes from this scholarship are introduced below.

The first and overarching theme is the general question of how military/security privatization affects the 'state monopoly on the legitimate use of force' (the SMLF). This question has become central because the SMLF is integral to the conceptualization of the modern state in political science/IR. In the sociological tradition of Weber, Elias, or Tilly it defines it. Discussing transformations of the SMLF therefore amounts to nothing less than to discussing changes in what the state is and what can be expected from it. Singer's (2003) pioneering work covered or hinted at many of the key ensuing issues that have later been discussed in detail elsewhere. Amongst other things it brings up the question of the implications of privatization for the global balance of power, for the balance between civil and military institutions at home and for the morality/ethics of warfare. Singer's conclusion is fairly straightforward: the SMLF is transforming profoundly but not disappearing. This conclusion is echoed by most scholars who have subsequently worked on the SMLF (Avant 2005; Krahmann 2007; Leander 2006). Scholars focusing on long-term transformation emphasize that the transformations are overstated and instead underline the stability of norms (Lynch and Walsh 2000; Percy 2007) and/or the historicity of the market (Milliard 2003). However, few deny that, taking the modern state and international state system as a reference point (i.e. not going back further than the 1850s), the surge in commercial activity since the end of the Cold War is a transformation.

This acknowledgment of transformation however merely raises a whole new range of issues about the extent and implications of the transformation of the SMLF. Two issues in particular have galvanized scholars. The first is the extent to which the transformation of the SMLF also entails a substantive change in politics inside states. It has for example been asked whether or not privatization alters the way that policy agendas are set (Leander 2005b), the way security policy is carried out and hence the provision of public security (Leander 2005a; Cockayne 2006; Spearin 2008) or the way democratic processes function (Avant 2007; Verkuil 2007). The second issue where concern is raised is whether or not privatization is altering the politics among states in the international system in significant ways. Does privatization make states more militaristic and war prone? For some it is clear that the market is merely a tool in the hands of the state (Shearer in *Cambridge Review* 1998), for others it is the sine qua non of contemporary militarism (Tiefer 2007). Or does privatization reshuffle hierarchies among states? Again answers vary. While some scholars have suggested that the market can be used by weak states to strengthen and develop their military forces (Howe 2001), critical voices have suggested that private markets open the way for new forms of decentralized imperialism weakening the weakest states (Francis 1999; Leander 2009; Musah 2002). The questions are clearly essential and the literature on security privatization has made an important contribution to public debate by raising them.

However at the same time, the literature on privatization has serious shortcomings that explain the importance of replacing the privatization terminology with a commercialization (or commodification) one. The most serious of these shortcomings is that the privatization terminology tends to underrate – not to say obscure – key political processes. Logically, in a discussion framed in terms of privatization there is a tendency to look for 'privatization' – i.e. shifts from a public to a private sphere. But this distracts attention from the most pressing political questions raised by privatization/commercialization. It is increasingly clear that the possibly most significant changes triggered by privatization/commercialization have little to do with shifts from the public to the private and much more to do with ways in which commercialization shapes how security is understood, how security spaces are delimited, and how security is practiced in public *and* private institutions. Commercialization matters mainly because of the shifts in substantive politics that span the public–private realms (Krahmann 2007; Leander 2003; Abrahamsen and Williams 2007). There is consequently an emerging research agenda where the focus of the discussion shifts as the discussion is framed in terms of commercialization and integrated with the broader 'new' or 'critical' security agenda.

Emerging Research Agendas and Issues

Instead of pitting the development of commercial security against the state—as the privatization terminology does—there is a growing strand of research conceptualizing it within a broader framework of societal change. From this perspective the commercialization of security should be read as part of the deepening of liberal or neo-liberal forms of government. Governance increasingly takes decentralized forms working through quasi-markets, distribution of responsibility, and empowerment. States rely on firms as partners in government. This is true of security governance where (at least in the EU) the public wish to set up such partnerships surpasses the willingness of private military/security actors to engage in them (Dorn and Levi 2007). More generally this is driven by the centrality of risk. Individuals and companies are expected to insure against risk, for example by acquiring protection in the open market. From this perspective it is inadequate to pit military markets against states and weight their significance by looking at their impact on the SMLF. To capture salience of these developments requires displacing attention from privatization and fixing it on the consequences of governing security through markets and quasi-markets. The literature on military/security privatization is taking this direction, as signaled by the focus on commercial practices and commodification. Simultaneously, scholars working on new and critical security approaches are beginning to integrate commercial practices in their work. Three themes emerging from the resulting research are introduced below: the commercial production of new insecurities, the commercial refashioning of security spaces, and the commercial everyday security practices.

Commercial Insecurities

One emerging theme is the study of how commercialization is (re)shaping the way (in)security is understood. This reflection is feeding into analysis of how (in)security is constructed, not necessarily through speech acts establishing it as an existential threat warranting emergency measures (Copenhagen School securitization) but also and more generally through practices, including routine practices, that frame specific issues as security issues and hence justify possibly equally routine like measures (Paris School securitization). Military/security commercialization might be expected to have implications for both types of construction of insecurities. It is hence being integrated in the study of these.

First, commercialization could be expected to alter both who is engaged in (speech act type) securitization and how. Private commercial military/security experts have established themselves as interlocutors in debates about insecurity and protection. As research on intelligence transformation testifies, private companies have established themselves as key sources not only of information but of analysis and agendas (Shorrok 2007). This raises the question about the extent to which commercial actors and markets have to be integrated in the study of securitization discourses. Are there new authorized speakers? Is there a need to move from the discourses of foreign ministers and high politics to one that includes markets? More than this, does the heavy presence of commercial actors change the way that securitization discourses work and hence demand revisions of the literature on the processes of securitization? Does an understanding of the Austinian 'felicity conditions' of securitizing speech acts increasingly pass through an understanding of the commercial security sector? Does commercialization tend to tilt the balance away from an emphasis on national interests and politics towards arguments about cost–effectiveness and feasibility? Research on these issues is emerging (Leander 2005b) but much work is needed to elaborate, contextualize, and refine understandings and arguments.

Second, commercialization might be expected to alter routine practice type securitizations. Not primarily because private security professionals are fundamentally more sanguine, more conspiring or less ethical than public ones. Security professionals more often than not share the same the training and professional background and the call on who is the most ethical and least conspiring is still open (Lynch and Walsh 2000; Singer 2007). However, as the broader literature on neo-liberal governance forms has persuasively shown for other areas, the shift in form and rationale of government also entails often unarticulated reshuffling of political priorities and aims as actors have to adjust their practices to suit new rules and requirements. How exactly this plays out in the security sphere is unchartered terrain. It has been argued that commercialization increases the pressure on public and private security professionals alike (as well as on all those in the enmeshed sphere where the two merge) to 'sell' their own message about insecurity and appropriate responses to an ever expanded number of potential clients/investors. As commercial indicators were introduced to govern armed forces and military/security in the wake of the cold war, both logically intensified their selling, striving to conquer new 'markets' for themselves. The consequence was a militarization of new geographic areas of the world (and especially of the NICs and China). It was also a militarization of new areas of public life as military technologies, techniques and knowledge were extended and adapted to new commercial employments. These processes have been traced for example in work on policing and justice (Haggerty and Ericson 1999; Haggerty and Ericson 2006). However, this work is more of a pointer in the direction of a vast potential area of research which is just beginning to emerge.

Most questions regarding the way commercial military/security alters (expands?) routine-based securitization across contexts and the reshuffling of political priorities and aims resulting from this still remain unanswered. The same can of course be said about the theme of the links between securitization and speech act type securitizations. In fact, one can see the two remaining emerging research themes partly as attempts to grapple with different aspects of these issues.

Commercial Security Spaces

The second emerging research theme where commercialization has entered directly into contact with new and critical security studies is in relation to its centrality for the reconfiguration of security spaces. Commercialization has been pulled into thinking about the processes through which boundaries and borders are produced and managed, i.e. about the way identities are stabilized and subjectivities produced. Commercialization plays a role in defining why and how some people become threatening outsiders while others are embraced as protection-worthy insiders.

Along these lines, the commercialization of security has been tied to the transformation of the practices upholding, managing and producing territorial borders. It has been suggested that commercialization is key in altering everything about territorial borders. At the most banal level it has altered who is engaged in ensuring that the border is respected. Private companies are hired into airports, border-crossings and checkpoints to take over context-defined parts of the border controls. This has altered how border controls are carried out and managed as new technologies to control travellers—profiling, biometric controls, data-mining and blacklists—and to control the controllers have altered who is likely to experience difficulties crossing a border and who is not. But more than this, policing the border has become largely separate from the state. Transport companies and in particular air and shipping companies shipping are held responsible through a range of (contextually varying) regulations for securing that the migrants they carry are 'legal' (Giraudon 2001; Salter 2008a). As these studies show, this change in who implements the border has entailed a change also in the practical exercise of authority; the decision to carry a person or not (and hence to grant access or refuse it) rests with a commercial actor. By the same token it has entailed a de-politicization of the criteria; actual decision-making is drifting outside the public sphere. Finally, it has changed the geographical location of the border as control is increasingly off-shored and de-territorialized (Gammeltoft-Hansen 2009).

The effects of commercialization on the production and upholding of the borders between social groups may be just as far-reaching. An explicit and key aspect of liberal thinking is that markets work effectively in part because they create incentive structures rewarding individuals who are efficient. The positive valuation of inequality implied has been amply discussed across politics in a variety of areas. With regard to the commercialization of security it has been showed to alter the practices of security professionals and to create justificatory discourses that, taken together, have profound implications for who can claim and expect to get what kind of security. Studies of the evolving urban security spaces where gated communities coexist with no-go zones have suggested that a deepening gap between insiders and outsiders rigidifies in time as the boundaries become increasingly difficult to cross (Bislev 2004). Analogous points have been made with regard the effects of commercializing the management of crime and punishment more generally (Harcourt 2006; Zedner 2006). The consequence is a redrawing but also a hardening of the boundaries between individuals cast as social insiders and those cast as social outsiders. This is a process with ramifications far beyond the national community as it directly feeds into the view of minorities, immigrants and migration in general. It is part and parcel of producing the 'ban-opticon' (a governance *dispositif* of bans, restrictions, and prohibitions) Bigo (2008a) suggests is increasingly central for governance in the contemporary world.

These explorations of how commercial security practices are refashioning security spaces are far from complete. There is ample scope for further work refining and differentiating our understanding of the processes at work in different contexts. More than this, thinking about strategies that might increase critical awareness of the role of commercialization in boundary-drawing processes is still sparse. Yet for practical reasons, including for example to protect the rights of travellers, or of football hooligans, it is vital to update the understanding of the location and underlying assumptions that govern the practices defining these spheres. Perhaps even more important, increasing awareness of the role of commercial practices in shaping boundary-drawing processes may be crucial for anyone striving to engage in the politics questioning these processes; that is, in politics regarding the inside/outside in the widest sense.

Commercial Everyday Security Practices

Finally, a third theme of research emerging from the current research on commercial security practices concerns the link between these practices and everyday (security) practices in different groups, including security professionals, public administrators, but also the private individual and citizen.

The consequence of commercialization on the institutional culture of security professionals (police and armed forces) is for example an issue of major importance that is beginning to receive attention among military sociologists and beyond. Some have taken the view that commercialization and the involvement of public security professionals in the market is most likely to lead to the spread of the prevailing public values and culture in the market as the actors there comply with a 'logic of appropriateness' (Avant 2005). However, there are good reasons to think that the processes are less straightforward. The market may well be developing its own professional security culture where customer service and contract fulfilment make choices by public and private security officials differ substantially. For example, the Blackwater employees killing 17 civilians in Nisour Square, Iraq (September 2007) clearly attached less importance to 'winning hearts and minds' and more to protecting their client than the American soldiers subsequently criticizing their behaviour. Even further, it has been argued that market culture (rather than public culture) might become the 'logic of appropriateness' fashioning the attitudes and behaviour of security professionals (Leander 2006, 2008). The consequence of this for issues as diverse as gender roles in the armed forces, the professional military ethos or the inscription of these changes in a broader social and political context remains all but unexplored. This discussion about changes in the everyday practices of security professionals and its consequences is no more than incipient. There is a blatant need for a better and contextualized understanding of these processes as they are bound to vary as much as does the culture of security professionals and commercialization.

This comment also pertains to the emerging research where the commercialization of security practices is brought into the study of everyday security practices in the broad public. First, commercialization has gone in parallel with the spread of images 'branding' issues as security issues and 'marketing' especially designed solutions to security problems. The consequence is a diffuse reshaping of visual culture. The development of video games, integrating pictures from real battles, and used both for simulation in the armed forces and sold on the open market (Der Derian 2001; Lenoir 2000) might be expected to contribute significantly to the 'militarization of visual culture' explored by for example Campbell and Shapiro (2007). Similarly, commercialization might be expected to be driving the designing of security into everyday practices (Weber and Lacy this volume). However, far more work needs to be done on these links and their significance. In addition, commercialization has engendered a wide range of new governance mechanisms – such as surveillance equipment, reporting schemes and bench-markings and risk-related concepts—that are promoted as providing protection against various risks. These mechanisms profoundly refocus everyday practices on security in areas as diverse as financial markets and local government (de Goede 2008a; Power 2007). Again, contextually anchored analysis of these processes is key to an assessment of the increasing role of security in everyday practices beyond the security sphere proper.

Conclusion

The privatization or commercialization (as this chapter suggests we should say) of security has been the subject of considerable scholarly, journalistic and media work. This chapter has sketched out some of the key debates and arguments. It has insisted first on the centrality of the practical challenges of understanding the market and sorting out accountability issues and, second, on the transformation of statehood. These two issues are usually framed in terms of privatization. However, the limits of this framing for understanding substantive changes in politics (as opposed to statehood) has led to a trend focusing on understanding the commercialization and commodification of security. This research agenda meets the new security research agenda as it feeds into discussions about the formation of (in) securities, the boundaries of (in)security spaces and about everyday (in)security practices. Like any sketching or 'overview' this one is simplifying. However, the intention with this simplification has emphatically not been to close down inquiry by suggesting that the issues have been exhaustively or satisfactorily covered. On the contrary, a very explicit effort has been made to underline the opposite, namely that there is plenty of work to be done and that most questions are still either unanswered or profoundly contested. By way of conclusion, it is appropriate to follow this up with an insistence that there are certainly innumerable important issues and questions that have not been given any space at all in this chapter. If the chapter has triggered awareness of such issues, it has done well.

22

Migration and Security

William Walters

Introduction

In this chapter I engage with a relatively new literature that has challenged the increasing tendency both within scholarship and public life more broadly to regard migration as a self-evident security problem. Identifying this literature as critical studies of migration-security, I examine how it poses a series of important questions: under what circumstances, with what effects and at what political and ethical cost does migration come to be framed and governed as a security issue rather than, say, a question of labour or cosmopolitical responsibility? Following a brief discussion of the relationship which critical studies bears to conventional approaches, the chapter observes that at least two strands can be identified within this critical perspective. I distinguish these as discursive and material-semiotic approaches. The chapter offers an assessment of some of the major accomplishments of critical approaches to migration-security. But it argues that, for all its obvious merits, critical scholarship has overlooked important work, both within migration studies and in other areas of the social sciences, work that could considerably enrich its critical project. I highlight three themes where the notion of the securitization of migration could be enhanced by forging closer connections to ongoing work in adjacent fields. These are: historical studies of the policing of mobility; critical studies of race, migration and postcoloniality; and geographies and sociologies that are charting new territories of power and governance.

Critical Studies of Migration-Security

Migration and security: the words seem to run together. They possess a certain mutual affinity and cohabit rather naturally. Like law and order, or peace and stability, they seem to belong together. One only needs to substitute democracy for security to realize this. Somehow the phrase 'migration and democracy' has a dissonant, jarring effect.[1] The terms are less commonly coupled. What possible connection could they have? Not so with migration and security. It's almost as though, like the proverbial happy couple, they were made for each other.

Why do migration and security seem to belong together, whether uttered in the context of political speeches by politicians (who would probably speak of *im*-migration and security), or by scholars and experts in security studies? What accounts for the existence today of this thing I shall be calling the migration–security nexus? One set of responses comes from the intellectual heartland of international relations (e.g. Adamson 2006; Rudolph 2003). Here it is observed that a whole series of elements and transformations have recently combined with the outcome that migration has been rendered as a security issue in a way that it was not before, at least not before the early 1990s. A typical rendering of these transformations would go something like this.

Globalization has changed the world. On the one hand it has meshed societies and economies ever closer together on a worldwide basis, set vast flows of investment, goods, ideas and images in circulation at dizzying speeds, and ended forever the possibility that states will function again as containers of their populations. But the global world is also a risky world, scarred with numerous regional instabilities and zones of disorder. With the fall of the Berlin Wall has come an upsurge in interethnic conflicts, civil wars and state implosions. It has generated refugees as well as impoverished persons scouring the world for work; often the two are blurred. Once this is coupled with the fact of the growing ease of movement and communication which globalization creates, it is not hard to see why there has been a dramatic increase in human movement. Globalization has placed the state in a new kind of environment, one in which it is seeking to recruit labour in its bid to remain competitive, but anxious about the kinds of threats that can move amidst these flows. The attacks of 9/11 are then read within this narrative as testament to the 'dark side' of globalization. They speak to the possibility that has for some time been debated amongst security experts, namely that this new global world has two faces: a world of benefits and opportunities, but also one that offers all manner of potential for fluid forms of crime, trafficking, drugs and terrorism. All of this has posed a new kind of security challenge for Western states. Read in this light, the migration–security nexus is nothing other than the expression of the state's response to this new situation, a situation where the gravest threats to the state and its population come not from enemy armies or rival geopolitical blocs but from these new flows, diffuse networks and mobile dangers.

But there is a second line of response to this question of migration-security. This response is far less inclined to accept the presumption that is embodied in the admittedly crude caricature I have just presented. This is the presumption that there is anything inevitable or necessary in the fact that migration has come to be widely perceived and governed as a matter of security. Whereas conventional international relations perceives migration-security as a *reaction* on the part of states to new situations and threats in their 'environment', this second position insists that we are facing not a general phenomenon but a particular social and political *construction* of migration in which, for complex reasons, migration is represented as a 'threat'. We are faced with a situation in which a whole series of dangers and fears come to find embodiment in the social figure of the immigrant, the refugee, the human smuggler, etc. By extension, the whole raft of measures now in place to police various spaces, expressions and flows of migration – from biometric passports to citizenship tests – only appear legitimate once this prior construction of migration is accepted. The problem for this critical perspective is not that identified by conventional approaches, namely how to design better security policies, or how to 'balance' security policies with other policy objectives such as free(r) trade and respect for human rights.

MIGRATION AND SECURITY

Instead, it is the recognition that the security perspective, deeply institutionalized as it is in this apparatus of control and advanced by innumerable vested interests, actually obstructs and marginalizes the space in which other imaginations and a different politics of migration might take shape. Security policy, in other words, is not the answer but the problem. For it impoverishes our ability to fashion a society that might actually overcome the debilitating dualisms which plague the present, binaries like us/them, national/foreigner, citizen/ illegal, worker/scrounger, etc.

It is this second line of investigation that interests me in the remainder of this chapter. It is this body of work which, it seems to me, can justly be associated with the idea of 'new security studies'. But while the above captures the broad outlook of critical approaches to migration-security, there are, it goes without saying, significant differences. For the purposes of exposition I propose to group critical approaches of migration-security into two broad families: discursive perspectives and material-semiotic perspectives. This is not a hard and fast distinction. There is a great deal of work that blurs this boundary, just as certain writers have moved back and forth across what is a permeable and in some ways fuzzy boundary. But for purposes of analysis this is a useful distinction to make. I shall deal first with discursive approaches.

Discursive Approaches

By a discursive approach to migration-security I mean studies which direct our attention to the particular ways in which migration comes to be represented within popular and official discourses, such as political debates and speeches or media frames. Discursive approaches insist that representation is not merely reflective but a set of active, performative, constitutive and productive processes. Hence we need to follow the ways in which 'immigration' is figured through representational processes into something dangerous, threatening, alarming and so on. A particularly influential example of this kind of work is provided by Wæver and his colleagues – retrospectively labelled as the 'Copenhagen School' – in their theorization of 'securitization' (Wæver 1995; Wæver et al. 1993). In this work securitization is modelled as a speech act. Whereas conventional and classical approaches treat security as a given threat that is immanent to the real world, whereas they make the understanding of that threat their central objective, securitization theory insists that it is the act of rendering something as a threat that should be treated as the site of investigation. Security is not a thing, a stable referent, but a practice. It is a way of framing things in ways that usually dramatize an issue and demand that it receives the utmost political priority and attention.

But in addition to Wæver's notion of speech acts, other theories and methodologies of discourse analysis have been important in studying the securitization of migration. These include Laclau and Mouffe's analysis of hegemonic formations and signifying chains (Buonfino 2004), Edelman's notion of symbolic politics (Ceyhan and Tsoukala 2002), and the work of Judith Butler and Homi Bhabha which sees discourse as a site of performativity (Doty 1996b). One aspect of securitization is the objectification of the migrant as one who has no political subjectivity. Hence special mention should be made of work that has developed Rancière's themes of disagreement and interruption to examine particular situations when the 'object' interrupts the security discourse and, through acts of political demonstration, claims a kind of political subjecthood, even a quasi-citizenship (Nyers 2003).

219

Discursive approaches reveal that the social construction of migration is actually quite complex. Certainly one sees negative and racialized strereotypes which 'other' the migrant, construing them as threats to hallowed institutions of national life, or a drain on scarce space and welfare resources. But there are other instances where the migrant is cast closer to the pole of victimhood, hence as a violated and often feminized subject who merits certain forms of protection from political authorities. This is especially clear in feminist and post-structuralist research into the discourse of 'anti-trafficking' (Andrijasevic 2007; Aradau 2004; Berman 2003). Such research shows how 'human trafficking' operates as a gendered site where 'illegal immigration', sex and crime are sutured together, and where the state will be performed as a protective, humanitarian agent. One conclusion to be drawn is that a range of contradictory identities circulate within the discursive field of migration: it is hence a field marked by considerable ambivalence (Ceyhan and Tsoukala 2002).

Discursive approaches have contributed many important insights into the phenomenon of migration-security. But if there is one I would single out for special attention it is the observation that it is not only the identity, and consequently the fate of the migrant that is at stake within these representational processes. Equally, it is the very identity of the state and the political community which is being (re)made (Doty 1996b). For any controversy about the presence of migrants in a particular society, their impact upon the culture, or about the challenge which migrant flows pose for the state, is invariably an occasion when the meaning and the boundaries of society, culture, sovereignty and much else besides come to be politically defined in particular ways. The 'us' is being manufactured at the same time as the 'them'. Perhaps Huysmans put it best when he observed that: 'Security policy is a specific policy of mediating belonging' (2000: 757).

A Material-Semiotic Turn?

If discursive approaches were among the first to challenge the hegemony of epistemological realism, and to explore the politics embedded in security practices, they are no longer alone. It is now possible to discern a second wave of research which has also taken up the theme of the securitization of migration. This is what I am calling material-semiotic approaches. I borrow this term from science and technology studies where it is used by scholars who refuse the ontological separation between the ideal and the material, discourses and institutions, and insist on the need to think of regimes and arrangements that are simultaneously material *and* semiotic (e.g. Law 2007). Taking a material-semiotic approach to migration-security entails that we cannot confine our analyses to the planes of speech, symbolism and language. Representational practice has to be studied in terms of its imbrication within a range of different practices that are not reducible to the linguistic model.

Just what these other practices are, of course, varies quite considerably. In a series of influential papers Bigo has demonstrated the benefits of connecting Foucauldian discourse and governmentality analyses to the kind of field analysis inspired by Bourdieu (Bigo 2001, 2002; see also Huysmans 2006). This means one has to take organizational practices very seriously: in his case the institutional and bureaucratic matrices (media, party politics, security agencies, etc.) within which discourses of in/security are generated. It means we must pay close attention to the dynamics of inter- and intra-agency competition which shape particular strategies and productions of migration as a security domain. Other researchers have focused the study of securitization around quite banal technological and technocratic practices operating in specific locales. These include the deployment of particular identification and authentication practices like passports and digital fingerprinting which attempt to fix identity in very material ways (Muller 2004; van der Ploeg 2005); technologies of human detection like the scanners that are marketed as security 'solutions' for the problem of stowaways in shipping containers (Verstraete 2001); the organizational and logistical planning of airport spaces (Salter 2008b); and the design of official forms and other inscription devices used to count and differentiate acts of border-crossing (Inda 2006; Walters 2002).

This turn towards the material-semiotic implies not so much a displacement as a broadening and reworking of discursive approaches. This move has enhanced the explanatory power of critical approaches. There are three points to be made in this regard. First, this reconsideration of discourses in relation to the space of institutions and technologies goes some way to explaining the durability of securitized framings of migration. For example, why is it that states persist with the militarization of borders as a 'solution' to illegal immigration, despite a great deal of anecdotal and scientific evidence pointing to the 'failure' of such policies. It is not just because of the potency and intrinsic threat value of the image of the illegal border-crosser, nor the functionality of illegalized and therefore highly vulnerable subjects to flexibilized regimes of capitalism. A material-semiotic approach would point in addition to the range of professional and bureaucratic actors, but also, for example, makers of surveillance hardware, who have a stake in this regime. As many politicians as much as retailers of detection machinery would no doubt recognize: whole careers can be built on the dual move that with one hand cultivates fear and unease while offering with the other a particular security 'fix'.

Second, these studies illustrate what we might call the *banality of security*. Wæver and others have tended to equate securitization with speech acts which dramatize a particular situation and make it a matter of existential survival. Hence, around the time of the fall of the Berlin Wall, there was much talk of massive 'flows' of migration from the East which, if they entered the European Union, would threaten the viability of welfare states and perhaps an entire way of life. This equation between securitization and dramatization has, of course, only been strengthened by the events of September 11, and theoretically glossed by the recent appropriation of Agamben's (1998) sometimes hubristic writing on the theme of sovereign power and bare life. Yet it has to be borne in mind that securitization has a second pole. It is the space where security measures and identities are made operable and normal precisely because they are inserted into daily regimes and routine behaviours, and enacted by a variety of subjects, including social workers, humanitarians, border guards and truck drivers. It is not a case of the banal versus the exceptional, Instead, one needs to observe how both poles interact in the production of security fields.

Finally, this material-semiotic turn alerts us to the *plurality of security*. As long as the debate remains at the level of the analysis of rhetoric, focused on the social construction of threats, and the deployment of the word 'security', we are likely to overlook the fact that there is no such thing as *security in general*. Instead, what exist are multiple practices which embody quite different meanings and logics of security. This becomes clear when we read laterally across the space of material-semiotic approaches. For instance, a series of studies point to the significant role which technologies of risk management now play in shaping the way security experts interpret and act on the problem of migration control (Amoore 2006; Aradau 2004; van Munster 2005). But contrast this with the way pastoral techniques of control are also evident in the management of migratory processes, especially in situations where migrants are placed in detention (Albahari forthcoming; Walters forthcoming), or place themselves in spaces of sanctuary (Lippert 2004). While risk management and pastoralism can certainly be combined in certain contexts, it is important to note that security is being imagined and enacted in different ways in different situations. Attending to such differences is important since it challenges the tendency to ontologize security.

It should be clear by now that critical studies of migration-security have not been content to merely criticize conventional approaches for their narrowness, or for their essentialization of security, statehood and much else besides. The strength of this work is that it has got on with the job of exploring, both theoretically and empirically, how different facets of migration are structured as questions of security. That said, it seems to me there are certain blindspots within the critical literature. In the remainder of this chapter I set out three areas where further research concerning the migration–security nexus could make significant advances. Of course, any such itemization is somewhat arbitrary. My claim is not that these themes will complete the bigger picture, or that they are tightly connected. But they are linked by at least one thing. In each case it is not a matter of developing a research agenda from scratch with an entirely new set of concepts. Instead, each theme represents a space of work that is already in certain respects well under way. Yet it is under way in fields and areas that seem to be, thus far at least, quite remote from scholarship in the area of security studies. Hence my remarks should be interpreted as a call for greater dialogue and connection with ongoing research at the edges of critical security studies.

The Mobilization of Security

What might critical studies of migration-security learn from the history of policing mobility? Quite early in his recently translated lectures on 'security, territory, population', Foucault uses the problem of towns to illustrate certain historical transformations related to the emergence of a modern conception of security. He notes how it was that surveillance became an issue in new ways for the typical European town during the eighteenth century. This was related to the fact that city walls were being suppressed to make way for economic development, to foster a greater circulation of goods and people between the town and the outlying countryside. But this meant in turn that it was no longer possible to close the town in the evenings or closely supervise 'daily comings and goings'. Motivated largely by economic considerations, the suppression of town walls created a situation in which 'the insecurity of the towns was increased by an influx of the floating population of beggars, vagrants, delinquents, criminals, thieves, murderers, and so on, who might come, as everyone knows, from the country' (Foucault 2007: 18).

Foucault's remark is interesting not least because it alerts us to the existence of a very long and complex history in which the question of how to police the mobility of population, and how to reconcile or adjust such mobilities to norms of settlement and sedentary life, has been posed. Certainly this theme of a dual movement that combines the removal of city walls with enhanced surveillance over perceived problems of vagrancy and crime powerfully anticipates current debates about border control under conditions of globalization. Indeed, there is surely a line one could draw between the remaking of towns in the period Foucault discusses, and the remaking of European space under the auspices of the Schengen agreement.

MIGRATION AND SECURITY

Historians of vagrancy, roguery and poor laws have carefully documented many of the ways in which the emerging states of the modern period sought to domesticate and pacify their interiors (Beier 1985; Feldman 2003; Lucassen 1997; Procacci 1991). Yet this rich history of the policing of mobility, and its relationship to later practices of security and surveillance, has been largely overlooked both by mainstream studies of migration–security, but also by critical research into security and policing. Perhaps it has been neglected because security studies has been somewhat presentist in its outlook. Drawn to pressing crises in the here and now it has rarely found the time for historical reflection. Perhaps it has been overlooked because the policing of towns, countrysides and highways has been deemed 'domestic' to the state, and therefore only peripheral to a field which has assumed the domain of the 'international' to be its proper space of inquiry. Whatever the reason, it is surely the case that our accounts of the migration–security nexus would be enriched by connecting them more fully to this history. It may well be true that migration has only recently been named as a 'security' issue. But the policing of mobility has a much older pedigree that most certainly does inform our current situation.

But Foucault's remark is interesting not just because it hints at an important but hitherto neglected historical field. It is also interesting because of the kinds of questions it opens up regarding the very meaning of security. As Foucault will explore at some length in these lectures, the idea of security he finds emerging in the eighteenth century – an idea he will come to associate closely with 'governmentality' as the lectures proceed – has an intrinsic and not merely incidental relationship to questions of mobility and circulation. Foucault develops this point by contrasting security and discipline as approaches to government. If discipline imagined an ideal state where everything – people, goods, places, etc. – could be accorded its rightful place, security abandons the dream of a fixed order. As Agamben (2002) notes, it is much closer to the idea of managing disorder. For security, as Foucault understands the term, is a way of governing which does not presume a stable terrain with fixed coordinates, but a world of flux and contradiction. It is a world of probabilities and risk. Put differently, movement, understood in its broadest sense, is immanent to modern ideas of security. For this reason we might say that a Foucauldian approach to security implies the *mobilization* of security.

To reiterate an earlier point, there exist multiple meanings and corresponding practices of security. Neocleous observes that the Englsh word 'security' derives from the Latin *securitas/securus*. 'As an explicitly political concept *securitas* became prominent with the motto *securitas publica* – the safety or defence of empire' (Neocleous 2000: 9). This idea of security was to be embodied in the Peace of Westphalia. And when certain US strategists coined the term 'national security' in 1945, an idea that would lie at the very heart of international relations as a discipline, it was this idea of security as the safety of the state that was being adapted and revived (Neocleous 2000: 9).

While any further elaboration of the kind of genealogy of security which Neocleous and others have undertaken would be beyond the scope of this chapter, this reflection on the multiple sources of the idea of security is pertinent to our discussion for the following reason. It suggests, I think, that what currently gets placed under the heading of 'the securitization of migration' actually involves the intersection of at least two currents within the history of security. As any attention to the long history of the policing of mobility suggests, our own time is not the first to see human movement as raising concerns about security. What is perhaps more novel about the present is the fact that political concerns and programmes concerning the policing of mobility have come to be overcoded by security as *securitas*. In other words, the securitization of migration is in actual fact a doubling of

223

security. It marks the point where the series circulation–population–security and state–security overlap and resonate, producing complex effects that are still far from clear.

Migration, Security, Post-coloniality

It should come as no surprise that in the sizeable body of work which has examined the politics and sociology of recent immigration in Western societies, questions of race and post-coloniality occupy a prominent if not always central place (e.g. Layton Henry 1992; Wrench and Solomos 1993). To date, debates about the securitization of migration have made surprisingly little connection with this work. But again, some kind of dialogue would be fruitful.

In the decades following the Second World War, 'immigration' marked a complex socio-political site where a series of racial dynamics were to play themselves out. This period saw on the one hand the withering within official state politics of the kinds of biological and supremacist conceptions of race which had underpinned not only the genocidal project of the Nazi regime but, in a somewhat different form, the colonial projects of most of the major European powers. The discrediting of the biological idea of race most certainly did not signal the disappearance of race as an element within politics or even as a category within administration. Against the backdrop of new flows of migration, this time moving from the newly independent ex-colonies to the metropoles and as such reversing the predominant direction which obtained before decolonization, the post-war period saw the crystallization of new forms of racism. These were racisms founded less in biology and more in assertions and assumptions about the fundamental incommensurability of certain 'cultures' and 'peoples' (Barker 1981) – positions which Balibar likens to a 'racism without races' (Balibar and Wallerstein 1991).

This racism without races often expressed itself, at least in its more public iterations, through a series of political codewords – 'immigrant', 'inner city', *'banlieu'*, or in the USA, 'urban problem'. But it goes without saying that this new racism was much more than a play of rhetoric. If a range of societal fears would cathect themselves around 'immigration', these fears were to find their institutional correlates within a whole series of governmental programmes and schemes focused upon the 'problem' of immigration. Duffield (2006) describes the administrative complex that would take shape in the British case, comprising a 'race relations industry' focused on the 'cohesion' and 'integration' of the national community, an overseas 'aid industry' tasked with the 'development' of decolonized regions, and a system of migration 'control'. The fundamental premise was that immigration was something risky that required careful management.

The political codewords may have changed – witness how it is not so much the immigrant but the 'illegal immigrant', 'asylum seeker' and 'terrorist' who now constitute the terrain of suspicion (Fekete 2001) or how talk of 'civilizations' now refigures the geopolitical imagination – but many of the basic features of this arrangement remain in place. For instance, the contemporary reassertion of a new civics and the fashion for citizenship tests are some of the more recent ways in which migration is marked as a site of racialized difference.

Critical studies of migration-security have not made as much connection with themes of race and post-coloniality as they might. As such, they have not adequately asked whether and how 'security' itself might now function as a site of racism without races. There are, of course, important exceptions (Ibrahim 2005), but in many of the attempts to theorize the securitization of migration, race is only accorded an incidental and not a theoretical status. The point is not, of course, that theorists of the securitization of migration fail to recognize that the various ways in which migrant communities might be negatively stereotyped, denigrated and alienated have a strong racial component. Nor is it that they have failed to note how antiterrorist measures unleashed in the wake of September 11 circle closely around Arab and Muslim communities (Cainkar 2004). My point here is somewhat different. It is that a fuller understanding of the security–migration nexus requires us to explore some of the less immediately visible, but much more subtle and enduring ways in which this space is marked out, subtended by and vitalized by colonial and post-colonial logics. And here I should stress that I understand the colonial and the post-colonial not as successive stages but, following Akhil Gupta, 'heterogeneous temporalities that mingle and jostle with one another to interrupt the teleological narratives that have served both to constitute and the stabilize the identity of "the West"' (cited in Gregory 2004: 7). The point is that the ways in which we imagine security, write its history, record its development, assess its costs and benefits, are much more profoundly shaped by colonial and post-colonial power relations and identities than is often acknowledged.

One example should make this abundantly clear. It has become a truism of writing on the theme of security and migration that '9/11' was a fundamental turning point. As commentators never tire of reminding us, the world changed that day. At one level this is of course absolutely true. The field of migration control, and more broadly the regulation of mobility, has changed quite dramatically. The war on terror has yielded unprecedented degrees of unease, surveillance, inspection and detention targeted at mobile populations. It has spawned gargantuan administrative agencies like the Department of Homeland Security, and everywhere accelerated and thickened international policing networks, to highlight just a few of its effects (De Genova 2007; Tirman 2004).

But as grotesque and dreadful as the mass murders of September 11 certainly were, and however profoundly the response to this event has reshaped the security world, there is a danger in blindly reproducing the line that we now inhabit a 'post-9/11 security environment'. September 11 was an exceptional event in all sorts of ways. But then so was Bhopal. Yet Western scholarship does not temporalize the present by reference to a post-Bhopal world. On a global scale, mass murder and mass suffering are not exceptional but somewhat normal. It is just that most lives and deaths are not marked, not *remembered*, in quite the same way. One thing 9/11 makes painfully clear is that a hierarchy of value continues to define the worth of human life on a planetary scale. It is not the same hierarchy as that which underpinned modern colonialism. But many of its most tangible expressions and outcomes are eerily similar. Consider, for instance, how every death of the 'coalition' troops occurring in the ongoing occupations of Iraq and Afghanistan is solemnly counted, and painfully remembered within media and state contexts. Compare this with the faceless, nameless, invisible and ignoble deaths suffered by most of those caught up on 'the other side' of these wars of occupation. Or compare it with the anonymity of death which befalls those thousands of migrants who drown in the Mediterranean and Atlantic, making desperate bids to evade detection in the EU's 'fight against illegal immigration' in order to reach European shores.

This is not to suggest that we should forget September 11. Nothing could be further from the point. It is to suggest instead that those deaths need to be remembered in a different way, one that, as Paul Gilroy has suggested, challenges 'the nationalist appropriation of the events' and 'remembers the dead on a different scale'. This would be a scale and a sensibility in which 'that [particular] injustice is required to be seen, felt and understood in the context of other similar and connected horrors that are more frequent, and less eventful, in other parts of the world' (Gilroy 2002).

All of this is to say that the very act of temporalizing and qualifying security in terms like 'September 11' can never be innocent or neutral. Logics of race and colonialism run deep, deep enough that they imbue the very narratives and categories that we commonly use to think the present.

New Territories of Power

My final case for broadening and deepening critical studies of migration-security concerns the theme of political transformation. It is, of course, a long-standing theme in the social sciences that in migration we find a force that is reshaping societies and cultures, challenging national, regional and other identities, and both undermining and generating new models of citizenship and belonging (Joppke 1999; Soysal 1994). But far less has been written about migration as a phenomenon around which we might observe a reshaping of state apparatuses and other machineries of rule. Compare international migration with global finance. The latter is deemed a weighty force, significant enough that it has compelled even the most powerful state actors on the world scene, albeit in complex and mediated ways, to reshape their very structures and operational logics. But the same is not usually said of migration. It is said to reshape identities, cultures and populations. But rarely is migration considered a phenomenon that transforms the very administrative structure or political logic of states, or even less the architecture of international order (but see Hollifield 2004). Migration is cast as altogether weaker.[2]

But this picture is beginning to change. One important point that can be drawn from many studies of the securitization of migration – and especially from semiotic-material approaches – is that the migration–security nexus needs to be understood not only as the *product* of state activity, but as a *site* of state and governmental transformation in its own right (Berman 2003; Doty 1996b). Put differently, we are not dealing here with a situation in which states engage in security practices, changing the meaning and experience of migration, while remaining themselves unchanged. On the contrary, the state itself is also being remade through its encounter with securitization. Just how it is remade depends very much on its insertion within the geopolitics of migration control (Samers 2004) and antiterrorism; whether, for instance, it is politically coded as a 'state of destination', of 'transit', of 'origin' or, perhaps, a 'failed state'. It goes without saying that the implications of securitization are very different for Germany or Britain compared with Morocco or Pakistan. But transformations are evident in each.

This theme of migration-security as a site of state transformation is present in the literature in several ways. State transformation is evident in all those instances where new statuses, linked to new forms of administration of migrants are being produced and put into service. For instance, in his discussion of the new 'homeland security state', de Genova (2007) examines the implications of a shift from the concept of 'illegal alien' to 'enemy alien'. State transformation is also there as a subtext in research that has developed the theme of the 'rebordering' of states and world-regions (Andreas and Biersteker 2003; Andreas and Snyder 2000). These studies suggest that, contrary to the prediction of a coming 'borderless world', the territorial state and the performance of sovereignty are alive and well, albeit if the borders do take new forms. And perhaps most interestingly, state transformation applies in the case of a range of studies which examine borders as the setting for new kinds of spaces and temporalities. Political geographers have been especially attuned to the fact that within contemporary strategies of migration and refugee deterrence we are seeing an alarming proliferation of territorial excisions, non-places and grey zones at borders (Davidson 2003; Lloyd 2002). Whether located in airports or on remote islands, these new spaces challenge norms of accountability and transparency and short-circuit the possibility of claiming asylum or seeking protection under various international rights protocols.

Ultimately, however, we can observe that research into the migration–security nexus would probably be limited in its understanding if it confined its conceptual language to that of *state* transformation. For clearly we are dealing not simply with transformations in the state, but the emergence of new territories of power that, while they may have states and their agencies as key nodes, are not really reducible to the old political maps of the international order. To take one example, consider the current turn towards biometric technology as a 'solution' for certain problems of surveilling, profiling and authenticating mobile populations. Certainly we could read the biometric as the latest development in a long line of instruments used by states to enhance the legibility of 'their' populations, a line that would include the passport (Salter 2003) but also, if we traced it back far enough, the political-administrative requirement that each of the sovereign's subjects possess a surname (Scott 1998). Yet the biometric is not simply an instrument wielded by state agencies. It is also the site of a burgeoning, multi-billion dollar techno-industry (Didier 2004). The biometric is taking shape in the midst of complex networks that include research laboratories, regulations and standards agencies, venture capitalists and investment consultants, and transnational corporations like Motorola, Sagem and Accenture. All of this is, in turn, unfolding around the search for new markets, markets which range from the development of entry and exit controls as part of the mandate of Homeland Security, to various local and national police and immigration agencies in countries like Croatia and Cyprus. In the latter cases, the quest to become fit to join the European Union, and participate in its intelligence networks, entails the purchase and implementation of new systems of biometric control and data-sharing. In the presence of dynamics like these, the old boundaries between public goods and private commodities, state and market, national and international, become blurred and complicated. One task of empirical research becomes that of tracing how such elements are being reassembled in new ways at different sites.

The challenge of mapping these new territories and configurations of power requires the invention of new methods and concepts. This point has not been lost on a number of writers who, working on themes of migration-security, have made the development of new concepts a matter of urgency. Whether one is talking of Bigo's idea of a 'möbius ribbon' that folds internal and external security into one another (Bigo 2001), or a series of studies which have found the Deleuzian idea of 'assemblage' useful for thinking irregularly shaped control systems and rhizomatic dynamics (Ong and Collier 2005), it is clear that the work of mapping new spaces is now being taken up, if not as extensively as it might.

But if there is one point that merits emphasizing in summing up this discussion of the migration–security nexus as a site of new territories of power, it is this: we should be cautious about placing these diverse new practices, sites and processes under the catch-all heading of 'globalization'. This is not to deny that recent studies of the 'globalization of migration control' (Duvell 2003), the 'globalization of enclosure' (Coward 2005), and 'global mobility regimes' (Shamir 2005) have produced very valuable and important insights. Nevertheless, there is perhaps something to be said for a more nominalist and less dramatized approach. Here it may well prove useful to follow the lead of those like

Sassen who writes of 'third spaces' (Sassen 2008b) or Barry who theorizes 'technological zones' (Barry 2006). Both offer us concepts to map processes that do indeed escape and transcend international systems of regulation – but do so without being properly global either. Whether we want to understand the biometricization of the policing of mobility and migration, the network of readmission agreements and practices which is giving rise to new geographies of expulsion in and from Europe, or many of the other perplexing phenomena that might be placed under the heading of migration-security, the chances are we will encounter emergent networks that, if they share nothing else, have in common this matter of being neither national nor global.

Notes

1 But for a study which insists on the integral and constitutive role which migration has played in the vitalization of democratic life see Honig (2001).
2 One exception is the literature which sees global migration as a movement that 'erodes' the sovereignty of states. But here change is modelled only as something negative – a subtraction from the (imagined) past of a fully sovereign state.

23

Security Technologies

Emmanuel-Pierre Guittet and Julien Jeandesboz

This chapter deals with the issue of security technologies, and the relationship between security and technology. We start by examining how the question of technology has become a stake for contemporary security studies, discussing in particular the so-called 'critical approaches' to security (CASE Collective 2006). We suggest that while the uses and effects of technological systems are increasingly scrutinized by security studies scholars, little work has been done on the practice of technology itself with regard to security. In the process, seemingly crucial issues, such as the role played by the private (industrial and commercial) technological sector in contemporary security practices, are left unattended – whereas such issues have been convincingly addressed for a long time in criminology for instance. The second part of the chapter then provides an overview of some of the insights that have been elaborated by scholars of the history and sociology of technology: we argue that these offer pertinent elements for understanding the relationship between security and technology. Accordingly, the last part of the chapter discusses the question of security technologies in relation to the argument, made by some journalists and commentators (e.g. Hayes 2006; Mac Donald 2006; Mills 2004; O'Harrow 2005), that transformations in the contemporary (in)security *doxa* as well as in existing and anticipated technological systems are leading to the constitution of a 'security-industrial complex' on the model of the notion of 'military-industrial complex' hammered out during the Cold War to frame the relationship between governments, security agencies and the industries of defence.

Security Studies and the Question of Technology

In recent years, scholars in international relations and security studies have increasingly emphasized the importance of the technological aspects of security practices. Whether this relates to the use of advanced biometrics, databases and risk models for the purpose of border protection, migration control, identification of individuals, crowd control and other concerns regarding population management or social control (e.g. Andreas 2000; Andreas and Snyder 2001; Amoore 2006; Amoore and De Goede 2005; Bonditti 2005; Ceyhan 2006; Marx 2001; Muller 2008; Salter and Zureik 2005), or to the transformation of warfare (e.g. Balzacq and De Nève 2003; Der Derian 1992, 2001; Rasmussen 2006), technological developments have been examined under different angles. In the process, international relations (IR) and security studies have come to overlap with concepts and concerns more familiar to other fields, such as criminology (on the study of technological transfers from the military to the police and the reframing of security expertise) and more recently surveillance studies. Technology, first, has been singled out as a crucial element of contemporary dominant narratives on (in)security. Secondly, it has been incorporated not as an instrument or outcome of security practices, but as one of their components.

Contemporary Discourses on (In)Security and Technology

With the end of the Cold War and the demise of strategic conceptions linked with nuclear dissuasion, a range of new doctrines and concepts came to the fore, particularly in the US, regarding first the conduct of military operations, and later on for the purpose of 'homeland security' (Mattelart 2007: 166–7). Acronyms such as C4ISR[1] or RMA,[2] notions of 'netwar', 'cyberwar' or 'global information dominance' were shaped to highlight the centrality of new technologies, in particular information and communications technologies (ICT) for the conduct of both external and internal security activities (Ackroyd *et al.* 1980, 1992; Dupont and Lemieux 2005; Ericson and Haggerty 1999; Kraska and Kappeler 1997). Of course, this does not mean that technology did not matter previously, or that the genealogy of these practices is limited to the 1990s.[3] At the end of the nineteenth century, technology was already a great concern to deal among others with the 'spread of anarchism'. Technological advances in forensic sciences significantly facilitated the internationalization of police operations (Deflem 2002; Cole 2001). However, technology mattered and was envisioned *differently* at the time, and the ways in which it mattered in the early 1990s also came to change in relation to the evolving *doxa* about threats and risks among professionals of security.

The evolution of this *doxa* can be seen as a movement from a set of discourses on *post*-bipolar[4] perils (Bigo 1995), generated by the demise of the bipolar order, to the formulation of a set of narratives on 'global (in)security' (Bigo 2006a), which was considerably accelerated with the 11 September 2001 attacks and the subsequent bombings in Madrid and London. Post-bipolar discourses focused on the disappearance of the 'enemy' of the Cold War, and on the consequences (unpredictability, resurgence of 'frozen conflicts', state failure and 'roguishness', proliferation of WMD) thereof. 'Global (in)security' narratives, on the other hand, encompass a move away from the notion that we live in a 'post' period: they stress, rather, that ours is an increasingly globalized world where liberal regimes, considered as the most committed to globalization and openness, are at risk because of a variety of unpredictable, transnational developments and operators. In this respect, the aim of security agencies is not so much to protect a given territory and a population, but to reduce vulnerability (Beck 1992; Bonditti 2008; Ericson and Doyle 2004; Ericson and Haggerty 1997), by anticipating potentially perilous occurrences. Hence the focus of some in the field of security studies on the progressive shift in the legitimization, meaning and practices of security from a logic of protection to a logic of 'risk management' (e.g. Aradau *et al.* 2008; Beck 2002; Bigo 2007; Ericson and Doyle 2004; Ericson and Haggerty 1997). The reliance on the notion of risk has been singled out as one of the driving factors of the transformation of security practices, both in the field of policing (e.g. Ericson and Haggerty 1997; Ericson and Stehr 2000) and of the military (e.g. Rasmussen 2006).

Technology plays a crucial part in this move. Despite strong criticism, in the wake of the 11 September 2001 attacks, of the heavy reliance of US security agencies on technological, rather than human, intelligence, the activities of the department of Homeland Security (DHS) established in 2002 have strongly focused on technological activities, with a budget of up to $50 bn in 2006 (Mattelart 2007: 174). Among the measures adopted to implement the contentious Patriot Act, one finds the Total Information Awareness (TIA) programme, initiated in 2002 and subsequently relabelled (in 2003) Terrorism Information Awareness, which aims at integrating the databases of various public and private bodies (local police, FBI, insurance companies, banks and so forth). In recent years, the European Union (EU), besides the increasingly technology-driven activities of its own security bodies (e.g. Bigo *et al.* 2009; Brouwer 2006; Jeandesboz 2008), has also been keen on providing financial and organizational support to research in the field of security technologies, as part of an effort to promote a 'security culture' (European Commission 2004: 2) within European industries and security agencies (Bigo *et al.* 2009; Preuss-Laussinotte 2006).

These activities have been justified under the claim that, despite its failings, technology is a mandatory prerequisite in a context of 'global (in)security' (Dupont 2005; Guittet 2008a): advanced technological systems are required to counter supposedly technology-savvy clandestine groups operating transnationally, to conduct 'asymmetric wars' in difficult environments, and most importantly to allow security bodies to gather and exchange information across professional (local and national/federal police, police and customs, police and border-guards, police and intelligence services, intelligence services and the military), sectoral (private/public) and national boundaries. Technology, then, is featured in contemporary (in)security discourses as a central solution to a range of claimed problems, with the key task to help master the uncertain and predict the unpredictable, to manage risks – in the words of Ulrich Beck, for 'calculating the incalculable, colonizing the future' (2002: 40). It is also, arguably, a crucial part of the claim made by some professionals of security (particularly among intelligence agencies) that they *know better* than professionals of politics, of the media, and than other professionals of security, because they have access to data-mining software and databases, which are stocked with an increased amount of information about an ever-growing collection of individuals.

Discourses about global (in)security then incidentally convey a certain understanding of technology and its dynamics. In these discourses, technology first emerges as a *fix*, a *solution* to a set of specific problems. It is ingenuous, in that it does not incorporate opinions and biases other than technical ones, and thus needs to be evaluated first in terms of efficiency (other considerations, such as civil liberties, being sometimes included, but almost as a second thought). Secondly, technology is evolutionary, in the Darwinian sense. Technological processes are cumulative and progress-driven: new technologies replace old ones primarily on the basis of them being more sophisticated and effective.

The Uses of Technology in Contemporary Security Practices

Jointly with the transformation of the *doxa* of security professionals since the end of the bipolar period, one key focus of security studies has been the study of security practices, that is, the various ways of doing and knowing of those who claim security to be their profession. The uses of technology by professionals of security count among the security practices that have been investigated in recent years: the use of technological systems involving biometrics, databases, information-sharing and data-mining procedures has emerged as a particular concern. Looking at security as a practice then shifts the attention to routines, daily surveillance and the everyday tracing of individuals and groups, allegedly to anticipate and sort out the dangerous, but in the process making insecure the totality of a given human collective (Bigo 2008b: 105–6). This has led in particular to an increased engagement with scholars in surveillance studies, who have in parallel been involved in a process of questioning some of the basics of their own field (e.g. the contributions to Lyon 2006, in particular Haggerty).

Of course, the recourse to technological systems, either for policing or military operations, is not new. As highlighted previously, the first large-scale communication interception systems were put to use by the US and UK intelligence services as early as the 1940s. In a similar vein, the nuclear arsenals of the Cold War period, and in fact the whole practice of deterrence and dissuasion, drew on advanced communication and computer systems, to the extent that they even inspired sizzling satires such as Stanley Kubrick's 1964 *Doctor Strangelove*. Police forces in the USA and Europe have been using electronic communications and computer systems for record-holding and surveillance purposes since the early 1970s, including in local contexts (Ericson and Haggerty 1997: 389). However, most studies agree on the notion that the use of technological systems in the management of (in)security has transformed in recent years.

Accordingly, a central dimension of recent research on security has been to incorporate technology not as a neutral factor or dependent variable of security practices, but as a key influence in the framing, layout and conduct of security policies:

> the modulation of insecurity domains … crucially depends on technological and technocratic processes. *The development and implementation of technological artefacts and knowledge*, such as diagrams, computer networks, scientific data, and even the specific forms that need filling in do more than simply implementing a policy decision … These solutions and instruments of policy implementation often precede and pre-structure political framing in significant ways. They are not just developed in response to a political decision but often already exist in one form or another within professional routines and institutional technology and evolve over time according to professional and bureaucratic or institutional requirements – such as the need to innovate.
>
> (Huysmans 2006: 8; our emphasis)

Technology, then, is not just a mere policy tool, or the outcome of a decision. We need to think of security and technology as interrelated: security practices play an important role in the framing, developing and promoting of technological systems, and in return, technology frames, shapes and channels security practices. There have, however, been very few discussions in IR and security studies about technology per se, and about the specific practices and processes associated with technology.

The Practice of Technology

Technology certainly stands as a central point and a major reference in our culture of modernity. There has been a considerable literature devoted to technology in history, philosophy or sociology (among who major figures such as Dewey, Heidegger, Marx or Weber). Each discussion on technology, however, seems to start anew with a preliminary clarification of the term and its intended use. The present section will provide an overview of recent debates on this topic among scholars of the history, philosophy and sociology of

SECURITY TECHNOLOGIES

science and technology, asking in particular how technology, technological change and 'progress' can be studied from the perspective of the social sciences.

Understanding Technology, Understanding Society

In its most direct understanding, technology can be conceived of as the realm of inert, manufactured objects. Of course, this is of little use for the social sciences: a device of any kind arguably matters insofar as it is embedded in human activities. The notion of technology thus also encompasses the ways in which devices are made and used, i.e. ways of doing. Furthermore, what we understand by inert manufactured devices needs to be specified. Manufactured objects which are considered as cutting-edge in one period become rudimentary contraptions in another. Some devices are only potentially in existence as we speak: they might, or might not, become commonplace in years to come. In addition, objects seldom constitute a totality: they are built out of a variety of components, a fact which we might not be aware of in the course of our daily lives, but of which we can be reminded. Technology then really involves technological *systems*. For instance, we conceive of a car as a whole, as one single object, until the moment when it stops to function: it is then broken down, metaphorically and literally, into its various components (e.g. engine, brakes, carburettor). Technology thus also encompasses ways of knowing: knowledge necessary to assemble and disassemble a device, to fix it, to invent it and so forth.

Beyond the materiality of artefacts, technology can therefore be conceived of as specific ways of doing and ways of knowing – in other words, as a *practice* (Franklin 1999: 6). This notion, under different guises, has been taken up by scholars who have sought, in the past three decades, to develop a history and sociology of technology which would move beyond the usual folk devils of classical analyses of technological developments, namely the interconnected argument and discussion on technological inertia, irreversibility and autonomy. *Technological inertia* involves the idea that once a given path is opened in technological change, other developments will inevitably follow in a linear fashion, building from the initial invention. *Irreversibility* coins the notion that there is no going back in technological development; this is also strongly connected with the conception that technological change represents progress. *Autonomy*, finally, encompasses the notions of inertia and irreversibility, but also comprises the idea that technological change somehow lies outside of society, and constitutes a driving evolutionary force for human collectivities.[5]

This threefold articulation has become a consistent target for critique, in particular by scholars who have contributed to the so-called 'SCOT' – social construction of technology – literature.[6] The editors of one of the most commented volumes in this thread of reflection argue:

> This new type of technology study can be characterized by three trends in the sort of analysis attempted. Authors have been concerned with moving away from the individual inventor (or 'genius') as the central explanatory concept, from technological determinism, and from making distinctions among technical, social, economic, and political aspects of technological development.
>
> (Bijker *et al.* 1987: 3)

Under this broad umbrella, one finds a variety of approaches and interests: the main point shared by these scholars is a loose commitment to a social constructivist methodology,

233

and a common interest in engaging critically with previous scholarship on the matter of technology (Hamlin 1992). Of course, these perspectives are not devoid of discrepancies, in particular as regards the difference between sociological and socio-technical analyses of technology. In the first perspective, the study of technology is approached by drawing on the research in the field of the sociology of science. While acknowledging that technology is a separate question (field) from science, these authors derive their concepts from studies in the constitution and elaboration of scientific knowledge. Their focus, then, is strongly on the sociology of technical knowledge and know-how, on the production of professional and lay knowledge about technology and the effects thereof (e.g. MacKenzie 1996b). Socio-technical approaches, on the other hand, while agreeing on the interest and importance of scrutinizing knowledge, also highlight that the practice of technology incorporates a very specific dimension, i.e. the relationship, the mediation, or indeed the negotiation, with the *technical*, with objects.[7]

Building on these elements from the sociology of technology, one can then oppose strong elements to the threefold argument of technological inertia, irreversibility and autonomy. The practice of technology, like any other socio-political process, is constantly in flux. Of course, some orientations consolidate over time. Ursula Franklin, in her elegant recapitulation of discussions on technology, suggests that, over time, a threefold shift can be observed in technological developments: a shift from work-related to control-related technologies, from holistic to prescriptive technologies, and from a growth-related to a production-related societal model (Franklin 1999: 9–26). This consolidation, however, is never the reflection of inevitability, of fate, but rather the end effect of complex dynamics in the evolving relations of power within human collectives. Technological developments, as Latour shows very well in his study of the rise and demise of the Aramis transportation system, are never linear, but constantly shaped and reshaped by negotiation between the local and the general, the social and the technical (Latour 1993). In other words, technology as a practice is neither revolutionary nor evolutionary in its operations, although in the final instance and in retrospect some developments might appear so: once one focuses on the nitty-gritty details of specific technological projects, technology appears in a constant state of flux, with some orientations being consolidated and others waning, but never according to some rational and linear process of technical progress.

The Question of Technological Change: Contesting Technological Ingenuity and Darwinism

The above-mentioned perspectives open up interesting perspectives as regards the twofold question of technological ingenuity and Darwinism. First, if technology constitutes a set of social processes and social practices, it cannot be considered ingenuous. Artefacts 'have politics' (Winner 1985), they incorporate social practices and representations. Latour, in his analysis of Aramis, a groundbreaking system of public transportation for the city of Paris which was studied, developed, but ultimately abandoned, highlights in this respect how the development of a specific technological system is based on 'chains of translation' and negotiation: translations between the concerns, ways of doing and interests, of the various actors which aggregate around a specific project, between local considerations and broader societal tendencies of a given period, as well as between human and non-human actors.

In view of these elements, technological Darwinism – i.e. the notion that technology is a forward-looking process, where archaic and inefficient systems are replaced by improved ones – does not hold. Certain technologies and projects, despite being more advanced

SECURITY TECHNOLOGIES

and groundbreaking, eventually end up in a dead-end, even if they are technically feasible. Others might be taken up, with massive amounts of funding going into them and backing from a whole range of actors, while being organizationally and technically fantasist, and still have effects, although not the ones intended initially – a case in point here is the Strategic Defence Initiative (SDI) launched under the Reagan presidency. Technological Darwinism, furthermore, conflates progress, sophistication and efficiency. Technological systems might grow more sophisticated, that is, more complex, involving more components and more technicalities, bigger machinery, but they might not be more advanced or more efficient.

What does this have in store for the study of the relationship between security and technology? First, it provides a strong counterpoint to narratives of technology as a fix and a solution, as an ingenuous component of security policies. Technology has an influence, it contributes actively to the definition of dangers and risks, and of (in)security practices. Secondly, it opens up new perspectives for the study of the relationship between security and technology, by means of opening it up to investigations of the practices of technology as a correlated, but autonomous, configuration. This involves examining the various logics and practices underpinning technological processes and the configurations of professionals that coalesce around given stakes.

Toward a 'Security-industrial Complex'?

As mentioned in the introduction, one question that has emerged in interrogations about the contemporary relationship between security and technology is whether we are currently witnessing the emergence of a 'security-industrial complex':

> The idea of a 'security-industrial complex' has gained currency for a number of reasons. First, state policy and security forces have increasingly been equipped with more and more military equipment, providing arms company with a growing sideline. More broadly, the traditional barriers between *internal* and *external* security, and *policing* and *military* operations, have been eroded. Secondly, arms companies are joined in the emerging 'security-industrial complex' by the burgeoning IT sector and its large multinationals, the IT revolution having thrown-up novel possibilities for the surveillance of public and private places, of communications, and of groups and individuals. Third, security-centric government responses to terrorism and the 'war on terrorism' have accelerated all these trends.
>
> (Hayes 2006: 4)

So the notion of a 'security-industrial complex' really encompasses three dimensions. First, the notion that security practices have been transformed: internal and external security activities are increasingly de-differentiated, and this has opened the way for new technological demands from security professionals and new ways of using technological systems. Secondly, a reframing of logics of competition among security professionals on security expertise and know-how occurs. The 'security-industrial complex' is the byproduct of a transformation in corporate logics: new entrants (such as IT companies), shifts in the activities of already-established organizations (arms companies) and new connections with the public sector. Finally, the constitution of a 'security-industrial complex' is tied to the emergence of the 'war on terror' which has spanned new perspectives and requirements for technological systems in the field of security.

235

Two aspects of this proposal need to be discussed. The first one is clearly the notion of the 'complex' by itself, its implications and the questions that it raises, particularly insofar as it shadows the actual dynamics (corporate, commercial, promotional) taking place around the issue of security technologies. The second is the corollary idea that a certain number of technological systems can be regrouped as 'security' technologies, that the de-differentiation of internal and external security practices is sustained by, and sustaining, a de-differentiation in technological systems.

Breaking Down the Complex

The notion of a 'security-industrial complex' as it is currently used by commentators, is derived from the discussions about the 'military-industrial complex' of the Cold War, introduced in the US political arena by the 1961 farewell speech of President Dwight Eisenhower. Five years earlier, sociologist C. Wright Mills, in his book *The Power Elite* (1956), had already coined the notion that American government and politics were dominated by a coalition of industrial and military groups, which were leading the country into dire straits. The 'military-industrial complex', in Mills's understanding, is backed by an oligarchic and institutionalist understanding of politics and government, whereby these are dominated and defined by the pre-existing relations (and competitions) between the predominant actors of different sectors of society.

The idea of a complex between the industry and the security professionals is however somewhat of an oversimplification. First, while it might be valid in the US context, it might not be so relevant in other settings – or at least, the logics and modalities of its functioning can be fairly different.[8] Secondly, the argument of the 'complex' is essentially conservative: if the complex is such a stable configuration, institutionalized by means of contracts, financial transfers and bureaucratic routines, then how can we account for change? How come, for instance, nuclear dissuasion and its technological corollaries (e.g. ballistic systems, satellite and computer networks for the detecting and tracing of launches) have, in recent years, seemingly faded away from discussions about security? Thirdly, while the distinction between, on the one hand, private corporate actors, and on the other, public actors from the military and government is to some extent pertinent, it greatly reduces the diversity of groups of professionals who actually intervene into technological development, the overlapping arenas through which technological systems are funded, developed, marketed, promoted and acquired, as well as the multiple logics which underpin these processes. In a similar vein, the distinction between technology designers (the industry) and users (here security professionals) is reductive: one needs for instance to distinguish between designers (e.g. engineers), marketers and promoters of technological systems, as well as between the agents responsible for acquiring technological systems (procurement administrations), for supporting research in the private and public sectors, and for using these systems – with the additional caveat that all of them intervene, through different arenas and interfaces, into technological processes. We must be wary, in this respect, of taking for granted the existence of a 'military-industrial', let alone of a 'security-industrial' complex.

Analytically, then, it seems fruitful and important to distinguish between several correlated logics such as the dynamics driving international strategic agendas and the market logics involving high levels of competition between major companies on the one hand, and the logics of merging of policing and surveillance technologies with military technologies – the resultant being the constitution of an apparent technological continuum regarding (in)security – on the other.

Security Technology as Knowledge Commodities: Corporate, Promotional and Market Logics

As mentioned earlier, the end of the Cold War resulted in a radical review of defence strategies, which stimulated development of RMA-related systems based on the combination of electronics, information and telecommunications technologies. One of the characteristic features of these technologies is their commercial origin: to a large extent they have not been developed by R&D departments within defence ministries but by civilian commercial firms. The most innovative contributions come from sectors on the periphery of the traditional defence industry, such as telecommunications, electronics, optronics and aerospace. It is the latter that have become the truly strategic sectors and the heart of the modern armaments industry (e.g. EADS, Hayes 2006). The growing role of civil technologies in the RMA represents one of the most fundamental changes that the defence industry has ever experienced, especially in Europe. The main firms involved in this process have become fewer and larger, partly because the global market shrank somewhat after the end of the Cold War, but even more because the escalating costs of research and development exclude all but companies with access to vast amounts of capital. In this regard, the concept of 'security industrial complex' does not take into account the logics of promotion, bargaining and competition among technology suppliers and their effects on demand (Bailes and Frommelt 2004). The 'complex' acts as a fog, veiling the processes through which technological systems are elaborated, marketed, promoted and acquired.

In this regard, the analysis of the logics and sites for the promotion of such technologies remains underdeveloped – and might constitute the missing link in security studies as regards technology. Beyond their material characteristics, security technologies are the embodiment of the ultimate expectations in terms of safety, predictability and reassurance – security technologies, then, are commoditized as knowledge (Neocleous 2007). Few scholars have paid attention to the increasing numbers of trade shows and trade fair exhibitions devoted to security, surveillance and defence since the beginning of the decade. In 2008, no less than 130 exhibitions specialized in technologies of surveillance, protection, police and weapons took place in different countries all over the world (Guittet 2008b). The study of those international security exhibitions might be very fruitful in order to understand the logics of competition and transfers of know-how on technologies related to the promotion of security. One effect of the securitization ('colonization' as Beck suggested) of the future, in this regard, is the business of security that it has contributed to expand. And one of the less investigated aspects of this business of security is the proliferation of international spaces of promotion of security technologies where new high-tech tools *available* to anticipate and fight uncertainty are presented. Paradoxically, these loci of promotion of high-tech security technologies create an increasing *expectation* of more efficient technologies for the purpose of achieving more security, more reassurance and as a way to reach the ultimate reduction of risk.

Lifting the Fog of (In)Security Technology

'Security' as a label for specific technological products has undoubtedly become a major business opportunity in the past two decades. Nevertheless, it is important to highlight the historical dynamics of this particular business that has grown in the shadow of major national and international trends of offer and demand for arms and other classical defence-related devices (armoured equipment, missiles and explosive materials, wheeled, tracked and amphibian transport equipments and other classical armaments). As a matter of fact, sites for the promotion of devices devoted to internal (domestic) security purposes were already in place back in the 1970s (e.g. the British internal security exhibition 'IFSEC', the German exhibition 'Security Essen', or EXPOL in France[9]), but were mostly kept confidential. At the time, markets for internal security technologies were referred to as markets for 'repression technologies' (Chomsky and Herman 1979; Klare and Arnson 1981; Stohl and Lopez 1984).

However, this business started to bloom in the 1990s, when internal security and the protection of the homeland became mobilizing issues in political discourses (Bigo 1995, 1996). In the process, internal security markets and industries have increasingly come to be seen as legitimate business because deemed to participate to the protection of societies. The notion has emerged in governmental arenas that we are currently observing the merging of policing and surveillance technologies with military technologies. For instance, the European Commission's insistence, in recent years, on funding and developing European research and development ventures in security technologies, has built from the notion that common technologies (dual or even triple use) can be elaborated in between the needs of the military and the civilian sectors (Bigo et al. 2009). A 'technological continuum' of security technologies seems to be, at least in the dominant narratives about (in)security, in the making, but this is shadowing the fact that this technological continuum for security is more a conjunction of the rediscovery of internal security and protection of the homeland by the military on the one hand and the development of security as a political virtue on the other (Bigo 2006a) than the outcome of technological convergence and functional rapprochement between internal ad external security. Certainly, the attacks of 9/11 created a space to strengthen the legitimacy of security technology industries, to reinforce the idea that politics is now all about expectation of hostility (past or forthcoming in a risk-based perception) and to promote security technologies as today's political imperative. Security technologies are the embodiment of the idea that we are everywhere under growing threat. They thus constitute a major asset for professionals of politics driven by the fear of the future. This particular relation between security technologies, their creators and promoters and social demands is certainly a constant and reciprocal one, but not the outcome of some 'continuum', practical or technological.

Conclusion

Security technologies are more than the sum of manufactured objects devoted to protection, safety and surveillance: they combine ways of designing, undertaking and practising security, and are both the support and the explanation of a certain *doxa* on security. They embody the contradiction of security practices themselves: the more security matters, the more we fear insecurity, and the more security technologies contribute to shape relentless expectations regarding a future always thought of as catastrophic. Ultimately, our alienation from technological devices is alienation from the belief of technology as salvation. Analytically speaking, this implies that we should be wary of *both* dystopian and utopian accounts of technology, let alone of narratives based on the twofold argument of technological ingenuity and efficiency. There is, however, important work to be conducted, in IR and security studies, on technology as a practice and an ideology, i.e. as an ensemble of social representations shaped by the activities of specific groups and generating effects of symbolic as well as material violence.

Notes

1 'Command, Control, Communications, Computing, Intelligence, Surveillance, Reconnaissance'
2 'Revolution in Military Affairs'
3 For instance, the US worldwide communications interception system ECHELON, which made the headlines in the late 1990s (when it was discovered by European citizens through a report commissioned by the European Parliament), forms part of what was initially known as the 'Brusa Comint' intelligence network (created in 1943), later codenamed 'UKUSA' (1948). See Bonditti 2008: 303–20, Mattelart 2007: 74–6.
4 On this notion of postness, see Huysmans 1996 (paras 160–7).
5 The argument of autonomy is often hastily associated with Marxist thinking (*contra*, see MacKenzie 1996a). For a critical perspective on autonomous technology, see Winner (1977).
6 In addition to the volume by Bijker *et al.* (1987), the interested reader can refer to the books by Laudan (1984), MacKenzie and Wajcman (1985) and Elliott (1988), for an overview of this literature.
7 The best illustration of this is the work undertaken by and with Bruno Latour, around the 'actor–network theory'. For a concise presentation, see Latour 1996. For fundamental developments on how such a socio-technical perspective operates, see Latour 1993.
8 For a general analysis on the case of France, see for instance Kolodziej 1987, as well as Genieys and Michel 2006 for an illuminating case study on the Leclerc battle tank.
9 EXPOL became MILIPOL, the French worldwide exhibition of Internal State Security, in 1984.

24

Designing Security

Cynthia Weber and Mark Lacy

> Modernity is a condition of compulsive, and addictive, designing.
> (Zygmunt Bauman)

Fears and anxieties over terrorism and crime are driving the design of new products, services, systems, and architectures to protect us. These attempts at 'designing out insecurity' and 'designing in protection' (Lacy 2008) are built on the assumption that new insecurities do not simply emerge from so-called great power politics, the traditional focus of international relations, particularly realism. Rather, insecurities increasingly emerge from attacks by state and non-state actors on our critical infrastructure – railways, airports, cyberspace, financial centers, and energy supplies – to the point where the traditional distinction between 'military' and 'civilian' zones and between perpetrators and victims is increasingly erased. The urbanist Paul Virilio describes this shift as the move from the geopolitical to the metro-political era (Lotringer and Virilio 2008: 209). Architectural critic Beatriz Colomina points out that this means that those objects that were designed to make our everyday lives more livable are being redeployed to take human life: 'If 9/11 in New York revealed the cell-phone as the last vestige of domesticity, 3/11 in Madrid revealed the cell-phone as a weapon, triggering the bombs in the trains. Personal defense became public attack. Once again, the intimate relationship between domesticity and war had evolved' (Colomina 2007: 302). With this shift in the use of everyday designs from objects that connect and comfort us into objects that carry the potential to attack us as we go about our everyday lives, we typically respond by creating new gadgets and new design solutions to protect us.

That's what is happening now, in our post-9/11, post-3/11, post-7/7 world. But despite our current feelings of insecurity, isn't it true that today we are safer than ever before? Haven't design solutions, technological advances, and policy innovations allowed us to manage (if not control) natural and human-made threats better than at any time in our history? And isn't it because of the success of security technologies that we continue to develop these technologies to further satisfy our expectations for higher and higher levels of safety and protection?

While the answer to these questions may be 'yes', it is most definitely a qualified 'yes'. For the seemingly unproblematic, progressive account of history this techno–optimistic story tells is complicated by several factors. One is our awareness that technological advancements (like the cell phones Colomina writes about) often carry unforeseen risks, dangers, and insecurities. Another is the recognition that these new risks, dangers, and insecurities no longer require the mobilization of armies but merely the mobilization of a few determined people to be realized. Andrew Marshall, an expert of security and technology at the Pentagon, explains it like this, 'A friend of mine, Yale economist Martin Shubik, says an important way to think about the world is to draw a curve of the number of people 10 determined men can kill before they are put down themselves, and how that has varied over time. His claim is that it wasn't very many for a long time, and now it's going up. In that sense, it's not just the US. All the world is getting less safe' (McGray 2003, www.wired.com).

It isn't just cell phones or determined individuals that can make us unsafe. Some new technologies themselves like nanotechnologies are potentially 'so much more powerful and invisible, uncontrollable, capable of creeping everywhere'. As radical philosopher Jacques Derrida explains, 'Our unconscious is already aware of this; it already knows it, and that's what's scary' (Derrida 2003: 102). Even those invisible technologies that we've gotten used to like electromagnetic technologies that give us everything from microwaves to TV broadcasts may be scarier than we realize. As designers Anthony Dunne and Fiona Raby note, the electromagnetic spectrum is fast becoming the 'central nervous system' of our modern lives not just by enabling communication and connection but also surveillance, detection, and disconnection (Dunne and Raby 2001: 15–18; see also Trüby 2008: 64–6). While new technologies definitely offer us some new material levels of security and safety compared to the past, then, they also make us insecure physically, socially, and psychologically in increasingly new and complicated ways (Thackera 2006). New technologies potentially increase our insecurity at the same time as they potentially increase our security. And this often fuels our desire to design out insecurity and design in protection even further. The dilemma, of course, is that because of the complex relationships between security and insecurity, security and safety, and security, safety, and design, these 'design solutions' create as much insecurity and danger as they eliminate.[1]

As scholars interested in contemporary security issues, we are asking questions about how design is being used to respond to real and imagined new insecurities and dangers and what new insecurities and dangers these 'design solutions' in turn create. How might we interrupt the seduction of politicians by technological fixes and by supposedly efficient design solutions to complex social, economic, and political problems? Certainly, governments are not going to stop marshaling the latest scientific expertise to try to make their citizens safer, nor should they. But we have concerns about how government desires for quick solutions, new technologies that promise these solutions at some future date, and designer expertise that makes these solutions saleable to citizens now mix into what for us in an uncomfortable and potentially dangerous new agenda for 'designing safe living',[2] an agenda that is being realized today with a very specific vision of tomorrow in mind.

This potentially dangerous new agenda for designing 'safe living' cannot be adequately interrogated from within a traditional security studies perspective. This is because of how traditional security studies understands security, technology, design, and their relationship. From a traditional security studies perspective, 'security' is typically about employing innovative problem-solving approaches to find the most efficient and effective answers to how might we best achieve security, without asking uncomfortable questions about how something gets designated as a 'problem' and a 'solution', by whom, and on whose behalf (Lacy 2005). While security experts provide the political/security problem and motivation for a security solution, it is technological innovation that holds the promise of solving these 'security problems'. From this perspective, technological innovation is understood as a process where inevitable accidents and flaws in a design drive the future refinement and progress of our society's ability to provide security (see Bauman 2004: 24). Finally, 'design' is where traditional security agendas, ever more powerful new technologies, and imagination meet to produce defense, safety, and security.

From a traditional security studies perspective, then, design is the creative link between preconceived 'security problems' and newly conceived 'technological fixes' to these problems. It is where imaginative problem-solving melds technology into a specific solution to a specific security problem by putting aesthetics in the service of policing and security (Igmade 2006). If it is successful, design does more than just imagine and manufacture solutions. It imagines and manufactures solutions in a manner that makes them acceptable, livable, and essential for our security, with the effect of depoliticizing security, technology, design, and their relationships. Design, then, is a space in which the political messiness of insecurity is reduced, stylized, and made ready to sell to sovereign nation-states, corporations, public policy-makers, and everyday citizens and consumers as a slick, seductive, effective product, service, or assemblage.

Sometimes policies implemented to make us secure do not work as intended; other times, they work exactly *as* intended, with destructive and exclusionary consequences for certain individuals and groups in society (Weizman 2007). Design can make these policies more acceptable, even seductive. However, instead of design functioning to smooth over the messiness of political life and render the security/technology relationship depoliticalized, the imaginative space of design in which security and technology meet can be mobilized to explore not only the operations of power and control in the present but to open up innovative and often troubling questions about the future consequences of new technologies in times of 'hype' about the promise of 'designing out insecurity'. A critical attitude toward design can illuminate the taken-for-granted assumptions, values, and projects designed into this relationship and throw them into doubt by raising questions like 'Why has this specific relationship between security and technology been designed?'; 'What are the political and economic projects inherent in this security/technology relationship?'; 'Who does this design empower, and who does it disempower?'; and 'What would its application mean for how we might live?'

From this critical perspective, then, design no longer necessarily functions as (just) an imaginative problem-solving space. Instead, design functions as an imaginative *problem-making* space, where concerns about the security/technology relationship can be rethought and reconfigured. In this way, design becomes a form of 'critical design' (Dunne and Raby 2001). And what are designed in this space of critical design are not techno-rational solutions to pre-given security problems but a whole range of political, social, and ethical questions/problems about how design works techno-rationally, techno-socially, and techno-psychically (Dunne and Raby 2001; also see Weber 2008).

Redesigning Security

It is precisely design's potential to critically interrupt the security/technology relationship that interests us. But how specifically can design be mobilized to enable a critical study of security? How can we apply the ideas, techniques, and methodologies of critical design to interrupt the often taken-for-granted relationship between security and technology? And, importantly, why should we make such a move?

In this chapter, we outline a new research agenda we call Redesigning Security. A Redesigning Security Approach begins from a recognition that the achievement of security is more often than not illusive, which means that the desire for security is itself problematic. Rather than encouraging the design of 'security solutions' – a securing by design (Weber and Lacy forthcoming) – a Redesigning Security Approach explores how we might *insecure security by design*. In other words, this approach uses design as a vehicle through which to raise questions about security problems and security solutions by designing concrete material objects that themselves embody questions about traditional security and about traditional design practices that use technology to depoliticize how technology is deployed by states and corporations to make us 'safe'.

Before we turn to this new research agenda, we first want to elaborate why we think it is important to rethink new securities through critical design. To do this, we discuss what intellectuals like Michel Foucault and Paul Virilio regard as the modern design problem that has generated and continues to generate some of the most politically and ethically far-reaching design 'solutions'. This problem is the management of circulation, a problem states and traditional designers have long been collaborating on to develop solutions to make us 'safe'. We have chosen this example because of how it highlights the need to rethink contemporarily designed policy problems and solutions through a Redesigning Security Approach. To make this point, we introduce several illustrations of political and critical design, discuss how they make visible the political and ethical assumptions bound up in these design 'solutions' and the technologies they are based upon, and analyze how they open up a new series of questions about the future of the security/design/technology relationship.

The Problem of Circulation

It has long been the case that the perception, emergence, and/or creation of new dangers have led policy-makers to turn to designers for technological fixes to security problems. What tend to be 'new' in this combination of new dangers, new securities, and new designs are what needs to be managed and what technological form design 'solutions' to management 'problems' take. As intellectuals like Michel Foucault and Paul Virilio argue, in modernity states have turned increasingly complex flows of 'circulation' into a management problem that states must administer and control (Bratton 2006; Foucault 2007; Virilio 2006). And so policy-makers and designers have long been collaborating on how to 'design out insecurities' and 'design in protection' with respect to circulation. But what circulates, how it circulates, where it circulates, why it circulates, and at what speed it circulates have all been changing. So finding the balance between making life livable and making life safe is an ongoing challenge for states, for citizens, and for designers.

In works like *Speed and Politics* and *Security, Territory, Population*, Paul Virilio and Michel Foucault respectively make a seemingly obvious point about the world we live in – that this world is only possible due to the complex forms of circulation that surround us, be these the circulation of money, goods, food, machines, armies, diseases, animals, or ideas. As such, circulation is vital to modern life and to modern living. Yet unregulated circulation is often perceived by states as a security problem. So states (often collaborating with designers and architects) step in to carefully and 'cost-effectively' manage circulation. As Virilio and

Foucault note, these management strategies are always political because they are always infused with the interests and desires of states.

Even so, some regulations on circulation seem to be unproblematic. For example, if we were allowed to drive our automobiles as fast as we wanted to, then fatalities on the roads would most likely increase. So it makes good sense to have enforced speed limits.[3] Yet other regulations are far more problematic. For example, many states currently justify the management of their territorial borders by arguing that, if the global circulation of people crossing borders were unregulated, then some countries would be 'swamped' with undocumented bodies that states claim threaten their economy, security, and health (Doty 2003, 2009).

States, then, face a predicament – how can states address the desires of their citizens for the accelerated mobility that modern circulatory systems can provide while at the same time putting in place controls devised to manage circulation that do not unduly irritate or impede the circulatory systems their citizens reply upon. One way is for states to regulate the speed of circulation. For example, the speed of the economic circulation of goods and services might be increased (through, for example, the quicker delivery of goods ordered online) while the speed of human circulation may be decreased at international borders to allow states to interrogate those people and packages whose transit the state may want to inhibit (whether they threaten to import disease, unemployment, or terror).

The management and control of circulation often relies upon 'low-tech' solutions, like speed bumps placed on roads or paper passports at border crossings. Yet as we move from a geopolitical to a metro-political era, increasingly powerful technologies are becoming part of our everyday lives, in part because our daily lives are constantly recontextualized through old dangers like crimes perpetrated by 'dangerous classes' and new dangers like threats created by 'terrorist networks'. This has the effect of increasing the number of products designed to protect our bodies and property from crime and terrorism through new 'networked' technology, smart materials, or biometric technologies like domestic surveillance, knife-proof clothing, or fingerprint-activated laptops. At the same time, these technologies enable new ways of monitoring the circulation of people and products while making circulation faster, more efficient, and more individualized by using everything from RFID devices to 'responsive environments' of the sort seen in films like *Minority Report* (see Sterling 2005; Weber 2005). In these ways, states attempt to 'design out' uncertainties, insecurities, and inconveniences while they 'design in' protection'.

Many of these designs have a connection to the military or the militarized mentality that modern citizens live with(in). For example, because the attainment of security seemed elusive for Cold War citizens, one of the prevailing images and technologies of 'safe living' during this period in US/Soviet history was for citizens to barricade themselves against a nuclear attack. On a low-tech level, school children were trained to 'duck and cover' when they saw a nuclear flash; on a high-tech level, nuclear shelters were built into backyards and mountain sides. In our contemporary world, though, moving around is often seen as safer than being a sitting duck (covered or not). As design theorist Susan Yelavich explains, 'In the end, mobility appeared the better course than perpetual internment [like in a nuclear fall-out shelter], and the shelter became just another decoy' (2005: 23). So new designs like Kosuke Tsumara's Final Home Jacket – a garment designed as a 'nomadic home' in times of disaster – were created that could protect mobile citizens from mobile dangers, something that makes more sense in our post-Cold War, post-9/11 era.

As Tsumara's Final Home Jacket illustrates, our relationships to everyday objects change when our military imaginaries and technologies change. The German designer and social theorist Stephan Trüby elaborates on this point:

> With the advent of the new wars 'things' have moved into our field of awareness more than ever before. An array of low-tech products such as rucksacks, carpet knives, soles of shoes, containers for liquids and so on have for some time now posed a considerable threat. Also high-tech products like iPods and other gadgets are inconceivable without the power of innovation which is to improve a MOUT [Israeli 'Military Operations in Urbanized Terrains'] agent's or IDF [Israel Defence Forces] soldier's chances of survival.
>
> (Trüby 2008: 92)

In addition to the everyday objects that we do see, there are everyday electronic impulses circulating through our environments and our bodies that we don't see – things like radio waves or microwaves that have their own spectral geography. These electromagnetic impulses make the circulation and exchange of data possible without us necessarily being aware of their invisible movements as they happen, yet we respond to them all the time – through broadcasts we watch, products we use to heat our food, and the weird buzz we sometimes pick up in our bodies. We are not just surrounded but permeated by these electromagnetic impulses, as we rely upon them to circulate the signals of modern life. Sometimes these signals have to do with security. In the USA, for example, television viewers are familiar with the Emergency Broadcasting System that tests whether or not radio and television signals could be transmitted during a national emergency. A more playful recent example is Future Farmers' Homeland Security Blankets. 'Each blanket is wirelessly networked to the internet and responds to the Homeland Security Acts fluxuating (sic) Color coded "Threat Levels". As a means to "disseminate information", these blankets disseminate temperature change and an indicating light which alerts the user of the current threat and comforts them accordingly' (Future Farmers 2008, www.futurefarmers.com).

What designs like the Homeland Security Blanket illustrate are how designers make security intelligible and accessible to us and livable for us, often through everyday objects that provide both information and comfort (Antonelli 2005: 15). But the Homeland Security Blanket does something else. It also makes us hyperaware of the invisible electromagnetic security-space we occupy and that occupies us. As such, it embodies two critiques of what attempts to 'design out insecurity' and 'design in protection' do in our daily lives. One critique suggests that new technologies are merely hype, designed to make everyday citizens aware of what their states designate as dangers and then to comfort citizens with their state's ability to provide them with 'safety' (Davis 2007; Nordstrom 2007).

Yet the possibility that new technologies of surveillance, control and protection could work leads to a second critique of the security/technology relationship – that new technologies introduce new dangers into our daily lives rather than (as promised) eliminate new dangers (like the danger of being forced to provide the state with our 'bio-political tattoos' like fingerprints when crossing international borders; see Agamben 2004a).

All this suggests that design 'solutions' may provide us with too much security and too much convenience, which can ultimately end up making us less secure and more inconvenienced. This is a common critique of large-scale modernist architectural projects like the city Brasilia that secured its citizens but also bored and frustrated them because of 'the absence of crowds and crowdiness, empty street corners, the anonymity of places and the facelessness of human figures, and a numbing monotony of an environment devoid of anything to puzzle, perplex or excite' (Bauman 1998: 43). Contemporary attempts to design in protection and create new controls for circulation generally lack the scale and ambition of such modern attempts to redesign life. However, with the move from the geopolitical to the metro-political and with the development of new technologies like biometrics, nanotechnology, and smart materials, an increasing number of 'small' everyday objects have security problems and solutions designed into them, as well as potential ethico-political dilemmas.

Making the ethico-political dilemmas designed into everyday objects and processes of safety visible is what political and critical designers do. In so doing, these designers help us to think about how security-obsessed objects, architectures, and impulses shape not only our environments but ourselves as contemporary subjects. For they present us with a whole new range of security questions, including 'Do we need protection from what the state designates as 'dangerous' or are we endangered by what the state tells us is 'safe'?

Consider the following examples – one having to do with the flow of undocumented bodies across international borders and one having to do with our everyday relationships with animals and food.

The first example is designer Robert Ransick's Casa Segura (Figure 24.1). Casa Segura (Safe House) is a small, solar-powered shed-like structure stocked with non-perishable

Figure 24.1 Casa Segura

DESIGNING SECURITY

food and water. Located on private land in the Sonora desert in Southern Arizona, this unmanned shack can be used by undocumented migrants crossing the US/Mexico border through the desert trying to avoid detection by US Border Patrol agents. Because of the harsh conditions of the Arizona desert and the general under-preparedness of crossers to make their journey, Casa Segura's shelter and provisions can mean the difference between life and death. But Casa Segura is more than just a transitional space that migrants can anonymously pass through. For Casa Segura also houses a computer touch screen that is linked (on a time delay) to the internet. Choosing between options 'to draw, write messages, or make a pictogram from a set of ready-made graphical icons', migrants using Casa Segura may not only mark their existence but also comment on their experience as they make their journey. By engaging 'Mexican migrants crossing the border through this dangerous landscape, the property owners whose land they cross, and members of the general public interested in learning more about border issues … Casa Segura offers a new method of engagement and free exchange. Shifting away from the abstract rhetoric of numbers, the project focuses on the anonymous – yet intimate – relationship between a property owner and the individual migrants walking their land' (Ransick 2008, www.casasegura.us).

The second example comes from James King's In-Vitro Meat Project, 'Dressing the Meat of Tomorrow' (Antonelli 2008: 106). King's interest is in how existing technologies make it possible to clone edible meat without the need to clone and then slaughter an entire animal. This leads him to speculate on 'how we might choose to give shape, texture and flavour to this new sort of food in order to better remind us where it came from' (King 2008, www.james-king.net). In his project, King designs in-vitro meat that in no way resembles the meat we are accustomed to eating these days, meat that is a discrete part of an animal like a leg or a breast. Instead, the meat King images might be served in the future is grown in-vitro in molds to resemble colorful (almost candy-like) cross-sections of an animal's inner organs, what he calls 'MRI steaks' (see Figure 24.2). By playing with ideas of taste and palatability, King's work challenges us to think about how existing technologies enable unforeseen relationships among humans, animals, and food. It raises questions like: 'Should cloning meat replace herding and slaughtering animals for food?'; 'If so, would cloning make animals safe from humans or would more species of animals become extinct because humans don't cultivate them?'; 'Is cloned meat safe for human

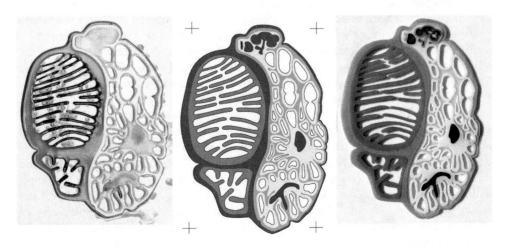

Figure 24.2 James King's In-Vitro Meat Project 'Dressing the Meat of Tomorrow'

247

consumption?'; 'If so, how might cloning meat introduce new practices of ethical eating beyond, say, vegetarianism?'; ' And how will designers make these developments normal and acceptable?'

Structures like Casa Segura and objects like MRI steaks are designed to hold social, cultural, political, and ethical values in ways that provoke questions. By building and/ or circulating these designed structures and objects, political and critical designers are effectively circulating their questions, about the normal and the abnormal, the real and the imaginary, the possible and the impossible. It is for this reason that critical designers sometimes refer to their work as 'design for debate' (Dunne and Raby 2008). Included in this debate are not just the intended uses of designed objects, but also their unintended uses. For one never really knows how an object will be used in a specific context by a specific individual with all sorts of emotions, desires, and needs that commodified technology cannot or will not recognize (Dunne and Raby 2001). Think again of Colomina's example of the cell phone, which was designed to enable communication and connection but which was used, misused, or abused to trigger destruction.

Overall, what these political and critical designs do is use the imaginative space of design in which security and technology meet to make politics, values, and ethics visible. They do this by illuminating many taken-for-granted assumptions, values, and utilities designed into this relationship and highlighting questions about why a particular security/technology relationship exists, on whose behalf, for what stated and unstated purpose, and for what intended and unintended use. In so doing, they allow us to think political, critically, and ethically about what the application of these everyday technologies of protection means for our 'safe living' right here and right now as we think about how we will live safely today and how we will live safely in the future.

'Do You Want to Replace the Existing Normal?'[4]

As the above discussion makes clear, the work of political and critical designers can embody unexpected and therefore disarming critiques of the relationship between security, technology, and design. It can do this by, in the words of critical designer Fiona Raby (2008), 'replacing the existing normal' in terms of what design is supposed to do. For critical designers like Raby, what traditional design is supposed to do is use technology to provide consumers with market-driven systems, services, and objects that are useful as well as aesthetically pleasing, rather than raise questions about new technologies. From our new securities perspective, what traditional design also does is smooth over and depoliticize the relationship between technology and security by providing slick, sellable technological 'solutions' to what states, corporations, and individuals designate as security 'problems'.

For the past few years, we have been working with political and critical designers to learn about the protocols and procedures of doing political and critical design and to expose these designers to how we think about safety and security.[5] Just as we would not claim any expertise in the area of design, none of the political and critical designers we work with would claim any expertise in the area of security studies. Nor would these designers necessarily appreciate all of the ways their work occasionally interrupts traditional and even new 'security dialogues'. So it is just as hit and miss that political and critical designers might direct their attention to 'security issues' as it is that security scholars might stumble upon the insights of political and critical designers to help them 'replace the existing normal' in terms of what security studies is supposed to do. The challenge, then, is to create a new, sustained dialogue among political and critical designers and security studies scholars and practitioners so that they might work together to influence public policy agendas that claim to 'design out insecurity' and 'design in protection' now and in the future and to expose dangerous contradictions bound up in these security agendas.

One of the ways we are taking up this challenge is by developing a new approach to security studies, what we call Redesigning Security. A Redesigning Security Approach combines the insights of new security studies and the insights of political and critical design to rethink the security/technology relationship in ways that may influence security policy. More specifically, it involves three moves: (1) interrupting the conventional conversation about security by broadening who takes part in this conversation; (2) identifying new research questions that emerge from this conversation; and (3) combining new security studies insights and political and critical design practices and research methods/attitudes as a way to explore these new research questions. We will elaborate on each of these moves in turn.

Conversations about security tend to be limited to social/political science academics, government policy-makers working directly on security issues, and scientists developing technologies that may be deployed to solve security problems. Occasionally, stakeholders like 'the public' or corporations are included. Our conversation about redesigning security draws upon these and three additional groups – (1) academics working on critical organizational management, critical science/technology studies, and critical humanities studies; (2) critical policy analysts working for independent public policy think tanks; and (3) design practitioners who understand themselves to be doing politically motivated design or to be employing 'critical design' methods in their practice of design. What these additional conversationalists add are alternative perspectives on what politics is and how it is practiced. They also broaden the resources we draw upon to reimagine and therefore rethink what security is, what technology is, what design is, and what the security/technology/design relationship should be. They do this through reference to aspects of the 'real world' that traditional security studies scholars, analysts, and practitioners often neglect and to 'other worlds' in film, literature, art, music, and performance.

What are emerging from this refigured conversation are a range of research questions that are markedly different to those found in traditional and new security studies because they require us to rethink security, technology, and design separately and together. These questions are:

1   What products, services and systems are designers, scientists and policy-makers imagining and proposing in order to 'design out' insecurity and 'design in' protection'?
2   How can we begin to use alternative practices and methods/attitudes – such as 'critical design' – to imagine how these new products, services, and systems will be used and (mis)used in the near future and to potentially interrupt and/or redirect these future applications of new technologies?
3   What are the ethico-political implications of these attempts to 'design out' insecurity and 'design in protection'?

How we investigate these research questions is by combining new securities insights with political and critical design methods/attitudes. As our earlier discussion pointed out, a new securities perspective offers a number of insights about the relationships between security and insecurity, security and fear, and security and politics/ethics. One of the mantras of new security studies is that attempts to increase security are often also accompanied by increases in insecurity. At the same time, though, multiplying insecurities can be a policy-making technique (as we've seen in the so-called war on terror). But it is a policy-making technique that always threatens to get out of hand. This is because the sorts of fears that bubble through all of the contemporary circulatory systems we discussed earlier are explicitly created, directed, containable, and predictable fears *as well as* unexpected, misdirected, uncontainable, and unpredictable fears. All responses to these insecurities and fears – whether we think they make us 'safe' or not – have ethico-political dimensions that are sometimes difficult to grasp when we are caught up in them (such as the complex architectural and technological developments in airport security and mobility, see Adey 2008; Jacobsen forthcoming).

Much of the work of political and critical designers engages (either explicitly or implicitly) the ethico-political issues circulating through contemporary networks of security and insecurity. What these designers are very good at is making visible the relationships between security and insecurity through the production of material objects (like Casa Segura or MRI steaks). The reason why these objects are so effective at materializing relationships between security and insecurity (particularly in the realm of science and technology) is because these objects embody paradoxes about the circulation of securities and insecurities through technologies that either exist today (border patrols) or that are being imaged to secure us in the future (Homeland Security blankets).

What we are calling 'political design' accomplishes its critique of the security/technology/design relationship by proposing self-consciously political designs that intentionally complicate prevailing knowledge about politics while (usually) offering alternative design solutions to political problems (as Casa Segura does, for example, in relation to the prevailing wisdom and practice of dealing with undocumented immigrants). How what designers Anthony Dunne and Fiona Raby call 'critical design' accomplishes its critique of the security/technology/design relationship is by standing outside the prevailing knowledge about design (that design should offer marketable 'solutions' to pre-given 'problems'). From this position, critical designers are able to design objects that are themselves questions about the ethico-political values and biases designed into everyday technologies, as well as questions about the traditional way of doing design. This position also allows critical designers to speculate not only about what appears to be normal in the present but also about what might become normal in the future, especially in relation to new sciences and technologies. And it also allows them to question how what is normal in the present is uncritically projected into the future by corporate (and we would add, state) futurologists (see Schwartz 2003). On this point, Dunne and Raby argue,

> Corporate [and state] futurologists force-feed us a 'happy-ever-after' portrayal of life where technology is the solution to every problem. There is no room for doubt or complexity in their techno–utopian visions. Everyone is a stereotype, and social and cultural roles remain unchanged. Despite the fact that technology is evolving, the imagined products that feature in their fantasies reassure us that nothing essential will change, everything will stay the same. … The resulting scenarios extend pre-existing reality into the future and so reinforce the status quo rather than challenging it.
>
> (2001: 6; our brackets)

Rather than buying into these conservative forecasting strategies, Dunne and Raby explore fantastical future scenarios that often have a bleaker quality, what they have sometimes referred to as 'design noir' (2001). Commenting on this practice, Anthony Dunne explains,

DESIGNING SECURITY

If we limit ourselves to only designing the present then the 'future' will just happen to us, and the one we get will be driven by technology and economics. We need to develop ways of speculating that are grounded in fact yet engage the imagination and allow us to debate different possible futures before they happen. The danger of course is that they become mere fantasies. So the challenge is how to maintain realism. Maybe it is related to the suspension of disbelief that filmmakers make use of. The social and ethical implications of technologies such as biotech and nanotech can only be explored through speculation.

(Quoted in Womack 2007)

Unconventional speculation and imagination about the future, then, are among the most important tools of critical designers. But, as Dunne points out, this speculation must be grounded in more than mere fantasy. For this reason, Dunne, Raby and their students in the Royal College of Arts' Design Interactions Programme team up with top-notch nano- and material scientists, bioengineers, and emerging technologists, with corporations like Microsoft and BT, and with government departments like the Department of Trade and Industry. By ensuring that the science and technology they engage with is on the drawing board (if not already in the marketplace) critical designers 'blur the boundaries between the real and the fictional, so that the conceptual becomes more real and the real is seen as just one limited possibility among many' (Dunne and Raby 2001: 65).

The results of critical design are objects that both fascinate and alienate, thrill and repel, aesthetically please and morally repulse. James King's MRI steaks are a good example of this. And all of this is, of course, intentional. It is what Fiona Raby calls 'the space of dilemma' (2008) and what we call 'thinking space'. It is in these sorts of spaces, through some very unexpected encounters with objects, that we might create new opportunities to think again about the security/technology/design relationship.

Conclusion

Design and security have a long and complex history. But integral to that history is a reliance upon technology to fix what states designate as security problems. As this chapter points out, sometimes states address the 'wrong' security problems, sometimes states proliferate insecurities in their development of new security technologies, and most of the time states along with corporate and scientific futurologists project a conservative understanding of security and technology into the future and ask design to merely confirm these scenarios.

The relationships among security, technology, and design can, however, be quite different, and these differences can have an impact on how security policy is conceived of and practiced today and in the future. Our goal in proposing a Redesigning Security Approach is to combine the 'very concrete and down to earth language' of design (Dunne quoted in Womack 2001) – a language articulated mostly through material objects – with the insights of new security studies. We recognize the potential for politics-as-usual to absorb the critiques offered by political and critical design and for design to shy away from doing politics (Weber and Lacy forthcoming). Yet at a time when policy-makers, futurists and designers are often seduced by the promise of 'securing through design', our engagements with political and critical design open up alternative ways of interacting with technology and design, potentially transforming us from policy analysts who uncritically

251

rely upon the latest technology to solve our security problems into 'scout[s] sent on ahead to see if the water is drinkable or not' (J. G. Ballard, quoted in Johnson 2008: 25).

Notes

1 This is what is known in the literature on safety and design as the principle of 'reverse risk compensation'. See Norman 2007: 82.
2 Our interest in 'designing safe living' has its roots in a programme we jointly ran with Adrian Mackenzie through the Institute of Advanced Studies at Lancaster University during the 2007–8 academic year called 'New Sciences of Protection: Designing Safe Living'. For more information about this programme and the issues it raised, see the program website at http://www.lancs.ac.uk/ias/annualprogramme/protection/ and see the program blog at http://safeliving.wordpress.com/.
3 For an alternative perspective, see Norman 2007.
4 This is a typical error message at comes up when using a computer, and it is also the title of designer Fiona Raby's presentation at the Lancaster University Institute for Advanced Studies' Annual Program Year Conference on 'New Sciences of Protection: Designing Safe Living', 10–12 July 2008.
5 See http://www.lancs.ac.uk/ias/annualprogramme/protection/ and http://safeliving.wordpress.com/.

25

New Mobile Crime

Monica den Boer

Introduction

There is a growing consensus among academics and law enforcement analysts that the volume of mobile and transnational crime keeps growing, due to globalization (Serrano 2002: 24), migratory patterns (Walters, this volume), technology, infrastructure, communication and market dynamics (Woodiwiss 2003: 25). Mobile crime has adopted a supra-local character, which necessitates information-exchange and operational cooperation between law enforcement agencies in different countries. The category of organized serious transnational crime includes fraud, forgery, money laundering, man-smuggling, trafficking in human beings, drugs trafficking, stolen vehicles, environmental crime, cyber-crime, child pornography, illegal arms trafficking and even terrorism. This wide list of criminal offences indicates that the label (transnational) 'organized crime' is imprecise and ambiguous. In fact, it has become more common to look at the causes of transnational crime.

In this chapter, I will seek to analyse and debate the field of mobile crime, that is to say, all crime that moves across jurisdictional borders, or even stronger, all crime that deliberately moves across borders for the purposes of exploitation or avoidance. Special attention is devoted to the role of technology, market dynamics and legal loopholes, as well as global connections, as they are deemed to be factors that accommodate and facilitate the mobility of crime. Furthermore, I will look at the challenge this poses to law enforcement organizations. With the growing acknowledgement that most organized crime and terrorism has adopted a transnational, fluid and networked character, the emphasis has gradually shifted from repressive policing to preventive, proactive and intelligence-based policing, which makes a tactical use of social network analysis, risk analysis, profiling and pattern detection. The final section of the chapter will look at the institutional and legal responses to mobile crime: while several international law enforcement agencies have been created such as Interpol and Europol, there is a growing reliance on 'mobile strategies' such as nodal policing, 'mobile squads' such as Joint Hit Teams and Joint Investigations Teams, as well as on movable liaison officers and mobile surveillance methods. The chapter closes by analysing the deeper tissue below the future development in mobile crime.

Analysing and Debating Mobile Crime

The first question to be tackled is the extent to which crime can be considered mobile. One definition is the label given by the Metropolitan Police who use the label 'mobile crime' for mobile phone crime, in other words the trade in stolen mobile phones.[1] The term 'mobile crime' has also been used to denote crime committed on mobile real estate. However, in this chapter I use a more encompassing definition, namely all crime that is mobile in character, especially crime of a transnational nature. In fact, the category of mobile crime is vast when taking into account that criminals are almost always on the go, whether they commit a petty crime like shoplifting, a capital crime like murder or rape, or crimes like piracy or cross-border brigandage. While a majority of all criminal offences takes place within small milieus, intimate communities or geographically confined spaces, several crime components may be defined as mobile, such as communication, transport logistics and trails left after the perpetration of a crime. Mobile transnational forms of organized crime are not new, but ancient (Woodiwiss 2003: 13). Studies which unravel itinerant crime in the Middle Ages, for instance, show how thieves and murderers exploited the limited competence of small state jurisdictions, and crossed the border to escape from the tentacles of the judicial authorities (Egmond 1994).

Global connections are an explanatory factor for the mobility of crime. All over the world, there are associations across large distances, demographic shifts and diasporas. Ethnic ties and knots are often anchored in durable family relationships, where common codes are cultivated and trust relations are developed over a longer period of time. In Europe, there are several ethnically homogeneous criminal associations (but many are also heterogeneously composed). Migratory movements across the world and large-scale demographic shifts (Walters this volume) are regarded as a key variable in crime dispersion (Bovenkerk *et al.* 1996).

Mobile crime also heavily exploits technological innovations. Virtual crime and cyber-crime, such as phishing, hacking, password-theft, electronic child pornography, industrial espionage, software piracy, fraudulent e-commerce transactions, digital money laundering, cyber-stalking, electronic infringement of intellectual property and several other crimes are examples enabled by computers and the internet. Innovations in communication technology are widely exploited by criminal groups to facilitate their exchanges (Thomas and Loader 2000). The internet has eroded the borders between nation states and their jurisdictions because of the emergence of so-called 'cyberspace'. Criminal offences can thus be committed in a nation state while remaining relatively unaffected by criminal prosecution (Den Boer 2002a: 436).

When analysing market dynamics as a crucial variable in mobile crime, analysts often refer to the notion of the (adjacency of) opportunities, opportunity structures (Klerks 2003: 99), market structures, 'criminogenic asymmetries' (Wright 2006: 206), or the 'proximity to source countries' (Von Lampe 2008: 9). Markets and market opportunities explain to some extent why there are regional variations in the prevalence of illegal markets within particular countries. Von Lampe (2008: 9) uses the example of the United Kingdom, which is Europe's largest retail market for contraband cigarettes, which shows a 'clear concentration in certain regions of the country, namely the northern parts of England … pointing to variations in socio-economic conditions and differential opportunities for link-ups in the distribution chain'. Failing and developing countries, or countries with a high poverty level, high unemployment rates, high levels of corruption, ample presence of weapons and low (post-conflict) morale generally have a relatively high propensity to function as facilitators for transnational organized crime.

Infrastructure (transport, roads, harbours, airports, communication infrastructure) is a crucial variable in the mobility of crime. Economic liberalization has reduced transportation costs, has encouraged improvement in transportation infrastructures, and has expanded distribution networks. Containerization 'has vastly increased the efficiency of transporting both legal and illegal goods' (Andreas 2002: 40). 'Smugglers have increasingly exploited the container revolution to camouflage their illicit cargo' (ibid. 41) Spain, for instance, 'serves as the main transshipment centre for Moroccan cannabis, accounting for about three quarters of the total quantity of cannabis resin seized in the EU' (Von Lampe 2008: 9). Famous is the Balkan route, which is used for the transportation of several illegal goods, ranging from drugs (notably heroin from Afghanistan via Turkey into Europe) and weapons to the trafficking in human beings, linking sources, markets and the activities (Köppel and Székely 2002; Netherlands Police Agency 2004: 14). Western Europe is the world market's major source of synthetic drugs, with the North–South connections between Europe and consumption markets in countries like Israel and Australia.

Legal loopholes and 'jurisdiction shopping' (Passas 2002: 27) are regarded as factors which may be beneficial to criminal entrepreneurship. Criminal organizations find the jurisdictions which allow conduct which has been criminalized in one's own state:

> Toxic waste may be dumped in countries with lax or no regulation of such waste. The bribery of foreign government officials (in order to ensure a contract is gained or renewed) has been treated by some countries as a tax-deductible business expense. Lawyers, accountants, former government or military officials often act as consultants or private businessmen after they leave public office and offer advice on how to engage in risky and harmful practices without breaking the laws of the countries where different operations take place.

Academic and crime analysts have established the emergence of strong interlinks between local and global economies (Hobbs 1998). Mutual connections between crime structures are considered to be symbiotic in nature, and this may also apply to criminal groups that become 'the crucial bases of support for governments and elites determined to hold on to power' (Berdal and Serrano 2002a: 199). Mobile, transnational organized crime is not only hard to quantify but semantically ambiguous. It is considered to be volatile, chameleon-like, and networked in character, whilst shifting across national, legal and jurisdictional borders as well as moving across volatile markets (Mitsilegas 2003; Sheptycki 2003). This reflects the analyses of national law enforcement authorities in the EU member states, which reveal that organized crime is not generally perceived to comprise large, monolithic and rigidly structured criminal organizations, but rather small organizations with a multinational orientation, few operating procedures, flexibility in their operations and the ability to adapt to changing markets and situations (Den Boer 2002b: 108).

When discussing 'transnational crime', we mostly refer to serious organized crime with a cross-border dimension. The focus in Europe has recently been on criminal groups that conduct criminal activities, but a problem for law enforcement remains the fuzzy definition, making the concept difficult to operationalize (Von Lampe 2008: 7): 'Myriad aspects of the social universe are lumped together in varying combinations within different frames of reference depending on the respective point of view of each observer.' Recently, there has also been growing attention on itinerant criminals who are reported to steal cars, cargo and burgle houses, and who move their activities from area to area, for example, from housing estates to industrial areas, facilitated by the fact that these criminal groups normally do not have a fixed residence. Mobile banditry has become a label more widely used for ram raids, coordinated shoplifting and fast crimes (robbery, burglary, car theft) (National Police Agency 2004: 30). The Polaris-project of the Dutch national police agency KLPD – replaced by the Monitor Supraregional Middle Crime – focuses on mobile banditry by East European criminal groups, notably Polish and Lithuanian criminals.

For the conceptualization of transnational organized crime, several (competing) paradigms have been used. Paradigms that come to mind are the hierarchy (also the Mafia paradigm), the Octopus, the Enterprise Paradigm, the Ad Hoc Coalition and the Network Paradigm (Von Lampe 2002: 193). The Mafia paradigm regards organized crime as relatively fixed, stable and durable structures of cooperation, and refers to characteristics which are derived from the analysis of crime families such as the Cosa Nostra, the Camorra or the 'Ndrangheta. These groups are also associated with internal distribution of tasks and disciplining. The potential emergence of an Octopus or the 'Pax Mafiosa' – which essentially means the cooperation among criminal organizations and the formation of global conglomerates of crime – has been extensively analysed (Wright 2006: 144ff.), but it is believed that instead a global web of criminal networks continue to build cooperative ventures (Williams 2002: 80).

A mobile crime dimension which has become subject of academic analysis is the entrepreneurial structure, defined as a non-economic structure that supports illegal economic activities indirectly (Liddick 1999). The entrepreneurs can often be seen on the intermediate level between the legitimate 'upperworld' and the illegitimate 'underworld', and often provide quasi-governmental services (see e.g. Netherlands Police Agency 2004: 51; Van Duyne 1993; Van Duyne *et al.* 2002). Examples are given by Von Lampe (2008: 11), who refers to the overlap between legal and illegal enterprise in the realm of VAT-fraud, investment fraud and subsidy fraud and private security firms that may offer illicit debt collection services or engage in extortion, or illegal gambling casinos that operate under the guise of a legally licensed casino. The enterprise paradigm puts forward a dynamic perspective of organized crime, where action and not the structure is taken as the starting point (Von Lampe 2002: 193): 'The question is not how criminal organizations take control of illegal markets, but how participants are *organizing* their crime-trade and adapt to and survive in illegal markets.' Increasingly also, organized crime is purported to be the work of so-called ad hoc coalitions, or opportunity-driven contractual enterprises between criminals, often based on relations of trust between employer and employee, and between supplier and consumer (Bovenkerk *et al.* 1996; Fijnaut and Paoli 2006).

Transnational organized crime in Europe has gained a more fluid and networked character, and the 'crime landscape' in Europe can be characterized by its 'patchwork character' (Von Lampe 2008: 9; see also Galeotti 2007). The diversification of contacts, relationships and criminal activities make criminal groups less permeable, and so it is more difficult for law enforcement to crack codes of communication, to identify membership, to establish evidence of a durable criminal enterprise, to delineate criminal activities within a geographically neatly delineated space and to find evidence of structured organized crime (Klerks 2003: 100). In other words, in order to prevent that these mobile criminal groups becoming relatively immune to law enforcement intervention, there is mounting pressure on law enforcement organizations to shift their focus from 'easily discernible organizational entities with some degree of formalization' to less easily recognizable collectives, such as local criminal milieus or cliques of individuals 'who share the same deviant values and socialize on a more or less continuous basis' (Von Lampe 2008: 12). The European Police Office Europol states that criminal groups evolve into 'oriented clusters' and that they strategically join each other on a temporary basis (Europol 2007: 9).

Edwards and Gill (2003: 270) state that law enforcement and researchers have gradually produced a different narrative about the formation and structure of transnational organized crime groups. Transnational crime is becoming restyled from immutable, pyramidical hierarchies to crime which is woven into the texture of ordinary social life, where contacts between criminals intermesh with habitual social patterns. This new narrative shifts the challenge for law enforcement intervention from targeted intelligence-gathering and interventions to even more encompassing crime control strategies (Grieve 2008: 19). Below, I will discuss how law enforcement agencies have revised their strategies on the relatively new network paradigm regarding transnational crime as predominantly fluid and mobile.

Targeting, Tracking and Tracing Mobile Crime

Under the assumption that transnational crime constitutes a real threat to legal economies and the integrity of governments (Berdal and Serrano 2002), the European Union has sought to flex its muscles by implementing a number of anti-organized crime strategies. The Action Plan on Organized Crime which was agreed in 1997 was an important step towards a common approach and demanded from the member states that they create central criminal investigation agencies, develop a multi-sectoral approach and adopt binding legislation for the criminalization of participation in a criminal organization (Den Boer 2001; 2002b: 108).[2] Meanwhile another significant step is the consolidation of the EU legal framework with regard to mutual assistance, in particular the adoption of the EU Convention on mutual assistance in criminal matters (Den Boer 2002b: 110: see also below). In response to the challenge of cross-border mobility of the crime economy (Vermeulen 2002: 124), new trends and cooperation mechanisms were laid down in this convention, including the interception of (GSM and satellite) telecommunications, controlled deliveries, covert investigations (infiltration), and joint (multi-national) investigation teams (see below). All these instruments point in the direction of increased surveillance and a predominantly proactive approach.

Together with several national criminal intelligence services, Europol has shifted its strategy from a retrospective reporting style to a more proactively geared risk assessment strategy. While the agency no longer highlights 'particular crime types since the replacement of the old "EU Organized Crime Report" by an annual "Organized Crime Threat Assessment"', it has also shifted its focus to five horizontal facilitating factors, which are document forger and identity fraud, technology, misuse of the transport sector, and globalization and borders (Von Lampe 2008: 8). Risk forecasting (Sheptycki 2003: 47) or risk assessment is a collective or corporate enterprise, embracing both the public and the private sphere (Ericson 2007).

Various methods of surveillance and data-collection fold into a 'surveillance assemblage' (Ericson 2007: 2; Shelley *et al.* 2005). Among these surveillance methods is the – among law enforcement authorities – rather popular Automatic Number Plate Recognition (ANPR), which entails that road cameras record all vehicle license plates of vehicles that pass a certain location (e.g. tunnel, bridge, motorway) which is placed under continuous surveillance. The technology – which is far removed from police officers' discretion to stop and search vehicle drivers – has the 'advantage' that it removes the guesswork from police intercepts (Corbett 2008: 137). However, the volumes of data retention are enormous as there can be 50 million 'reads' on just one day in a country like the United Kingdom. The monitoring of traffic makes retrospective revisiting by the police possible, and by the Association of Chief Constables it has been claimed as a technology which 'will revolutionize arrest, intelligence and crime investigation opportunities' (ibid. 138). Large-scale data collection and data-storage allows for data-mining, text-mining and pattern-detection. At the policy level of the European Union, new legislation has been adopted to allow for extensive data-retention,[3] as well as for the communication of Passenger Name Records (PNR) to some third countries (USA, Canada and Australia) (Kuipers 2008).[4]

Several preventive methods also have an active, operational dimension: transport of illegal goods may be interrupted, disrupted (Dorn 2003: 230), seized or simply the flow of goods and services may be 'choked off' (Sheptycki 2003: 63). Hence, the 'strike' is essential, and it is supposed to flow from good-quality intelligence-gathering (Phillips 2008: 34). However transnational organized crime groups may simply write off the loss of a shipment as a company risk. With the creation of a surveillance assemblage (Ericson 2007) and the convergence of intelligence systems, 'conjoining information across the categories of criminal law, disruption, administrative action and regulation of markets' (Dorn 2003: 237), there is a growing need for oversight and accountability (Passas 2002: 33), as the value of intelligence and the effect of surveillance may eventually be (con)tested in court.

Until now, there has been insufficient reflection as to how preventive intervention by law enforcement may itself be responsible for shifts in crime patterns and unforeseen effects which may ultimately be in favour of the illegal market. In other words, law enforcement interventions in mobile crime may create a waterbed effect by means of which crime itself is merely transposed from one area to another (Stelfox 2003: 120). A similar analysis applies to the criminalization of certain activities. According to Baker (2003: 191), criminals easily adapt their laundering patterns, which is described as 'displacement activity': 'Instead of channelling capital through banks and other primary financial agencies, once these became subject to effective regulation, the launderers adapted to the new conditions of the marketplace by investing in other forms of property.'

Crime on the Move: Law Enforcement on the Move

Mobile transnational organized crime is regarded as a concern that transcends national law enforcement concerns (Woodiwiss 2003: 21). With the gradual acknowledgement that crime is increasingly adopting a mobile and transnational character, law enforcement organizations have also sought to revise their structures. In most European countries, this has culminated in some degree of centralization and specialization (Den Boer 2005: 199; Harfield 2008: 68). Countries with a traditionally decentralized police force, like the United Kingdom and the Netherlands, for instance, have created a national crime investigation facility, which is co-equivalent to the regional forces but responsible for all forms of supra-regional and international crime. Also at the governance level of the European Union, we have witnessed the creation of agencies such as Europol and Eurojust, which deal with serious organized crime that harms the interests of a minimum of two EU member states.

However, the creation of agencies is not always deemed to be the appropriate or only answer to the growing mobility of crime. Instead, much more emphasis has lately been shifted to a flexible, smart, professional and multilateral type of law enforcement (Wright

2006: 201). This shift was to some extent already noticeable in the 1997 EU Action Plan on Organized Crime. As is described below, police processes are increasingly often shifted towards the proactive domain, although at the same time there is still a strong repressive reflex within any police organization. However, in the realm of preventive and proactive policing, there is far more attention to the mapping and analysis of the manœuvring of criminals: 'Thinking about crime more in terms of opportunity, of risk mechanisms, of personal motives, co-optation and seduction demands a willingness to depart from the familiar patterns and usual suspects' (Klerks 2003: 99).

The shift towards intelligence-led policing (ILP) – which is not necessarily integrally endorsed by all law enforcement agencies across the European Union member states – implies a shift from the crime to the criminal and his or her network. In several countries, work is under way to implement a National (Crime) Intelligence Model, which 'defines ways in which intelligence would drive prioritization and define responsibilities' (Harfield 2008: 67). The emergence of ILP and the NIM and ECIM are regarded as a step that will make a difference in the control of transnational organized crime (Gregory 2003: 93), however a challenge resides in the hierarchical relationships in the National Intelligence Model which do not match the networked and fluid character of transnational mobile crime.

The flexible response to crime means that within police services old but successful recipes are cultivated, such as stationing liaison officers at locations which are seen as crime hubs, but also the introduction of new recipes, such as nodal policing. Below, I will discuss several strategies of mobile law enforcement intervention –liaison officers, mobile patrols, flying squads, hotspot policing, roads policing, nodal policing, cyber policing, joint hit teams and joint investigation teams – in more detail.

The use of liaison officers or 'missions' by European countries only emerged in the 1970s (Block 2008b: 184). Liaison officers are usually police officers who act as intermediaries between the law enforcement authorities of two countries. They are stationed in a foreign jurisdiction without enjoying formal powers. Instead, they are tasked with the maintenance of contacts, but their role can be quite ambiguous, because they can also 'fix things' and facilitate the execution of mutual legal assistance requests (Nadelmann 1993). Usually, liaison officers are stationed from one country in another, or placed within an organization like Europol, but the Nordic Union model allows liaison officer presentation on behalf of a number of countries. This relatively flexible way of law enforcement operation – in which a liaison officer is seconded to another country for a few years – had its precedent in the United States. Nadelmann (1993) disentangled the global dispersion of American law enforcement liaison officers from various agencies, ranging from the Drug Enforcement Administration (DEA) to the CIA and FBI. Originally, liaison officers primarily undertook activities in the field of drugs trafficking, but their remit has in many instances been expanded to other forms of crime and also counter-terrorism (Block 2008a: 77; Bigo 1996; 2000: 74). Block (2008b: 185) reckons there are about 100 liaison officers on behalf of European law enforcement agencies deployed within Europe, whereas in 'third countries', this number approaches about 250.

Several other mobile methods of crime control have become part and parcel of the law enforcement response to transnational organized crime. After the implementation of the Schengen Agreement, for instance, several European countries abolished their internal border controls and hence felt they had lost an effective instrument to control crime (Den Boer 1994). Border filtering was no longer within the terms of the international agreement, and this was perceived as a security deficit. Soon after 'Schengen' entered into force,[5] police and military forces introduced mobile controls on the motorways, which made use of selective targeting and stop and search facilities. In the Netherlands, for instance, mobile patrols on the A16 motorway – which runs from Rotterdam to Antwerp and on to Brussels – are a well-known feature and are used to clamp down on drug runners. Additional methods of mobile crime control include selective (border) control, hot-spot policing and targeted policing.

A strategy which gained ground in some national police forces, notably the Dutch and the British police, is the strategy of 'nodal policing' which is inspired by the acknowledgement that societies are increasingly networked in character: in this model, crimes and criminals are predominantly seen as 'movable' targets and law enforcement activity focuses on the flows of illegal goods and transactions. These flows come together in so-called nodes, which represent a density of contact between criminals (e.g. in terms of communication or infrastructure). Another definition of nodal policing is its multi-agency perspective. In other words, law enforcement efforts against transnational organized crime are no longer regarded as successful if there is no cooperation with a range of other partners in the public and private sphere. Examples of nodal, multi-agency cooperation are combined efforts of police, customs and other agencies in the monitoring of containers that are shipped through the Rotterdam and Antwerp harbours (Dorn 2003: 229; Netherlands Police Agency 2004: 13).

At the European level, several forms of multi-agency cooperation have been encouraged, facilitated or institutionalized. Europol for instance accommodates liaison officers and analysts from several disciplinary backgrounds, ranging from police to customs, immigration services, special investigation services and the secret service. Moreover, Europol cooperates with other agencies in the field, namely SitCen (Joint Situation Centre which produces risk assessments for the European Council), the European Police Chiefs Task Force, the European Agency for the Management of External Border Controls (FRONTEX) and the European Anti-Fraud Office (OLAF). There is also an increased effort to allow agencies to communicate the data that are held in the various European databases in Europe, which include the Schengen Information System (SIS), the Customs Information System (CIS), and the Europol Information System (EIS). Hence, 'nodal policing' or multi-agency cooperation against transnational crime is an emerging practice, both at the European level as well as within some EU member states.

'Cyber-policing' – which can be volatile in nature – has also become an accepted form of policing, both in view of computer-crimes and crimes conducted on the internet, but also with regard to telecommunication and internet traffic between criminals or terrorists. Cyber-forensics can be conducted on the internet and within virtual space, however, consideration has to be given to privacy interests and ethical codes of conduct, particularly in order to avoid the solicitation or provocation of internet crime when a law enforcement officer presents himself or herself in an undercover capacity.

Within the European Union, there has also been reflection on the way in which the gap between formal 'vertical' policing and spontaneous policing can be closed, or rather, how formal intergovernmental police governance can be complementary to informal bilateral police governance (Den Boer 2005: 192). The model of the internationally and multi-disciplinarily composed Joint Investigation Teams was already adopted in 1999, with the conception of the so-called 'Tampere Programme' to deepen the EU Area of Freedom, Security and Justice.[6] Originally, the concept of JITs in the EU was introduced by Article 13 of the 2000 EU Convention on Mutual Assistance in Criminal Matters.[7] According to Block (2008a: 79), a Joint Investigation Team in the EU is understood to be a team consisting of representatives of law enforcement and judicial authorities from different member states and possibly from other organizations such as Europol and Eurojust: 'Based on an agreement, they jointly investigate cases of cross-border and international crime' (Block 2008a: 79). An important innovative feature of the JIT is that it is created for a single purpose within a limited time-frame, and that all information and evidence obtained during the operation of a JIT is fully shared between the participating countries. Despite their relatively flexible character, JITs have not been set up under the EU Framework Decision, but there have however been several bilateral JITs, e.g. between France and Spain on drug trafficking and terrorism.

Outside the formal scope of the European Union, but strongly cultivated in border regions and Euroregions, are the operational Joint Hit Teams, which can be considered as another 'mobile' and flexible answer to transnational organized crime. These teams are usually composed of law enforcement officials from different countries and operate in border regions in a fast and flexible mode. Joint patrols, joint information rooms and joint policy forums are other examples of close cooperation between law enforcement agencies in border areas, with a status that is quasi-institutional (Den Boer 2005: 202; Nogala 2001). At the external borders of the European Union, the EU Agency for the Integrated Management of External Borders (FRONTEX) also performs joint operations. Moreover, Rapid Border Intervention Teams (RABITs) have been introduced to assist member states of the EU when 'they are faced with sudden large influxes' of (illegal) migrants (Beuving 2008: 12); in 'less urgent situations and when a situation is still relatively in control, Frontex can also deploy so called Frontex Joint Support Teams (FJSTs)' (Beuving 2008: 13). In summary, the law enforcement community has sought to adapt its strategies to the relatively fluid and mobile character of crime and terrorism. This formula transgresses the traditional institutional law enforcement borders. Such new strategies, models and compositions pose a tremendous challenge to traditional accountability frameworks.

Conclusion

Mobile transnational crime is embedded in the deeper tissue of society and is strongly facilitated by processes of globalization, de-territorialization, immigration, networked economies, and distribution logistics (Wright 2006). Criminal groups have developed methods to reduce their vulnerability by acting in a volatile manner: they change their internal composition, diversify their illegal activities, spread themselves out and communicate in a concealed way. Hence, criminals become smarter, modify their modus operandi and prefer impermeable communication such as skyping (Arsovska 2008: 52). Law enforcement agencies no longer want to bring sand to the beaches and have sought to develop anticipatory and proactive methods of screening, surveillance and intervention. Gradually, however, they have also become more aware of the potential 'cat and mouse' effect of their interventions. In other ways, a causal, networked and strategic orientation on markets, prices and opportunities is required in cooperation with several other agencies, in the public as well as in the private sphere. The danger of this modern multi-disciplinary and multi-agency style of thinking is however that again the focus may be lost and that responsibility for action may be shifted from one actor to another.

Law enforcement agencies at various levels have sought to develop flexible, preventive and shrewd methods against the displacement of transnational organized crime. These methods range from increased surveillance such as automatic number plate recognition to mobile patrols, and from multi-agency policing to intelligence-led policing which analyses the formation of crime networks and their movements on the markets.

The ultimate method is to prevent transnational mobile crime from gaining ground, for instance by assisting weak states to bolster their authorities and to improve the integrity of government (security sector reform), and by building stronger economies and employment opportunities. These long-term preventive strategies are not primarily a responsibility of law enforcement organizations, but for politicians and civil society alike. But they also need police forces to adopt a reflexive attitude about their role in the control of transnational organized crime, and to continue to invest in professionalization, knowledge-management and the pairing of police forces with legal specialists. The effectiveness, efficiency and legitimacy of mobile methods of investigating transnational organized crime will – in the end – be subjected to political and legal scrutiny.

Notes

1 http://www.met.police.uk/campaigns/call_time.htm, and the Immobilise Campaign at: http://www.t-mobile.co.uk/help-and-advice/advice-for-parents/preventing-crime/. The UK has a National Mobile Phone Crime Unit (NMPCU): http://www.mobilenewscwp.co.uk/archive/7710/crackdown_on_london_mobile_crime_gangs.html
2 In the meantime, a new Action Programme has been adopted, see Council Decision 2007/125/JHA of 12 Feb. 2007 establishing for the period 2007–13, as part of the General Programme on Security and Safeguarding Liberties, the Specific Programme 'Prevention of and Fight against Crime' (http://europa.eu/scadplus/leg/en/lvb/l33263.htm).
3 Directive 2006/24/EC of the European Parliament and of the Council of 15 March 2006 on the retention of data generated or processed in connection with the provision of publicly available electronic communications services or of public communications networks and amending Directive 2002/58/EC, OJ L 105/54, published on 13 April 2006.
4 Agreement between the European Union and the USA on the processing and transfer of Passenger Name Record (PNR) data by air carriers to the US Dept of Homeland Security (DHS) (2007 PNR Agreement). For the history of this agreement, see EU Commission (6 Nov. 2007), 'Proposal for a Council Framework Decision on the Use of Passenger Name Records for Law Enforcement Purposes', COM (2007) 654/F; Council Decision 2007/551/CFSP/JHA of 23 July 2007 on the signing, on behalf of the European Union, of an Agreement between the European Union and the United States of America on the processing and transfer of Passenger Name Record (PNR) data by air carriers to the United States Department of Homeland Security (DHS) (2007 PNR Agreement) (OJ L 204 of 4 Aug. 2007).
5 Convention implementing the Schengen Agreement of 14 June 1985 between the Governments of the States of the Benelux Economic Union, the Federal Republic of Germany and the French Republic on the gradual abolition of checks at their common borders, 19 June 1990 (http://www.unhcr.bg/euro_docs/en/_schengen_en.pdf).
6 Presidency Conclusions, Tampere European Council, 15 and 16 Oct. 1999: http://www.consilium.europa.eu/ueDocs/cms_Data/docs/pressData/en/ec/00200-r1.en9.htm
7 Convention on Mutual Assistance in Criminal Matters between the Member States of the European Union (OJ C 197 of 12 July 2000). A separate and more elaborate legal instrument was adopted after 9/11 and was formally adopted the following summer: Council Framework Decision of 13 June 2002 on JITs (OJ L 162 20 June 2002).

References

Abraham, I. (1998) *The Making of the Indian Atomic Bomb: Science, Secrecy and the Postcolonial State,* New York: Zed Books.

Abraham, T. (2007) *Twenty-First Century Plague: The Story of SARS,* Baltimore, MD: Johns Hopkins University Press.

Abrahamsen, R. and Williams, M. C. (2007) 'Introduction: the privatisation and globalisation of security in Africa', *International Relations,* 21(2): 131–41.

Abrahamsen, R. and Williams, M. C. (2007) 'Selling security: assessing the impact of military privatization (book review essay)', *Review of International Political Economy,* 15(1): 131–46.

Abu-Lughod, J. L. (1989) *Before European Hegemony: The World System AD 1250–1350,* Oxford: Oxford University Press.

Acharya, A. (1998) 'Collective identity and conflict management in Southeast Asia', in E. Adler and M. N. Barnett (eds) *Security Communities,* Cambridge: Cambridge University Press.

Acharya, A. (2001) *Constructing a Security Community in Southeast Asia: ASEAN and the Problem of Regional Order,* London: Routledge.

Ackroyd, C., Margolis, K., Rosenhead, J. and Shallice, T. (1980) *The Technology of Political Control,* London: Pluto Press.

Ackroyd, S., Harper, R. H. R., Hughes, J. A., Shapiro, D. and Soothill, K. (1992) *New Technology and Practical Police Work,* London: Open University.

Adamson, F. (2006) 'Crossing borders: international migration and national security', *International Security,* 31(1): 165–99.

Adelman, H. (2001) 'From refugees to forced migration: the UNHCR and human security', *International Migration Review,* special issue: 'UNHCR at 50: Past, Present and Future of Refugee Assistance', 35(1): 7–32.

Adey, P. (2006) 'If mobility is everything then it is nothing: towards a relational politics of (im)mobilities', *Mobilities,* 1: 75–94.

Adey, P. (2008) 'Airports, mobility and the calculative architecture of affective control' *Geoforum,* 39(1): 438-451.

Adler, E. and Barnett, M. N. (1998) *Security Communities,* Cambridge: Cambridge University Press.

Agamben, G. (1991) *Language and Death: The Place of Negativity,* trans. K. E. Pinkus and M. Hardt, Minneapolis, MN: Minnesota University Press.

Agamben, G. (1993) *Stanzas: Word and Phantasm in Western Culture,* trans. R. M. Martinez, Minneapolis, MN: Minnesota University Press.

REFERENCES

Agamben, G. (1998) *Homo Sacer: Sovereign Power and Bare Life,* trans. D. Heller-Roazen, Stanford, CA: Stanford University Press.

Agamben, G. (1999a) *Remnants of Auschwitz : The Witness and the Archive*, trans. D. Heller-Roazen, New York: Zone Books.

Agamben, G. (1999b) *Potentialities: Collected Essays in Philosophy,* trans. D. Heller-Roazen, Stanford, CA: Stanford University Press.

Agamben, G. (1999c) *The End of the Poem: Studies in Poetics*, trans. D. Heller-Roazen, Stanford, CA: Stanford University Press.

Agamben, G. (2000) *Means Without End : Notes on Politics*, trans. V. Binetti and C. Casarino, Minneapolis, MN: Minnesota University Press.

Agamben, G. (2001) 'Giorgio Agamben: On Security and Terror', trans. Soenke Zehle, *Frankfurter Allgemeine Zeitung* (20 Sept.).

Agamben, G. (2002) 'Security and terror', *Theory and Event,* 5(4): 1–6.

Agamben, G. (2004a) 'No to bio-political tattooing', *Le Monde* (10 Jan.): online <http://www.ratical.org/ratville/CAH/totalControl.pdf> (accessed June 2009).

Agamben, G. (2004b) *The Open: Man and Animal*, trans. K. Attell, Stanford, CA: Stanford University Press.

Agamben, G. (2005a) *State of Exception*, trans. K. Attell, Chicago: Chicago University Press.

Agamben, G. (2005b) *The Time That Remains. A Commentary on the Letter to the Romans*, trans. P. Dailey, Stanford, CA: Stanford University Press.

Agar, N. (2004) *Liberal Eugenics: In Defence of Human Enhancement*, Oxford: Blackwell.

Agathangelou, A. and Ling, L. H. M. (2004) 'Power, borders, security, wealth: lessons of violence and desire from September 11', *International Studies Quarterly,* 48: 517–38.

Agathangelou, A. and L. H. M. Ling (2005) 'Power and play through poisies: reconstructing self and other in the 9/11 Commission Report', *Millennium: Journal of International Studies,* 33: 827.

Aggestam, L. and Hyde-Price, A. G.V. (2000) *Security and identity in Europe: Exploring the New Agenda,* New York: St Martin's Press.

Agnew, J. (2003) *Geopolitics: Re-Visioning World Politics,* London: Routledge.

Agosín, M. (ed.) (2001) *Women, Gender, and Human Rights: A Global Perspective*, Piscataway, NJ: Rutgers University Press.

Aitken, R. (2005) '"A direct personal stake": cultural economy, mass investment and the New York Stock Exchange', *Review of International Political Economy,* 12(2): 334–63.

Aitken, R. (2006) 'Capital at its fringes', *New Political Economy,* 11(4): 479–96.

Aitken, R. (2007) *Performing Capital: Toward a Cultural Economy of Popular and Global Finance,* New York: Palgrave Macmillan.

Aitken, R. (2003) 'The democratic method of obtaining capital: culture, governmentality and ethics of mass investment', *Consumption, Markets and Culture,* 6(4): 293–317.

Albahari, M. (forthcoming) 'Charitable borders? Religion, policing and belonging on the Italian maritime edge', in J. L. Bacas and W. Kavanagh (eds) *Asymmetry and Proximity in Border Encounters*, New York: Berghahn Books.

Alkire, S. (2003) 'A conceptual framework for human security', working paper 2, Centre for Research on Inequality, Human Security and Ethnicity (CRISE), University of Oxford : online <http://www.crise.ox.ac.uk/pubs/workingpaper2.pdf> (accessed June 2009).

Allen, L. H. and Gillespie, S. R. (2001) *What Works? A Review of the Efficacy and Effectiveness of Nutrition Interventions,* ADB's Nutrition and Development Series, United Nations Administrative Committee on Coordination Sub-Committee on Nutrition (ACC/SCN) in collaboration with the Asian Development Bank (ADB), Manila: ADB.

Al-Sowayegh, A. (1984) *Arab Petropolitics*, London: Croom Helm.

Alvarez, J. (2005) *International Organizations as Law-makers*, Oxford and New York: Oxford University Press.

Amnesty International (2004) *Sudan, Darfur, Rape as a Weapon of War: Sexual Violence and its Consequences*, online <http://www.amnesty.org/en/library/asset/AFR54/076/2004/en/dom-AFR540762004en.pdf> (accessed Sept. 2008).

REFERENCES

Amnesty International (2008) *Displaced in Darfur: A Generation of Anger*, online <http://www.amnesty.org/en/library/asset/AFR54/001/2008/en/f2b06a31-caa3-11dc-b181-d35374267ce9/afr540012008eng.pdf> (accessed Sept. 2008).

Amoore, L. (2006) 'Biometric borders: governing mobilities in the War on Terror', *Political Geography*, 3(25): 336–52.

Amoore, L. and de Goede, M. (2005) 'Governance, risk and dataveillance in the war on terror', *Crime, Law and Social Change*, 43: 149–73.

Amoore, L. and de Goede, M. (eds) (2007) *Risk and the War on Terror*, London: Routledge.

Amoore, L. and de Goede, M. (2008) 'Transactions after 9/11: the banal face of the preemptive strike', *Transactions of the Institute of British Geographers*, 33: 173–85.

Anderson, B. (2007) 'Hope for nanotechnology: anticipatory knowledge and the governance of affect', *Area*, 39(2): 156–65.

Andreas, P. (2001) *Border Games: Policing the US–Mexico Divide*, Ithaca, NY: Cornell University Press.

Andreas, P. (2002) 'Transnational crime and economic globalization', in M. Berdal and M. Serrano (eds) *Transnational Organized Crime and International Security: Business as Usual?*, London: Lynne Rienner Publishers.

Andreas, P. (2003) 'Redrawing the line: borders and security in the 21st century', *International Security*, 28: 78–112.

Andreas, P. and Biersteker, T. J. (eds) (2003) *The Rebordering of North America: Integration and Exclusion in a New Security Context*, New York: Routledge.

Andreas, P. and Snyder, T. (eds) (2000) *The Wall around the West: State Borders and Immigration Controls in North America and Europe*, Lanham, MD: Rowman & Littlefield.

Andrews-Speed, P., Liao, X. and Dannreuther, R. (2002) *The Strategic Implications of China's Energy Needs*, Oxford: Oxford University Press.

Andrijasevic, R. (2007) 'The spectacle of misery: gender, migration and representation in anti-trafficking campaigns', *Feminist Review*, 86: 24–44.

Anghie, A. (1996) 'Francisco de Vitoria and the Colonial Origins of International Law', *Social and Legal Studies*, 5/3: 332–3.

Anghie, A. (1999) 'Finding the peripheries: sovereignty and colonialism in nineteenth-century international law', *Harvard International Law*, 40/1: 1–80.

Annan, K. (1999) *Report of the Secretary-General to the Security Council on the Protection of Civilians in Armed Conflict*, New York: United Nations.

Annan, K. (2000) *We the People: Report of the Secretary-General*, New York: United Nations.

Anonymous (2003) *Maximum Security: A Hackers Guide to Protecting your Internet Site and Network*, Indianapolis, IN: Sams Publishing.

Antonelli, P. (2005) 'Grace under pressure', in P. Antonelli (ed.) *Safe: Design Takes on Risk*, New York: MoMA.

Antonelli, P. (ed.) (2008) *Design and the Elastic Mind*, New York: MoMA.

Applebaum, A. (2006) *Gulag: A History of the Soviet Camps*, London: Allen Lane.

Aradau, C. (2004) 'The perverse politics of four-letter words: risk and pity in the securitization of human trafficking', *Millennium*, 33(2): 251–77.

Aradau, C. and van Munster, R. (2007) '*Governing terrorism through risk: taking precautions, (un)knowing the future*', *European Journal of International Relations*, 13(1): 89–115.

Aradau, C., Lobo-Guerrero, L. and Van Munster, R. (eds) (2008) 'Security, technologies of risk, and the political', *Security Dialogue*, 39(2–3): 147–154.

Architecture for Humanity. (ed.) (2006) *Design like you Give a Damn: Architectural Responses to Humanitarian Crises*, London: Thames & Hudson.

Arevena, F. R. and Goucha, M. (2001) 'Human security, conflict prevention and peace in Latin America and the Caribbean', in M. Goucha and J. Cilliers (eds) *Peace, Human Security and Conflict Prevention in Africa*, Pretoria: Proceedings of the UNESCO–ISS Expert Meeting.

Arevena, F. R. and Goucha, M. (eds) (2001) *Human Security, Conflict Prevention and Peace in Latin America and the Caribbean*, Paris: UNESCO.

Aristotle (1912) *The Politics*, London: J. M. Dent & Sons.

REFERENCES

Arnoldi, J. (2004) 'Derivatives: virtual values and real risks', *Theory, Culture and Society,* 21(6): 23–42.

Arsovska, J. (2008) 'Decline, change or denial: human trafficking and EU responses in the Balkan Triangle', *Policing: A Journal of Policy and Practice,* 2(1): 50–62.

Atia, M. (2007) 'In whose interest? Financial surveillance and the circuits of exception in the War on Terror', *Environment and Planning D: Society and Space,* 25(3): 447–75.

Atkins, P. J. (1993) 'How the West End was won: the struggle to remove street barriers in Victorian London', *Journal of Historical Geography,* 19: 265–77.

Atlas, R. M. and Dando, M. (2006) 'The dual-use dilemma for the life sciences: perspectives, conundrums, and global solutions', *Biosecurity and Bioterrorism: Biodefense Strategy, Practice, and Science,* 4(3): 276–86.

Australia Group, online <http://www.australiagroup.net/en/index.html> (accessed Oct. 2008).

Avant, D. (2005) *The Market for Force: the Consequences of Privatizing Security,* Cambridge: Cambridge University Press.

Axworthy, L. (2001a) 'Human security and global governance: putting people first', *Global Governance,* 7(1): 19–23.

Axworthy, L. (2001b) 'Comments to UBC Human Security Graduate Course, Liu Institute for Global Issues, Vancouver, BC, November'.

Ba, O., O'Regan, C., Nachega, J., *et al.* (2008) 'HIV/AIDS in African militaries: an ecological analysis', *Medicine, Conflict and Survival,* 24(2): 88–100.

Baechler, G. (1999) *Violence through Environmental Discrimination: Causes, Rwanda Arena, and Conflict Model,* Dordrecht: Kluwer.

Bah, A. (2004) *Toward a Regional Approach to Human Security in Southern Africa,* Kingston: Centre for International Relations, Queen's University.

Bailes, A. and Frommelt, I. (eds) (2004) Business and Security. Public–Private Sector Relationships in a New Security Environment, Oxford: Oxford University Press.

Bajpai, K. (2004) 'An expression of threats versus capabilities across time and space', *Security Dialogue,* 35(3): 360–1.

Baker, T. and Simon, J. (eds) (2002) *Embracing Risk: The Changing Culture of Insurance and Responsibility,* Chicago: University of Chicago Press.

Baldwin, D. A. (1995) 'Security studies and the end of the cold war', *World Politics,* 48: 117–41.

Baldwin, D. A. (1997) 'The concept of security', *Review of International Studies,* 23: 5–26.

Balibar, E. and Wallerstein, I. (1991) *Race, Nation, Class; Ambiguous Identities,* London: Verso.

Ballentine, K. and Sherman, J. (eds) (2003) *The Political Economy of Armed Conflict: Beyond Greed and Grievance,* Boulder, CO: Lynne Rienner.

Balzacq, T. (2005) 'The three faces of securitization: political agency, audience, and context', *European Journal of International Relations,* 11: 171–201.

Balzacq, T. and De Nève, A. (eds) (2003) *La révolution dans les affaires militaires,* Paris: Economica.

Barker, M. (1981) *The New Racism: Conservatives and the Ideology of the Tribe,* London: Junction Books.

Barlow, E. (2008) *Executive Outcomes: Against All Odds,* Alberton: Galago Publishing.

Barlow, J. P. (1994) 'The economy of ideas: selling wine without bottles on the global net', *Wired Magazine,* 2(3) (March): online <http://www.wired.com/wired/archive/2.03/economy.ideas.html> (accessed Nov. 2008).

Barlow, J. P. (1996) *A Declaration of the Independence of Cyberspace,* Electronic Frontier Foundation Website: online <http://homes.eff.org/~barlow/Declaration-Final.html> (accessed Nov. 2008).

Barnett, J. (2001) *The Meaning of Environmental Security: Ecological Politics and Policy in the New Security Era,* London and New York: Zed Books.

Barnett, J. and Adger, N. (2003) 'Climate dangers and atoll countries', *Climatic Change,* 61(3): 321–37.

Barnett, J, and Adger, N. (2007) 'Climate change, human security and violent conflict', *Political Geography,* 26(6): 639–55.

Barnett, M. and Finnemore, M. (2004) *Rules for the World: International Organizations in Global Politics,* Ithaca, NY: Cornell University Press.

Barnett, M. N. (1998) *Dialogues in Arab Politics: Negotiations in Regional Order,* New York: Columbia University Press.

Barrett, C. and Maxwell, D. (2005) *Food Aid After Fifty Years: Recasting its Role,* Abingdon, Oxon.: Routledge.

Barry, A. (2006) 'Technological zones', *European Journal of Social Theory*, 9(2): 239–53.

Barton, B., Redgewell, C., Ronne, A. and Zillmnan, D. (eds) (2004) *Energy Security: Managing Risk in a Legal and Regulatory Framework*, Oxford: Oxford University Press.

Bartram, J., Lewis, K., Lenton, R. and Wright, A. (2005) 'Focusing on improved water and sanitation for health', *Lancet*, 365: 810–12.

Bastick, M., Grimm, K. and Kunz, R. (2007) *Sexual Violence in Armed Conflict: Global Overview and Implications for the Security Sector*, Geneva: Democratic Control of Armed Forces.

Bauman, Z. (1995) *Life in Fragments: Essays in Postmodern Modernity*, Oxford: Blackwell.

Bauman, Z. (1998) *Globalization: The Human Consequences*, Cambridge: Polity Press.

Bauman, Z. (2004) *Wasted Lives: Modernity and Its Outcasts*, Cambridge: Polity Press.

Baylis, J. (1997) 'International security in the post-cold war era', in J. Baylis and S. Smith (eds) *The Globalization of World Politics*, Oxford: Oxford University Press.

Beck, U. (1992) *Risk Society: Towards a New Modernity*, London: Sage.

Beck, U. (2002) 'The terrorist threat: world risk society revisited', *Theory, Culture and Society*, 19(4): 39–55.

Beck, U. (2003) 'The silence of words: on terror and war', *Security Dialogue*, 34(3): 255–67.

Beck, U. (2007) *Die Weltrisikogesellschaft*, Frankfurt/Main: Suhrkamp.

Bedeski, R. E. (2007) *Human Security and the Chinese State: Historical Transformations and the Modern Quest for Sovereignty*, New York: Routledge.

Behrman, J. R., Alderman, H. and Hoddinott, J. (2004) 'Hunger and malnutrition', paper for the Copenhagen Consensus : Challenges and Opportunities, 19 Feb.

Beier, A. L. (1985) *Masterless Men : The Vagrancy Problem in England 1560–1640*, London and New York: Methuen.

Bellamy, A. (2004) *Security Communities and their Neighbours: Regional Fortresses or Global Integrators?*, London: Palgrave.

Bellamy, A. (2006) *Just Wars: From Cicero to Iraq*, Cambridge: Polity.

Bellamy, A. J. and McDonald, M. (2002) '"The Utility of Human Security": Which Humans? What Security? A Reply to Thomas and Tow', *Security Dialogue*, 33(3): 373–7.

Benedictow, O. J. (2004) *The Black Death 1346–1353: The Complete History*, Rochester, NY: Boydell & Brewer.

Benjamin, W. (2004) 'Critique of Violence', in M. Bullock and M. W. Jennings (eds) *Walter Benjamin Selected Writings*, vol. 1, *1913–1926*, Cambridge, MA: Harvard, Belknap Press.

Bennett, C. (2008) 'Unsafe at any altitude: the comparative politics of no-fly lists in the United States and Canada', in M. B. Salter (ed.) *Politics at the Airport*, Minneapolis, MN: University of Minnesota Press.

Bennett, C. and Lyon, D. (eds) (2008) *Playing the Identity Card: Surveillance, Security and Identification in Global Perspective*, London: Routledge.

Benveniste, E. (1971) 'Civilization: a contribution to the history of the word', in *Problems in General Linguistics*, trans. M. E. Meek, Coral Gables, FL: University of Miami Press.

Bequai, A. (1986) *Technocrimes: The Computerization of Crime and Terrorism*, Lexington: Lexington Books.

Berdal, M. and Malone, D. (eds) (2000) *Greed and Grievance: Economic Agendas in Civil Wars*, Boulder, CO: Lynne Rienner.

Berdal, M. and Serrano, M. (eds) (2002) *Transnational Organized Crime and International Security. Business as Usual?*, London: Lynne Rienner Publishers.

Berdal, M. and Serrano, M. (2002a) 'Transnational organized crime and international security: the new topography', in M. Berdal and M. Serrano (eds) *Transnational Organized Crime and International Security: Business as Usual?*, London: Lynne Rienner Publishers.

Berman, J. (2003) '(Un)popular strangers and crises (un)bounded: discourses of sex-trafficking, the European Political Community and the panicked states of the modern state', *European Journal of International Relations*, 9(1): 37–86.

Best, J. (2008) 'Why the economy is often the exception to politics as usual', *Theory, Culture and Society*, 24(4): 83–105.

Best, J. (2003) 'Moralizing finance: the new financial architecture as ethical discourse', *Review of International Political Economy*, 10: 579–603.

REFERENCES

Beuving, M. (2008) *FRONTEX: Its Role and Organization*, Working Papers Series on EU Internal Security Governance, 8, Strasbourg: SECURINT.

Bhattacharya, P. and Hazra, S. (2003) *Environment and Human Security*, New Delhi: Lancers' Books.

Biersteker, T. J. (2004) 'The return of the state? Financial re-regulation in the pursuit of security after September 11', in J. Tirman (ed.) *The Maze of Fear: Security and Migration After 9/11*, New York: New Press.

Biersteker, T. J. and Eckert, S. E. (eds) *Countering the Financing of Terrorism*, London: Routledge.

Bigo, D. (1995) 'Grands débats dans un petit monde: les débats en relations internationales et leur lien avec le monde de la sécurité', *Cultures et Conflits*, 19–20: 7–48.

Bigo, D. (1996) *Polices en réseaux: L'expérience européenne*. Paris: Presses de Sciences Po.

Bigo, D. (2000) 'Liaison officers in Europe: new officers in the European security field', in J. Sheptycki (ed.) *Issues in Transnational Policing*, London: Routledge.

Bigo, D. (2001) 'Internal and external securities: the Möbius ribbon', in M. Albert, D. Jacobson and Y. Lapid (eds) *Identities, Borders, Orders: Rethinking International Relations Theory*, Minneapolis, MN: University of Minnesota Press.

Bigo, D. (2002) 'Security and immigration: toward a critique of the governmentality of unease', *Alternatives: Global, Local, Political*, 27(1): 63–92.

Bigo, D. (2006a) 'Protection: security, territory and population', in J. Huysmans, A. Dobson and R. Prokhovnik (eds) *The Politics of Protection, Sites of Insecurity and Political Agency*, London: Routledge.

Bigo, D. (2006b) 'Security, exception, ban and surveillance', in D. Lyon (ed.) *Theorizing Surveillance: The Panopticon and Beyond*, Cullompton: Willan Publishing.

Bigo, D. (2007) 'Proactivity, profiling and prevention in regard to privacy and freedom', Paris, unpublished manuscript.

Bigo, D. (2008a) 'Globalized (in)security: the field and the ban-opticon', in D. Bigo and A. Tsoukala (eds) *Terror, Insecurity and Liberty: Illiberal Practices of Liberal Regimes*, London: Routledge.

Bigo, D. (2008b) 'Security: a field left fallow', in M. Dillon and A. W. Neal (eds) *Foucault on Politics, Security and War*, Houndmills, Basingstoke: Palgrave Macmillan.

Bigo, D., Bonditti, P., Jeandesboz, J. and Ragazzi, F. (2008) 'The ethics and politics of security technologies in the management of Europe's borders', Brussels: CEPS, paper given at the INEX Kick-Off meeting.

Bigo, D., Bonditti, P., Olsson, C. (2009) *Synthesis Report of the "Mapping the European Field of Security Professionals Project"*, CHALLENGE, forthcoming.

Bijker, W. E., Hughes, T. P. and Pinch, T. J. (1987) *The Social Construction of Technology: New Directions in the Sociology and History of Technology*, Cambridge, MA: The MIT Press.

Bilgin, P. (2005) *Regional Security in the Middle East: A Critical Perspective*, London: Routledge.

Bilham, R. (2004) 'Urban earthquake fatalities: a safer world, or worse to come?', *Seismological Research Letters* 75: 706–12.

Biological and Toxin Weapons Convention (BWC) (1972) Online <http://www.unog.ch/80256EDD006B8954/(httpAssets)/C4048678A93B6934C1257188004848D0/$file/BWC-text-English.pdf> (accessed June 2009).

Bissel, W. C. (2000) 'Conservation and the colonial past: urban planning, space and power in Zanzibar', in D. Anderson and R. Rathbone (eds) *Africa's Urban Past*, Oxford: James Currey, pp. 246–61.

Black, J. (1998) *War and the World: Military Power and the Fate of Continents, 1450–2000*, New Haven, CT: Yale University Press.

Black, R. E., Allen, L. H., Bhutta, Z. A., Caulfield, L. E., de Onis, M., Ezzati, M., Mathers, C. and Rivera, J. (2008) 'Maternal and child undernutrition: global and regional exposures and health consequences', *Lancet*, 371: 243–60.

Bleiker, R. (2005) *Divided Korea: Toward a Culture of Reconciliation*, Minneapolis, MN: University of Minnesota Press.

Block, L. (2008a) 'Combating organized crime in Europe: practicalities of police cooperation', *Policing: A Journal of Policy and Practice*, 2(1): 74–81.

Block, L. (2008b) 'Cross-border liaison and intelligence: practicalities and issues', in C. Harfield, A. MacVean, J. G. D. Grieve and D. Phillips (eds) *The Handbook of Intelligent Policing: Consilience, Crime Control and Community Safety*, Oxford: Oxford University Press.

REFERENCES

Body-Gendrot, S. (2000) *The Social Control of Cities? A Comparative Perspective,* Oxford: Blackwell.

Body-Gendrot, S. and Spierenburg, P. (eds) (2008) *Violence in Europe: Historical and Contemporary Perspectives,* New York: Springer.

Bonditti, P. (2005) 'Biométrie et maîtrise des flux: vers une "géo-technopolis du *vivant-en-mobilité*"?', *Cultures et Conflits,* 58: 131–54.

Bonditti, P. (2008) *L'antiterrorisme aux Etats-Unis (1946–2007),* Paris: Sciences Po.

Bonner, D. (1985) *Emergency Powers in Peacetime,* London: Sweet & Maxwell.

Booth, K. (1979) *Strategy and Ethnocentrism,* New York: Holmes & Meier.

Booth, K. (1991a) 'Security and emancipation', *Review of International Studies,* 17(4): 313–26.

Booth, K. (ed.) (1991b) *New Thinking about Strategy and International Security,* London: HarperCollins Academic.

Booth, K. (ed.) (2005) *Critical Security Studies and World Politics,* Boulder, CO: Lynne Rienner.

Booth, K. (2007) *Theory of World Security,* Cambridge: Cambridge University Press.

Booth, K. and Wheeler, N. J. (2007) *The Security Dilemma: Fear, Cooperation, and Trust in World Politics,* Basingstoke: Palgrave Macmillan.

Booth, K. and Wheeler, N. J. (2008) *The Security Dilemma: Fear, Cooperation and Trust in World Politics,* Basingstoke: Palgrave.

Bosold, D. and Werthes, S. (2005) 'Human security in practice: Canadian and Japanese experiences', *International Politics and Society,* 1: 84–101.

Botsman, D. V. (2005) *Punishment and Power in the Making of Modern Japan,* Princeton, NJ: Princeton University Press.

Bougen, P. D. (2003) 'Catastrophe risk', *Economy and Society,* 32(2): 253–74.

Bovenkerk, F., Bruinsma, G., van de Bunt, H. and Fijnaut, C. (1996) 'Eindrapport onderzoeksgroep Fijnaut', *Inzake Opsporing,* Enquêtecommissie opsporingsmethoden, Bijlage 7, Tweede Kamer der Staten-Generaal, 24072/16.

Bowden, B. (2004a) 'In the name of progress and peace: the "standard of civilization" and the universalizing project', *Alternatives: Global, Local, Political,* 29(1): 43–68.

Bowden, B. (2004b) 'The ideal of civilisation: its origins and socio-political character', *Critical Review of International Social and Political Philosophy,* 7(1): 25–50.

Bowden, B. (2005) 'The colonial origins of international law: European expansion and the classical standard of civilisation', *Journal of the History of International Law/Revue d'histoire du droit international,* 7(1): 1–23.

Bowden, B. (2007) 'Civilization and savagery in the crucible of war', *Global Change, Peace and Security,* 19(1): 3–16.

Bowden, B. (2009a) *The Empire of Civilization: The Evolution of an Imperial Idea,* Chicago, IL: University of Chicago Press.

Bowden, B. (ed.) (2009b) *Civilization: Critical Concepts in Political Science,* 4 vols, London: Routledge.

Boyden, S. (1987) *Western Civilisation in Biological Perspective: Patterns in Biohistory,* New York: Oxford University Press.

Boyer, P. (1978) *Urban Masses and Moral Order in America: 1820–1920,* Cambridge, MA: Harvard University Press.

BP (2008) *Statistical Review of World Energy 2008,* online <http://www.bp.com/productlanding.do?categoryId=6929&contentId=7044622> (accessed Oct. 2008).

Bracewell, W. (2000) 'Rape in Kosovo: masculinity and Serbian nationalism', *Nations and Nationalism,* 6(4): 563–90.

Brady, H. (2008) 'Europol and the European criminal intelligence model: a non-state response to organized crime', *Policing: A Journal of Policy and Practice,* 2(1): 103–9.

Bratton, B. (2006) 'Introduction: logistics of habitable circulation' in Paul Virilio, *Pure War,* Los Angeles: Semiotexte, pp. 7–25.

Brauch, H. G. (2005) *Environment and Human Security: Towards Freedom From Hazard Impacts,* Bonn: Institute for Environment and Human Security (UNU-EHS).

Braudel, F (1986 [1979]) *The Perspective of the World (Civilisation and Capitalism 15th to 18th Century,* vol. 3), New York: Harper & Row.

269

REFERENCES

Braudel, F. (1980) *On History*, trans. S. Matthews, London: Weidenfeld & Nicolson.

Brauer, J. and Muggah R. (2006) 'Completing the circle: building a theory of small arms demand', *Contemporary Security Policy*, 27(1): 138–54.

Brecke, P. (2002) *Notes on Developing a Human Security/Insecurity Index*, Atlanta, GA: Sam Nunn School of International Affairs, Georgia Institute of Technology: online <http://www.inta.gatech.edu/peter/hsi.html> (accessed June 2009).

British Foreign and Commonwealth Office, 'Counter-proliferation: Academic Technology Approval Scheme (ATAS)', online <http://www.fco.gov.uk/en/fco-in-action/counter-terrorism/weapons/atas/> (accessed June 2009).

Brock, L. (1992) 'Security through defending the environment: an illusion?', in E. Boulding (ed.) *New Agendas for Peace Research: Conflict and Security Reexamined*, Boulder: Lynne Rienner, pp. 79–102.

Brouwer, E. (2006) 'Datasurveillance and border control in the EU: balancing efficiency and legal protection', in T. Balzacq and S. Carrera (eds) *Security versus Freedom? A Challenge for Europe's Future*, London: Ashgate.

Brown, L. (1977) *Redefining National Security*, Worldwatch Paper, 14. Washington, DC: Worldwatch.

Brown, M. E. (1993) *Ethnic Conflict and International Security*, Princeton, NJ: Princeton University Press.

Brown, S. and Sherry, J. F. (2005) *Time, Space and the Market: Retroscapes Rising*, New York: M. E. Sharpe.

Bruderlein, C. (2000) 'The role of non-state actors in building human security', *Centre for Humanitarian Dialogue*, Geneva: HD Centre.

Brumfiel, G. (2007) 'Foreign students face extra UK security check', *Nature*, online <http://www.nature.com/news/2007/071107/full/450140a.html> (accessed June).

Bryce, J., Boschi-Pinto, C., Shibuya, K., Black, R. E. and the WHO Child Health Epidemiology Reference Group (2005) 'WHO estimates of the causes of death in children', *Lancet*, 365: 1147–52.

Brzoska, M. (2003) 'Development donors and the concept of security sector reform', *Occasional Paper*, 4: 1–61.

Brzoska, M. (2006) 'Collective violence beyond the standard definition of armed conflict', in Stockholm International Peace Research Institute, *SIPRI Yearbook 2006*, Stockholm: SIPRI.

Buhaug, H., Gleditsch, N. and Theisen, O. (2008) 'Implications of climate change for armed conflict', paper presented at the World Bank Workshop on the Social Dimensions of Climate Change, Washington, DC: World Bank, March.

Bull, H. (1977) *The Anarchical Society: A Study of Order in World Politics*, London: Macmillan.

Bulletin of the Atomic Scientists: online <http://www.thebulletin.org/content/doomsday-clock/overview> (accessed May 2009).

Buonfino, A. (2004) 'Between unity and plurality: the politicization and securitization of the discourse of immigration in Europe', *New Political Science*, 26(1): 23–49.

Burch, K. (1998) *'Property' and the Making of the International System*, London: Lynne Rienner.

Burgess, J. P. and Owen, T. (2004) 'Special section: what is human security?', *Security Dialogue*, 35(3): 73–115.

Burgess, J. P., Amicelle, A., Bartels, E. *et al.* (2007) *Promoting Human Security: Ethical, Normative and Educational Frameworks in Western Europe*, Paris: UNESCO.

Burke, A. (2001) *Fear of Security: Australia's Invasion Anxiety*, Annandale: Pluto Press ; repr. Cambridge: Cambridge University Press, 2008.

Burke, A. (2005) 'Against the new internationalism', *Ethics and International Affairs*, 19(2): 73–89.

Burke, A. (2007a) 'What security makes possible: some thoughts on critical security studies', *Working Paper 1/2007*, Canberra: Department of International Relations, ANU.

Burke, A. (2007b) *Beyond Security Ethics and Violence: War Against The Other*, London and New York: Routledge.

Burke, A. and McDonald, M. (2007) 'Introduction', *Critical Security in the Asia-Pacific*, Manchester: Manchester University Press, pp. 1–21.

Bush, G. W. (2001) Address to a Joint Session of Congress and the American People, 20 Sept. 2001 : online <http://www.archive.org/details/gwb2001-09-20.flac16> (accessed May 2009).

270

REFERENCES

Bush, G.W. (2002) 'President Bush delivers graduation speech at West Point', Office of the Press Secretary, White House, 1 June: online <http://www.whitehouse.gov/news/releases/2002/06/20020601-3.html> (accessed June 2009).

Butler, J. (1993) *Bodies that Matter: On the Discursive Limits of 'Sex'*, London: Routledge.

Butler, J. (1999) *Gender Trouble*, rev. edn, London: Routledge.

Butler, J. (2004) *Precarious Life: The Powers of Mourning and Violence*, London: Verso.

Buttedahl, P. (1994) *Viewpoint: True Measures of Human Security*, Ottawa: IDRC.

Buur, L. (2006) 'Reordering society: vigilantism and sovereign expressions in Port Elizabeth's townships', *Development and Change*, 37(4): 735–57.

Buzan, B. (1991a) 'New patterns of global security in the twenty-first century', *International Affairs*, 67: 431–51.

Buzan, B. (1991b) *People, States and Fear: An Agenda for International Security Studies in the Post-Cold War Era*, New York: Harvester Wheatsheaf.

Buzan, B. (1997) 'Rethinking security after the cold war', *Cooperation and Conflict*, 32(1): 5–28.

Buzan, B. (1999) 'Change and insecurity revisited', *Contemporary Security Policy*, 20: 1–17.

Buzan, B. and Wæver, O. (1997) 'Slippery? Contradictory? Sociologically untenable? The Copenhagen School replies', *Review of International Studies*, 23: 241–50.

Buzan, B. and Wæver, O. (2003) *Regions and Powers: The Structure of International Security*, Cambridge: Cambridge University Press.

Buzan, B., Kelstrup, M., Lemaityre, P., Tromer, E. and Wæver, O. (1990) *The European Security Order Recast: Scenarios for the Post-Cold War Era*, London and New York: Pinter.

Buzan, B., Wæver, O. and de Wilde, J. (1998) *Security: A New Framework for Analysis*, Boulder, CO: Lynne Rienner.

BWC Meeting of States Parties (2008) 'Report of the Meeting of States Parties', document BWC/MSP/2008/5, 12 Dec.

CASE Collective (2006) 'Critical approaches to security in Europe: a networked manifesto', *Security Dialogue*, 37: 443–87.

Cainkar, L. (2004) 'The impact of the September 11 attacks on Arab and Muslim community in the United States', in J. Tirnan (ed.) *The Maze of Fear: Security and Migration after 9/11*, New York: New Press.

Caldeira, T. (2001) *City of Walls: Crime, Segregation and Citizenship in Sao Paulo*, Berkeley: University of California Press.

Calder, K. E. (1996) *Asia's Deadly Triangle: How Arms, Energy and Growth Threaten to Destabilize Asia Pacific*, London: Nicholas Brealey.

Cambridge Review of International Affairs (1998) 'Special Issue on Private Military Companies', 13(1).

Campbell, C. (1997) *The Coming Oil Crisis*, Brentwood: Multi-Science.

Campbell, C. and Laherrere, J. (1998) 'The end of cheap oil?', *Scientific American*, 278(3): 78–84.

Campbell, D. (1982) *War Plan UK: The Truth about Civil Defence in Britain*, London: Burnett Books.

Campbell, D. (1992) *Writing Security: United States Foreign Policy and the Politics of Identity*, Minneapolis, MN: University of Minnesota Press.

Campbell, D. (1993) *Politics without Principle: Sovereignty, Ethics and the Narratives of the Gulf War*, Boulder, CO: Lynne Rienner.

Campbell, D. (1994) 'The deterritorialization of responsibility: Levinas, Derrida, and ethics after the end of philosophy', *Alternatives*, 19: 455–84.

Campbell, D. (1998) *National Deconstruction: Violence, Identity and Justice in Bosnia*, Minneapolis, MN: University of Minnesota Press.

Campbell, D. (2005) 'The biopolitics of security: oil, empire and the sports utility vehicle', *American Quarterly*, 57(3): 943–72.

Campbell, D. and Dillon, M. (1993) 'The end of philosophy and the end of international relations', in D. Campbell and M. Dillon (eds) *The Political Subject of Violence*, Manchester: Manchester University Press.

Campbell, D. and Shapiro, M. (eds) (1999) *Moral Spaces: Rethinking Ethics and World Politics*, Minneapolis, MN: Minnesota University Press.

REFERENCES

Campbell, D. and Shapiro, M. J. (2007) 'Introduction to special issue on securitization, militarization and visual culture in the worlds of post 9/11', *Security Dialogue*, 38(2): 131–7.

Campbell, D. B. (2006) *Besieged: Siege Warfare in the Ancient World*, Oxford: Osprey Publishing.

Campbell, J., Webster, D., Koziol-McLain, J. *et al.* (2003) 'Risk factors for femicide in abusive relationships: results from a multisite case control study', *American Journal of Public Health*, 93(7): 1089–97.

Canguilhem, G. (1988) *Ideology and Rationality in the History of the Life Sciences*, Cambridge: MIT Press.

Canguilhem, G. (1991) *The Normal and the Pathological*, with an introduction by Michel Foucault, New York: Zone Books.

Capgemini and Merrill Lynch, Pierce, Fenner and Smith Incorporated (2008) *World Wealth Report 2008*, New York: Capgemini and Merrill Lynch.

Caprioli, M. (2004a) 'Democracy and human rights versus women's security: a contradiction?', *Security Dialogue*, 35: 411.

Caprioli, M. (2004b) 'Feminist IR theory and quantitative methodology: a critical analysis', *International Studies Review*, 6(2): 253–69.

Caprioli, M. (2005) 'Primed for violence: the role of gender inequality in predicting internal conflict', *International Studies Quarterly*, 49(2): 161–78.

Caprioli, M. and Boyer, M. (2001) 'Gender, violence and international crisis', *Journal of Conflict Resolution*, 45(4): 503–18.

Carr, E. H. (1969) *The Twenty Years' Crisis, 1919–1939*, New York: Harper & Row.

Carruthers, B. G. and Babb, S. (1996) 'The color of money and the nature of value: greenbacks and gold in postbellum America', *American Journal of Sociology*, 101(6): 1556–91.

CBACI (2000) *Contagion and Conflict: Health as a Global Security Challenge,* Washington, DC: Chemical and Biological Arms Control Institute.

Center for Humanitarian Dialogue (2003) 'Small arms and human security: a snapshot of the humanitarian impacts', Geneva: HD Briefing Paper, online <http://se1.isn.ch/serviceengine/FileContent?serviceID =ISN&fileid=C08FD2B4-184F-7FAF-F55A-A3DEC6E62065&lng=enhttp://www.google.com/ url?sa=t&source=web&ct=res&cd=3&url=http%3A%2F%2Fhdcentre.org%2Ffiles%2FRXbriefing. pdf&ei=AM01SsOOJY3-sgPkiPTHDg&usg=AFQjCNFXjHWCvY4TE4m4okwrrotihWl_HQ> (accessed June 2009).

Ceyhan, A. (2006) 'Technologie et sécurité: une gouvernance libérale dans un contexte d'incertitudes', *Cultures et Conflits*, 64: 11–32.

Ceyhan, A. and Tsoukala, A. (2002) 'The securitization of migration in western societies: ambivalent discourses and policies', *Alternatives*, 27: 21–41.

Chancellor, E. (1999) *Devil Take the Hindmost: A History of Financial Speculation*, London: Macmillan.

Changming, L. And Shifeng, Z. (2002) 'Drying up of the Yellow River: its impacts and counter-measures', *Mitigation and Adaptation Strategies for Global Change*, 7(3): 203–14.

Chen, L. and Vasant, N. (2003) 'Human security and global health', *Journal of Human Development and Capabilities*, 4(2): 81–190.

Chen, S. and Ravallion, M. (2008) The Developing World is Poorer than we Thought, But No Less Successful in the Fight Against Poverty, Washington, DC: World Bank Development Research Group WPS4703.

Chester, D. K. (2001) 'The 1755 Lisbon earthquake', *Progress in Physical Geography*, 25: 363–83.

Chesterman, S. and Lehnardt, C. (eds) (2007) *From Mercenaries to Markets: The Rise and Regulation of Private Military Companies*, Oxford: Oxford University Press.

Chin, J. (2007) *The AIDS Pandemic: The Collision of Epidemiology with Political Correctness,* Abingdon: Radcliffe.

Chinkin, C. and Charlesworth, H. (2000) *The Boundaries of International Law: A Feminist Analysis*, New York and Manchester: Juris Pub. and Manchester University Press.

Chiozza, G. (2002) 'Is there a Clash of Civilizations? Evidence from Patterns of International Conflict Involvement, 1946–97', *Journal of Peace Research*, 39: 711.

Chomsky, N. and Herman, E. (1979) *The Washington Connection and Third World Fascism*, Boston: South End Press.

272

Chyba, F. and Greninger, A. L. (2004) 'Biotechnology and bioterrorism: an unprecedented world', *Survival*, 46(2): 143–62.

Clark, G. W. (1999) *Betting on Lives: The Culture of Life Insurance in England, 1695–1775,* Manchester: Manchester University Press.

Clark, M. A. (2003) 'Trafficking in persons: an issue of human security', *Journal of Human Development*, 4(2): 247–63.

Clay, E. and Stokke, O. (2000) *Food Aid and Human Security*, London: Portland, EADI.

Clevestig, P. and Hart, J. (2008) 'Microbial forensics', *Jane's Intelligence Review*, 20(11): 48–51.

CNA Corporation (2007) *National Security and the Threat of Climate Change*, Alexandra, VA : CNA Corporation.

CNN (2008) Transcript of Second McCain Obama debate, online <http://edition.cnn.com/2008/POLITICS/10/07/presidential.debate.transcript> (accessed June 2009).

Coady, C. A. J. (2008) *Morality and Political Violence*, Cambridge: Cambridge University Press.

Coaffee, J. and Murakami Wood, D. (2006) 'Security is coming home: rethinking scale and constructing resilience in the global urban response to terrorist risk', *International Relations*, 20: 503–17.

Coaffee, J., Murakami Wood, D. and Rogers, P. (2008) *The Everyday Resilience of the City: How Cities Respond to Terrorism and Disaster*, Basingstoke: Palgrave Macmillan.

Cockayne, J. (2006) *Commercial Security in the Humanitarian Space*, New York: International Peace Academy.

Cockburn, C. (2001) 'The gendered dynamic of armed conflict and political violence', in C. Moser and F. Clark (eds) *Victims, Perpetrators or Actors? Gender, Armed Conflict and Political Violence*, London: Zed Books.

Cockburn, C. and Zarkov, D. (eds) (2002) *The Postwar Moment: Militaries, Masculinities, and International Peacekeeping*, London: Lawrence & Wishart.

Cohen, B. (1996) 'Phoenix risen: the resurrection of global finance', *World Politics*, 48: 268–96.

Cohn, C. (1987) 'Sex and death in the rational world of defence intellectuals', *Signs: Journal of Women in Culture and Society*, 12(4): 687–718.

Cohn, C. and Ruddick, S. (2003) 'A feminist ethical perspective on weapons of mass destruction', *Boston Consortium on Gender, Security and Human Rights Working Paper*, 104, online <http://www.genderandsecurity.org/cohnruddick.pdf> (accessed July 2008).

Cohn, N. (2001) *Cosmos, Chaos and the World to Come: The Ancient Roots of Apocalyptic Faith*, London: Yale University Press.

Coker, C. (2002) *Globalisation and Insecurity in the Twenty-first Century: NATO and the Management of Risk*, Adelphi Paper, 345, Oxford: Oxford University Press.

Cole, S. A. (2001) *Suspect Identities: A History of Fingerprinting and Criminal Identification*, Cambridge, MA: Harvard University Press.

Coleman, J. R. (2004) 'Constraining modern mercenarism', *Hastings Law Journal*, 55(June): 1493–1537.

Coleman, M. (2003) 'The naming of "terrorism" and evil "outlaws" geopolitical place-making after 11 September', *Geopolitics*, 8(3): 87–104.

Coleman, M. (2007) 'A geopolitics of engagement: neoliberalism, the war on terrorism, and the reconfiguration of US immigration enforcement', *Geopolitics* 12(1): 607–34.

Collier, P. (2000) *Economic Causes of Civil Conflict and their Implications for Policy*, Working Paper, New York: World Bank.

Collier, P. and Hoeffler A. (2001) *Greed and Grievance in Civil Wars*, Washington, DC: World Bank.

Collier, S. and Lakoff, A. (2008) 'The vulnerability of vital systems: how "critical infrastructure" became a security problem', in M. Dunn Cavelty and K. S. Kirstensen (eds) *The Politics of Securing the Homeland: Critical Infrastructure, Risk and Securitisation*, London: Routledge.

Colomina, B. (2007) *Domesticity at War*, Cambridge: MIT Press.

Colvin, C. J. (2004) 'Ambivalent narrations: pursuing the political through traumatic story telling', *PoLAR (Political and Legal Anthropology Review)*, 27(1): 72–89.

Commission of the European Communities (2007) *Green Paper on Biopreparedness*, Brussels: Commission: online <http://eur-lex.europa.eu/LexUriServ/site/en/com/2007/com2007_0399en01.pdf> (accessed Oct. 2008).

Commission on Human Security (2003) *Human Security Now*, New York: United Nations.

REFERENCES

Committee on Research Standards and Practices to Prevent the Destructive Applications of Biotechnology (2004) *Biotechnology in an Age of Bioterrorism*, Washington, DC: National Academies Press.

Committee on Science, Engineering, and Public Policy (1982) *Scientific Communication and National Security*, Washington, DC: National Academy Press.

Computer Science and Telecommunications Board (1989) *Growing Vulnerability of the Public Switched Network: Implications for National Security Emergency Preparedness,* Washington, DC: National Academy Press.

Connolly, W. E. (1991) *Identity/Difference : Democratic Negotiations of Political Paradox,* Ithaca, NY: Cornell University Press.

Conrad, P. (2007) *The Medicalization of Society: On the Transformation of Human Conditions into Treatable Disorders,* Baltimore, MD: Johns Hopkins University Press.

Conteh-Morgan, E. (2002) 'Globalization and human security: a neo-Gramscian perspective', *International Journal of Peace Studies:* online <http://www.google.com/url?sa=t&source=web&ct=res&cd=1&url=http%3A%2F%2Fwww.gmu.edu%2Facademic%2Fijps%2Fvol7_2%2FContech-Morgan.htm&ei=UtE1Svm_EoKwsgPY4YTNDg&usg=AFQjCNHzv4BO1R9uJpsLNXauPmFoGNvGdg> (accessed June 2009).

Conteh-Morgan, E. (2005) 'Peacebuilding and human security: a constructivist perspective', *International Journal of Peace Studies*: online < http://www.google.com/url?sa=t&source=web&ct=res&cd=1&url=http%3A%2F%2Fwww.gmu.edu%2Facademic%2Fijps%2Fvol10_1%2FConteh-Morgan_101IJPS.pdf&ei=aNI1StPzAYvcswO_1OX9Dg&usg=AFQjCNFSNZdNyBzyStmpSOSHl2NwFhLbRQ > (accessed June 2009).

Cook, P., Ludwig, J., Venkatesh, S. and Braga, A. A. (2007) 'Underground gun markets', *Economic Journal,* 117: 588–618.

Cooper, M. (2006) 'Pre-empting emergence: the biological turn in the War on Terror', *Theory, Culture and Society*, 4(23): 113–35.

Corbett, C. (2008) 'Roads policing: current context and imminent dangers', *Policing: A Journal of Policy and Practice*, 2(1): 131–42.

Corrin, C. (2000) 'Post-conflict reconstruction and gender analysis in Kosova', *International Feminist Journal of Politics*, 3(1): 73–93.

Corrin, C. (2003) 'Developing policy on integration and re/construction in Kosova', *Development in Practice*, 13(2): 189–207.

Coward, M. (2005) 'The globalisation of enclosure: interrogating the geopolitics of empire', *Third World Quarterly*, 26(6): 105–34.

Cowen, D. and Emily G. (eds) (2008) *War, Citizenship, Territory,* New York: Routledge.

Craven, M., Marks, S., Simpson, G. and Wilde, R. (2004) 'We are teachers of international law', *Leiden Journal of International Law*, 17: 363–74.

Crawford, A. (2002) *Crime and Insecurity: The Governance of Safety in Europe,* Cullompton: Willan.

Crooks, E. (2007) 'ExxonMobil attacks US energy drive', *Financial Times* (13 Nov.).

Crutzen, P. J. and Steffen, W. (2003) 'How long have we been in the Anthropocene Era? An editorial comment', *Climate Change*, 61: 251–7.

CSIS (1994) *Global HIV/AIDS: A Strategy for U.S. Leadership,* Washington, DC: Center for Strategic and International Studies.

CSIS (2002) *The Destabilizing Impacts of HIV/AIDS,* Washington, DC: Center for Strategic and International Studies.

CSIS (2007) *The Age of Consequences: The Foreign Policy and National Security Implications of Global Climate Change,* Washington, DC: Centre for Strategic and International Studies.

Culpeper, R. and Baranyi, S. (2005) *Human Security, Sustainable and Equitable Development: Foundations for Canada's International Policy,* Ottawa: North-South Institute.

Cunningham, K. (2007) 'Countering female terrorism', *Studies in Conflict and Terrorism*, 30(2): 113–29.

Curley, M. and Thomas, N. (2004) 'Human security and public health in Southeast Asia: The Sars outbreak', *Australian Journal of International Affairs,* 58(1): 17–22.

Daase, C. and Kessler, O. (2007) 'Known and unknowns and the political construction of danger', *Security Dialogue*, 38(4): 411–34.

274

REFERENCES

Dalby, S. (1990) *Creating the Second Cold War: The Discourse of Politics,* London: Pinter.

Dalby, S. (1992) 'Ecopolitical discourse: "environmental security" and political geography', *Progress in Human Geography,* 16(4): 503–22.

Dalby, S. (1997) 'Contesting an essential concept: reading the dilemmas in contemporary security discourse', in K. Krause and M. C. Williams (eds) *Critical Security Studies: Concepts and Cases,* Abingdon, Oxon.: Routledge.

Dalby, S. (2000) *Geopolitical Change and Contemporary Security Studies: Contextualizing the Human Security Agenda,* Working Paper, 30, Institute of International Relations, University of British Columbia, April.

Dalby, S. (2002a) 'Environmental change and human security', *Canadian Journal of Policy Research,* 3(3): 71–9.

Dalby, S. (2002b) *Environmental Security,* Minneapolis, MN: University of Minnesota Press.

Dalby, S. (2003) 'Calling 911: geopolitics, security and America's new war', *Geopolitics* 8(3): 61–86.

Dalby, S. (2005) 'Political space: autonomy, liberalism and empire', *Alternatives: Global, Local, Political,* 30(4): 415–41.

Dalby, S. (2007) 'Regions, strategies, and empire in the global war on Terror', *Geopolitics* 12(4): 586–606.

Dalby, S. (2008a) 'Imperialism, domination, culture: the continued relevance of critical geopolitics', *Geopolitics* 13(3): 413–36.

Dalby, S. (2008b) 'Warrior geopolitics: *Gladiator, Black Hawk Down* and the *Kingdom of Heaven*', *Political Geography* 27(4): 439–55.

Dalby, S. (2009) *Security and Environmental Change,* Cambridge: Polity.

Dam, K. W. and Lin, H. S. (eds) (1996) *Cryptography's Role in Securing the Information Society,* Washington, DC: National Academy Press.

Dando, M. and Rappert, B. (2005) 'Codes of conduct for the life sciences: some insights from UK Academia', *Bradford Briefing Paper,* 16 (2nd series).

Dando, M. and Revill, J. (2006) 'A Hippocratic-style oath in the life sciences could help educate researchers about the dangers of dual-use research', *EMBO Rep,* 7: 55–60.

Dannreuther, R. (2007) *International Security: The Contemporary Agenda,* Cambridge: Polity.

Das, R. (2002) 'Engendering post-colonial nuclear policies through the lens of Hindutva: rethinking the security paradigm of India', *Comparative Studies of South Asia, Africa and the Middle East,* 22(1–2): 76–89.

Daston, L. (1988) *Classical Probability in the Enlightenment,* Princeton, NJ: Princeton University Press.

Dauphinée, E. (2007) *The Ethics of Researching War,* Manchester: Manchester University Press.

Dauphinée, E. and Masters, C. (eds) (2007) *The Logics of Biopower and the War on Terror,* Houndmills and New York: Palgrave Macmillan.

Davidson, R. (2003) 'Spaces of immigration «prevention»: interdiction and the non-place', *Diacritics,* 33(3–4): 3–18.

Davis, J. K. (1992) *Spying on America: The FBI's Domestic Counterintelligence Program,* Westport, CT: Praeger.

Davis, M. (1998) *Ecology of Fear: Los Angeles and the Imagination of Disaster,* London: Picador.

Davis, M. (2007) *Buda's Wagon: A Brief History of the Car Bomb,* London: Verso.

Davis, M. and Monk, D. B. (eds) (2007) *Evil Paradises: Dreamworlds of Neoliberalism,* New York: New Press.

De Boer, J. Z, and Sanders, D. T (2005) *Earthquakes in Human History: The Far-Reaching Effects of Seismic Disruption,* Princeton, NJ: Princeton University Press.

De Boer, J. Z. and Sanders, D. T. (2002) *Volcanoes in Human History: The Far-Reaching Effects of Major Eruptions,* Princeton, NJ: Princeton University Press.

De Cauter, L. (2004) *The Capsular Civilization: On the City in the Age of Fear,* Rotterdam: NAi Publishers.

De Genova, N. (2007) 'The production of culpability: from deportability to detainability in the aftermath of «homeland security»', *Citizenship Studies,* 11(5): 421–48.

De Goede, M. (2001) 'Discourses of scientific finance and the failure of long-term capital management', *New Political Economy,* 6(2): 149–70.

De Goede, M. (2005) *Virtue, Fortune and Faith: A Genealogy of Finance,* Minneapolis, MN: University of Minnesota Press.

De Goede, M. (2008a) 'Beyond risk: premeditation and the post-9/11 security imagination', *Security Dialogue,* 39(2–3): 155–76.

REFERENCES

De Goede, M. (2008b) 'Money, media and the anti-politics of terrorist finance', *European Journal of Cultural Studies,* 11(3): 289–310.

de Soysa, I. (2000) 'The resource curse: are civil wars driven by rapacity or paucity?', in M. Berdal and D. Malone (eds) *Greed and Grievance: Economic Agendas and Civil Wars,* Boulder, CO: Lynne Rienner, pp. 113–36.

de Waal, A. (1989) *Famine that Kills: Darfur, Sudan, 1984–1985,* Oxford: Oxford University Press.

de Waal, A. (2006) *AIDS and Power: Why there is No Political Crisis – Yet,* London: Zed Books.

de Waal, A. and Tumushabe, J. (2003) 'HIV/AIDS and food security in Africa: a report for DFID', report for the United Kingdom Department for International Development : online <http://www.sarpn. org.za/documents/d0000235/P227_AIDS_Food_Security.pdf> (accessed June 2009).

de Wolf, A. H. (2006) 'Modern condottieri in Iraq: privatizing war from the perspective of international and human rights law', *Indiana Journal of Global Legal Studies,* 13(2): 315–56.

Debiel, T. and Werthes, S. (eds) (2006) *Human Security and Foreign Policy Agendas: Changes, Concepts and Cases,* INEF Report 80, Duisberg: Institute for Development and Peace.

Debrix, F. (2008) *Tabloid Terror: War, Culture and Geopolitics,* New York: Routledge.

Debrix, F. and Lacy, M. (eds) (2009) *Insecure States: Geopolitical Anxiety, the War on Terror, and the Future of American Power,* London: Routledge.

Deflem, M. (2002) 'Technology and the Internationalization of policing: a comparative historical perspective', *Justice Quarterly,* (19)3: 453–75.

Deleuze, G. (1990) 'Post-scriptum sur les sociétés de contrôle', *L'autre journal,* 1 (May) 240–7.

Den Boer, M. (1994) 'The quest for international policing: rhetoric and justification in a disorderly debate', in M. Anderson and M. den Boer (eds) *Police Co-operation across National Boundaries,* London: Pinter.

Den Boer, M. (2001) 'The fight against organised crime in Europe: a comparative perspective', *European Journal on Criminal Policy and Research,* 9: 259–72.

Den Boer, M. (2002a) 'Cybercrime', in B. de Ruyver, G. Vermeulen and T. Vander Beken (eds) *Strategies of the EU and the US in Combating Transnational Organised Crime,* Antwerp and Apeldoorn: Maklu.

Den Boer, M. (2002b) 'Law-enforcement cooperation and transnational organized crime in Europe', in M. Berdal and M. Serrano (eds) *Transnational Organized Crime and International Security: Business as Usual?,* London: Lynne Rienner Publishers.

Den Boer, M. (2005) 'Copweb Europe: venues, virtues and vexations of transnational policing', in W. Kaiser and P. Starie (eds) *Transnational European Union: Towards a Common Political Space,* Abingdon: Routledge.

Department of Foreign Affairs and International Trade (2002) *Freedom From Fear: Canada's Foreign Policy for Human Security,* Ottawa: DFAIT.

Der Derian, J. (1992) *Anti-diplomacy: Spies, Speed, Terror and War,* Oxford: Blackwell.

Der Derian, J. (2001) *Virtuous War: Mapping the Military-Industrial-Media-Entertainment Network,* Boulder, CO: Westview Press.

Der Derian, J. and Shapiro, M. (eds) (1989) *International/Intertextual Relations: Postmodern Readings of World Politics,* Lexington: Lexington Books.

Derian, J. D. (1993) 'The value of security: Hobbes, Marx. Nietzsche, and Baudrillard' in D. C. M. Dillon (ed.) *The Political Subject of Violence,* Manchester and London: Manchester University Press.

Derrida, J. (1992) 'Force of law: the "Mystical Foundations of Authority"', in D. Cornell and M. Rosenfeld (eds) *Deconstruction and the Possibility of Justice,* London: Routledge.

Derrida, J. (2003) 'Autoimmunity: real and symbolic suicides – a dialogue with Jacques Derrida', in G. Borradori (ed.) *Philosophy in a Time of Terror,* Chicago: University of Chicago Press.

Deudney, D. (1990) 'The case against linking environmental degradation and national security', *Millennium: Journal of International Studies,* 19(3): 461–76.

Deudney, D. (1991) 'Environment and security: muddled thinking', *Bulletin of Atomic Scientists,* 47(3): 23–8.

Deudney, D. and Matthew, R. (eds) (1999) *Contested Grounds: Security and Conflict in the New Environmental Politics,* Binghamton, NY: State University of New York Press.

Devereux, S. (2002) 'The Malawi famine of 2002', *IDS Bulletin,* 33(4): 70–8.

Dhillon, G. (2007) *Principles of Information Systems Security: Text and Cases,* New York: John Wiley & Sons.

REFERENCES

Dickson, P.G.M. (1967) *The Financial Revolution in England: A Study in the Development of Public Credit 1688–1756,* London: Macmillan.

Didier, B. (2004) 'Biometrics', in OECD (ed.) *The Security Economy,* Paris: OECD.

Diehl, P. and Gleditsch, N. (eds) (2001) *Environmental Conflict: An Anthology,* Boulder, CO: Westview Press.

Diffie, W. and Hellman, M. E. (1976) 'New directions in cryptography', *IEEE Transactions on Information Theory,* (22) 6: 644–54.

Diken, B. and Lausten, C. (2005) *The Culture of Exception :- Sociology Facing the Camp,* London: Routledge.

Dillon, M. (1996) *Politics of Security: Towards a Political Philosophy of Continental Thought,* London and New York: Routledge.

Dillon, M. (2005) 'Global security in the 21st century: circulation, complexity and contingency', in ISP/NSC Briefing Paper 05/02, *The Globalization of Security* (Oct.), <http://www.chathamhouse.org.uk/files/3281_bpsecurity2.pdf>.

Dillon, M. (2006) 'Governing through contingency: the security of biopolitical governance', *Political Geography,* 26(1): 41–7.

Dillon, M. (2007) 'Governing terror: the state of emergency of biopolitical emergence', *International Political Sociology,* 1(1): 7–28.

Dillon, M. (2008a) 'Underwriting security', *Security Dialogue,* 39(2–3): 309–32.

Dillon, M. (2008b) 'Security, race and war', in M. Dillon and A. Neal (eds) *Foucault on Politics, Security and War,* London: Palgrave/Macmillan.

Dillon, M. and Lobo-Guerrero, L. (2008) 'Biopolitics of security in the 21st century: an introduction', *Review of International Studies,* 34(2): 265–92.

Dillon, M. and Neal, A. (eds) (2008) *Foucault on Politics, Security and War,* London: Palgrave/Macmillan.

Dittmer, J. (2005) 'Captain America's empire: reflections on identity, popular culture and post 9/11 geopolitics', *Annals of the Association of American Geographers,* 95(3): 626–43.

Dittmer, J. (2009) 'Maranatha! Premillennial dispensationalism and the counter-intuitive geopolitics of (in)security', in A. Ingram and K. Dodds (eds) *Spaces of Security and Insecurity,* Aldershot: Ashgate.

Dittmer, J. and Dodds, K. (2008) 'Popular geopolitics past and future: fandom, identities and audiences', *Geopolitics,* 13(3): 437–57.

Dodds, K. (1997) *Geopolitics in Antarctica: Views from the Southern Oceanic Rim,* Chichester: John Wiley.

Dodds, K. (1998) 'Enframing Bosnia: the geopolitical iconography of Steve Bell', in G. Ó Tuathail and S. Dalby (eds) *Rethinking Geopolitics,* London: Routledge.

Dodds, K. (2003) 'Licensed to stereotype: popular geopolitics, James Bond and the spectre of Balkanism', *Geopolitics,* 8(2): 125–56.

Dodds, K. (2006) 'Popular geopolitics and audience dispositions: James Bond and the Internet Movie Database (IMDb)', *Transactions of the Institute of British Geographers,* 31(2): 116–30.

Dodds, K. (2007) *Geopolitics: A Very Short Introduction,* Oxford: Oxford University Press.

Dodds, K. and Atkinson, D. (eds) (2000) *Geopolitical Traditions: A Century of Geopolitical Thought,* London: Routledge.

Donnelly, J. (1992) 'Twentieth-century realism', in T. Nardin, and D. R. Maple (eds) *Traditions of International Ethics,* Cambridge: Cambridge University Press.

Dorn, N. (2003) 'Proteiform criminalities: the formation of organised crime as organisers' responses to developments in four fields of control', in A. Edwards and P. Gill (eds) *Transnational Organised Crime: Perspectives on Global Security,* New York: Routledge.

Dorn, N. and Levi, M. (2007a) 'European private security, corporate investigation and military services: collective security, market regulation and structuring the public sphere', *Policing and Society,* 17(3): 213–38.

Dorn, N. and Levi, M. (2007b) 'Private–public or public–private? Strategic dialogue on serious crime and terrorism in the EU', *Security Journal* (Aug.).

Doty, R. L. (1996a) *Imperial Encounters: The Politics of Representation in North–South Relations,* Minneapolis, MN : University of Minnesota Press.

Doty, R. L. (1996b) 'The double-writing of statecraft: exploring state responses to illegal immigration', *Alternatives,* 21(2): 171-189.

Doty, R. L. (1998–9) 'Immigration and the politics of security', *Security Studies,* 8(2–3): 71–93.

REFERENCES

Doty, R. L. (2003) Anti-immigrantism in Western Democracies: Statecraft, Desire, and the Politics of Exclusion, New York: Routledge.

Doty, R. L. (2009) *The Law into their own Hands: Immigration, and the Politics of Exceptionalism*, Tucson, AZ: University of Arizona Press.

Douglas, M. and Wildvasky, A. (1992) *Risk and Blame: Essays in Cultural Theory*, London: Routledge.

Douzinas, C. (2007) *Human Rights and Empire, the Political Philosophy of Cosmopolitanism*, Abingdon and New York : Routledge-Cavendish.

Dowdney, L. (2003) *Children of the Drug Trade*, Rio de Janeiro: Viva Rio/ISER.

Dowler, L. and Sharp, J. (2001) 'A feminist geopolitics?', *Space and Polity*, 5(3): 165–76.

Doyle, M.W. (1997) *Ways of War and Peace: Realism, Liberalism and Socialism*, New York: W.W. Norton & Co.

Dregne, H. E. and Chou, N.T. (1994) 'Global desertification dimensions and costs', in H. E. Dregne (ed.) *Degradation and Restoration of Arid Lands*, Lubbock, TX: Texas Technical University, pp. 249–81.

Drèze, J. and Amartya, S. (1989) *Hunger and Public Action*, Oxford: Clarendon Press.

Droege, C. (2007) 'The interplay between international humanitarian law and international human rights law in situations of armed conflict', *Israel Law Review*, 40(2): 310–55.

Dudai, R. (2008) 'Can you describe this?' Human rights reports and what they tell us about the human rights movement', in R. D. Brown and R. A. Wilson (eds) *Humanitarianism and Suffering: The Mobilization of Empathy*, Cambridge: Cambridge University Press.

Duffield, M. (2001) 'Governing the borderlands: decoding the power of aid', *Disasters*, 25(4): 308–20.

Duffield, M. (2006) 'Racism, migration and development: the foundations of planetary order', *Progress in Development Studies*, 6: 68–79.

Duffield, M. (2007) *Development, Security and Unending War*, London: Polity.

Duffield, M. and Waddell, N. (2004) *Human Security and Global Danger: Exploring a Governmental Assemblage*, Economic and Social Science Research Council (ESRC) New Security Challenges Programme, RES-223-25-0035, London: British Overseas NGOs for Development.

Dunbar, N. (2000) *Inventing Money: The Story of Long-Term Capital Management and the Legends Behind it*, New York: John Wiley.

Dunn Cavelty, M. (2008) *Cyber-Security and Threat Politics: US Efforts to Secure the Information Age*, London: Routledge.

Dunne, A. and Raby, F. (2001) *Design Noir: The Secret Life of Electronic Objects*, Basel: Birkhauser.

Dupont, A. (2001) *East Asia Imperilled: Transnational Challenges to Security*, Cambridge: Cambridge University Press.

Dupont, A. and Pearman, A. (2006) *Heating up the Planet: Climate Change and Security*, Sydney: Lowy Institute for International Policy.

Dupont, B. (2005) 'Les morphologies de la sécurité après le 11 septembre: hiérarchies, marchés et réseaux', *Criminologie*, 38(2): 123–55.

Dupont, B. and Lemieux, F. (2005) *La militarisation des appareils policiers*, Quebec: Presses Universitaires de Laval.

Durkheim, E. and Mauss, M. (1971) 'Note on the notion of civilization', *Social Research*, 38(4): 808–13.

Duvell, F. (2003) 'The globalization of migration control', *openDemocracy*, online <http://www.opendemocracy.net/content/articles/PDF/1274.pdf> (accessed June 2009).

Dynes, R. R. (1997) *The Lisbon Earthquake In 1755: Contested Meanings in the First Modern Disaster*, Disaster Research Center Preliminary Papers, 255, University of Delaware.

Dyson, E., Gilder, G., Keyworth, G. and Toffler, A. (1994) 'Cyberspace and the American dream: a Magna Carta for the knowledge age', *Future Insight*, release 1.2 (Aug.), online <http://www.pff.org/issues-pubs/futureinsights/fi1.2magnacarta.html> (accessed Nov. 2008).

Eberstadt, N. (2002) 'The future of AIDS', *Foreign Affairs*, 81(6): 22–45.

Eckersley, R. (2009) 'Environmental security, climate change, and globalizing terrorism', in D. Grenfell and P. James (eds) *Rethinking Insecurity, War and Violence: Beyond Savage Globalization*, London: Routledge.

Eckert, S. E. (2008) 'The use of financial measures to promote security', *Journal of International Affairs*, 62(1): 103–11.

Edkins, J. (2003) *Trauma and the Memory of Politics*, Cambridge: Cambridge University Press.

REFERENCES

Edwards, A. and Gill, P. (2003) 'After transnational organised crime? The politics of public safety', in A. Edwards and P. Gill (eds) *Transnational Organised Crime: Perspectives on Global Security*, New York: Routledge.

Egmond, F. (1994) *Op het verkeerde pad: Georganiseerde misdaad in de Noordelijke Nederlanden 1650–1800*, Amsterdam: Bert Bakker.

Elbe, S. (2002) 'HIV/AIDS and the changing landscape of war in Africa', *International Security*, 27(2): 159–77.

Elbe, S. (2005) 'AIDS, security biopolitics', *International Relations*, 4(19): 403–19.

Elbe, S. (2006) 'Should HIV/AIDS be securitized? The ethical dilemmas of linking HIV/AIDS and security', *International Studies Quarterly*, 50: 119–44.

Elbe, S. (2008a) 'Our epidemiological footprint: the circulation of avian flu, SARS, and HIV/AIDS in the world economy', *Review of International Political Economy*, 15: 116–30.

Elbe, S. (2008b) 'Risking lives: AIDS, security and three concepts of risk', *Security Dialogue*, 39(2–3): 177–98.

Elbe, S. (2009) *Virus Alert: Security, Governmentality and the AIDS Pandemic*, New York: Columbia University Press.

El-Bushra, J. (2000) 'Transforming conflict: some thoughts on a gendered understanding of conflict processes', in S. Jacobs, R. Jacobson and J. Marchbank (eds) *States of Conflict: Gender, Violence and Resistance*, London: Zed Books.

Elden, S. (2007) 'Blair, neo-conservatism and the war on territorial integrity', *International Politics*, 44: 37–57.

Electronic Privacy Information Center (1998) *Critical Infrastructure Protection and the Endangerment of Civil Liberties: An Assessment of the President's Commission on Critical Infrastructure Protection (PCCIP)*, Washington, DC: EPIC.

Electronic Privacy Information Center (2007) 'Iraqi Biometric Identification System' (17 Aug.), online <http://epic.org/privacy/biometrics/iraq.html> (accessed June 2009).

Elias, N. (2000 [1939]) *The Civilizing Process*, Oxford: Wiley-Blackwell.

Elliott, B. (ed.) (1988) *Technology and Social Process*, Edinburgh: Edinburgh University Press.

Ellison, R. J., Fisher, D. A., Linger, R. C., Lipson, H. F., Longstaff, T. and Mead, N. R. (1997) *Survivable Network Systems: An Emerging Discipline*, Technical Report, CMU/SEI-97-TR-013, ESC-TR-97-013 <www.cert.org/research/97tr013.pdf> (accessed Nov. 2008).

Elshtain, J. B. (2003) 'International justice as equal regard and the use of force', *Ethics and International Affairs*, 17(2): 63–75.

Elshtain, J. B. (2004) *Just War Against Terror*, New York: Basic Books.

Elshtain, J. B. (2007) 'Against the new utopianism', *Studies in Christian Ethics*, 20(1): 44–54.

Enloe, C. (1989) *Bananas, Beaches, and Bases: Making Feminist Sense of International Relations*, Berkeley, CA: University of California Press.

Ericson, R. V. (2007) *Crime in an Insecure World*, Cambridge: Polity Press.

Ericson, R. V. and Doyle, A. (2004) *Uncertain Business: Risk, Insurance, and the Limits of Knowledge*, Toronto: Toronto University Press

Ericson, R. V. and Haggerty, K. D. (1997) *Policing the Risk Society*, Oxford: Oxford University Press.

Ericson, R. V. and Haggerty, K. D. (1999) 'The militarization of policing in the information age', *Journal of Political and Military Sociology*, 27: 233–55.

Ericson, R. V. and Stehr, N. (2000) *Governing Modern Societies*, Toronto: Toronto University Press.

Esposito, R. (2008) *Bios: Biopolitics and Philosophy*, trans. T. Campbell, Minneapolis, MN: Minnesota University Press.

Ethics and International Affairs (2005) Special section on intervention after Iraq, 19(2).

European Commission (2004) *On the Implementation of the Preparatory Action on the Enhancement of the European Industrial Potential in the Field of Security Research: Towards a Programme to Advance European Security through Research and Technology*, Brussels, COM (2004) 72 final.

European Commission (2006) *An External Policy to Serve Europe's Energy Interests*, Brussels : EC.

Europol (2007) *Organised Crime Threat Assessment*, The Hague: Europol.

REFERENCES

Evans, G. (2008) *The Responsibility to Protect: Ending Mass Atrocity Crimes Once and for All*, Washington, DC: Brookings Institution Press.

Ewald, U. (2002) 'Victimization in the context of war : some aspects of a macro-victimological research project', *European Journal of Crime, Criminal Law and Criminal Justice*, 10(2–3): 90–7.

Ewald, U. (2006) 'Large-scale victimisation and the jurisprudence of the ICTY-victimological research issues', in U. Ewald and K. Turković (eds) *Large-Scale Victimisation as a Potential Source of Terrorist Activities Importance of Regaining Security in Post-Conflict Societies*, NATO Security through Science, vol. 13. Series E: Human and Societal Dynamics, Amsterdam: IOS Press.

Fagan, J., Wilkinson D. and Davies, G. (2007) 'Social contagion of violence', in Daniel Flannery, A. Vazsonyi and I. Waldman (eds) *The Cambridge Handbook of Violent Behavior*, New York: Cambridge University Press.

FAO (Food and Agriculture Organisation of the United Nations) (1996) *Rome Declaration on World Food Security*, Rome: FAO, online <http://www.fao.org/docrep/003/w3613e/w3613e00.HTM> (accessed June 2009).

FAO (2006a) *The State of Food Insecurity in the World 2006 : Eradicating World Hunger – Taking Stock Ten Years After the World Food Summit*, Rome: FAO.

FAO (2006b) *The Right to Food in Practice: Implementation at the National Level*, Rome: FAO.

FAO (2008) *The State of Food Insecurity in the World 2008: High Food Prices and Food Security – Threats and Opportunities*, Rome: FAO.

Farer, T. J. (ed.) (2005) 'Roundtable on Humanitarian Intervention After 9/11', *International Relations*, 19(2): 211–50.

Farish, M. (2003) 'Disaster and decentralization: American cities and the Cold War', *Cultural Geographies*, 10: 125–48.

Febvre, L. (1973) '*Civilization*: evolution of a word and a group of ideas', in P. Burke (ed.) *A New Kind of History: From the Writings of Febvre*, trans. K. Folca, London: Routledge & Kegan Paul.

Federation of American Scientists (FAS), online <http://www.fas.org/biosecurity/education/dualuse/> (accessed June 2009).

Fekete, L. (2001) 'The emergence of xeno-racism', *Race and Class*, 43(2): 23–40.

Feldman, D. (2003) 'Was the nineteenth century a golden age for immigrants? The changing articulation of national, local and voluntary controls', in A. Fahrmeir, O. Faron and P. Weil (eds) *Migration Control in the North Atlantic World*, New York: Berghahn.

Ferguson, N. (2008) *Geopolitical Consequences of the Credit Crunch*, Hoover Institution, online <http://fora.tv/2008/10/21/Geopolitical_Consequences_of_the_Credit_Crunch> (accessed April 2009).

Fidler, D. (2004) *SARS: Governance and the Globalization of Disease*, New York: Palgrave.

Fidler, D. (2004) 'Germs, norms and power: global health's political revolution', *Law, Social Justice and Global Development Journal, online*, <http://www2.warwick.ac.uk/fac/soc/law/elj/lgd/2004_1/fidler/> (accessed May 2009).

Fierke, K. M. (2007) *Critical Approaches to international Security*, Cambridge: Polity.

Fijnaut, C. and Paoli, L. (2006) *Organised Crime in Europe: Concepts, Patterns and Control Policies in the European Union and Beyond*, Dordrecht: Springer.

Fischer, Eric A. (2005) 'Creating a national framework for cyber-security: an analysis of issues and options', CRS Report for Congress, order code RL32777, online <http://www.usembassy.it/pdf/other/RL32777.pdf> (accessed Nov. 2008).

Fischer, J. E. (2006) *Stewardship or Censorship: Balancing Biosecurity, the Public Health and the Benefits of Scientific Openness*, Washington, DC: Henry L. Stimson Center.

Flint, C. (2005) *The Geography of War and Peace: From Death Camps to Diplomats*, Oxford: Oxford University Press.

Florquin, N. and Stoneman, S. (2004) '*A House isn't a Home Without a Gun*':- *SALW Survey of Republic of Montenegro*, Belgrade: SEESAC.

Floyd, R. (2007) 'Towards a consequentialist evaluation of security: bringing together the Copenhagen and the Welsh schools of security studies', *Review of International Studies*, 33(2): 327–50.

Flusty, S. (1994) *Building Paranoia: The Proliferation of Interdictory Space and the Erosion of Spatial Justice*, Los Angeles Forum for Architecture and Urban Design, 11.

280

REFERENCES

Focarelli, C. (2008) 'The responsibility to protect doctrine and humanitarian intervention: too many ambiguities for a working doctrine', *Journal of Conflict and Security Law*, 13(2): 191–213.

Forced Migration Review (2008) *Ten Years of the Guiding Principles on Internal Displacement*, online <http://www.fmreview.org/GuidingPrinciples10.htm> (accessed June 2009).

Foucault, M. (1975) *Surveillir et punir: Naissance de la prison*, Paris: Gallimard.

Foucault, M. (1976) *Histoire de la sexualité*, Paris: Gallimard.

Foucault, M. (1977a) *Discipline and Punish: The Birth of the Modern Prison*, New York: Vintage.

Foucault, M. (1977b) *Discipline and Punishment*, New York: Pantheon.

Foucault, M. (1977c) 'In the Flesh', in C. Gordon (ed.) *Power/Knowledge: Selected Interviews and Other Writings*, New York: Pantheon.

Foucault, M. (1981) *The History of Sexuality*, vol. 1, *An Introduction*, trans. R. Hurley, London: Penguin.

Foucault, M. (1984) 'What is enlightenment?', in P. Rabinow (ed.) *The Foucault Reader*, New York: Pantheon Books.

Foucault, M. (1987) *The History of Sexuality*, vol. 1, New York: Peregrine Books.

Foucault, M. (1989) *The Order of Things: An Archaeology of the Human Sciences*, London: Tavistock/Routledge.

Foucault, M. (1997) 'The birth of biopolitics', in P. Rabinow (ed.) *Ethics: Subjectivity and Truth: Essential Works of Foucault 1954–1984*, vol. 1, trans. Robert Hurley, New York: New Press, pp. 73–9.

Foucault, M. (2002) 'The political technology of individuals', in J. D. Faubion (ed.) *Power: Essential Works of Foucault 1954–84*, vol. 3, New York: Open Press.

Foucault, M. (2003a) *Abnormal*, trans. G. Burchell, New York: Picador.

Foucault, M. (2003b) *Society Must Be Defended: Lectures at the Collège de France 1977–78*, London: Allen Lane.

Foucault, M. (2007) *Security, Territory, Population: Lectures at the Collège de France 1977–78*, trans. G. Burchell, Basingstoke and New York: Palgrave.

Foucault, M. (2008) *The Birth of Biopolitics: Lectures at the Collège de France 1979–80*, trans. G. Burchell, Basingstoke and New York: Palgrave.

Fourie, P. and Schenteich, M. (2001) 'Africa's new security threat: HIV/AIDS and human security in Southern Africa', *African Security Review*, 10(4): 35–6.

Franceschet, A. (2006) 'Global legalism and human security', in S. J. MacLean, D. R. Black and T. M. Shaw (eds) *A Decade of Human Security, Global Governance and New Multilateralisms*, Aldershot and Burlington, VT: Ashgate Publishing, pp. 31–8.

Francis, D. J. (1999) 'Mercenary intervention in Sierra Leone: providing national security or international exploitation?', *Third World Quarterly*, 20(2): 319–38.

Franklin, U. (1999) *The Real World of Technology*, rev. edn, Toronto: House of Anansi Press.

Freedman, L. (2003) *The Evolution of Nuclear Strategy*, 3rd edn, Basingstoke: Palgrave Macmillan.

Frieden, J. A. (1993) 'Capital politics: creditors and the international political economy', in J. A. Frieden and D. A. Lake (eds) *International Political Economy*, London: Unwin Hyman.

Friman, H. R. and Reich, S. (2007) *Human Trafficking, Human Security, and the Balkans*, Pittsburgh, PA: University of Pittsburgh Press.

Froud, J., Johal, S., Leaver, A. and Williams, K. (2006) *Financialization and Strategy: Narrative and Numbers*, London: Routledge.

Fu, G. and Chen, S. (2006) 'Water crisis in the Yellow River: facts, reasons, impacts, and countermeasures', *Water Practice and Technology*, 1(2): doi10.2166/wpt.2006.0028.

Fukuyama, F. (1989) 'The end of history?', *National Interest*, 16: 3–18.

Fukuyama, F. (1992) *The End of History and the Last Man*, London: Penguin.

Fuller, J. F. (1992 [1961]) *The Conduct of War, 1789–1961: A Study of the Impact of the French, Industrial, and Russian Revolutions on War and Its Conduct*, New Brunswick, NJ: Da Capo Press.

Future Farmers (2008) 'Homeland security blanket', online <http://www.futurefarmers.com/survey/homeland.php> (accessed June 2009).

Galbraith, J. K. (1993) *A Short History of Financial Euphoria*, London: Whittle Books in association with Penguin.

Galeotti, M. (ed.) (2007) *Global Crime Today: The Changing Face of Organized Crime*, London: Routledge.

281

REFERENCES

Gammeltoft-Hansen, T. (2009) 'The refugee, the sovereign and the sea: European Union interdiction policies', in R. Adler-Nissen and T. Gammeltoft-Hansen (eds) *Sovereignty Games: Instrumentalising State Sovereignty in Europe and Beyond*, London: Palgrave.

Garfinkel, M. S., Endy, D., Epstein, G. L. and Friedman, R. M. (2007) *Synthetic Genomics: Options for Governance*, Cambridge, MA: J. Craig Venter Institute, Center for Strategic and International Studies and the Massachusetts Institute of Technology's Department of Biological Engineering.

Gartzke, E. and Gleditsch, K. S. (2006) 'Identity and conflict: ties that bind and differences that divide', *European Journal of International Relations,* 12: 53–87.

Gathii, J. T. (2000) 'Rejoinder: Twailing international law', *Michigan Law Review,* 98: 2066.

Geithner, T. (2009) Prepared Statement by Treasury Secretary Tim Geithner at the G-20 Finance Ministers and Central Bank Governors Meeting, 14 March, online <http://www.ustreas.gov/press/releases/tg56.htm> (accessed April 2009).

Gellman, B. (2000) 'The belated global response to AIDS in Africa: world shunned signs of the coming plague', *Washington Post* (5 July).

Genel, K. (2006) 'The question of biopower: Foucault and Agamben', *Rethinking Marxism,* 18(1): 43–62.

Geneva Declaration (2008) *Global Burden of Armed Violence,* Geneva: Geneva Declaration Secretariat, online <http://www.genevadeclaration.org/pdfs/Global-Burden-of-Armed-Violence-full-report.pdf> (accessed June 2009).

Genieys, W. and Michel, L. (2006) 'Au-dela du complexe militaro-industriel: Le rôle d'une élite sectorielle dans le programme du char Leclerc', *Revue française de sociologie,* 47: 117–42.

George, S. and Sabelli, F. (1994) *Faith and Credit: The World Bank's Secular Empire,* London: Penguin.

Germain, R. D. (1997) *The International Organisation of Credit: States and Global Finance in the World-Economy,* Cambridge: Cambridge University Press.

Gershenfeld, N., Krikorian, R. and Cohen, D. (2004) 'The internet of things', *Scientific American,* 291: 76–81.

Gever, J. (1986) *Beyond Oil: The Threat to Food and Fuel in the Coming Decades,* Cambridge: Ballinger.

Giddens, A. (1985) *The Nation-State and Violence,* Berkeley and Los Angeles, CA: University of California Press.

Gill, S. (1990) *American Hegemony and the Trilateral Commission,* Cambridge: Cambridge University Press.

Gill, S. (1995) 'The global panopticon? The neoliberal state, economic life, and democratic surveillance', *Alternatives,* 20(1): 1–49.

Gill, S. and Law, D. (1993) 'Global hegemony and the structural power of capital', in S. Gill (ed.) *Gramsci, Historical Materialism and International Relations,* Cambridge: Cambridge University Press.

Gillespie, S. (ed.) (2006) *Aids, Poverty and Hunger: Challenges and Responses,* Washington, DC: International Food Policy Research Institute (IFPRI).

Gillespie, S. and Haddad, L. R. (2003) *The Double Burden of Malnutrition in Asia: Causes, Consequences, and Solutions,* New Delhi and London: Sage Publications.

Gilroy, P. (2002) 'Raise your eyes', *openDemocracy,* online <http://www.opendemocracy.net/conflict-911/article_249.jsp> (accessed June 2009).

Gioia, G. (2007) 'Victims' rights overview under the ICC legal framework: a jurisprudential analysis', *International Criminal Law Review,* 7: 531–47.

Giraudon, V. (2001) *Controlling a New Migration World,* London: Routledge.

Glasius, M. and Kaldor, M. (2006) *A Human Security Doctrine for Europe: Project, Principles, Practicalities,* New York: Routledge.

Glazovsky, N. F. (1995) 'The Aral Sea Basin', in J. X. Kasperson, R. E. Kasperson and B.L. Turner II (eds) *Regions at Risk: Comparisons of Threatened Environments,* Tokyo: United Nations University Press, pp. 92–139.

Gleditsch, N. (1998) 'Armed conflict and the environment: a critique of the literature', *Journal of Peace Research,* 35, 381–400.

Goldmann, M. (2008) 'Inside relative normativity: from sources to standard instruments for the exercise of international public authority – part II', *German Law Journal,* 9(11): 1865–1908.

Goldstein, J. L., Kahler, M., Keohane, R.O. and Slaughter, A. (2000) 'Introduction: legalization and world politics', *International Organization,* 54(3): 385–99.

REFERENCES

Gong, G.W. (1984) *The Standard of 'Civilization' in International Society*, Oxford: Clarendon Press.

Goodwin-Gill, Guy S. (1996) *The Refugee in International Law*, Oxford: Clarendon Press.

Gordon, L. and Loeb, M. (2006) *Managing Cybersecurity Resources: A Cost-Benefit Analysis*, New York: McGraw-Hill.

Gore, A. (2008) Speech to Democratic National Convention, 28 Aug.

Gostin, L. (2004) 'International infectious disease law: revision of the World Health Organization's international health regulations', *Journal of the American Medical Association* 291(21): 2623–7.

Gottron, F. and Shea, D. A. (2009) *Oversight of High-Containment Biological Laboratories: Issues for Congress*, report R40418, Washington, DC: Congressional Research Service.

Government of Japan (2008) 'National, regional and international measures for improving biosafety and biosecurity with a focus on the safety of pathogens and toxins at the laboratory level', national paper presented at BTWC Meeting of Experts, Geneva, 18–22 Aug., <http://daccessdds.un.org/doc/UNDOC/GEN/G08/627/13/PDF/G0862713.pdf?OpenElement> (accessed March 2009).

Graham, D.T. and Poku, N. (2000) *Migration, Globalisation, and Human Security*, New York: Routledge.

Graham, S. (ed.) (2004) *Cities, War and Terrorism: Towards an Urban Geopolitics*, Oxford: Blackwell.

Graham, S. (2006a) '"Homeland" insecurities? Katrina and the politics of "security" in metropolitan America', *Space and Culture*, 9: 63–7.

Graham, S. (2006b) 'Surveillance, urbanization, and the "revolution in military affairs"', in D. Lyon (ed.) *Theorizing Surveillance: The Panopticon and Beyond*, Cullompton: Willan Publishing, pp. 245–67.

Graham, S. (2008) 'Imagining urban warfare: urbanization and U.S. military technoscience', in D. Cowen and E. Gilbert (eds) *War, Citizenship, Territory*, New York: Routledge.

Graham, S. (2010) *Cities Under Siege: The New Military Urbanism*, London: Verso.

Graham, S. and Marvin, S. (2003) *Splintering Urbanism*, London: Routledge.

Grayson, K. (2004a) 'A challenge to the power over knowledge of traditional security studies', *Security Dialogue*, 35(3): 357.

Grayson, K. (2004b) 'Branding "transformation" in Canadian foreign policy: human security', *Canadian Foreign Policy*, 11(2): 41–68.

Greenfeld, K.T. (2006) *China Syndrome: The True Story of the 21st Century's First Great Pandemic*, New York: HarperCollins.

Gregory, D. (2004) *The Colonial Present: Afghanistan, Palestine and Iraq*, Malden, MA: Blackwell.

Gregory, D. (2006a) 'The black flag: Guantanamo Bay and the space of exception', *Geografiska Annaler B*, 88(4): 405–27.

Gregory, D. (2006b) '"In another time zone, the bombs fall unsafely": targets, civilians and late modern war', *Arab World Geographer*, 9(2): 88–111.

Gregory, D. and Pred, A. (eds) (2007) *Violent Geographies: Fear, Terror and Political Violence*, New York: Routledge.

Gregory, F. (2003) 'Classify, report and measure: the UK Organised Crime Notification Scheme', in A. Edwards and P. Gill (eds) *Transnational Organised Crime: Perspectives on Global Security*, New York: Routledge.

Grieve, J. (2008) 'Lawfully audacious: a reflective journey', in C. Harfield, A. MacVean, J. G. D. Grieve and D. Phillips (eds) *The Handbook of Intelligent Policing: Consilience, Crime Control and Community Safety*, Oxford: Oxford University Press.

Groebner, V. (2007) *Who are You? Identification, Deception and Surveillance in Early Modern Europe*, New York: Zone.

Grusin, R. (2004) 'Premediation', *Criticism*, 46(1): 17–39.

Grygiel, J. J. (2006) *Great Powers and Geopolitical Change*, Baltimore, MD: Johns Hopkins University Press.

Guittet, E.-P. (2008a) 'Military activities inside national territory: the French case', in D. Bigo and A. Tsoukala (eds) *Terror, Insecurity and Liberty*, London: Routledge.

Guittet, E.-P. (2008b) 'Promoting high tech security: mapping the international security and defence exhibitions', unpublished manuscript, Montreal.

Gurr, T. R. (1994) 'Peoples against states: ethnopolitical conflict and the changing world system', *International Studies Quarterly*, 38: 347–77

REFERENCES

Gusterson, H. (1999) 'Missing the end of the cold war in international security', in J. Weldes, M. Laffey, H. Gusterson and R. Duvall (eds) *Cultures of Insecurity: States, Communities and the Production of Danger,* Minneapolis, MN: University of Minnesota Press.

Gusterson, H. (2004) *People of the Bomb: Portraits of America's Nuclear Complex,* Minneapolis, MN: University of Minnesota Press.

Hables Gray, C. (1997) *Postmodern War: The New Politics of Conflict,* New York: Guilford Press.

Hack FAQ (2004) Online <http://www.nmrc.org/pub/faq/hackfaq/index.html> (accessed Nov. 2008).

Haggerty, K. D. (2006) 'Tear down the walls: on demolishing the panopticon', in D. Lyon (ed.) *Theorizing Surveillance: The Panopticon and Beyond,* Cullompton: Willan.

Haggerty, K. D. and Ericson, R. V. (1999) 'The militarization of policing in the information age', *Journal of Political and Military Sociology,* 27(winter): 233–55.

Haggerty, K. D. and Ericson, R. V. (2000) 'The surveillant assemblage', *British Journal of Sociology* 51: 605–22.

Haggerty, K. D. and Ericson, R. V. (eds) (2006) *The New Politics of Surveillance and Visibility,* Toronto: University of Toronto Press.

Haldon, J. (1999) *Warfare, State and Society in the Byzantine World, 565–1204,* London: Routledge.

Haldrup, M., Koefoed, L. and Simonsen, K. (2008) 'Practicing fear: encountering O/other bodies', in R. Pain and S. Smith (eds) *Fear: Critical Geopolitics and Everyday Life (Re-Materialising Cultural Geography),* London: Ashgate.

Hall, S. and Winlow, S. (2005) 'Anti-nirvana: crime, culture and instrumentalism in an age of insecurity', *Crime, Media, Culture,* 1: 31–48.

Halperin, M. H. (1987) *Nuclear Fallacy,* Cambridge: Ballinger.

Hamlin, C. (1992) 'Reflexivity in technology studies: towards a technology of technology (and science)?', *Social Studies of Science,* 22: 511–44.

Hampson, F. O. and Daudelin, J. (2001) *Madness in the Multitude: Human Security and World Disorder,* Oxford: Oxford University Press.

Hampson, F. O. and Hay, J. (2002) 'Human security: a review of the scholarly literature', paper presented to the annual meeting of the Canadian Consortium on Human Security, Ottawa, April.

Hamre, J. J. (1998) 'Critical infrastructure protection: information assurance', Hearing on Intelligence and Security, Testimony of the Deputy Secretary of Defense, 11 June, House Military Procurement and Military Research & Development Subcommittees. Online <http://www.fas.org/irp/congress/1998_hr/98-06-11hamre.htm> (accessed Nov. 2008).

Han, B. (2002) *Foucault's Critical Project: Between the Transcendental and the Historical,* trans. E. Pike, Stanford, CA: Stanford University Press.

Handrahan, L. (2004) 'Conflict, gender, ethnicity and post-conflict reconstruction', *Security Dialogue,* 35(4): 429–45.

Hannah, M. (2006) 'Torture and the ticking bomb: the war on terrorism as a geographical imagination of power/knowledge', *Annals of the Association of American Geographers,* 96(3): 622–40.

Hansen, L. (2000) 'Gender, nation, rape: Bosnia and the construction of security', *International Feminist Journal of Politics,* 3(1): 55–75.

Hansen, L. (2006) *Security as Practice: Discourse Analysis and the Bosnian War,* New York: Routledge.

Haraway, D. (1991) *Simians, Cyborgs, and Women: The Reinvention of Nature,* New York: Routledge.

Harbom, L. (ed.) (2007) *States in Armed Conflict 2006,* Uppsala: Uppsala University.

Harcourt, B. (2006) *Language of the Gun: Youth, Crime and Public Policy,* Chicago: University of Chicago Press.

Hardt, M. and Negri, A. (2000) *Empire,* Cambridge, MA: Harvard University Press.

Hardt, M. and Negri, A. (2004) *Multitude,* Harmondsworth: Penguin.

Harfield, C. (2008) 'Paradigms, pathologies, and practicalities: policing organized crime in England and Wales', *Policing: A Journal of Policy and Practice,* 2(1): 63–73.

Harfield, C. (2008a) 'Introduction: intelligent policing', in C. Harfield, A. MacVean, J. G. D. Grieve and D. Phillips (eds) *The Handbook of Intelligent Policing: Consilience, Crime Control and Community Safety,* Oxford: Oxford University Press.

REFERENCES

Harmes, A. (2009) 'Imagined futures: anticipatory visuality and the political economy of corporate scenario planning', paper presented to the Annual Meeting of the International Studies Association, New York.

Harrison, G. (2004) *The World Bank and Africa: The Construction of Governance States,* London: Routledge.

Hart, J. and Kuhlau, F. (2005) 'Codes of conduct for scientists in the biological field', paper presented by Frida Kuhlau at the conference Meeting the Challenges of Bioterrorism: Assessing the Threat and Designing Biodefence Strategies, 22–3 April, Fürigen (Nidwalden), Switzerland (conference organized by the Center for Security Studies (CSS) at the Swiss Federal Institute of Technology, ETH Zurich).

Hartmann, B., Subramaniam, B. and Zerner, C. (eds) (2005) *Making Threats: Biofears and Environmental Anxieties,* Lanham, MD: Rowman & Littlefield.

Harvey, P. (2007) *Cash-Based Responses in Emergencies,* Humanitarian Policy Group (HPG) Report, 24, London: Overseas Development Institute.

Hastrup, K. (2001) 'Representing the common good, the limits of legal language', in R. A. Wilson and J. Mitchell (eds) *Human Rights in Global Perspective: Anthropological Studies of Rights, Claims and Entitlements,* London and New York: Routledge.

Hauge, W. and Ellingsen, T. (2001) 'Causal pathways to conflict', in P. Diehl and N. Gleditsch (eds) *Environmental Conflict: An Anthology,* Boulder, CO: Westview Press, pp. 36–57.

Hayek, F. A. Von (1945) 'The use of knowledge in society', *American Economic Review,* 35(4): 519–30.

Hayes, B. (2006) *Arming Big Brother: The EU's Security Research Programme,* Amsterdam: Transnational Institute and Statewatch.

Headrick, D. (1981) *Tools of Empire,* Oxford: Oxford University Press.

Heberer, T. and Jakobi, S. (2000) *Henan – the Model: From Hegemonism to Fragmentism. Portrait of the Political Culture of China's Most Populated Province,* Duisburg Working Papers on East Asian Studies, 32, Duisburg: Gerhard-Mercator-Universität.

Heffernan, M. (1998) *The Meaning of Europe: Geography and Geopolitics,* London and New York: Arnold and Oxford University Press.

Helleiner, E. (1994) *States and the Reemergence of Global Finance: From Bretton Woods to the 1990s,* Ithaca, NY: Cornell University Press.

Helleiner, E. and Gilbert, E. (1999) *Nation-States and Money: The Past, Present and Future of National Currencies,* London: Routledge.

Helm, D. (ed.) (2007) *The New Security Paradigm,* Oxford: Oxford University Press.

Henderson, E. A. (1997) 'Culture or contiguity: ethnic conflict, the similarity of states, and the onset of war, 1820–1989', *Journal of Conflict Resolution,* 41: 649.

Henderson, E. A. and Tucker, R. (2001) 'Clear and present strangers: the clash of civilizations and international conflict', *International Studies Quarterly,* 45: 317–38.

Heng, Y. and McDonagh, K. (2008) 'The other war on terror revealed: global governmentality and the financial action task force campaign against terrorist financing', *Review of International Studies,* 34(3): 553–73.

Herbert S. (2007) 'The "Battle of Seattle" Revisited: or, seven views of a protest-zoning state', *Political Geography,* 26: 601–19.

Herz, J. (1950) 'Idealist internationalism and the security dilemma', *World Politics,* 2(2): 157–180.

Hilferding, R. (1981) *Finance Capital: A Study of the Latest Phase of Capitalist Development,* online <http://www.marxists.org/archive/hilferding/1910/finkap/index.htm> (accessed April 2009).

Hinsely, F. H. and Stripp, A. (2001) *Codebreakers: The Inside Story of Bletchley Park,* Oxford: Oxford University Press.

Hirst, P. Q. and Thompson, G. F. (1996) *Globalization in Question: The International Economy and the Possibilities of Governance,* Cambridge: Polity Press.

Hobbes, T. (1985 [1651]) *Leviathan,* ed. C. B. MacPherson, Harmondsworth: Penguin.

Hobbs, D. (1998) 'Going down the glocal: the local context of organised crime', *Howard Journal,* 37: 407–22.

Hogan, M. J., Chiricos, T. and Geertz, M. (2005) 'Economic insecurity, blame and punitive attitudes', *Justice Quarterly* 22: 392–412.

285

Hollifield, J. (2004) 'The emerging migration state', *International Migration Review*, 38 (3): 885–911.

Homer-Dixon, T. F. (1991) 'On the threshold: environmental changes as causes of acute conflict', *International Security*, 16(2): 76–116.

Homer-Dixon, T. F. (1994) 'Environmental scarcities and violent conflict: evidence from cases', *International Security*, 19(1): 5–40.

Homer-Dixon, T. F. (1999) *Environment, Scarcity and Violence*, Princeton, NJ: Princeton University Press.

Homer-Dixon, T. F. (2001) *Environment, Scarcity, and Violence*, Princeton, NJ: Princeton University Press.

Honig, B. (2001) *Democracy and the Foreigner*, Princeton, NJ: Princeton University Press.

Hoogensen, G. and Stuvoy, K. (2006) 'Gender, resistance and human security', *Security Dialogue*, 37(2): 207–28.

Hopf, T. (1998) 'The promise of constructivism in international relations theory', *International Security*, 23: 171–200.

Hopf, T. (2002) *Social Construction of International Politics: Identities and Foreign Policies, Moscow, 1955 and 1999*, Ithaca, NY: Cornell University Press.

Horowitz, D. L. (1985) *Ethnic Groups in Conflict*, Berkeley, CA: University of California Press.

Horsnell, P. (2000) *The Probability of Oil Market Disruption: With an Emphasis on the Middle East*, Houston, TX: James A. Baker III Institute for Public Policy.

House of Lords (2007) *Schengen Information System II (SIS II): Report with Evidence*, 9th Report of Session 2006–07, European Union Committee, HL Paper 49, London: Stationery Office.

Howe, H. M. (2001) *Ambiguous Order: Military Forces in African States*, Boulder, CO: Lynne Reider.

Hoyes, C. (2008) 'Running on empty? Fears over oil supply move into the mainstream', *Financial Times* (20 May).

Hudson, H. (2005) '"Doing" security as though humans matter: a feminist perspective on gender and the politics of human security', *Security Dialogue*, 36(2): 155–74.

Hudson, H. (2006) *Human Security and Peacebuilding Through a Gender Lens: Challenges of Implementation in Africa*, DIIS Working Paper, 37.

Human Rights First (2008) 'Private security contractors at war: Ending the culture of impunity' available online at www.humanrightsfirst.org.

Human Security Center (2005) *Human Security Report 2005*, ed. Human Security Center and UBC, New York: Oxford University Press.

Hunt, A. (1999) *Governing Morals: A Social History of Moral Regulation*, Cambridge: Cambridge University Press.

Hunter, S. S. (2003) *Black Death: AIDS in Africa*, Basingstoke: Palgrave Macmillan.

Huntington, S. P. (1993a) 'Clash of civilizations?', *Foreign Affairs*, 72: 22–8.

Huntington, S. P. (1993b) 'If not civilizations, what-paradigms of the post-cold war world', *Foreign Affairs*, 72: 186–94.

Huntington, S. P. (1996) *The Clash of Civilizations and the Remaking of World Order*, New York: Simon & Schuster.

Huntington, S. P. (2004a) 'The Hispanic challenge', *Foreign Policy*, 141: 30–45.

Huntington, S. P. (2004b) *Who Are We? The Challenges to America's National Identity*, New York: Simon & Schuster.

Huysmans, J. (1996) *Making/Unmaking European Disorder: Meta-Theoretical, Theoretical and Empirical Questions of Military Stability after the Cold War*, Leuven: Katholieke Universiteit Leuven.

Huysmans, J. (1998) 'Security! What do you mean? From concept to thick signifier', *European Journal of International Relations*, 4: 226–55.

Huysmans, J. (2000) 'The European Union and the securitization of migration', *Journal of Common Market Studies*, 38(5): 751–77.

Huysmans, J. (2006) 'Agency and the politics of protection: implications for security studies', in J. Huysmans, A. Dobson and R. Prokhovnik (eds) *The Politics of Protection: Sites of Insecurity and Political Agency*, London: Routledge.

Huysmans, J. (2006) *The Politics of Insecurity: Fear, Migration and Asylum in the EU*, London: Routledge.

Huysmans, J. and Tsoukala, A. (2008) *Special Issue of Alternatives: Global, Local, Political: The Social Construction and Control of Danger in Counterterrorism, London:* Lynne Rienner Publishers.

REFERENCES

Hyndman, J. (2001) 'Towards a feminist geopolitics', *Canadian Geographer*, 45(2): 210–22.

Hyndman, J. (2008) 'Conflict, citizenship and human security: geographies of protection', in D. Cowen and E. Gilbert (eds) *War, Citizenship and Territory*, London: Routledge.

Ibrahim, M. (2005) 'The securitization of migration: a racial discourse', *International Migration*, 43(5): 163–87.

ICDSI (Independent Commission on Disarmament and Security Issues) (1982) *Common Security: A Blueprint for Survival*, New York: Simon & Schuster.

ICG (2001) *HIV/AIDS as a Security Issue*, Washington, DC, and Brussels: International Crisis Group.

ICG (2004) *HIV/AIDS as a Security Issue in Africa: Lessons from Uganda*, Kampala and Brussels: International Crisis Group.

ICIDI (Independent Commission on International Development Issues) (1980) *North–South: A Programme for Survival*, London: Pan Books.

IDMC (2009) 'Report internal displacement: global overview of trends and developments in 2008', online <http://www.internal-displacement.org/> (accessed June 2009).

Igmade (ed.) (2006) *5 CODES: Architecture, Paranoia and Risk in Times of Terror*, Basel: Birkhäuser.

IISI (International Iron and Steel Institute) (2007) *Steel Statistical Yearbook 2007*, Brussels: IISI.

Inda, J. I. (2006) *Targeting Immigrants: Government, Technology, and Ethics*, Oxford: Blackwell.

Ingram, A. (2008) 'Pandemic anxiety and global health security', in R. Pain and S. Smith (eds) *Fear: Critical Geopolitics and Everyday Life (Re-Materialising Cultural Geography)*, London: Ashgate.

Ingram, A. and Dodds, K. (eds) (2009) *Spaces of Security and Insecurity*, Aldershot: Ashgate.

Institute of International Relations (2000) *Contextualizing the Human Security Agenda*, Working Paper, 30, Vancouver: University of British Columbia.

Interacademy Panel on International Issues (2005) A Global Network of Science Academies, 'Statement on biosecurity', online <http://www.knaw.nl/nieuws/pers_pdf/IAP_Biosecurity_statement.pdf> (accessed Aug. 2008).

International Energy Agency (IEA) (2002) *World Energy Outlook, 2002*, Paris: OECD/IEA.

Jackson, R. H. (1993) *Quasi-States: Sovereignty, International Relations and the Third World*, Cambridge: Cambridge University Press.

Jacobsen, K. (forthcoming) 'Making design safe for living: a case of humanitarian experimentation', *Citizenship Studies*.

Jacobson, R. (2000) 'Women and peace in Northern Ireland: a complicated relationship', in S. Jacobs, R. Jacobson and J. Marchbank (eds) *States of Conflict: Gender, Violence and Resistance*, London: Zed Books.

Jacobson, R. (2005) 'Gender, war and peace in Mozambique and Angola: advances and absences', in D. Mazurana, A. Raven-Roberts and J. Parpart (eds) *Gender, Conflict and Peacekeeping*, Plymouth and Lanham, MD: Rowman & Littlefield.

Jaffe, A. M. and Manning, R. A. (2000) 'The shocks of a world of cheap oil', *Foreign Affairs*, 79(1): 16–29.

Jayne, T. S., Villarreal, M., Pingali, P. and Hemrich, G. (2004) 'Interactions between the agricultural sector and the HIV/AIDS pandemic: implications for agricultural policy', *ESA Working Paper No. 04-06*, March, Agricultural and Development Economics Division, Rome: FAO.

Jeandesboz, J. (2008), *Reinforcing the surveillance of EU borders: the future development of FRONTEX and EUROSUR*, CHALLENGE Research Papers 11, Brussels: CEPS.

Jervis, R. (1978) 'Cooperation under the security dilemma', *World Politics*, 30(2): 167–214.

Jervis, R. (1982) 'Security regimes', *International Organization*, 36: 357–78.

Johnson, D. (2008) 'J. G. Ballard: the glow of the prophet', *New York Review of Books*, 55(15): 25.

Johnson, N. P. and Mueller, J. (2002) 'Updating the accounts: global mortality of the 1918–1920 "Spanish" influenza pandemic', *Bulletin of the History of Medicine*, 76(1): 105–15.

Jones, A. (2002) 'Gender and genocide in Rwanda', *Journal of Genocide Research*, 4(1): 65–94.

Jones, G. S. (1971) *Outcast London: A Study in the Relationship between Classes in Victorian Society*, Oxford: Clarendon Press.

Joppke, C. (1999) 'How immigration is changing citizenship: a comparative view', *Ethnic and Racial Studies*, 22(4): 629–52.

Juncosa, P. (2005) Plate description of Dunne and Raby's Faraday Chair, in *Safe: Design Takes on Risk*, New York: MOMA, p. 73.

287

REFERENCES

Kabay, M. E. (1998) *ICSA White Paper on Computer Crime Statistics,* online <http://www.amc.army.mil/amc/ci/matrix/documents/white_papers/computer%20crime%20stats.pdf> (accessed Nov. 2008).

Kahn, M. E. (2005) 'The death toll from natural disasters: the role of income, geography, and institutions', *Review of Economics and Statistics,* 87(2): 271–84.

Kaldor, M. (1990) *The Imaginary War: Understanding the East–West Conflict,* Oxford: Blackwell.

Kaldor, M. (2000) *Global Insecurity: Restructuring the Global Military Sector,* London: Pinter.

Kaldor, M. (2007) *Human Security: Reflections on Globalization and Intervention,* Cambridge: Polity.

Kaldor, M. and Glasius, M. (2004) *A Human Security Doctrine for Europe: The Barcelona Report of the Study Group on Europe's Security Capabilities,* London: LSE.

Kaldor, M., Albrecht, U. and Schméder, G. (eds) (1998) *Restructuring the Global Military Sector: The End of Military Fordism,* London: Pinter.

Kalicki, J. H. and Goldwyn, D. L. (2005) *Energy Security: Toward a New Foreign Policy Strategy,* Washington, DC: Woodrow Wilson Center Press.

Kandiyoti, D. (2004) 'Post-conflict reconstruction, "democratisation" and women's rights', *IDS Bulletin,* 35(4): 134–6.

Karl, T. L. (1997) *The Paradox of Plenty: Venezuela, and Other Petro-States,* Berkeley, CA: University of California Press.

Karns, M. P. and Mingst, K. A. (2004) *International Organizations, the Politics and Processes of Global Governance,* Boulder, CO: Lynne Rienner Publishers.

Katzenstein, P. J. (ed.) (1996) *The Culture of National Security: Norms and Identity in World Politics,* New York: Columbia University Press.

Kearns, G. (2009) *Geopolitics and Empire: The Legacy of Halford J. Mackinder,* Oxford: Oxford University Press.

Keen, D. (1998) *The Economic Functions of Violence in Civil Wars,* Oxford: Oxford University Press.

Kellermann, A. L., Rivara, F. P., Rushforth, N. B. *et al.* (1993) 'Gun ownership as a risk factor for homicide in the home', *New England Journal of Medicine,* 329(15): 1084–91.

Kelling, G. L. and Wilson, J. Q. (1982) 'Broken windows: the police and neighbourhood safety', in *The Atlantic* (March), online <http://www.theatlantic.com/doc/198203/broken-windows > (accessed Nov. 2008).

Kelly, L. (2000) 'Wars against women: sexual violence, sexual politics and the militarised state', in S. Jacobs, R. Jacobson and J. Marchbank (eds) *States of Conflict: Gender, Violence and Resistance,* London: Zed Books.

Kennan, G. (1954) *Realities of American Foreign Policy,* Princeton, NJ: Princeton University Press.

Kennedy, D. (2005) 'Challenging expert rule: the politics of global governance', *Sydney Journal of International Law,* 27(1): 5–28.

Keohane, R. O. (1986) 'Realism, neorealism and the study of world politics', in R. O. Keohane (ed.) *Neorealism and its Critics,* New York: Columbia University Press.

Keohane, R. O. (1988) 'International institutions: two approaches', *International Studies Quarterly,* 32: 379–96.

Kern, P. B. (1999) *Ancient Siege Warfare,* Bloomington, IN: Indiana University Press.

Kessler, O. and Werner, W. (2008) 'Extra juridical killing as risk management: the breakdown of legal rationalities in the fight against terrorism', *Security Dialogue,* 39(2): 299–322.

Keynes, J. M. (1937) 'The general theory of employment', *Quarterly Journal of Economics,* 51(2): 209–23.

Khagram, S. and Clark, W. (2001) *Gendering Human Security: From Marginalization to the Integration of Women in Peace-Building,* Oslo: NUPI.

Khatib, L. (2009) 'Satellite television, the war on terror and political conflict in the Arab world', in A. Ingram and K. Dodds (eds) *Spaces of Security and Insecurity,* Aldershot: Ashgate.

Kierpaul, I. (2008) 'The rush to bring private military contractors to justice: the mad scramble of Congress, lawyers, and law students after Abu Ghraib', *University of Toledo Law Review,* 39: 407–35.

Killias, M. (1993) 'International correlations between gun ownership and rates of homicide and suicide', *Canadian Medical Association Journal,* 148: 1721–5.

King, G. and Murray, C. (2002) 'Rethinking human security', *Political Science Quarterly,* 116(4): 585–610.

REFERENCES

King, J. (2008) 'Dressing the meat of tomorrow', online <http://www.james-king.net/projects/meat> (accessed June 2009).

Kingham, R. (ed.) (2006) *Inventory of Environmental Security Policies and Practices*, The Hague: Institute for Environmental Security.

Kissinger, H. (1969) *American Foreign Policy: Three Essays,* London: Weidenfeld & Nicolson.

Kitiyadisai, K. (2005) 'Privacy rights and protection: foreign values in modern Thai context,' *Ethics and Information Technology,* 7: 17–26.

Klare, M. (1995) *Rogue States and Nuclear Outlaws: America's Search for a New Foreign Policy*, New York: Hill & Wang.

Klare, M. (2001) *Resource Wars: the New Landscape of Global Conflict,* New York: Henry Holt.

Klare, M. T. and Arnson, C. (1981 [1978]) *Supplying Repression*, Washington, DC: Institute for Policy Studies.

Klein, B. (1997) 'Every month is "security awareness month"', in K. Krause and M. Williams (eds) *Critical Security Studies: Concepts and Cases*, Minneapolis, MN: University of Minnesota, pp. 359–68.

Klein, B. S. (1990) 'How the West was one: representational politics of NATO', *International Studies Quarterly,* 34: 311–25.

Klein, N. (2008) *The Shock Doctrine*, London: Penguin.

Klerks, P. (2003) 'The Network Paradigm applied to criminal organizations: theoretical nitpicking or a relevant doctrine for investigators? Recent developments in the Netherlands', in A. Edwards and P. Gill (eds) *Transnational Organised Crime: Perspectives on Global Security*, New York: Routledge.

Kneebone, S. (2005) 'Women within the refugee construct, exclusionary inclusion in policy and practice, the Australian experience', *International Journal of Refugee Law*, 17(7): 7–42.

Knezo, G. (2003) '*Sensitive But Unclassified' and Other Federal Security Controls on Scientific and Technical Information: History and Current Controversy*, Congressional Research Report for Congress, RL31845, 20 Feb., Washington, DC: Congressional Research Service.

Knight, F. (1921) *Risk, Uncertainty and Profit*, Chicago: Chicago University Press.

Kolodziej, E. A. (1987) *Making and Marketing Arms: The French Experience and its Implications for the international system*, Princeton, NJ: Princeton University Press.

Kontopoulos, K. (1993) *The Logics of Social Structure,* Cambridge: Cambridge University Press.

Koo, K. L. (2002) 'Confronting a disciplinary blindness: women, war and rape in the international politics of security', *Australian Journal of Political Science*, 37(3): 525–37.

Koonings, K. and Kruijt, D. (eds) (2007) *Fractured Cities: Social Exclusion, Urban Violence and Contested Spaces in Latin America,* London: Zed Books.

Köppel, T. and Székely, A. (2002) 'Transnational Organized Crime and Conflict in the Balkans', in M. Berdal and M. Serrano (eds) *Transnational Organized Crime and International Security: Business as Usual?*, London: Lynne Rienner Publishers.

Kotsopoulos, J. (2006) 'A human security agenda for the EU?', *EPC Issue Paper,* 48.

Krahmann, E. (2007) 'Security: collective good or commodity?', *European Journal of International Relations*, 14(3): 379–405.

Kraska, P. B. and Kappeler, V. E. (1997) 'Militarizing American police: the rise and normalisation of paramilitary units', *Social Problems*, 44(1) 1–18.

Krause, K. (1992) *Arms and the State*, Cambridge: Cambridge University Press.

Krause, K. (1996) 'Insecurity and state formation in the global military order: the Middle Eastern case', *European Journal of International Relations*, 2(3): 319–54.

Krause, K. (2008) 'New forms of violence', in P. Cronin (ed.) *The Impenetrable Fog of War*, London: Praeger.

Krause, K. and Williams, M. C. (1996) 'Broadening the agenda of security studies: politics and methods', *International Studies Quarterly,* 40: 229–54.

Krause, K. and Williams, M. C. (eds) (1997) *Critical Security Studies: Concepts and Cases,* Minneapolis, MN: University of Minnesota Press.

Kraynak, R. P. (1983) 'Hobbes on barbarism and civilization', *Journal of Politics*, 45(1): 86–109.

Kretzmer, D., Giladi, R. and Shany, Y. (2007) 'Introduction: international humanitarian law and international human rights law: exploring parallel application', *Israel Law Review*, 40: 306.

289

REFERENCES

Krishna, S. (1999) *Postcolonial Insecurities: India, Sri Lanka, and the Question of Nationhood*, Minneapolis, MN: University of Minnesota Press.

Kristensen, K. S. (2008) '"The absolute protection of our citizens": critical infrastructure protection and the practice of security', in M. Dunn Cavelty and K. S. Kirstensen (eds) *The Politics of Securing the Homeland: Critical Infrastructure, Risk and Securitisation*, London: Routledge.

Kristoffersson, U. (2000) 'HIV/AIDS as a human security issue: a gender perspective', paper presented at the Expert Group Meeting on the HIV/AIDS Pandemic and its Gender Implications, Windhoek, Namibia.

Kuhlau, F. (2006) 'Disease outbreaks: managing threats to health and security', in A. Mellbourn (ed.) *Health and Conflict Prevention*, Anna Lindh Programme on Conflict Prevention, Hedemora: Gidlunds Förlag.

Kuhlau, F. (2007) *Countering Bio-threats: EU Instruments for Managing Biological Materials, Technology and Knowledge*, SIPRI Policy Paper, 19, Stockholm: SIPRI.

Kuhlau, F., Eriksson, S., Evers, K. and Höglund, A. T. (2008) 'Taking due care: moral obligations in dual use research', *Bioethics*, 22(9): 477–87.

Kuipers, F. (2008) *No Dream Ticket to Security: PNR Data and Terrorism*, Clingendael Security Paper, 5, The Hague.

Kuus, M. (2007) *Geopolitics Reframed: Security and Identity in Europe's Eastern Enlargement*, New York: Palgrave Macmillan.

Kwik, G., Fitzgerald, J., Inglesby, T. V. and O'Toole, T. (2003) 'Biosecurity: responsible stewardship of bioscience in an age of catastrophic terrorism', *Biosecurity and Bioterrorism: Biodefense Strategy, Practice and Science*, 1(1): 27–35.

Lacina, B. (2004) 'From side show to centre stage: civil conflict after the cold war', *Security Dialogue*, 35: 191–205.

Lacina, B. A., Gleditsch, N. P. and Russett, B. M. (2006) 'The declining risk of death in battle', *International Studies Quarterly*, 50(3): 673–80.

Lacy, M. J. (2005) *Security and Climate Change: International Relations and the Limits of Realism*, London: Routledge.

Lacy, M. J. (2008) 'Designer security: MoMA's safe: design takes on risk and control society', *Security Dialogue*, 39(2–3): 333–57.

Lal, R. (1995) 'Erosion–crop productivity relationships for soils of Africa', *Soil Science Society of America Journal*, 59(3): 661–7.

Landau, S. (1994) *Codes, Keys, and Conflicts: Issues in U.S. Crypto Policy*, New York: Association for Computing Machinery Press.

Langley, P. (2007) 'The uncertain subjects of Anglo-American financialization', *Cultural Critique*, 65 (Winter): 66–91.

Langley, P. (2008) *The Everyday Life of Global Finance: Saving and Borrowing in Anglo-America*, Oxford: Oxford University Press.

Lapid, Y. and Kratochwil, F. V. (1996) *The Return of Culture and Identity in IR Theory*, Boulder, CO: Lynne Rienner.

Lash, S. and Urry, J. (1994) *Economies of Signs and Space*, London: Sage.

Latour, B. (1993) *Aramis ou l'amour des techniques*, Paris: La Découverte.

Latour, B. (1996) 'On actor–network theory: a few clarifications', *Soziale Welt*, 47: 369–81.

Laudan, R. (ed.) (1984) *The Nature of Technological Knowledge: Are Models of Scientific Change Relevant?*, Dordrecht: D. Reidel.

Lautsen, C. B. and Wæver, O. (2003) 'In defense of religion: sacred referent objects for securitization', in P. Hatzopoulos and F. Petito (eds) *Religion in International Relations: The Return from Exile*, London: Palgrave Macmillan.

Law, J. (2007) 'Actor–network theory and material semiotics', draft paper 25 April, Dept of Sociology, Lancaster University, online <http://www.heterogeneities.net/publications/Law-ANTandMaterialSemiotics.pdf> (accessed June 2009).

Layton, H. Z. (1992) *The Politics of Immigration: Immigration, 'Race' and 'Race' Relations in Post-war Britain*, Oxford: Blackwell.

REFERENCES

Le Billon, P. (2001) 'Angola's political economy of war: the role of oil and diamonds, 1975–2000', *African Affairs*, 100(398): 55–80.

Le Billon, P. (2008) 'Diamond wars? Conflict diamonds and geographies of resource wars', *Annals of the Association of American Geographers*, 98(2): 345–72.

Leander, A. (2003) 'The commodification of violence: private military companies and African states', in M. Muchie (ed.) *The Making of the Africa-Nation: Pan-Africanism and the African Renaissance*, London: Adonis-Abbey.

Leander, A. (2005a) 'The market for force and public security: the destabilizing consequences of private military companies', *Journal of Peace Research*, 42(5): 605–22.

Leander, A. (2005b) 'The power to construct international security: on the significance of private military companies', *Millenium Journal of International Studies*, 33(3): 803–26.

Leander, A. (2006) *Eroding State Authority? Private Military Companies and the Legitimate Use of Force*, Rome: Centro Militare di Studi Strategici.

Leander, A. (2007) 'The impunity of private authority: understanding the circumscribed efforts to introduce PMC accountability', paper presented at ISA Conference, Chicago, 28 Feb.–3 March, online <http://www.cbs.dk/content/view/pub/38570> (accessed June 2009).

Leander, A. (2008) 'Portraits in practice: the politics of outsourcing security', online <http://www.cbs. dk/content/view/pub/38570> (accessed June 2009).

Leander, A. (2009) 'Securing sovereignty by governing security through markets', in R. Adler-Nissen and T. Gammeltoft-Hansen (eds) *Sovereignty Games: Instrumentalising State Sovereignty in Europe and Beyond*, London: Palgrave.

Leaning, J. and Arie, S. (2001) *Human Security: A Framework for Analysis in Settings of Crisis and Transition*, Cambridge, MA: Harvard Center for Population and Development Studies, Working Paper, 8.

Lebow, R. N., Gross Stein, J. and Risse-Kappen, T. (eds) (1994) *We All Lost the Cold War*, Princeton, NJ: Princeton University Press.

Lederberg, J., Shope, R. E. and Oaks, S. C. Jr. (eds) (1992) *Emerging Infections: Microbial Threats to Health in the United States*, Committee on Emerging Microbial Threats to Health, Institute of Medicine, Washington, DC: National Academy Press.

Lee, S. (2006) *When the Levees Broke: A Requiem in Four Acts*, film, 40 Acres & A Mule Filmworks/HBO Documentary Films.

Leitenberg, M. (2004) *The Problem of Biological Weapons*, Stockholm: Swedish National Defence College.

Leitenberg, M. (2007) 'Evolution of the current threat', in A. Wenger and R. Wollenmann (eds) *Bioterrorism: Confronting a Complex Threat*, London: Lynne Rienner Publishers.

Lemmers, E. (1999) *Refugees, Gender and Human Security: A Theoretical Introduction and Annotated Bibliography*, Utrecht and Chipping Norton: International Books.

Lenoir, T. (2000) 'All but war is simulation: the military-entertainment complex', *Configurations*, 8: 289–335.

Leverett, F. and Noel, P. (2006) 'The new axis of oil', *The National Interest* (Summer): 62–70.

Levine, D. H. (1986) *Religion and Political Conflict in Latin America*, Chapel Hill, NC : University of North Carolina Press.

Levitt, M. and Jacobson, M. (2008) 'The US campaign to squeeze terrorist' financing', *Journal of International Affairs*, 62(1): 67–85.

Lewis, M. W. and Wigen, K. E. (1997) *The Myth of Continents: A Critique of Metageography*, Berkeley, CA: University of California Press.

Leyshon, A. and Thrift, N. (1997) *Money/Space: Geographies of Monetary Transformation*, London: Routledge.

Liddick, D. (1999) '"The enterprise model" of organized crime: assessing theoretical propositions', *Justice Quarterly*, 16(2): 404–30.

Ling, L. H. M. (2002a) 'Cultural chauvinism and the liberal international order: "West vs Rest" in Asia's financial crisis', in G. Chowdhry and S. Nair (eds) *Power in a Postcolonial World: Race, Gender and Class in International Relations*, London: Routledge.

Ling, L. H. M. (2002b) *Postcolonial International Relations : Conquest and Desire between Asia and the West*, New York: Palgrave.

REFERENCES

Liotta, P. H. (2003) *The Uncertain Certainty: Human Security, Environmental Change, and the Future Euro-Mediterranean*, Lanham, MD: Lexington.

Lippert, R. (2004) 'Sanctuary practices, rationalities, and sovereignties', *Alternatives,* 29: 535–55.

Lipschutz, R. (ed.) (1995) *On Security,* New York: Columbia University Press.

Lipuma, E. and Lee, B. (2005) 'Financial derivatives and the rise of circulation', *Economy and Society,* 34(3): 404–27.

Lloyd, J. (2002) 'Departing sovereignty', *e-borderlands,* 1(2).

Lobo-Guerrero, L. (2007) 'Biopolitics of specialized risk: an analysis of kidnap and ransom insurance', *Security Dialogue,* 38(3): 315–34.

Lobo-Guerrero, L. (2008) 'Pirates, stewards, and the securitization of global circulation', *International Political Sociology,* 2(3): 219–35.

London, J. P. and the CACI Team (2008) *Our Good Name: A Company's Fight to Defend its Honour and Get the Truth told about Abu Ghraib,* Washington, DC: Regenery Publishing.

Lonergan, S. (2000) 'The index of human insecurity', *Aviso Bulletin,* 6, online <http://www.google.com/url?sa=t&source=web&ct=res&cd=1&url=http%3A%2F%2Fwww.gechs.org%2Faviso%2F06%2F&ei=0tc1SvuALYT-tQP6tsSrDg&usg=AFQjCNFpfbslcVzKkL2KcEm8Z0sEXKAEvA> (accessed June 2009).

Loo, D. and Grimes, R. (2004) 'Polls, politics, and crime: the "law and order" issue of the 1960s', *Western Criminology Review,* 5: 50–67, online <http://wcr.sonoma.edu/v5n1/loo.htm> (accessed Nov. 2008).

Lotringer, S. and Virilio, P. (2008) *Pure War: Twenty Five Years Later,* Los Angeles: Semiotext.

Lowenheim, O. (2008) 'Examining the state: a Foucauldian perspective on international "governance indicators"', *Third World Quarterly,* 29: 255–74.

Lucassen, L. (1997) 'Eternal vagrants? State formation, migration, and travelling groups in Western Europe, 1350–1914', in L. Lucassen and J. Lucassen (eds) *Migration, Migration History, History : Old Paradigms and New Perspectives,* Berne: Peter Lang.

Lugar Letter (2008) Richard G. Lugar, United States Senator for Indiana. Online <http://lugar.senate.gov/newsletter/2008/02/feature.html> (accessed June 2009).

Luhmann, N. (1993) *Sociology of Risk,* New York: Walter de Gruyter.

Luhmann, N. (1996) *Social Systems,* Princeton, NJ: Princeton University Press.

Luhmann, N. (1997) *Die Gesellschaft der Gesellschaft,* Frankfurt/Main: Suhrkamp.

Lynch, T. and Walsh, A. J. (2000) 'The good mercenary', *Journal of Political Philosophy,* 8: 133–53.

Lyon, D. (2001) *Surveillance Society: Monitoring Everyday Life,* Buckingham: Open University Press.

Lyon, D. (ed.) (2003) *Surveillance as Social Sorting: Privacy, Risk, and Digital Discrimination,* London: Routledge.

Lyon, D. (ed.) (2006) *Theorizing Surveillance: The Panopticon and Beyond,* Uffculme: Willan Publishing.

Lyon, D. (2007) *Surveillance Studies: An Overview,* Cambridge: Polity.

McCamley, N. J. (1988) *Secret Underground Cities: An Account of Some of Britain's Subterranean Defence, Factory and Storage Sites in the Second World War,* Barnsley: Pen & Sword Books.

McConnell, J. M. (2008) *Annual Threat Assessment of the Director of National Intelligence for the Senate Select Committee on Intelligence,* online <intelligence.senate.gov/080205/mcconnell.pdf> (accessed Oct. 2008).

McCulloch, J. and Pickering, S. (2005) 'Suppressing the financing of terrorism', *British Journal of Criminology,* 45: 470–86.

Mac Donald, H. (2006) 'The security-industrial-complex', *Wall Street Journal* (7 Sept.).

McDonald, M. (2002) 'Human security and the construction of security', *Global Society,* 16(3): 277–95.

MacFarlane, N. and Khong, Y. F. (2005) *Human Security and the UN,* Bloomington and Indianapolis, IN: Indiana University Press.

McGray, D. (2003) 'The Marshall Plan', *Wired,* 11.02 (Feb.), online <http://www.wired.com/wired/archive/11.02/marshall.html> (accessed June 2009).

McGrew, A. and Poku, N. (eds) (2007) *Globalization, Development and Human Security,* Cambridge: Polity.

McGuire, W. J., Griffiths, D. R., Hancock, P. L. and Stewart, I. S. (2000) *The Archaeology of Geological Catastrophes* (Special Publication, 171), London: Geological Society.

REFERENCES

McIlwaine, C. and Moser, C. O. N. (2007) 'Living in fear: how the urban poor perceive violence, fear and insecurity', in K. Koonings and D. Kruijt (eds) *Fractured Cities: Social Exclusion, Urban Violence and Contested Spaces in Latin America,* London: Zed Books, pp. 117–37.

McInnes, C. (2006) 'HIV/AIDS and security', *International Affairs,* 82(2): 315–26.

Mack, A. (2002) *A Report on the Feasibility of Creating an Annual Human Security Report,* Program on Humanitarian Policy and Conflict Research, Harvard University, online < http://www.hsph.harvard. edu/hpcr/FeasibilityReport.pdf> (accessed June 2009).

McKay, S. (2004) 'Women, human security, and peacebuilding: a feminist analysis', in H. Shinoda and H. Jeong (eds) *Conflict and Human Security: A Search for New Approaches of Peacebuilding,* Hiroshima: Institute for Peace Science, Hiroshima University.

MacKenzie, D. (1996a) 'Marx and the machine', in D. MacKenzie (ed.) *Knowing Machines: Essays on Technical Change,* Cambridge, MA: MIT Press.

MacKenzie, D. (ed.) (1996b) *Knowing Machines: Essays on Technical Change,* Cambridge, MA: MIT Press.

MacKenzie, D. (2006) *An Engine, Not a Camera: How Financial Models Shape Markets,* Cambridge, MA: MIT Press.

MacKenzie, D. (2007) 'The material production of virtuality', *Economy and Society,* 36(3): 355–76.

MacKenzie, D. and Wajcman, J. (eds) (1985) *The Social Shaping of Technology: How the Refrigerator Got its Hum,* Milton Keynes: Open University Press.

McLagan, M. (2005) 'Circuits of suffering', *PoLAR (Political and Legal Anthropology Review),* 28(2): 223–39.

MacLean, G. (2000) 'Instituting and projecting human security: a Canadian perspective', *Australian Journal of International Affairs,* 54(3): 269–75.

MacLean, S. J., Black, D. R. and Shaw, T. M. (2006) *A Decade of Human Security: Global Governance and New Multilateralisms,* Aldershot: Ashgate.

McLuhan, M. (1964) *Understanding Media: The Extensions of Man,* New York: McGraw-Hill.

McNamara, R. S. and Blight, J. G. (2003) *Wilson's Ghost,* New York: Public Affairs.

McNeil, M. (2007) *Feminist Cultural Studies of Science and Technology,* London: Routledge.

McNeill, J. R. (2000) *Something New Under the Sun: An Environmental History of the Twentieth Century,* New York: Norton.

McNeill, W. H. (1984) *The Pursuit of Power: Technology, Armed Force, and Society since A.D. 1000,* Chicago: University of Chicago Press.

McNeill, W. H. (1994 [1976]) *Plagues and Peoples,* Harmondsworth: Penguin.

McRae, R. G. and Hubert, D. (2001) *Human Security and the New Diplomacy: Protecting People, Promoting Peace,* Montreal: McGill-Queen's University Press.

McSweeney, B. (1999) *Security, Identity and Interests: A Sociology of International Relations,* Cambridge: Cambridge University Press.

Manning, R. A. (2000) *The Asian Energy Factor: Myths and Dilemmas of Energy, Security and the Pacific Future,* Basingstoke: Palgrave.

Markusen, A. R. (2003) 'The case against privatizing national security', *Governance: An International Journal of Policy, Administration, and Institutions,* 16(4): 471–501.

Markusen, A., DiGiovanna, S. and Leary, M. C. (eds) (2003) *From Defense to Development? International Perspectives on Realizing the Peace Dividend,* London: Routledge.

Marples, D. (1993) 'Chernobyl's lengthening shadow', *Bulletin of the Atomic Scientists,* 49(7): 38–43.

Marten, K. (2006–7) 'Warlordism in comparative perspective', *International Security,* 31(3): 41–73.

Martin, R. (2007) *An Empire of Indifference: American War and the Financial Logic of Risk Management,* Durham, NC: Duke University Press.

Marx, G. T. (2001) 'Technology and social control: the search for the illusive silver bullet', in P. B. Baltes and N. J. Smelser (eds) *International Encyclopedia of the Social and Behavioral Sciences,* Amsterdam and New York: Elsevier Publishing, pp. 15506–12.

Masters, C. (2005) 'Bodies of technology', *International Feminist Journal of Politics,* 7(1): 112–32.

Masters, C. and Dauphiné, E. (eds) (2007) *The Logics of Biopower and the War on Terror,* London: Palgrave/ Macmillan.

Mathews, J. T. (1989) 'Redefining security', *Foreign Affairs,* 68(2): 162–77.

REFERENCES

Mattei, U. (2003) 'A theory of imperial law: a study on U.S hegemony and the Latin resistance', *Indiana Journal of Global Legal Studies*, 10(1): 383–448.

Mattei, U. and Nader, L. (2008) *Plunder: When the Rule of Law is Illegal*, Malden, MA: Wiley-Blackwell.

Mattelart, A. (2007) *La globalisation de la surveillance : Aux origines de l'ordre sécuritaire*, Paris: La Découverte.

Mattern, J. B. (2000) 'Taking identity seriously', *Cooperation and Conflict*, 35: 299–308.

Mattern, J. B. (2001) 'The power politics of identity', *European Journal of International Relations*, 7: 349–97.

Mattern, J. B. (2005) *Ordering International Politics: Identity, Crisis, and Representational Force*, New York: Routledge.

Matthew, R. (2000) 'Environment and security in an international context: critiquing a pilot study from NATO's Committee on the Challenges of Modern Society', *Environmental Change and Security Project Report*, 6: 95–8.

Matthew, R., McDonald, B, and Rutherford, K.R. (2004) *Landmines and Human Security: International Politics and War's Hidden Legacy*, Albany, NY: State University of New York Press.

Maxwell, S. and Fernando, A. (1989) 'Cash crops in developing countries: the issues, the facts, the policies', *World Development*, 17(11): 1677–1708.

Maxwell, S. and Slater, R. (2003) 'Food policy old and new', *Development Policy Review*, 21: 5–6.

Mazurana, D., Raven-Roberts, A. and Parpart, J. (eds) (2005) *Gender, Conflict and Peacekeeping*, Plymouth and Lanham, MD: Rowman & Littlefield.

Mearsheimer, J. (2001) *The Tragedy of Great Power Politics*, New York: Norton.

Mearsheimer, J. and Walt, S. (2003) 'An unnecessary war', *Foreign Policy* (Jan.–Feb.).

Mearsheimer, J. and Walt, S. (2007) *The Israel Lobby and U.S. Foreign Policy*, New York: Farrer, Strauss & Giroux.

Melander, E. (2005) 'Gender inequality and intra-state armed conflict', *International Studies Quarterly*, 49(4): 695–714.

Meron, T. (2000) 'The humanization of humanitarian law', *American Journal of International Law*, 94(2): 239–78.

Merry, S. E. (2006) 'Transnational human rights and local activism: mapping the middle', *American Anthropologist*, 108(1): 38–51.

Merton, R. C. (1998) 'Application of option-pricing theory: twenty-five years later', *American Economic Review*, 88(3): 323–49.

Metz, S. (2000) 'The next twist of the RMA', *Parameters*, 30(3) (Autumn): 40–53.

Miguel, E., Satyanath, S. and Sergenti, E. (2004) 'Economic shocks and civil conflict: an instrumental variables approach', *Journal of Political Economy*, 112(4): 725–53.

Millard, A. and Stevenson, C. (2009) *Guatemala Armed Violence Mapping*, Geneva: Small Arms Survey.

Miller, P. and Rose, N. (1990) 'Governing economic life', *Economy and Society*, 19(1): 1–31.

Milliard, M. T. S. (2003) 'Overcoming post-colonial myopia: a call to recognize and regulate private military companies', *Military Law Review*, 176(1): 19-76.

Mills, C. (2009) *The Philosophy of Agamben,* London: Acumen.

Mills, C. W. (1956) *The Power Elite,* New York: Oxford University Press.

Mills, M. P. (2004) 'The security-industrial complex', *Forbes* (29 Nov.).

Ministry of Foreign Affairs of Japan (MOFA) (2007) *The Trust Fund for Human Security: For the 'Human-Centered' 21st Century*, online <http://www.mofa.go.jp/policy/human_secu/t_fund21.pdf> (accessed June 2009).

Mitchell, J. K. (1999) *Crucibles of Hazard: Mega-cities and Disasters in Transition*, New York: United Nations University Press.

Mitsilegas, V. (2003) 'Countering the chameleon threat of dirty money: "hard" and "soft" law in the emergence of a global regime against money laundering and terrorist finance', in A. Edwards and P. Gill (eds) *Transnational Organised Crime: Perspectives on Global Security*, New York: Routledge.

Mitzen, J. (2006) 'Ontological security in world politics: state identity and the security dilemma', *European Journal of International Relations*, 12: 341–70.

Mmbembe, A. (2003) 'Necropolitics', *Public Culture*, 15(1): 11–40.

Molloy, P. (2009) 'Zombie democracy', in F. Debrix and M. Lacy (eds) *Insecure States: Geopolitical Anxiety, the War on Terror, and the Future of American Power,* London: Routledge.

294

Monahan, T. (ed.) (2006) *Surveillance and Security: Technological Politics and Power in Everyday Life*, New York: Routledge.

Montag, W. (2005) 'Necro-economics: Adam Smith and death in the life of the universal', *Radical Philosophy*, 134 (Nov./Dec.): 7–17.

Montgomery, M. R., Stern, R., Cohen, B. and Reed, H. E. (eds) (2004) *Cities Transformed: Demographic Change and its Implications in the Developing World*, London: Earthscan.

Moore, H. and Vaughan, M. (1987) 'Cutting down trees: women, nutrition and agricultural change in the Northern Province of Zambia, 1920–1986', *African Affairs*, 86(345): 523–40.

Morgenthau, H. J. (1964 [1948]) *Politics among Nations: The Struggle for Power and Peace*, New York: Knopf.

Morse, E. L. (1999) 'The new political economy of oil', *Journal of International Affairs*, 53(1): 1–29.

Morse, E. L. (2003) 'Personal commentary', *Oxford Energy Forum*, 54: 17–19.

Moser, C. and Clark, F. (2001) 'Gender, conflict and building sustainable peace: lessons from Latin America', *Gender and Development*, 9(3): 29–39.

Moser, C. and Clark, F. (eds) (2001) *Victims, Perpetrators or Actors? Gender, Armed Conflict and Political Violence*, London: Zed Books.

Moser, C. O. N. (2004) 'Urban violence and insecurity: an introductory roadmap', *Environment and Urbanization*, 16(3): 3–16.

Mueller, J. (2004) 'A false sense of insecurity', *Regulation* (Fall): 42–6, Washington, DC: Cato Institute.

Muller, B. (2004) '(Dis)qualified bodiers: securitization, citizenship and "identity management"', *Citizenship Studies*, 8(3): 279–94

Mumford, L. (1961) *The City in History: Its Origins, its Transformations, and its Prospects*, Harmondsworth: Penguin.

Muppidi, H. (1999) 'Postcoloniality and the production of international insecurity: the persistent puzzle of US–Indian Relations', in J. Weldes, M. Laffey, H. Gusterson and R. Duvall (eds) *Cultures of Insecurity: States, Communities, and the Production of Danger*, Minneapolis, MN: University of Minnesota Press.

Musah, A. (2002) 'Privatization of security: Arms proliferation and the process of state collapse in Africa', *Development and Change*, 33(5): 911–33.

Musah, A. and Fayemi, K. J. (eds) (2000) *Mercenaries: An African Security Dilemma*, London: Pluto Press.

Mutimer, D. (2000) *The Weapons State: Proliferation and the Framing of Security*, Boulder, CO: Lynne Rienner.

Myrttinen, H. (2003) 'Disarming masculinities', *Disarmament Review*, 4: 37–46.

Myrttinen, H. (2004) '"Pack your heat and work the streets": weapons and the active construction of violent masculinities', *Women and Language*, 27(2): 29–34.

Mythen, G. and Walklate, S. (2006) *Beyond the Risk Society: Critical Reflections on Risk and Human Security*, Maidenhead: Open University Press.

Nadelmann, E. (1993) *Cops Across Borders: The Internationalization of US Law Enforcement*, University Park, PA: Pennsylvania State University Press.

Nader, L. (2005) 'The Americanization of international law', in F. Benda-Beckmann, K. Benda-Beckmann, and A. Griffiths (eds) *Mobile People, Mobile Law*, Aldershot and Burlington, VT: Ashgate Publishing.

Nadig, A. (2002) 'Human smuggling, national security, and refugee protection', *Journal of Refugee Studies*, 15(1): 1–25.

Naess, A. (1989) *Ecology, Community and Lifestyle: Outline of an Ecosophy*, trans. D. Rothenberg, Cambridge: Cambridge University Press.

Naidoo, S. (2001) 'A theoretical conceptualization of human security', paper presented at the Peace, Human Security and Conflict Prevention in Africa Proceedings of the UNESCO–ISS Expert Meeting held in Pretoria, 23–4 July.

Nardin, T. (ed.) (1998) *The Ethics of War and Peace: Religious and Secular Perspectives*, Princeton, NJ: Princeton University Press.

National Academy of Sciences, Computer Science and Telecommunications Board (1991) *Computers at Risk: Safe Computing in the Information Age*, Washington, DC: National Academy Press.

National Intelligence Council (2004) 'Mapping the global future', Report of the National Intelligence Council's 2020 Project, online <http://www.foia.cia.gov/2020/2020.pdf> (accessed Oct. 2008).

National Science Advisory Board for Biosecurity (NSABB) Online <www.biosecurityboard.gov> (accessed June 2009).

REFERENCES

National Science Advisory Board for Biosecurity (NSABB), National Institutes of Health, Office of Science Policy, online <http://oba.od.nih.gov/biosecurity/> (accessed June 2009).

Nchinda, T. (1998) 'Malaria: a reemerging disease in Africa', *Emerging Infectious Diseases*, 4: 398–403.

Neal, A. (2004a) 'Cutting off the king's head: Foucault's society must be defended and the problem of sovereignty', *Alternatives: Global, Local, Political*, 29(4): 373–98.

Neal, A. (2006) 'Foucault in Guantanamo: towards an archaeology of the exception', *Security Dialogue*, 37(1): 31–46.

Neal, A. and Dillon, M. (eds) (2008) *Foucault on Politics, Security and War*, London: Palgrave.

Neal, L. (1990) *The Rise of Financial Capitalism: International Capital Markets in the Age of Reason*, Cambridge: Cambridge University Press.

Nel, E. and Ringharts, M. (2008) 'Natural disasters and the risk of violent civil conflict', *International Studies Quarterly*, 52(1): 159–85.

Neocleous, M. (2000) 'Against security', *Radical Philosophy*, 100: 7–15.

Neocleous, M. (2007) 'Security, commodity, fetishism', *Critique*, 35(3): 339–55.

Neocleous, M. (2008) *Critique of Security*, Edinburgh: Edinburgh University Press.

Nesvetailova, A. and Palan, R. (2008) 'A very North Atlantic credit crunch: geopolitical implications of the global liquidity crisis', *Journal of International Affairs*, 62(1): 165–85.

Netherlands Police Agency (2004) *National Threat Assessment of Serious and Organised Crime in the Netherlands*, Zoetermeer: National Criminal Intelligence Department.

Neumann, I. B. (1999) *Uses of the Other: 'The East' in European Identity Formation*, Minneapolis, MN: Minnesota University Press.

Newman, E. (2001) 'Human security and constructivism', *International Studies Perspectives*, 2(3): 239–51.

Newman, E. and Richmond, O. P. (2001) *The United Nations and Human Security*, Houndmills, Basingstoke: Palgrave.

Newman, O. (1972) *Defensible Space: Crime Prevention through Urban Design*, New York: Macmillan.

NIC (2000) *The Global Infectious Disease Threat and Its Implications for the US*, Washington, DC: National Intelligence Council, online <http://www.fas.org/irp/threat/nie99-17d.htm> (accessed May 2009).

NIC (2003) *SARS: Down But Still a Threat*, Washington, DC: National Intelligence Council, ICA 2003-09.

Nogala, D. (2001) 'Policing across a dismorphous border: challenge and innovation at the French-German border', *European Journal of Crime, Criminal Law and Criminal Justice*, 9(2): 130–43.

Nordstrom, C. (2007) *Global Outlaws: Crime, Money, and Power in the Contemporary World*, Berkeley, CA: University of California Press.

Norman, D. A. (2007) *The Design of Future Things*, New York: Basic Books.

Norris, C. and Armstrong, G. (1999) *The Maximum Surveillance Society: The Rise of Closed Circuit Television*, Oxford: Berg.

Notestein, R. B. (1968) 'The patrician', *International Journal of Comparative Sociology*, 9: 106–20.

Noxolo, P. (2009) 'Negotiating security: governmentality and asylum/immigration NGOs in the UK', in A. Ingram and K. Dodds (eds) *Spaces of Security and Insecurity*, Aldershot: Ashgate.

NSS (2006) *The National Security Strategy of the United States*, Washington, DC: White House.

NSS (2008) *The National Security Strategy of the United Kingdom: Security in an Interdependent World*, London: Cabinet Office.

Nuruzzaman, M. (2006) 'Paradigms in conflict: the contested claims of human security, critical theory and feminism', *Cooperation and Conflict*, 41(3): 285–303.

Nye, J. S. Jr. and Owens, W. A. (1996) 'America's information edge', *Foreign Affairs*, 75(2): 20–36.

Nyers, P. (2003) 'Abject cosmopolitanism: the politics of protection in the anti-deportation movement', *Third World Quarterly*, 24(6): 1069–93.

Obama, B. (2008a) Speech in Berlin, 24 July.

Obama, B. (2008b) Remarks of Senator Barack Obama: National Security Avail, Richmond, VA, 22 Oct., online <http://www.barackobama.com/2008/10/22/remarks_of_senator_barack_obam_144.php> (accessed April 2009).

Obama, B. and Lugar, R. (2005) 'Grounding a pandemic', *New York Times* (6 June).

Oberleitner, G. (2005) 'Human security: a challenge to international law?', *Global Governance*, 11: 185–20.

REFERENCES

Odell, K. A. and Weidenmier, M. D. (2004) 'Real shock, monetary aftershock: the 1906 San Francisco earthquake and the panic of 1907', *Journal of Economic History*, 64: 1002–27.

Office of Technology Assessment (1987) *Defending Secrets, Sharing Data: New Locks and Keys for Electronic Information*, OTA-CIT-310, Washington, DC: US Government Printing Office.

Ogata, S. (1999) 'Human security: a refugee perspective', Keynote Speech at the Ministerial Meeting on Human Security Issues of the 'Lysoen Process' Group of Governments, Bergen.

Ogata, S. (2004) 'The Human Security Commission's strategy', *Peace Review*, 16(1): 25–8.

Ogata, S. and Cels, J. (2003) 'Human security: protecting and empowering the people', *Global Governance*, 9(3): 273–82.

Ogata, S. and Sen, A. (2003) *Human Security Now: Commission on Human Security, Final Report*, New York: United Nations.

O'Harrow, R. (2005) *No Place to Hide*, New York: Free Press.

Ojakangas, M. (2005) 'Impossible dialogue on bio-power: Agamben and Foucault', *Foucault Studies*, 1(2): 5–28.

O'Malley, P. (2004) *Risk, Uncertainty and Govern*ment, London: GlassHouse Press.

Onduku, A. (2004) 'Human security dilemma in Nigeria's Delta', *Human Security Perspectives*, 1(1): 45–50.

Ong, A. and Collier, S. J. (eds) (2005) *Global Assemblages : Technology, Politics, and Ethics as Anthropological Problems*, Malden, MA: Blackwell Publishing.

Oquist, P. (2008) 'Basic elements of a policy framework for human security', *International Social Science Journal*, 59(1): 101–12.

Organization for Economic Co-operation and Development (2007) *OECD Best Practice Guidelines on Biosecurity for BRCS*, Paris: OECD, online <http://www.oecd.org/dataoecd/6/27/38778261.pdf> (accessed Oct. 2008).

Osgood, R. E. and Tucker, R. W. (1967) *Force, Order and Justice*, Baltimore, MD: Johns Hopkins University Press.

Ostergard, R. L., Jr. (2002) 'Politics in the hot zone: AIDS and national security in Africa', *Third World Quarterly*, 23(2): 333–50.

Ostergard, R. L., Jr. (ed.) (2005) *HIV, AIDS and the Threat to National and International Security*, London: Palgrave.

Ó Tuathail, G. (1996a) *Critical Geopolitics: The Politics of Writing Global Space*, Minneapolis, MN: University of Minnesota Press.

Ó Tuathail, G. (1996b) 'An anti-geopolitical eye? Maggie O'Kane in Bosnia, 1992–94', *Gender, Place and Culture*, 3: 171–85.

Ó Tuathail, G. (2003) '"Just out looking for a fight": American affect and the invasion of Iraq', *Antipode*, 35(5): 856–70.

Ó Tuathail, G. and Agnew, J. (1992) 'Geopolitics and discourse: practical geopolitical reasoning in American foreign policy', *Political Geography*, 11(2): 190–204.

Ó Tuathail, G. and Dalby, S. (eds) (1998) *Rethinking Geopolitics*, London: Routledge.

Ó Tuathail, G. and Luke, T. W. (1994) 'Present at the (dis)integration: deterritorialization and reterritorialization in the new wor(l)d order', *Annals of the Association of American Geographers*, 84(3): 381–98.

Ó Tuathail, G., Dalby, S. and Routledge, P. (eds) (1998) *The Geopolitics Reader*, London: Routledge.

Owen, T. (2002) 'Body count: rationale and methodologies for measuring human security', *Human Security Bulletin*, 1(3): 1–18.

Owen, T. (2003) 'Measuring human security: overcoming the paradox', *Human Security Bulletin*, 2(3): 1–11.

Owens, E. J. (1999) *The City in the Greek and Roman World*, London: Routledge.

Owens, P. (2008) 'Humanity, sovereignty and the camps', *International Politics*, 45(4): 522–30.

Oye, K. A. (ed.) (1986) *Cooperation under Anarchy*, Princeton, NJ: Princeton University Press.

Page, E. and Redclift, M. R. (2002) *Human Security and the Environment: International Comparisons*, Northampton, MA: Edward Elgar.

Pain, R. and Smith, S. (eds) (2008) *Fear: Critical Geopolitics and Everyday Life*, Aldershot: Ashgate.

REFERENCES

Palmer, S.H. (1988) *Police and Protest in England and Ireland, 1780–1850*, Cambridge: Cambridge University Press.

Parker, D. B. (1976) *Crime by Computer*, New York: Charles Scribner's Sons.

Parker, D. B. (1980) *Computer Security Management*, Reston, VA: Reston Publishing Co.

Parker, D. B. (1983) *Fighting Computer Crime*, New York: Charles Scribner's Sons.

Parker, G. (1996) *The Military Revolution: Military Innovation and the Rise of the West, 1500–1800*, Cambridge: Cambridge University Press

Parra, F. (2004) *Oil Politics: A Modern History of Petroleum*, London: I. B. Tauris.

Parry, M., Rosenzweig, C. and Livermore, M. (2005) 'Climate change, global food supply and risk of hunger', *Philosophical Transactions of the Royal Society B*, 360: 2125–38.

Passas, N. (2002) 'Cross-border crime and the interface between legal and illegal actors', in P. Van Duyne, K. von Lampe and N. Passas (eds) *Upperworld and Underworld in Cross-Border Crime*, Nijmegen: Wolf Legal Publishers.

Pauly, L. (1997) *Who Elected the Bankers?*, Ithaca, NY: Cornell University Press.

PCCIP, President's Commission on Critical Infrastructure Protection (1997) *Critical Foundations: Protecting America's Infrastructures*, Washington, DC: US Government Printing Office.

Peach, L. (2004) 'A pragmatist feminist approach to the ethics of weapons of mass destruction', in S. Hashmi and S. Lee (eds) *Ethics and Weapons of Mass Destruction: Religious and Secular Perspectives*, Cambridge: Cambridge University Press.

Pearson, L. B. (1955) *Democracy in World Politics*, Princeton, NJ: Princeton University Press.

Pelletier, D. L. (2002) 'Toward a common understanding of malnutrition: Assessing the contribution of the UNICEF framework', Background Paper, World Bank/UNICEF Nutrition Assessment, 2–24 Sept.

Pelling, M. (2003) *The Vulnerability of Cities: Natural Disasters and Social Resilience*, London: Earthscan.

Pelton, R. Y. (2006) *Licensed to Kill: Hired Guns in the War on Terror*, New York: Crown Publishers.

Peluso, N. and Watts, M. (eds) (2001) *Violent environments*, Ithaca, NY: Cornell University Press.

Percy, S. (2007) 'Mercenaries: STRONG NORM, WEAK LAW', *International Organization*, 61(2): 367–97.

Persaud, R. B. (2002) 'Situating race in international relations: the dialectics of civilizational security in American immigration', in G. Chowdhry and S. Nair (eds) *Power, Post-Colonialism and International Relations*, New York: Routledge.

Petersen, K. L. (2008a) 'When risk meets security', *Alternatives: Global, Local, Political*, 33(2): 173–90.

Petersen, K. L. (2008b) 'Risk, responsibility and roles redefined: is counter-terrorism a corporate responsibility?', *Cambridge Review of International Affairs*, 21(3): 403–20.

Pettman, R. (2005) 'Human security as global security: reconceptualising strategic studies', *Cambridge Review of International Affairs*, 18(1): 137–50.

Phillips, D. (2008) 'Police intelligence systems as a strategic response', in C. Harfield, A. MacVean, J. G. D. Grieve and D. Phillips (eds) *The Handbook of Intelligent Policing: Consilience, Crime Control and Community Safety*, Oxford: Oxford University Press.

Picciotto, R., Olinisakin, F. and Clarke, M. (2007) *Global Development and Human Security*, New Brunswick, NJ: Transaction Publishers.

Podesta, J. and Ogden, P. (2007) 'The security implications of climate change', *Washington Quarterly*, 31(1): 115–38.

Ponting, C. (1998) *Progress and Barbarism: The World in the Twentieth Century*, London: Chatto & Windus.

Porter, B. (1987) *The Origins of the Vigilant State: The London Metropolitan Police Before the First World War*, London: Weidenfeld & Nicolson.

Porter, D. (1999) *Health, Civilization and the State: A History of Public Health from Ancient to Modern Times*, London: Routledge.

Posen, B. (1993) 'The security dilemma and ethnic conflict', *Survival*, 35(1): 27–47.

Potter, C. W. (2001) 'A history of influenza', *Journal of Applied Microbiology*, 91(4): 572–9.

Power, M. (2005) 'The invention of operational risk', *Review of International Political Economy*, 12(4): 577–99.

Power, M. (2007) *Organized Uncertainty: Designing a World of Risk Management*, Oxford: Oxford University Press.

REFERENCES

Power, M. and Crampton, A. (eds) (2007) *Cinema and Popular Geo-Politics*, London: Routledge.

PRB (Population Reference Bureau) (2008) *2008 World Population Data Sheet*, Washington, DC: PRB.

Preuss-Laussinotte, S. (2006) 'L'Union européenne et les technologies de sécurité', *Cultures et Conflits*, 64: 97–108.

Price, R. (1997) *The Chemical Weapons Taboo*, Ithaca, NY: Cornell University Press.

Privacy International (2007) 'Satellite surveillance', 18 Dec., online <http://www.privacyinternational.org/article.shtml?cmd%5B347%5D=x-347-559095> (accessed June 2009).

Procacci, G. (1991) 'Social economy and the government of poverty', in G. Burchell, C. Gordon and P. Miller (eds) *The Foucault Effect: Studies in Governmentality*, Chicago: University of Chicago Press.

Public Health Security and Bioterrorism Preparedness and Response Act of 2002, law 107-188, 12 June 2002.

Quah, E. (2002) 'Transboundary pollution in Southeast Asia: the Indonesian fires', *World Development*, 30(3): 429–41.

Raby, F. (2008) 'Do you want to replace the existing normal?', keynote address delivered at the Lancaster University Institute for Advanced Studies Annual Program Year conference on New Sciences of Protection: Designing Safe Living, Lancaster, 10–12 July.

Raco, M. (2003) 'Remaking place and securitising space: urban regeneration and the strategies, tactics and practices of policing in the UK', *Urban Studies,* 40: 1869–87.

Raco, M. (2007) 'The planning, design and governance of sustainable communities in the UK', in R. Atkinson and G. Helms (eds) *Securing and Urban Renaissance: Crime, Community and British Urban Policy*, Bristol: Policy Press, pp. 39–56.

Raeff, M. (1975) 'The well-ordered police state and the development of modernity in seventeenth and eighteenth-century Europe: an attempt at a comparative approach', *American Historical Review*, 80: 1221–43.

Rajagopal, B. (2003) *International Law from Below, Development, Social Movements and Third World Resistance*, Cambridge: Cambridge University Press.

Rajasingham-Senanayake, D. (2004) 'Between reality and representation: women's agency in war and post-conflict Sri Lanka', *Cultural Dynamics*, 16(2–3): 141–68.

Ransick, R. (2008) 'Casa segura', online <http://www.casasegura.us/?q=en/project_description> (accessed June 2009).

Rappert, B. (2007) *Biotechnology, Security and the Search for Limits: An Inquiry into Research and Methods*, Basingstoke and New York: Palgrave Macmillan.

Rasmussen, V.B. (2006) *The Risk Society at War: Terror, Technology and Strategy in the Twenty-First Century*, Cambridge: Cambridge University Press.

Rasor, D and Bauman, R. (2007) *Betraying our Troops: The Destructive Results of Privatizing War*, New York: Palgrave.

Rattray, G. (2001) *Strategic Warfare in Cyberspace*, Cambridge, MA: MIT Press.

Raustiala, K. (1997) 'States, NGOS, and international environmental institutions', *International Studies Quarterly*, 41(4): 719–40.

Ravid, B. C. I. (1976) 'The first charter of the Jewish merchants of Venice', *Association for Jewish Studies Review*, 1: 187–222.

Reagan, R. (1982a) *National Security Information*, Executive Order 12356, Washington, DC, 2 April.

Reagan, R. (1982b) *President's National Security Telecommunications Advisory Committee*, Executive Order 12382, Washington, DC, 13 Sept.

Reagan, R. (1984) *National Policy on Telecommunications and Automated Information Systems Security*, National Security Decision Directive NSDD 145, 17 Sept.

Reid Sarkess, M., Whelon Wayman, F. and Singer, J. D. (2003) 'Inter-state, intra-state, and extra-state wars: a comprehensive look at their distribution over time, 1816–1997', *International Studies Quarterly*, 47(1): 49–70.

Reid, J. (2004) 'War liberalism and modernity: the biopolitical provocations of empire', *Cambridge Review of International Affairs*, 1(17): 63–79.

Reid, J. (2007) *The Biopolitics of the War on Terror: Life Struggles, Liberal Modernity and the Defence of Logistical Societies*, Manchester: Manchester University Press.

REFERENCES

Renner, M. (1991) 'Assessing the military's war on the environment', in L. Brown (ed.) *State of the World 1991,* New York: W. W. Norton, pp. 132–52.

Reno, W. (1999) *Warlord Politics and African State,* Boulder, CO: Lynne Rienner.

Restrepo, J. and Spagat, M. (2004) 'Civilian casualties in the Colombian conflict: a new approach to human security', Royal Holloway College, online <http://eprints.rhul.ac.uk/439/1/HS_in_Colombia_ Civil_Conflict.pdf> (accessed June 2009).

Richelson, J. (1999) *America's Space Sentinels: DSP Satellites and National Security,* Kansas City, KS: University Press of Kansas.

Roberts, D. (2008) *Human Insecurity: Global Structures of Violence,* London: Zed Books.

Roberts, P. (2004) *The End of Oil,* London: Bloomsbury.

Roe, P. (1999) 'The intrastate security dilemma: ethnic conflict as a "tragedy"?', *Journal of Peace Research,* 36: 183–202.

Roffey, R. (2005) 'From bio threat reduction to cooperation in biological proliferation prevention', paper presented at the Conference on Strengthening European Action on WMD Non-proliferation and Disarmament: How Can Community Instruments Contribute?, Brussels, 7–8 Dec., p. 3. Online <http://www.sipri.org/contents/expcon/euppconfmaterials.html> (accessed Sept. 2008).

Roffey, R. and Kuhlau, F. (2006) 'Enhancing bio-security: the need for a global strategy', *SIPRI Yearbook 2006: Armaments, Disarmament and International Security,* Oxford: Oxford University Press.

Rogers, P. (2002) *Losing Control: Global Security in the Twenty-First Century,* London: Pluto Press.

Rogers, P. and Dando, M. (1992) *A Violent Peace: Global Security after the Cold War,* London: Brassey's.

Rose, N. (2000) 'Government and control', *British Journal of Criminology* 40: 321–39.

Rosén, F. (2008) 'Commercial security: conditions of growth', *Security Dialogue,* 39(1): 77–97.

Rosenberg, E. S. (1999) *Financial Missionaries to the World: The Politics and Culture of Dollar Diplomacy 1900– 1930,* Cambridge, MA: Harvard University Press.

Ross, M. L. (1999) 'The political economy of the resource curse', *World Politics,* 51(2): 297–322.

Ross, M. L. (2001) 'Does oil hinder democracy?', *World Politics,* 53(3): 325–61.

Rothschild, E. (1995) 'What is security?', *Daedalus,* 124(3): 53–98.

Routledge, P. (1998) 'Going globile: spatiality, embodiment, and mediation in the Zapatista insurgency', in G. Ó Tuathail and S. Dalby (eds) *Rethinking Geopolitics,* London: Routledge.

Rudolph, C. (2003) 'Security and the political economy of international migration', *American Political Science Review,* 97(4): 603–20.

Rumelili, B. (2004) 'Constructing identity and relating to difference: understanding the EU's mode of differentiation', *Review of International Studies,* 30: 27–47.

Ruttan, V. W. (2006) *Is War Necessary for Economic Growth? Military Procurement and Technology,* New York: Oxford University Press.

Sachs, J. D. and Warner, A. M. (2000) 'Natural resource abundance and economic growth', in G. M. Meier and J. E. Rauch (eds) *Leading Issues in Economic Development,* Oxford: Oxford University Press.

Safir, H. and Whitman, E. (2003) *Security: Policing Your Homeland, Your City, Yourself,* New York: Thomas Dunne Books.

Said, E. (1978) *Orientalism,* New York: Vintage.

Said, E. (2001) 'The clash of ignorance', *The Nation,* 273/12 (22 Oct.): 11–14.

Salter, M. (2003) *Rights of Passage: The Passport in International Relations,* Boulder, CO: Lynne Rienner.

Salter, M. (2008a) 'Imagining numbers: risk, quantification, and aviation security', *Security Dialogue,* 39(2–3): 243–66.

Salter, M. (ed.) (2008b) *Politics at the Airport,* Minneapolis: University of Minnesota Press.

Salter, M. (2008c) 'Risk and imagination in the war on terror', in L. Amoore and M. de Goede (eds) *Risk and the War on Terror,* London: Routledge.

Salter, M. and Zureik, E. (eds) (2005) *Global Surveillance and Policing: Borders, Security, Identity,* Portland, OR: Willan Publishing.

Samers, M. (2004) 'An emerging geopolitics of illegal immigration in the European Union', *European Journal of Migration and Law,* 6(1): 27–45.

REFERENCES

Sandia National Laboratories (2005) *Laboratory Biosecurity Implementation Guidelines*, Sandia Report SAND 2005-2348P, online <http://www.mipt.org/pdf/Laboratory-Biosecurity-Implementation-Guidelines.pdf> (accessed Oct. 2008).

Sandvik, K. B. (2008) 'The physicality of legal consciousness: suffering and the production of credibility in refugee resettlement', in R. D. Brown and R. A. Wilson (eds) *Humanitarianism and Suffering: The Mobilization of Empathy*, Cambridge: Cambridge University Press.

Sapone, M. (1999) 'I have rifle with scope, will travel: the global economy of mercenary violence', *California Western International Law Journal*, 30 (Fall): 1–43.

Sassen, S. (2008a) 'Mortgage capital and its particularities: a new frontier for global finance', *Journal of International Affairs,* 62(1): 187–212.

Sassen, S. (2008b) 'The world's third spaces', *openDemocracy,* online <http://www.opendemocracy.net/node/35523> (accessed June 2009).

Sassen, S. (2009) 'Too big to save: the end of financial capitalism', *OpenDemocracy* (2 April), online <http://www.opendemocracy.net/article/too-big-to-save-the-end-of-financial-capitalism-0> (accessed April 2009).

Savage, C. C. (1987) *Architecture of the Private Streets of St. Louis: The Architects and the Houses they Designed*, Columbia, MO: University of Missouri Press.

Savitch, H.V. (2008) *Cities in a Time of Terror: Space, Territory and Local Resilience*, New York: M. E. Sharpe.

Scahill, J. (2007) *Blackwater: The Rise of the World's Most Powerful Mercenary Army*, Washington, DC: Nation Books.

Schelling, T. (1966) *Arms and Influence*, New Haven, CT, and London: Yale University Press.

Schmitt, C. (1996) *The Concept of the Political*, Chicago and London: University of Chicago Press.

Schmitt, C. (2005) *Political Theology: Four Chapters on the Concept of Sovereignty*, trans. G. Schwab, Chicago: Chicago University Press.

Schmitt, C. (2007) *The Concept of the Political,* expanded addition, Chicago: Chicago University Press.

Schmitt, C. (2008) *Political Theology*, vol. 2, *The Myth of the Closure of any Political Theology*, Cambridge: Polity.

Schroeder, E., Farr, V. and Schnabel, A. (2005) *Gender Awareness in Research on Small Arms and Light Weapons*, swisspeace Working Paper Series, Berne: swisspeace Foundation.

Schroeder, G. A. (1982) 'An Overview of Executive Order 12356', *FOIA Update*, 3(3) (June).

Schwartz, P. (2003) *Inevitable Surprises: A Survival Guide for the 21st Century*, London: Simon & Schuster.

Schwartz, P. and Randall, D. (2003) *An Abrupt Climate Change Scenario and its Implications for United States National Security*, San Francisco, CA: Global Business Network.

Schwarzenberger, G. (1955) 'The standard of civilisation in international law', in G. W. Keeton and G. Schwarzenberger (eds), *Current Legal Problems*, London: Stevens & Sons.

Scott, J. (1998) *Seeing like a State: How Certain Schemes to Improve the Human Condition have Failed*, New Haven, CT: Yale University Press.

Scruton, R. (2002) *The West and the Rest: Globalization and the Terrorist Threat*, London and New York: Continuum.

Seaman, J. (1993) 'Famine mortality in Africa', *IDS Bulletin*, 24b(4): 27–32.

Segall, K.W. (2002) 'Postcolonial performatives of victimization', *Public Culture,* 14(3): 617–19.

Sekula, A. (1986) 'The body and the archive', *October*, 39: 3–64.

Sembacher, A. (2004) 'The contribution of the International Criminal Court (ICC) to an improvement of human security in a post-conflict situation', *Human Security Perspectives*, 1(1): 51–7.

Sen, A. (2002) 'Basic education and human security', Report of the Kolkata Meeting in Commission on Human Security Bangkok, compiled by Center for Social Development Studies, Faculty of Political Science, Chulalongkorn University.

Sen, A. (1981) *Poverty and Famines: An Essay on Entitlement and Deprivation*, Oxford: Clarendon Press.

Sen, A. (2002) 'Global inequality and human security', Ishizaka Lectures, 2, Tokyo, 18 Feb.

Sen, A. (2006) *Identity and Violence: The Illusion of Destiny*, New York: W. W. Norton & Co.

Seng, T. S. (2001) *Human Security: Discourse, Statecraft, Emancipation*, Institute of Defense and Strategic Studies Working Paper, 11.

REFERENCES

Serrano, M. (2002) 'Transnational organized crime and international security: business as usual?', in M. Berdal and M. Serrano (eds) *Transnational Organized Crime and International Security: Business as Usual?*, London: Lynne Rienner Publishers.

Seul, J. R. (1999) '"Ours is the way of God": religion, identity, and intergroup conflict', *Journal of Peace Research*, 36: 553.

Shamir, R. (2005) 'Without borders? Notes on globalization as mobility regime', *Sociological Theory*, 23(2): 197–217.

Shapiro, M. J. (1990) 'Strategic discourse/discursive strategy: the representation of "security policy" in the video age', *International Studies Quarterly*, 34: 327–40.

Shapiro, M. J. (2007) 'The new violent cartography', *Security Dialogue*, 38(3): 291–313.

Sharp, J. (1998) 'Reel geographies and the new world order: patriotism, masculinity and geopolitics in post cold war American movies', in G. Ó Tuathail and S. Dalby (eds) *Rethinking Geopolitics*, London: Routledge.

Sharp, J. (2000) *Condensing the Cold War: Reader's Digest and American Identity*, Minneapolis, MN: University of Minnesota Press.

Shaw, M. (2003) *International Law*, 5th edn, Cambridge: Cambridge University Press.

Shaw, R. and Goda, K. (2004) 'From disaster to sustainable civil society: the Kobe experience', *Disasters*, 28: 16–40.

Shelley, L., Picarelli, J. T., Irby, A., Hart, D. M., Craig-Hart, P., Williams, P., Simon, S., Addullaev, N., Stanislawski, B. and Covill, L. (2005) *Methods and Motives: Exploring Links between Transnational Organized Crime and International Terrorism*, Washington, DC: US Department of Justice, research report, award no. 2003-IJ-CX-1019, online <http://www.ncjrs.gov/pdffiles1/nij/grants/211207.pdf> (accessed May 2009).

Shepherd, B. (2008) *The Circuit: An Ex-SAS Soldier's True Account of One of the Most Powerful and Secretive Industries Spawned by the War on Terror*, London: Macmillan.

Shepherd, L. J. (2005) 'Loud voices behind the wall: gender violence and the violent reproduction of the international', *Millennium: Journal of International Studies*, 34(2): 377–401.

Shepherd, L. J. (2006) 'Veiled references: constructions of gender in the Bush administration discourse on the attacks on Afghanistan post-9/11', *International Feminist Journal of Politics*, 8(1): 19–41.

Shepherd, L. J. (2008a) 'Power and authority in the production of United Nations Security Council Resolution 1325', *International Studies Quarterly*, 52(2): 383–404.

Shepherd, L. J. (2008b) *Gender, Violence and Security: Discourse as Practice*, London: Zed Books.

Sheptycki, J. (2003) 'Global law enforcement as a protection racket: some skeptical notes on transnational organised crime as an object of global governance', in A. Edwards and P. Gill (eds) *Transnational Organised Crime: Perspectives on Global Security*, New York: Routledge.

Sherry, M. S. (1987) *The Rise of American Air Power: The Creation of Armageddon*, New Haven, CT: Yale University Press.

Shorrok, T. (2008) *Spies for Hire: The Secret World of Intelligence Outsourcing*, New York: Simon & Schuster.

Shukla, A. (2008) 'India's gated townships can induce psychological barriers', *News 24* (India, 8 April), online <http://www.news24online.com/ViewDetails.aspx?NewsID=7054> (accessed Nov. 2008).

Sieber, U. (1986) *The International Handbook on Computer Crime: Computer-Related Economic Crime and the Infringements of Privacy*, Chichester: John Wiley & Sons.

Siegel, M. (2006) *Bird Flu: Everything you Need to Know about the Next Pandemic*, Hoboken, NJ: John Wiley & Sons.

Sinclair, T. J. (2005) *The New Masters of Capital: American Bond Rating Agencies and the Politics of Creditworthiness*, Ithaca, NY: Cornell University Press.

Singel, R. (2003) 'JetBlue shared passenger data', *Wired* (18 Sept.), online <http://www.wired.com/politics/security/news/2003/09/60489> (accessed June 2009).

Singer, P. (2002) 'AIDS and international security', *Survival*, 44(1): 145–58.

Singer, P. W. (2003) *Corporate Warriors: The Rise of the Privatized Military Industry*, Ithaca, NY: Cornell University Press.

Singer, P. W. (2007) 'Can't win with 'em, can't go to war without 'em: private military contractors and counterinsurgency', *Foreign Policy at Brookings, Policy Papers*, 4.

REFERENCES

Sjoberg, L. (2006) *Gender, Justice and the Wars in Iraq: A Feminist Reformulation of Just War Theory*, Lanham, MD: Lexington Books.

Sjoberg, L. and Gentry, C. (2008) *Mothers, Monsters, Whores: Women's Violence in Global Politics*, London: Zed.

Skaine, R. (2006) *Female Suicide Bombers*, Jefferson, NC: McFarland.

Skinner, Q. (1988) 'Language and social change', in J. Tully (ed.) *Meaning and Context: Quentin Skinner and his Critics*, Cambridge: Polity.

Skinner, Q. (1999) 'Rhetoric and conceptual change', *Finnish Yearbook of Political Thought*, 3: 60–72.

Skjelsbæk, I. and Smith, D. (2001) (eds) *Gender, Peace and Conflict*, London: SAGE.

Sklair, L. B. (2001) *The Transnational Capitalist Class*, Malden, MA: Blackwell Publishers.

Slater, R., Sharp, K. and Wiggins, S. (2008) 'Food security' in V. Desai and R. Potter (eds) *The Companion to Development Studies*, 2nd edition, London: Hodder Education

Slyomovics, S. (2008) 'Financial reparations, blood money, and human rights witness testimony: Morocco and Algeria', in R. D. Brown and R. A. Wilson (eds) *Humanitarianism and Suffering: The Mobilization of Empathy*, Cambridge: Cambridge University Press.

Small Arms Survey (2005) *Small Arms Survey 2005: Weapons at War*, Oxford: Oxford University Press.

Small Arms Survey (2006) *Small Arms Survey 2006: Unfinished Business*, Oxford: Oxford University Press.

Small Arms Survey (2007) *Small Arms Survey 2007: Guns and the City*, Cambridge: Cambridge University Press.

Small Arms Survey (2008) *Small Arms Survey 2008: Risk and Resilience*, Cambridge: Cambridge University Press.

Small, I., van de Mer, J. and Upshur, R. E. G. (2001) 'Acting on an environmental health disaster: the case of the Aral Sea', *Environmental Health Perspectives*, 109(6): 547–9.

Smillie, I., Gberie, L. and Hazelton, R. (2000) *The Heart of the Matter: Sierra Leone, Diamonds and Human Security*, Ottawa: Diane Publishing.

Smith, C. (1995) *Urban Disorder and the Shape of Belief: The Great Chicago Fire, the Haymarket Bomb, and the Model Town of Pullman*, Chicago: University of Chicago Press.

Smith, L. C. and Haddad, L. (2002) 'How potent is economic growth in reducing undernutrition? What are the pathways of impact? New cross-country evidence', *Economic Development and Cultural Change*, 51(1): 55–76.

Smrkolj, M. (2008) 'International institutions and individualized decision-making: an example of UNHCR's refuge status determination', *German Law Journal*, 9(11): 1779–1804.

Solove, D. J., Rotenberg, M. and Schwartz, P. M. (2006) *Privacy, Information, and Technology*, New York: Aspen Publishers Online.

Somerville, M. A. and Atlas, R. (2005) 'Ethics: a weapon to counter bioterrorism', *Science*, 307(5717): 1881–2.

South Eastern and Eastern Europe Clearinghouse for the Control of Small Arms and Light Weapons (2006) *The Rifle has the Devil Inside: Gun Culture in South Eastern Europe*, Belgrade: SEESAC.

Soysal, Y. N. (1994) *Limits of Citizenship: Migrants and Postnational Membership in Europe*, Chicago: University of Chicago.

Sparke, M. (1998) 'Outsides inside patriotism: the Oklahoma bombing and the displacement of heartland geopolitics', in G. Ó Tuathail and S. Dalby (eds) *Rethinking Geopolitics*, London: Routledge.

Sparke, M. (2005) *In the Space of Theory*, Minneapolis, MN: University of Minnesota Press.

Sparke, M. (2007) 'Geopolitical fears, geoeconomic hope and the responsibilities of geography', *Annals of the Association of American Geographers*, 97(2): 338–49.

Spearin, C. (2008) 'Private, armed and humanitarian? States, NGOs, international private security comapnies and shifting humanitarianism', *Security Dialogue*, 39(4): 363–82.

Spengler, O. (1926–8) *The Decline of the West*, vol. 1, *Form and Actuality;* vol. 2, *Perspectives of World History*, trans. Charles Francis Atkinson, London: George Allen & Unwin.

Spicer, T. (1999) *An Unorthdox Soldier: Peace and War and the Sandline Affair*, Edinburgh: Mainstream.

Starobinski, J. (1993) 'The word civilization', in *Blessings in Disguise; or The Morality of Evil*, trans. A. Goldhammer, Cambridge, MA: Harvard University Press.

Steele, B. J. (2007) *Ontological Security in International Relations: Self-Identity and the IR State*, New York: Routledge.

REFERENCES

Steiner, H. J., Alston, P. and Goodman, R. (2008) *International Human Rights in Context*, Oxford: Oxford University Press.

Steinhardt, N. S. (1999) *Chinese Imperial City Planning,* Honolulu: University of Hawaii Press.

Stelfox, P. (2003) 'Transnational organised crime: a police perspective', in A. Edwards and P. Gill (eds) *Transnational Organised Crime: Perspectives on Global Security*, New York: Routledge.

Sterling, B. (2005) *Shaping Things*, Cambridge, MA: MIT Press.

Stevens, P. (2008) 'Oil wars: resource nationalism and the Middle East', in P. Andrews-Speed (ed.) *International Competition for Resources: the Role of Law, the State and of Markets*, Dundee: Dundee University Press.

Stevens, P. (2008) *The Coming Oil Supply Crunch*, London: Royal Institute for International Affairs

Stocker, J. (2004) *Britain and Ballistic Missile Defence, 1942–2002*, London: Frank Cass.

Stohl, M. and Lopez, G. (1984) *The State as Terrorist: The Dynamics of Governmental Violence and Repression*, Westport, CT: Greenwood Press.

Stoler, A. L. (1995) *Race and the Education of Desire: Foucault's History of Sexuality and the Colonial Order of Things*, Durham, NC: Duke University Press.

Stoll, C. (1989) *The Cuckoo's Egg: Tracking a Spy through the Maze of Computer Espionage*, New York: Doubleday.

Stoneburner, G. (2001) *Computer Security: Underlying Technical Models for Information Technology Security. Recommendations of the National Institute of Standards and Technology*, NIST Special Publication 800-33, Washington, DC: US Government Printing Office.

Strange, S. (1986) *Casino Capitalism*, London: Basil Blackwell.

Strange, S. (1998) *Mad Money*, Manchester: Manchester University Press.

Strong, M. F. (2002) Statement at hearing of the United States Senate Committee on the Environment and Public Works and the Committee on Foreign Relations, 24 July. Online <http://epw.senate. gov/107th/Strong_072402.htm> (accessed May 2009).

Struckman, S. (2006) 'The veiled women and the masked men of Chechnya: documentaries, violence conflict and gender', *Journal of Communication Enquiry*, 30(4): 337–53.

Sturm, T. (2006) 'Prophetic eyes: the theatricality of Mark Hitchcock's premillennial geopolitics', *Geopolitics*, 11: 231–55.

Suchman, L. (2007) *Human–Machine Reconfigurations: Plans and Situated Actions*, 2nd edn, Cambridge: Cambridge University Press.

Suhrke, A. (1999) 'Human security and the interests of states', *Security Dialogue,* 30(3): 265–76.

Susman, G. and O'Keefe, S. (eds) (1998) *The Defense Industry in the Post-Cold War Era: Corporate Strategies and Public Policy Perspectives*, Oxford: Pergamon.

Suteanu, C. (2005) 'Complexity, science and the public: the geography of a new interpretation', *Theory, Culture and Society*, 22(5): 113–40.

Svedberg, P. (1999) '841 million undernourished?', *World Development*, 27(12): 2081–98.

Tadjbakhsh, S. and Chenoy, A. M. (2007) *Human Security: Concepts and Implications*, London: Routledge.

Tannewald, N. (2005) 'Stigmatizing the bomb: origins of the nuclear taboo', *International Security*, 29(4): 5–49.

Taylor, D. (1997) *The New Police in Nineteenth-Century England: Crime, Conflict and Control*, Manchester: Manchester University Press.

Taylor, M. C. (2004) *Confidence Games: Money and Markets in a World without Redemption*, Chicago: University of Chicago Press.

Teitel, R. (2002) 'Humanity's law: rule of law for the new global politics', *Cornell International Law Journal*, 35: 355–87.

Tenet, G. (2003) Testimony of Director of Central Intelligence George J. Tenet before the Senate Select Committee on Intelligence, Washington, DC, 11 Feb.

Thackera, J. (2006) *In the Bubble: Designing in a Complex World*, Cambridge, MA: MIT Press.

Thakur, R. (1997) *From National to Human Security*, Sydney: Allen & Unwin.

The Economist (1999) 'Survey: The New Geopolitics' (31 July).

Thomas, C. (1992) *The Environment in International Relations*, London: Royal Institute of International Affairs.

Thomas, C. (2001) 'Global governance, development and human security: exploring the links', *Third World Quarterly*, 22(2): 159–75.

Thomas, C. (2004) 'A bridge between the interconnected challenges confronting the world', *Security Dialogue*, 35(3): 353.

Thomas, D. and Loader, B. D. (eds) (2000) *Cybercrime. Law Enforcement, Security and Surveillance in the Information Age*, London and New York: Routledge.

Thomas, N. and Tow, W. T. (2002) 'The utility of human security: sovereignty and humanitarian intervention', Security Dialogue, 33(2): 177–92.

Tickell, A. (2000) 'Dangerous derivatives: controlling and creating risks in international money', *Geoforum*, 31: 87–99.

Tickner, J. A. (1992) *Gender in International Relations: Feminist Perspectives on Achieving Global Security*, New York: Columbia University Press.

Tickner, J. A. (1995) 'Re-visioning security', in K. Booth and S. Smith (eds) *International Relations Theory Today*, Oxford: Polity.

Tiefer, C. (2007) 'The Iraq debacle: the rise and fall of procurement-aided unilateralism as a paradigm of foreign war', *University of Pennsylvania Journal of International Economic Law*, 29 (Fall): 1–56.

Tilly, C. (1992) *Coercion, Capital, and European States, AD 990–1992*, Oxford: Blackwell.

Tirman, J. (ed.) (2004) *The Maze of Fear: Security and Migration after 9/11*, New York: New Press.

Torrence, R. and Grattan, J. P. (2002) *Natural Disasters and Cultural Change*, London: Routledge.

Tow, W. (2000) *Asia's Emerging Regional Order: Reconciling Traditional and Human Security*, New York: United Nations University Press.

Toynbee, A. J. (1934–61) *A Study of History*, 12 vols, London: Oxford University Press.

Toynbee, A. J. (1948) *Civilization on Trial*, New York: Oxford University Press.

Toynbee, A. J. (1953) *The World and the West*, London: Oxford University Press.

Toynbee, A. J. (1972) *A Study of History*, rev. and abridged edn, London: Thames & Hudson and Oxford University Press.

Tracy, J. D. (ed.) (2000) *City Walls: The Urban Enceinte in Comparative Perspective*, Cambridge: Cambridge University Press.

Trüby, S. (2008) *Exit-Architecture: Design between War and Peace*, New York: SpringerWien.

Tucker, J. and Sands, A. (1999) 'An unlikely threat', *Bulletin of the Atomic Sciences*, 55(4): 46–52.

Tucker, J. B. (2001) *Scourge: The Once and Future Threat of Smallpox*, New York: Atlantic Monthly Press.

Turshen, M. (2001) 'The political economy of rape', in C. Moser and F. Clark (eds) *Victims, Perpetrators or Actors? Gender, Armed Conflict and Political Violence*, London: Zed Books.

Ullman, R. H. (1983) 'Redefining security', *International Security*, 8(1): 129–53.

UN SCN (2004) *5th Report on the World Nutrition Situation: Nutrition for Improved Development Outcomes*, New York: United Nations System, Standing Committee on Nutrition (SCN), March.

UNAIDS (2001) *AIDS Epidemic Update*, Geneva: UNAIDS, Dec.

UNAIDS (2007) *2007 AIDS Epidemic Update*, Geneva: UNAIDS and World Health Organization.

UNDP (1994) *Human Development Report: New Dimensions of Human Security*, New York: Oxford University Press.

UNDP (2002) *World Energy Assessment*, New York: UNDP.

UNDP (2007) 'Fighting climate change: human solidarity in a divided world', *Human Development Report 2007/2008*, New York: UNDP.

UNEP (United Nations Environment Program) (2002) *Global Mercury Assessment*, Geneva: UNEP Chemicals.

UNESCO (2005) *Promoting Human Security: Ethical, Normative and Educational Frameworks in the Arab States*, Paris: UNESCO.

UNOHCHR (United Nations Office of the High Commissioner for Human Rights) (2007) *Sexual violence during attacks on villages in East Jebel Marra, Darfur*, New York : United Nations, online <http://www.unhchr.ch/huricane/huricane.nsf/0/46aa541d34b02a41c12572b50033edf9/$FILE/SexualViolence.doc> (accessed Sept. 2008).

REFERENCES

UNSC (United Nations Security Council) (2000) *Resolution 1325,* New York: United Nations, online <http://daccessdds.un.org/doc/UNDOC/GEN/N00/720/18/PDF/N0072018.pdf?OpenElement> (accessed Sept. 2008).

UNSC (2008) *Resolution 1820,* New York: United Nations, online <http://daccessdds.un.org/doc/UNDOC/GEN/N08/391/44/PDF/N0839144.pdf?OpenElement> (accessed Sept. 2008).

UNSC (2004) *Resolution 1540,* online <http://daccessdds.un.org/doc/UNDOC/GEN/N04/328/43/PDF/N0432843.pdf?OpenElement> (accessed April 2008).

United Nations (1993) *Declaration on the Elimination of All Forms of Violence Against Women,* New York: United Nations, online <http://daccessdds.un.org/doc/UNDOC/GEN/N94/095/05/PDF/N9409505.pdf?OpenElement> (accessed Sept. 2008).

United Nations (2004) 'A more secure world: our shared responsibility', Report of the High-level Panel on Threats, Challenges and Change, online <http://www.un.org/secureworld/report3.pdf > (accessed 2 Oct. 2008).

United Nations (2007) *The Millennium Development Goals Report 2007,* New York: UN.

United Nations (2008) *The Millennium Development Goals Report 2008,* New York: UN.

United States Congress (1979) *The Effects of Nuclear War,* Washington, DC: Office of Technology Assessment, United States Congress.

University of Bradford, 'The biological and toxin weapons website', <http://www.opbw.org/> (accessed June 2009).

University of Exeter and University of Bradford, 'Biological weapons and codes of conduct', <http://www.ex.ac.uk/codesofconduct/Examples/> (accessed June 2009).

US Centers for Disease Control and Prevention (CDC), <http://www.cdc.gov/od/sap/> (accessed Oct. 2008).

US National Academy of Sciences (2008) *Emerging Cognitive Neuroscience and Related Technologies,* Washington, DC: National Academies Press.

Vale, J. L., and Campanella, J. T. (eds) (2005) *The Resilient City: How Modern Cities Recover from Disaster,* Oxford: Oxford University Press.

Vale, L. J. (1987) *The Limits of Civil Defence in the USA, Switzerland, Britain and the Soviet Union,* Basingstoke: Macmillan.

van Aken, J. (2006) 'When risk outweighs benefit: dual-use research needs a scientifically sound risk-benefit analysis and legally binding biosecurity measures', *EMBO Report,* 7: 10–13.

Van den Berg, L., Pol, P. M. J., Mingardo, G. and Speller, C. J. M. (2006) *The Safe City: Safety and Urban Development in European Cities,* Aldershot: Ashgate.

van der Pijl, K. (2006) *Global Rivalries: From the Cold War to Iraq,* London: Pluto.

Van der Ploeg, I. (2005) *The Machine-Readable Body: Essays on Biometrics and the Informatization of the Body,* Maastricht: Shaker.

Van Duyne, P. (1993) 'Organised crime and business crime-enterprises in the Netherlands', *Crime, Law and Social Change,* 19: 103–42.

Van Duyne, P., von Lampe, K., and Passas, N. (eds) (2002) *Upperworld and Underworld in Cross-Border Crime,* Nijmegen: Wolf Legal Publishers.

van Houtum, H. Henk and Pijpers, R. (2008) 'On strawberry fields and cherry picking: fear and desire in the bordering and immigration politics of the European Union', in R. Pain and S. Smith (eds) *Fear: Critical Geopolitics and Everyday Life,* Aldershot: Ashgate.

van Munster, R. (2004) 'The war on terrorism: when the exception becomes the rule', *International Journal for the Semiotics of Law,* 17(2): 141–53.

van Munster, R. (2005) *The EU and the Management of Immigration Risk in the Area of Freedom, Security and Justice,* University of Southern Denmark, Political Science Publications, 12, online <http://www.sdu.dk/~/media/Files/Om_SDU/Institutter/Statskundskab/Skriftserie/05Rens12%20pdf.ashx> (accessed June 2009).

Vanderbilt, T. (2002) *Survival City: Adventures among the Ruins of Atomic America,* New York: Princeton Architectural Press.

Vatis, M. A. (1998) 'National infrastructure protection', Michael Vatis, Deputy assistant director and chief of the Federal Bureau of Investigation's National Infrastructure Protection Center (NIPC) before the

Senate Judiciary Subcommittee on Terrorism, Technology and Government Information, 10 February 1998.

Venzke, I. (2008) 'International bureaucracies from a political science perspective: agency, authority and international institutional law', *German Law Journal*, 9(11): 1401–28.

Verkuil, P. (2007) *Outsourcing Sovereignty: Why Privatization of Government Functions Threatens Democracy and What we Can Do about it*, Cambridge: Cambridge University Press.

Vermeulen, G. (2002) 'New developments in EU criminal policy regarding cross-border crime', in P. Van Duyne, K. von Lampe and N. Passas (eds) *Upperworld and Underworld in Cross-Border Crime*, Nijmegen: Wolf Legal Publishers.

Verrastro, F. and Ladislaw, S. (2007) 'Providing energy security in an interdependent world', *Washington Quarterly,* 30(4): 95–104.

Verstraete, G. (2001) 'Technological frontiers and the politics of mobility in the European Union', *New Formations,* 43: 26–43.

Verwimp, P. (2006) 'Machetes and firearms: The organization of massacres in Rwanda', *Journal of Peace Research*, 43(1): 5-22.

Virilio, P. (2006) *Speed and Politics*, Los Angeles: Semiotexte.

Virno, P. (2004) *A Grammar of the Multitude*, New York: Semiotext(e).

von Braun, J. (1995) 'Agricultural commercialization: impacts on income and nutrition and implications for policy', *Food Policy*, 20(3): 197–202.

Von Lampe, K. (2002) 'Afterword: organized crime research in perspective', in P. Van Duyne, K. von Lampe and N. Passas (eds) *Upperworld and Underworld in Cross-Border Crime*, Nijmegen: Wolf Legal Publishers.

Von Lampe, K. (2008) 'Organized crime in Europe: conceptions and realities', *Policing: A Journal of Policy and Practice*, 2(1): 7–17.

Von Tigerstrom, B. (2007) *Human Security and International Law: Prospects and Problems,* Studies in International Law, Oxford and Portland, OR: Hart Publishing.

Wacquant, Loic (2008) *Urban Outcasts: A Sociology of Advanced Marginality,* Cambridge: Polity.

Wæver, O. (1993) 'Societal security: the concept', in O. Wæver, B. Buzan, M. Kelstrup and P. Lemaitre (eds) *Identity, Migration, and the New Security Agenda in Europe,* London: Pinter.

Wæver, O. (1995) 'Securitization and desecuritization', in R. D. Lipschutz (ed.) *On Security*, New York: Columbia University Press.

Wæver, O. (1997) *Concepts of Security,* Copenhagen: University of Copenhagen.

Wæver, O. (1998) 'Insecurity, Security, and Asecurity in the West European Non-War Community', in E. Adler and M. N. Barnett (eds) *Security Communities,* Cambridge: Cambridge University Press.

Wæver, O. (2000) 'What is security? The securityness of security', in B. Hansen (ed.) *European Security Identities: 2000,* Copenhagen: Copenhagen Political Studies Press.

Wæver, O., Buzan, B., Kelstrup, M. and Lemaitre, P. (1993) *Identity, Migration and the New Security Agenda in Europe,* London: Pinter.

Walby, S. (1989) 'Theorising patriarchy', *Sociology,* 23(2): 213-34.

Walker, A. F. and Pavitt, F. (1989) 'Energy density of Third World weaning foods', *Nutrition Bulletin*, 14(2): 88–101.

Walker, R. B. J. (1988) *One World, Many Worlds: Struggles for a Just World Peace*, Boulder, CO: Lynne Rienner.

Walker, R. B. J. (1993) *Inside/Outside: International Relations as Political Theory,* Cambridge: Cambridge University Press.

Walker, R. B. J. (1997) 'The subject of security', in M. C. Williams and K. Krause (eds) *Critical Security Studies*, Minneapolis, MN: University of Minnesota Press.

Walkowitz, J. R. (1992) *City of Dreadful Delight: Narratives of Sexual Danger in Late-Victorian London*, Chicago: University of Chicago Press.

Wallerstein, I. M. (1989) *World System III: The Second Era of Great Expansion of the Capitalist World-Economy, 1730s–1840s*, San Diego, CA: Academic Press.

Walt, S. (1987) *The Origins of Alliances*, Ithaca, NY: Cornell University Press.

Walt, S. (1991) 'The renaissance of security studies', *International Studies Quarterly*, 35(2): 211–39.

Walt, S. (2005) *Taming American Power: The Global Response to U.S. Primacy*, New York: W.W. Norton.

REFERENCES

Walters, W. (2002) 'The power of inscription: beyond social construction and deconstruction in European Union studies', *Millennium: Journal of International Studies,* 31: 83–108.

Walters, W. (forthcoming) 'Foucault and frontiers: notes on the birth of the humanitarian border', in U. Bröckling, S. Krasmann and T. Lemke (eds) *Governmentality: Current Issues and Future Challenges,* New York: Routledge.

Waltz, E. (1998) *Information Warfare: Principles and Operations,* Boston, MA: Artech House.

Waltz, K. N. (1959) *Man, the State, and War: A Theoretical Analysis,* New York: Columbia University Press.

Weber, C. (2005) 'Securitizing the unconscious: the Bush doctrine of preemption and *Minority Report*', *Geopolitics,* 10: 1–18.

Weber, C. (2008) 'Designing safe citizens', *Citizenship Studies,* 12(2): 125–42.

Weber, C. and Lacy, M. (forthcoming) *Securing by Design.*

Weber, M. (1996 [1921]) *The City,* New York: Free Press.

Weins, L. (2005) 'US-VISIT accuracy could be better', *Biometric Technology Today,* 13(2): 5–12.

Weiss, T. and Gordenker, L. (1996) *NGOs, the UN, and Global Governance,* Boulder, CO: Lynne Rienner.

Weizman, E. (2007) *Hollow Land: Israel's Architecture of Occupation,* London: Verso.

Weldes, J. (1999a) *Constructing National Interests: The United States and the Cuban Missile Crisis,* Minneapolis. MN: University of Minnesota Press.

Weldes, J. (1999b) 'The cultural production of crises: US identity and missiles in Cuba', in J. Weldes, M. Laffey, H. Gusterson and R. Duvall (eds) *Cultures of Insecurity: States, Communities, and the Production of Danger,* Minneapolis, MN: University of Minnesota Press.

Weldes, J., Laffey, M., Gusterson, H. and Duvall, R. (1999) 'Introduction: constructing insecurity', in J. Weldes, M. Laffey, H. Gusterson and R. Duvall (eds) *Cultures of Insecurity: States, Communities, and the Production of Danger,* Minneapolis, MN: University of Minnesota Press.

Wendt, A. (1992) 'Anarchy is what states make of it: the social construction of power politics', *International Organization,* 46: 391–425.

Wendt, A. (1994) 'Collective identity formation and the international state', *American Political Science Review,* 88: 384–96.

Wendt, A. (1999a) 'Anarchy is what states make of it: the social construction of power politics', *Theory and Structure in International Political Economy: An International Organization Reader,* 46: 391–425.

Wendt, A. (1999b) *Social Theory of International Politics,* Cambridge and New York: Cambridge University Press.

Wetzell, R. F. (2000) *Inventing the Criminal: A History of German Criminology, 1880–1945,* Chapel Hill, NC: University of North Carolina Press.

Wheelis, M. and Dando, M. (2005) 'Neurobiology: a case study of the imminent militarization of biology', *International Review of the Red Cross,* 87(859): 553–71.

Wheelis, M. and Sugishima, M. (2006) 'Terrorist use of biological weapons', in M. Dando, L. Rózsa and M. Wheelis (eds) *Deadly Cultures: Biological Weapons since 1945,* Cambridge, MA: Harvard University Press.

Whiteside, A., de Waal, A. and Gebre-Tensae, T. (2006) 'AIDS, security and the military in Africa: a sober appraisal', *African Affairs,* 105(419): 210–18.

Whitman, M. E. and Mattord, H. J. (2002) *Principles of Information Security,* Boston, MA: Thomson Course Technology.

Wilkinson, D. (2003) *Guns, Violence and Identity among African American and Latino Youth,* El Paso: LFB Scholarly Publishing.

Williams, A. (1979) *The Police of Paris, 1718–1789,* Baton Rouge, LA: Louisiana State University Press.

Williams, M. C. (1998a) 'Identity and the politics of security', *European Journal of International Relations,* 4: 204–25.

Williams, M. C. (1998b) 'Modernity, identity and security: a comment on the "Copenhagen Controversy"', *Review of International Studies,* 24: 435–9.

Williams, M. C. (2003) 'Words, images, enemies: securitization and international politics', *International Studies Quarterly,* 47(4): 511–31.

Williams, M. C. (2007) *Culture and Security: Symbolic Power and the Politics of International Security,* London: Routledge.

Williams, P. (1994) 'Transnational criminal organizations and international security', *Survival*, 36: 96–113.

Williams, P. (2002) 'Cooperation among Criminal Organizations', in M. Berdal and M. Serrano (eds) *Transnational Organized Crime and International Security: Business as Usual?*, London: Lynne Rienner.

Wilson, R. (2001) *The Politics of Truth and Reconciliation in South Africa*, Cambridge: Cambridge University Press.

Winner, L. (1977) *Autonomous Technology: Technics-out-of-Control as a Theme in Political Thought*, Cambridge, MA: MIT Press.

Wolf, A. (1999) 'Water and human security', *Aviso*, 3(2), online <http://www.google.com/search?hl=en&rlz=1B3GGGL_en___CA217&q=Water+and+Human+Security'%2C+Aviso&cts=1245045088160&aq=f&oq=&aqi=> (accessed June 2009).

Wolstein, B. (1987) 'Anxiety and the psychic center of the psychoanalytic self', *Contemporary Psychoanalysis*, 23: 631–58.

Womack, D. (2007) 'Uncertain futures: a conversation with Professor Anthony Dunne', *Think Tank* (21 Feb.), online <http://www.adobe.com/designcenter/thinktank/dunne_02.html> (accessed June 2009).

Wood, D. M. (ed.) (2006) *A Report on the Surveillance Society*, Report for the Information Commissioner by the Surveillance Studies Network, online <http://www.ico.gov.uk/upload/documents/library/data_protection/practical_application/surveillance_society_full_report_2006.pdf> (accessed June 2009).

Woodiwiss, M. (2003) 'Transnational organised crime: the global reach of an American concept', in A. Edwards and P. Gill (eds) *Transnational Organised Crime: Perspectives on Global Security*, New York: Routledge.

World Bank (2000) *Energy Services for the World's Poor*, Washington, DC: World Bank.

World Energy Council (1999) *The Challenge of Rural Energy Poverty in Developing Countries*, London: World Energy Council.

World Health Organization (WHO) (2006) 'Biorisk management: laboratory biosecurity guidance', Geneva: WHO, online <http://www.who.int/csr/resources/publications/biosafety/WHO_CDS_EPR_2006_6.pdf> (accessed Sept. 2008).

Wrench, J. and Solomos, J. (eds) (1993) *Race and Migration in Western Europe*, Oxford: Berg.

Wright, A. (2006) *Organised Crime*, Cullompton: Willan Publishing.

Wright, Q. (1964) *A Study of War*, 2nd edn, Chicago: University of Chicago Press.

Wright, R. (1992) *Stolen Continents: The Americas through Indian Eyes since 1492*, New York: Houghton Mifflin.

Wyn Jones, R. (1999) *Security Strategy and Critical Theory*, London: Lynne Rienner.

Yeager, R. and Kingma S. (2001) 'HIVAIDS: destabilizing national security and the multi-national response', *International Review of the Armed Forces Medical Services*, 74(1–3): 3–12.

Yelavich, S. (2005) 'Safety nets', in P. Antonelli (ed.) *SAFE: Design Takes on Risk*, New York: Museum of Modern Art.

Yergin, D. (1991) *The Prize: The Epic Quest for Oil, Money and Power*, New York: Simon & Schuster.

Yergin, D. (2006) 'Ensuring energy security', *Foreign Affairs*, 85(2): 69–82.

Yergin, D. (2008) 'Oil has reached a turning point', *Financial Times* (28 May).

Zalewski, M. (1995) 'Well, what is the feminist perspective on Bosnia?', *International Affairs*, 71(2): 339–56.

Zamparelli, S. J. (1999) 'Competitive sourcing and privatization: contractors on the battlefield', *Air Force Journal of Logistics*, 23(3): 1–17.

Zanders, J. P. (1999) 'Assessing the risk of chemical and biological weapons proliferation to terrorists', *Non-Proliferation Review*, 6(4): 17–34.

Zanders, J. P. (2002) 'Weapons of mass disruption?', *SIPRI Yearbook 2002: Armaments, Disarmament and International Security*, Oxford: Oxford University Press.

Zedner, L. (2006) 'Liquid security: managing the market for crime control', *Criminology and Criminal Justice*, 6(3): 267–88.

Zehfuss, M. (2007) 'The tragedy of violent justice: the danger of Elshtain's just war against terror', *International Relations*, 21(4): 493–501.

Zuckerman, E. and Greenberg, M. (2005) 'The gender dimensions of post-conflict reconstruction: an analytical framework for policymakers', in C. Sweetman (ed.) *Gender, Peacebuilding and Reconstruction*, Oxford: Oxfam GB.

Index

3/11: Madrid   240
7/7: London   188
9/11   12, 13, 24, 225–6, 230–1; effect of   17, 18, 54

Academic Technology Approval Scheme (ATAS)   179
Adler, E.   84, 85, 87, 92
Afghanistan   54, 55, 78
Africa: food security   135, 136
Agamben, Giorgio   96–7, 223, 245; biopolitics   61–71; urban insecurity   197, 202, 204
Agnew, John   51
AIDS   141; pandemic   164–7
Aitken, Rob   102, 103, 105
Alkire, Sabine   41, 43, 44
al-Qaeda   90, 175–6, 183n1, 189
America   10, 102; 2008 Presidential campaign   90, 100; biosecurity   178–9; cyber-security   154–62; 'dollar diplomacy'   101; environmental security   126; foreign policy   90; geopolitics   52; identity   52; national security   92; Saudi alliance   149–50; small arms   30, 36; surveillance   191–2, 194; technological intelligence   231; war on terror   53
Anghie, A.   13
Angola: civil war   149
Annan, Kofi   44, 47
Antarctica: geopolitics   52
anthrax letter attacks   178
Antonelli, P.   247–8
Arabs, relations between   82
Aradau, C.: financial security   107; migration and security   220, 221; risk   17, 18, 20–1; security technologies   230; surveillance   193

Aramis: security technologies   234
Arie, S.   39, **41**, 45, 47
Aristotle   10, 65, 66, 67
armed forces   31, 165–6
armed violence   **35**
Atkinson, D.   50
Australia Group (AG)   178
Automatic Number Plate Recognition (ANPR)   257–8
avian flu   170–1
Axworthy, Lloyd   39, 43, 47

Bajpai, Kanti   **41**, 45, 47
Baldwin, Stanley   199
banality of security   221
Bangladesh famine 1974   136
Barnett, Jon   124, 126, 127, 128, 129, 130
Barnett, Michael   82, 84, 85, 87, 92, 112
Bauman, Zygmunt   240, 245–56
Beck, U.   18–20, 23, 105–6, 197, 230, 231
Bengal famine   137, 138–9
Benjamin, W.   62, 69
Benveniste, E.   7
Best, Jacqueline   108
Bigo, D.   24, 214; cyber-security   156, 162; migration and security   220, 227; security technologies   230, 231–2, 238; surveillance   187, 190, 192
Bijker, W. E.   233
bioethics   174–5
Biological and Toxic Weapons Convention (BWC)   173, 177–8
biological warfare, international prohibition against   177–8
biomass fuel   147
biometric technology   190, 227

310

INDEX

biopolitics 61–71

biosafety 173, 174

biosecurity 173–83, 190–1; codes of practice 182; definitions of 174–5; international prohibition against chemical and biological warfare 177–8; laboratory and facility-level 180–1; life sciences and dual use research 181–2

biotechnology 181

bioterrorism 175, 176–7, 183n1

bird flu 170–1

The Birth of Biopolitics (Foucault) 63

Blackwater 208, 210, 215

Bleiker, Roland 83

Block, L. 259, 260–1

Booth, Ken 82, 85, 89; ethics 92, 93, 95, 99

border security 214, 221, 226–7, 261

boundaries 214–15

Bowden, B. 7, 9, 14

Brasilia: designing security 245–6

Braudel, F. 9, 199

Bretton Woods 102

Britain 144, 201, 205, 224

Brzoska, M. 33, 47

Burch, K. 106

Burke, Anthony 107; ethics 92; security as ethics 93, 94, 96, 97, 98

Bush, G.W. 12, 54, 118, 145, 189

Butler, Judith 72, 219

Buzan, B. 2, 40; cyber-security 162n1; energy security 146; ethics 93; financial security 100; identity/security 84, 86; pandemic security 171; societal security 148; urban insecurity 202–3

Canada **41**, 43, 47

Casa Segura **246**, 247

Casino Capitalism (Strange) 104

CCTV 188, 190, 193, 204, 206

chemical and biological warfare (CBW) 175–6, 177–8

Chemical Weapons Convention (CWC) 175, 177

China 138, 143n3, 167–8

cities: contemporary insecurities 202–6; insecurity in 200–2; insecurity of 198–200

civilian weapons **29**, 29–32

Civilization 9–10, 11

civilization: concept 7–16; ethnographic 10; and security 10–11; security as a result of 12–14; security of 14–15

civilizations, security of 11–12

The Clash of Civilizations (Huntington) 12

climate change 14–15, 130, 141

coal 151

Cohn, Carol 78, 79, 82

Cold War 14, 17, 52, 110; cities after 202–6; commercial security after 209; conflicts since 30, 33; environmental concerns since 126; environmental security after 39–40; identity since 81–3; identity/security nexus 82, 84, 88–9; liberal internationalists after 40; post 2, 31, 39; security technology since 230

Colomina, Beatriz 240, 241, 248

The Colonial Present (Gregory) 53–4

colonialism 53–4, 106

commercial security practices 208–16; everyday practices 215–16; insecurities 212–13; market size 209; practical challenges 209–10; privatization 208–9; research issues 212; security spaces 214–15; transformation of states 211–12

Commission on Human Security **41**, 44, 93–4

computer security 154–62

consumption 124

Copenhagen School 28, 86, 93, 212–13, 219

cosmopolitanism 93, 94–5

courts of human rights 113

credit crisis 2008-9 100–1, 105, 106

crime 204–5, 253–62

criminal violence 32–5

critical design 242–3, 246–51

critical geopolitics 50–8; global war on terror 53–5; history 50–3; popular culture 56–8

Critical Geopolitics (Ó Tuathail) 51

critical infrastructure protection (CIP) 159, 161–2

cryptography 158–9

Cuban Missile Crisis 87, 189

'culture of violence' 36–8

cyber-crime 157–8

'cyber-policing' 260

cyber-security 154–62; definition 155–6; distributed security 160–2; encryption 158–9; and national security 156; threat clustering 157; threats and critical infrastructures 159–60

Daase, C. 17, 18, 20, 26n5

Dalby, S. 50–1, 53, 54, 56, 57, 96; environmental security 125, 126

danger, social construction of 18–20

Darfur: famine 1984–5 135, 137; sexual violence 72, 75–6

databases, private 188, 192–3

data-mining 190, 191, 192, 231, 258

Daudelin, Claude 42, 47

Dauphinée, Elizabeth 97

Davis, Mike 204, 205, 245

De Cauter, Lieven 204

de Waal, A. 135, 137, 141, 166

deaths: small arms 32–5

Debrix, F. 57, 58

Declaration on the Elimination of Violence Against Women (DEVAW) 73–4

Den Boer, M. 254, 255, 257, 258, 259, 260, 261

311

INDEX

Derrida, Jacques 97, 241
designing security 240–52, **246**, **247**; problem of
    circulation 243–51
Dillon, M. 54, 96, 107, 193; biopolitics 63–4,
    65, 66; risk 20, 25
disease 15, 135, 137, 163–72
dispositif, risk as 20–1
'distributed security' 161
Do you want to replace the existing normal?
    248–51, 252n4
Dodds, K. 50, 52, 53, 54, 56, 58
'dollar diplomacy' 101, 107
Doomsday Clock 14
Doty, R. L. 85, 93, 219, 220, 226, 244
Duffield, M. 48, 103, 224
Dunne, Anthony 241, 242, 248, 250–1

Eberstadt 165, 166
'Echelon' 188, 191, 239
economy and security 100–1
Ecuador 204
Elbe, S. 18, 67, 165, 166, 192–3
Elden, Stuart 54, 55
Electronic System for Travel Authorization
    (ESTA) 194
Elshtain, Jean Bethke 90, 98, 99
encryption 158–9
energy security 144–53; challenges 152–3;
    conventional approach 145–6; demand and
    supply 149–52; and environmental security
    150–1; and human security 147; scarcity
    151–2; and societal security 148–9
Environment and Conflicts Project (ENCOP)
    127–8
environmental and human securities 93–6
environmental change: human security 129–30;
    territorial integrity 129; and violent conflict
    127–8
environmental insecurity 123–5
environmental risks 127
environmental security 95, 123–31; and end
    of Cold War 39–40; and energy security
    150–1; policy 125–7
Ericson, R.V. 213; crime 257, 258; surveillance
    193, 194; technologies 230, 232; urban
    insecurity 181, 197, 204, 207
ethico-political dilemmas 246–8, 250
ethics, security as 90–9; human and
    environmental securities 93–6; post-
    structuralism 96–8; statism 91–3; war and
    security 98–9
Europe: biosecurity 178; borders security 261;
    identity 51, 84; transnational crime 255–6;
    urban insecurity 205–6
European Union (EU) 231
Europol 257–8, 260–1
extraordinary rendition 192

Fagan, J. 37
famines 135–6
FAO (Food and Agriculture Organisation of the
    United Nations) 133, **134**
fear of others 54–5
Febvre, L. 8–9
feminism 93
Fidler, David 169
Final Home Jacket 244–5
finance: colonialism 106; interrelationship with
    security 106–8; *securitization* 104; security
    aspects of 103–6; surveillance 191, 192
financial security 100–9
flu pandemic 169–71
food crises 136
food policies 138–9
food prices 136–7, 140
food security 132–43; access to food 138–9;
    availability of food 137; causes of insecurity
    136–7; definitions 133; global production
    136–7; insecurity 133, **134**, 139–41; and
    security 142–3; temporary insecurity 135–6
food utilization 139
Foreign Affairs (Eberstadt) 166
Foreign Affairs (Huntington) 11–12, 81
foreign intelligence threat 157–8
foreign policy 46–7, 101–3
Foucault, Michel 53, 63; biopolitics 61–71;
    designing security 243–4; ethics 96–7, 98,
    99; finance 106, 107; migration and security
    222–3; risk 20, 23; surveillance 193, 194,
    196; urban insecurity 201, 204
Franklin, Ursula 233, 234
Fukuyama, F. 11

Garland, David 203
gated communities 54–5, 205, 206, 214
Gellman, B. 164, 166
gender 53, 118; issues 72–80; violence 115
gendering security 72–89; gender violence
    74–6, 115; violence against women 73–4;
    violent reproduction of gender 76–9
gendering violence 76–9
geographical theories/global insecurities 57–8
geopolitics, critical 50–8; definition 50; identity
    52–3; popular culture 56–7; states 52
GHECHS (Global Environmental Change and
    Human Security project) **41**, 45
Gillespie, S. 133, **134**, 140, 141
Gilroy, Paul 225–6
Global Environmental Change and Human
    Security project (GHECHS) **41**, 45
global food production 136–7
global governance, legalization of 110–11
global insecurities 57–8, 230
global war on terror 17, 53–5, 108, 191–2
globalization and migration 218
Goldmann, M. 112

312

INDEX

Gore, Al 95
Graham, S. 54, 55, 195–6, 203
Gregory, D. 53–4, 55, 58
Guantanamo Bay 55, 62
'gun culture' **35**, 36
Gupta, Akhil 225

H1N1 swine flu 171
H5N1 avian flu 170–1
Haddad, L. R. 133, 139
Haggerty, K. D. 193, 194, 213, 230, 232
Hall, S. 204, 205, 206
Hampson, Fen Osler 47
Hanshin earthquake 203
Hardt, M. 61, 102
Hayes, B. 229, 235, 237
Headrick, D. 30–1
health 124, 130, 139, 168–9; pandemic security 163–72
health programmes 140
Herz, J. 22, 91
HIV/AIDS 141; pandemic security 164–7
Hobbes, T. 10, 67, 96, 106
homeland security 230–1
Homeland Security Blanket 245
Homer-Dixon, T. F. 14, 40, 127, 147
human and environmental securities 93–6
human rights: International Law 112–17
human security 39–49, 94; categories of use 46–8; contested concept of 48–9; definitions **41**, 42–6, 93–4; and energy security 147; environmental change 129–30; and foreign policy 46–7; and international institutions 47; as issues label 47; measuring 47; post Cold War 39–40; state power 48; and state security 39–42, 94–5
Human Security Report Project 94
human–environment interactions 123–5
humanitarian law 114
Huntington, S. P. 7, 9, 11, 12, 81
Hurricane Katrina 203
Huysmans, Jef 162, 205; financial security 100; identity/security nexus 17, 85, 87, 88; migration and security 220; security politics 96; security technologies 232

identity 221; geopolitics 52–3; return of since cold war 81–3; as social construct 84–5
identity documents 190
identity/security nexus 81–9; literature 82; source of identity 83–5; studying 85–8
immigrants 10, 214, 250
immigration 97, 219 *see also* migration
Indonesia: flu 171
infectious disease, pandemic security 163–72
infrastructure: and crime 255
infrastructures, critical: cyber-threats 159–60
Ingram, A. 53, 54, 56, 58

intelligence gathering 231
internally displaced people (IDP) 115–16
International Court of Justice 114
International Health Regulations 168–9
international institutions: human security 47
international law 110–19; humanization of 112–14; knowledge construction 117–18
international oil companies (IOCs) 144, 150, 152, 153
international organizations (IO): global governance 111–12
international political economy (IPE) 101, 102
international prohibition against chemical and biological warfare 177–8
interventionism 13–14
Iraq 54, 55, 78, 144, 208, 215

Japan 41, 44, 47, 180–1, 199
Joint Investigation Teams 260–1
Jones, Adam 75
just war theory 90, 91, 98–9

Kazakhstan: biosecurity 179
Kelly, Liz 73
Kessler, O. 17, 18, 25, 26n5, 107, 187
Keynes, J. M. 23
Khong, Yeun Foong **41**, 46
King, James **247**, 248
Kitiyadisai, K. 193
Klerks, P. 254, 256, 259
Knight, F. 23
knowledge commodities 237
knowledge construction: international law 117–18
Krause, K. 28, 29, 34, 40, 82, 83
Kuhlau, F. 174, 177, 180, 181, 182, 192

laboratories: biosecurity 180–1
Lacy, M. 58, 215, 240, 241–2, 243, 251
Latour, B. 234
law enforcement: structure 257–8
Le Billon 53, 149
Leaning, J. 39, **41**, 45, 47
Lederberg, J. 163–4
liaison officers 259
liberal internationalists: end of Cold War 40
life sciences: dual use research 181–2
Lobo-Guerrero, L. 20, 25, 64, 65, 105
Lodgaard, Sverre **41**, 46
Los Angeles: urban insecurity 204
Lugar, Richard 170, 179
Luhmann, N. 21, 23–4

MacFarlane, Neil **41**, 46
Mack, Andy **41**, 45, 47
McNeill, J. R. 144–5
McNeill, W. H. 24, 27
McSweeney, Bill 82, 84, 86, 87, 88

313

Madrid: 3/11   240
Mafia paradigm   256
malnutrition   **134**, 135
Markusen, A. R.   209, 210
Marshall, Andrew   240–1
Masters, C.   78, 97
Mattern, J. B.   82, 85, 86, 87
medicalization   171–2
Mexican migrants   246–7
Mexico: violence   33
Middle East, energy security   145–6
migration   214, 217–28, 244; critical studies
   217–19; discursive approaches   219–20;
   material-semiotic approach   220–2;
   mobilization of security   222–4; state
   transformation   226–8
migration–security nexus   218–28
military   31, 165–6
military-industrial complex   236
Millennium Development Goal (MDG)   135
Mills, Catherine   62, 66, 68, 69
mobile crime   253–62; analysing and debating
   254–7; definitions   254; investigating   257–8;
   policing   258–61
Morgenthau, H. J.   22, 92
Moser, Caroline   204–5
Mozambique: rape   75
Mueller, J.   181, 206–7

Nadelmann, E.   259
Naidoo, Sagaren   42
national securities, ethics   91–3
national security   170
National Security Advisory Board for Biosecurity
   (NSABB)   179
National Security Agency (NSA)   157, 158
NATO   126
natural disasters   135, 136, 138, 191, 198–9, 203
Neal, A.   20, 24, 25, 65
Neal, L.   106
Negri, A.   61, 102
Neocleous, M.   96, 223, 237
Netherlands: policing   260
New Orleans   201, 203
Newman, E.   42, 47, 48
nodal policing   260
non-combatant men   75
non-knowledge   19, 23
Norway: conflict negotiation   46–7
nuclear threat   14, 244
nutrition   133, **134**, **135**, 140, 141

Ó Tuathail, G.   51, 52, 56
Obama, Barack   90, 100, 154, 170
oil crisis 1970's   144
oil prices   144, 151
oil supply   151
oil-producing states   145–6, 148

'ontological security'   87–8
Oquist, P.   42–3
The Order of Things (Foucault)   70, 71n1
organized crime   255–7
The Origins of Alliances (Walt)   82

pandemics   15, 163–72; flu   169–71; HIV/AIDS
   164–7; SARS   167–9
panopticon   194
Paris School securitization   213
Passas, N.   255, 258
Passenger Name Records (PNR)   188, 258,
   262n4
Patriot Act (2001)   179, 230–1
Payatas landslide   203
Pearson, L. B.   12
personnel: biosecurity   180
Pirbright, Surrey: biosecurity   180
plurality of security   221–2
policing mobility   222–3
political stability: HIV/AIDS   166–7
pollution   124
popular culture   52–3, 56–7
population   123–4
Posen, Barry   33, 83
postcoloniality   224–6
post-structuralism, security politics   96–8
poverty   124, 140, 200–1, 202–3, 205
power   63
preemption   191–2, 193
*President's Commission on Critical Infrastructure
   Protection (PCCIP)*   161–2
privatization: security practices   208–9

Raby, Fiona   241, 242, 248, 250, 251
race   10, 224
radio-frequency identification (RFID)   190
Ransick, Robert   246–7
rape   46, 72–7
redesigning security   242–52
Redesigning Security Approach   243, 249–51
refugees: international law   115–16
'rentier state'   148
'resource curse'   148
Responsibility to Protect (R2P)   116
risk   17–26; cyber-security   160–2; and danger
   19; as dispositif   20–1; finance and security
   107; management of   24–5; as mode of
   observation   21–2; and uncertainty   18–20,
   22–4
risk management   54, 193–4, 230–1
RMA (Revolution in Military Affairs)   230, 237
Roberts, D.   197, 206
Roffey, R.   174, 176, 177, 180
Rome Statute of the International Criminal
   Court   116
Rosenberg, E. S.   101, 107
Ruddick, S.   78

Rwanda 116, 117; genocide 31, 32; rape 75

Said, Edward 50, 53
Sandvik, K. B. 117
SARS 167–9
Sassen, Saskia 104, 105, 108, 228
Saudi Arabia: energy security 149–50
Savitch, H.V. 205
Schengen Agreement 259–60, 262n5
Schengen Information System (SIS) 50, 107,
   187, 188, 194, 215
'SCOT' literature 233–4
securitization 192–3, 212–13, 219; theory 2,
   100
securitization: finance 104
security: business of 237; definitions 103, 223;
   exhibitions 237, 238; and finance 101–3;
   mobilization of 222–4; as result of civilization
   12–14; "saying and doing of" 24–5
Security Dialogue 40–2
'security dilemma' 85
security politics: post-structuralism 96–8
security practices: use of technology 231–2
security privatization: practical challenges 209–
   10; transformation of states 211–12
security professionals 215
security spaces 226–7
security technologies 229–39; contemporary
   discourses 230–1; knowledge commodities
   237; in practice 231–2; 'security-industrial
   complex' 235–8; technological Darwinism
   234–5
security technology 103
security/identity nexus 81–9
'security-industrial complex' 235–8
Sen, Amartya 41, 44, 45, 47, 81; food security
   137, 138–9
September 11, 2001 12, 13, 24, 225–6, 230–1;
   effect of 17, 18, 54
Shaffer, Richard 166
Shapiro, M. J. 50, 56, 82, 215
Sharp, Joanne 52, 53
Shepherd, L. J. 72, 73, 77, 78
Singer, P.W. 209, 211, 213
Sjoberg, Laura 80, 93, 98
Slater, R. 135, 136, 141, 142
small arms 27–37, 38n4; deaths by 32–5;
   distribution of **29**, 29–32; etiology of
   violence 35–8
Small Arms Survey 29, 30–1
smuggling 255
social systems 124
societal security 86, 148–9
sociology of technology 233–4
sovereignty 10–11
Spanish flu 181
Sparke, M. 53, 57–8
Starobinski, J. 8

state arsenals 31
'state monopoly on the legitimate use of force'
   211
state power and human security concept 48
state security versus human security 39–42, **40**
state transformation: migration and security
   226–8
states: geopolitics 52
statism 91–3
Stevens, Paul 150, 151–2
Strange, Susan 102, 104, 105
Strong, M. F. 15
Study of History (Toynbee) 9
surveillance 187–96, 232; internationalization
   191–2; mobile crime 257–8; modes of
   194–5; preemption 191–2; research program
   195–6; securitization 192–3; strategies of
   193–4
swine flu 171
systemic shift 23–4, 26n1
systems theory 23–4

tabloid geopolitics 57
Taft, President 101
technical innovations 240–2
technological Darwinism 234–5
technological intelligence 231
technologies, security 229–39, 244;
   contemporary discourses 230–1; in practice
   231–2; practice of 232–5; since Cold War
   230; sociology of 233–4
technology: and security studies 229–32
territorial entities 52, 54, 55
territorial integrity: environmental change 129
'terror laws' 117–18
Terrorism Risk Insurance Act (TRIA) 20
testimonials: of victims 116–17
Thailand: ID cards 193
Thomas, Caroline 45, 47, 48, 94
threat clustering 157
Tickner, J. Ann 82, 86, 93
Toynbee, A. J. 9–10, 11–12, 16n6
transnational crime 253, 254–6
traveller information 188, 195, 214, 258, 262n4
Trüby, Stephan 245
Trust Fund for Victims 116
truth commissions 117
Tsumara, Kosuke 244–5
Turshen, Meredeth 75

UN human rights bodies 113
uncertainty and risk 22–4; and risk 19–20
UNDP **41**, 42, 43, 93–4, 124, 147
UNHCR: refugees 115–16
United Nations Conference on Environment and
   Development (UNCED) 126
United Nations Development Program *see*
   UNDP

United States *see* America
UNSC 1540 177
UNSC 1820 72
urban insecurity 197–207, 214, 222;
    contemporary 202–6; insecurity in cities
    200–2; insecurity of cities 198–200
US National Intelligence Council 175
US National Security Strategy 170
US Presidential Campaign 2008 100
US Terrorism Screening Centre 188
USA *see* America
US-VISIT 188, 190, 191–2

Van den Berg, L. 205–6
van Munster, R. 20–1, 24, 193, 221
victims: definitions and categories 114–15
violence: contemporary small arms 27–37;
    energy security 148–9; small arms and
    etiology of 35–8; against women 46, 72–7,
    79
violent conflict and environmental change
    127–8
violent deaths **34**, 38n8
Virilio, Paul 240, 243–4
virtual crime 254
Von Lampe, K. 254, 255, 256–7

Wæver, O. 2, 93, 99; identity/security nexus 86,
    87, 88; migration and security 219, 221
Walby, S. *see also* migration

Walt, S, 27, 82, 83, 84, 92
war: cities 198–200; definitions 27, 38n1; and
    security 98–9
war bonds 102
war on terror 17, 53–5, 108, 191–2
warlordism 33
weapons: small arms 27–37
Weberian state 29, 37, 55
Weberian triangle 28
Weldes, Jutta 82, 87
Wendt, Alexander 74–5, 84, 85, 86
Werner, W. 25
Wheeler, Nicholas J. 85, 92, 99
Williams, Michael C. 24, 40, 54, 57, 100, 212;
    identity/security nexus 82, 83, 86
Winlow, S. 204, 205, 206
women: violence against 73–4
'Women-at-Risk' 115
women's rights 110
Wood, D. M. 191, 205
World Commission on Environment and
    Development Report 125–6
World Health Organization (WHO) 168–9, 174
world risk society 18–19

Yelavich, Susan 244
Yugoslavia: witness accounts 116, 117

Zanders, J. P. 176–7